Also by
WILLIAM L. SCOTT

INVESTING AT THE RACE TRACK
(Simon & Schuster, 1981)

HOW WILL YOUR HORSE RUN TODAY?
(Amicus Press, 1984)

Total Victory At The Track

THE PROMISE AND THE PERFORMANCE

by
William L. Scott

Author of
Investing at the Race Track
and
How Will Your Horse Run Today?

AMICUS PRESS
Baltimore, MD

Published by: Amicus Press
                  4201 Underwood Road
                  Baltimore, Md. 21218

Distributed by: Liberty Publishing Co.
                  440 S. Federal Highway
                  Deerfield Beach, FL 33441

Library of Congress Cataloging in Publication Data

Scott, William L.
Total Victory at the Track:
The Promise and the Performance

1. Horse race betting—United States. 2 Scott, William L.
3. Horse players—United States.

ISBN 089709-183-3

Printed in the United States of America

Cover Photograph by Skip Dickstein

Table Of Contents

1 The Promise

THIS BOOK WILL undertake to set forth the soundest, safest and most comprehensive program for making money at the race track that has ever been published to this time. In the process it will explore new methods and concepts never before set forth for handicapping thoroughbred racing. It will combine these new methods and concepts with some careful revisions of earlier ideas, and then provide guidelines for a method of play that, since its development and testing at the race track, has provided consistent substantial profits for the player.

In this considerable undertaking, we are here to improve upon what this writer has previously set forth. In my first book on handicapping the horses to make a profit, *Investing at the Race Track*, there was a method of play that used two major devices, both of which had not been previously employed by anyone, to achieve an overall profit. The first was to confine selections of winning horses to the first three betting choices in a race, because statistically, year in and year out, two thirds of all races run were won by a horse that was one of the first three betting choices of the public. With only three horses from which to choose, the task could be profitable based upon sound separation principles.

That same winning percentage of low odds horses continues to hold true, and perhaps that will always be the case. This limitation of selections, however, as some sharp critics were quick to point out, had the obvious drawback of ignoring potential winning horses that paid high prices and brought far greater returns to the player, as long as he was able to choose them in advance. We shall employ no such limitation in this book, prepared as we now are to take advantage of every sound opportunity to enhance profits at the track.

The second highly original device in Investing at the Race Track was to employ an altogether new and different method of rating horses in order to select the one of the first three favorites that would likely defeat the other two. This device was called Ability Times, based upon a selected construction of an artificial time for a critical portion of a race as a determinant of a horse's ability. The best two races out of the horse's published past performances were used to calculate these times and the highest rated horse then became the choice for your·investment. There were also necessary additional qualifications based upon current form.

This method achieved a measure of success. Many readers and players wrote glowing accounts of what they had been able to achieve. A number of others even developed programs for personal computers based upon the rules and guidelines in the book. On the other hand, there were some who experienced difficulty in making it work, yielded in frustration and despair, and even vented their displeasure on the author whom they believed had misled them.

Whatever its merits, or even lack of them, Investing at the Race Track will not take you nearly as far as what you will find in this book. You will readily learn why as you move deeper into this work.

Our second book, *How Will Your Horse Run Today?*, was primarily devoted to a study and analysis of current form, which was then considered to be the one handicapping factor that, comparatively speaking, is more important than any of the other vital factors. It still is. In researching and writing that book, we found that there was another sound flat bet profit to be obtained at the race track. If one confined his plays only to horses that were favorites, provided they did not have any of the form defects that were identified in that book, there was a profit to be made—not a great one, but a profit nonetheless.

Just as confining one's play to the three lowest priced horses in the race was a limitation on profit possibilities, so was the even more restricted play on qualified favorites, who, in every case, would return the lowest price of any horse in the race. Of course, that was not the main point of *How Will Your Horse Run Today?*, which was far more concerned with current form as an indicator of any horse's chances to win or lose.

Are the concepts developed in those two books still valid? And if so, how are we using them here in this broader and more profitable work to obtain the Total Victory at the Track that we must have?

The concept of ability times was no more than a method among many others of rating horses. In any form of play at the race track, there must be some kind of measurement to enable you to select one horse over another. Whether this measurement is based upon adjusted speed figures, which is probably the most prominent and widely used, or upon class comparisons, consistency, money earnings, or upon any number of other varieties of ways of comparing thoroughbreds, it is nonetheless necessary to have some hopefully reliable device to select one or more as a probable winner.

Ability times, as developed in *Investing at the Race Track,* are still a sound method of rating horses. Here, we will use an improved and modified version of ability times as a key ingredient in this book. But an entirely new and original rating method which we call Performance Class Rating will be introduced as an integral part of a rating process that leads to a final selection.

No single isolated rating method can be expected to bring unrequited happiness and financial joy. If one were to proclaim a new rating method, tell you that all that was necessary was to apply it, place your money on the highest rated horse, and sit back to rake in the profits, you might be, and should be, skeptical enough to dismiss the claim as just another fantasy for getting rich at the race track.

That is why the Performance Class Rating that you will read about and learn to apply is primarily only one part of a totally new comprehensive handicapping line. The other part of the total line will take into account form factors as they were developed in *How Will Your Horse Run Today?* and then add revised ability times as an integrated whole. The blending of ability and performance with the power of current form is the fundamental strength of this book, and is the foundation upon which its program for selecting winning horses is based.

Thus, we are bringing forth two completely original and never before presented elements of rating horses: 1. performance class ratings, and 2. a comprehensive revised ability time rating. They will be used together with the key factors of current form that we have used for several years, and integrated into the most effective combination of ratings that has yet been provided to any handicapper.

Notice that we have said: *combination of ratings.*

You will be shown a handicapping line with three essential ratings: 1. performance class ratings, or PCR; 2. last race form factor ratings; and 3. last race revised ability time ratings. All three must be taken into account. Any one of the three in isolation cannot thrive without the other.

The most original aspect of this book is the creation and adoption of the never-before presented method of combining performance and class into a mathematical evaluation of a thoroughbred. But this evaluation does not stop with an adoption of a number. If it did, it would be less than complete. For when you have it, you will be able to read new comparisons of competing horses that you never had previously. As you will see later, it likewise establishes a horse's running style from the internal totals we compile, and allows you to integrate what you are able to see in the PCR lines with track bias and last race form. This last function may well be its most important contribution.

We believe you will find this new comprehensive method of rating thoroughbreds to select a winner not only exciting and rewarding, but incredibly useful in all its aspects. It is now a fundamental part of our program for Total Victory at the Track.

In developing this comprehensive method of play, we also intend to take into account the enormous difficulty in winning money at the track, and turn those core problems to our advantage. Of course, everyone recognizes that it is extremely hard to win money, regularly and consistently, at the track. No one should ever even try to tell you otherwise. The old bromide, chronicled over and over again by innumerable observers, "you can't beat the races," has almost become an American commonplace. The man or woman who tries to do so is viewed with skepticism and sometimes scorn. Even skilled experienced handicappers may have their days of disaster when losses pile up, eating away at the profits that are made when all goes well, making the whole enterprise a frustrating up and down way of life.

If one is able to search out and isolate a key factor or factors which causes most of the difficulty and then attack that factor head on with a strategy to overcome it, then the mountain may be truly moved. Thus, a complete recognition of what is at the heart of the peril is your first step toward overcoming it.

There are two great battlefields. The first is found in the race itself, which we will identify and intend to overcome. The second is in you. This book will have greater success in coping with the first than with the second.

As to the race, what is the great unmanageable, the massive obstacle, the seemingly impenetrable barrier to economic success at the track?

The central key begins with how the competition is put together and what happens thereafter. Individual horse races are constructed by racing officials to provide as wide an opportunity as possible for each horse entered to win. Old hands at the track recognize that it is the job of the racing secretary at each racing plant to try to establish conditions for races that will give owners and trainers some reason to enter their animals. The better the racing secretary is able to "bring them all together," the more difficult it is for you to predict which one will win.

If ten horses are entered in a race, and all ten have a realistic chance to win (which, happily for us, almost never happens), you might as well draw numbers from a hat and rely upon your mathematical one chance in ten of winning.

The job of rating, or handicapping, these horses to provide a better predictor of which one might win is what all of us strive to achieve. We are confronted with the reality that because of the necessity to equalize the competition, there are several horses in the race that do have a realistic chance to win. When you understand that there may be four or five or six horses that, because of a particular aptitude that may emerge that day, chance and circumstance in the running of the race, mistakes of jockeys and other horses, and the infinite varieties of events that can dominate a race, do have that opportunity to win, you can better appreciate that your task is formidable indeed.

Thus, it is this number of opportune horses that is at the heart of the problem. If there were always a single standout in every race, all the players would rush to place their bets accordingly, and the whole sport would be reduced to nothing. This varying number of opportune horses can arise equally where all the horses entered are very good or where all the horses entered are very bad. Even among the worst of competitors, one of them must win. Where well bred animals with class and speed and stamina come together in stakes races, there is too often no outstanding choice. The Kentucky Derby, the Preakness, and the Belmont, our three most prestigious Triple Crown races, are often extremely difficult to predict.

As an example, a writer and racing scholar that I consider as knowledgeable and perceptive as any person in the field is Andrew Beyer of the Washington Post. In 1987, Beyer wrote that in 17 years, he had never once been able to pick the winner of the Kentucky Derby. Does that give you some indication of how difficult it is?

On the other end of the spectrum, at every track, races must be carded for the cripples, the slow, the unwilling, the bottom of the barrel, whose owners have to pay their feed bills just as do the owners of the Secretariats and the Seattle Slews. The common question among these lower class creatures is often which one is the least likely to falter today. While the running of their race in slow time may be as exciting to watch as a contest among superior animals, the difficulty of successfully predicting the winner is frequently too much for even the best of handicappers.

Ordinarily, I consider races among the best horses at the track and races among the worst horses at the track equally the most difficult of all to play. Of course, in some of them, you will be able to find a horse that stands out, and a major goal of this book will help you in that direction. But even then, because where there are other good horses one of them might display an outstanding performance, and where there are other bad horses one of them may shake off his aches and pains for one brief moment of equine glory, your best laid plans may be defeated.

It is never easy. But it can be done.

We do have some allies in the process. While the racing secretary often does an admirable job of writing conditions for a race to equalize the competition, he can only accept those horses that are actually entered. The trainer is usually the person who selects the race in which he wishes to enter his horse. In doing that, because he not only needs to win but is required to do so often enough to stay in business, he is always searching, just as you or I would do, for an edge of some kind, or an advantage.

Consequently, we can often depend upon the maneuvers of trainers, in their own attempts to find an advantage, to create imbalances among the contenders. These efforts may not always be soundly based, but they do create jagged departures from the smooth flow of evenly matched competition that the racing secretary desires.

For example, in a typical ten horse field, there are usually at least four or more horses that have little or no chance. A trainer may enter his horse primarily for conditioning, or for testing a new distance or class, or for evaluating suspect physical condition, or even for reasons of desperation. And, of course, the trainer may have grossly miscalculated, believing that his horse has a chance to win when the realities are otherwise. Trainers are human—they make mistakes and misjudgments as well as brilliant coups. These horses will seldom measure up to the standards we demand for the location of the horse with an advantage.

In addition to the actions of the trainers who actually enter the horses that cause some to be more opportune than others, there is the further reality that the entry process is never perfect. All horses are not created equal in every race to be run, although some times they may appear to be. Some of them are bound to possess advantages over the others because of this natural irregularity in the entry process. It is our job to find them.

This will become the key theme of this book to overcome the inherent difficulty of selecting the winning horse. We must find the horse that shows the advantage. Therefore, we must play only those races where you can find a demonstrable, recognizable advantage of one kind or another. We shall find it through the use of the complete handicapping equation of PCR and current form, which includes last race ability times. This two-part equation will identify the horse or horses that have this absolutely necessary advantage.

We will search for it in every race we review. It will occur often enough for you to achieve the result that we must have.

On the other hand, if a sufficient advantage of one or more horses over the others cannot be found, and that, too, will often occur, you must resolutely learn to pass the race. If you cannot do so, and cannot attend the race track without playing every race, you may want to read this book for entertainment and enlightenment, but surely not for profit. You must either bypass those races where no demonstrable and recognizable advantage can be found, or remain forever among the ranks of the losers. And to me, losing is totally unacceptable.

Throughout all the rest of this book, we will be constantly searching for those signs of advantage. We will define them, identify them, and learn to recognize them. Equally, we will be patient and careful to curb our desires for a "sure thing" sufficient to recognize the situations where there is no measurable difference between contenders sufficient to have any confidence that any one of them will emerge from the pack, even though you know one of them will prevail at the wire.

When you have identified the horses that possess the kind of advantage we must have in order to be successful, then you must confine your play to these animals and manage your wagering properly.

This is where the second monumental difficulty of winning money at the race track emerges to loom in front of you like a monster gorilla in the jungle. Exercising the self-discipline that is so necessary is so hard that it is almost beyond belief. This is separate and apart from the mistakes that you will surely make in your handicapping that are comprehensible aspects of human endeavor. Sloppy calculating and overlooking a key factor are usually fatal when they occur, as they do, but it is the failure to supply the rigid control over what you plan to do that can insure your deflation over the long haul.

A prime single selection method is set forth later in this book, designed to produce at least 50% winners and so reliable that we have even been presumptious enough to call it social security. But there may be days at the track when these plays are fewer in number than you expect. One or more of these selections may lose, as almost half of them surely will, and plunge you into a loss situation earlier in the day than you expect. You may not be able to resist shaving your standards, pumping up an exacta race that carries its own built-in dangers, and wind up betting more on losing horses than on winning horses. Your plan for profit begins to evaporate. Good night, sweet prince.

Your own inner capacity to prevail cannot be treated, of course, in this book. That is equally as important as the knowledge and decisiveness of the selection process that is the first essential.

As we move forward, we shall, as indicated, fully set forth and explore the new basic method of Performance Class Rating which becomes the first part of our total handicapping equation. When that is complete, and you are ready to employ it, we shall take up the profit-sustaining factor of current form.

The form factors that were so thoroughly discussed in *How Will Your Horse Run Today?* will now be re-shaped to conform with what we have discovered in our PCR lines and the new changes we have made in ability times as well, and thus improved over their considerable efficiency of the past. These form factors will be enrolled as the beginning of the second part of the total handicapping equation that is devoted to current form.

Thereafter, the new revised ability time concept for the last race only will be inserted as a part of the entire handicapping equation. Those horses that do not have measurable last race form and ability times must be treated in some manner in the total equation, and that, too, will be set forth.

When all of these applications are mastered, you will then be ready to recognize the horses that possess the handicapping advantages that are necessary for success.

In doing all this, we must be frank about what is required. It is first of all hard work. Considerable time is necessary to prepare yourself for the track. How much is needed depends upon how fast and how accurately you are able to work. The methods shown here lend themselves to the making of a worksheet, which should be prepared before you leave for the track, and which will usually cover every horse in every race. Your reading and understanding of that worksheet is vital. It is even hard work after you get to the track, for you are required both to pay attention and analyze what is happening, as you will learn.

We have already spoken sufficiently of the self-discipline and determination that is required, and without which you may be better off staying at home.

But the reward is sweet indeed.

The entire framework of evaluating and selecting horses with advantages is done without inclusion of three factors that are both important and successfully used by many perceptive players around the country. They are trainers, trips, and body language.

At every track, there are trainers who dominate the results and there are trainers who show wretched records. Knowing the habits and patterns of these trainers who win can be an enormously useful guide and a helpful supplement to what is set forth in this book. Trainer statistics and patterns are not available in the Daily Racing Form, outside of the standings for most winning horses, which are of minimal use.

Trip handicapping, as it is called, requires rather constant attendance at the track and skilled observation. Its validity as a handicapping factor is unquestioned. When you observe a horse in trouble in a race and understand that his performance is not truly representative of what you can expect from him in his next effort, you will have gained an additional edge. You can sometimes, but not always, find some references to trouble in the Daily Racing Form, but this is far less useful than actual observation.

There are those experts who can learn much from observing a horse in the paddock and in the post parade before the race to form opinions about his readiness to run. They call this "body language," and it, too, has substantial validity. I am still working to learn more about it. Because it is beyond the scope of this work, there is little more that I can say about it.

But even without these admittedly helpful tools, we are still able to work from what we find in the Daily Racing Form to construct the total handicapping lines we need to accomplish our necessary goal: Total Victory at the Track.

All that has been said to now is about the promise. What is the performance?

In the last portion of this book, we have set forth three full racing cards at three different tracks, all from the same day, January 21, 1987, in order to guard against picking and choosing the good racing cards and forgetting to tell you about the bad ones. This was a mid-week day when poorer and less predictable horses could be expected to run. It was at a time when weather conditions would not likely have been at their optimum. Yet these days will be encountered by every committed player, and they, too, must be conquered if Total Victory is to be achieved.

In these three racing days, we have applied the principles of this book in race after race. This is done for two purposes. The first is as a review and reminder of how to apply every method shown in the book. And the second, quite obviously, is to show you the actual performance of what occurred there, and what should occur for you from now on.

2 Performance Class Ratings

WHAT ARE THESE Performance Class Ratings, how do they work, and more important, why do they work?

When you compile them, you will then be able to use them in three major ways: 1. as a basic comparison rating in itself, 2. as a comparison of running style to coordinate a horse's running habits with the track flow, or track bias of the day, and 3. a class factor that provides added insight into how a horse might run today.

The basic rating itself is founded on the simple principle of measuring how a horse has performed in his available reported races within the class, or level of competition, in which he has run. To arrive at the figure, we use all the races shown in his past performances in the Daily Racing Form, which are usually ten races for seasoned horses. If the horse has run less than five times, or if there is a field of lightly raced horses, such as two-year-olds or young three-year-olds, the rating method is either not useable at all or should be used only as an advisory guide line.

To obtain this rating, the first task is to add the number of horses in the listed races of each horse's past performances, which indicates the total number of horses that have run in the races that are shown. This involves no more than simple addition, and after we go through the entire method, we shall provide some easy guidelines to make this kind of calculation quick and accurate, because it is the most time-consuming of all that you will be required to do.

In doing this addition, you will find you can mentally add a column of figures, where no more than 10 numbers are involved, far quicker than you can punch in each number on your calculator, where you have the added burden of tapping the plus button each time. Then, when you have acquired the total number of horses in competition, the most practical thing is to enter it on your Racing Form at a convenient space.

The second step is to add up the number of horses shown in the second call of all the listed races.

The third step is to add up the number of horses shown in the finish position of all races.

You are now ready to perform class calculations, which is the only element of the entire task that requires some racing or handicapping knowledge.

For each race in his past performances where the horse has run at the same class level as today's race, there will be no class points awarded.

There are higher class points and lower class points, which may be added and compared with each other.

For each race in his past performances where the horse has run at a higher class level than today's race, we shall award Higher Class points as follows: 1 point for a class level of competition immediately higher than the class of today's race, 2 points for class levels that are more than one level above today's race, and finally, and rarely, 3 points for races "substantially far higher" than the class of today's race. An illustration of what is "substantially far higher" would be where today's race is an allowance event and a horse shows a Grade I stakes race in his past performances. There is such a wide class gap when a horse is performing in Grade I compared to allowance and lower rated races that we must accord the higher points for the maximum accuracy in our ratings. There will be other examples as we move along, which will enable you to make the determination without too much difficulty of when to award 3 Higher Class Points.

Lower Class Points are done in exactly the reverse fashion. Where a horse ran at a class level immediately below the class of today's race, there is 1 Lower Class point. For lower class races of more than the next immediate level, 2 Lower Class points, and finally, where a horse has run "substantially far lower" in class than today's race, we may assess 3 Lower Class Points.

Let's assume the horse has 8 Higher Class points and 3 Lower Class points. This would leave us a net figure of 5 Higher Class points.

Now comes the important reverse point that you must absorb. When we go to add the three figures which we now call "internal figures," i.e., the second call total, the finish total, and the class total, we will *subtract* Higher Class points and *add* Lower Class points. The reason for this is that the lower the internal figures are, the higher the Performance Class Rating will turn out to be. Again, you will see how this works when we begin to do our calculations.

You will now have three internal totals to add: second call position, finish position, and class (plus or minus). You can easily add them laterally across your Racing Form, and when you have this total, you are ready to do the final long division calculation to obtain the actual Performance Class Rating.

With your pocket calculator, you will divide the number of total horses by the combined total of the three class performance figures, i.e., the total of second call positions, finish positions, and class points. The resulting figure is the Performance Class Rating. Let's assume you are dividing 89 by 62. The calculator shows this number: 1.4354838. We are only interested in the number to the left of the decimal and the two numbers to the right of the decimal. If the extended numbers are greater than one half, we would record the result as 1.44 as above. You will then find it convenient to drop the decimal and write the horse's PCR as simply 144.

To demonstrate how quickly and easily this works, we shall now go through the exercise on past performances of a few horses. Any horse in any race will do, because the process works on all races at all tracks at any time.

From an old back issue of the Daily Racing Form, California edition, the seventh race at Hollywood Park on December 5, 1985, provides a good example to show how we develop the PCR for those horses under review. The race was a six furlong claiming event with a claiming price of $32,000. For the purposes of our calculations, the distance is not important, nor the date of the last race, nor anything else except the figures we shall use. We shall get into handicapping later when we deal with final application of these formidable PCRs.

Both to provide sufficient examples for you to learn from this one race how to do the calculations, and to show you the munificent effectiveness of it, we shall run figures on five horses of the eight entered, leaving out the three longest priced horses except for one in the examples we have provided.

The favorite at a flat 2-1 on the board was Danish.

We first add the total numbers in the final column of the past performances to the far right, which shows the number of horses competing in each race, which gives us a total of 89. We find a convenient blank space near the top of the p.p., which could be almost any place, but here we can do it just under the $32,000 claiming price where we can run our entire line of figures, and start there by enter-

```
Danish                               Ro. f. 3, by Bold 'n Rulling—Kamarish, by Silver Shark
                                     Br.—The Hat Ranch West (Cal)          1985 21 3 5 2    $53,185
  CASTANON A L                  115  Tr.—Stute Gary             $32,000    1984  5 1 1 0    $16,125
Own.—The Hat Ranch                   Lifetime   26 4 6 2    $69,310
17Nov85-3Hol   6f :22^1 :46 1:11^1ft      2 115  6^7½ 6^4¾ 4^2 2^1      Castanon AL^2 Ⓕ 25000 87-10 Al'sBigTime,Danish,FightirgMriett 6
      17Nov85—Lost whip at 3/16
7Nov85-2SA     6½f:21^4 :45^1 1:17^4ft   3 116  8^11 8^7¾ 7^9¾ 3^4     Castanon AL^7 Ⓕ 32000 77-18 Tammy Lu, Third Marriage, Danish 8
      7Nov85—Very wide stretch
25Oct85-7SA    6f :22 :45^3 1:11^1ft     4½ 116  9^10 7^6 5^8 3^2½      Castanon AL^5 Ⓕ 40000 79-23 Mind Storm, Jigalores, Danish    9
      25Oct85—Steadied start
14Oct85-7SA    6f :21^3 :44^4 1:10^4ft   24 118  12^9½ 11^11 7^3¾ 2^1¼  CastanonAL^11 Ⓕ 32000 83-17 FireMissLeader,Dnish,MindStorm 12
      14Oct85—Very wide into stretch
27Sep85-10Pom  6½f:21^3 :45^1 1:17^2ft   3¾ 117  9^13 8^12 5^6¾ 4^2½   Ortega L E^2  Ⓕ 32000 — —   TrickyTurn,MindStorm,SlfSustinng 9
      27Sep85—Wide late
20Sep85-11Pom  1 1/16:46^2 1:12^2 1:45 ft 10 117 9^9½ 7^10 6^11 6^13   CstAL^6 ⒻⓈC TBAMrn — — Bold Vegas, Fleet Rain, KindaBeau 9
31Aug85-3Dmr   6½f:22^2 :45^4 1:17^4ft   3¾ 116  8^9¾ 8^7¼ 4^2¾ 1^1¼   Stevens G L^3 Ⓕ 32000 87-11 Danish, Ritzy Chick, Clearway   8
      31Aug85—Wide final 3/8
12Aug85-1Dmr   6f :22^2 :46^1 1:11 ft    5½ 118  8^6½ 8^8¼ 7^7¼ 4^3½   Solis A^8     Ⓕ 25000 79-17 RitzyChick,KindOfMgic,GoodStyle 10
      12Aug85—Broke slowly; lugged out backstretch, wide final 3/8
26Jly85-1Dmr   6f :21^4 :45^2 1:10 ft    3½ 118  10^13 9^14 8^14 6^12  Castaneda M^9 Ⓕ 32000 76-13 Spirited Madam,Yampa,StarPirate 10
      26Jly85—Rough trip
12Jly85-3Hol   6f :22^2 :45^4 1:11^2ft    3 115  7^8 7^13 5^6½ 6^5½     Pedroza M A^8 Ⓕ 40000 84-09 MindStorm,CostumeBll,Al'sBigTim 8
      12Jly85—Lugged out drive
  ●Nov 26 Hol 3f sy :36 h      Nov 3 SA 4f ft :47^1 h      Oct 22 SA 5f gd 1:03 h      Oct 6 SA 5f ft 1:00^1 h
```

ing the 89. Because this is the number into which the final total will be divided, it is convenient and practical to separate the numbers by a slash, as we have done here.

The second step is the easy one of adding the number of positions where the horse was running at the second call. As you note, we are not concerned about lengths behind, but only the placement of the horse in the field at the second call. The total here is 79 and when you become familiar with the significance of these totals, you will realize that the favorite is in trouble already. More about that later. Write in the 79 after the slash beyond the 89.

Third step: add the finish positions, where the total is 37, and again, we place this number in the space alongside the 79.

Now we come to our final assessment for class, and here, for consistent useage, we have adopted the practice of when a horse has run at a higher class, we enter the High Class points at the left of the class figure, and when at a lower class, we write the Lower Class points on the right hand side of the class figure.

You will see five races where Danish ran at the same $32,000 claiming race as today, and where no points are awarded. In his last race of Nov. 17, he ran at $25,000, and since this represents the first class level below the $32,000 claiming figure on the southern California circuit, we place "1" on the right hand side for a Lower Class point. On Oct. 25, Danish ran for $40,000, which is the class level immediately higher than $32,000, and thus we write a "1" on the left hand side of the class figure for a Higher Class point. On Sept. 20, Danish ran at Pomona in a state-bred named stakes. Southern California players know that Pomona is a minor track, but here we make our first comparison judgment and decide that a state-bred named stakes race is at least at the next higher class level above a $32,000 claiming race on the major circuit, and accordingly, we place "1" to the left.

On Aug. 25 at Del Mar, there was a $25,000 claiming race, one level below, and on July 12 at Hollywood, a $40,000 claimer, the next highest, where we place a "1" on the higher side. We thus have three points for higher class and two points for lower class, leaving a total of 1 Higher Class point. Because we subtract higher class points, we enter -1 alongside the 79 and the 37, which, when added together, come out like this, $79 + 37 + -1 = 115$. We can separate this calculation by another slash, because the three internal numbers have substantial significance later on which we will use.

We can now divide the total number of horses, which is 89, by 115, (or, stating it the other way around if you wish, 115 divided into 89). Our calculator quickly reads out 0.773913. We are only concerned about the first number to the left of the decimal and the two numbers to the right. We now have .77, or just plain 77. As you will later learn, such a low number is almost always a formula for disaster, and you can quickly realize that here is a 2-1 favorite that has practically no chance of winning, unless all the other horses are also similarly rated.

You should also be reminded again that in these ratings, we are not separating distances. While today's race is a sprint at six furlongs, and Danish ran once, on Sept. 20, at a mile and a sixteenth, we are concerned about competitive performances in these ratings, and we use the second call of every race, no matter what the distance.

To complete the process, my own practice is to write on a separate comparison sheet, or in my workbook or notebook for the day, the name of each horse and the numbers thereafter, which will be used in many later ways, as you shall see. Our PCR line for Danish now looks like this:

Danish 89 / 79 37 -1 / 115 = 77

Let's try the second choice in the betting, which is Al's Big Time, at 5-2 on the board.

As usual, we again start with the numbers at the end of each racing line, which show the number of horses in the race. We add up 86 and find a convenient space for entering our numbers above the $32,000 figure this time. The second call total is 40 and the finish total

```
Al's Big Time                    B. f. 3, by O Big Al—Time Rolls By, by Time Tested
 VALENZUELA P A          115    Br.—Ross A (Cal)                        1985 18 3 3 1   $47,950
Own.—Ross A or Mildred          Tr.—Manzi Joseph           $32,000      1984  4 1 1 1   $13,700
                                Lifetime  22 4 4 2  $61,650              Turf 1 0 0 0
17Nov85-3Hol  6f :22^1 :46 1:11^1ft      6¼ 115 4^2 3^2 1^hd 1^1   ValenzuelPA^4 Ⓕ 25000 88-10 Al'sBigTime,Danish,FightirgMriett 6
 7Nov85-2SA  6½f :21^4 :45^1 1:17^4ft     3 117 3^3 3^2 56½ 6^7    Pincay L Jr^6 Ⓕ 32000 74-18 Tammy Lu, Third Marriage, Danish 8
25Oct85-7SA   6f :22 :45^3 1:11^1ft      6¼ 115 43½ 4^4 4^5 4^3    ValenzuelPA^7 Ⓕ 35000 79-23 Mind Storm, Jigalores, Danish     9
14Oct85-7SA   6f :21^3 :44^4 1:10^4ft    3¾ 116 95¾ 86¾ 62¾ 42¼    ValenzuelPA^3 Ⓕ 32000 82-17 FireMissLeader,Dnish,MindStorm  12
     14Oct85—Fanned wide into stretch
 5Sep85-5Dmr  1 :46 1:10^4 1:36^1ft       7 116 2^1 2^3 3^6 46¾    ValenzuelPA^5 Ⓕ 40000 80-15 I'm Sizzling,DonATop,Neumie'sGirl 9
19Aug85-3Dmr  6f :22^1 :45^2 1:09^4ft  *6-5 116 4^3 21½ 22½ 23½    ValenzuelPA^5 Ⓕ 35000 85-10 Yampa, Al's Big Time, Mind Storm 8
 5Aug85-3Dmr  6f :22^1 :45^4 1:11 ft      8 116 75¾ 86¾ 5^5 5^3    Hawley S^4    Ⓕ 40000 80-16 TmmyLu,SpiritedMdm,CountOnLyn 8
     5Aug85—Clipped heels, bobbled start
12Jly85-3Hol  6f :22^2 :45^4 1:11^2ft    6¼ 115 66½ 34½ 33½ 32¾    Hawley S^2    Ⓕ 40000 87-09 MindStorm,CostumeBll,Al'sBigTim 8
26Jun85-4Hol  6f :22^3 :46^2 1:12^1ft     3 115 54½ 43½ 41¼ 2^1    Hawley S^1    Ⓕ 40000 85-08 CostumeBelle,Al'sBigTime,Nit'sJwl 7
 6Jun85-6Hol  1 :45^2 1:10^3 1:35^4ft    7¾ 115 31½ 3^1 4^3 4^7    Hawley S^8    Ⓕ 40000 87-05 Clearway, I'm Sizzling, Iva's Rich 11
   Nov 28 Hol 4f ft :49^1 h      Nov 3 SA 4f ft :46^2 h      Oct 11 SA 4f ft :47^2 h      Oct 5 SA 5f ft :59^1 h
```

is 35, and we write these numbers in after our slash mark following the number 86.

We are now ready for the class calculation. The last race at $25,000 is again at the next lower level, and we enter "1" alongside the class figure. This is easy enough, but for the Oct. 25 race at $35,000, we are required to apply some handicapping knowledge. The conditions of our race show $32,000 as the top claiming price, at 121 pounds, with a claiming price reduction to $25,000 with only one pound off. No trainer was willing to lower the claiming price for only one pound off in a sprint, and every horse ran for $32,000. But the point is that $32,000 was the exact top price in this race.

When we see the $35,000 claiming price for Oct. 25, this is obviously higher, but not much. We don't know the conditions of the Oct. 25 race at Santa Anita without a Racing Form for that occasion, but we really don't need it. We may readily recognize that the race was very likely one for a $40,000 tag, with lower prices for weight off, and thus Al's Big Time was most likely running in a $40,000 claiming race. But whatever, since $32,000 is the absolute high for today's race, we may resolve our doubts and award "1" on the left hand side as a Higher Class point. We shall do the same thing for the Aug. 19 race at Del Mar, recognizing that we may be wrong there, and that the Del Mar race could be for a top figure of $35,000. But we can live within these parameters. The $40,000 claiming races shown all warrant "1" for higher class and we wind up with 7 points on this side against one Lower Class point. This gives us a net of 6 Higher Class points, to be entered as a minus six after our other additions.

We now add the numbers between the slashes, 40+35+ −6, and

we come up with 69. We next go to the calculator, divide 86 by 69 and read the screen at 1.2463768, an easy 1.25, or 125. Our line reads like this:

Al's Big Time: 86 / 40 35 −6 / 69= 125

You should be readily getting the hang of it by now. The third betting favorite is Pauline Revered, showing on the board at 7-2.

Pauline Revered

SOLIS A   **118**

Own.—Belles H

Ch. f. 3, by Unconscious—Ms Canyon, by Dusty Canyon
Br.—Miller & Belles (Ky)   1985 8 1 0 1 $10,775
Tr.—Manzi Joseph $32,000   1984 0 M 0 0

Lifetime   8   1   0   1 $10,775

8Nov85-9SA	1	:464 1:113 1:371ft	2½ 116	2hd 2hd 2½	76¾	ValenzuelPA4 ⓕ 40000	75-13 Pet Bird, Jigalores, Ed's Bold Lady 8
19Oct85-3SA	6f :22 :451 1:101ft	3 118	3nk 12½ 17	19	VlenzuelPA6 ⓜM32000	87-13 PulineRevered,PrincessLrk,Cutnss 12
29Aug85-2Dmr	6f :221 :453 1:112ft	*2½ 116	2hd 1hd 21	57¾	McCrrnCJ11 ⓜM32000	73-17 Hydro Jet, Revista, Riviera Racer 11
16Aug85-4Dmr	6½f :221 :454 1:182ft	2½ 117	2hd 11 14	31½	McCrrnCJ11 ⓜM32000	83-12 SmnthSue,SweetDeeDe,PulinRvrd 12
29Jly85-6Dmr	6f :221 :454 1:113ft	9 116	1hd 2hd 813 915½		McCrronCJ2 ⓜM50000	65-17 FightingMriett,LorOfZorro,Chrysili 9
18Jly85-6Hol	6f :223 :46 1:11 ft	*3-2 115	3nk 21½ 35½ 48½		McCrronCJ5 ⓜM50000	84-11 MontiLynn,Chrysili,FightingMriett 12
9Mar85-3SA	6f :213 :443 1:094ft	12 117	74½ 78½ 813 1017½		Hawley S6 ⓜMdn	72-14 MyVrgnRl,GrbYorSocks,DsrtSnds 11
18Feb85-6SA	7f :224 :453 1:244ft	6½ 117	107 107½ 89 89½		Pincay L Jr6 ⓜMdn	67-18 Rose Cream,SoftDawn,SereneFire 11

18Feb85—Took up sharply at 3/4

Nov 29 Hol 5f sy 1:02² h   Nov 23 Hol 4f ft :464 h   Nov 17 Hol 6f ft 1:13³ h   Nov 4 SA 4f ft :463 h

While Pauline Revered shows only 8 races in her past performances, since this is her total number of efforts, compared to the 10 races shown for Al's Big Time, we see that the total number of horses adds to the same 86 that we found for Al's Big Time. The second call total, however, is down to 26, while the finish total comes to 47. For our class calculation, we have some new problems.

For the last race for $40,000, we easily write "1" to the left of the class figure. Below that we are confronted with maiden races. Later on, when we discuss class evaluation in greater detail, I will try to provide guidelines for rating maidens, as well as other races, but here, I will consider that maiden claimers for $32,000 are one level below winners for $32,000. One might argue that a maiden claimer for the same claiming price should be at least two levels below winners for $32,000, and keen students of Southern California class might know one way or the other. But here, I will use the next lower level for our purposes. Thus, we have five races for $32,000 maiden claiming, all where we award "1" Lower Class point.

Pauline Revered's first two races were straight maiden. Class at this point is extremely difficult to judge, for one hardly knows how these untested nonwinners will turn out until they develop a more complete history. For our purposes here, we will call a straight maiden equivalent to claiming $32,000 for winners and award no points either way. We now have 1 Higher Class and 5 Lower Class points, or a net of 4 Lower Class, which requires us to write in a +4 above. Our total now is 26 + 47 + +4=77. We divide 86 by 77 and read 1.12, or 112. We no longer need to show all the extended numbers. Here is the line on Pauline Revered: 86 / 26 47 +4 / 77 = 112.

Now, when we compare the numbers on Al's Big Time with those of Pauline Revered, we can make a powerful point on class. With no class calculations, relying only on the two totals of second call and finish, Al's Big Time should show 40 and 35 for a total of 75. We would then divide 86 by 75 and Al would have a performance rating (without class) of 115. With Pauline Revered, excluding the class rating, the internal numbers would be 26 and 47, or a total of 63. We would divide 86 by 63 and come up with a bare unadjusted performance rating of 137. Pauline with 137 would thus be higher rated than Al at 115 without the class rating formula.

Factoring class figures into the calculation, which is an absolutely essential part of the process, and one of the reasons why it works as it does, we find that Al's Big Time carries a higher PCR than Pauline Revered, attributable to his races at a higher class level. Of course, as you will find, these essential class ratings may not be sufficient to give a higher class horse a higher rating than a cheaper horse who may have far more impressive internal figures. But again, that is one of the strengths of the method.

Let us do two more horses and then see what happened in this particular race. The highest rated horse in the field is easily Committee Girl, who went off at the surprising odds of 9-1.

In reviewing her six listed races, we see the most recent one on Oct. 31 at Santa Anita showing the filly as "Eased." When a horse is eased, or pulled up, or the jockey fell, the race itself is not a fair comparison effort. So we strike it out, and draw a line all across, using none of the numbers. Consequently, we add the totals for only

Committee Girl

WALKER R		115	B. f. 3, by House Committee—Gifted Girl, by Golden Eagle II		
Own.—Santero M D			Br.—Santero M D (Cal)	1985 6 1 2 0	$12,550
			Tr.—Bellasis Richard L $32,000	1984 0 M 0 0	
			Lifetime 6 1 2 0 $12,550		

31Oct85-7SA 6½f :22 :45² 1:16³ft 11 114 3½ 3½ 7¹⁴ — Hawley S⁷ ⓐAw25000 — — Miss O.B.E,FireMissLeader,Zythum 7
　31Oct85—Eased
20Oct85-8SA 6f :21⁴ :45 1:10³ft 7½ 114 2½ 2¹ 2³ 66½ Hawley S⁹ ⓐAw24000 79-17 NotAllFoolish,DrmFthr,MyVirginiRl 9
23Mar85-4SA 6½f :21³ :44⁴ 1:16²ft 2½ 118 1hd 1½ 2hd 54½ McHargueDG⁵ ⓒ 50000 79-14 Al'sBigTime,CountOwlyn,SwtPtuni 7
6Mar85-7SA 6½f :21³ :45 1:17³ft 4 120 1½ 1½ 1³ 2² McHrDG⁶ ⓒⓢAw23000 88-19 Nn'sCreer,CommitteeGirl,Pirt'sGlow 9
16Feb85-4SA 6f :21² :44² 1:10³ft 9 114⁵ 2hd 1½ 12½ 2nk DmngRE² ⓒⓢAw26000 85-16 Danuta, Committee Girl, Jingle 8
3Feb85-8AC 6f :22⁴ :46¹ 1:11²sy ⁴1 118 1½ 11½ 1⁶ 112 Espindola MA⁴ ⓒMdn 82-25 CommittGirl,SouthrnFir,Shirl'sGrl 11
Dec 1 Hol 5f sy :59³ h　　Nov 28 Hol 3f ft :35⁴ h　　Nov 24 Hol 5f ft 1:00⁴ h　　Nov 18 Hol 3f ft :35² h

five races and get 44. The second call total is the very low number of 6, and the finish total is 17.

When we come to class, we see excellent numbers. The Oct. 20 allowance race is more than one level about a $32,000 claimer and thus gets 2 points. Next, we look at the $50,000 claimer. Since we have determined that a $40,000 claimer is the next level of competition above $32,000, this means that a $50,000 claiming race is more than one level above the $32,000 event, and consequently, we again count up 2 Higher Class points. Equating the maiden race as even, we have four higher class races for 8 points. The line comes out this way: 44 / 6 + 17 + −8 / 15 = 293. This is an extremely high figure.

The next horse, Precious Martini, ran a dismal last at 17-1, but we wanted to run through her figures to show how we do class evaluations outside the southern California circuit.

Precious Martini

FERNANDEZ A L		115	Bk. b. or br. f. 3, by Right Cross—Julie's Martini, by Third Martini		
Own.—Watkins-Weiss-et al			Br.—McKahan R B (Cal)	1985 11 3 2 1	$22,605
			Tr.—Taliaferro Charles L $32,000	1984 0 M 0 0	
			Lifetime 11 3 2 1 $22,605		

15Nov85-5Hol 6f :22² :45⁴ 1:11²ft 9 115 2hd 2hd 66½ 913½ FernandezAL⁶ ⓒ 40000 74-22 Quil'sLovebug,TmmyLu,LorOfZorro 9
　15Nov85—Lugged out
6Oct85-9Cby 5f :22 :45³ :58¹ft 3½ 114 53½ 54½ 56 24½ Hansen RD² Hennepin 99-13 NobleScrtry,PrciousMrtini,SpdyPln 5
28Sep85-4Cby 6f :22¹ :45¹ 1:10³ft 4-5 112 12 12½ 13 1⁴ FernandezAL³ ⓒ 22500 95-08 PrcosMrtn,LmttdLss,Sh'sALckyPly 6
15Sep85-5Cby 6f :21⁴ :44² 1:11¹ft 2 114 11½ 12 12 13½ FernandezAL⁴ ⓒ 20000 92-11 PrcousMrtn,Sh'sALckyPly,LttlCool 6
2Sep85-2Cby 6f :22 :44⁴ 1:11¹gd 5 114 1¹ 11½ 11½ 31½ FernaandezAL³ ⓒ 25000 90-04 OnClirDy,Drconic'sMrk,PrcousMrtn 7
14Aug85-1Cby 6f :23² :46³ 1:13 ft ⁴2 113 12 12 12 21½ Fernandez Al⁹ ⓒ 28000 81-16 OnaClaireDy,PreciousMrtini,Simliot 8
27Jly85-9Cby 6f :21³ :44³ 1:11²ft 10 113 11 13 21½ 67½ FernndzAl⁸ ⓒAw11000 — — LilPreppy,HoistHerFlag,Adaplable 10
30Jun85-6Cby 5½f :22⁴ :46² 1:05²ft 3½ 117 43½ 66½ 81⁴ 816½ Fernandez A⁷ ⓒSplW — — SmoothRb,Tohppyfrwrds,PrtasD'Or 8
10May85-4Hol 6f :22² :45³ 1:10³ft ⁴3 115 11½ 1⁴ 16 19½ Sibille R³ ⓒⓢM32000 94-08 PrcsMrtn,EglsGldnLdy,Mm'sTwst 12
28Feb85-3SA 6f :22 :45³ 1:12¹ft 2½ 117 1hd 2hd 2² 54½ Lauzon JM¹² ⓒM32000 73-17 SearchForHeaven,LaMurd,DrkLilc 12
Nov 26 Hol 5f sy 1:01² h　　Nov 18 Hol 5f ft 1:03¹ h

Total horses were 83, the second call total the very good 21, and the finish total was 38. We have the makings of a reasonably high rating. The races at Santa Anita and Hollywood are easily rated for class, but the "Cby" becomes something quite different. "Cby" is Canterbury Downs, the reasonably new Minnesota track, fairly unfamiliar to the mass of racing fans in other areas of the country. Where we have an unfamiliar track, we again must use track comparisons, claiming prices, and an awareness that named stakes races at second or third tier tracks do not always equate with high priced claiming races in New York and southern California.

The Oct. 5 race was a named stakes at Canterbury, and while we have no more knowledge about the race than what is shown here, we shall put it·at one higher class level than a $32,000 claimer in southern California. We really don't know whether this is accurate or not, but we have to make some decision. The four claiming races are easy, with 2 Lower Class points awarded for each. We will have awarded 1 Higher Class point for the $40,000 claiming race at Holly-wood. The allowance race and the Special Weight are not too familiar, either, but they are very likely one level below the $32,000 claiming race for winners at Hollywood. Thus, we score another 1 Lower Class point for each, and extend this likewise to the $32,000 maiden claim-ing events. This brings us down to the maiden claiming races at Hollywood and Santa Anita, where we award one lower class point each. We now have 2 Higher Class points against 12 Lower Class points, leaving us with a net of 10 Lower Class Points. We place the +10 figure alongside the other numbers. We now have 83 / 21 + 32 + +10 / 69 = 120, after our division on the calculator.

Let's now place all five horses alongside and see what we have for this race. As we do this, we must pause for another reminder on an absolutely vital point. These are PCR ratings only. They are merely one-half of the total rating process. When we extend our work sheet lines for a total evaluation of a horse, we will add the necessary form ratings that are the second half of what we must always do.

Danish	89/	79	37	–	1/	115	=	77
Al's Big Time	86/	40	35	–	6/	69	=	125
Pauline Revered	86/	26	47	+	4/	77	=	112
Committee Girl	44/	6	17	–	8/	15	=	293
Precious Martini	83/	21	38	+10/		69	=	120

Before we show you the result of the race, the outcome of which may becoming more apparent to you by now, it is important to look at what comparing these horses, line by line, and number by number, is able to tell us. The first column, representing the total number of horses, tells us at a glance that Committee Girl is lightly raced in comparison with the others, having competed in races involving only 44 horses as compared to the 83 to 89 of the others. But, as we have earlier stated, five races are enough for the use of the PCR rating.

Next, the second column of numbers, representing the second call of all races, gives us a valuable piece of important information to compare early speed. In a six furlong sprint race, we pointed out in *How Will Your Horse Run Today?* that an animal whose total lengths behind at the first call exceeded 60 for 10 races was almost certain to lose. Danish shows 97+ total lengths behind at the first call under that standard. Here, using the second call, however, ignoring lengths behind and totalling only horses, the number is still astronomically high, telling us at a glance that Danish has very little chance if there is any other early speed in the race.

We can see, again at a glance, that the early speed factor is very good for Committee Girl and respectable for the other horses we have studied.

The third column of numbers, representing the finish position, shows the strength of a horse in closing to the finish, as compared to early speed. Danish, with 37 in this column as compared to the 79 for the second call, is obviously a strong closer. Any comparison where the finish total is less than the second call total indicates that a horse likes to close in a race. Al's Big Time, with a 35 total which is less than the 40 at the second call, runs more evenly with a slight edge to closing. The other three, showing greater totals in the finish column than in the second call column, are not closers, and thus, rely far more on early speed.

The third column, representing class ratings, provides a quick comparison of class for the horses entered. Larger minus totals represents greater class; higher plus totals represents lower class. In assessing these figures, we must also take into account the number of races a horse has run. Accordingly, the minus 8 for Committee Girl, acquired in only five races, shows that she has an enormously higher class rating than her competitors. Precious Martini and Pauline Revered show lower class ratings.

Then, why did the crowd make the slow starting Danish such a favorite and allow Committee Girl to go off at an incredible 9-1? Perhaps the fact that Committee Girl had not run since Oct. 31 when she was eased was the factor that caused the ordinarily sharp southern California players to discount her chances. But when you see that she worked five furlongs on Dec. 1 at :59.3 at the end of three other good works in close succession, you have a shouting indication of a horse back in good form. Again, we must remind you that our research in *How Will Your Horse Run Today?*, which will be of great use to us in this book, revealed that a very fast five furlong workout before a race was a sure sign of fitness.

Anyway, look at the result chart.

SEVENTH RACE
Hollywood
DECEMBER 5, 1985

6 FURLONGS. (1.08⅘) CLAIMING. Purse $15,000. Fillies. 3-year-olds. Weight, 121 lbs. Non-winners of two races since September 15 allowed 3 lbs.; a race since then, 6 lbs. Claiming price $32,000; if for $28,000 allowed 1 lb. (Races when entered for $25,000 or less not considered.)

Value of race $15,000; value to winner $8,250; second $3,000; third $2,250; fourth $1,125; fifth $375. Mutuel pool $144,715. Exacta Pool $188,037.

Last Raced	Horse	Eqt.	A.	Wt	PP	St	¼	½	Str	Fin	Jockey	Cl'g Pr	Odds $1
31Oct85 7SA	Committee Girl		3	115	3	3	1 1½	1 hd	2 1½	1½	Walker R	32000	9.00
17Nov85 3Hol2	Danish		3	115	1	8	8	8	5 1½	2½	Castanon A L	32000	2.00
5Aug85 3Dmr7	Search For Heaven	b	3	115	2	7	7 3	5 1½	3 1½	3½	McCarron C J	32000	9.30
17Nov85 3Hol1	Al's Big Time	b	3	115	5	5	5 4	3 3	1 hd	4 5	Valenzuela P A	32000	2.50
16Nov85 4Hol3	J. D. Canyon	b	3	115	6	6	6½	7 hd	7 3	5¾	Hernandez R	32000	11.50
15Nov85 5Hol7	Chrysilia	b	3	118	8	1	3½	4½	6 1	6 1¾	Kaenel J L	32000	43.50
8Nov85 9SA7	Pauline Revered		3	118	4	4	4 hd	2 hd	4 hd	7 4½	Solis A	32000	3.50
15Nov85 5Hol9	Precious Martini	b	3	115	7	2	2½	6 hd	8	8	Fernandez A L -	32000	17.50

OFF AT 4:29. Start good. Won driving. Time, :22⅕, :45⅗, :58, 1:11 Track fast.

$2 Mutuel Prices:				
	3-COMMITTEE GIRL	20.00	8.60	5.00
	1-DANISH		4.20	2.80
	2-SEARCH FOR HEAVEN			4.40

$5 EXACTA 3-1 PAID $182.00.

Committee Girl used her early speed to get out in front, battle with Al's Big Time in the stretch, and hold on nicely to finish ahead of the fast closing Danish and return an even $20 up front to win. Danish, as our line of figures showed, was decidedly a closer, and was last by 5 lengths at the second call, somewhat nearer than we would have thought. But closers seldom win sprint races on normal tracks against strong early speed horses.

Committee Girl was easily an outstanding play. If you think we have just singled out this race merely to show off the method, just stay around for a while. You will see this kind of outcome repeated over and over again. And over and over again, we continue to say. And, of course, this race does illustrate the power of this totally new rating method of Performance Class Rating. But this is how it works so often, as you will find. When we combine it with the invaluable handicapping factor of form in the manner we intend to show you hereinafter, and use it at the track in the hard world of practicality, we will let results speak for themselves.

Before dealing with other major factors which we must take into account, we shall next turn to an explanation of why this method, compared to other methods of rating contenders, carries with it such exciting effectiveness, and how it can best be used.

3 How and Why PCR Works as a Rating Method

We have already stated that our new PCR ratings are but one part of the thoroughbred handicapping process, and standing alone without the vital other parts, would not be enough to carry you to total victory at the track. In fact, as you will discover, our new last race ability times are the single most formidable part of the overall rating method.

With that concession, important questions immediately arise. Is this new method of rating horses worth using at all? Should we go so far as to scrap what we have been doing in the past and bring in something entirely different? Is it practical within the time frame in which all handicappers must labor, in view of what it requires us to do?

Or, as some of you will surely say, "Running all these numbers is too much work. Who needs it? The hell with it."

Accordingly, many experienced handicappers, who have struggled for years with speed figures, track variants, velocity, ability times, innumerable kinds of point ratings, and the like, may have an immediate reaction that this addition and division is all too simple and means so little that it won't work at all. Dismiss it as another fantasy on how to rate the horses, and go on to something more substantial. Besides, what is wrong with what we have been doing all these years? Perhaps nothing, but if we can increase our handicapping skills, and wind up with selecting more winners at higher prices, then let us do it.

Why is this concept of Performance Class Ratings a sound enough method for rating thoroughbreds so as to make it important that we change what we have been doing in the past and use it as one of our major rating methods? How can it be superior to tried and true methods of adjusted speed and adjusted variants and other methods of measuring speed to establish a horse's possibility of winning today's race? Again, you will ask the question over and over again, as you ought to do, is it worth the effort of adding columns of figures, establishing totals, and pumping numbers into a calculator while engaging in a grammar school process of long division?

The fundamental strength of this new process is based upon this theory: how a horse runs against his competitors at comparable class levels is as accurate a test of his ability as you are likely to find. It is the competition over a representative series of races that counts, regardless of distance or surface, and regardless of all the other countless intervening circumstances that make horseracing such a volatile, unpredictable adventure.

The formula to make the theory work comes from a percentage performance based upon class of competition. Rating a horse in this fashion has never been seriously attempted before. One of its essential keys is the use of the total number of horses in listed races as a basis for comparison. When this base is found, the other totals are fed into it by the process of long division, which essentially provides us with the percentage figure that we can use, one horse against the other.

Use of the finish position, since it is the one from whence the money comes, is too obviously necessary to be disputed. But why use the second call position as an essential element in the ratings and even go so far as to give it equal weight to the finish?

We can begin an answer to this question by stating that if the finish position were used by itself, you would be leaving out every consideration in a race except how horses finished. It would be leaving out internal performance, such as early speed, which so often affects the outcome of a race. It is this "affecting the outcome of a race" that cannot be ignored.

We have tested and experimented over and over again, and it has become inescapable that one may not rely exclusively upon finish position, but that, somehow, elements that "affect the outcome of the race" must be factored into any formula that has a chance to be effective over a long run. The element we have chosen here is a comparison of performance taking into account the pace of the race, which is, for our purposes, best represented by the second call position.

The second call establishes both a measure of early speed and an ability to be competitive against the pressures of a race. In sprints, early speed has been shown by every scholar of handicapping to be vitally important. Most of us thus far have usually relied on the time shown at the second call in the running line to determine true early speed. Time is an indicator of early speed all right, as it is affected by track surface and its variant, by the pace at which leaders choose to run, by tactics and strategy, and by numerous other factors that influence horse races. But position, unvarnished by these other factors, is clean and certain. A horse running first or second, no matter what the clock may show, is evidencing some early speed as well as an ability to be out there ahead of his rivals.

In distance races where the second call position is usually shown after horses have run six furlongs, actual running position is equally important. By the time the competitors have run three-quarters of a mile, position has been established, and a horse should by that point be taking measure of his rivals. However, as you shall see later, the second call in distance races, for PCR rating purposes, does not have the same clout as it does in sprint races. But we will take that into account, of course, in our total rating methods.

The importance of internal positions in winning races may be tested in a number of ways. But before proceeding to do this, you may wish to raise the question, if early speed is so important in sprint races, why not use the first call position instead of the second call? When I first began to experiment with these ratings, I did use the first call position, but later testing convinced me that the second call was better, as I will now indicate from the tests I have run.

From past performances and running lines, I began to study winning horses in both sprint races and route races, marking the diversion with the usual line of one mile or longer for routes. After a few hundred were tabulated, the patterns became clear.

In sprint races of 6½ furlongs and less, I found that winning horses ran either first, second, or third at the second call in their last race 79% of the time, almost four times out of five. Closing horses who were not among the first three thus managed to win only 21% of these races. On the other hand, using the first call as an indicator, for purposes of our comparison for effectiveness, horses running first, second, or third won only 67% of the races. Horses farther behind at the first call thus had a better chance of winning than horses farther behind at the second call. Running position at the second call was clearly superior over the first call as a potential indicator of final outcome. And when a winning horse is within the first three leaders at the second call almost four times out of a five, then this internal figure becomes of first rate importance.

This "up close" formulation in distance races, while not as effective as in shorter races, still is significant enough to require us to pay considerable attention. In races of more than one mile, the winning horses were running either first, second, or third at the second call of their last race 75% of the time, three out of four. This is somewhat different from running style as revealed in the lines, because in the actual winning race, the victor managed to be up nearer the lead than in losing efforts. You will see how this distinction works in the many examples that are set forth in this book.

At 7f and one mile there were far fewer races to study, but in the comparison period, there was not enough evidence to suggest that any substantial changes were needed. Reliance on the second call still stands.

In turf races of a mile or more, early running position was shown to be not nearly so important. Only 61% of the winners were among the three leaders at the second call, and back at the first call, only 49% of winners were first, second, or third.

With these realities before us, none of which should be surprising to any seasoned handicapper, the next question is whether we should give equal credit to second call positions with that of finish positions. For example, we might give only 80% credit to these positions in sprint races and 75% credit in distance races. And even less credit in turf races.

For a time, I experimented with devaluating the second call position in distance races as compared to the finish position. This involves adopting a formula and doing considerably more calculating. I then compared results with races where full credit was given. Only occasionally was a final PCR changed enough to affect the outcome of a race. I then concluded that the time and effort in the extra calculations, making the process more complicated, could be waived in favor of simplicity and especially the saving of much-needed time. In other words, while there was some difference, I concluded it wasn't worth the effort, especially in view of other adjustments that we will be using, which we will discuss later in this work.

Therefore, we fixed on the formula in the method shown in the previous chapter. Second call positions do exert a powerful influence on the outcome of races, and when used with the finish position, affected by the class of the race, we have a rating method that is highly successful for our purposes.

And, as we have tried to state earlier, the use of class ratings is the glue that makes it work, more so in distance races than in sprints, but there, also, it has its worth. A cheap horse may slaughter his opposition, and turn out a string of low figures for both second call and finish positions. But when his class rating is added, he will ordinarily be brought back down with his competitors in today's race.

In our ratings for class, how did we come up with 1, 2, and 3 points, both higher and lower? These numbers also came out of a process of experimentation and careful evaluation. When we began running tests with this method, we used 2 points for all class differences, regardless of the span. While this was workable in a rough way, its deficiencies soon became apparent. A horse in today's cheap $5,000 claiming race who previously ran for a $6,500 tag was competing against only marginally better horses. But back in his past performances, some months previously, he may have been running for $18,000, where his rivals were far superior to those who are entered into today's rock bottom affair. Thus, there was a need to separate the points, and the use of 1 was adopted for the next immediate level, higher or lower.

And by the same token, when a horse has run at a vastly different price, higher or lower, the constant use of a common 2 is not enough to reflect the difference, so a further adjustment had to be made, and 3 was selected.

One may ask, why not use 4 points or 5 or 6?

The answer to that question fits easily within the confines of our numbers. The common denominator is the number of horses entered. It cannot cover more than 10 races, since that is the maximum shown in any past performances. The Daily Racing Form even shows only eight races at some lesser tracks, and here, we must make do with what we have. When we deal with 10 races, the total number of horses entered is usually under or around 100, and even if there were an average of 12 horses in every race (which sometimes occurs), the number would top out at around 120. Accordingly, internal class numbers that grow too large in comparison would begin to have an inordinate effect.

This is particularly so since we are comparing positions in a race which can never exceed the number of horses running. Even if our entry was last at both second call and the finish in every race, the number could not exceed twice the number of horses running. Any additional numbers, such as those for class, must fit somewhere within in a relative fashion. The higher the class number, the more influence on the final outcome, and once again, we strive for a measured relativity which can be relied on. The 1, 2, 3 formula thus appears as soundly comparative as we can get.

In this light, you will see that when a higher class horse sometimes gets 20 points deducted internally for class that this has an enormous effect on the final figure. And likewise, when points are added in any meaningful number, the result is altered downward. You saw in the last chapter how only a few class points raised the PCR of Al's Big Time above that of Pauline Revered.

Thus, the more you evaluate these class points, the more apparent it becomes that the figure of 2, which is most common, is quite effective, tempered by the 1's and 3's that must also be used.

In view of the reliance on finish positions, one may ask whether this entire method is no more than a revised kind of consistency ratings? Consistency became a much publicized staple handicapping factor many years ago when it was first popularized by Robert Saunders Dowst. But it should be evident by now that the PCRs we use here go far beyond the old consistency ratings of the past. Consistency, as it has been used by handicappers for many years, usually related to how many times a horse ran first, second, or third in the number of races he had run.

Here, we depart from "number of races" run to "number of horses in competition." There is a vast difference. For example, a horse may have a good number of in the money finishes in races where there are short fields. An animal that finishes third in a 6-horse field has beaten only three other horses, and may have run poorly in the process. A horse that finishes third in a 12-horse field has come in ahead of 9 rivals, and must have done reasonably well to have accomplished this. In our method of rating, the number "3" in the finish position therefore takes on far more significance when it is compared to the "12" in the field than when it is compared with "6" in a field.

In addition, when we end up with a rating, we are able to know how many horses an animal surpassed at an internal point in a race, the second call, as well as many horses he defeated at the end of the race, weighted against the total number of his competitors. If he ran at higher class than today's race, he may be able to defeat more of

them at today's lower class than in the previous race where his competition was more severe. And likewise on the lower class side, he
may find it harder today to outrace superior animals. The old consistency ratings did not deal with class, which was often treated in
the form of average earnings, or earnings based upon size of purses.
One aberrant high-priced result could distort the entire process.

With class factored in, the final number in the PCR, whether it be
1.27 or 127, or .98 or 98, represents a kind of average of performance,
just as a major league baseball player compiles a batting average over
a span of time as a percentage of his ability to produce. In some instances, we all know that a .350 hitter may strike out and a .240 hitter may wallop a drive off the wall, as individual human performances vary just as individual horse performances vary. Performance
Class Ratings tend to level off at comparable figures for each class
of race, just as a player's batting average in the major leagues of .282
may be a superior performance to his average of .341 made in a Class
AAA minor league. For example, a horse in a $5,000 claiming race
may have a PCR of 168 while on the same card, you may find horses
in the featured stakes race with PCRs of 108. The higher number in
the lower class would mean no more than that the horse carries a
high rating within the particular class in which he is competing today.

You may be able to think of each horse's PCR then as his batting
average for the class in which he competes. Horses with higher
averages tend, on the whole, to defeat horses with lower averages,
just as a team of baseball players with very high batting averages,
such as the famed Yankee Murderers' Row of years gone by, would
ordinarily defeat the weak hitting St. Louis Browns of yore.

What do these ratings mean as compared to other ratings? As
always, I have the utmost respect for those who labor so intensely
and even effectively with adjusted speed ratings. My approach is
always to try to build a better mousetrap, to keep experimenting,
to try to find ways of rating horses in a better, quicker, and more efficient manner.

In that spirit, I took a long critical look at the ability times I had
developed in *Investing at the Race Track*. They, just as adjusted speed
ratings are, represent a sound way of rating a horse. One of the problems I had with my own ability times, and perhaps the major one,
was how to correctly factor in a track variant. In *Investing at the Race
Track*, the solution was to disregard variants altogether and maintain that sound ability times could be extracted from the listed races

where variants had little effect on the measured quotient. This, of course, was not fair to the race where a varying track surface may have had a considerable effect on the times involved, and where a horse had performed extremely well.

After a considerable period of time, I tried to improve upon the no-variant approach by using my own adjusted variants, which had been demonstrated to also carry a good measure of effectiveness. Because I was not a full-time professional handicapper, as most of you are not, I could not compute the daily variants that are used by those who spend all their work time at the track. At the same time, my experience over the years, particularly trying to be, perhaps not always successfully, a scholar of handicapping had led me to considerable doubt about the total reliability of any track variants I have seen. However, even with all the many unknowns that go into them, we are compelled to use them, as we shall see at a later point in this book.

However, one of the advantages of using the PCR method for an overall rating is that we don't care what the variant was at any time over a particular span of races, nor are we concerned with time figures, which also carry their own deficiencies. When a horse performs in any particular race, the same track variant applies to his competitors as well, and the test we use is how well he did against his rivals, slow track, fast track, muddy track, or what have you.

The same is true as to speed, as represented by time. One of the great defects of speed handicapping, where time is used, is that it cannot be accurate enough with sufficient precision for us to totally vest our handicapping fortunes in it alone. This comes about for one great reason. The only true time that can be shown for any horse is when the horse wins a race wire to wire, establishing absolutely correct clock time at each call in the race. The time for each and every other horse that did not win wire to wire is only an estimate, based upon estimated lengths behind, or upon estimated lengths gained from points that are simply not precise.

For example, one writer (supported by a number of others) has argued that the standard measurement of using one length as equivalent to a fifth of a second is grossly erroneous. It is claimed that a length is more equivalent to 1/6 of a second. But even that depends on the segment of race in which the measurement is taken. Horses in sprint races in particular run much faster in the first two furlongs of a race than they do in the last two furlongs. Is the deceleration worth 1/6 of a second per length or even 1/7 of a second? Horses gaining ground are particularly difficult to properly evaluate in terms of time and lengths gained. A gaining horse may be zeroing in on a rival that has begun to creep. What is a length worth then in terms of time? It also has been pointed out that different horses have different measurements. A length for one horse is not the same as a length for another horse. Yet most rating methods still cling to the 1/5 of a second per length formula. When your entire justification for risking your money on one horse as compared to another is based on those slender fifths of seconds, you are wandering in the ozone of the unknown. As my past readers know, and as I will again do in this book, I have tried to take some of all this into account in the adjustments I make for lengths gained.

These problems are not nearly so great when we rely entirely upon positions in a race. It is far easier for the Daily Racing Form's chart caller to identify who is second or third or sixth or eighth in a race with accuracy than it is to determine whether the horse running fourth or sixth at any point of call is five lengths behind or six and a half lengths behind. Thus, we repeat, all length figures are estimates, even to the fractional time allowed for a length. True, position calls may sometimes be erroneous also, such as when two horses noses apart at the second call may be incorrectly slotted for third or fourth positions, but this does not occur very often. These numbers, in the occasional occurrences when they are wrong, would have an influence on the totals. But my point is that, on the whole, running positions are likely to be far more accurate than time represented by lengths behind, lengths gained, and lengths lost as they are shown in the running lines in the Daily Racing Form. And "far more accurate" is something that must be seriously taken into account.

Another substantial problem in rating horses by speed, ability times, or any other method, is the variety of the kinds of races in which they have competed. Distance is our first example. Take a look at Texola Joe, running in the 11th race at Hialeah on January 24, 1987.

This horse has run at six different distances in the ten races shown in his past performances: 6f, 7f, one mile, a mile seventy, a mile sixteenth, and a mile and one-eighth. How do you accurately compare times at one distance with times compiled at an altogether different distance? The added varieties of class in these events, running styles, and the like, as to how they may have influenced time, are all speculative. But somehow, this horse must be rated.

Texola Joe — Ch. c. 4, by Sauce Boat—Lady Bahia, by Royal Note
Own.—Hough S M — $25,000 — Br.—Hamilton & Humphrey Jr (Ky) — Tr.—Hough Stanley M — 120

Lifetime	1987	1	1	0	0	$5,700
19 4 1 4	1986	14	1	1	1	$19,437
$38,437	Turf	4	1	1	0	$15,892

9Jan87- 4Hia	fst	7f	:23	:45⅗	1:23⅖	Clm 20000	10	3	63½	51½	2½	1no	Romero R P	116	8.20	86-20	Texola Joe 116no Katzenjammer1161ItsHardtoBelive116hd	Driving	12
27Dec86- 8Crc	sly	1⅛	:51⅕	1:17	1:56⅖	3↑Clm 25000	1	2	22	21	2½	812	Velez J A Jr	114	4.60	56-27	[D]SprucKing1164TimlssGust1141½PositvInfluncl114½	Tired mid str	8
18Dec86- 4Crc	fst	7f	:23	:47	1:26	3↑Clm 32500	10	2	41½	4¾	55	87½	Velez J A Jr	113	7.50	78-23	Shy Gold 112nk Commander Cal 1151 All Sincerity 114½	Faltered	10
6Dec86- 8Crc	sly	6f	:22	:46	1:13⅗	3↑Clm 30000	1	7	56½	56	21½	52½	Velez J A Jr	115	4.50	80-22	Naughty At Night 116no Commander Cal 1151ShyGold1161½	Tired	10
27Nov86- 7Crc	fst	6f	:22⅖	:45⅘	1:11⅘	3↑Clm 35000	4	3	32½	44	45½	55	Paynter L A5	111	17.20	87-11	Guyana 1131 Hypnotized 121½ Party Breaker 1162	Tired	6
11Oct86- 4Bel	fst	1 1/16	:45⅗	1:10	1:43	Clm 80000	4	6	74¾	914	931	—	Romero R P	114	26.50	— —	Golden Olden 1124¾ Macbest 1161¾ Make A Decision 1181¼	Eased	9
2Oct86- 2Bel	gd	1	[T]:46⅘	1:12⅖	1:39	Clm 95000	5	9	95½	118¼	1023	928¾	Maple E	120	3.70	41-28	Kruckel 1122¼ Mr. Van Dell 113no Arrived On Time 1141¾	Outrun	11
11Jun86- 5Crc	fst	170	:47⅕	1:11⅘	1:43⅘	3↑Alw 14500	1	2	23	26	413	617½	Espinoza J C	111	4.10	73-14	Indio Lobo 1189 Peaceful Arab 120¾ Act Upon 1204½	Faltered	6
1Jun86- 9Crc	fst	7f	:22⅘	:46	1:25⅘	Carry Back	9	7	71½	65½	1116	1216	Espinoza J C	112	13.00	71-18	Kid Colin 116hd Big Jolt 1165 Lucky Rebeau 116hd	Outrun	13
24May86- 9Hia	gd	*1⅛ [T]			1:50⅘	Citation	5	2	25	21½	1hd	43½	Espinoza J C	112	4.00	74-21	Annapolis John 1121 Lyphard Line 122½Dr.DanEyes1171½	Faltered	6

LATEST WORKOUTS ●Jan 22 Hia 4f fst :48 b Jan 17 Hia 4f fst :50 b Jan 6 Hia 5f fst 1:01⅗ b Dec 26 Crc 3f fst :39⅗ b

In all these different distances, however, Texola Joe was forced to be competitive. How well he ran against his rivals at any distance is shown by the positions he was in, both at the second call and the finish. And since the class can be readily calculated, it is not too difficult to obtain a PCR on Texola Joe in which we can place some reliance, in comparison with the rating on each of his opponents.

Variety of tracks, as well as variety of distances, also presents enormous problems in standard handicapping. Winter cards at Hialeah, where horses come from many tracks, are typical. Silver Surfer, entered in the 6th race at Hialeah on January 24, 1987, presents an abundance of tracks.

Silver Surfer — B. h. 6, by Second Bar—Exclusive Lady, by Exclusive Native
Own.—Petelain Stable — Br.—Bryant J C H (Va) — Tr.—Byrne Patrick J — 113

Lifetime	1987	1	0	0	0	$1,150
30 9 5 2	1986	6	0	2	1	$22,514
$247,895	Turf	7	1	2	0	$23,620

9Jan87- 9Hia	yl	*1 1/16 [T]			1:45⅘	Alw 23000	4	4	43	43	31½	42	Romero R P	113	11.30	69-34	Purple Comet 113½ Single Solo 1131 Tonzarun 114½	Weakened	8
16Dec86- 9Crc	fm	*1 1/16 [T]			1:43	3↑Alw 17000	3	6	56½	53½	42½	54	Lester R N	114	6.10	88-12	Plum Wine 1141½ Iroko 1141½ Purple Comet 119¾	Weakened	9
8Nov86- 9Lrl	my	1⅛	:47⅘	1:12⅗	1:51⅗	3↑W Haight H	5	4	64	912	915	925¾	Saumell L	115	7.10	64-25	Sparrowvon117hdAlongCmeJones1094¾WrmSeson1121½	Fin. early	9
20Oct86- 3Bel	fm	1	[T]:47	1:11	1:35⅘	3↑Alw 40000	3	2	22	21	2½	2nk	Migliore R	115	6.10	86-19	My ManJohn115nkSilverSurfer1154¾CornishGemII1157¾	Game try	6
26Mar86- 8Aqu	fst	1⅛	:48⅕	1:12⅕	1:51⅗	Handicap	1	2	53	77½	68	512	Ward W A	113	9.70	65-27	BrodwyTommy112¾[D]ImportntBusiness122nkJudgCost1146½	Tired	7
17Feb86- 8GS	fst	1	:46⅕	1:11⅗	1:37⅗	3↑Carry Bck H	3	6	77½	32	32	33½	Ward W A	113	2.60	84-22	Indian Detail 1121½ Land of Believe1161¾SilverSurfer113½	Rallied	8
1Feb86- 8Pha	fst	1 1/16	:45⅘	1:10⅕	1:42⅘	3↑Gettysburg H	5	5	65¾	64¾	33½	22½	Wilson R	114	2.90	90-11	Derby Hat 1152½ Silver Surfer 114nk Double No 1152	Up for place	10
23Dec85- 8Aqu	fst	1⅛	[•]:47⅘	1:12⅕	1:52⅕	3↑Handicap	3	3	37	37	43½	34½	Decarlo C P	110	7.50	77-25	Waitlist 122½ Strong Dollar 1143¾ Silver Surfer 1101¾	Even try	7
13Dec85- 8Aqu	fst	1 1/16	[•]:47⅗	1:12	1:43⅗	3↑Handicap	8	2	31½	43½	67½	69¾	Davis R G	112	19.20	82-16	Artichoke 1201½ Badwagon Harry 120hd Waitlist 1222	Used early	8
16Nov85- 8Med	sly	1⅛	:47⅕	1:11⅕	1:49⅘	3↑Paterson H	5	3	36	46½	814	816¾	Antley C W	116	18.20	67-23	[DH]Skip Trial 1175 [DH]Fighting Fit 1225 Artichoke 117no	Tired	8

16Nov85-Grade II

LATEST WORKOUTS Dec 25 GP 3f sly :37⅗ b Dec 13 GP 4f fst :48⅗ b

Count them: nine different tracks and track surfaces out of ten races shown. Going down the list, you find Hialeah, Calder, Laurel, Belmont, Aqueduct main track, Garden State, Philadelphia Park, Aqueduct inner track, and Meadowlands. Leaving out varieties in distance, surface, and class, all these tracks are indeed different in and of themselves. How do you compare speedy Garden State with the grass at Calder, or Belmont's turf with Laurel's mud?

We return again to our thesis. In every one of these races, regardless of where they were, Silver Surfer attempted to be competitive. Rating him by his finishing positions and second call positions in each of these races, along with class figures, at least gives us again a meaningful yardstick for today's race. We don't have to worry about differences in tracks, only differences in performances, where it counts.

That is the beauty of the Performance Class rating. No longer do you need to be internally harassed by the problem of how to compare Calder's surface with that of Hialeah, or even Del Mar with Hollywood Park, Churchill with Keeneland, Fairgrounds with Oaklawn, or even Hawthorne with Sportsman's in Chicago, the latter being a six and a half furlong track. For example, Calder, with its slow surface that produces extremely slow times, drove me to distraction when I tried to handicap horses coming from races at that track. When I spent two successful days at Hialeah in early January, 1987, before the big snows wiped out eastern racing, I could happily calculate my PCRs without any worries about Calder's incredibly puzzling surface. And do very well, thank you.

As we glanced at both Texola Joe and Silver Surfer, we saw turf races intermingled with dirt races. We shall discuss this divergence in detail later on, showing you how to use both dirt and grass running lines, what races to use and not to use, and providing a complete, workable formula for computing the PCR when difference surfaces are involved.

In this entire discussion of "new ways of rating horses," acknowledging some deficiencies in every method we know, including our own, where and how do we use, if at all, the ability time rating concept that was first developed in *Investing at the Race Track*? As you will read before too long, we have vastly revised this concept to make it far more effective. The theory is still sound. We will, however, rather than use even these new ability times as the total rating, as did previously, use this as a part of form in the last race, and as a helpful further guide to performance.

But before we do that, we must further evaluate the effectiveness of PCR ratings in the context of the three major ways of using them that we mentioned in the first chapter. Just what role do they play in the final evaluation of a horse and his rivals? In other words, how do they help us win and save us from losing?

4 Making PCR Work for You

WE HAVE TAKEN considerable effort to point out that Performance Class Ratings, standing alone, are not enough to lead you to the promised land of consistent profits at the race track. In fact, as we have said, it is but one of three key elements in a total handicapping line. Consequently, if you relied upon PCR exclusively, such as for example simply betting the highest PCR horse in every race, you would surely fail. Their great value, however, that makes them so worthwhile and so inherently useful, is in what they add to the total handicapping process, and how they, in conjunction with form and other ingredients, can set up a foundation for the selection process that is so critical.

(a) *PCR as a Rating Guide in Itself*

First of all, there is an enormous value in the rating, even standing alone. Hearken back to the second chapter when we began the explanation of how PCR works. We showed you a race at Hollywood Park where one horse, Committee Girl, was rated far higher than any other in the field and won the race at odds of 9-1 with a mutuel of a flat $20.00. Back in *Investing at the Race Track*, we built an entire method of play on choosing between the first three favorites, because statistics told us that two-thirds, or 67% of all races, were won by one of the three lowest odds horses in the race. Some critics snorted at relying exclusively on this concept, because it obviously eliminated many high priced winners. When you use a PCR, you will frequently pick up price bonanzas like Committee Girl.

This alone makes it truly worthwhile. I cannot stress it enough. During my use of PCRs over the last few months at the Maryland tracks, where I am usually able to attend only on Saturdays, it has turned up winners paying $74, $80, and then, only two weeks ago before writing this, a top rated horse at Pimlico that paid an incredible $148.40 to win. But I would never want to include or rely upon such bombs as a demonstration effort at what a great method of play this is. These bonanzas do not come along very often. You have to be alert to finding them. All I am saying here is that they do happen. When you hit them, they are a splendid bonus. And I suppose I would have the right to ask, in what other method of play will such astounding long shots be uncovered?

As a comparison standard, you may ask what if you confined your selection process to the three highest PCR horses in comparison with confining it to the first three favorites? I have run comparative figures, which reveal that the first three favorites, still producing at the same steady approximate rate of winning two races out of every three, will win more often than the first three PCR horses. The three highest PCR horses, regardless of form and regardless of all other handicapping factors, usually run somewhere in the neighborhood of winning 55 to 60% of all races. That, of course, as we want to emphasize, is regardless of form and other factors.

But what they do is return more money. If you added up the gross returns of all three top betting choices and added up the gross returns of all three highest PCR horses, with no handicapping eliminations at all, the PCR horses would substantially surpass the total mutuel earnings of the three favored horses. You already know the reason: those box car priced winners, such as Committee Girl and the Maryland horses that brought home the big balloons, and even moderately priced $12 and $14 horses, will push your returns upward far beyond what the three lowest odds horses will produce.

The ultimate key, of course, is handicapping, selecting out the winners and staying away from the losers. When we come to adding the vital other parts of the handicapping equation and use them along with PCR, you will have the capacity to regularly pick solid plays like Committee Girl and stay away from doomed favorites like Danish in that race. This is the major strength of this book.

We will use it, however, not only to point out possible winners with high return, but as a base point from which to look at all the horses in the race. We will start our evaluation, not with the first three favorites, as we used to do, but with the first three PCR horses, and then go from there. It is a new foundation, therefore, upon which we can rely to select potential winners, low priced and high priced alike, especially including those that might otherwise be overlooked. In every race, we will thus include the three top PCR horses as initial contenders and eliminate them only when the remaining parts of the handicapping equation show that they literally have no chance to win.

(b) *Running Style, or Reading the Numbers*

The second great value of compiling the PCR lines is that it provides the most incisive and reliable comparison of the running styles of all the horses in the race. You may then integrate this with the critical factor of what I sometimes call track flow, and what has often been called track bias. This use is so vital that it can by itself win races for you and lose races for you.

We also can call it: Reading the Numbers. Here, we read the numbers off the PCR line. Of course, we shall read all the numbers across the line when we later reach full development of our final selection methods, but for here, our concentration is on the PCR numbers alone. We have already done some of that in the previous chapter when we analyzed the Hollywood race, but now the time has come to develop the full potential of the PCR line.

Again, almost any race will do, but we can use the sixth race at Hollywood Park on June 20, 1987, where I happened to be that afternoon. It was a six furlong sprint for three-year-old fillies at a claiming price of $40,000. We can readily analyze the race by Reading the Numbers. To do this, we will set out only the PCR lines, with closing tote board odds, of the entries.

Odds	Horse	Performance Class Rating							
8-5	Live by the Sword	91/	53	46	+ 2/	101	=	90
(e)	Folia	105/	12	23	+ 3/	38	=	276
6	Hoofer's Brew	45/	8	18	– /	26	=	173
25	Clements Creek	65/	19	35	+ 3/	57	=	127
60	Cherokee Gladys	48/	31	36	– 6/	61	=	79
60	Spectacular Moment	91/	39	31	– /	70	=	130
5-2	Plans Awry	83/	39	26	+11/	76	=	109
5	Dandy Ruth	82/	44	33	– 7/	70	=	117
7-2	My Proper Gal	LRH						
90	Flying Up	107/	49	42	+15/	106	=	100

We are now ready to begin Reading the Numbers.

The important numbers in all cases are the three internal numbers: second call totals, finish totals, and class totals. But as a preliminary, we can always see from the first column the activity of the horse. One, My Proper Gal, is not rated at all, since she has had but two races, and thus is called a Lightly Raced Horse. I must repeat: when there are less than five races showing for a horse, we can use PCR only as advisory, and when there are two or less, there is not much value in even listing it at all. However, at a glance, we can see two other somewhat lightly raced horses whose numbers we can use: Hoofer's Brew who has been in fields with 45 total horses and Cherokee Gladys in fields of 48 horses. If you had the past performances, you would see that Hoofer's Brew had run five times and Cherokee Gladys on six occasions.

But now to the important internal numbers for running style. Their greatest use is to identify horses with early speed, horses that run evenly, and horses that are closers. Horses usually run to a pattern. Those that show substantially lower numbers in their second call totals, which is the internal first column after the first slash, as compared to higher numbers in the second internal column, which is the finish total, are likely to run to early speed. On the other hand, horses that show lower finish call totals than second call totals, are usually closers and will come off the pace. Where these two internal totals are within a close range of each other, it usually means that a horse runs evenly and in some races, depending upon circumstances, will be up front and in other races, is capable of closing. There is much to be said for this kind of runner.

Reading the Numbers here immediately shows us who are the early speed horses and who are the closers. The entry of Live by the Sword and Folia at 8-5 is the heavy favorite. Folia, with an extremely high PCR, has consistent and powerful early speed, with the number of 12 when she has run in fields totalling 105 horses. This means that she is almost always in or near the lead and will surely be up there today.

Hoofer's Brew, lightly raced, also shows strong early speed, with a number of 8 against 18. Clement's Creek is the other horse with strong early speed with 19 as compared to 35, along with Cherokee Gladys with a slightly lower second call figure of 31 as against 36. Cherokee Gladys comes off a layoff, and with board odds of 60-1 and her low PCR, is not likely to concern anyone in this race.

The closers are identified as easily. Plans Awry, the 5-2 second choice, shows a second call total of 39 compared to 26 at the finish, letting us know she will be trailing the leaders at the second call and moving toward the front in the latter stages of the race. Dandy Ruth, the fourth betting choice, shows a 44 over 33, and will be doing likewise. Two far-out longshots, Spectacular Moment and Flying Up, both with wretched last race form, are also closers who will have little impact on the outcome of this race. The second half of the favored entry, Live by the Sword, is also a closer.

These key numbers will help you analzye every race. Their enormous importance cannot be understated. However, we do recognize there are other ways of evaluating early speed. Most experienced handicappers, by merely looking at a past performance listing, can tell early speed horses from closing horses. But what is so helpful here is to set forth the precise numbers involved and use them far more comprehensively than if you confine your knowledge to "the No. 2 horse has early speed and No. 7 is a closer."

Look again at the numbers in the race we are using. You are now almost certain that in the early stages of the race, Folia and Hoofer's Brew can be counted on to be up there, with Clements Creek and even Cherokee Gladys having an opportunity to run with the leaders. You know that Dandy Ruth will not be there and that highly regarded Plans Awry is not likely to press the front runners. Some of the newspaper analysts that day put forth the pre-race opinions that the early speed would set the race up for closers like Dandy Ruth to come on and win.

The real key to a prediction like that almost becomes the condition of the track surface. In a few pages from now, we will come to the major topic of track bias, how to Read the Numbers to identify it, and how PCR is affected by it. But how the track is running affects every race. When a track favors early speed, horses with lower internal numbers at the second call will be the major threats. When the track is favoring horses that close, the low finish position numbers may be your key to victory.

Tracks may have a heavy bias for early speed, may favor early speed somewhat, may appear reasonably neutral, may favor closing speed somewhat, or may have a heavy bias for closers, as almost as if there were five divisions, or five categories of track condition. I have largely found this to be true. Every time you go to the track, you must absolutely evaluate how the track surface itself is affecting the runners, and PCR internal numbers provide us the best tool I know for making these determinations.

Based upon my observations at Hollywood Park on June 20, I rated the track in the second category of "early speed somewhat," based on what I had seen prior to the sixth race. This meant that early speed would do quite well indeed. There really wasn't much question about it.

Once having established the track surface as favoring early speed somewhat, you could now make the next step toward predicting the outcome of the race. Folia, with good form and a strong last race ability time, which we will come to in a later part of this book, was sure to be a prime contender. It appeared that the only other horse with any real chance to defeat her was Hoofer's Brew, with the second highest PCR. Based upon this analysis, the second favorite, Plans Awry and the well-regarded Dandy Ruth, stamped as closers after Reading the Numbers, had very little chance at all.

This gives me another opportunity to respectfully disagree with those who believe that an abundance of early speed in a sprint race will result in a closer coming on to win. It almost never happens. When two or more strong early speed horses move out in front *on a track that is hospitable to early speed,* one of them will win almost every time. On the other hand, when the track favors closers, the early speed animals will die and the closers will likely prevail. But it is the receptivity of the track that influences the outcome, not that two speed horses will burn each other out and allow the closer to win.

In distance races, of course, that is not the case, and we must emphasize that here. All of us know that two speed horses fighting for the lead in the early stages of a route race will often "cook" each other and will fall back to the rear when the tough time of stretch call arrives. But not so with sprints. And of course, even in distance races, if you have a strong track bias up front, one of the speedsters is likely to go all the way.

But back to our sixth race at Hollywood. Because the track was conducive to the kind of speed that was out there, the race indeed was a two horse event. Hoofer's Brew was coming off a 45-day layoff, but had the favorable series of reasonably strong five furlong workouts. She was a dangerous foe for Folia. The two of them went out in front as expected, battled each other all the way, with Hoofer's Brew winning the race to pay $15.80 up front.

Reading the Numbers properly was the key to handicapping this race.

How did I come to rate the track at Hollywood on June 20 as favoring early speed somewhat? Where does one draw the line between categories of track ratings for bias? How do we detect the all-important condition of track bias that is such a vital part of any program of successful handicapping?

Recognition of track bias as an important handicapping factor has come to the fore only in recent years. That insightful writer and two-fisted bettor, Andrew Beyer of the Washington Post and handicapping book fame, was one of its earliest proponents and helped enlighten us all as to its major importance. Track bias has been generally considered in two areas: one, position bias (whether the rail is dead or fast or whether outside post positions are more or less favorable in comparison with inside post positions), and two, surface bias (whether the track favors early speed or late speed). The bias we are talking about here is surface bias, which we think is far more important than position bias. This is so because whether an entire track surface is fast or slow often affects how horses do in their post positions. A watchful jockey can often overcome position bias by moving his horse in or out from the rail as the race unfolds. But surface bias cannot be so easily overcome, as it dominates all positions and affects all horses.

The most recent outstanding examples of surface bias, both early and late, came prominently to the fore in the 1987 runnings of the Kentucky Derby and the Preakness at Churchill Downs and Pimlico, respectively. The early speed bias at Churchill was so pronounced that early speed horses dominated every race but the Derby itself. Horses with late speed, or closing habits, had virtually no chance whatever. On the other end of the spectrum, the late speed, or closing, bias dominated every race run at Pimlico on Preakness Day so much so that the winner of every one of the 10 races on the card showed a lower number in the finish column than in the second call column. Horses with early speed should have been pronounced as dead before they left the starting gate.

Reading the Numbers in the PCR lines quickly and readily identified these biases at both tracks.

This leads us into how we go about rating the track surface every time we attend the races. It is an absolute essential that must be undertaken.

One must obviously begin with the first race, which now assumes far more importance than merely being the first part of the daily double. You may want to pass the first race at the windows, but never give it short shrift in Reading the Numbers. Just as one swallow does not a summer make, the first race may not always be the definitive guide to the track surface for the day, but you can learn a great deal from it by using PCR lines, and when you add the second and third races, you should have a fully developed defined rating line on the track surface.

At Churchill Downs on Derby Day, 1987, the first race was a maiden special six furlong sprint, filled with lightly raced horses. Where horses have not yet run often enough to have established racing patterns, it becomes far more difficult to evaluate their reaction to track surface than if a group of experienced runners are in the field. But you can easily see if a horse wins wire to wire or whether someone from back in the pack is able to move past the others in the stretch. While there were a number of horses in the race that demonstrated some early speed in their few starts, the heavily favored winner, Chitter Chatter, raced far out in front to move away from the field. So far, not much to guide us, except for the fact that strong early speed did run very well. Otherwise, there weren't enough numbers to read.

When you have a first race situation where there is not enough on which to form an opinion, you naturally watch the second race with considerable interest. The two outstanding early speed horses in the 6½ furlong allowance event gave us these PCR lines to read:

| Mr. Biscuit | 91/ 23 41 | −/ 64 | = 142 |
| Sovereign Swing | 83/ 18 25 | +4/ 47 | = 177 |

Mr. Biscuit was an overwhelming favorite at 4-5 on the board. Sovereign Swing was hardly regarded at all at 15-1. The second choice, Groom, was lightly raced with only two starts, but showed some early speed. The third rated horse, Fast Reputation, was strictly a closer, with a second call total of 43 as compared to a finish total of 26. How would he fare against the speedballs?

Mr. Biscuit romped easily, wire to wire. What was significant was that the early speed longshot, Sovereign Swing, ran second. Fast Reputation closed slightly for third, but far up the track. It now could be said that early speed was definitely a very strong factor, and perhaps even into a pronounced bias. Although one would have expected Mr. Biscuit to do extremely well, the fact that a rank outsider with strong early speed was far ahead of the next runner was very helpful in establishing a bias toward early speed.

The third race, although it was becoming apparent by now, removed any doubts that may have remained. There were two strong contenders, Baby It's You, at 1.4-1 and You Make Me Happy at 1.6-1, almost identical in the odds. Internal figures for Baby It's You were 12 and 15 against 50 runners and for You Make Me Happy, it was 38 to 36 against 83 runners. Baby It's You was positively a strong early speed horse, as gleaned from Reading the Numbers, and You Make Me Happy was evenly to a slight closer. If the bias was as strong toward early speed as the first two races indicated, it would be Baby It's You all the way and so long, it's been good to know you, for You Make Me Happy. That was exactly what happened. Baby It's You was ahead by three lengths at the first call and ran away with the race. His supposedly strong competitor, You Make Me Happy, ran a good second, four lengths behind at the finish.

Early speed dominated the entire day at Churchill, as horse after horse won wire to wire. Only in the Derby when Alysheba came on to defeat Bet Twice did the early speed fail.

While I have not calculated PCRs for the Churchill card that day, a comparison of second call totals of winners with their finish totals further demonstrates the dominance of early speed that day and the favorable bias that made it possible. We now list each of the winning horses on the card with these comparison totals, second call and then finish.

Race	Dist.	Winner	2C	Fin	Comment
1CD	6.0	Chitter Chatter	1	7	Lightly Raced
2CD	6.5	Mr. Biscuit	28	41	Wire to wire
3CD	8.5	Baby It's You	12	13	Wire to wire easily
4CD	5.0	Twice Around	3	4	Lightly Raced
5CD	7.0	Lazer Show	21	22	Big win, very strong
6CD	7.0	Sovereign's Ace	23	29	Wired big win
7CD	8.5	Fast Forward	22	26	Another wire big win
8CD	10.0	Alysheba	37	24	Derby, of course
9CD	6.0	Dial Home	22	24	Wired as usual
10	8.5	Charging Falls	40	32	Wire to wire also

Aside from the Derby, every race was won wire to wire except for the fourth and fifth where the winners were a close up second at the first call and in front at the second call to go all the way from there. Aside from the Derby, you can see that the only other horse that did not have a lower second call total was Charging Falls in the tenth race. He had been showing early speed, however, in his later races, and he did win wire to wire, never challenged. The strong favorite in the race, Blandford Park, had internal totals of 83 and 49, leaving him no chance whatever. And yet, after witnessing so many wire to wire races, fans not aware of the importance of track surface poured enough money on this horse to make him a 7-5 choice. It was like throwing money in the gutter. No player who uses the numbers in PCR lines, along with track style, would ever make such a mistake.

Now, let's look at Pimlico on Preakness Day for just the opposite. Since I was there, I was able to make my PCR lines for all horses in all the races, and thus learn a lot by Reading the Numbers. Once again we can start with the first race to show you what so quickly became apparent. The first race was a six furlong claimer with these numbers (again, I have omitted the form ratings, since we have not yet arrived at that point, and since Reading the Numbers for track bias is primarily a function of what we have learned thus far):

Odds	Horse	PCR								
7-2	Cracked Diamond	75/	24	47	−	8/	63	=	119
5	Roll Dem Bones	74/	15	39	−	6/	48	=	154
40	Uncle Bentley	77/	35	47	−	16/	66	=	117
6-5	Mortgage Man	69/	35	42	−	17/	60	=	115
7	T. Farnon	70/	28	43	−	17/	54	=	130
35	Gangway Jack	79/	35	34	+	5/	74	=	107
9-2	Aprils Son	82/	53	37	−	1/	89	=	92
12	Zen Again	78/	23	63	−	16/	70	=	111

Look at the early speed showing when we read the numbers. Roll Dem Bones, with the highest PCR in the race, showed outstanding early speed, and had won his last race. Cracked Diamond, T. Farnon, and Zen Again all had low second call numbers, while the heavy favorite, Mortgage Man at 6-5, also ran forwardly more often than not. Mortgage Man had a serious form defect in lack of recent action, but there was such an abundance of early speed showing that any number of early runners could win.

What happened? There was but a single closer in the race, Aprils Son, and he passed them all in the stretch. Since we must always caution about drawing final conclusions from one race, we have to see more, and there was plenty to unfold quickly at Pimlico on Preakness Day. The second race was also at six furlongs, filled with lightly raced horses, including four first time starters in this maiden event. There can be little reading of the numbers in races like this, but we can still study the actual running for evidence of bias. A strong favorite, Beth's Bonus, with a powerful five furlong workout, rallied on the rail to come off the pace to win.

By the finish of the third race on any card, you should be able to fully evaluate the track's surface, rate it for early speed bias or late bias, or somewhere in between. Let's do the numbers on the third at Pimlico that day, a cheap router for $5,000 claimers at a mile and a sixteenth, and that will be it.

Odds	Horse	PCR Line
25	Just De Spook	74/ 45 33 + 4/ 82 = 90
6	Colonel Law	91/ 58 37 + 2/ 97 = 94
25	Ofa's Image	78/ 47 30 −14/ 83 = 124
5-2	Gopher Baroque	78/ 34 39 − 5/ 68 = 115
25	Rightful Speaker	92/ 42 42 + 1/ 85 = 108
2	Off the Vine	89/ 48 51 − 6/ 93 = 96
3	Pyrite Star	88/ 45 43 + 1/ 89 = 99
17	Cornish Recipe	80/ 44 43 + 1/ 88 = 91
30	Boza	84/ 53 46 −15/ 84 = 100
15	Seniah	87/ 61 34 + 2/ 97 = 90

None of the first three favorites, all well backed, was a confirmed closer. Two of them, Off the Vine and Gopher Baroque, had lower second call numbers, although not by much. Pyrite Star would be classed as an even runner with no pronounced inclination. None of the horses was particularly strong in PCR.

The most confirmed closer in the field, Seniah, at 15-1, charged home to win. Ofa's Image, another late finisher, steamed in to finish second. Closing was the established order of the day. Say goodbye to all early speed and look for the horses with finish position numbers that were lower than second call numbers.

Just to illustrate the point, I will show you the PCR line numbers for the winners of the next five races prior to the running of the Preakness, where you can see the influence of finish position totals.

Odds	Horse	PCR Line
4Pim	Cutlasee	75/ 41 21 +4/ 66 = 114 (6f)
5Pim	Minute N' Change	88/ 44 34 +3/ 81 = 109 (6f)
6Pim	Green Book	89/ 52 42 −6/ 88 = 101 (1 1/16)
7Pim	Bagetelle	71/ 54 31 +4/ 89 = 80 (1 1/16)
8Pim	Willowy Mood	70/ 41 30 −6/ 65 = 108 (6f)

Not one of these winners had the highest PCR in the race, as did neither Aprils Son nor Seniah in the first and third races. In only two of the seven races we have discussed was the winner even among the first three PCR-rated horses. There were short-priced favorites like Minute N' Change and Green Book and long shot winners like Seniah and Bagetelle at 25-1, but they all had one thing in common: their finish call totals were markedly lower than their second call totals.

Now you should be able to see why PCR ratings alone do not turn out as many winners among the three highest rated as do the first three favorites in a race. In the same seven Pimlico races we have discussed, five of them were won by one of the first three betting choices.

All this reinforces the conclusion that PCR ratings are weighted toward early speed and are weakest when late speed, or closing speed, is predominant.

But this reality actually helps guide us toward a more effective use of PCR as such. When tracks are biased toward early speed, or favor early speed somewhat, or are even neutral, PCR ratings are very effective. When tracks are biased toward closing horses, or somewhat toward closers, PCR ratings will not do nearly as well. When we learn to adjust our PCR concepts, based upon how the track is responding, they can continue to be a potent handicapping force.

More needs to be said about track surface response before we leave the subject. We have stressed the importance of analyzing the first race on every card, and following it by keeping close watch on both the second and third races, because by that time you should have an excellent idea of how the track is "running" on any day. Sometimes, however, a track surface begins to switch during the day, becoming faster or slower as the races unfold. This can create difficult problems for the thoughtful handicapper, as it can sometimes leave you one race behind all day, to the gross misfortune of your pocketbook.

You must also face the realities that good horses can sometimes overcome even a pronounced bias, and this can lead you astray in rating a track. For example, a high PCR horse with good early speed may still have enough strength and class to defeat all his rivals. You are required to take other factors into account, such as last race form and particularly last race ability times, which will help you enormously in rating any race, regardless of track bias.

What do you do if your observation of the first race leads you to no conclusion at all? Or, what do you do when you strongly favor a horse in the first race, want to place a bet on him, but have no idea of how the track is running? One obvious approach, of course, is to be aware of how races were run on the previous day, and assume that early speed or late speed or a relatively neutral surface will carry forward into the following day. You might also conservatively lower your size of bet in the early races until you are more certain of how the track is running.

But on the whole, if there is a strong horse in the first race that I like, and a look at yesterday's charts reveals that the track is not hostile to my choice's running style, then I will play him. Bear in mind that tracks are far more often neutral or speed favoring than they are favorable to closers. All of you have probably seen many days in a row at your track where one kind of bias or another is pronounced, and have watched it continue for a substantial period of time. In the early winter of 1987 at Laurel, for example, there was a sustained period of time where the track was almost as biased toward closers as was Preakness Day at Pimlico, and where high PCR horses were not strong plays at all.

But Reading the Numbers off the PCR lines is your most important tool for determining how the track is running. When horses with lower second call numbers and reasonably high PCR figures are winning or running well, you can be sure the track is favorable to early speed. You can adjust all your handicapping accordingly. And when the reverse occurs, as it did at Pimlico on Preakness Day, and on hosts of other occasions, you must make your adjustments accordingly. All this is necessary to achieve Total Victory at the Track.

There is yet another major lesson in early speed and closing speed to be found in Reading the Numbers insofar as sprint and route races are concerned. In an intensive study of 119 races, almost equally divided between sprints and routes, I found that in sprint races, regardless of track bias, 70% of all sprint races were won by one of the three horses with the lowest second call totals as compared to the finish totals. This demonstrates the dominance of early speed in sprints, and makes PCR ratings more effective in sprints than in route races. If early speed horses did not die so readily on tracks heavily biased toward closers, the percentage would be even higher.

In the distance races, on the other hand, approximately 68% of all races were won by one of the three horses with a lower finish total compared to the second call total. Early speed prevails in route races usually when the track is slanted strongly toward speed or where a power horse is able to play with his opposition throughout an entire race.

(c) *Using Numbers to Understand the Class Factor*

The third important internal number in the PCR formula is the class rating figure. A lower class horse with a plus number will have his PCR downgraded. The higher class horse with a minus number will have his PCR increased. But within those simple arithmetical realities, aside from the totals they produce on which we rely, astute handicappers should be able to further evaluate these numbers and treat class more incisively in each race.

The effectiveness of class in sprints and in routes, I have found, is incredibly different. Class alone in sprints is not nearly as effective as it is in distance events, as a class plus number in a sprint often shows in the winner's line. But beyond that, here is an important new concept that I learned in developing this entire method of play:

Horses with lower second call numbers in sprints who have a minus class number (which indicates a higher class animal) are strong candidates to win. On the other hand, in routes, it is the opposite. Horses who have a minus class number along with a lower finish position are strong candidates to win.

Think of why this is so. A sprinter who shows an early running style while competing at a higher class than today's race is more likely to carry his speed to the wire against animals of lesser class. A router who shows a late running style while competing at a higher class than today's race, where he was able to gain on higher class animals, is more likely to come strongly to the wire against lower class animals today, who should not have the finishing kick of the more valuable horses.

With that in mind, you can use the class number effectively in both sprints and routes. Your sprint winner is more likely to come from the three best lower second call numbers *reduced by the class factor.* Your route winner is more likely to come from the three best lower finish call numbers *reduced by the class factor.* This shading in one direction or another can often be an improvement in the naked final number of PCR.

On the whole, however, based upon my use of class numbers within these PCR ratings, it is safe to say that class in sprint races as compared to the effect of class in distance races is not as effective standing alone. Even with factoring in class with the second call numbers as a tool of comprehension, the reality is that a lower class horse with strong early speed has a far better chance of winning at six furlongs than a lower class horse with lower second call figures in a distance race, who may be wiped out by the class factor.

Analzying the same races that I used to determine the effect of lower internal numbers at second call and finish positions, I looked at class ratings to see how the better class horses fared. In sprint races, the three best class numbers won only 46% of the time, a surprisingly low figure. But this was not integrated with the early speed-class factor. Horses that had run for higher dollars and did not win because of their lack of early effort could not compensate for this with a class drop against a sharp animal that had run well in lower class events.

In distance races however, one of the three top rated class horses won 61% of the time. Using these comparisons, you can see that early speed is more powerful than class in sprints and that higher class and closing ability are more powerful in distance races. In Reading the Numbers, you must always take these realities into consideration.

I have experimented with devaluating the second call number in distance races, for example, which would in turn elevate the finish call number and the class number to a higher degree of numerical standing, and result in higher PCRs for closers and class horses. You may even want to do the same. However, this leads to a great deal of more intricate calculations, and there comes a time when some slight improvement in the result is not worth the precious time expended on it. As you become more experienced, you can mentally elevate the class number horse in distance races slightly above what his PCR shows, and in sprint races, slightly elevate the low class horse in your final comparisons.

But because class ratings have such an important bearing on the final PCR, and in particular have a strong influence on distance races, we are obliged to return to some of the difficult and finer analyses that are necessary in arriving at class points, higher and lower. We must complete that part of our exposition before we come to the major area of form ratings and last race ability times.

5 How To Make Class Determinations

BECAUSE CLASS RATING points are not only important in the final determination of Performance Class Ratings, but carry their own consequences as a rating factor, we need to review some of the problem areas that we will encounter. In the second chapter, when we first explained how PCRs are compiled, we provided the basic outline of class points for higher class and lower class races. But there are innumerable situations where problems arise, where decisions must be made, where some handicapping judgment must be exercised. Consequently, it is important to be able to deal with these situations and arrive at class points that are as nearly accurate as we can make them.

The examples we will give may not solve all your class rating problems, but hopefully, they will provide an adequate basis and understanding of the process so that you will be able to properly assign class ratings in most of the handicapping situations confronting you.

(a) *Claiming Races*

Assessing class points in cheaper claiming races is one of the relatively easy tasks we confront, since the claiming price itself is the primary standard from which we work. A horse running for a $20,000 price is obviously a higher class rated horse than one running for $10,000.

To do what is necessary as an essential part of the process we must evaluate levels of class, because we award only 1 point, up or down, for the class level immediately above or below the class level of today's race. This requires you to have a general knowledge of the class levels at the track where you play. Using the Maryland circuit as an example, the lowest claiming price there is $5,000. In southern California, it may be $10,000 and in New York, it may be $12,000.

The next level above the bottom rung in Maryland is a $6,500 claiming price. If today's race is for horses at a $6,500 price and there is a $5,000 line in the past performances, that will be graded with 1

Lower Class point because it is the next level immediately below $6,500. Horses who have run at the next higher level than $6,500, which happens to be $8,500, would receive 1 Higher Class point.

Consequently, a horse running for $5,000 today would receive 2 Higher Class points for each $8,500 race (or higher) that shows in his past performances. The horse running for $6,500 today would receive only 1 Higher Class point for each $8,500 race, and would have had to run at at even higher level to obtain 2 Higher Class points.

In Maryland, as in most racing jurisdictions, there is a step-by-step claiming price ladder. After the $5,000, the next level, as we have said, is $6,500, then $8,500, followed by $11,500, and then further upward to $14,500. Above this rung of the ladder comes the $18,500 claiming race, and then $25,000. The gap becomes wider as we move into upper levels. You must therefore know each class level at your track, for you have to compare each race listed as to whether it is one level or two levels higher or lower, in order to properly award points.

Therefore, check your own local track to establish the price ranges for each rung of the claiming ladder. This is relatively easy at home. But when you deal with horses coming from unfamiliar tracks, you may not be certain of the various claiming price ranges, up or down. But here is where actual claiming price is so helpful. While horses running for $10,000 at different tracks may not be equal in class in every situation, you can still use the dollar figures as a workable guide.

Where does the 3 point award come in? If, for example, today's race was for $8,500 claiming and one of the entrants had run in a reasonably high grade allowance race or a named stakes (unlikely, or else what is he doing in an $8,500 claiming race), we could award 3 points. We will have a later discussion of this question in greater depth than this.

As claiming prices go upward, your problems increase. Horses at higher claiming levels frequently switch from allowance races back into higher priced claimers, and may often come from other tracks as well when purses become attractive. Even in cheaper races, trainers often come in from neighboring tracks, hoping to hide the class of their horse, in an effort to come away with a purse.

However, we can illustrate the problem of class evaluations in higher priced claiming events by looking at the 9th race at Hollywood on December 4, 1985, a one mile event out of a chute for a claiming price of $50,000. Here, as in every race, you must—and we add, *absolutely must*—look at the conditions of the race, even though they are primarily controlled by a price tag. They are always shown in the Daily Racing Form under the listing of the race itself, after the track symbol that indicates the distance.

12   **DAILY RACING FORM, WEDNESDAY, DECEMBER 4, 1985**

9th Hollywood

1 MILE. (1.32⅗) CLAIMING. Purse $22,000. Fillies and mares. 3-year-olds and upward. Weights, 3-year-olds, 119 lbs.; older, 122 lbs. Non-winners of two races at a mile or over since September 15 allowed 3 lbs.; such a race since then, 6 lbs. Claiming price $50,000; for each $2,500 to $45,000 allowed 1 lb. (Races when entered for $40,000 or less not considered.)

As you see, in addition to the claiming price, there are weight allowances for age and past winning performances. These kinds of allowances do not concern us here, only those affecting actual claiming price. After you see the listing of the claiming price of the race, you read the following: "for each $2,500 to $45,000 allowed 1 lb." This means that the trainer can obtain one pound off any of the other weight assignments that are made in the conditions if he will lower the cost of claiming his horse down by $2,500. A $45,000 bottom is established, which means that the maximum weight off a trainer could obtain would be 2 lbs. At this price level, this is not much of a bargain, but two of the nine horses entered in the race carried lesser weights and resultant lowered claiming prices.

The most important information for our purposes, however, is that this is a $50,000 claiming race, and even though a horse may have run for $45,000, it is still, for class level purposes, a $50,000 claiming race. This issue becomes further important in looking at other races in a horse's past performance, where claiming prices may be slightly lowered and you may need to determine whether they are lower because of class level or because of weight off. Comparison of weights carried in other races may be very helpful in most situations where you have any difficulty in making this determination.

Accordingly, when you see any claiming price across a line in the past performances that does not fit the price pattern of the rungs of the claiming ladder, you may assume that the horse's lowered claiming price is based on weight off allowances. For example, in Maryland, where we have pointed out that the common claiming prices are usually fixed at established numbers, such as from $6500 to $8500 to $14,500, and so on, you may often see a horse's claiming price listed at $7500 or $13,500. In each case, since you know what the established claiming prices are, you can be certain that the horse ran in an $8500 or $14,500 claimer, and that the reduced price was due to weight off allowances. In all cases, we are concerned only about the true claiming class level, which in the two examples, would be $8500 and $14,500.

The problem becomes far more difficult, of course, when you evaluate races from other tracks. A horse shipping into Maryland may have run at nearby Delaware Park for $7500, which does not fit in the established Maryland price brackets. This same problem can occur wherever you are throughout the entire country. How do you compare the $7500 Delaware race against the $8500 Maryland race in class rating purposes? The only sensible approach is to try to evaluate the class of the track itself, and those of us who live nearby readily know that Delaware, once upon a time a splendid track, does not possess the same class, dollar for dollar, as does Maryland. Therefore, the $7500 Delaware race would be one class level below the $8500 Maryland race, and would require adding one point.

We shall now run through the first three favorites in the Hollywood race for the primary purpose of awarding class points in a higher priced claiming race, and demonstrating the process of solving some of the class rating problems in races of this kind. We can start with Tamure, the third favorite showing at 7-2 on the board with that grand old favorite of everyone, William Shoemaker himself, as the rider.

The last race on Nov. 22 shows at $45,000. Is that one level below the class of today's race? You will quickly note that the claiming tag

Tamure

Gr. f. 4, by Navajo—Tahitian Chant, by Distinctive
Br.—Manderly Farms (Ky)
Tr.—Vienna Darrell

SHOEMAKER W   114

Own.—Hadley Jean B

Lifetime 17 2 4 3 $59,075

on Tamure for today's race is $45,000, which means that his trainer chose to take advantage of the weight off possibilities and lowered the price tag to $45,000 to remove two pounds from the horse's back. While we do not have the conditions of the Nov. 22 race before us, we may readily and correctly conclude that the $45,000 tag there was in a race of exactly the same class level as today's race, and award no points either way. You may note that the weight carried on Nov. 22 was 114, the same as the load in today's race. At this point, we can repeat some of what has been said in our previous books, small weight adjustments in no way will influence our judgment on the race itself, but paying attention to weight allows us to make comparisons and because trainers still seek every weight advantage they can find, we can use variations in weight to at least get some idea of trainer intentions.

Now, back to assessing the other races in Tamure's past performances for class points. The Nov. 6 race at Santa Anita was for $50,000, and again, no points need be awarded. When we encounter the race of Oct. 20 at Santa Anita for $40,000, we must make another decision on awarding points. We assume class levels at Hollywood and Santa Anita to be the same, as they usually are. Since the bottom possible claiming price in today's race can go no lower than $45,000, and the Oct. 20 race was at $40,000, we may now assume one level lower, and award 1 Lower Class point.

As we drop to the next race below, we see that it was run on the turf. In this particular situation, I would omit it, as I will set forth when we deal with mixtures of turf and dirt racing. But for our lesson in class, let's evaluate the Oct. 2 grass event, an allowance race for a purse of $30,000. The purse of today's claiming race, as you will see when you look again at the conditions, is $22,000. Allowance races, where horses run without carrying a purchase price, are generally a level higher than claimers, except the very high claiming races that we will talk about later on. This race is more than one level higher than the $50,000 claimer, and if we were to include it, we would award 2 Higher Class points.

Let's keep going. The next race down was run on Sept. 15 at Pomona, which is a track of lower caliber than Hollywood and Santa Anita. But the race was a restricted named stakes, and even with Pomona's lesser clout, we can safely give 2 more Higher Class points.

The remaining allowance races present a new set of problems. The Aug. 29 race at Del Mar had a purse of $24,000. Today's claiming race has a purse of $22,000. Del Mar, while possibly a shade under Santa Anita and Hollywood Park in track stature, is still a part of the southern California circuit. Within the same circuit, because allowance races are generally a level higher than claimers, even when the money is the same, we can give 1 Higher Class point here. The same would follow for the July 27 race at Del Mar (assuming we would include it) and both the March 1 and Feb. 8 races at Santa Anita. The remaining race is the July 6 start at Hollywood in another $30,000 allowance race, which we have already determined to be two levels higher with 2 Higher Class Points.

Let's keep going. The next race down was run on Sept. 15 at Pomona, which is a track of lower caliber than Hollywood and Santa Anita. But the race was a restricted named stakes, and even with Pomona's lesser clout, we can safely give 2 more Higher Class points.

The remaining allowance races present a new set of problems. The Aug. 29 race at Del Mar had a purse of $24,000. Today's claiming race has a purse of $22,000. Del Mar, while possibly a shade under Santa Anita and Hollywood Park in track stature, is still a part of the southern California circuit. Within the same circuit, because allowance races are generally a level higher than claimers, even when the money is the same, we can give 1 Higher Class point here. The same would follow for the July 27 race at Del Mar (assuming we would include it) and both the March 1 and Feb. 8 races at Santa Anita. The remaining race is the July 6 start at Hollywood in another $30,000 allowance race, which we have already determined to be two levels higher with 2 Higher Class Points.

Summarizing, we have one Lower Class point (Oct. 20), two races with 2 Higher Class points each (Oct. 2 and July 6) for 4, and 5 more Higher Class points for the 1's awarded. This would ordinarily come out to 8 net Higher Class points, where we would subtract 8 from the second call and finish position totals. If you are grading this race with us, omit the two turf races of Oct. 2 and July 27, which takes away 3 Higher Class points, leaving a net of 5 for subtraction.

Let's next move to Jigalores, the co-favorite with Positioned, both showing on the board at 5-2.

Rating the class of this horse brings us back to the problem of integrating different tracks. This necessarily results in rounds of assumptions and some subjective evaluations, but it cannot be avoided. So, let's get going.

Dropping down below the last easy race at the same $50,000 price,

```
Jigalores                         Ro. f. 3, by Jig Time—Maria Delores, by Rey Clare II
  BLACK C A                       Br.—Epstein K (Fla)                    1985 15 6 5 0   $62,920
                            1145  Tr.—Feld Jude T              $50,000   1984  7 1 3 1   $11,242
Own.—Conway & Feld                Lifetime  22 7 8 1  $74,162            Turf  1 0 0 0      $270
20Nov85-4Hol  1  :463 1:113 1:36 ft   6½ 1135  31 21 2½ 1hd  Black C A3  Ⓕ 50000 83-15 Jigalores, Alitina, B. Elite 9
8Nov85-9SA    1  :464 1:113 1:371ft  *2½ 1135  1hd 1hd 1½ 21½  Black C A2  Ⓕ c40000 80-13 Pet Bird, Jigalores, Ed's Bold Lady 8
   8Nov85—Bobbled start
25Oct85-7SA   6f :22  :453 1:111ft    3½ 1136  32½ 33½ 35 22½  Black C A8  Ⓕ 40000 79-23 Mind Storm, Jigalores, Danish 9
12Oct85-2SA   1  :46  1:111 1:38 ft   2½ 118   31½ 22 32 21½  ShoemakerW1 Ⓕ 40000 76-18 Clearway, Jigalores, Don A Top 8
   12Oct85—Altered course, bumped at 3 1/2
18Sep85-6BM   1  :454 1:101 1:363ft  *3-2 114  21½ 3½ 21½ 1hd  Baze R A4  ⒻAw15000 85-19 Jigalores, Normira, Falcon'sReward 6
1Sep85-11Sac  1  :45  1:093 1:353ft   2 118    75½ 63½ 45½ 46  Baze RA4 Ⓕ[R]Camelia 90-11 Pirte'sReglt,SplndidPrid,ScrnDoor 8
21Jly85-9Aks  1⅛ :483 1:131 1:533ft   8 113    65½ 79½ 713 714½  CptNM7 ⒻAks Oaks 55-30 LdyDomAlrc,MyInhrtnc,JstAnythng 8
   21Jly85—Grade III
13Jly85-5Aks  170:472 1:113 1:43 ft  *2-3 121  2hd 2½ 2½ 1nk  Lively J1  ⒻAw16900 82-21 Jigalores, Brooke Marie, Lip Gloss 7
29Jun85-3Aks  6f :223 :454 1:113ft   *2-3 118  51½ 41½ 2½ 22  Lively J4  Ⓕ c27500 77-20 C. P.Smarty,Jigalores,ExpressSuzie 6
31May85-8Aks  170:472 1:12  1:43 ft   2½ 112   31½ 31 2½ 2½  Lively J3  ⒻAw16000 81-28 Envy Me Fool,Jigalores,GoGoHasIt 8
  Nov 7 SA 3f ft :364 b        Oct 11 SA 3f ft :364 h        Oct 5 BM 6f ft 1:14 h
```

we hit three $40,000 claiming races in a row, all of which merit 1 Lower Class point each for the next immediate level below today's race. On Sept. 18, Jigalores ran at Bay Meadows in a $15,000 allowance race, and with the purse substantially lower than the $22,000 offered today, we have to give one more Lower Class point, even though it was an allowance race. Thus, here you see the phenomenon of an allowance race being rated lower in class than a claiming race. Bay Meadows events do not approach the class level of southern California, and this kind of race is a good example.

On Sept. 1, there was a restricted stakes race at Sacramento, another lesser track, which raises yet another class rating problem. Since it is a northern California restricted stakes race, we can readily rate it as even in class to a $50,000 claimer in southern California, and award no points either way. The last four races shown were at Ak-sar-ben in Omaha, and once again, we are called upon to do some subjective class evaluation. It will help to know that Ak-sar-ben, while not of the stature of southern California or New York, is a reasonably high class track with many good purses, attracting many first rate horses.

The July 21 event is rather easy, since it was a graded stakes race at Grade III. This confirms something about the general class level of Ak-sar-ben. Therefore, it is easily worth 2 Higher Class points, and had it been a Grade I stakes, we would have raised the result to 3. Below that is the July 13 allowance at a purse of $16,900, and since it is an allowance race from where the horse went to compete in a graded stakes, we shall call it even with the $50,000 claimer in southern California.

On June 29, Jigalores was claimed for $27,500, and that race readily gets 2 Lower Class points. The last race shown on May 31 carried an allowance purse of $18,000, and since this is higher than the $16,900 purse (although not by much), and since it came prior to the July 13 race, we can safely give 1 Higher Class point.

Thus, we have 3 Higher Class points (2 for July 21 and 1 for May 31), and 5 Lower Class points (1 each for Nov. 8, Oct. 25, Oct. 12, Sept. 18, and June 29). The net is 2 Lower Class points, and in calculating the PCR, we will add these 2 points to the second call and finish position totals.

Positioned, the co-favorite with Jigalores, presents similar class rating problems.

The last two races, both at $40,000, are awarded 1 Lower Class point each, while the third race down at today's price is passed. On Sept. 16 there was another restricted named stakes at Pomona, which we will rate even in class, just as we did in the race where Tamure ran. The Aug. 9 race at Del Mar will be skipped, even though it was at the same class, because the horse was eased. As earlier stated, we do not count any race where a horse's effort cannot be fairly compared, which includes "eased" when there is some mishap involved.

On July 16, Positioned was running on the summer circuit at Solano, another minor California track, for an allowance purse of $16,000, and because it is below the $22,000 claiming purse of today's race, we rate it one level below and give 1 Lower Class point. On June 26, the horse ran at Pleasanton, across the bay from San Francisco, where we also give 1 Lower Class point for the same reasons that we have stated. Below that are three turf races at Golden Gate, the sister circuit track to Bay Meadows, and using these races, again we award 1 Lower Class point for each. The net total is 7 Lower Class points which must be added to the other totals.

Now that we have run through three horses in a high priced claiming event to demonstrate how we deal with some of the problems involved in making class ratings, let's review and summarize some guidelines for evaluating class in claiming races.

1. At your track, you must know and be aware of the various prices of claiming races offered. You will then be in a position of determining the levels of claiming prices so you can know when a race is one claiming price level above or below the price of today's race.

2. Read and become familiar with the conditions of each race. Even where our major reliance is on claiming price, you need to know what lower prices are available for weight off allowances to enable you to compare races.

3. When you encounter higher priced claiming races, many of the horses entered may have run in allowance races at your track or other tracks. Therefore, you must learn to compare class levels of claiming races with those of allowance races.

4. One helpful measuring device when races are within the same racing circuit is comparison of purses, using the size of the purse of the claiming race against the size of the purse of the allowance race. This was shown in the example of Tamure, where we evaluated the allowance races with purses roughly equal to the purse of the claiming race under study as one class level higher.

5. When allowance races at tracks outside your racing circuit show up in past performances of a high priced claiming race at your track, you are required to know something about the class levels of tracks outside your circuit. For example, every knowledgeable southern California racing fan knows that the northern California circuit around San Francisco, where Bay Meadows and Golden Gate are the dominant tracks, are considerably below the southern California tracks of Santa Anita, Hollywood Park, and Del Mar in class value. In the east, New Yorkers know that their circuit is composed of Aqueduct, Belmont, and Saratoga, and that all other tracks in the northeast, even though of good quality, are below the class structure provided in New York.

Consequently, in comparing allowance races at tracks outside your circuit with high priced claiming races within your circuit, you can make some evaluations based upon purses, starting with a general rule of this kind: an allowance race at a lower circuit with a purse lower than the purse of the your claiming race is very likely one level below in class. We applied this guideline in Positioned's past performances above, where we found the Golden Gate races with purses of $15,000 and $16,000 to be one class level below the $50,000 claimer at Hollywood with a $22,000 purse.

Following this structure, where an allowance race at a track outside your circuit has a purse reasonably equal to, or higher than, the purse in your claiming race, you may rate the out- circuit track race as equal to, or one level higher. This guideline is compounded by the problem shown in Jigalore's past performances, where the filly ran in Nebraska at Ak-sar-ben. At tracks like this, which are of reasonably high quality, and which are far removed from the two major racing circuits in New York and southern California, the class of horses is usually higher than the actual purse level, and for that reason, we slightly up- graded the Ak-sar-ben races in comparing them with the Hollywood claiming race.

The problem here for many of you is that you are not expected to be scholars of insular race tracks. A regular racing fan in either Los Angeles or New York might say, "Where in the hell is Aks?" Or "LaD," or "Tdn," or "Rkm" for that matter. And even knowing where these tracks are, you may have no way of knowing about their purse structures.

These kinds of situations relegate you to guess work. If you have absolutely no idea of the value of allowance races at these out-circuit tracks, aside from the purses shown, you may be better off rating the off-circuit race, even where purses are comparable, as one level lower, and let it go at that.

6. Finally, there is the question about what to do about maiden races, both maiden claimers and maiden special races. We shall defer discussing these situations until the next chapter.

(b) *Evaluating Class in Allowance Races*

Awarding class points in allowance races is in many respects similar to arriving at class points in high priced claiming races. However, for a comprehensive understanding of class levels in allowance races, every reader is urged to become familiar with and understand the single outstanding work in the field, *The Handicapper's Condition Book*, by James Quinn.

Since we have the Daily Racing Form for Dec. 4, 1985 so readily available, let's use the 8th race on the same Hollywood card that we have previously used. Your first assignment is to again carefully read the conditions, which are even more important in allowance races than in claiming races.

8th Hollywood

7 FURLONGS. (1.20%) ALLOWANCE. Purse $20,000. 3-year-olds and upward. Non-winners of $3,000 other than maiden, claiming or starter. Weights, 3-year-olds, 120 lbs.; older, 122 lbs. Non-winners of a race other than claiming since September 15 allowed 3 lbs.; such a race since August 15, 6 lbs.

The purse of $20,000 is your first consideration. Quickly, you see that the purse in the feature event of the day is slightly under the $22,000 purse in the claiming race that completed the card. We have previously told you that an allowance race with a purse roughly equivalent to the purse of a claiming race should be rated one level higher in class because the horses entered are not subject to claim. This might not apply, of course when claiming prices rise exceptionally high, with very high purses to go with them. For example, when you see a $100,000 claiming race in New York or California, you may quickly realize that this is a high class race indeed, superior in class to many allowance races.

The other conditions shown will further help you evaluate this race, which must be done fully because your task is to compare all the races shown in the past performances of all the entries with the class of this event. The conditions show the race is not restricted by age, since it is for 3-year-olds and upward. The favorite, Odysseus, who did not win, by the way, was a 6-year-old who had run all but his last race in South America. We will come to the problems in evaluating him shortly.

Continuing with the conditions of this race, we see that it is limited to non-winners of $3,000 other than maiden, claiming, or starter. This is a very cheap allowance race, which accounts for the rather low California purse, and in fact, is so cheap that we become very uncomfortable in rating it one level above a claiming race with a similar purse structure. But we are trying to formulate a rule that will work in most instances, and we are not ready to deviate from it at this point. In evaluating past earnings, any money won in any claiming race is not counted. These conditions mean that a winner of any high priced claiming race could still be eligible for this race, if not otherwise restricted.

Likewise, any money won in a maiden race would not be counted insofar as eligibility was concerned. The "non-winners of $3,000" refers to the proportionate share of a winning purse, where you can usually figure that the winning horse is awarded 60% of the purse.

We can test the purse size of such a race by calculating that $3,000 is 60% of $5,000, which would be the amount of the allowance purse that would make the winner ineligible for this race. Now, you can see why this is an incredibly cheap allowance race.

In races of this kind, as students of class such as James Quinn would tell you, it is best to start looking for a winning horse out of high claiming ranks. But we are not here to handicap this race as such, but to deal with problems in class evaluations. A good place to start is with Verbatim's Pride, the second choice who scored a relatively easy victory, again with the highest PCR of any of the rateable horses.

The last previous race was at a claiming price of $62,500. We have seen on the same card that a $50,000 claimer carried a $22,000 purse, and we may assume, without knowing, that the $62,500 race would carry an even higher purse, probably at a $25,000 figure. Here is where knowing claiming and purse levels at your own track is important. Fortunately for us, the earlier 7th race on the card was a claiming event for $62,500, where the purse was the same $22,000 that was offered in the 9th race where the claiming price was $50,000. Whoever said this game was easy?

Therefore, we reluctantly give 1 Lower Class point for the race of Nov. 21. We have to award 2 Lower Class points for the cheaper claiming races of Oct. 13 and Sept. 1, and one more Lower point for the Aug. 3 race at Del Mar where the price tag was again $62,500. Hereafter, we can pick up a little steam. On July 14, Verbatim's Price ran in an allowance event where the purse was $28,000, and since it is considerably above the $20,000 offered today (despite other leveling conditions), we can rate it a Higher Class race. Whether it should have 1 point or 2 becomes a tough question, but we will give it 2 for this reason: there was a $22,000 allowance purse on May 3, and because today's race at $20,000 is so classless, we think the May 3 race may be a shade higher at the next level which would merit 1 point. If the May 3 race with a $22,000 purse gets 1 point, we can then extend the July 14 race to 2 points. We shall not consider the May 23 Hollywood race on the grass, based on the guidelines we shall give you later.

We also have not yet discussed maiden races, but we will cross them off here as even, with no points, plus or minus, and now total up the class rating of Verbatim's Choice. There are 5 High Class points (2 for July 14 and June 30, and 1 for May 3). There are 6 Low Class points (1 for Nov. 21, 2 each for Oct. 13 and Sept. 1, and 1 more for Aug. 3), leaving us with a net low of 1, which must be added to the totals of second call positions and the finish positions. Just for fun, they are 22 for second call and 25 for finish out of 82 total horses (leaving out the race of May 23. We can write Verbatim's Pride's PCR line in this manner: 82 / 22 25 + 1 / 48 = 171, a cracking good figure in a race of this kind. The horse paid $6.40 to win.

We may have shown you enough at this point to start to help formulate guidelines for comparative class in allowance races. But before we set them out, let's look at the favorite, Odysseus, who presents some additional problems.

First of all, you will not be able to run a PCR line on this horse, because he has run but one race in the United States. There are no available figures on internal positions in foreign races. When we move to evaluating class, you can see that Odysseus ran in Grade 1 stakes in Argentina and Brazil, and even scored a victory in a Grade 3 stake. Then, how he is eligible for a cheap allowance race like this one? Conditions again, please. "Non-winners of $3,000 other than..." lets this horse in this race because of the puny purses in South America. Look at the earnings box, where you see that the horse, even though winning five out of nine races in 1984, won only $11,063. Not one of his winning races had a purse high enough to give him a winner's share of $3,000.

We don't really know what the class of his opposition was in the South American races. But because he ran in graded stakes and because he ran a very strong race on Nov. 24 for a $20,000 allowance purse similar to the one before us, the crowd sent him off at odds of 3-2, not at all unreasonable. Verbatim's Pride was simply better that day, as were two other horses who finished ahead of the fourth place position of Odysseus.

Since you have a race where the favorite cannot be given a PCR, what do you do? If you wish to play the race, you are invited to make your selection by other handicapping methods. In doing so, you could run a PCR on some of the other horses, but not all. You would have to take into account the high PCR of Verbatim's Pride in any evaluation of the race. Because of his impressive Big Win on Nov. 21 and strong early speed, and the dubious class of the race itself, you might well have had no hesitation whatever in backing him to win.

To this point, we have dealt only with evaluating class in mixed-bag allowance races at levels comparable to high priced claiming races. We must reiterate that in all allowance races, conditions are critically important, and it is from these conditions, along with the purse structure, that we award points for Higher Class and Lower Class in allowance races.

We could rather easily extend analysis of class ratings to the length of half a book, but our purpose here must be focused on practicality and setting forth enough to enable you to make reasonably sound ratings, although in some spots tinged with both speculation and subjective evaluations. While we strive to be as accurate as possible in all situations, if you are off by one point in one race, the overall figures will not be too distorted.

It may be helpful before we conclude to run through class ratings of some of the animals in one more allowance race to further illustrate both how-to-do-it and deal with problems encountered. We have selected the past performances from the 7th race at Aqueduct on January 23, 1987, a race that was not run because of snow cancellation, so we are not talking about winners or losers, but only examples of class ratings.

7th Aqueduct

6 FURLONGS. (InnerDirt). (1.08⅗) ALLOWANCE. Purse $29,000. Fillies and Mares, 4-year-olds and Upward which have never won three races other than Maiden, Claiming or Starter. Weights, 122 lbs. Non-winners of two races other than Maiden or Claiming since December 15, allowed 3 lbs. Of such a race since then 5 lbs.

We start, as always, with these important conditions. The basic eligibility limitation for these fillies and mares is that they cannot have won three races other than maiden, claiming, or starter. Experienced handicappers know that the next allowance lower than this is non-winners of two "other than," which is a phrase we can use to describe conditions. Below that level is non-winners of one "other than," which means primarily that the entries would have won only a maiden race, and no more, except for forays into the claiming ranks. In all these cases, the purses may be approximately the same, or only slightly different, but at each higher level of competition, the class of the race is slightly higher.

Our first horse is All for London out of the Wayne Lukas stable.

All For London — **B. m. 5, by Danzig—Full Card, by Damascus**
Own.—Allen J — **117** — **Br.—Allen Joseph (Ky)** — **Tr.—Lukas D Wayne**

Lifetime	23	3	2	4	$38,665
1986	17	1	2	4	$30,528
1985	3	0	0	0	
Turf	9	2	1	0	$12,027

15Dec86-5Aqu	1 1/16 [•]:47^{3}1:13^{1}1:46^{3}ft	30	110^7	4$^{2\frac12}$	4^4	7$^{8\frac14}$	5$^{15\frac14}$	RomeroJA^5	Ⓕ Aw31000	62-20	Ecorche,HppyCherok,PltinumPostr	8
30Nov86-6Aqu	7f :22^4 :45^4 1:24^{2}ft	14	117	6^7	6^9	6^8	6$^{10\frac34}$	RomeroRP^1	Ⓕ Aw29000	68-24	NotchsTrc,PltinumPostr,SucyMissy	9
23Nov86-6Aqu	7f :22^1 :45^3 1:23^{3}ft	6½	115	2$^{\frac12}$	1^{hd}	5^8	6$^{15\frac14}$	RomeroRP^3	Ⓕ Aw36000	58-23	SherryMary,BarbicueSuce,DmeGris	7
12Sep86-6Bel	7f [T]:23^1 :46 1:22^{4}fm	21	115	1^{hd}	2^{hd}	7^8	9^{10}	Romero R P^8	Ⓕ Manta	80-08	Duckweed, Top Issue, Tarifa	9
12Sep86—Run in Divisions												
30Aug86-9Atl	5½f [T]:22 :45^{3}1:04^{3}fm	*3¼	112	4^4	3$^{2\frac12}$	3$^{\frac12}$	2^{nk}	BilbyJA^2	Ⓕ Ocean City	90-15	LdyInBlue,AllForLondon,Chrmful	10
16Aug86-8Atl	6f :21^4 :45 1:09^{2}ft	3¾	112	5$^{1\frac34}$	5^5	3^5	3$^{2\frac34}$	Lopez C^2	Ⓕ Margate	92-12	Aldn'sAmbton,PsWho,AllForLondn	8
2Aug86-6Mth	5f :22 :45 :57^{3}ft	23	113	5^4	4^4	3$^{2\frac12}$	2$^{\frac12}$	LpzC^8	Ⓕ Platnum Blle	95-12	QuitPnsy,AllForLondon,FstrThnFst	8
26Jly85-5Mth	170 :46 1:11^2 1:41^{4}sy	11	113	3$^{1\frac12}$	2$^{\frac12}$	4$^{3\frac12}$	4$^{4\frac12}$	LpC^4	Ⓕ Ambssdr Luck	82-15	Top Issue, Four Flings,MissNataLu	6

Jan 10 Bel tr.t 3f ft :38 b

This mare shows three lifetime victories and you may quickly and correctly assume that one of these was the traditional maiden win and the two others were in allowance races for non-winners "other than" at the appropriate level, which qualifies her for the conditions of this race. Our problem, of course, is with class ratings, as always.

Look at the last three races, allowance events with three different purse structures. How do you rate them? Are they all the same or is the race of 23Nov86 with a $36,000 purse at a higher level? Because there are no wins showing in the eight races set forth above, you can now be reasonably sure that in each of the last three allowance races, the conditions were very likely the same as those for the Jan. 23, 1987 race which we are reviewing. If the conditions are approximately the same, the class of the race would be approximately the same, despite the $36,000 purse on 23Nov86. The purse in today's conditions is $29,000, the same as on 30Nov86. The judgment call here is that there is not sufficient class difference involved, and therefore, all three of these races would be rated approximately even in class to today's races, and no points, up or down, would be involved.

On 12Sept86 there is a named stakes at Belmont, which we would rate as roughly equivalent to the next class level above, and award one Higher Class point. Can an argument be made for two points? Perhaps, but again in this wide range of class, we need more assurance of higher class before we can go to two points.

There are two stakes shown at Atlantic City. Again, we have to resort to conjecture, since we must assume that none of us have a record of those August races to determine the purse values and conditions. Again, the safe, conservative thing to do is to rate the two Atlantic City races, because the track itself is considerably below the New York circuit in class value, as relatively even to the "non-winners of three other than" in New York and again award no points.

On the other hand, the two Monmouth stakes races shown for 2Aug86 and 26Jly86 may be a shade higher. Monmouth (as well as its sister track at the Meadowlands) is a much better track than Atlantic City, but not as classy as New York. Here we can make an argument for 1 Higher Class point for each race, and act accordingly.

We can next look at My Virginia Reel, who last ran for a claiming tag of $100,000.

My Virginia Reel — **B. m. 5, by Roanoke Island—Tizonada, by Tinajero**

Br.—Dodderidge R R (Va) — 1987 2 0 0 0 $960

Own.—Dodderidge R R — **117** — **Tr.—Fernandez Floreano** — 1986 2 2 0 0 $29,700

Lifetime 14 3 4 3 $74,610 — **Turf** 2 1 0 0 $18,400

15Jan87-7Aqu	170 ⊡ :48^2 1:13 1:43^1 ft	6	122	1^1	1^{hd}	6^6	7^{9½}	Davis R^1	Ⓕ 100000	74-19	BthsSong,HppyChrok,VntgChmpgn	7
4Jan87-8Lrl	6f :22^4 :47 1:12 ft	4½	114	2^{hd}	1^{hd}	2^3	4^{5¼}	McCrronG^3	ⒻAw16000	78-19	FrndlyTony,WorthyWorthy,GldKss	8
18Jan86-5SA	a6½f Ⓣ:22 :44^4 1:16 fm	8½	120	5^{1¾}	5^{4¼}	3^{nk}	1^{¾}	StevensGL^3	ⒻAw28000	79-16	My Virginia Reel, Miranda,InNeon	12
4Jan86-6SA	1 1/16 :47 1:11 1:42^4 ft	3¾	117	1^{½}	1^1	1^3	1^3	StevensGL^1	ⒻAw26000	87-13	MyVirgnRl,Sr'sNwHop,Vronc'sQust	7
26Dec85-6SA	6f :21^4 :44^1 1:09^2 ft	2¾	115	5^{1¾}	5^{7½}	6^{9¼}	4^{10¼}	McCrrnCJ^7	ⒻAw24000	81-13	Doff, SoulLight,HappyEveraftering	8
6Dec85-8Hol	1 :44^3 1:10 1:35^1 ft	*4-5	114	2^{½}	1^{½}	2^{½}	2^6	McCrrnCJ^1	ⒻAw22000	81-17	VividDncer,MyVirginiRel,NtliKnows	6
30Oct85-3SA	1 1/16 :45^4 1:10^4 1:44 ft	2	114	1^{hd}	1^{hd}	2^{½}	3^{2½}	McCrrnCJ^2	ⒻAw27000	78-14	RsUpAndDnc,Vronc'sQst,MyVrgnRl	7
20Oct85-8SA	6f :21^4 :45 1:10^3 ft	*9-5	114	3^2	3^{2½}	3^3	3^{4¼}	Meza R Q^5	ⒻAw24000	81-17	NotAllFoolish,DrmFthr,MyVirginiRl	9

Jan 14 Bel tr.t 4f ft :51^1 b — Dec 27 Mid tr.t 5f ft 1:03^4 b

Our first decision compels us to compare the $100,000 claimer with today's allowance race. It may have attracted entries of higher class than today's race, but we cannot be sure without going back to that race of 15Jan87. Again, we solve our problem by the conservative tack of the rating the races as even, where we lack sufficient facts upon which to make a judgment. The California races may be rated also as approximately the same in class, but how about the lower purse allowance race at Laurel on 4Jan87?

The Maryland tracks, which have advanced immeasurably in the last two years under dynamic leadership, still rate below the New York circuit in general class of racing. The Laurel race, therefore, with lower purse value, even assuming the same conditions of "nonwinners of three other than," would have to receive 1 Lower Class point.

Let's do one more from this same race to illustrate yet another point. We can use Just Gorgeous for this example.

Just Gorgeous — **Ch. f. 4, by Princely Pleasure—Bluegrass Ball, by Young Emperer**

Own.—Gold-N-Oats Stable — 114^5 — **Br.—Edwards Mr-Mrs K J (Va)** — **Tr.—Lenzini John J Jr**

Lifetime	25	5	6	3	$99,175		
1987	2	2	0	0	$33,600		
1986	18	1	5	3	$36,820		
Turf	1	0	0	0			

14Jan87-5Aqu	6f	[•]:22^2 :45^{2}1:11^{1}ft	*6-5	112^5	$1^{\frac12}$	$1^{1\frac12}$	1^1	$1^{\frac12}$	Ortiz E Jr^3	[F]Aw27000	88-16	JustGorgous,Blm'sMjsty,MssScndl	7
2Jan87-1Aqu	6f	[•]:22^1 :45^{2}1:11 m	3e	108^5	1^{hd}	1^{hd}	$1^{\frac12}$	$1^{\frac12}$	Ortiz E Jr^2	[F] 75000	89-21	JustGorgeous,Robin'sRob,T.V.Snow	8
20Dec86-1Aqu	6f	[•]:22^2 :45^{2}1:10^{2}ft	2	116	1^1	1^{hd}	1^{hd}	2^2	Cordero A Jr^4	[F] 50000	90-09	Spiriting, JustGorgeous,Doonesday	9
7Dec86-4Aqu	6f	[•]:22^2 :45^{4}1:11^{1}ft	*3	107^7	1^{hd}	1^1	1^1	2no	Ortiz E Jr^7	[F] 45000	88-18	ARILulu,JustGorgous,Blum'sMjsty	10
22Nov86-1Aqu	7f	:23^2 :46^3 1:25 ft	$4\frac14$	116	$3^{\frac12}$	$6^{1\frac34}$	$7^{6\frac34}$	7^{12}	Lovato F Jr^1	[F] c35000	64-18	Quillo's Love,TorridZone,Pia'sBaby	8
7Nov86-5Aqu	6f	:22^1 :45^4 1:10^{3}ft	28	116	2^1	1^1	1^{hd}	2^3	Ward W A^3	[F] 35000	85-21	SondRsonng,JstGorgos,Blm'sMjsty	8
24Sep86-9Bel	6f	:22^2 :46 1:10^{4}ft	29	116	5^5	9^{11}	$6^{5\frac14}$	$7^{10\frac34}$	Santagata N^8	[F] 35000	78-16	Spiriting, Cherokee Chill, Grotona	11
3Sep86-9Med	6f	:22^2 :45^3 1:11^{1}ft	19	113	$6^{6\frac12}$	$6^{6\frac34}$	$6^{5\frac34}$	$6^{6\frac34}$	McClyWH^1	[F]Aw16000	79-18	Glide Along, Star Brilliant,Spiriting	7

Dec 17 Aqu [•] 4f ft :49 b   ●Dec 1 Aqu [•] 5f ft 1:03^1 b

We wanted to show you this filly because of her claiming race background. Since she has five lifetime victories and is still eligible for this race, we know that some of these triumphs were scored in claiming races, and we can see at least one of them in the line of 2Jan87, where she won for a tag of $75,000. Her last race of 14Jan87 where she won under allowance conditions with a purse of $27000 tells us that this was very likely for "nonwinners of two other than. . ." This would make it a shade below the class of today's race, but some of the other entries also show allowance races which were very likely under similar conditions. All of these animals would have been ordinarily climbing the same class progression ladder.

But our task here is to assign class points, up or down, and no more. Because no horse in the race has won three times in allowance company, and every one of them (I have not shown all of them for reasons of space, but this is the case) has won at least two in allowance company, and show similar climbs up the class ladder, we can rate all the allowance races as basically even in class, and award no points at all. Back to Just Gorgeous, the $75,000 claiming race would likely be of the same class as the $100,000 claimer in which My Virginia Reel ran, so we can treat it the same way and award no points either way. But when we come to the $50,000 claimer, we assess 1 Lower Class point, and so the same for the $45,000 race. We are next confronted with a string of three races where the claiming price was $35,000, and here we can step down the price ladder one rung, and assess 2 Lower Class points for each of these three races. That about does it.

Now, let's see if we can summarize some guidelines for evaluating class in allowance races. We have tried to stress that it is literally impossible to discuss all the various situations you will encounter without writing half a text or more on the subject, and that is beyond the range of what we are trying to do here. We re-state the purpose of this chapter: to provide you enough principles and guidelines to enable you to reasonably assess class ratings in past races, not perfectly, but close enough so your tallies will be as useful and reliable as the average good player can make them. Some of this may be repetitious and some of it may be restatements of what has been set forth above.

1. In any situation, when in doubt or when knowledge is lacking about a track, be conservative in assigning class points. Remember, on any difficult individual line, not more than one point is at stake either way. Although we strive at all times for accuracy, one point will not substantially alter a PCR. What is important is to be correct in rating enough running lines that your class ratings will have overall significance.

2. Learn the standard claiming price levels at your track, up and down, in order that you may compare races at claiming levels.

3. High priced claiming races may be as good or better than some allowance races. Use purse structures as a helpful comparison factor.

4. When horses have run races at other tracks, which will show in the vast majority of all past performances, try to evaluate the class of the outside track itself, higher or lower, and integrate general track class with claiming price.

5. Be alert to claiming prices that are reduced because of weight-off allowances. Horses should be rated off the top claiming price shown in the conditions of the race.

6. When comparing claiming races with allowance races, look for guidance in the purse of the claiming race where it is known. Ordinarily, an allowance race with a purse approximately the same as that of a claiming race is one class level higher merely because none of the horses in the allowance race are subject to being claimed.

7. In evaluating class in allowance races, study carefully the con-

ditions of the race before you, and try to evaluate other allowance races in the past performances, where you will not necessarily have access to the conditions, in the framework of the class of today's allowance race.

8. Named but ungraded stakes races at the same track are usually one class level above higher allowance races, and may be even two levels above the cheaper allowance races or those for very limited winners.

6 Solving Additional Class Rating Problems

WHILE THE PREVIOUS chapter dealt with most of the primary class rating problems that you will normally encounter in claiming and allowance races, there are a number of remaining areas that will arise from time to time. Because every race you will ever handicap makes an important contribution to your bankroll, up or down, and you need to know all that is possible, and more, it is essential to be able to deal with occurring problems beyond the ordinary. None of these is especially difficult. All them contribute to your class ratings.

(a) *Starter Allowance or Starter Handicap Races*

At many tracks in the United States, there are races known as Starter Allowance (west coast) or Starter Handicaps (east coast). These races protect ordinary claiming horses from being subjected to claim. Eligibility conditions are written with reference to horses having started for a certain claiming price, usually quite low, within a specified back period of time. These races provide trainers with a variety of opportunities for class maneuvers, and such events must be watched carefully in evaluting class.

For example, a trainer may enter an animal whose true value may be at a $10,000 level into a lowly $5,000 claiming race when the horse is off form, or at a stage where the trainer is reasonably confident he can risk running the horse without having it claimed. After the "risk" race is run without a claim, the trainer may then elevate the horse back to his truer class level of $10,000. Then, at some later time, when a starter race is carded for horses that have run for a $5,000 claiming price within the past year (or eight months or whatever), the trainer can happily enter his charge, a normal $10,000 claiming horse, in this event without running another risk of a claim in the hope that he will meet a string of inferior competitors.

It doesn't always work that way, of course, primarily because these starter races are commonly filled with a number of horses of higher value that have run at one time for the bottom figure. But for handicappers comparing class ratings, we must know how to treat these occasional races. Because the major line of comparison for class ratings is the class of today's race, you must compare the value of previous running lines with the class of the starter race before you.

We can begin by looking at the conditions of the 9th race at Bay Meadows on January 23, 1987.

9th BayMeadows

1 $\frac{3}{16}$ MILES. (1.52⅗) STARTER ALLOWANCE. Purse $7,000. 4-year-olds and upward which have started for a claiming price of $6,250 or less since January 1, 1985 and since that start have not won a race other than maiden, starter or claiming or a claiming or starter race exceeding $6,250. Weights, 4-year-olds, 121 lbs., older, 122 lbs. Non-winners of two starter races since December 15 allowed 3 lbs.; two such races since November 15, 5 lbs.; one such race since December 15, 7 lbs. (Maiden, starter and claiming races for $5,000 or less not considered.)

It is listed as a Starter Allowance with a variety of conditions. The key claiming price situation is that the eligible horse must have started for a regular claiming price of $6,250 or less since January 1, 1985 to the date of today's race, which is an unusually long two-year period. All this means is that somewhere back in the past performances within the previous two years, that animal must have run for a $6,250 claiming price. The other conditions in the race which deal with winning performances and weight are not as important at this moment as the class ratings that we are required to make for each entry in the race.

Running through some necessary examples will get us started. The first horse is Rainbow Ridge.

Rainbow Ridge — Ch. g. 5, by Cloudy Dawn—Swinging Sara, by Nearctic
MAPLE S — 115 — Br.—Rancho Del Charro (Cal) — 1987 1 1 0 0 $3,300
Tr.—Arterburn Jack — 1986 10 0 0 2 $7,265
Own.—Wong Tai Sang — Lifetime 16 2 2 2 $19,760

10Jan87-3BM	$1\frac{1}{16}$	:47^4	1:13^2	1:47^{3}sl	$4\frac{3}{4}$	115	2^{hd}	1^1	1^2	$1\frac{1}{2}$	Maple S^1	6250	54-34	RinbowRidge,FletBlldir,Promptnss	8
21Dec86-9BM	$1\frac{1}{16}$	:48^3	1:14	1:47^{4}m	$7\frac{1}{2}$	114	$5^{2\frac{1}{2}}$	$4^{3\frac{1}{2}}$	$6^{9\frac{1}{4}}$	$6^{12\frac{3}{4}}$	Schacht R^8	[S] 8000	40-35	PcosExprss,BorrgoSn,MovYorAsst	8
22Nov86-5BM	6f	:23	:46^1	1:11^{1}ft	36	114	11^{12}	11^{13}	11^{10}	$8^{5\frac{1}{4}}$	Schacht R^7	10000	78-24	DustyTrader,DownRange,FireyStr	12
1Nov86-9BM	6f	:22^3	:45^3	1:10^{1}ft	40	114	12^{15}	12^{15}	12^{13}	10^9	Schacht R^7	12500	79-21	Pensr,UnitedVictory,PlentyBrown	12
1Nov86—Ducked in start															
4May86-1GG	$1\frac{1}{16}$	:46^4	1:11^1	1:44^{4}ft	$3\frac{1}{4}$	109^5	5^{11}	$5^{7\frac{1}{2}}$	$4^{4\frac{1}{2}}$	3^3	Yamamoto T J^3	16000	76-19	Vronic'sMrk,Exclusion,RinbowRidg	6
12Apr86-6GG	$1\frac{1}{16}$	:46^3	1:11^1	1:43 ft	*$2\frac{1}{4}$	114	9^{15}	10^{15}	10^{14}	10^{11}	Baze R A^1	25000	77-17	FlyingBob,Dave'sReality,WhtAPly	10
26Feb86-6GG	$1\frac{1}{16}$	:46^4	1:11^2	1:43^{2}ft	16	114	$6^{7\frac{1}{2}}$	$5^{3\frac{3}{4}}$	$8^{9\frac{3}{4}}$	4^2	Schacht R^6	Aw17000	84-18	Witin'ForBevr,BroomBuck.GtMEvn	8
12Feb86-8GG	$1\frac{1}{16}$	:47^2	1:11	1:42^{2}sy	26	114	7^{16}	6^{14}	5^9	3^7	Schacht R^2	Aw16000	84-20	RetsinLdr,BroomBuck,RinbowRidg	8
30Jan86-8BM	$1\frac{1}{16}$	:47^2	1:11^3	1:43^{2}m	$7\frac{1}{2}$	114	$3\frac{1}{2}$	$6^{6\frac{1}{2}}$	7^{12}	6^{19}	Schacht R^7	Aw16000	56-23	Dominant, Get MeEven,PorchLight	7
18Jan86-9BM	1	:47^4	1:13^3	1:39^{1}gd	4	120	$5^{5\frac{1}{2}}$	$8^{6\frac{1}{2}}$	$5^{8\frac{1}{2}}$	$4^{10\frac{1}{2}}$	Ives T A^8	Aw17000	61-24	Julie'sMark,GallntHwk,GetMeEven	8

Jan 8 BM 3f m :37^3 h   Dec 31 BM 5f ft 1:02^3 h   Dec 14 BM 1 ft 1:39^4 h   Dec 8 BM 6f gd 1:16^2 h

This horse is eligible because he ran in his last race for $6250. You can also see that this horse has been sliding steadily down the class ladder from allowance races down to higher priced claimers to the $6250 figure last out.

The very last race was a straight claiming race for $6250. Is it equivalent in class to the $6250 starter race before us? Not at all, for the reason that these starter races, whatever the price may be, will almost always rank higher in class than an ordinary claiming race at the same price. Therefore, we would award 1 Lower Class point for the last claiming race.

The next race down, that of 21Dec86, was an $8000 statebred claiming race. Is it the same class as today's race, or inferior, or superior? Because I attend races in the east, even though I read and try to study racing all around the United States, I am not as fully knowledgeable about northern California tracks as the scholars who reside there, but my general awareness tells me that a race limited to California-bred horses is lower in class than the same priced event open to horses bred anywhere. If the $8000 state bred is equivalent in class to a $6250 open claiming race, and a $6250 open claiming race is not equal in class to a $6250 starter race, then the state-bred event would receive the same 1 Lower Class point that the $6250 race received. This is an example of the kind of judgments and calculations you will be required to make in many situations. It thus presents the principles on which you will have to work in making these class evaluations yourself, when you read and study your Racing Form for the races you are going to play.

Our next problem comes in the very next line below as we have to decide where to slot the $10,000 claiming race. Because you will see in other past performances in this race that there is a level of $8,000 open claiming races at Bay Meadows, which is the next level above the $6250 claiming race, you must also rate the $8000 race and use it as a base for comparison with the $10,000 race. We can safely adopt a rule in starter races that the next higher claiming price level is approximately even in class with the lower priced starter race. Accordingly, the $8000 race, which you will see in the next past performances that we will show, is awarded no class points up or down.

Therefore, if the $8,000 race is even, the $10,000 race becomes the very next level above, and for a $10,000 race, we can assign 1 Higher Class point.

As for the remainder of the races of Rainbow Ridge, the $12,500 race would then merit 2 Higher Class points, as would all the others shown. We may now move to the next horse, which will only require the briefest of comments.

West Side Willie — Dk. b. or br. g. 7, by No Prevue—McLass, by McTavish
TOHILL K S — 115 — Br.—Clement Mr–Mrs J C (Cal) — 1987 1 0 0 0
Own.—Shoua D & Silva — Tr.—Silva Neal — 1985 14 3 1 2 $15,894
Lifetime 37 7 3 5 $54,504 — Turf 4 1 0 0 $6,050

11Jan87-5BM	6f	:23	:47	$1:12^2$gd	22	115	9^{12}	$99\frac{1}{4}$	$87\frac{1}{2}$	$76\frac{1}{4}$	Tohill K S^5	8000	71-27	Pro Am, Pensar, Fleet Waver	10
20Dec85-9BM	$1\frac{1}{4}$	:46	$1:37^2$	$2:04^2$ft	$5\frac{1}{2}$	115	6^{13}	$74\frac{3}{4}$	$2\frac{1}{2}$	$1\frac{3}{4}$	Tohill K S^7	A5000	80-24	WstSdWll,‡Bn'sDncr,GongFrAStrll	8
20Dec85—Wide into stretch															
6Dec85-9BM	$1\frac{1}{4}$	$:51^2$	$1:44^2$	$2:11^4$sl	5	115	$31\frac{1}{2}$	2^{hd}	3^1	$22\frac{1}{2}$	Tohill K S^4	A5000	40-41	Cat Isle Don, West Side Willie,Pow	6
22Nov85-10BM	$1\frac{1}{4}$	$:47^1$	$1:37^1$	2:03 ft	$8\frac{1}{2}$	115	$79\frac{1}{2}$	$44\frac{1}{2}$	$46\frac{1}{2}$	4^{11}	Tohill K S^1	A5000	76-20	Pow, O' Lucky Pet, Bini's Dancer	11
8Nov85-9BM	$1\frac{1}{4}$	:48	$1:37^3$	$2:02^1$ft	4	119	3^5	5^7	5^{10}	$514\frac{1}{2}$	Tohill K S^3	A5000	76-25	Pow, Bini's Dancer, First Amour	6
25Oct85-10BM	$1\frac{3}{16}$	$:47^4$	$1:12^3$	$1:57^1$ft	11	122	3^{nk}	$2\frac{1}{2}$	$2\frac{1}{2}$	$31\frac{3}{4}$	Tohill K S^3	A5000	76-27	Pow, Bini'sDancer,WestSideWillie	12
11Oct85-9BM	$1\frac{3}{16}$	:47	$1:11^4$	$1:55^2$ft	$9\frac{1}{2}$	117	$32\frac{1}{2}$	$31\frac{1}{2}$	$4\frac{3}{4}$	1^{hd}	Tohill K S^7	A5000	87-20	WestSidWilli,BlckMrktr,Bini'sDncr	7
27Sep85-9BM	$1\frac{1}{8}$	$:46^1$	$1:10^3$	$1:50^2$ft	$9\frac{3}{4}$	117	6^{12}	4^7	4^3	$51\frac{1}{2}$	Tohill K S^6	A5000	77-20	Bini'sDncer,Bnker'sPyoff,CrditKing	8
27Sep85—Far wide stretch															
14Sep85-12Bmf	$1\frac{1}{4}$	$:45^3$	$1:36^2$	$2:02^2$ft	45	113	5^{13}	$43\frac{1}{4}$	$3\frac{1}{2}$	1^{hd}	Tohill K S^{10}	A5000	90-25	WestSideWillie,Bini'sDncer,PlnFst	10
6Sep85-12Bmf	$1\frac{1}{8}$	$:46^2$	$1:10^4$	1:49 ft	23	116	7^5	$65\frac{1}{2}$	6^8	$77\frac{3}{4}$	Munoz E^8	A5000	78-14	Bini's Dancer, Pow, Plane Fast	9

Jan 3 BM 6f sy $1:18^4$ h   Dec 28 BM 6f ft $1:15^4$ h   ●Dec 20 Sac 6f sy 1:21 h (d)   Dec 13 Sac 6f ft $1:14^3$ h

In the discussion above, we have disposed of the $8000 claiming question. Every other race shown is a $5000 starter allowance race, and this, in comparison with today's $6250 event, would be one class level below, and 9 Lower Class points would follow.

That just about covers the basic principles. To walk through all the other entries in that race would be largely repetitive. At your own track, you should be able to adequately deal with rating problems, as long as you bear in mind that the starter allowance or starter handicap at a particular claiming price is ordinarily higher in class by at least one level than a straight claiming race at the same price.

(b) *Rating Maiden Running Lines*

Rating past maiden running lines for class in races for winners is a quite different proposition from rating running lines in actual maiden races. In races for these non-winners of anything, comparisons of running lines for class is comparatively easy. If you have a field of straight maidens or maiden special entrants who have always run in such races, which is common, there would be no class points, up or down, for any of them. A horse rising from the maiden claiming ranks would be assessed lower class points just as in any other race, while a precocious maiden that may have competed in stakes races may receive higher class points when it is back in maiden company. Likewise, maiden claiming prices may be compared to each other.

However, because many horses entered in races for winners show in their past performances many past efforts in maiden ranks, these races must be evaluated for class, up or down. How do you compare the class of a race in a straight maiden against a low priced claiming race, or how many maiden races may you tolerate before downgrading for class? These, and many other questions, will frequently arise.

Let's return to Bay Meadows for the 10th race on the same January 23 card that we have previously reviewed. We start, as always, with the conditions of the race.

10th BayMeadows

1 1/16 MILES. (1.38⅖) CLAIMING. Purse $10,000. 4-year-olds. Weight, 120 lbs. Non-winners of two races at one mile or over since December 1 allowed 3 lbs.; one such race since then, 6 lbs. Claiming price $16,000. (Maiden, starter and claiming races for $12,500 or less not considered.)

You can see that this is an ordinary claiming race for a $16,000 claiming price, nothing unusual, no different from many that are run at tracks everywhere. Quite a number of the entries show maiden races in their p.p.'s. We can look at Super Charge to deal with some of the situations that arise.

Super Charge — Gr. g. 4, by Native Charger—Superiority, by Bold Ruler
Br.—Reed Dr W O (Ky) — 1987 1 0 0 0 $900
TOHILL K S — **114** — Tr.—Murphy Chuck — $16,000 — 1986 12 1 2 1 $10,759
Own.—4-Fun Stable & Maybury — Lifetime 13 1 2 1 $11,659

4Jan87-5BM	1 1/16	:46^3	1:12	1:46 m	26	114	7$^{8\frac{1}{2}}$	5^5	6$^{3\frac{1}{2}}$	4^3	Tohill K S^8	10000	59-30	WonderPlum,YeahMeDo,ChinaSag	10
19Dec86-9BM	1 1/16	:48^2	1:13^3	1:47 m	13	114	11^{12}	9$^{9\frac{1}{2}}$	8^{10}	6$^{5\frac{1}{4}}$	Grable T C^{11}	16000	52-29	YehMeDo,NightSwope,CptinO'Dsy	11
5Dec86-10BM	1 1/16	:46^1	1:12^1	1:45^{3}sl	16	114	7^{15}	6^6	5$^{4\frac{1}{2}}$	4^5	Grable T C^{10}	16000	59-26	Boundround,CloudBstr,Ddthbllrng	11
21Nov86-10BM	1 1/16	:46^3	1:11^3	1:43^{2}ft	23	114	1^{hd}	1^{hd}	4^2	4$^{5\frac{1}{4}}$	Grable T C^6	16000	70-23	Mr.Hugh,CutHimFree,Didthbllring	12
21Nov86—Lost whip 3/16															
7Nov86-4BM	1 1/8	:47	1:11^4	1:52^{3}ft	2$\frac{1}{2}$	117	5^5	3^4	1$^{\frac{1}{2}}$	1^{nk}	Grable T C^1	Mc12500	68-24	SuprChrg,WondrPlum,ThGoldGuy	12
30Oct86-4BM	1 1/16	:46	1:11^1	1:45 ft	*2$\frac{1}{4}$	116	7^{14}	5^{11}	4$^{6\frac{1}{2}}$	3^2	Grable T C^4	M16000	65-24	MovYorAsst,DynstcPckt,SprChrg	11
30Oct86—Bobbled start															
17Oct86-4BM	1 1/16	:47^1	1:11^4	1:44^{1}ft	3$\frac{3}{4}$	116	4$^{1\frac{3}{4}}$	1^{hd}	1$^{\frac{1}{2}}$	2$^{1\frac{1}{2}}$ ♦	Grable T C^8	M16000	69-16	RtonlApproch,MovYrAsst,SprChrg	10
♦17Oct86—Dead heat															
3Oct86-4BM	1 1/16	:46^3	1:11^4	1:44^{3}ft	13	116	9^{12}	7$^{5\frac{3}{4}}$	3$^{4\frac{1}{2}}$	2^3	Grable T C^2	M16000	66-21	TheRammer,SuperCharge,Zafirino	10
3Oct86—Hopped in air															
20Sep86-9BM	1	:46^4	1:11^1	1:36^{3}ft	35	115	10^{13}	9^{11}	8^{16}	8$^{17\frac{3}{4}}$	Grable T C^2	Mdn	67-19	AcksMlesin,ArtOfDwn,SplitWinnrs	10
29Aug86-4Dmr	1 1/16	:46^1	1:12^3	1:44^{1}ft	8$\frac{1}{2}$	111^5	8^{10}	7$^{6\frac{1}{2}}$	8^{18}	8$^{18\frac{1}{2}}$	Black C A^5	M32000	60-15	CodeDeInterpol,BlckStel,Yippyyo	12

Jan 15 BM 4f ft :51^3 h   Jan 2 BM 3f gd :39 h   Nov 30 BM 4f ft :53 h

His four most recent races are easily rated at the same claiming price of today's race. Then we are back to the race of 7Nov86, a maiden claimer with a $12,500 price. If the horse had run in an open claiming race for $12,500, we would rate it as one level below today's $16,000 event. But a maiden race at the same price is not equal in class to races for winners. Therefore, we would assess 2 Lower Class points.

The next three races were all maiden claimers at $16,000. As we have just indicated, this would be one class level below the open $16,000 claimer, for 1 Lower Class point. But as maiden claiming prices rise, the problems get stickier. We see a straight maiden at Bay Meadows and a $32,000 maiden claimer at Del Mar. How do we rate these races?

Again, general judgment and knowledge of class comparisons must be invoked. A straight maiden at Bay Meadows should be sufficient to place at one class level higher than a $16,000 open claiming race, because such races will ordinarily attract well bred animals who are considered by their handlers to have both a racing future and a high value. One point here for higher class, but not two points, because of the unproven quality of non-winners of any class. As to the race of 29Aug86 at Del Mar, we begin with the proposition that the track, being on the much higher class southern California circuit, would generally field higher class animals than the northern California circuit. Thus, a maiden claiming event at the reasonably high price of $32,000 would rank one class level above the $16,000 claimer, or roughly equivalent to the straight maiden at Bay Meadows.

A different kind of problem occurs in lower class allowance races for "non-winners other than." Let's compare two hypothetical horses, both of which show ten races in their past performances, which totals their lifetime starts. Horse A, in his last race, at straight maiden or maiden special, scored his first victory and thus graduated to the next class level of non-winners other than maiden, claiming, or starter. All his previous races were in straight maiden or maiden special where he was unable to win.

Horse B, on the other hand, broke his maiden in his second start, and has run his last eight races against winners. Because of the conditions of the race before you, which we still are assuming to be an allowance race for non-winners of a race other than maiden, claiming, or starter, all the horses would be theoretically equal in class, because none of them would have ever beaten allowance winners, and all of them would have won at the same maiden level.

Yet we accept the reality that races for winners are higher in class than races at the same price for non-winners. How we do we class-rate the string of maiden races showing for Horse A as against the races for winners shown by Horse B?

At this point, I have adopted an arbitrary rule which we are going to use. We will assume that any horse is entitled to four maiden efforts before it can be subjected to class penalties. After four losing efforts, the remaining maiden races would receive 1 Lower Class point. Thus, Horse A in our example would wind up with 6 Lower Class points for each of the six maiden races showing after forgiving his first four efforts. Horse B, which had only two maiden races before he moved upward to run against winners, would not be awarded class points either way in any of his efforts.

This rule may be usefully applied in other situations: no class penalty for a horse's first four maiden races, but after that, maiden efforts will have to be assessed generally lower as against races for winners. The more times a horse runs in the maiden ranks without winning, the more times we add on 1 Lower Class point. It works very well.

(c) *Class Ratings of Stakes Races*

In many allowance races in particular, many of the entrants will have run in named stakes races, or even up into graded stakes. On the other hand, in such stakes races, many entrants will have run in high class allowance races. How do we rate class lines, up or down, in these situations?

Again, we start with general principles. A named stakes race can be one level higher than a higher priced allowance race and two levels higher than lower priced allowance races. A Grade III stakes race is ordinarily a notch above ungraded stakes. And likewise it follows that Grade II stakes are a shade higher than Grade III, and Grade I stakes are at the very highest level of all. Again, demonstrations from a graded stakes and an allowance race can give us the sound applications. In making these comparisons, we must keep in mind at all times the class of the race that is being run and the general class experience of the contestants.

1 $\frac{1}{16}$ MILES. (1.40$\frac{1}{5}$) 23rd Running of The EL ENCINO STAKES (Grade III). $100,000 added. Fillies. 4-year-olds. (Allowance). By subscription of $50 each to accompany the nomination, $1,000 additional to start, with $100,000 added, of which $20,000 to second, $15,000 to third, $7,500 to fourth and $2,500 to fifth. Weight, 122 lbs. Winners of $100,000 twice at one mile or over in 1986–87, 2 lbs. additional Non–winners of $90,000 at one mile or over or two such races of $40,000 in 1986–87 allowed 3 lbs; of $60,000 at one mile or over or $30,000 twice at any distance in 1986–87, 5 lbs.; of $30,000 at seven furlongs or over since December 25, or $25,000 at one mile or over at anytime, 8 lbs. Starters to be named through the entry box by the closing time of entries. A trophy will be presented to the owner of theClosed Wednesday, January 14, 1987 with 17 nominations.

This Grade III stakes on the dirt was for 4-year-old fillies and drew a sparkling field, including two stars from the talent-rich Wayne Lukas stable, Life at the Top and Family Style. Family Style, for example, shows races in only Grade I, II, and III level stakes. We would give her 1 Higher Class Point for Grade II and 2 Higher Class points for Grade I, which takes care of her ratings. We can learn better from other animals where we can find a greater mixture of races. Out of the barn of the renowned Charlie Whittingham, we can look at Kraemer, whose past efforts all show turf races. We will deal with turf racing shortly, but for now, we will rate all these turf races for class only.

```
Kraemer                              B. f. 4, by Lyphard—Rich and Rietous, by Empery
 BAZE G                              Br.—Hunt N B (Ky)                       1986 12 3 2 2   $160,375
                               119   Tr.—Whittingham Charles                 1985  4 1 0 1    $10,440
Own.—Hunt N B                      Lifetime  16 4 2 3  $170,815              Turf 15 4 2 2   $166,915
13Dec86-8BM  a1⅛(T)        1:48 fm 6½ 117    69½ 65½ 45½ 23½   CstdM1 (F)Ca Jky CbH 91-05 Solva, Kraemer, Bonne Ile  7
    13Dec86—Grade III
23Nov86-8Hol  1⅛(T):473 1:113 1:48 fm 9¼e120  1214 129¾ 117¼ 109¼  BazeG11 (F)Mtrarch Iv 79-13 Auspiciante, Aberuschka, Reloy 12
    23Nov86—Grade I; Very wide into stretch; bumped early drive
1Nov86-10BM  1 1/16(T):474 1:123 1:434fm *6-5 117  107¾ 84¼ 11½ 17  BazeG9 (F)B M Oaks H 84-16 Kremer,Chnngo'sAlibi,BlckSophie 12
8Oct86-8SA   a6½f (T):213 :443 1:144fm 15 113  95½ 94¼ 72¾ 51¾  BlckCA9 (F)Atm Dys H 83-14 Shywing,HerRoyalty,WaterCrystals 9
    8Oct86—Blocked into stretch; Run in divisions
7Sep86-8Dmr  1⅛(T):471 1:11 1:482fm 5 109  65½ 73¼ 810 89½  BlcCA4 (F)Ramona H 82-08 Auspiciante, Justicara, Sauna 9
    7Sep86—Grade I
24Aug86-8Dmr  1⅛(T):471 1:11 1:474fm 5¼ 114  510 37½ 22½ 2¾  BlcCA3 (F)Dmr Oaks 94-04 HiddenLight,Krmr,ShotgunWdding 7
    24Aug86—Grade II
14Aug86-5Dmr  1 1/16(T):471 1:112 1:42 fm *9-5 1115  64¾ 53¼ 11½ 14  Black C A3 (F)Aw23000 96-04 Kremer,T.V.Rsidul,ShotgurWdding 8
    14Aug86—Crowded 3/8 turn
26Jly86-8Dmr  1 1/16(T):474 1:113 1:421fm 6¼ 111  109¾ 88½ 99 85¾  SolsA2 (F)(R)Osunitas H 89-05 FlyingGirl,Cnyk'sStr,MssBvrlyHlls 11
    26Jly86—Run in divisions
2Jly86-7Hol   1 1/16(T):473 1:111 1:413fm 7 1095  41½ 1hd 11 3½  Black C A1 (F)Aw25000 95-07 Rekindling, T. V. Residual,Kraemer 9
22May86-9Hol  1 1/16(T):454 1:102 1:413fm 2¼ 1095  35½ 2hd 12 12  Black C A1 (F)Aw22000 96-04 Kraemer,OurLutka,WeddingDancer 9
  Jan 20 SA 5f ft 1:012 h    ●Jan 15 SA 1 ft 1:402 h    Jan 10 SA 6f gd 1:133 h    ●Jan 3 SA 6f ft 1:123 h
```

We may move quickly from the graded stakes to the other races showing. As we do this, we must bear in mind that we are not talking about the inherent class of Kraemer, but about comparisons of performance in past races. A horse that ran seventh at the second call and sixth at the finish in a Grade I race might run third at the second call and third at the finish in a Grade II or Grade III race.

There is the 1Nov86 ungraded stakes at Bay Meadows. We would have to place it one level below for 1 Lower Class point. The next decision areas come in the allowance races shown, which, because of the size of their purses, are reasonably strong. Here, we would assess 2 Lower Class points, and that is it.

Another entry in the race, Seldom Seen Sue, whose record we do not need to show, ran in two Del Mar allowance races at $19,000 immediately after she broke her maiden in 1986. Not only is the purse size below that of the higher allowance races, but you may be sure that these allowances were for "non-winners other than maiden, claiming, or starter," and thus of considerably lower quality than what is before us today. However, just as we limit class points to no more than 2, except in the vastly different and limited situations where we award 3, we will not award more than 2 Lower Class points otherwise.

Now, let's move to Bay Meadows for a lesser quality race on January 24, 1987, the Atherton Stakes, carrying a purse of $50,000 added.

This is a rather typical Saturday ungraded stakes race at good tracks of the level of Bay Meadows, Hialeah, Meadowlands, Hawthorne,

8th BayMeadows

1 1/16 MILES. (1.38⅘) 8th Running of THE ATHERTON STAKES. $50,000 added. 3-year-olds. (Allowance). By subscription of $50 each, which shall accompany the nomination, $200 to pass the entry box, and $250 additional to start, with $50,000 added, of which $9,000 to second, $6,500 to third, $4,000 to fourth, $1,750 to fifth and $1,250 to sixth. Weight, 120 lbs. Non-winners of a race of $20,000 at one mile or over since September 1 allowed 3 lbs.; of $12,000 any distance since July 1, 5 lbs.; of $8,500 at any distance since May 1, 8 lbs. Starters to be named through the entry box Thursday, January 22 by the usual time of closing. A trophy will be presented to the owner of the winner. Closed Thursday, January 15, 1987 with 21 nominations. Winners of a sweepstakes preferred. (Maiden and claiming races not considered).

Laurel, and similar tracks. You will find horses ranging up and down the class ladder from graded stakes to cheap allowances, and in some cases, even claiming races. This race is limited to 3-year-olds early in the year, which means that all of the entries are not far removed from their 2-year-old seasons and are not likely to show a wide range of experiences. From the record of Thunder Cat, we can extract a few instances that require us to make class rating judgments.

Thunder Cat — Gr. c. 3, by Storm Bird—Salud, by Raise a Cup
BAZE R A — 115 — Br.—Thmas-Partnrs-Ashfrd Stud (Ky) — 1987 1 0 0 0 $4,500
Tr.—Drysdale Neil — 1986 6 2 1 0 $25,150
Own.—Farish-Hudson Jr-Kilroy — Lifetime 7 2 1 0 $29,650

14Jan87-8SA	1	:46^2	1:10^3	1:36^{2}ft	6¼	116	$6^{3\frac{3}{4}}$	5^5	$5^{7\frac{1}{2}}$	$4^{9\frac{3}{4}}$	DlhossyE^2	[R]Los Feliz	76-20	MsterfulAdvocte,RdAndBlu,Tlinum	6
14Dec86-8Hol	1	:44^4	1:09^3	1:36^{1}ft	18	121	$11^{6\frac{1}{4}}$	$11^{9\frac{3}{4}}$	$8^{9\frac{1}{2}}$	$8^{13\frac{1}{4}}$	OlivaresF^{10}	Hol Fut	69-18	TempertSil,Alyshb,MstrfulAdvoct	12
14Dec86—Grade I; Wide final 3/8															
26Nov86-7BM	1	:45^4	1:10^2	1:36 ft	*2-3	120	$4^{4\frac{1}{2}}$	3^1	1^3	$1^{3\frac{1}{2}}$	Baze R A^5	Aw16000	88-20	ThundrCt,CourtWizrd,I'mNotorious	8
8Nov86-5Hol	1	:45^1	1:10^1	1:36 ft	*7-5	118	4^5	2^2	1^1	$1^{3\frac{1}{2}}$	Pincay L Jr^7	Mdn	83-13	ThunderCat,Barb'sRelic,LightSabre	9
25Oct86-6SA	1 1/16	:46^4	1:11^2	1:44^{2}ft	*9-5	117	$3^{\frac{1}{2}}$	1^{hd}	1^{hd}	2^{nk}	Delahoussaye E^5	Mdn	79-17	On The Line, Thunder Cat, Fiction	8
3Oct86-6SA	6f	:21^4	:44^3	1:09^{2}ft	9	118	$12^{9\frac{1}{2}}$	6^{10}	5^{11}	$4^{14\frac{1}{2}}$	DelahoussayeE^{10}	Mdn	76-17	Cpot,WndwoodLn,BooBoo'sBckro	12
3Oct86—Hopped in air															
24Aug86-6Dmr	6f	:22^3	:46^1	1:10^{4}ft	*9-5	117	1^{hd}	3^1	7^{11}	$8^{13\frac{1}{4}}$	McCarron C J^3	Mdn	71-12	ExbrntFlng,BooBoo'sBckro,Prmtng	8
24Aug86—Broke slowly															

Jan 22 SA 3f ft :35^2 hg   Jan 9 Hol 6f ft 1:14^3 h   ●Jan 3 SA 1 ft 1:40^2 h   Dec 29 SA 7f ft 1:27^2 h

Down at the bottom of his past performances, we can invoke our 4-race maiden rule, and award no points either way. We would rate the allowance race of 26Nov86 at Bay Meadows, because it was obviously for "nonwinners other than maiden. . ." as two class levels below today's named stakes event.

Now we can come to our first 3-point play. Thunder Cat ran in the Grade I Hollywood Futurity on 14Dec86, one of the premier two-year-old races late in the season. The class of this race is so vastly above the level of an ungraded stakes at Bay Meadows that we can safely award the 3 Higher Class points that we have been looking for. Of course, Thunder Bay didn't so very well in that kind of company, but his internal numbers of 11 and 8 are somewhat compensated for by the subtraction of the number of 3, based upon the Higher Class points.

The other race that we will rate, the 14Jan87 restricted stakes at

Santa Anita, may be a shade better than today's Bay Meadows stake, but here again, we are back to nebulous class lines involving lightly raced horses. I would be very conservative here and award no points either way, but if our knowledgeable handicapping experts on the west coast would want to overrule me and award 1 Higher Class point, the ultimate rating would not be too distorted either way. We are only trying to show how to handle situations of this kind.

Let's do one more from that race, using the erstwhile claimer, Hot and Smoggy, shipped up from southern California by Mel Stute, who became nationally known in 1986 as the handler of Snow Chief.

Hot And Smoggy

CHAPMAN T M		112	Ch. c. 3, by Singular—Marselar, by Selari				
			Br.—Siegel Jan (Fla)		1987 2 2 0 0	$26,950
Own.—Magee & Stute			Tr.—Stute Melvin F		1986 6 2 1 1	$19,225
			Lifetime 8 4 1 1 $46,175			

16Jan87-5SA	1½ :46⁴ 1:11¹ 1:43³ft	13 116	2½ 2hd 12 1⁶	ValenzuelPA⁵ Aw28000	83-18 Hot AndSmoggy,Reland,JustBobby 9
1Jan87-2SA	1 :46⁴ 1:12¹ 1:38³ft	*9-5e114	3¹ 2hd 1hd 1hd	Meza R Q¹⁰	c40000 75-19 HotAndSmoggy,Rkposh,SprActon 10
1Jan87—Wide 7/8 turn					
6Dec86-1Hol	7f :22¹ :45 1:25²gd	4½ 117	4² 3¹ 1½ 11½	Meza R Q⁶	32000 77-16 HotAndSmoggy,SolnBoostr,NomdB 7
20Nov86-3Hol	6f :22 :45⁴ 1:12¹ft	4½ .117	67½ 47½ 46 4⁴	Meza R Q⁴	32000 78-16 TheQuipper,Rakaposhi,DoubleSong 8
7Nov86-3Hol	6f :22² :46¹ 1:12²ft	*6-5 118	31½ 2hd 1hd 1½	Meza R Q⁴	M32000 81-18 HtAndSmggy,HllywdSrnd,NvrSmk 12
7Nov86—Lugged out backstretch					
24Oct86-2SA	6f :22 :45³ 1:11¹ft	*2½ 118	53½ 42½ 34½ 32¾	Stevens G L⁹	M40000 79-20 P.T.Hustlr,Grnspn,HotAndSmoggy 12
15Sep86-4Pom	6f :22² :46 1:11²ft	*2-3 118	2³ 23½ 22 2½	Vergara O⁷	M32000 93-08 Mr.ToBWon,HotAndSmoggy,Smdn 9
27Aug86-4Dmr	6f :22¹ :46² 1:14⁴ft	8½ 116	52½ 41½ 22 1½	† Vergara O⁹	M35000 79-14 ‡HotAndSmoggy,Bwn'sFld,Frcflly 12
27Aug86—Wide 3/8 turn, lugged in 1/8. ; †Disqualified and placed seventh					
● Jan 22 SA 4f ft :46⁴ h	Jan 15 SA 3f ft :36³ h	Jan 9 SA 5f sl 1:01⁴ h	Dec 28 SA 5f ft 1:02⁴ h		

We have two problems here, track class, and claiming class. Is an ungraded stakes at Bay Meadows equal or superior to the 16Jan87 allowance at Santa Anita? You will encounter similar problems wherever you are, where a horse who has run in an allowance race at a higher class track comes in to run at an ungraded stakes at a slightly lower class track. In happens all the time in the east between New York, New Jersey, and Maryland, and in some of the midwestern and southern tracks. Our purpose here is not to make the reader in Illinois or New Jersey an expert on California racing but to provide guidelines for you to apply whether you are at Oaklawn, Churchill, Pimlico, Canterbury, Calder, or Arlington. Thus, we re-emphasize that this California situation is only an example that is hoped to be illustrative of what you might encounter almost anywhere.

Back to the last Santa Anita race and our efforts to give it a running line class rating. As a rule, a strong allowance race from a higher level track would be equal to an ungraded stakes at a lesser quality track. But again, it would appear obvious that the Santa Anita allowance race was probably for non-winners other than maiden or claiming. So, once again, we have a close call that could be decided either way without offending our concepts. For our purposes here, I would make the hard decision of awarding 1 Lower Class point for the Santa Anita allowance race only because I have concluded that it was a lower grade allowance race. Then, for the remaining claiming races showing for Hot and Smoggy, we can award 2 Lower Class points each, and finish it off that way.

Obviously, other kinds of individual problems will arise, where we can only ask you to use your general knowledge and reasoning power, and come up with a solution as reasonably sound as you can. It will work remarkably well.

(d) *The Three-Point Play*

We have shown one example already where 3 points may be awarded, up or down, in class evaluations. We repeat the general standard: where the class of a race is vastly higher or lower in class than the race before you, where an ordinary 2-point difference is not sufficient to take into account the enormous difference in class, you should award 3 points up or down. Obviously, you will be called upon to exercise more general handicapping judgment in cases like this than in ordinary situations. We have already provided the example of the much higher class of a Grade I stakes race in comparison to ungraded stakes races or allowance races.

Now, we can look at a situation on the downside. On January 24, 1987, in New York, trainer Oscar Barrera, whose maneuvers up and down are often confusing, inexplicable, and sometimes incredibly

7th Aqueduct

1 1/16 MILES. (InnerDirt). (1.41⅘) ALLOWANCE. Purse $45,000. 4-year-olds and upward which have not won a race of $18,650 at a mile or over in 1986–87. Weight, 122 lbs. Non-winners of two raes of $17,500 at a mile or over since November 1 allowed 3 lbs.; of such a race since September 1 5 lbs.; of such a race since July 1 7 lbs. (Maiden, claiming, starter and restricted races not considered.)

Coupled—Proud And Tall and The Rogers Four.

Proud And Tall

Ch. c. 4, by Private Account—Deep Dish Pie, by George Lewis

Br.—Jones W L Jr P Farish W S (Ky) 1987 3 1 0 0 $9,060

Own.—Barrera O S **110^5** **Tr.—Barrera Oscar S** 1986 23 4 3 2 $68,040

Lifetime 32 6 4 2 $84,920 Turf 2 0 0 0

21Jan87-5Aqu	6f	[•]:22^2 :45^{4}1:10^{1}sy	11	113	10 7¾ 9 7¾ 6 8¾ 4 10¾	Bailey J D^6	45000	82-17	AswnHigh,FlyingSkipper,Dl'sFolly	11
16Jan87-2Aqu	6f	[•]:23^1 :47^{2}1:12^{1}ft	8¾	117	8^5 7 6¼ 5 2¾ 1^{nk}	Murphy D J^7	c17500	83-18	ProudAndTll,Chrsmo,HowofWnloc	10
8Jan87-1Aqu	6f	[•]:23^1 :47 1:12^{2}ft	20	117	9^9 9 5¼ 6^8 6 5¼	Murphy D J^9	17500	77-24	GoldenChief,Strtop,BetterBeSingl	10
31Dec86-2Aqu	1 3/16	[•]:47^{1}1:12^{2}1:57^{2}ft	10	115	2 1½ 5^5 7^{15} 7 16¾	Vasquez M M^5	25000	74-13	ArcticSong,LedTheWy,OurTriumph	9
11Dec86-2Aqu	1⅛	[•]:48^{2}1:13 1:51^{3}ft	20	113	6^6 10 8½ 10^{16} 10 18¼	Vasquez M M^9	45000	65-16	Alioth, Addison Steele, Dalmatian	10
23Nov86-9Aqu	1	:46^2 1:11 1:37^{1}ft	10	113	9 6¾ 8^{10} 7^8 7^9	Vasquez M M^5	45000	71-23	Sky Raider, Lord's Wish,LeVroom	11
9Nov86-3Aqu	1⅛	:48^1 1:12^1 1:52 sy	*3-2	110^7	1^{hd} 1^{hd} 2^2 2no	Nuesch D^4	35000	75-22	Concatinate,ProudAndTll,FlyGryFly	6
20Oct86-5Bel	1⅛	:46^3 1:11^1 1:49^{2}ft	29	114	3^2 5 6½ 7^{17} 7^{13}	Vasquez M M^5	Aw25000	67-16	WickedWike,Michel'sDncer,Hudcek	8

Dec 7 Bel tr.t 4f ft :49^3 b

successful, has entered Proud and Tall in the 7th at Aqueduct. We will show you the combined conditions and record of Proud and Tall.

The conditions of the race show that it is a high quality allowance event, with a purse of $45,000. You can see that it is restricted to horses that have not won at a mile or longer back through Jan. 1, 1986, in races where the winner's share would be $18.500 or more. You may quickly calculate that this would mean races where the purse was greater than $30,000, because the 60% winner's share of $30,000 would be a flat $18,000. The $500 thrown in makes it necessary for the horse to have won where the purse was higher than $30,000. You may expect to find some high- powered horses in a race of this kind.

We are only concerned here with class ratings for the running lines of 8Jan87 and 16Jan87, where Proud and Tall was entered in a $17,500 claiming race. You can see that Barrera claimed him in the January 16 race for that price, and ran the horse back five days later in a $45,000 claimer, where he ran dismally. Undaunted, Oscar is back again in three days boosting the horse farther up the ladder to the kind of allowance event you see before you. Unorthodox, yes, but New York players have long dropped their astonishment at the strange maneuvers of this trainer. But these are only asides, as our concern now rests solely with the class ratings of the two $17,000 claiming events as compared to the $45,000 high quality allowance race before us.

There is such a vast difference in class between these two kinds of races that you may easily and readily award 3 Lower Class points for each of the two claiming races. The 20Oct86 Belmont allowance race at a $25,000 purse would get 1 Lower Class point, and all the remaining races showing would receive the more traditional 2 Lower Class points.

At this point, we will digress for a moment from our 3-point discussion of class to show you how trainers carefully monitor and shave the conditions in these races. There were two horses entered in the same race above that just slide within the outer limits of these conditions. We will show only one of them, Alioth.

Look at the second line down in his p.p., the race of 30Dec86, where Alioth won an allowance event with a purse of $31,000. Sixty percent of $31,000 comes out to $18,600. The conditions provide that a horse must not have won $18,650. So you can see how the conditions are tailored to Alioth, with the extra $50 thrown in by the rac-

Alioth — Ch. c. 4, by Vigors—Bright Reflection, by Reneged
Own.—Harp Angel Stable — 1145 — Br.—Vogel W M Jr (NJ) — Tr.—O'Connell Richard
Lifetime 15 6 0 1 $75,532 — 1987 1 0 0 0 — 1986 14 6 0 1 $75,532 — Turf 2 0 0 0

7Jan87-8Aqu	1 1/16 ⊡:47⁴1:11¹1:44³ft	5	117	54¾ 52¾ 55 66	Davis R G6	Aw45000	81-21	Synastry, Grand Rivulet, Khozaam 11
30Dec86-6Aqu	170 ⊡:48 1:12²1:41 ft	12	117	31 2hd 13½ 16	Santagata N6	Aw31000	95-16	Alioth, I'm Ahead, Faraway Island 6
19Dec86-5Aqu	1 1/16 ⊡:46⁴1:11 1:44 m	5	115	33½ 42½ 44¼ 45¾	Santagata N7	70000	84-20	AlbertClipper,ClssicMov,BoldMrudr 8
11Dec86-2Aqu	1⅛ ⊡:48²1:13 1:51³ft	5	1107	43 53 2hd 1¾	Nuesch D4	47500	84-16	Alioth, Addison Steele, Dalmatian 10
24Nov86-8Med	1 :47² 1:11⁴ 1:38¹m	*6-5	1117	1hd 13 13½ 12½	Nuesch D5	Ⓢ Aw21200	84-27	Alioth, Drewster, Ernie'sSugarBowl 7
14Nov86-8Med	1 :47¹ 1:12 1:36²ft	5	1077	51¾ 52½ 31½ 12¼	Nuesch D7	Ⓢ Aw17500	93-12	Alioth, Talk Nice, Klassy Serenade 7
8Nov86-2Aqu	6f :22 :45³ 1:11¹sy	34	113	73¾ 53 21½ 1nk	Bailey J D10	15500	85-22	Alioth,MajesticDncer,Jugglebucks 11
18Sep86-8Med	1 Ⓣ:46³1:10⁴1:36 fm	40	112	41½ 68 611 720¼	Melendez JD9	Aw15000	78-09	LoomngLbr,SmmrColony,Woodcck 9

Dec 5 Bel tr.t 4f ft :48¹ h

ing secretary to require higher priced races. The trainer thus squeaked under the line and has entered his horse for more money against lesser class competition of the likes of Proud and Tall and a flock of others in the race.

(e) *Dirt to Turf and Turf to Dirt*

Most of you have learned that for many horses, there is a vast difference between performances on the grass and on the dirt. A good dirt runner may be a dismal performer on the turf. A strong turf horse may just never make it on the dirt. And, of course, there are versatile runners that can perform ably no matter what the surface. In making Performance Class Ratings, we would need to properly evaluate a horse and take into account how he is able to perform when we see both turf and dirt races in his past performances.

Experience has taught us to adopt these guidelines. If today's race is on the dirt, and the horse you are reviewing shows very bad lifetime performances on the grass, you should eliminate the grass races altogether, not counting the number of horses in the race in that total nor any of the second call or finish positions. From the 9th race at Santa Anita on January 24, 1987, a mile and a sixteenth claiming race on the dirt at a claiming price of $25,000, we can look at Sir Lyon.

Sir Lyon — Dk. b. or br. g. 4, by Leather Lyon—Kitch, by Petrone
STEVENS G L — 115 — Br.—Roche J & Mary (Wash) — Tr.—Chambers Mike — $25,000
Own.—Cross-Roche-Wright — Lifetime 17 3 2 1 $63,642 — 1986 9 1 0 1 $36,200 — 1985 8 2 2 0 $27,442 — Turf 1 0 0 0

28Dec86-8SA	1 1/16 :47 1:12 1:44 ft	5½	115	88¾ 65¼ 65½ 66¾	Stevens G L4	32000	74-14	Chili Hill, Cojak Man, Bruli's Ante 8
13Dec86-7Hol	1 1/16 Ⓣ:47²1:11¹1:41¹fm	39	116	104¾109¾1015 915	McHrgueDG7	Aw27000	73-08	Rai Den, Truth, Coasting Cougar 10
13Dec86—Wide backstretch								
12Oct86-9Lga	1 1/16 :46 1:10 1:42²ft	*2	116	914 89½ 712 66¼	LsthC3	Ⓢ Wash Chp H	81-16	Sissy'sHllr,CptnCondo,BgEdBombr 9
21Sep86-9Lga	1⅛ :45⁴ 1:09² 1:48²ft	6¾	114	717 715 79½ 1¾	† Best F7	Seattle H	91-17	‡SirLyon,Mandtory,UncleBrrydown 8
†21Sep86—Disqualified and placed fourth								
1Sep86-9Lga	1 1/16 :45⁴ 1:10² 1:42²ft	17	115	1011 95½ 31½ 12	HnsRD10	Labor Day H	87-19	SirLyon,CurrencyControl,KentGrn 11
22Aug86-9Lga	1 :45³ 1:10¹ 1:35¹ft	3¼	115	77 86¼ 610 43¾	Hansen R D5	Aw10000	89-17	Sssy'sHllr,CrrncyContrl,BrndyRsrv 10
10Aug86-7Lga	1⅛ :47 1:11³ 1:50²ft	7	121	77 74½ 85 52½	Hansen R D5	SplW	78-13	HousSpcilty,Sssy'sHllr,Hll'sCrossng 8
26Jun86-9Lga	1 :47² 1:11 1:35⁴ft	11	117	41¼ 2hd 34 34½	Steiner J J5	Aw10000	85-14	CurrncyControl,BlckBllmy,SirLyon 8
19Jun86-9Lga	1 :46² 1:10⁴ 1:36¹ft	17	117	1014 1011 911 85¼	GonsalvesFA4	Aw11100	83-17	SuperSevn,BlckBllmy,HousSpcilty 10
10Nov85-8BM	1 1/16 :46³ 1:11² 1:45²m	12	115	814 816 819 724	DelgdilloC6	Cal Juv	41-28	Darby Fair, JaySwift,LadyMaxineD. 8
10Nov85—Grade III								

Dec 24 SA 5f ft 1:04 h — Dec 10 SA 5f ft 1:03 h — Dec 5 SA 7f ft 1:33 h — Nov 29 SA 6f ft 1:17¹ h

Focus your attention on the race of 13Dec86 at Hollywood, where this gelding made his only start on the grass. You can tell this from looking at the lifetime turf record that is always shown under the performance boxes of the two preceding years. The performance of Sir Lyon was horrendous. Therefore, because today's race is on the dirt, you should excuse the terrible grass race showing and rate Sir Lyon off 9 races rather than 10. You would not count the number of 10 horses running, nor the 10th and 9th running positions at second call and finish. Easy enough.

The record of Oak Tree II in the same race illustrates the other side of the coin. While his grass record is not spectacular, he does show one victory, two seconds, and five thirds in 21 lifetime starts on the grass. This is easily sufficient to show that he can handle the grass. His dirt record is even better, for you can subtract the 21 grass starts from the total of 31 lifetime starts showing, which gives you 10 races run on the dirt.

***Oak Tree II** — B. h. 7, by Vacilante II—Oak Leaf, by Val de Loir
BAZE G — 118 — Br.—Haras Santa Maria de Araras (Brz) — 1986 13 1 0 4 $26,950
Tr.—Whittingham Charles $25,000 — 1985 3 1 1 0 $727
Own.—Haras Santa Maria de Araras — Lifetime 31 6 5 5 $33,470 — Turf 21 1 3 5 $20,069

26Dec86-9SA	1 1/16 :45^4 1:10^2 1:43 ft	6	118	9^{15}	8^{8½}	7^{7½}	5^5	Baze G^3	25000	81-13	Cold,TommyThoms,BoncngBttons	11
7Dec86-6Hol	1⅛ :47^2 1:12^1 1:51^{4}gd	5	119	7^{13}	7^{10}	5^{3¾}	5^{5½}	Baze G^6	32000	72-18	VlintGeorge,GumFleet,ForignLgion	9
20Nov86-5Hol	1⅛ :46^4 1:11^4 1:51^{2}ft	23	116	7^{8½}	6^{6½}	3^{nk}	1^{hd}	Baze G^{10}	32000	80-16	Oak TreeII,Bedouin,ValiantGeorge	11
20Nov86—Wide												
5Nov86-7Hol	1⅛ Ⓣ:47^3 1:11^3 1:48^{3}fm	21	114	5^7	6^{6½}	6^{8¼}	6^{5½}	Baze G^2	45000	79-14	Too Much For T. V.,Massera,Tarver	8
7Sep86-9Dmr	1 1/16 Ⓣ:47^1 1:11 1:42^{3}fm	11	114	5^{14}	5^{13}	4^{8½}	3^5	Stevens G L^5	45000	88-08	EmperadorAlNorte,Msser,OkTreeII	8
18Jly86-9Hol	1 Ⓣ:46^4 1:10^4 1:35^{3}fm	*2¾	116	5^{3½}	4^{¾}	2^{½}	3^{¾}	McCarron C J^3	40000	— —	North Of Lake, Rushad, Oak TreeII	7
6Jly86-10Hol	1⅛ Ⓣ:47^3 1:11^4 1:48^{2}fm	3	116	7^{6¾}	7^{3½}	5^{5½}	5^6	McCarron C J^1	50000	84-07	TooMuchForT.V.,Rajhn,IronLeder	10
19Jun86-7Hol	1 1/16 Ⓣ:46^2 1:10 1:40^{3}fm	*2¾	116	6^{4½}	6^{4¾}	3^{4½}	3^{2¾}	McCarron C J^2	50000	98 —	PlentyConscious,SuperNobl,OkTrII	8
1Jun86-7Hol	1⅛ Ⓣ:47^3 1:12^1 1:48^{4}fm	6	116	7^8	7^{3½}	6^{3¾}	6^{4¼}	McCarron C J^6	62500	84-07	IronLeder,Monno,SuccessfulBidder	8
17May86-6Hol	1⅛ Ⓣ:47^4 1:11 1:48 fm	5½	111^5	7^{4½}	7^{3¾}	4^{2½}	3^2	Black C A^4	62500	90-02	Piper John, TulsaFlyerII,OakTreeII	8

Jan 22 Hol 4f ft :48 h — Jan 16 Hol 7f ft 1:27^4 h — Jan 11 Hol 6f ft 1:13^4 h — Jan 6 Hol 6f gd 1:16^4 h

Therefore, with Oak Tree II, because he has shown an ability to win on both grass and dirt, you would rate every one of his races, whether grass or dirt, in computing his PCR rating.

Now, let's try a grass race to see how we similarly handle previous outings on the dirt. The 7th race on the same Santa Anita card of January 24, 1987, shows a mile and an eighth allowance event on the turf. When we look at Blushing Redhead, we can see that he is strictly a grass runner.

Out of 27 lifetime starts, this horse has run 25 of them on the grass. He has never won a single race on the dirt in his entire career. We can see that he tried the dirt on New Year's Day at Santa Anita and we can also see how he ran—dismally. Therefore, we would strike

Blushing Redhead — B. m. 5, by Blushing Groom—Foolish Redhead, by Nijinsky II
MCHARGUE D G — 116 — Br.—Knott Virginia M (Ky) — 1987 1 0 0 0
Own.—Brillembourg J D — Tr.—Sullivan John — 1986 14 1 2 1 $35,025
Lifetime 27 4 5 1 $50,715 — Turf 25 4 5 1 $50,715
11Jan87-6SA 7f :223 :451 1:221ft 38 116 1hd 21½ 811 817¾ DlhoussyE3 ⒻAw33000 72-21 SldomSnS,TwlghtRdg,OnY-OwnTm 9
28Dec86-3SA 1⅛Ⓣ:4641:11 1:483fm 20 116 33 32 41¾ 54½ VlenzulPA7 ⒻAw36000 79-16 Felliniana,Cruell,AffectionAffirmed 7
10Dec86-8Hol 1 1/16Ⓣ:4721:11 1:422fm 2½ 117 54 32½ 54 610½ Pincay LJr6 ⒻAw31000 71-18 AmbraRidge,AffectionAffirmed,Rea 7
30Nov86-8BM 7½fⓉ:23 :4621:293fm 15 114 1013 87¼ 66 810 JdcJC1 ⒻMs UnvrseH 86-04 Goldenita,TxDodge,AbstrctEnergy 10
21Nov86-8Hol 1 Ⓣ:4811:1221:37 fm 3½ 116 31 41½ 31½ 32½ ShoemkrW1 ⒻAw35000 79-18 FruAltv,Rock'nRollLdr,BlshngRdhd 6
7Nov86-7Hol 1 1/16Ⓣ:4721:1121:42 fm 6¾ 117 78 63 41½ 21¾ ShoemkrW5 ⒻAw30000 82-16 StllCloud,BlushingRedhd,Rkindling 8
7Nov86—Broke slowly
25Oct86-5SA 1⅛Ⓣ:4711:1141:484fm 19 114 73¼ 62¼ 43½ 51½ ShoemkrW7 ⒻAw35000 81-17 PerfectMtchII,Rekindling,StllCloud 9
25Oct86—Crowded 3/8 turn
10Oct86-8SA 1⅛Ⓣ:4641:1041:481fm 7½ 116 612 69½ 68 611 DlhoussyE1 ⒻAw45000 75-14 Bonne Ile, Miss Clipper, StallCloud 6
30Aug86-5Dmr 1 1/16Ⓣ:4631:1121:43 fm 7¼ 118 53½ 51½ 31 53 Toro F6 ⒻAw28000 88-11 ShortSleeves,PlumTasty,MngezLes 8
30Aug86—Wide 3/8 turn, into stretch
7Aug86-8Dmr 1 1/16Ⓣ:4721:1211:432fm 6 120 96 94½ 72¼ 41¼ ShoemkrW7 ⒻAw27000 88-11 PerfectMatchII,Miranda,P'umTasty 9
7Aug86—Wide into stretch
Jan 3 SA 3f ft :363 h — Dec 26 SA 3f ft :351 h — Dec 20 Hol 3f ft :354 h

out that one dirt effort and rate Blushing Redhead off the 9 grass races showing.

Another horse in the same race, Annapurna, in 10 lifetime races, had never run on the grass. This would not deter us from making a PCR off all the dirt races showing. You may want to share our judgment that a horse that has never run on the grass has a very poor chance against some power-house grass runners, and eliminate her altogether on that handicapping ground.

Therefore, in summary, when you are handicapping a race, whether turf or dirt, and a horse shows winning efforts on both surfaces, you may rate all his races. Likewise, if a horse has shown promise on the grass without winning, such as a second or a third in a reasonably low number of starts, his grass efforts should likewise be included. Only when a horse's record shows that his performances on one surface or the other are simply not representative of his ability in any meaningful way should his prior efforts be scratched off and not counted.

7 Adding Numbers In Lightning Style

THIS VERY SHORT chapter is not about handicapping at all, but about addition. It will show you how to save enormous amounts of time, turn the process of adding columns of numbers into an exercise of ease, and move you rapidly along the way toward getting faster and better ratings of horses. Skip it at your peril.

To do Performance Class Ratings, you have to add numbers, three columns of them for every horse. If you laboriously punch out numbers on your pocket calculator, which you may think you have to do, you will consume a great amount of unnecessary time. The long division in your final computation is different—here the calculator becomes an essential and vital tool, allowing you to do division with a quickness and accuracy that would not otherwise exist, because division is not amenable to easy shortcuts and quick accuracy as is addition.

But if you are going to use up great gobs of valuable time in slow, agonizing addition, many of you out there will likely throw up your hands and say it is not worth it. You will learn, however, in this chapter, with the use of a few sound techniques, you can add by calling out a column of 10 numbers immeasurably faster than you can do it on a calculator, and be just as accurate about it. If fact, you are more likely to make a mistake in touching the wrong number on the calculator than you are to err in the open addition process.

There are several techniques you can use. The first one we will call, "Multiplying the same numbers and adding to the base." You start by looking down the column to be added to see if there are at least three numbers or more that are the same. If you find them, then you would multiply the same numbers, and then add the remaining numbers to that first total. This way, you can get a running start on adding the entire column. We can return to the same Santa Anita card of January 24, 1987, that we have been using, and work on the record of Decontrol to establish this point.

```
Decontrol                          Ch. g. 8, by Majestic Light—La Fantastique, by Le Fabuleux
 VALENZUELA P A           116      Br.—Pinewood Stable (Ky)                 1987  1 0 0 0       $525
                                   Tr.—Stute Warren              $25,000    1986  2 0 0 0     $2,350
Own.—Diamant-Harris-Morningstar   Lifetime  36 9 6 1  $140,300              Turf  8 2 2 0    $44,550
11Jan87-9SA   1 1/16:473 1:113 1:443ft  *2 1/2 116  1 1/2 1hd 2 1/2 53  Valenzuela P A7 25000 75-21 Impulsively, Pegus, Bedouin  9
    11Jan87—Wide 7/8 turn
21Dec86-7Hol  6f :22 :452 1:101ft        25 116  75 1/4 64 3/4 54 57 1/2  Castanon A L4 32000 85-15 Romaxe, Ondarty, EllsBravestSong 8
8Jan86-9SA    1 1/16:464 1:113 1:432ft    5 116  42 41 1/4 43 45 1/2  Sibille R2 50000 78-16 VigorousVigors,Swivel,TrusT.Danus 8
14Dec85-1Hol  1 :462 1:113 1:363ft     *7-5 116  11 1 1/2 1 1/2 1hd  Sibille R1 40000 80-14 Decontrol, Juntura, Preprint  8
6Dec85-9Hol   1 :453 1:094 1:351ft     2 1/4 116  42 44 1/2 43 43  Sibille R7 50000 84-17 Menswear, Amarone, Hydrostatic  7
    6Dec85—3 wide into drive
11Aug85-9Dmr  1 1/8(T):5021:1421:50 fm*9-5 115  42 31 1/2 25 45 1/2  Toro F3 62500 82-05 Dumant, Fabuleux Prince,Tyrabellor 9
24Jly85-9Dmr  1 (T):4641:1131:363fm*8-5 116  2hd 1hd 11 1/2 21  Sibille R3 62500 88-09 Nonno, Decontrol, Super Noble  9
30Jun85-6Hol  1 1/16(T):4641:1021:411fm 5 1/2 116  11 1/2 1hd 2hd 22 3/4  Sibille R5 62500 90-09 Sagamore, Decontrol, Viron  12
16Jun85-3Hol  1 1/8:464 1:102 1:481ft      4 116  1hd 11 1/2 1hd 11 1/2  Sibille R4 40000 108-02 Decontrol, Golden E., Stickette  6
17Feb85-7SA   1 1/8(T):4631:1021:481fm 5 3/4 118  21 2 1/2 45 1/2 77 1/2  ValenzuelPA4 Aw33000 78-14 Champion Pilot, Penzance Byron  9
  Jan 22 SA 4f ft :48 h     Jan 17 SA 5f ft 1:011 h     Jan 8 SA 6f m 1:163 h     Jan 2 SA 1 ft 1:431 h
```

We shall first add up the total number of horses. In every such column of figures, you should first look for frequency of numbers. Running your eye down the column before you add anything, you can see that there are 4 races where the number of horses entered was 9. Your grade school multiplication tables tell you without a second thought that 9 times 4 equals 36. But we are not not done yet. There are also three races where 8 horses ran. We can now multiply $8 \times 3 = 24$. Adding any two numbers together is much, much easier than adding a string of 10. You don't need a calculator to tell you that $36 + 24 = 60$. After you do it a few times, just looking at numbers like $36 + 24$ tells you the total is 60, particularly when we call into play the "Rule of 10," which will be our second major shortcut to fast addition. But we are not yet finished with the techniques for multiplication of numbers.

To complete your work on Decontrol, you now have a total of 60. As you run up and down the remainder of the column, you will automatically skip each 9 and each 8 that you see, and just add the other numbers to 60. There are only 3 more remaining, 7 and 12 and 6, which add up to 25, and 25 plus 60 equals 85, and there you have it, fast and efficient.

The "total horses" column is in many ways the easiest one of all to add, because you are more likely to find duplicate races where the same number of entrants are found. The numbers of 8 and 9 are probably the most frequent you will find, although you will also pick up the frequent number of 12 where there are reasonably full fields available. When you deal with 9, you will seldom have to know more than what 9×3 or 9×4 equals, and likewise, with 8, the same. These totals will become so quickly fixed in your awareness that you will soon obtain the figure almost as fast as you see the relationships.

The number of 7 will also come up frequently, and here again, 7×3 and 7×4 get very easy to multiply.

You should also look for duplicate numbers in the internal columns, although you are not as likely to find them in groups as common as in the total horses column. Furthermore, many of the internal numbers are very low ones, such as in Decontrol's record, making them easier and quicker to add. However, in his finish column, you find the number 4 occurring three times, and if you wish, you can multiply 4×3 for 12, and add the others off that base. Going from the top down and skipping the three 4's where you see them, add the two 5's for 10 to the 12 for 22, plus 1 and 2 and 2 and 1 and 7 for a quick total of 35, and there you have it.

This covers our first rule of multiplication of same numbers. We can now apply our second rule for quick and easy addition, which we will call, "Combining numbers to make 10 and 20."

This simple and easy technique allows us to us to group numbers together that add up to 10, or 20. Usually this means only two numbers, such as 6 and 4 internally, or 12 and 8 or 11 and 9 to make 20 in the total horses column. To make this process the most useful, the two numbers should be clustered together, or very close together, if your eye is trained to scan upward and downward. Adding 10 and 20 to the existing added numbers is about the easiest thing known, and tremendously speeds up the entire process. Sometimes, in the internal columns, where smaller numbers are involved, you can be able to cluster three or four together to make a total of 10.

Let's do quick numbers on Miss Alto from the 7th race at Santa Anita on the same day to get a good example of how this technique works.

We first add up the total horses. You may want to start from either the top or the bottom, it doesn't matter. Sometimes when I want to check accuracy, if I went first from top to bottom I will do the checkup from bottom to top. But here, to apply our Rule, let's start at the top, going down from number to number.

We can start our addition with two numbers that do not fit within our rule, as we encounter 7 and 8, which we can quickly add to get a starting total of 15. After you do additions like this for a while, you will become extremely familiar with these common numbers and how they add together, because they usually fall within the limited range of from 6 to 12. In other words, you will know by sight that 7 + 8 is 15 or 8+7 = 15 in a flash. You next add 10, which is our easiest number of all, where you are adding 1 to the first of two numbers, and where 25 becomes our running total as we move downward.

Now you are ready for grouping, 12 and 8, together they make 20, always and always, and you will learn to look for them. Adding 20 to an existing number is as easy as adding 10, because you're adding small numbers to the first digit. So, as you call them out, you can say "25 plus 20 is 45," and just keep rolling.

There are two nines that follow. The first 9 we will add to the 45 to get 54. Now, we are ready for another application of the Rule (to get 20) as we bunch 9 and 11 together for the 20 to add to our 54, which now comes to 74. The rest is easy. Ten more for 84 and a final 12 for 96 and you have your total. The more you do it, the faster you will become.

The key here is to always look for the groups of 12 and 8 and 11 and 9. Rarely you will hit a 13 and a 7, but the common and most useful combinations are 12 and 8 (or 8 and 12) and 11 and 9 (or 9 and 11). Use them always and they will zoom your speed upward.

When we go to internal numbers, this rule works extremely well for grouping numbers to total 10. When we begin to do the second call numbers for Miss Alto, we can return to our first rule of multiplying the equals, since as we scan up and down, we can quickly see that this filly has run 6th at the second call on five occasions. We thus start with $6 \times 5 = 30$, and add from there. Just as you do when multiplying equal numbers in the total horses column, you will bypass the number 6 when do you the remaining addition.

Next, if you use your eye scan downward correctly, you will see a 3 and a 5 and a 3 and a 5 later on in the column. Pick out the numbers that add up to 10. The two 5's together are an obvious 10, and when you add 10 to the 30, you now have 40 and you can then pick up 3 and 3 and quickly get to 46. Your last number is 9, and you finish with 55 as a second call total.

The finish total is easier, because they are all small numbers, and the smaller a number is, the easier it is to add. Even here, in rapid fire style, with a little practice, you will be able to spot a string of numbers that add up to 10. For example, if you were starting from the bottom upward for Miss Alto's finish numbers, you could put the 3 and 1 and 3 together to make 7 and before you know it, the next two numbers, 2 and 1 make 3, and 7 and 3 make 10 and you're rolling upward. That's what we mean by looking for clusters of low numbers to add to 10.

We are going to limit these rules to three, which are sufficient to do what we need to do. We will call our third rule, "Adding by subtracting off the number 10." My own grammar schooling occurred so long ago that I can hardly remember it, and in later years, I heard something about "new math," which was never explained to me, and which may have had semblances of what we are going to set forth here. But adding by subtracting from the number 10 is a technique that seemed obvious to me long years ago, and I always use it.

As we go down a column of numbers, we may look for isolated 9, 8, and 7. Subtracting 9 from 10 is easy: the answer is 1. Likewise, it is almost as easy to recognize that 8 is 2 less than 10 and that 7 is 3 less than 10. We only use three numbers, 7, 8, and 9, and no more, because they lend themselves so easily to this technique. Let's look at the record of Annapurna for a fresh start on adding our columns.

```
Annapurna                           B. m. 5, by Raja Baba—Glinka, by Sir Iver
  MEZA R Q                          Br.—Warner M L (Ohio)                 1987  1 1 0 0   $17,050
                              118   Tr.—Gosden John H M                   1986  6 1 1 0   $25,825
Own.—Getty–Phillips–Rierdan         Lifetime  10 3 2 0   $61,625
 1Jan87-7SA  1 1/16:461 1:113 1:443ft  16 118  67¼ 52½ 1½ 12¼  Meza R Q8  ⒻAw31000 78-19 Annapurna, Python, La Codorniz  9
11Dec86-8Hol 1  :464 1:114 1:361ft   8 122  32 31 43 49¼  Meza R Q3  ⒻAw27000 72-21 OnYourOwnTim,FlightAbov,Python 6
19Nov86-9Hol 1  :462 1:112 1:371ft   5 122  44 35 36 25   Sibille R6  ⒻAw26000 72-21 Mirculous,Annpurn,DremAboutYou 7
26Oct86-5SA  1 1/16:463 1:111 1:433ft   5 118  43½ 54 45½ 44  Sibille R1  ⒻAw30000 79-16 Fairly Old, Python, Petillante  9
17Oct86-7SA  1 1/16:463 1:112 1:434ft   6 116  45½ 43 21½ 12  Sibille R2  ⒻAw27000 82-21 Annpurn,LCodorniz,Veroni:'sQuest 8
14Aug86-7Dmr 1 1/16:454 1:104 1:432ft  7¾ 118  74¼ 64½ 65½ 64  VlenzulPA2 ⒻAw20000 79-17 MargretBooth,Plumpetr,DonATop 10
    14Aug86—Bumped start, lugged in stretch
26Jly86-7Dmr 1  :452 1:11  1:371ft  3¼ 118  89 77 56 46½  DlhoussyE5 ⒻAw20000 75-13 Beulhlnd,Bggr'sWllt,RoylDrby'sLov 8
26Jun85-1Hol 1  :461 1:114 1:371ft  2½ 115  2hd 3nk 11 13  McCarron C J4 ⒻMdn 87-08 Annpurn,ReigningMlody,FtchNCrry 7
 9Jun85-5Hol 1  :45  1:101 1:362ft  34 115  56½ 55 32 2nk  McHargue DG2 ⒻMdn 91-02 MgnfcntEncor,Annprn,RgnngMlody 8
    9Jun85—Bumped late
18May85-3Hol 1  :461 1:111 1:363ft  32 120  1012 1021 917 816¾  Toro F4  ⒻMdn 73-06 Ice Stealer, KindaBeau,StopQuick 10
   Jan 18 SA 6f ft 1:14 h      Jan 12 SA 3f ft :363 h      Dec 29 SA 4f ft :491 h      Dec 23 Hol 6f ft 1:141 h
```

To do the "number of horses" total for Annapurna, we would quickly note there are three 8's in the column, and then start our addition from the top off the base total of 24. Our first number is 9. Rather than adding 9 to 24, we can do it faster and easier by adding 10 to 24, which makes 34. We then subtract 1, because 9 is one less than 10, and 33 becomes a quick answer. Most of us can add 10 and subtract 1 quicker than we can add 9 because we can recognize instantly that a 10 added to a 24 jumps to 34. You will learn to call out the numbers, "24 and 33," and move on to the next one.

We can then add 6 by itself, which makes 39. Again, we come to one of our three subtraction numbers, which is 7. We add 10 to the 39 to get 49 and subtract 3, which gives us 46 as fast as a wink. We hit 9 again as we go down and we just automatically say 55. We then skip the number 8, pick up the 10 for 65, skip another 8 as we keep moving down the column, reach another 7, subtract our 3 from 75 (65 + 10) to get 72. We skip 8 again and wind up with a final 10 for a total of 82.

When you look at the two internal columns for Annapurna, you will find that the technique of adding by subtracting from 10 is not nearly so useful, again because of the infrequency of the key numbers 7, 8, and 9. And when those numbers do appear, you can often cluster them with a low number to make 10 and pick up speed in that fashion. For example, whether you are going up or down the second call numbers for Annapurna, you can see a 6 and a 4 next to each other and a 7 and a 3 likewise, and you have the number 10 twice as quick as a flash.

These three rules, or guidelines, are not only useful for you as a handicapper, but if you master them, as you should, they will assist you in every numerical exercise of addition and subtraction that you will use in every endeavor. Let's restate them again as we close out this little lesson.

(1) Multiply same numbers when you find three or more in a column. Thereafter, use the total as a base upon which to add the other numbers in a column.

(2) Combine numbers that total 20 and 10 whenever you encounter clusters together that easily add up to these totals. The most common for our use in the total horses column are the combinations of 12 and 8 and 11 and 9. The most common in the internal columns are 5 and 5, 6 and 4, and 7 and 3.

(3) Add by subtracting from the number 10, using three numbers only, 9, 8, and 7. You will add 10 to your previous total and subtract 1, 2, or 3, as the case may be for the key numbers we use.

We repeat: when you use these techniques for only a few times, you will become so adept at using them that you will literally be amazed. You will be able to add the three columns of figures we must use immeasurably faster in this manner than if you laboriously punch each number and a plus button on a calculator. My own experience is that I can add the three necessary columns for approximately 100 horses, which are usually the maximum number you will find on any full racing card, in one hour or less. Perhaps you can do even better.

8 The Vital Form Factors

WE ARE NOW ready to move to the next part of our handicapping equation, current form, surely the factor that is singularly more important than any other, especially when it is combined with the revised last race ability times that we will be using in this book for the first time. Yes, standing in comparison, more important than speed ratings, class ratings, Performance Class Ratings, or any other method of ranking race horses for the important selection process. While each and every aspect of rating horses is extremely important —we emphasize again and again that no single isolated factor is alone enough to produce Total Victory at the Track—one cannot hope to prevail unless current form (which also embraces last race figures) is recognized as the foremost ingredient.

The major reason why this is so is that when races are put together by a racing secretary, as we have previously stated, whether they be stakes races or for the cheapest maidens on the grounds, the constant goal is to always match horses as nearly equal in class and ability as possible. While we know that this cannot always be done, a competent racing secretary will usually come reasonably close to achieving it. Consequently, you are likely to find that in almost any race, the majority of the entrants, but not all, are usually within some measurable range of each other in class and ability.

The one element the racing secretary cannot control in establishing conditions for a race is current form. Two competing horses may fit the conditions of the race perfectly, but how they come into the race in terms of form, preparation, or readiness is beyond the range of the person who makes the rules for who is entitled to run.

The job of the successful handicapper is to make his own evaluation of a horse's current form, his readiness to run, his chances of winning today's event, not the one of yesterday or tomorrow. Even the horse that is able to fit into a race with superior class and ability is not likely to win unless he is form-ready to do so. However, the fact that so many horses in a race are so often relatively equal in class and ability makes the task of selecting winners all the more difficult and elevates form analysis into the primary position it must occupy in any program of successfully handicapping the races.

This is why in this book we have divided the overall selection process into two analytical parts: (1) using Performance Class Ratings as a combination class and ability rating in conjunction with race analysis and track surface, and (2) integrating this with form ratings which will in the future consist of establishing both form factors and last race ability times, where possible.

Establishing form factors is the first essential step. This was done in substantial detail in my first major study of current form in How Will Your Horse Run Today? We are now prepared to redefine these form factors and make certain adjustments to them in view of what has been learned in the development of Performance Class Ratings.

In the previous book, I isolated four form factors, calling them (1) Recency, for recent action, (2) Running Line, which meant how a horse performed at the various calls in his last race, (3) Improvement or Decline, which sought to measure a horse's form cycle as to whether he was improving or declining, and (4) Stretch Performance. How a horse performed in each of these categories merited three basic ratings: Plus, for the prime kind of performance; Neutral or Non-Applicable, for a factor that did not significantly impact the race one way or the other; and Minus, for the negative factor that would either disqualify a horse as a contender or cause us to considerably downgrade his chances. For symbols to record these form factors, we used the common plus sign (+), a capital letter N, and a zero (0) as short form identifications as we underwent our handicapping.

We also identified a last race win, while not a form defect as such, as a hindering factor, or blemish, that would discount a horse's chance to win a second time in succession, unless it was a Big Win that entitled the horse to a + factor in Stretch Performance.

In the approximate 5-year period since the form research was done, we have continued, year after year, to keep close watch on these form factors, to constantly evaluate their effectiveness, to determine if they continue to give us top flight guidance in determining how a horse will run in his race today. I am delighted to tell you that I consider these same form factors still highly relevant, still reliable, and absolutely essential ingredients in seeking to predict the outcome of a race.

That same continuing evaluation led us into comparisons of these form factors for effectiveness. Which ones were the strongest? Where were the borderline factors? Could one factor be elevated over another as an indicator?

In following up these studies, I made the decision to make one major change. The third form factor of Improvement or Decline, while useful, was not always easy to establish. Some of the most loyal followers of our form factors complained about the complexity and difficulty of the methods we used in comparing the last two races. I was constantly trying to simplify this factor and make it more useful.

At the same time, I began to study last race form in light of time-based performance as well as form factors. This brought me into the use of the ability times for the last race as a part of current form. The use of these ability times for the last race only will be fully discussed later, but for now, when I began to integrate them into current form, I could see that they could eliminate the need for using improvement or decline as a form factor. The last race performance was thus an overriding factor and led to the conclusion that the difficult, complex, and time-consuming calculation of improvement or decline could be abandoned without any dilution of the final product.

That we have done. The last race ability time that you will be using hereinafter is a superior substitute for improvement or decline, since the figure itself will show the condition of the horse. As a result, we are now going to rely entirely on the three factors of Recency, Running Line, and Stretch Performance, with their derivations, which will be sufficient for us to establish the form priorities that will be so important in the selection process.

We will move through each of them quickly, as a review for old readers and as a guideline for new readers.

Recency. Any horse coming back to the races in seven days or less is awarded a plus (+) for recent action. Eight days won't do—we must have a cut off line. Some horses return in six days, all to the good, and those that come back in five days with good current form are powerful candidates for a good performance today.

If a horse returns from eight to 21 days, even without a workout, he receives a Neutral, or N rating. If a horse has not run in 21 days, or three weeks, without a workout, he receives a Minus, or 0 rating, and absent unusual circumstances, is almost sure to lose.

If a horse has not run within 21 days, he must have a workout of at least four furlongs within ten days of the race (or a four furlong work within the 21-day period, followed by one or more three furlong works). A three furlong workout, standing alone, is insufficient, and will leave a horse with a 0 rating for Recency. A five furlong workout is much preferable to one of four furlongs. We wrote of the "Fabulous Five Furlong Workout" in How Will Your Horse Run Today? because a bullet five furlong workout or one in less than one minute was an unusual sign of readiness for a returning horse.

(An exception to the workout rule would have to apply to cheap tracks with low purses and low claiming prices. If you happen to be playing there, you know that horses at these lower levels are rarely able to navigate workouts longer than three furlongs. A trainer is not likely to risk injury to his questionable horse by putting him through a strenuous work. Thus, a three furlong workout at these tracks may be sufficient. And if a horse shows four furlongs or even five (which may never occur, or if so, only rarely), you can know he is ready to run. At better tracks, the lowest priced claiming horses on the grounds may also be lightly worked for the same reasons.)

A horse returning between 22 and 28 days, if he showed the requisite four or five furlong workout within 10 days, would receive an N for recency and you could thereafter rate his entire last race running line.

However, no matter how long a horse would be away from the races, if he showed a recent five furlong workout, or a meaningful four furlong workout, I gave him in the past an N, or Neutral, rating for Recency. Of course, a horse away more than 28 days would not receive any other form ratings for either Running Line or Stretch Performance.

In the use of our symbols for current form, rather than use the N rating for horses that have not run within 28 days, we will now call these animals "Layoff Horses" and will use the letter "L" in all cases. This is extremely helpful in evaluating form, because where a horse comes off a layoff, we cannot use his last race, no matter when it was, to set forth form factors or last race ability times.

Running Line. The last useable race within a 28 day period is rated. A horse that was within less than three lengths of the lead at the stretch call in a sprint race was given an N rating. This was called being Up Close. This same standard of being less than three lengths from the lead was applied to all calls, and if a horse qualified as Up Close at all four calls in his last race, he would receive a + for Running Line. In races of one mile or more, Up Close for an N rating was considered to be less than five lengths from the lead at the stretch call.

Your biggest problem in this area is what to do about the horse in a sprint race that is shown to be three lengths or 3½ lengths from the lead at the stretch call, and 5 or 5½ in a route race. This is too close for comfort, and you should be accorded some leeway here if otherwise a horse has shown some life. We adopted a "close" symbol here by writing a zero with a diagonal through it (ϕ), which would allow us to keep considering such a horse.

A horse could also receive an N rating for running "evenly" without being Up Close at the stretch call. This will often show up in the comment, or trouble, line in your Racing Form.

In *How Will Your Horse Run Today?* we gave N ratings for horses that were not Up Close at the stretch call who were dropping in class or running a shorter distance today by at least one furlong, as long as they were Up Close at the second call. Because we are using form factors in a slightly different fashion here, treating a reading of form factor symbols as a part of the whole process of Reading the Handicapping Line, we will now make some slight adjustments for our recording purposes, but still maintain the same principles that have proved so effective in the past.

Where a horse that was not Up Close at the stretch call in his last race is dropping in class and he was Up Close at any of his earlier calls, we will still record him as having an N running line, but will write the small letters "cd" alongside which tell us he is dropping in class. If he is within our recency guidelines and has the Up Close rating, we will write the form rating in this fashion: NNcd. If he is not up close at any call, even though he is dropping in class, we write it: NOcd.

For the horse that is running at a shorter distance today by at least one furlong, such as from 7 furlongs down to 6, or from 1 1/8 miles down to one mile or less, we look to the second call for the Up Close decision. However, if he was up close at the second call and lost ground by a length or more to the third call, which is the stetch call, he would still get a form defect for stretch loss, as we shall review in a moment.

We will also make additional concessions to an N running line where there are defineable internal gains. A horse with a gain of five in horses and lengths in his last race must be given an N. This means he must pass at least one horse and pick up any combination of horses and lengths totalling five (with the proviso that the starting point for measuring lengths gained cannot extend beyond eight). We can also write the small letters, "ig," for internal gain into his form ratings. A horse that falls back and then gains is showing some life in his running line, as well as a horse that shows a gain of three from any one call to the next. We can thus award an N for any of these efforts.

In rating running lines, as I have earlier indicated, we cannot rate any horse that has not run within 28 days. A horse that has not raced or worked in 21 days receives a zero for Recency, but we can rate his last race running line if he has run within 28 days. Otherwise, he is a Layoff horse and cannot be rated for running line at all.

Failure to be Up Close at the stretch call, without any of the exceptions, will ordinarily bring a minus, or 0, rating and will indicate a serious form defect.

Stretch Performance. The highest accolade for stretch performance is the Big Win, which is the only + rating we can award. A horse must have won his last race by three lengths or more without losing ground in the stretch to be awarded a plus form factor, and must not have led at the second call by more than two lengths. If a horse is ahead of his field by more than two lengths at the second call, he is not being pushed sufficiently to merit a Big Win. I have seen too many early speed horses pull far away from their opponents and then fail to produce the next time around. When a horse is more than two lengths ahead at the second call, and goes on to win, he is entitled to only an N for stretch performance, even though he may get a + for Running Line.

The more common use of Stretch Performance as a form factor comes when a horse that is Up Close at the stretch call loses one or more lengths from the stretch to the finish. This brings the unwelcome 0 as a form defect, and makes such a horse a prime candidate for defeat in today's race, as was explained in *How Will Your Horse Run Today?* Because some horses do occasionally win, however, carrying this form defect, we continued to study the whys, and when we reach a later point in this work, we will provide helpful insight into when a stretch loss defect may be overcome and when an animal with that kind of defect may be able to win today.

When a horse that is not Up Close at the stretch call loses ground in the stretch, and already has a form defect because of it, he is not charged further and is given an N rating for non-applicable.

There are a few other exceptions. A horse running in his first race after a layoff of more than 28 days is not given a form defect for Stretch Performance if he loses ground in the stretch on the theory that he is "running short" because of his absence from competition. Also, a horse running at a shorter distance today by one furlong or more than in his last race will be given a stretch loss form defect only if he lost a length between the second call and the stretch call.

One of the elements of stretch performance that we have not fully considered in the past is the stretch gain where a Big Win is not involved. While a stretch gain as such may denote a running style, such as one which comes from having lower finish position totals in his PCR line than at the second call, a gain in the stretch is too often favorable enough that it cannot be ignored. In recent years, we have developed the habit of writing the small letters "sg" at the end of our form symbols to denote any stretch gain or two or more in either lengths or horses. If your track is favoring late speed today, you need to be aware of this circumstance.

Winners of the Last Race. A horse that won his last race is hardly an animal that is deficient in form. Yet, as our research in *How Will Your Horse Run Today?* demonstrated, horses that won their last races without a Big Win usually have considerable difficulty in repeating at the same or higher class. We can label this as a form hindrance, and will also note it hereafter in our form symbols by the small letter "w" at the end of the form ratings. There are a number of reasons even apart from statistical improbability that these last race winners have difficulty, and at a another later point, we will attempt to demonstrate instances where they are likely to lose and situations where they have a reasonably good opportunity of repeating.

Now that we have run through these form factors, it should be helpful to demonstrate these ratings in lines from past performances. Again, almost any will do, and for this purpose, we have before us the record of Lovers Native from the Daily Racing Form of Jan. 21, 1987.

Today's race on Jan. 21 would be form rated off the previous race of Jan. 14, which is the top one shown. This would read: + + +, a powerful showing indeed. The Jan. 14 race was within 7 days, so there would be a + for recency. The running line is + because the horse was Up Close or better at every call. A Big Win + is scored because Lovers Native won by more than three lengths and was not two lengths or more ahead at the second call.

Lovers Native

MEZA R Q

Own.—Miller & Warner

114

B. f. 4, by Raise a Native—Miss Gallivant, by Gallant Man
Br.—Miller L R (Ky)
Tr.—Ellis Ronald W
Lifetime   8   3   4   0 $62,400

1987	2	1	0	0		$15,950
1986	5	2	3	0		$42,650

14Jan87-3SA	7f :223 :453 1:224ft	*8-5 115	2hd 1hd 13 15¼	Meza R Q⁵	ⒻAw29000	86-20	LovrsNtiv,LCodorniz,DrmAboutYou 8
1Jan87-7SA	1₁₁₆:461 1:113 1:443ft	*8-5 116	2hd 1½ 31 610¼	DlhoussyE²	ⒻAw31000	67-19	Annapurna, Python, La Codorniz 9
29Nov86-3Hol	7f :222 :451 1:23 ft	2 117	11½ 1¹ 1hd 2hd	Pincay LJr⁶	ⒻAw26000	89-12	Symboliclly,LoversNtiv,FlightAbov 6
29Nov86—Brushed late							
2Nov86-5SA	6f :212 :441 1:102ft	*6-5 117	44½ 43 42 21¾	Pincay LJr¹	ⒻAw28000	84-10	StridingEsy,LoversNtive,FlyingJuli 9
2Nov86—Lugged out							
7Mar86-6SA	1 :452 1:093 1:361ft	*2-3 117	14½ 16 15 15	Pincay LJr¹	ⒻAw31000	87-14	LovrsNtv,WondrfulFrnd,ArctcMoon 7
16Feb86-6SA	6f :22 :451 1:103gd	*1-2 117	12½ 16 18 15½	Pincay L Jr¹	ⒻMdn	85-14	LoversNative,ExcellentSpirit,Mgri 12
25Jan86-3SA	6½f:214 :443 1:16 ft	*1 117	1½ 2hd 2hd 2no	Pincay L Jr¹	ⒻMdn	90-11	WinterTresur,LovrsNtiv,Mirculous 12
29Dec85-4SA	6f :212 :441 1:093ft	3½ 117	11½ 1¹ 1¹ 2½	Meza R Q⁶	ⒻMdn	89-12	SldomSnS,LovrsNtv,SptmtrShwrs 12

Jan 10 SA 4f gd :49 h   Dec 28 SA 5f ft :59³ h   Dec 22 SA 1 ft 1:39³ h   Dec 15 SA 7f ft 1:27⁴ h

The form rating for the Jan. 14 race would be taken from the race of Jan. 1 and would read like this: NNN. Recency is easy enough, with the last race being 14 days ago. For running line, we see that today's race (Jan. 14) at 7 furlongs is more than one furlong shorter than the 1 1/16 event of Jan. 1. Consequently, we would disregard the finish position and look for Up Close at the earlier calls. We cannot award a + because Lovers Native was not up close at all four calls, but we would give an N. As for stretch performance, even though there was a loss of more than a length between the two pertinent calls, the second and the stretch call, we now note that this came after a layoff of more than 28 days. Thus, there is another N.

For the Jan. 1 race, we would look at the race of November 29 and having noted that it was more than 28 days earlier, the form line would get an L and nothing more.

To form rate the November 29 race, we would look at the previous race of Nov. 2, some 27 days earlier. Because our workout lines do not go back that far, we will assume a qualifying workout and post an N for recency. The same would follow for the running line, not quite Up Close at all four calls, as well as for stretch performance. Since there was a gain of two (for horses), we would note this as we write the form line in this fashion: NNNsg.

The November 2 race would show as L, the March 7 race as N+Nw (no Big Win because more than two lengths in front at the second call of the Feb. 16 race, and a small "w" for the last race win), the February 16 race as N+N off the Jan. 25 event, and the Jan. 25 line would be N+0 off the Dec. 29 effort (noting the stretch loss of more than one length).

Let's do another one where the horse's performances were not nearly as good. From the same edition of the Daily Racing Form, we can look at Charsky, who was running at Aqueduct.

Charsky — Ch. m. 8, by Surge Ahead—Cal Chance, by Stepfather

Br.—Richard Mr-Mrs B C (Va) — 1987 2 0 0 1 $2,520

Own.—Spiegel R — 117 — Tr.—Schaeffer Stephen $35,000 — 1986 10 2 2 3 $44,300

Lifetime 83 21 5 14 $274,258 — Turf 3 . 0 0 0

15Jan87-3Aqu	$1\frac{1}{16}$ ⊡:48 1:12^{4}1:45^{4}ft	$4\frac{1}{2}$	117	8^{9}	8^{10}	$8^{7\frac{3}{4}}$	$5^{4\frac{3}{4}}$	Santagata N^{1}	Ⓕ 35000	76-19	Sea Trip,Lou'sLogic,HonestNickle	10
7Jan87-1Aqu	$1\frac{1}{16}$ ⊡:50 1:14^{4}1:47^{4}ft	$3\frac{1}{4}$	117	5^{3}	$3^{2\frac{1}{2}}$	3^{3}	3^{3}	Santagata N^{7}	Ⓕ 35000	68-21	Crown Piper, Kathy W., Charsky	7
27Dec86-3Aqu	$1\frac{1}{16}$ ⊡:49^{1}1:14^{1}1:46 ft	$3\frac{3}{4}$	117	$7^{4\frac{1}{2}}$	$6^{3\frac{3}{4}}$	$4^{3\frac{1}{2}}$	2^{2}	Santagata N^{6}	Ⓕ 35000	78-11	ImbicPentmtr,Chrsky,BllOfWstviw	8
15Dec86-3Aqu	1^{70} ⊡:47^{4}1:13^{3}1:44^{3}ft	$4\frac{3}{4}$	113	8^{14}	$8^{8\frac{3}{4}}$	$5^{4\frac{3}{4}}$	$3^{1\frac{3}{4}}$	Antley C W^{3}	Ⓕ 30000	75-20	ImbcPntmtr,MrryWdwWltz,Chrsky	9
23Nov86-2Aqu	1 :46 1:11^{1}1:38 ft	13	117	$9^{8\frac{1}{4}}$	$8^{7\frac{3}{4}}$	$7^{5\frac{3}{4}}$	$6^{5\frac{3}{4}}$	Migliore R^{1}	Ⓕ 35000	70-23	PltinumPoster,FinlStrok,SoloEnrgy	9
14Apr86-1Aqu	$1\frac{1}{8}$:51^{2} 1:16 1:53^{3}ft	$3\frac{1}{2}$e	119	$8^{7\frac{3}{4}}$	$7^{7\frac{1}{2}}$	5^{11}	4^{11}	Migliore R^{2}	Ⓕ 35000	56-24	Kouklamou,BoatHook,HrlemQueen	8
1Apr86-5Aqu	$1\frac{1}{8}$:50^{2} 1:15 1:53^{2}ft	4e	113	9^{12}	$7^{4\frac{3}{4}}$	4^{3}	4^{5}	Migliore R^{5}	Ⓕ 45000	63-27	Oceanic View,Athabasca,BoatHook	9
25Mar86-2Aqu	$1\frac{1}{8}$:49^{2} 1:14^{2} 1:55^{2}ft	*8-5	117	6^{12}	$5^{6\frac{1}{2}}$	$2^{1\frac{1}{2}}$	$1^{2\frac{1}{4}}$	Migliore R^{3}	Ⓕ 35000	58-26	Charsky, New Poems,HarlemQueen	8

Dec 11 Bel tr.t 4f ft :51 b — Dec 4 Bel tr.t 4f ft :50^{2} b

In rating today's race for form, we would use the last race of Jan. 15 and record it like this: +0sg. The last race six days ago would bring a + for recency, the poor running line would get a zero, and the stretch gain could be noted. For the Jan. 15 race, we would rate form off the Jan. 7 race and get a much better result like this: N+N. Because a distance race was involved, Charsky was Up Close at every call by being less than 5 lengths from the leader.

The Jan. 7 race, being rated off the Dec. 27 line would get the same N+N, while the Dec. 27 race off the Dec. 15 line would be shown as: NNsg. The Dec. 15 race off the Nov. 23 line would show as NON. The November 23 race would show an L.

We would rate the April 14 race off the April 1 line to read: NNOig. The N for running line would come from the stretch call position or the internal gain, and the loss of two lengths in the stretch would require 0. However, we would note the internal gain with the small letters "ig" as an important guiding signal. The form rating for the April 1 race off the March 25 line would read: NNNw.

While these few examples show far less than you will encounter in the races you handicap, they are meant to provide a quick helpful showing to illustrate what we have set forth. As we go into other races in fuller detail, we will be constantly illustrating the application of form factor ratings that will cover many other situations that you will be facing from time to time.

To this point, we have undertaken to provide only a highlight digest of what was contained in a full study of current form in our last work. In some situations here, we have diverged slightly to conform to the entire spectrum of PCR-form handicapping, which we have called the method we advocate for Total Victory at the Track.

In an effort to continually follow up on the effectiveness of these form ratings, and determine where winners emerged, I have undertaken additional studies of some 2000 winning horses. Rather than boring you with all the statistical details, I do want to provide some highlights for your further use in your handicapping.

The most surprising thing I learned from looking at 2000 winning horses in every kind of race was the high number that had not run in 28 days or more. While this included first time starters, horses which I now label as "L" in form for Layoff won almost 17 per cent of all races recorded. I still suspect this was abnormally high, but a point has been made that many many horses do win off layoffs, and must be taken seriously in any race where they show any positive signs.

One of the reassuring things about the study was that there was some kind of legitimate handicapping positive sign for winning horses in an extremely high percentage of the races. A horse would either have good current form, be returning off a layoff, show early speed with a drop in class, or post an impressive gain somewhere in his running line. For winners where there was no defineable explanation, the percentage fell somewhere between four and five percent. And I can assure you that for the most part, these winning efforts came at the lowest rungs of the class ladder. In most cases of even extremely high paying long shots, there was some legitimate sign of some kind that an astute handicapper could recognize.

Another factor that interested me was early speed. In the 2000 race study, I placed approximately 18% of the winners in a separate early speed category that would not ordinarily show an N for running line, distinguishing them from the early speed winners that showed good form. In other words, 18% of the winning horses, a very substantial number, were winning with what might be called a form defect, but which was being overcome by strong early speed.

But we need to break that down a bit further into two more separate groups. I separated early speed with a drop in class and found that 60% of these early speedsters came in this category. We now had 11.6% of all winners showing early speed with a drop in class. This is a formidable factor that cannot be overlooked. You will find that when this is associated with a high PCR that you may have a very substantial play.

Many of the other early speed winners came from a shorter distance. And some of the others not in these categories very likely scored on days when the track was unusually conducive to early speed, a factor that we were unable to incorporate into our study.

All this again was a splendid reaffirmation of the importance of form as a handicapping factor and a further support for applying knowledge, experience, and observation research to the enjoyable but difficult task of selecting winning horses.

When these form factor lines are written, I place them to the right of the PCR numbers as one moves to a laying out of the key factors we must take into account in handicapping a race. When you do this, and when you enter into your final and overall evaluation of the entries in any race, you may want to consider which form factors are superior in weight and importance to others.

As research and study in *How Will Your Horse Run Today?* established, the Plus form factors are the most positive. A plus form factor in itself is an advantage for you to savor. The Big Win is perhaps the most powerful statistically, closely followed by a + for Recency. A + running line ranks ahead of a running line filled with NNN, of course, and thereafter, we encounter form defects. Here, we can readily assess the negative side. A zero rating for recency is the most deadly, where it is almost safe to say the forbidden word, "never." A zero for stretch performance is extremely unfavorable, but can be overcome in some situations, as we will demonstrate later. A 0 running line where a horse is reasonably close is the least fatal, although a terrible running line of far back at all calls is usually disastrous, as all of you surely know. We will also undertake to show you many races where horses have won with zero running lines and then provide an explanation of why.

We are now at the point of readiness to complete the important second part of current form by going beyond form ratings to setting forth last race ability times for horses that have run within the last 28 days. Where a horse is given an L for layoff, we shall have to look at other factors in the handicapping process. When all of this is done, we will at last be prepared to make selections in races and put our money on the line where it counts.

9 The Troublesome Problem Of the Track Variant

HAVING DEALT WITH the development of PCRs and our new revised form factors, we can now approach the last critical element of the total handicapping line we will use in every race wherever possible. We have developed entirely new and revised ability times, as you will see in the next two chapters, which are substantially superior to those that have been used in the past. While one of the great advantages of using PCRs as a rating is that they do not take time into consideration, when we go beyond a base rating to deal with last race form, we are compelled to consider how fast a horse ran.

Because we had to rate the last race as a component of both form and ability, we were back to finding a workable standard. That brought us back to ability times with the new revisions that we have structured.

But to get the best line possible on an ability time, or any kind of time for that matter, we are dragged back, even though partially kicking and screaming, to the ever troublesome problem of the track variant.

I tried to ignore the variant altogether in Investing at the Race Track. Sometimes, when tracks appear to be running "normal," one can get away with ignoring variants. But as I continued to study and analyze and ask questions, it became always apparent that differences in the surface of the track, or how it varied, from day to day had an influence on running times that could not be ignored. Even with the adjustments one could make in any effort to construct meaningful comparative times, there was always the specter of the variant out there to haunt us.

It simply has to be factored in. But how do we do it? What variants? Whose variants?

No one can make a persuasive argument that the variants published in the Daily Racing Form are reliable enough to be used without some tampering or adjustment. Yet, with all their weaknesses, which all of us recognize, they still are able to show us something about how a track has been running.

For example, when you see a number like a 33 track variant in the Daily Racing Form, you immediately know that a deep slow track is having a tremendous impact upon times of the horses running. At the other end of the spectrum, when you see track variants with such low numbers as 10 or 11, even with high caliber horses performing, you know that a very fast track on that day is producing some speedy times. The question of how you compare times of a horse running on a track with a Racing Form variant of 33 with a horse running off a line showing a variant of 10 in the Racing Form is always a difficult one. But it has to be done.

Every experienced player knows that different tracks can show widely varying times when the abilities of the horses may be approximately the same. Different surfaces, different distances, and different conditions may all account for key defects in track variants. One of the critical items that every astute scholar has pointed out is that variants in the Daily Racing Form are influenced greatly by the class or caliber of the horse running on any given day. Variants on Saturdays, for example, where races are run with horses that are generally superior to those that are entered on Monday, will usually be lower than those on Monday, even if the track surface was the same. If on a particular day the majority of the races on a card are sprints, variants will be lower than on a day when the majority of races run are distance races.

In an effort to try to solve these kinds of problems, other writers and dedicated, full-time handicappers developed the par time technique, comparing times in each race with what might be expected of horses of similar class at the same distance, and rating the track fast or slow accordingly. There is little doubt but that variants off par times are superior to the raw variants that we find in the Daily Racing Form.

But the player who does not spend full time at handicapping horses, which probably covers more than 99% of you, would have neither the time, the resources, nor the data banks to be able to cope with all the problems of track variants that one will inevitably encounter. What is he, and you and I, to do?

While I greatly respect the efforts of all the compilers of par time variants, I am still unpersuaded that they are totally accurate or reliable, or even close enough to consistent reliability to allow you to live or die with them. Notice that I used the term, "consistent reliability." Some of the par time variants I have tested may be reliable on some days and on other cards, be terribly out of line. This kind of inconsistency will produce a speed figure for one horse that may be grossly out of line in comparison with the speed figure of another animal that ran on a different day.

How do I know this? On what basis do I make these observations?

They come from hours of comparing commercial variants both with what is shown in the Daily Racing Form, and what my own adjustments show, which will be given to you shortly. If a horse is rated the highest off my artificial variant and wins the race and would be rated much lower (and would thus not be selected) with a comparison commercial variant, then I have to believe that something is wrong with the commercial product. On the other hand, I have found examples where the commercial kind would place the horse higher than I have rated him, and the horse lost. Same conclusion. But to be fair, and perfectly frank, there are other examples I have found which are the opposite: the horse ranks highest off the commercial variant and wins, and under my figures, he would not be selected.

But that is precisely the point: inconsistency. If Product A is inconsistent and my own Product B is inconsistent as well, and assuming ultimate results are approximately the same, I will stick with my method. Reasons: I still have room to tinker and experiment and my method doesn't cost anything. But I am saying a little more than that: I am not even persuaded at this point about approximately the same results. I may be persuaded some day, but as I continue to compare the commercial variants with my own observations of the track, I continue to see enough holes and gaps in them that I have to stay with what I am doing.

Why is this so?

The major reason is that horses of the same class vary very much in their individual winning efforts, no matter how the track surface might be flowing. I pointed this out in Investing at the Race Track as an argument against using any variants. A good example is where an ungraded stakes race may be split into two divisions. The class factor would be the same for both races. Yet, one winner will invariably run faster than the other winner at the same class level.

Which one sets the correct variant?

I have seen claiming horses at $12,500 run faster than claiming horses at $25,000 on the same day. What does that do to the par time variant? Let me give you an example you can read in the Daily Racing Form, Eastern Edition, of Oct. 2, 1987. On the night of Sept. 30, 1987, in the fourth race at the Meadowlands, the winner in a lowly $5,000 claiming race won a six furlong sprint in 1:11.3. In the eighth race on the same card, a claimer for 3-year-old fillies with a $50,000 tag, the winning time was 1:12, two full ticks slower. Now, you may say that 3-year-old fillies are quite different from open entries who may have greater age and seasoning, but really, $50,000 and $5,000 is such a gap in class value that the crippled old bottom-of-the-barrel claimers can hardly be rated the same. They were all running on the same track surface. How does this affect the track variant for the commercial sellers, the Daily Racing Form, or the reconstructed numbers that I will use?

With a recognition of these problems and a healthy skepticism about the precise reliability of any particular variant, I set out to make artificial variants which, as long as they are consistently applied, would be as generally reliable as any others that may be constructed. Because the published variants in the Daily Racing Form, even with all their defects, are there for all to see and use, I have tried to work off them as a base for factoring in differences in track surfaces.

The underlying consideration is to roughly work off a concept of 50% reliability for Daily Racing Form variants, and fine tune them from that point.

I first tried this concept several years ago when I published a small work called "The Improvement Factor." A conscientious racing scholar on the west coast who was one of the earlier pioneers in feeding racing data into computers, and who used his own computerized par time variants which he deemed highly reliable, undertook to compare my artificial variants with what he considered the more scientific version that he had developed on his computer.

I was delighted when this much respected scholar put forth his results, which were not issued until a long time after both my earlier books had been published. This devoted researcher wrote that while he still did not understand how I arrived at these variants, he found them very close in reliability with what he considered the "real thing." Not only had experience taught me that these artificial variants worked reasonably well, but now someone had run a critical test and had come to the same conclusion.

When it became apparent that it was absolutely necessary to use some kind of variants in constructing ability times, and impressed by the finding of the west coast scholar (about which I was not too terribly surprised), I went back to these artificial variants again. Now, I have made minor adjustments to these original artificial variants, and will now set them forth fully with a thorough explanation of the theory behind them and how they are expected to work.

We start with our own concept of "average" or "normal." At the eastern tracks, a Daily Racing Form variant of 18, 19, or 20 usually indicates that the track surface has relatively little influence on the times that are run. But even if they do have some slight influence, as long as we apply these numbers to all horses at all times, the consistency itself is a leveling factor. Consequently, when the numbers of 18, 19, and 20 show, we make no adjustment at all in a published time.

As the Daily Racing Form variant increases, we begin to accept that a slower track is influencing the variant, and accordingly, we will deduct fifths of seconds accordingly. To make a deduction of one for one is far too influential, and again, we seek an estimated span that will be workable and effective. Thus, back to our general 50% consideration, for the most part, we can equate two numbers in the variant as the proper measuring device for adjustment upward, one for track surface and another for the many different influences on the way a race is run. Accordingly, where the published variant shows 21 and 22, we can deduct one tick off the time we are using. (You can then say the track is slow by one, but you need not bother, since the numbers give us what we use.)

We continue the same process as the totals move upward. A published variant of 23 and 24 requires us to conclude that the track is running slow by 2 and we can deduct two ticks from our adjusted ability time. At 25 and 26, we go to 3, at 27 and 28 we use 4, and so on upward, 2 at a time.

The process is somewhat the same on the faster side, but with some very important variations that also must be consistently applied. We start with the same span of two, and where a Racing Form variant is 16 or 17, we add one tick. At 14 and 15, we add two ticks. But as we drop below 14, experience has taught me that when DRF variants get that low, the track surface is beginning to exert an unusually speedy influence. As a result, we revert to one for one to account for the speeded-up surface. A 13 variant requires us to add 3, a 12 for 4, and an 11 for 5. When you see a Racing Form variant as low as 10, where we will begin to add 6, you are usually dealing with a lightning track so fast that cheap horses will run incredibly quick times.

With this explanation, here is our Variant Table:

Racing Form	Our Adjustment
09	Add seven fifths, or ticks
10	Add six
11	Add five
12	Add four
13	Add three
14-15	Add two
16, 17	Add one
18, 19, 20	None
21, 22	Subtract one
23, 24	Subtract two
25, 26	Subtract three
27, 28	Subtract four
29, 30	Subtract five
31, 32	Subtract six
33, 34	Subtract seven

As variants balloon upward, you keep on the two-for-one track. As they expand so greatly, however, they become less and less reliable. Fortunately, there should not be too many of these except where a track is exceptionally heavy and bogged down, and when that happens, you may be far better off ignoring the race altogether.

These are the adjusted variants we will use hereafter. They are totally artificial. But they do come from a most valuable source: experience and observation, testing and re-testing, comparison and more comparison. You will find them, I repeat, as comparably reliable as almost any other brand of track variant.

In all of this, however, there is one major exception. This entire method of constructing variants does not work in turf races. So, a warning and a direction: do not use them in turf races.

The major reason is the total unreliability of published Daily Racing Form variants in grass races. Frequently, there may not be more than one grass race on a particular racing card. Since the track variant is computed separately for turf and dirt races, the variant may represent the result of only one race. If the winner had a speed rating of 88, for example, the variant would be 12, as the total figure would always come out to 100 when there is but one turf race on the card.

When you see a turf race in a horse's past performances, you can add the speed rating, the variant, and the lengths behind at the finish, and if the total comes out to 100, as it often does, you will know that there was only turf race on the card that day. On the other hand, if adding these three numbers gives you a different total than 100, you will then know that there was at least two races on the grass that day.

But no matter, the unreliability is basically the same. With only one or two turf races on a particular day, the variant will almost always reflect the class and speed of the horse that won, and have very little to do with the kind of racing surface. Oh, sure, most of you have at one time or another seen turf variants as high as 30 or even 40 when there was a soft turf, and this, too, leaves you guessing.

Thus, when you are trying to construct figures for grass racing, you are limited to two alternatives. One is to handicap without figuring variants at all, which is all I am able to do in grass races. Of course, you should pay attention to the DRF variant, for if it is very low or very high, you will know that the running times shown are most unreliable. I have, however, found some very solid plays in turf races without using the variant in any manner.

The other alternative is to try to construct your own par time variants. This will require you to have a set of turf only par times for each distance at the track where you play. This may simply be too big a task without some unusual resources, which will bring you back to the unhappy method of totally ignoring turf variants. And, as I have just said, you can still do reasonably well with some sound handicapping judgments that you are qualified to make.

These are the basics that we will use in dealing with track variants. When we go to use them in constructing ability times, they will be applied differently in sprint races and in distance races. This comes about because of the substantial changes we have made in our adjusted ability times. We are now ready for that important next step.

10 Ability Times In Sprint Races

WHILE PERFORMANCE CLASS Ratings have become a first step as a base rating, we know that PCR is still only a portion, albeit a very important one, of a comprehensive handicapping line. The element carrying the most isolated power is the last race ability time as we have re-constructed this rating as a combined ingredient of both form and ability. We have referred to the last race repeatedly, without yet considering what we do if the last race is non applicable, or not useable, as will be the case in many situations. We will come to dealing with that problem later, but for now, our concentration will be on the formula itself, and how to do the calculations.

Therefore, before we reach the final analysis of integrating PCR, form, and last race ability times into the selection process itself, we must re-evaluate the ability time and set forth the new and far more effective structure that we have developed. Because sprint races and route races are run differently, we will further divide ability times into sprints and routes, with a somewhat different formula for each of them. You will find this far stronger than anything we have used in the past.

The concept of Ability Times, as we developed it in Investing at the Race Track, was at that time a new effort at another method of rating a thoroughbred as a means of making a sound selection. It was centered upon adjusted time compiled by the horse between the four furlong call and the six furlong call, and was used in both sprint and distance races. This meant that in the ordinary six furlong sprint race, we were measuring from the second call to the finish. In longer sprint races, such as those at six and one-half furlongs or seven furlongs, we would be compelled to adjust the time to a six furlong figure to obtain consistent comparative measurements. We will still use that same technique in sprints.

This concept needed some important adjustments to make it work effectively. The major adjustment that was made, after any alterations for distance, was to add fifths of seconds, or ticks, to the in-between times based upon how slow the reported time at the second call in sprint races appeared to be, and likewise, doing the same thing with the first call in distance races. This was referred to as "Energy Adjustment." Its theory was simple: if a horse ran slower in the earlier part of his race, his use of energy was less than if he had burned up a strong early pace. This left him free to run the next portion of his race in a stronger comparative time than he would otherwise have done. Accordingly, there should be some adjustment in the actual ability time based upon how fast or how slow he ran the first part of his race.

Because these ability times were used as the essential rating of the horse, we would go over the entire past performance listing to search for the two best times, give them point figures, add them together, and see who was the highest rated horse. Now that we are using Performance Class Ratings as the base rating, it is no longer necessary to search up and down to compute the two best ability times.

But throughout all of this study and re-study, analysis and re-analysis, I was still confronted with the reality that the last race was ordinarily the most important one to evaluate, even though there are some occasions when we have to disregard the last race shown because it is unuseable. Insofar as the importance of the last race itself is concerned, as long ago as 1968, that perceptive patron of all struggling handicappers, Tom Ainslie, relying primarily on the last race, developed a figure rating method which combined the Daily Racing Form speed rating and track variant along with a number of other adjustments which brought in class and weight. Just as Ainslie wrote, it was reasonably effective. Others developed some similar programs, but what was significant about all of them was that they were primarily using the last race (with only rare deviation) as the basis for an entire rating of a horse.

Then, it occurred to me that if we looked only at the last race for ability times, supplemented with form factors, we might have a very powerful rating device. The strength of the closing horse would be given full measure, along with current form, and we would no longer have to pore over all the other races shown in the past performances to try to extract the best ability times. The use of Performance Class Ratings would tell us what we needed to know about ability and consistency, early speed and late speed, and how a horse could be expected to perform within his own class level.

Therefore, if we use ability times off the last race when possible as a combination of ability, current form, and actual speed as we have adjusted it, we may be nearer to the better rating that we have always sought. That is, as long as we are able to come up with superior last race ability times. We will also be able to forego conversion to points, which may no longer be necessary, and merely select the lowest ability times as the best.

In the sprint race, just as in the past, we will continue to compute the time between the second call and the finish that our horse has run. If the race we are handicapping is a six-furlong race, and the majority of horses ran at 6 furlongs in their last effort, we will have to convert such distances as 6½ and 7 furlongs back to 6-furlong time. We will do the same, of course, when the last race was at 5½ furlongs with a conversion extension.

If the race we are handicapping is either at 6½ or 7 furlongs, and a majority of the horses have run at one of those distances, we can convert the ability times to the distance that is most common, because this makes our task easier. There was a comparative time chart for sprint races only that was set forth in How Will Your Horse Run Today?, which we will repeat here for conversion of shorter and longer sprint distances to the base six furlong time that we will use most often.

We are now ready to compute the sprint ability time. We start with the second call. We first establish the horse's running time by calculating the lengths off the leader, where on the downside, we stick with the consistency of the much maligned one fifth of a second for each length behind. As an example, if the lead time is shown at 46.2 and our horse is 4½ lengths behind, his base time would be 47.2. We would write the 47.2 on our Racing Form (or on a work sheet) at some appropriate place, probably in the area where the first three finishers are shown.

We are ready for the second step that was a staple of our computation in the past. After our time is converted to six furlongs (which must be done in 6½ and 7 furlong races), we subtract the lead time at the second call from the lead time at the finish. For example, if the horse in the lead shows a 46.2 time at the second call and the winning time showed 1:12.1, we would subtract the 46.2 from 1:12.1 to obtain a 25.4 base ability time before adjustment. In using these numbers, bear in mind we are using fifths of seconds, not tenths. The 46.2 means 46 and two-fifths seconds, the 1:12.1 means one

Comparative Time Chart for Sprint Races Only

5 f	5½ f	6 f	6½ f	7 f
:57.1	1:03.2	1·09.2	1 15.3	1.21.4
:57.2	1:03.3	1.09.3	1.15.4	1:22 0
:57.2	1:03.4	1.09 4	1.16.0	1.22.1
:57.3	1·04 0	1.10.0	1.16 1	1:22.2
:57.3	1.04 0	1.10 1	1.16 2	1:22.3
.57.4	1:04.1	1.10 2	1.16.3	1.22 4
:57.4	1.04 1	1 10 2	1 16.4	1.23 0
:58.0	1:04 2	1.10 3	1 17 0	1.23.1
:58 1	1.04.3	1 10 4	1:17 0	1:23.2
:58 1	1.04.3	1 10,4	1.17 1	1:23.3
:58 2	1:04 4	1 11'0	1 17.2	1:23.4
:58 2	1 04 4	1 11 0	1·17 3	1:24.0
.58.3	1:05 0	1 11 1	1.17.4	1:24.1
.58.4	1·05 1	1.11 2	1.18.0	1.24.2
:59.0	1.05 2	1·11.3	1 18 1	1 24 3
:59.1	1 05 3	1 11 4	1.18 2	1 24.4
.59.1	1.05.3	1.12 0	1.18 3	1 25.0
:59.2	1.05 4	1 12 1	1:18.4	1.25 1
:59.3	1:06.0	1.12.2	1:19 0	1.25.2
:59.3	1 06 0	1 12 2	1 19.0	1 25 3
:59 4	1:06.1	1 12.3	1.19 1	1 25 4
1.00.0	1:06 2	1 12 4	1 19.2	1.26 0
1.00.0	1:06.2	1.12 4	1.19 2	1.26 1
1:00.1	1.06 3	1.13 0	1 19.3	1.26.2
1.00.2	1:06 4	1.13 1	1 19 4	1.26 3
1:00.2	1:06.4	1.13 2	1.20 0	1 26.4
1:00.3	1:07.0	1 13.3	1:20 1	1.27 0
1.00.4	1:07 1	1.13.4	1.20.2	1.27 1
1:00.4	1:07.2	1·14 0	1·20 3	1.27.2
1.01.0	1:07.3	1·14 1	1:20.4	1.27.3
1.01.1	1:07.4	1:14.2	1:21.0	1:27 4
1:01.1	1:07.4	1:14.2	1 21 0	1.28 0
1:01.2	1:08 0	1 14 3	1 21 1	1.28.1
1:01.3	1:08.1	1.14.4	1.21.2	1:28.2
1:01.3	1:08.1	1:14.4	1:21.3	1.28.3
1:01.4	1:08.2	1.15.0	1:21 4	1:28.4
1:02.0	1:08.3	1.15.1	1.22 0	1.29.0
1:02.1	1:08.4	1:15.2	1.22 1	1.29.1
1:02.1	1:09.0	1.15.3	1 22 2	1.29 2
1:02 2	1:09.1	1.15.4	1.22 3	1 29 3

minute, twelve and one- fifth seconds, and 25.4 means twenty-five and four-fifths seconds.

The next step is to deal with lengths gained or lost in computing the base ability time. We repeat what has been said many times: the only true, accurate time published in the Daily Racing Form is that posted by a horse that was in the lead at both the second call and the finish. This is true clock time, because the same horse is activating the timer at both the critical points. All other times that handicappers are compelled to use are based upon lengths gained or lengths lost as gleaned from the running line in the Daily Racing Form.

Positions in lengths as shown in the Form are based upon the chart caller's estimate of where each particular horse was at a point of call. These estimates, which admittedly come from experienced eyes, are still only estimates. Even a half-length off can influence the times that we are called upon to use. Lengths behind at the finish are usually more accurate than lengths behind at any internal call, because the horses are in direct line of vision of the chart caller in the press box. Also, lengths can be measured off the rail, and video replays can help erase doubts. But they are still estimates. But even the more accurate lengths behind at the finish cannot solve the problem of estimated times at the first and second calls, where it is far more difficult for the chart caller to be precisely accurate. All this, of course, is another reason why we make the adjustments we do.

Here is the Lengths Gained Adjustment table that we used in Investing at the Race Track, which is as sound and valid today as then:

Gain in Lengths	Gain in Fifths of Seconds
Less than 1	None
1 to 1¾	One
2 to 2¾	Two
3 to ¾	Three
4 to 4¾	Three
5 to 5 ¾	Four
6 to 6¼	Four
6½ to 7¼	Five
7½ to 8	Six
8 and more	Six

You may be surprised at drawing the line at a six-fifths time gain after 8 lengths when the Racing Form running line may show a gain of 10 lengths, 12 lengths, or more. But the reason for this has an important foundation. First of all, the farther back a horse is in the pack, the more difficult it becomes to even closely estimate his true lengths behind, in keeping with what we said earlier. Accordingly, inaccurate estimates are far more likely to occur back in the crowd, which we can hardly afford when we deal with the important element of lengths gained. Secondly, horses making up enormous chunks of ground are likely to be gaining lengths on horses who are decelerating, thus reducing time spans between the two at such a rapid rate that we have no way of knowing what actual time gain there was.

We are thus back to the hazardous endeavor of estimating, which plagues every student of the game, every handicapper, and every rating method known, no matter what it is. We are compelled to invest our money on unreliable estimates, not precisely accurate realities. We must therefore do the best we can to make these estimates as workably useable as possible. Experience and study has convinced us that the Lengths-Time Gained table set forth above is as reliable a device as we have been able to find.

We shall use this Adjustment for Lengths Gained table in both sprints and distance races.

Thus far, we know of no other handicapping scholar who has set this forth in this fashion, or has even relied upon this. But even with all our respect for our fellow writers, I am compelled to argue that any method of rating horses that relies on the usual one tick for each length gained as shown in the Form will produce some unreliable figures that can cost you a great deal of money.

Thus, in fixing a raw ability time for the sprint race that shows a lead time of :46.2 and a finish time of 1:12.1, as long as the horse we are rating was not in the lead at both these two positions, we must use our table. If the horse was 3 ¾ lengths behind at the second call and 1 ½ lengths behind at the finish, we would subtract an additional two ticks from the lead time of 25.4 to award our horse a 25.2 raw ability time.

Accordingly, using the same 46.2 and 1:12.1 lead times, if another horse in the same race was two lengths behind at the second call and 5 ½ lengths behind at the finish, we would add four ticks to the 25.4 base time and give this horse a 26.3 ability time. In this process, we are compelled to use ½ length and more as a whole length for time purposes, with less than a half length being disregarded.

We are now at the point where we will make a substantial major departure from how we calculated ability times in Investing at the Race Track and how we will calculate them here. We will do away with the Energy Adjustment we used in the former process, because we have substituted something else for it. As a result, the whole process will be much easier, faster, and more reliable.

We will write this new time number for the span of the race between the second call at four furlongs and the finish call at six furlongs (or the adjustment to six furlong time) alongside the time number for the second call. If the second call time was 47.2 and the adjusted time span between the second call and the finish was 25.4, we would have these numbers listed side by side and would be ready to add them together for a new figure. If you added 47.2 and 25.4, you would get 73.1.

When you add these figures in any race that is based on six furlong time, your new total will almost always be in the 70's, and that makes it much easier to add. You will be in effect adding only the last numbers, such as 7.2 and 5.4 in the example above, which gives you 13.1, which can be added on to the constant 60 to get 73.1. In fact, if you wanted to make the task easier, you could always use these smaller number combinations. My reason for sticking with the full numbers of 47.2 and 25.4 is that they give you a familiar reading on how the horse has performed, especially as to the pace of the race.

Now you may see why it was easy to eliminate the energy adjustments that we had used before when we relied only on the last fractional time. Resurrecting an old example in simple form, if a horse ran 48.0 and 1:12.0, he would have a last quarter fraction of 24.0, very good. If a horse ran 46.0 and 1:10.0, he would also have a last quarter fraction of 24.0, also very good. But the horse that ran six furlongs in 1:10.0 compared to the horse than ran in 1:12.0 was demonstrably a faster horse. To use ability times effectively, I made the energy adjustment for the 48.0 runner, which caused his ability time to be higher than his 1:10 competitor.

But now that we are giving full measure to the second call time, the energy adjustment is no longer necessary. If we use the 48.0 and the 1:12.0 for the horse that ran the 24.0 final quarter, we would have a new total number of 48.0 + 24.0, or 72.0. When we add the 46.0 to the 24.0 for the faster horse, we would have a total of 70.0, which readily demonstrates the superiority of the last horse.

Now, it is highly possible, of course, that the final times in both instances, 1:12.0 against 1:10.0 were influenced by the track variant, and this brings us to our final adjustment from the track variant table that we have presented earlier.

We will apply the track variant adjustment in all cases.

Let us assume the horse that ran 48.0 and 1:12.0 did it on a day when the Daily Racing Form variant was 27. Under our figures, this would require a subtraction of 4 from his tentative ability time of 72.0 (for 48.0 + 24.0), thus reducing his final ability time to 71.1.

Let us assume that the horse that ran the 46.0 and 1:10.0 times with a tentative ability time of 70.0 (46.0 + 24.0) did it on a day when the track was so fast that the DRF variant stood at 10. We would add 6 ticks to the tentative ability time of 70.0 to give us a final ability time of 71.1.

The two horses would thus wind up with exactly the same ability times. This is remarkably effective, despite all the estimates and rule-of-thumb calculations. All the adjustments that may go into these calculations may be off here and there, and for those reasons, as we will state again and again, a horse that shows a final number one tick better than his rival is probably nearly even. If there is a 2-tick difference, we can approach it warily. We now will look for as much as a 3-tick difference (which we can do now because two sets of numbers are involved) in order to find any meaningful span in ability times between competing horses.

Let us now take note of several points before we go to practice exercises to further show you how to do it. The use of two time figures is, as we have said, a drastic change from the old ability times, where we relied solely on the adjusted portion between the second call and the finish. The advantage of the new combined figures gives us a better indication of the pace of the last race, how the horse coped with it, and a new total that my research and testing has shown to be more reliable. The frantic closer who would pick up a sparkling ability time will now have it leveled off with the addition of a slow second call time, as further adjusted by the track variant.

Let us now repeat, step by step, how we now calculate ability times in sprint races.

1. We begin with the second call time of our horse, adjusting it for lengths behind. We write it down.

2. Assuming that the race is a six furlong race, we next calculate the lead time as the difference between the second call time and the finish time as shown in the running line of the race. We do this by subtracting the second call lead time from the finish lead time. If our horse gained lengths from the second call to the finish, we subtract from the lead time as we use the Lengths Gained Adjustment table. When the horse lost ground from the second call to the finish, we add one-fifth of a second, or tick, for each length and half-length shown to the lead time. We write this number down alongside the second call time number.

3. We add the two numbers together for a total that will always (except for very, very fast races and very, very slow races) will be

in the 70's. The internal numbers will also give you guidance as to the pace of the race and the closing efforts.

4. To this tentative total of the two times, we will make an adjustment for track variant, either adding or subtracting or making no change at all when the variant so indicates.

This will be our final ability time in a sprint race.

It is artificial, constructed, and meant only to be a method of comparing one horse against another. When it is applied consistently, as it must be, it is a highly reliable rating. When we recognize that all ratings are based upon estimates and perhaps some kinds of adjustments, and further recognize that no horse may run to any particular rating at any particular time, we can comfort ourselves with the pattern of reliability that the use of this method will show.

With all the information now set forth, let's run through some ability times in sprint races, using the tables that are shown in this chapter which, by the way, will fall into your memory quicker than you can imagine once you use them a few times.

From the Daily Racing Form of Jan. 24, 1987, we can compute for practice purposes the ability times for all three races shown for Princess Mercedes, although in comparing her with today's entries, we would use only the last race. She was an Also Eligible in the first race at Santa Anita that day.

Princess Mercedes
STEVENS G L
Own.—Sofro D I   114

B. f. 3, by The Irish Lord—My Mercedes, by Doc Scott J
Br.—Parrish & Navert (Cal)
Tr.—Canani Julio C $40,000
Lifetime   3 2 1 0 $17,050

			1987	1 0 1 0	$4,400
			1986	2 2 0 0	$12,650

9Jan87-1SA   6f :22³ :46⁴ 1:124sl   *1 115   11½ 1½ 11½ 2ʰᵈ   ValenzuelPA⁸ ⓕ 50000 74-26 Trcy'sTrck,PrncssMrcds,BtflBrook 8
20Dec86-5Hol 6f :22 :46 1:113ft   *6-5 116   2ʰᵈ 1¹ 14 1⁶   ValenzuelPA⁴ ⓟ 25000 85-15 PrncssMrcds,HvyWthr,IDon'tNLcy 6
14Nov86- Hol 6f :22 :46 1:122ft   — 118   1ʰᵈ 1¹ 1ʰᵈ 11½ McHrgDG² ⓔMc32000 81-16 PrncssMrcds,Lf'sSng,LvByThSrd 10
  14Nov86—No wagering
Jan 17 SA 4f ft :50⁴ h   Jan 2 SA 5f ft 1:03² h   Dec 17 Hol 4f ft :48¹ h   Dec 10 Hol 5f ft 1:02 h

This is an easy one, because this young filly was in the lead at the second call in each of her races. But beginning with the last race of Jan. 9, we have a second call time of :46.4 and a finish of 1:12.4 on a slow track. Thus, we have a base unadjusted time of :26.0. We add the 46.4 to the 26.0 and come up with a tentative ability time of 72.4. Now we factor in the variant, and from the DRF number of 26, we subtract 3, and have an ability time for Princess Mercedes of 72.1.

Continuing for practice, we try the race of Dec. 20, 1986 at Hollywood. There is a 46.0 second call and a finish of 1:11.3, which are the lead times. The difference is 25.3, which you will be able to snap off by sight after you do it a few times. We add 46.0 and 25.3

and come up with 71.3. Off the DRF variant of 15, we add 2, bringing the final ability time to 72.0, not much different from the Jan. 9 race at Santa Anita. For the third race, you can quickly see 46.0 and 26.2 for 72.2, plus 1 for variant, for a final figure of 72.3.

Let's do a few that require a little more than the easy run we have just shown. Take a look at the past performances of Count Geiger, entered in the second race at Santa Anita on January 24, 1987, at six furlongs.

Count Geiger * — Dk. b. or br. h. 6, by Bold Bidder—Lady Leallah, by Sir Ivor

FERNANDEZ A L — 116 — Br.—Firman Mrs Pamela H (Ky) — 1987 1 0 0 0

Own.—Etter R L — Tr.—Pew Karl — $32,000 — 1986 5 0 2 0 $10,300

Lifetime 14 2 4 0 $51,225 — Turf 4 1 1 0 $20,175

17Jan87-2SA	6f	:21^4	:45	1:10^{3}ft	13	116	6$^{5\frac{1}{2}}$	7^7	7$^{6\frac{1}{2}}$	8$^{9\frac{1}{4}}$	Valenzuela P A^4	40000	76-18	Ondarty, Romaxe, Rivets Factor	11
17Jan87—Rough start; came in, bumped, took up 5/8															
31Dec86-5SA	6½f	:22	:45^3	1:17^{2}ft	13	116	4$^{1\frac{3}{4}}$	1^{hd}	2$^{\frac{1}{2}}$	6$^{4\frac{3}{4}}$	Fernandez AL^{12}	40000	78-20	Watch'n Win, Angle Arc, I:Idol	12
13Apr86-3SA	6½f	:21^4	:44^4	1:16^{4}ft	2¾	117	3$^{1\frac{1}{2}}$	1^{hd}	2^{hd}	2^2	Pincay L Jr^9	c32000	84-15	Paskanell, Count Geiger, ‡Timlin	12
21Mar86-7SA	6f	:21^2	:44	1:09^{2}ft	6¼	117	8$^{5\frac{3}{4}}$	8$^{7\frac{1}{4}}$	8$^{6\frac{1}{4}}$	5$^{2\frac{3}{4}}$	Pincay L Jr^5	50000	88-15	KingOfCliforni,Cryptrch,Menswer	12
31Jan86-5SA	6½f	:22^1	:45^4	1:18^{3}sy	*2½	117	3^{nk}	1$^{\frac{1}{2}}$	2^2	2^2	Pincay L Jr^6	Aw28000	75-29	Amnothrbrothr,ContGgr,VrgnPrvtr	6
31Jan86—Wide into turn															
8Jan86-5SA	a6½f Ⓣ	:21	:43^3	1:15 fm	*2¼	117	8$^{9\frac{3}{4}}$	8^{12}	8^{10}	7$^{9\frac{1}{4}}$	Pincay L Jr^3	Aw28000	75-17	All Hands OnDeck,BlueRazor,Hatim	8
13Dec85-8Hol	1$\frac{1}{16}$ Ⓣ	:49^2	1:13^2	1:43^{1}fm	3	116	1^{hd}	1^{hd}	1^{hd}	4^3	McCarronCJ^5	Aw27000	— —	Rivlia, Barland, Faridpour	8
13Dec85—Bumped start; wide into drive															
28Nov85-7Hol	7f	:22	:44^2	1:21^{1}ft	6¾	122	4^3	5$^{4\frac{1}{2}}$	6^7	5$^{10\frac{1}{2}}$	Pincay L Jr^3	Aw22000	87-12	Crcksmn,PrideOfOurs,UltimtePlsur	9
7Nov85-8SA	a6½f Ⓣ	:21^4	:44^4	1:15^{4}fm	*1	118	4^4	4$^{4\frac{1}{2}}$	3^1	1^{nk}	Pincay L Jr^7	Aw25000	80-20	CountGeiger,MyGallntGme,QuipStr	9
7Nov85—Bumped 3/16															
28Mar85-6SA	1$\frac{1}{16}$	:47^3	1:14^1	1:48^{2}sl	*3-5	118	1^1	1$^{\frac{1}{2}}$	1^1	1$^{1\frac{1}{2}}$	Pincay L Jr^5	Mdn	59-31	Count Geiger, Kinetic, Adclfo	9

Jan 12 SA 4f ft :47^4 h   Dec 26 SA 4f ft :48 h   Dec 19 SA 6f ft 1:14^1 h   Dec 12 SA 5f ft :59^4 h

Because this is for practice, we will ignore the last race and assume the races we point out are the ones we would be calculating on any particular day. We can start with the race of Dec. 31 at 6½ furlongs because it requires us to make a comparison adjustment to 6 furlongs. Since the lead time (or winning time) is 1:17.2, we would subtract 6.2 based upon our comparison table, which would give us a 6 furlong time of 1:11.0. We then do our calculations off that figure. The second call time is 45.3, and subtracting this from 1:11.0 gives us a 25.2 lead time. There was a 4 ¾ length loss, which requires us to add 5 to the 25.2 to end up with 26.2. We now add 45.3 + 26.2 to come up with 72.0. The variant of 20 requires no adjustment, so the final ability time is fixed at 72.0.

Let's next do the 7 furlong race down on November 28, 1985. Our first adjustment is off the very fast winning time, which runs us off our chart. But we can see that we subtract 12.2, which would give us the astonishing figure of 1:08.4 as an adjusted 6 furlong time. The lead time for the measured quarter would thus be 1:08.4 minus 44.2, or 24.2. Now, to the adjustments for our horse. To the 44.2 we add 4 lengths to 45.1, which we write down. Off the 24.2 lead preliminary ability time, Count Geiger lost 6 lengths, pushing the figure up to 25.3. We can now add 45.1 and 25.3, leaving us with 70.4. The variant is next, and off the 12 showing, we add 4 more ticks to come up with a final ability time of 71.3.

Now look at the bottom race in the past performances, the mile sixteenth event of March 28, 1985, at Santa Anita. When you calculate a sprint ability time off a distance race, the process is basically the same, except that you use the first call and the second call as the 6 furlong point. In this case, Count Geiger set the lead times of 47.3 and 1:14.1. We write down the 47.3, and then subtract that number from the 1:14.1 to get a 26.3 preliminary ability time. Adding the two numbers brings us to 74.1 for a preliminary. The variant is almost out of sight at 31, which allows us to deduct 6 ticks to wind up with a 73.0 final ability time. Because of the very slow track that day and the extremely high variant, any figure would be questionable.

But the technique of using the first two calls in a distance race, where a horse is running today at a sprint, to obtain the ability time, is a very useful device that will lead you to some surprisingly good figures and some excellent numbers on the tote board. Many handicappers simply miss those strong sprint figures that may be overlooked because of a poor finishing performance in a distance race.

We could show even more races as practice examples, but we think the principles are now well established. If you have any difficulty in doing these new sprint ability times, which we believe are now both far easier than the old and more effective, look back at the summary of how to do it that is in this chapter.

If you have a 6½ furlong race, for example, where half or more than half the entries last ran at 6½ furlongs, you can extend the figures to the final 6½ furlong time. For those horses that last ran at 6 furlongs, you would add on the comparison numbers to get the figure from which you work. Let's go back to Count Geiger again and do a practice run on his race of Jan. 31, 1986 as if the majority of the horses in the race last ran at the 6½ distance.

We would first do our lead time, subtracting 45.4 from the final time figure of 1:18.3, which would leave us with 32.4 as the unadjusted lead ability time. We then write down the 45.4 second call time for Count Geiger. Since he lost two lengths in the final portion of the race, the 32.4 base figure would rise to 33.1. We now add 45.4 + 33.1, where we have the new unfamiliar number of 79.0 as a preliminary ability time. This may be a little awkward, but only because we are not too familiar with these kinds of calculations. All that we have to do now is factor in the variant, which shows at 29, allowing us to deduct five ticks from 79.0 to wind up with 78.0 as the final ability time. This isn't too bad in itself. You can then compare this final ability time with those of the other horses, all calculated at the same distance. It's relatively easy to do.

With sprint races under control, we next turn to ability times in distance, or route, races, which will always produce a quite different kind of number.

11 Ability Times In Distance Races

OUR NEW REVISED ability times in distance races will now conform in method along the same lines as those we do in sprints. But there is just enough difference to warrant this separate treatment. We have previously mentioned that our original ability times for distance, or route races, as we used them in Investing at the Race Track, were compiled between the same four furlong and six furlong distance span inside a race as we used in sprints. There was a theory behind it that made some sense, and to a limited degree, these times were effective. But the new method here, factoring in the second call and the adjusted time from the second call to the finish, is far, far more realistic and effective.

We shall use this calculation method in all races of one mile or more where the second call time is shown in the running line at the six furlong position. Where the races extend to as long as a mile and a quarter and longer, the second call time is often shown at the one mile position. Once we give you the complete method here, you will be able to adapt it to those marathon events by adding the second call time to the difference between the second call and finish times, as you also undertake to make whatever distance adjustments are necessary.

In route races, one of the major problems you will encounter is the difference in distances which will require you to use comparison times for the finish time. In these longer races, and let's start with the common example of an event at a mile and one-sixteenth, it is not unusual to have horses that have run at a great variety of distances. A horse's last race could have been at 6 furlongs, or 6½, or 7, or a mile, a mile forty, a mile seventy, a mile and one-eighth, and even a mile and three-sixteenths. Yet you are trying to adjust times so that they all come out at the same distance, in order to use common figures.

Once again, the ever occurring comparison table must be used.

First, let us establish the basic formula, as we did in sprints, and then work toward the comparison distances.

We will first write down the time of the horse at the second call, which will always be at six furlongs in the races that we will be reviewing in this manner. Let us assume our race is at a mile and one-sixteenth. Assume further that the lead time at 6f was 1:12.1. Because we are trying to save time and lop off unnecessary numbers, we will write this figure on our Racing Form or in our workbook as simply 12.1. All times would be in excess of one minute, so you are dealing in blessed uniformity. You will quickly learn to accept that the 12.1 time is really the 1:12.1 that the lead horse turned in.

Our next hypothetical is that our horse was 5½ lengths behind, which would give him a 1:13.2 second call time, which we would write as 13.2. This is quick, easy, and uniform.

The next step would be to subtract the second call lead time from the finish lead time to obtain the span time. Let us assume the winning time was 1:44.3. Subtracting the lead time of 1:12.1 from the finish time of 1:44.3 would give us a span time of 32.2. Now, we would work off that figure for our horse, who was 5½ behind at the second call and finished 1¼ off, according to the chart. We would credit him with a gain of 3, and subtracting the 3 from the lead span time of 32.2 would give our horse a 31.4.

We would then add the 13.1 for the second call to the 31.4 and get a preliminary total of 45.0.

The final step is to add or subtract the variant, just as we do in sprint races, using the same formula. If the DRF variant was 16, we would add 1 to the 45.0 and write in the final adjusted ability time as 45.1.

To do this kind of simple exercise, let's work off the record of Vysotsky, entered in the 4th race at Santa Anita on Jan. 24, 1987, at a mile sixteenth.

Vysotsky — B. c. 4, by Sassafras—Karetch, by Karabas
VALENZUELA P A 119 — Br.—Gordon Mrs Rachel (Ky) — 1987 1 M 0 0 $1,725
Tr.—Ippolito Steve — 1986 4 M 1 1 $6,360
Own.—Green Thumb Farm Stable — Lifetime 5 0 1 1 $8,085

9Jan87-6SA	1 1/16	:47^{2}	1:12^{4}	1:46^{4}sl	3½	119	$7^{7\frac{1}{2}}$	7^{10}	$5^{7\frac{1}{2}}$	$4^{9\frac{3}{4}}$	Valenzuela P A^{9}	Mdn	57-26	Jack McCoy, Centenary, Rewana	11
9Jan87—Rough start															
28Dec86-4SA	1 1/16	:46	1:10^{2}	1:42^{4}ft	7¾	117	3^{6}	2^{7}	2^{8}	$2^{7\frac{1}{2}}$	Valenzuela P A^{5}	Mdn	79-14	Valiant Cougar,Vysotsky,Centenary	8
31Mar86-10Hia	1⅛	:47^{1}	1:11^{4}	1:51 ft	3½	119	6^{8}	$6^{8\frac{1}{2}}$	6^{13}	5^{15}	Mayorga W^{7}	Mdn	62-15	Dearborn, LarryAtLaw,PassTheLaw	7
21Mar86-8Hia	1⅛	:46^{1}	1:11^{4}	1:52^{1}sy	*2½	119	$4^{4\frac{1}{2}}$	$3^{1\frac{1}{2}}$	2^{2}	$4^{3\frac{1}{2}}$	Mayorga W^{2}	Mdn	68-17	Cox'sBest,PillrOfStrength,Owr'sHll	8
8Mar86-5Hia	1⅛	:47^{1}	1:12^{2}	1:50^{3}ft	45	119	11^{13}	$8^{9\frac{3}{4}}$	4^{11}	$3^{10\frac{1}{2}}$	Mayorga W^{3}	Mdn	68-16	ComHomBoy,LklyKnght,Vysotsky	12

Jan 18 SA 5f ft 1:01^{1} h   Jan 5 SA 4f sy :48^{2} h   Dec 25 SA 4f ft :48^{1} h   Dec 18 SA 5f ft 1:00^{4} h

In the last race, the lead time was 1:12.4, and with Vysotsky 10 lengths behind, his second call time would be 1:14.4, which we would write down as 14.4. The lead time span between the second call and the finish was 34.0, which we obtain by subtracting the 1:12.4 from the 1:46.4, or 12.4 from 46.4. Since Vysotsky neither gained nor lost measurable ground, his preliminary span time would be the same 34.0. We would next add: 14.4 + 34.0 = 48.4. For the variant, off the DRF 26, we subtract 3 from 48.4, leaving us with a final ability time of 48.1.

That is the easy kind.

We must next learn to compile extended or estimated final times in route races with varying distances. The most common back and forth distances are 1 1/16 to 1 1/8. But we need to be prepared for all varieties. This brings us to another comparison line, which is to be used in most "normal" (if that condition ever exists) situations. Here are estimated times between varying distances:

Mile to 1-40	Mile to 1-70	Mile to 1 1-16	1-70 to 1 1-16	1 1-16 to 1 1-8
:02.2	:04.2	:06.3	:02.4	:06.3

This kind of extrapolation can vary from day to day at any particular track. It can also be different from track to track. We repeat that it is no more than an estimate that must be applied because we can never know the accurate figure because it is ordinarily not available to us.

When a track is running unusually fast, you would do well to subtract one tick off those numbers. Likewise, if a track is running unusually slow, as it may in the winter, you would add one tick to those numbers. You might be guided again by the general usefulness of the Form variants. If you see DRF variant numbers as low as 10, 11, and 12, for example, you can be reasonably sure the track was running fast and you could deduct one tick off from each of the above projected time span figures. Likewise, if the Form variant shows at 29 or 30 or upward, you should add at least one tick across the board to those numbers.

Let's now go back to Vysotsky and practice with the 21Mar86 race at Hialeah at 1 1/8. We will convert it to the 1 1/16 distance, which is the first assignment on this kind of computation of the ability time. We work off the lead time at the finish, which in this case was 1:52.1. We subtract the 6.3 that we would expect, giving us an estimated 1 1/16 time of 1:45.3. (A quick easy way to deal with different fifths of time would be to always subtract 7 from the base time, such as 7 from 1:52, which would give 1:45, and then add the difference between the 7 and the 6.3, which is 2, to the extra tick for a total of 3 and the same 1:45.3. Try it, you may like it, for it is sometimes quicker and easier).

With the lead times at 1:11.4 and 1:45.3, we can now compute the span time as 33.4. Vysotsky had a 1:12.1 second call time, which we write in as 12.1, lost two in last portion of the race, which we add to the lead time span to get 34.1. We next add 12.1 to 34.1 to get 46.2, and add 1 more for variant for a 46.3 ability time. If we wanted to do it the other way, from 1 1/16 to 1 1/8, we could go back up to the 9Jan87 event and add 6.3 to the finish time of 1:46.4, which would give us 1:53.2. This would increase the span time to 40.3, and our line would read this way: 14.4 + 40.3 −3, or 54.4 for a final ability time. All other horses in the race would have to be rated at the same distance, of course.

The same technique follows at any distance from one mile to a mile and three-sixteenths. We will do a few more examples shortly. This will be the method on all occasions when we are constructing ability times for a distance race off a distance race.

But because many horses stretch out from sprints in their last race to run a route today, we have a new set of problems. We have to find a way to convert to comparable route times using a similar set of figures that will always be comparable. And even when we are able to do that, we cannot escape the recognition that because sprint races are run differently and that a bigger span of estimation goes into our construction, we will have to use the converted sprint time as advisory only. When these times are constructed, I will regularly place a parenthesis around them to show two things: one, that they are based upon a sprint race last out and two, they should be used with caution and thus are advisory only. Of course, when a reconstructed time off a sprint is far and away better than the times off route races, you can and should use it, because the wide span creates the advantage we seek.

The common sprint distances that have to be converted to route distances for span times are ordinarily 6f, 6½ f, and 7f. Each of them has to be handled in its own way.

When a horse last ran at 6f and today is running at 1 1/16, here is how we start our projected method. We first write in the horse's 6f time (not the lead time or finish time), as if it were the second call in a sprint race. We will then have to compute the span time in the sprint race between the second call and the finish as we normally do it, and then we add an estimated time for a half furlong, which would be the 6.3 that we ordinarily use. Therefore, if the span time was 26.0, the 6.3 to be added to it would be 32.3. A 1:12.1, or 12.1, off the 6-furlong time would be further added for a 44.4 (with a hypothetical variant of 19 which would require nothing further), which would be our adjusted ability time for a mile and one-sixteenth.

Here is where we run into a new problem which requires us to take on another step, which I admit is burdensome, but we have to do it in order to qualify our projected time off a sprint as comparable to the ability time off a last race route. When we use the span time between the second call and the finish in the ordinary sprint race, we are back to the framework of sprint ability times. How fast a horse is able to run the last two furlongs in a sprint race depends a great deal on how fast or how slow he runs the first four furlongs to get to the second call. In other words, a horse that loafed to the second call could wind up with a sparkling two furlong final span time, which, if carried over to a distance race that would be run in a different manner, would result in a distorted figure.

Let's use an actual race which will bring up again later to illustrate the point. In the sixth race at Pimlico on August 1, 1987, an allowance event at a mile and a sixteenth for some rather high quality fillies and mares, all the major contenders except one had last run at the same 1 1/16 distance of that day's race. Masked Barb, a tough old competitor on the Maryland circuit, had last raced at 6 furlongs. She had loafed to the second call in 48.2 and without the strain of a fast early pace, was able to turn on a powerful kick to the wire for a 24.1 adjusted time off my figures. If we wrapped that 24.1 into our calculated extensions, we would be giving her an unbalanced competitive edge on the others in the race. We thus have to find a way to account for that.

We do it by a simplified version of the old energy adjustments we used to make for slow second calls. After we compute the span time from the second call to the finish in a sprint, we will tack on penalty ticks for a slow second call. We will start the penalty running at 47.0 and add one tick when a horse's second call time is either 47.0 or 47.1. We then go upward with one penalty tick for each additional two ticks showing. Here is how it comes out:

Second call time: 47.0 and 47.1 – Add one penalty tick
47.2 and 47.3 – Add two penalty ticks
47.4 and 48.0 – Add three
48.1 and 48.2 – Add four

Continue to add an additional penalty tick, or fifth of a second, for every two as the time moves upward after 48.2. In the case of Masked Barb, the sprint lead time in her race was 25.1. She gained five allowable lengths from the second call to the finish, reducing her final span time to 24.1. But because she turned in a 48.2 second call time, we would add a four tick penalty to convert it to 25.0. We would then add 6.3 to get the comparison 2½ furlong time for the last portion of the 1 1/16 race, which would give us 31.3. Off her 1:12.0 finish time, we would add 12.0 to the 31.3 and have a powerful 43.3. The variant in her last race was 19, which required no further action, and we would then call her advisory last race ability time as 43.3.

To show the sprint calculation to a mile sixteenth time in general, let's look at the last race of Mondanite, who was entered in the same 1 1/16 race at Santa Anita from which we have taken Vysotsky's record to analyze.

Mondanite B. g. 5, by Lyphard—Social Column, by Sween's Son or Vaguely Noble
DELAHOUSSAYE E 120 Br.—Gainesway Farm & Hart (Tenn) 1987 1 M 0 1 $3,150
Own.—Juddmonte Farms Tr.—Gosden John H M 1986 8 M 2 2 $13,075
Lifetime 14 0 3 3 $17,477 Turf 7 0 1 0 $1,252

8Jan87-6SA	6f	:22	:45^4	1:11^{2}m	2¾	120	6^6	45½	3^4	3^6	Delahoussaye E^6	Mdn	75-30	Svnfvndchng,Dn'sIrshMldy,Mndnt	10
8Jan87—Bumped hard start															
27Dec86-6SA	6f	:22	:45^3	1:11 ft	7½	120	6^3	3^2	41¼	32½	Delahoussaye E^9	Mdn	80-19	General At War,Rufjan,Mondanite	12
10Aug86-4Dmr	6½f	:21^4	:44^4	1:15^{1}ft	16	121	2^{hd}	21½	54½	711¾	Lipham T^{10}	Mdn	84-08	OurLordship,Extrnix,NorthernBlzr	11
16Jly86-7Hol	6f	:22^3	:46^2	1:12 ft	4¾	122	2^1	2½	3^1	32¾	Lipham T^3	Mdn	81-15	Miocene, Outer Limits, Mondanite	7

We first write down Mondanite's actual 6f time, which in the 8Jan87 race would be 1:11.2 plus the 6 lengths behind, or 1:12.3. We would then write 12.3 on our Form or in our workbook. Now we will compute the last portion span time in the sprint race off the lead times, which gives us a 25.3. We will add 1 to that total because of the ½ length loss of Mondanite, which gives us 25.4. Now, we will look to see if a penalty is required. Mondanite's second call time would be 47.0, and that would require adding a penalty tick to make her span time at 26.0. Now, we are ready to add the estimated last half furlong time. Notice that the track variant was 30 and the track was muddy, which would then require us to add 6.4 rather than the normal 6.3. We add 6.4 to 26.0 and we have 32.4. We then add 12.3 to 32.4 for 45.2. Next, it's variant time, and we subtract 5 to get a 44.2

ability time, which would be advisory only because it is off a sprint race. If we were converting to a 1 1/8 distance, instead of adding one 6.4, we would add two, or 13.3 to the 26.0 for 39.3. Then 12.3 + 39.3 −5 = 51.1, which is 6.4 greater than the time for the 1 1/16 distance.

To repeat and summarize for conversion of 6 furlong time to the 1 1/16 or 1/8 distances (or any of the others for that matter), we first record the actual 6f time of the horse, and write it down. Then, we compute the sprint last portion time between 4f and 6f. We next check the second call time, and if it is 47.0 or higher, we add one penalty tick for every two ticks from 47.0 upward. To the new adjusted span total, we add the time for an extra half furlong or a full furlong (or other distance) as the case may be. We then add this span figure to the 6f (or equivalent to second call time) number, and add or subtract the variant to get a final adjusted ability time.

Next, let's do the conversion off a 6½ furlong sprint race to the 1 1/16 distance. This launches us into a time conversion at the very outset to get an equivalent 6f time. From the 6½f final time, we would subtract 6.3 in most cases to give us an estimated 6f time which we would use as our equivalent second call time, and as our first number in the line calculation.

Now, we save a step. We can compute the last portion time between the second call and the finish just as it is without adjustment, because the distance between 4f and 6½ furlongs is the same 2½ furlong distance between 6 furlongs and the 8½ furlongs that is involved in the 1 1/16 race. Once again, we will have to check the second call time to see if penalty ticks are to be added. Thereafter, we do our calculations in the same manner. We will show an example shortly.

But when we convert from 6½f to 1 1/8, or 9f, we have to go back to more extensions. We are required, of course, to first compute the 6f time by subtracting from the final time of the 6½f race. We would do it the same way as if the race were at the 1 1/16 distance, and then add 6.3 to get it up to the 1 1/8 comparison. Now, that really isn't so difficult, is it?

We have yet a third exercise when the last race was at 7f and we want to convert to 1 1/16. We first subtract from the 7f final time to obtain an estimated 6f time, which we will write down and use. Our next step is to compute the last portion span time between the second call in the sprint race to the finish at 7f, which will give us a 3f figure. Again, we check for penalty times. We would then have the equivalent time if today's race was at 1 1/8, and we would use it without further conversion. But if today's race is at 1 1/16, we would then have to subtract 6.3 from the inner span time and would wind up with the usual addition of the 6f time (for second call) with the adjusted estimated final portion time with the variant.

To show how these conversions work, we can use the record of Onnagata, entered in the first race at Belmont on June 20, 1987, as shown in the Daily Racing Form.

Onnagata — Ch. g. 4, by Wajima—Saturday Matinee, by Silent Screen

Own.—Gold N Oats Stable — 115 — Br.—DiMaure S A (Ky) — Tr.—Martin Gregory — $32,500

1987 8 3 1 0 $41,820
1986 16 1 0 2 $13,800
Lifetime 30 5 2 3 $70,580

10Jun87-1Bel	6½f	$:22^4$	$:45^3$	$1:15^4$ft	*9-5	117	1½	1^4	1^7	$1^{6\frac{3}{4}}$	Santos J A 7	17500	96-17	Onnagata, Truth Be Told, IrishIrish	9
1Jun87-1Bel	7f	$:23^1$	$:46^1$	$1:23^4$ft	8½	117	$6^{3\frac{1}{2}}$	$6^{3\frac{1}{2}}$	5^2	$5^{2\frac{3}{4}}$	Santos J A 3	25000	80-20	SntlyChf,Rxson'sQll,CorncobsRylty	7
17Apr87-3Aqu	1⅛	$:46^4$	1:12	$1:51^1$gd	5	117	$3^{3\frac{1}{2}}$	2^1	$7^{5\frac{1}{2}}$	$7^{13\frac{3}{4}}$	Migliore R 8	35000	65-23	No Ski, Classic Move, GoldenChief	9
26Mar87-3Aqu	1	$:45^3$	$1:09^4$	$1:35^2$ft	7¾	112^5	$6^{4\frac{1}{2}}$	$6^{5\frac{1}{2}}$	$7^{6\frac{1}{4}}$	$7^{7\frac{1}{4}}$	Ortiz E Jr 9	50000	82-25	Revelrout, Keep It Easy,Dale'sFolly	9
7Mar87-3Aqu	1⅛ ⊡	$:48^1$	$1:12^3$	$1:50^2$ft	*9-5	117	$6^{2\frac{1}{4}}$	3^1	$2^{\frac{1}{2}}$	$2^{1\frac{1}{4}}$	Cordero A Jr 3	35000	89-13	IamCharlesPet,Onnagata,FstPhillip	9
7Mar87—Taken up															
5Feb87-7Aqu	1⅛ ⊡	$:46^3$	$1:11^3$	$1:50^4$ft	8	117^5	$1^{2\frac{1}{2}}$	$1^{\frac{1}{2}}$	12^{19}	12^{30}	Ortiz E Jr 8	Aw28000	58-24	Belocolus, Tull, Curtin	12
28Jan87-9Aqu	1 3/16 ⊡	$:47^2$	$1:21^1$	$1:58^2$ft	3½	112^5	$1^{1\frac{1}{2}}$	1^2	1^3	$1^{3\frac{3}{4}}$	Ortiz E Jr 5	Aw27000	85-18	Onnagt,ProudAndTll,RreWelshBit	10
17Jan87-2Aqu	1^{70} ⊡	$:47^3$	$1:13^4$	$1:43^2$ft	*7-5e	108^5	4^3	$3^{1\frac{1}{2}}$	$1^{1\frac{1}{2}}$	$1^{1\frac{1}{2}}$	Ortiz E Jr 3	30000	83-20	Onnagata, Quiet Royalty, Sir Keys	10

●Jun 18 Bel tr.t 3f ft :35 h   Jun 8 Bel tr.t 4f ft :48 h   May 30 Bel tr.t 3f ft :38 b   May 25 Bel tr.t 6f ft $1:17^1$ b

We can begin with his last race, which was outstanding, and convert it as if he were running at a mile sixteenth. Our first job would be to reduce the 6½f time to 6f, where in this case, we would subtract only 6.2, because of the fast time involved. This would give us 1:09.2, and we would write 9.2 in our workbook. The time span between the second call and the finish would require us to subtract 45.3 from 1:15.4, which would be 30.1. Because of the speed involved, there would be no need for second call penalty ticks. The 9.2 + 30.1 is 39.3, to which we add 1 for variant, or an estimated ability time of 39.4, incredibly good. If this speedster, who turned in this time in a $17,000 claiming race, which is a very low price in New York, were running out at 1 1/8, we would add 6.3 to come up with 46.2, again most impressive.

Now, let's do the next race down at 7f and convert it to a 1 1/16 ability time. Working off the 7f time, using our sprint conversion table, we would subtract 13.0 from the 1:24.2 actual time, which would give us 1:11.2, where we would write down 11.2. We can go back to calculating the final portion time in the sprint race, where the lead times were 46.1 and 1:23.4, which would give us 37.3. Onnagata didn't pick up anything for gain, so we would work off the 37.3. When we check for penalty ticks, we find the second call time at 47.0, which requires us to add one for 37.4. We would subtract 6.3, giving us a 31.1 to add to the 11.2 for a 42.3. That would be it, because the variant required no change. If we were converting to a 1 1/8 race, we would add the 37.4 to the 11.2 for a 49.1, still very impressive.

While we're using this horse's past performances for practice examples, drop down to the 26Mar87 race at one mile. This one is relatively easy, also. If the next race was at one mile, the second call time of 1:11.0 or 11.0 would be recorded. The difference between the second call lead time and the mile finish was 25.2, our horse lost 2, so we would have 25.4 to add to 11.0 for 36.4. We would subtract 3 off the variant for a one-mile ability time of 36.1.

If we converted the mile race to a mile sixteenth, we would add another 6.3 and if to a mile and an eighth, we would add 13.1.

If you look further down to the 28Jan87 race at 1 3/16, you would have a different final figure for an ability time. You would record the 1:12.1 of course, and then subtract that figure from 1:58.2 to get a final portion time of 46.1. With no adjustment for variant, your ability time at 1 3/16 would be 12.1 + 46.1, or 58.2.

This horse's record gives us an opportunity to do yet another distance, that of a mile seventy from the 17Jan87 race. The same easy procedure would be followed. We would write down the second call time of 1:14.1 for our horse. We would then compute the final portion lead time by subtracting 1:13.4 from 1:43.2 to get 29.3. We would have to add 2.4 to convert it to a mile sixteenth, which would give us 32.2. We would reduce 1 for the gain to 32.1, which added to 14.1 would give us 46.2. With no adjustment for variant, that would be the final ability time.

This is primarily how we do ability times in distance races. These examples should readily provide all the skills you need. As we work in the last chapters on the cards at Aqueduct, Santa Anita, and Bay Meadows, where you will see all the past performances, you will have further opportunity to practice your computations.

12 Reading The Entire Handicapping Line In The Selection Process

NOW THAT WE have developed Performance Class Ratings and have set forth form rankings, supplemented with last race ability times, we will have a full, complete handicapping line to read from which we can make the final selection and decision on where to put our money in a race, or decline to play any horse at all.

In this entire process, however, we will sometimes come up with blanks on both sides of our two-sided handicapping equations. As to PCR ratings, they will not be available at all where horses have run fewer than three times. When a horse has run three or four times, they can only be used as advisory because of the insufficient history. As to form ratings, where the last race is the handicapping key to the entire second half of our equation, there will be some horses coming off layoffs or horses whose last races were not run under similar conditions to those in the race before you. We will therefore not have any form ratings to compare. We shall provide guidelines at a later point for dealing with these situations.

Our most frequent race, however, is the one on which our bread and butter is based: races where we can rely upon the entire handicapping equation, where sufficient PCR and form- ability time ratings are available to provide maximum useable data for a full comparative evaluation of every horse in the race, or on almost every horse in the race. This full handicapping equation is our major tool for achieving Total Victory at the Track.

When we encounter the situation, which occurs far more often than a skilled handicapper would like, where a race is filled with lightly raced horses, or even first time starters, we must turn to other handicapping tools if we are to wager at all. As long as there is some data available on which to make sound judgments, these races may be cautiously played. In some of them, you may sometimes find an outstanding play, as we will discuss at a later point. There is no reason not to take advantage of any such opportunity when it rises up out of the weeds.

The most baffling and most difficult race for me is a turf race where all, or nearly all, the entries are running on the grass for the first time. This kind of race comes up frequently with young horses that are getting their early exposures to the grass. Perhaps your best way of playing these races, if you choose to do so, is to consult the works of Dr. William Quirin, who has demonstrated that certain sires produce strong grass runners, and if you find one of these offspring in a race, you may wind up with an excellent play.

(a) *Combining PCR and Form Lines*

Before beginning the handicapping process as to any race on the card, a necessary early assignment is to rate the track surface. Previously, we have pointed out that it may require analysis and study of as many as the first three races on a given card for you to be sure how the track is running. We also said that when studying the first race of the card, you are justified in considering it from yesterday's base, with a reasonable expectation of the likelihood that the track may not have changed overnight. Even though you start with the first race under that conception, you can never be sure, and the reality is that you absolutely must rate a track every day for its surface reaction. Not only that, but you must be continuously alert throughout the day for shifts and movements from one kind of bias to another.

In our normal, stable situation, we return first to reading the PCR lines, as we have previously shown. Then, we follow that immediately with a reading of the total form lines, integrating the two into an overall composite to see if any entry in the race possesses the strong advantage over the others that we are looking for in order to make a single selection play.

Since we will be looking first at PCR ratings, and will focus our primary consideration upon the three highest rated animals in that category, what kind of separation lines do we use in choosing one over the other? Obviously, a PCR rating that is but one point higher than another, such as 123 against 122, is of very little significance, if any at all.

Accordingly, then, how large a difference are we looking for? In most cases, it is helpful to have wide disparities between numbers, such as 20, 30, 40 and upward in point totals. A general thumb rule is to look for percentages of differences which can usually be determined through glance comparison, which will eliminate the need for any calculation comparison.

After a lot of thought and experimentation, I have concluded that a 10% difference in PCR is too much to ask and a 5% difference is not quite enough. But splitting the difference, halfway in between, at about 7½% is like little Baby Bear's porridge, just right.

You can even mentally calculate this spread without too much difficulty. You start with 10%, which is the easiest number in the world to calculate, cut it in half to get 5%, and quickly pick up the number that is half way between the two. For example, if one horse has 142 and the other has 131, you could quickly take 10% of the 142 to get 14. Then reduce it in half for 5% and you have 7. The half-way point between 7 and 14 would be your 7½%, and your number could be at 10 (or more accurately 10½, but we would have to play the half-number in one direction or the other) and since 142 is 11 more than 131, you would have a significant difference between the two ratings. I have found this highly workable and very easy to handle.

Accordingly, when two horses have basic PCR ratings that are less than 7½% apart, I will call them relatively equal and consider them basically the same as I move to the form half of our handicapping equation. A good example is where one horse had 142 and the other 137, and are thus close enough together to be rated relatively equal. And, of course, if one of these two closely rated PCR horses has deficient form, he is very, very likely not to defeat the other, and can be discarded.

Sometimes, of course, a horse may have a PCR so much greater than any other horse in the race, or his class may be so dominant, that he will overcome any form defect and may be expected to win. Another kind of example is a strong early speed horse with a big advantage in PCR but with an otherwise disabling form defect that is running on a speed favoring track against a gang of slow starters. His PCR and the race matchup will mandate his selection, even with bad form.

What we are always looking for to establish our required advantage in making any selection is a horse that is high in PCR and strong in form. A prime selection is always the highest rated PCR horse that also has no form defects and possesses the best last race ability time. When you come upon such a horse, and you will find them, of course, you have a double advantage that should always be strongly and confidently played. In Investing at the Race Track, I identified a Double Advantage horse as one whose two best ability times surpassed the best ability time of any other horse in the race, and pointed out that these animals consistently turned in high profits. Since we are not using ability times here as our base rating, we can identify our Double Advantage horses as those that are both highest in PCR and highest in form. You will find that they will win consistently more than 50% of the time. They can be counted on to place around 80% of the time. Any failure is usually due to bad racing luck.

As far as last race form is concerned, we have already spoken on the higher priorities of horses with plus form factors. But what about last race ability times? How effective are they in the selection process?

At the outset in evaluating last race ability times, you must always consider that a difference of only one tick means that the two affected horses are approximately even. This is necessary because of the manifold estimations that we not only have made, but that are also contained in the Daily Racing Form numbers. In addition, a careful wariness must now be extended to a two-tick difference because we are combining three figures to make up the ability time. In *Investing at the Race Track*, we required a two-tick margin to establish a necessary advantage. But the time there was based upon a single number, not the addition of three that are involved here, which contain second call time, the last portion time, and the track variant.

Accordingly, we will consider a two-tick difference as a slight advantage but will have no hesitancy in giving the lesser numbered horse full consideration.

The real breaking point is the three-tick advantage. Even considering all the built-in estimates, when a horse in a sprint race shows a 3-tick margin over his competitor, we have the advantage that we are seeking. This kind of advantage is always a strong play, *even if his PCR is low and he carries a last race form defect in his running line or even in the stretch.* We can ordinarily play a three-tick advantaged horse as a single selection play or certainly as a part of a multiple selection in almost every race where he is found.

Before we leave last race ability times, there is one further caution in our comparisons. A horse may have had a woeful trip in his last race which may have caused his reading to be not representative at all, or he may have become bogged down in a muddy surface that he could not handle. When I have enough information to conclude that his last race ought not be held against him, I write "n/a" for non-applicable in his ability time rating. I will then look back for a more representative race and enclose its calculations within a parenthesis, just as I do when a layoff is involved. This can save us enormous grief.

Let's take sprint races first. We have done some studies that show the effectiveness in sprint races of last race ability times alone, without any other handicapping factors whatever. In an analysis of 60 races where all factors could be evaluated, horses whose ability times were among the three highest in the race won 44 times, or at a 73% rate. When you consider that some of the other 16 winning horses came from layoffs and there were other critical intervening factors, such as class drops and unexpected performances, a figure this high is truly remarkable.

In 13 of these 60 races, one horse had the desired advantage of three ticks or more over his rivals. Nine of them won. You may want to argue back that this is a sample so small that it has little significance. I will respectfully disagree, because over and over again, in many months of study and analysis, I have seen the effectiveness of these last race times, particularly in sprints.

Another area in which they are extremely effective is when we see, by reading all the handicapping numbers, that a horse possesses early speed and combines this with a sparkling ability time, regardless of his PCR rating. An outstanding example comes from the fourth race at Pimlico on April 25, 1987, which was a strong $35,000 claiming race for older horses at six furlongs, and where the track was rated neutral to perhaps a slight leaning toward early speed.

While I have already shown you how to write PCR lines, we can now fully develop the entire handicapping line. I write this out on my worksheet before I leave for the track, leaving a space to the left of the entries for writing in the final tote board odds, which I do immediately after the race is run as a measure of good record keeping. Here is what the six entries in this race revealed.

Odds	Horse	Perf. Class Rating						Form A/Time	
7-2	Trial Flight	78/	40	35	−10/	65	= 102	L	(47.2 24.2−2/ 71.2)
7	Titan Ribot	65/	32	24	+ 2/	58	= 112	NNsg	48.0 24/4−1/ 72.3
15	Lydian's Touch	88/	30	29	+11/	70	= 126	NO	47.4 25.1−4/ 72.1
9-5	Hawaiian Cop	78/	40	52	+ 1/	93	= 84	NNsg	47.3 23.4−3/ 70.4
6	Top Appeal	97/	24	32	− 6/	50	= 194	NNO	47.2 25.3−1/ 72.4
2	Drat Foot	71/	47	24	− 2/	69	= 103	NOsg	47.4 24.1−3/ 71.2

We immediately see a horse with a three-tick last race advantage, Hawaiian Cop, even though the low odds as a 9-5 favorite are not exactly inspiring. But the real question is whether he is so likely to win that even the 9-5 odds are generous, and should be happily accepted.

We can answer this question, and almost every other one by a reading of the total handicapping line. When we do this, we should be able to identify the contenders in every race. We should likewise be able to foretell with a great degree of probability how the race will unfold, who will be out early, who will be able to keep up, who will come on at the end. In short, we submit that this layout of the total handicapping equation, fortified on one end by PCR and on the other by last race ability times, comes together in the most powerful evaluative tool that you will have ever used. This is inherent in the promise in this book. You will see it over and over again in the performance.

We will make it a practice, or confirmed habit, to start our reading of the crucial numbers with a consideration of the three highest PCR horses. This will insure that you will never overlook any of the high priced bonanzas that sometimes lurk there. We have Top Appeal as the highest, with Lydian's Touch and Titan Ribot to follow.

With Top Appeal, we must, of course, read the entire line. After his strong PCR, he has a form defect of a stretch loss in his last race. Is there anything there to make up for it? We see that his ability time is 72.4, the lowest in the race. We have already determined that the track is either neutral or with a slight leaning to early speed, and Top Appeal is clearly the leading early speed horse in the race. Is this enough to save him? To help us answer this question, there is another comparison reading in the lines that we can use as a guide. We will return to it when we look at the other horses.

Lydian's Touch, with the highest odds in the race, also has a form defect, even though his ability time is decent. This one is doubtful. Titan Ribot stands a little better, with no form defect, but when you see that his ability time is the second weakest in the field and that he is not an early runner, you can now be reasonably sure he won't be there.

After we take our first preliminary reading on the three top PCR horses, it is a sound approach to next study the strong form horses, with emphasis on ability times. We are impressed with Hawaiian Cop with no form defect and that wholesome three-tick advantage over the field.

The next horse to be considered is Drat Foot, who is pressing Hawaiian Cop in the odds, and who went off as a strongly backed 2-1 second choice. His last race ability time is a good four ticks better than any of his other rated rivals. We see the last race form defect and the reality that he is indeed a closer. Even with his good last race ability time, which is still three ticks behind Hawaiian Cop, he will have a hard time winning today.

What do we do about Trial Flight? As the third choice in the betting and with the best class figure in the race, we have to evaluate him. You will notice in the ability time column that we have entered a figure for him, which is enclosed in parentheses.

We said a few pages back that we handle all horses whose last race ability times are not measurable by looking down their past performances to find a reasonably late representative race and we run an ability time on that one, to see if a horse is competitive in today's field. Often we can see that he is not, and can discard him with confidence. When a horse does show a strong ability time down in his record, we have to keep him under our watchful eye, using the time as advisory. We see that Trial Flight does have an impressive ability time. But, as we have tried to indicate, horses coming back off layoffs must have a very strong workout for us to factor them in, unless their ability times are so outstanding that they cannot be disregarded.

Having taken our first run through the field, we can look again at the internal numbers. In addition to Top Appeal, our power horse, Hawaiian Cop, despite his low PCR, has a smaller second call number than his finish number, indicating that he can run forwardly.

Now, we go to the next critical reading that is so helpful, the first number in the ability time line, representing the actual running time (with all its unreliabilities) in the last race. None of the horses is outstanding. Top Appeal with 47.2 is one over Hawaiian Cop. But one tick, as we have said, in any situation is not enough to sway us. We see second call times reasonably bunched, but note that Titan Ribot looks out of it.

With all these readings, we can summarize and readily reach a decision. Hawaiian Cop, with the three-tick advantage, can run forwardly, will not be disadvantaged by the track flow or bias, if any, is in good form, and has a competitive first figure in his ability time numbers. He is truly a powerful single play selection under these circumstances, as nearly everything comes together for him. He has the big advantage that we seek.

Hawaiian Cop's low PCR, his only disadvantage, is no longer so troubling because we have now shown that reading the entire handicapping line reveals enough to overcome this one single blot. And the other horses, of course, reveal their deficiencies as well. Drat Foot, heavily played, was far too much of a closer to have much of a chance. Top Appeal, despite his attractiveness otherwise, is held back by a bad ability time. Trial Flight, off a layoff, is still a question-mark. A questionable horse against a known quantity like Hawaiian Cop is never a sound play. We are fortified in our decision. At the track that day, I bet Hawaiian Cop with great confidence.

The race was only slightly more difficult than I would have expected, but the outcome was never too much in doubt. Top Appeal, using his strong early speed to good advantage, held close and tough down the lanes, but Hawaiian Cop, already in front at the second call, was steady and solid down the stretch where it counted. And where that last race ability time said he would be performing. The $5.60 winning ticket, considering its safety, was hardly a weak investment. Top Appeal held on for second and late closing Drat Foot, running just the way his internal numbers said he would run, rallied to finish third.

This race was run almost as a reading of the lines indicated. This happens time after time. It is the great strength of this new total method of analyzing a race and selecting the probable winning horse or horses.

This race was a sprint. How about the effectiveness of last race ability times in distance races? My studies have shown that they are both sound and reliable, but are not quite as potent as they are in sprint races. I have found, first of all, that there is often not such a disparity between these last race times in routes as there is in sprints. In other words, they are usually far more closely bunched after all adjustments are made, and perhaps that is a correct reflection of reality. However, when one horse stands out with a considerable advantage, such as three ticks or more, treat him with the same respect that you treat his dangerous cousin in a sprint race.

In looking for horses with a sufficient advantage to warrant being backed at the window in both sprints and routes, I undertook to integrate the handicapping factors of PCR, class, and last race ability times, singly and collectively, to try to find out where the strength was based. To isolate class, I selected horses with the three best low class numbers in my PCR lines. In each category thereafter, I evaluted the top three in each of these categories: PCR, class, and last race ability times.

I had full details on 119 races where all these factors could be evaluated. The prime choice was the horse that stood among the first three in all three categories, as you might expect. Then I undertook to try to find out how important it was whether a winning horse was rated among the top three in two or more of these categories. He could either be among the three highest in PCR and class, or PCR and ability times, or class and ability times.

Of the 119 winners, 80 of them were in the top three of two or more categories, which amounts to 67% of these winners. In the total of 119 winners, only 11 horses managed to win who were not in one of the top three in at least one of the categories, which is only 9% of the time.

While I have previously given you some rough figures on the effectiveness of last race ability times in sprint races only, these 119 races combined both sprints and route races. In this particular collection, 79 of the 119 horses, or 67%, were among the three highest rated in last race ability times. This was the most effective factor of all. The most effective double factor was a combination of last race ability times and PCR, with class only slightly behind.

This brings us back again to what is most effective when we are dealing with horses with an L for layoff and lightly raced horses with no PCR rating. In the race we have just discussed, we showed how we dealt with the layoff situation as to Trial Flight. We uncovered a recent running line to get an ability time to see if it were competitive with the field in the race. That will be one of our first principles, which we will use regularly.

Of course, when you have a horse in a race off a layoff, you will obviously pay close attention to his PCR line. You will want to classify him for early speed or late speed and see how this fits with how the track is running today.

But the key ingredient is the workout. Unless a layoff horse has an outstanding PCR, I am hesitant to play him unless he shows an exceptional workout. The five furlong bullet is what I am looking for, or a five furlong work in less than one minute. An exceptional four furlong work of less than :48.0 will also get my attention.

But again, you cannot always isolate a layoff horse as to what he does show. He must be compared with the other horses in the race. If all of them show form defects, for example, the layoff horse has a good chance, but I would not be playing any of them. Even when a layoff horse shows good possibilities, he is a doubtful play if you find a horse rated high within at least two of the three strong categories that we mentioned earlier.

At this point, we may look at another example, which shows how we can utilize these factors to look for potential winners as we once more read the entire handicapping line for all the horses in the race. On Derby Day, May 2, 1987, I was at Pimlico where I found a splendid opportunity in the fourth race at six furlongs, where three-year-old allowance horses, non-winners of two other than maiden or claiming, went to the post. I will show my usual worksheet lines.

Odds	Horse	Perf. Class Rating					Form A/Time	
3	Darknesian	51/ 21 19	+5/	45	=	113	N+w	46.3 25.2−1/ 71.4
3	Ringing	25/ 7 7	−/	14	=	(179)	N+w	47.3 25.2−1/ 72.4
6	Smart Mover	34/ 7 16	−3/	20	=	(179)	L	(46.2 26.2−3/ 72.1)
9-5	Judge's Dream	76/ 38 39	−7/	70	=	109	NNN	47.0 25.0+1/ 72.1
12	Negative Cap/	53/ 16 31	−/	46	=	115	NNO	46.1 26.2+1/ 72.4
10	Gala Gold Dust	78/ 17 45	−3/	59	=	132	NNN	46.3 25.4−1/ 72.1
9	Roman Mist	35/ 12 16	+1/	29	=	(121)	N0N	48.2 25.4−3/ 73.3

Properly evaluating our PCR ratings is somewhat hobbled by the fact that three of our seven entries are lightly raced horses. We have shown PCRs for Ringing with three races and Smart Mover and Roman Mist, who had run four times, as advisory guides. But we are able to read and use their internal numbers.

Consequently, in looking at the PCRs, we have to put those of the three lightly raced horses on a temporary shelf. Gala Gold Dust commands the highest acceptable figure at 132, but with only four fully rated horses, who is in the first three doesn't mean very much. We wanted to show you this race for this reason, where obviously, other form factors will have to be carefully integrated along with the PCRs, which will still be of some use, especially where the internal numbers are concerned.

We have evaluated the track as hospitable to early speed, in great contrast to what it was two weeks later on Preakness Day when all early speed horses died. With that in mind, we can look at the PCR numbers to see how the horses look in early running style. We are immediately struck by the low second call numbers which tell us that there is a lot of forward speed in the race. There is not a confirmed closer in the field. Gala Gold Dust has the strongest comparative number, which accounts for his high PCR, although we can see that Smart Mover in his few races is a tiger in the early part of any field.

How do we make eliminations from this field? We can quickly see that Judge's Dream, the strong 9-5 favorite, and Gala Gold Dust have no form defects, and cannot be eliminated. But there are three that can go quickly, off the total lines. Roman Mist has both a form defect and the weakest ability time in the race. That is an automatic elimination. Negative Capital has a form defect and an ability time that sags badly against the others. Out. And then Ringing, well played at 3-1, comes off two successive last race victories, which is a handicap in itself. But the major factor that eliminates him is his last race ability time, which is too far back from the others to give him much of a shot. We also note that his internal PCR numbers show that he has run evenly in his few races, and with strong early speed and a track that is hospitable to front runners, his task would be difficult indeed.

This is how we go about it when there is no marked PCR advantage and no horse with a three-tick ability time advantage. We therefore make those clearly defined eliminations at the outset based upon the total handicapping lines. We have four horses remaining in the seven horse field, and from among them we must find the winner. Does our total handicapping line lead us to enough of an advantage that we can find some kind of play?

While there is no three tick ability time advantage, we see Darknesian off a last race win with a strong 71.4. Judge's Dream and Gala Gold Dust both have 72.1, and Smart Mover likewise has that figure off an advisory race, and has a series of good workouts as well.

Not one of these four is an automatic elimination. This makes it on the surface a very tough race to pick. We can see that last race ability times among these four will not give us the guidance we need.

When you see a group of horses as contenders in a race that all have a sound chance to win, by far and away your soundest approach is multiple selection play, as we will discuss in a later chapter. And when you are engaged in multiple selection play, you should look for healthy odds to compensate for the losing part of the proposition. But first you have to make a decision.

How do we make that decision in circumstances like this? We have to look for areas inside the handicapping lines that do provide an advantage to one horse or another. And we are able to find precisely that advantage. It comes from the track's receptivity to early speed. Gala Gold Dust and Smart Mover are the two strongest early speed runners. We conclude that one of them is the most likely winner. When we compare Smart Mover with a layoff to the known quantity of Gala Gold Dust's last race, we have our decision. Gala Gold Dust turned in a 46.3 second call time, both competitive and strong, and when we integrate that with the early speed habit, we will then choose Gala Gold Dust off Smart Mover as a primary win prospect.

Darknesian troubles us very much. He, too, had a 46.3 second call last time out, with a strong finish to turn in a 71.4 figure. Only his last race win is a blemish. And what do you do about the strong favorite, Judge's Dream, who has no form defect? Again, the internal numbers tell us that both Judge's Dream and Darknesian are even runners and where a track is strongly leaning toward early speed, the horse with the front running habit, as long as his ability time does not fall away, is a powerful play.

Therefore, the advantage in this race is the forward running habit on a track conducive to that style, as long as ability times are within the relatively equal range. We have already selected Gala Gold Dust as a play for this reason. Because we are so certain that one of the other three remaining contenders will run one-two, because they stand out over the others, exacta play looks like our best multiple selection opportunity. We will then use our most preferred exacta play, two on top to win and three to run second, which will cost $12 at the $2 price in this combination.

To go with Gala Gold Dust on top, we choose Smart Mover because of his early speed habit, his workouts, and his ability time showing. We cross each horse for second, and add both Darknesian and Judge's Dream as the second horses in our $12 spread. We are confident that we will have an excellent exacta payoff, because both our top horses have healthy odds. An exacta box would have been wasteful because it would have required the elimination of one of these horses unless we wanted to put three on top and four on the bottom—too much money.

Again, our numbers led the way to the promised land. Gala Gold Dust, with that good front speed, moved out quickly and not only won wire to wire, but romped to a Big Win! And who came in second? Smart Mover, at 6-1, with all the potential that our numbers revealed, was home second.

The exacta paid $200.80 for a $2 ticket!

This was the kind of result that makes all the work and analysis so worthwhile—adding the numbers, as laborious as it may appear, going through the adjustments to make the ability times, and studying them all, line by line. As I happily cashed my ticket, I not only reveled in the result, but took considerable satisfaction in being able to compile data that led to a reasoned outcome.

Oh, but were it that all races would be run so beautifully. Actually, you will find that more of them are than you might otherwise imagine. Those that are not are usually loaded with varieties of conflicting factors, all of which give us the message to be very careful and most likely stay away. But in this process of recognizing these races, it is the reading of the internal numbers that give us the warning signals.

There are a vast number of other important situations that we will encounter when we read the entire handicapping line, some of which we have mentioned earlier. A second look at some of these and an analysis of some of others is warranted to try to frame appropriate responses to problems that we will frequently encounter in reading the lines.

(b) *The Lightly Raced Horse and First Time Starter*

When we are dealing with lightly raced horses, last race form is all-important since we have no PCR upon which we can rely. If a lightly raced horse shows a last race ability time that stands out over his rivals, he can be played with reasonable confidence, because young horses lightly raced who bring good form into a race are more likely to improve than decline. If a last race ability time is in the middle of the pack, a horse's rating on form factors will provide some guidance. A form defect that also brings with it a so-so ability time makes the lightly raced horse a dubious play indeed.

In addition, when a lightly raced horse is climbing the class ladder after winning his last race, you must be very watchful. In the previous race that we have analyzed, this was the situation with both Ringing and Darknesian.

On the other hand, you must always compare the entire line of the lightly raced horse with the entire lines of the other horses in the race. If all of them are uniformly lacking in some area, and a lightly raced horse shows strong credentials, you know what to do.

As to first time starters, especially two-year-olds, most of the story is in what is shown on the workout line. I have had considerable success in playing first time starters off sparkling workouts. And when you find two youngsters in a race with outstanding works, you can almost bet the family jewels that one of them will win. Where there is no horse among first time starters with a workout that is impressive, I have no hesitancy in passing the race altogether.

(c) *Reading the Lines in Turf Races.*

Where most of the horses in a turf race are experienced grass runners and show a turf race in their last effort, you can read the lines just as you would in a dirt race. Problems begin to arise when a horse that is predominantly a grass runner has turned in his last effort on the dirt within the last 28 days. In such a situation, if he has not run on the grass within 28 days of today's effort, he should be treated as if he were a layoff horse and given an L as a form factor. We would then look down to preferably his last grass race to do ability times, hampered as they will be because of the inability to apply a meaningful variant. In this situation, because the horse was not a true layoff horse, we would place greater reliance on the recorded ability time, and essentially make our final decisions accordingly.

If a horse entered in a turf race has not run on any surface in the last 28 days, he will have to be assessed as in our normal layoff situation.

(d) *Compensation for Form Defects*

In our extended studies of form defects in *How Will Your Horse Run Today?* we acknowledged the reality that some horses with form defects do win. We did not go extensively into all of the whys, resting instead on presenting the facts surrounding form defects as they affected a horse's chances of winning.

As we go into a reading and study of total handicapping lines which integrate form factors into the important second part of the across-the-line equation, we will be constantly confronted with horses that reveal form defects in either recency, last race running line, stretch loss, and in the semi-defect of having won the last race with something less than a Big Win. It is in these situations that the remaining portions of the total handicapping line will assist us enormously in dealing with form defects. This is a further advantage of having both PCR lines and last race ability times as comparative devices and accordingly becomes the very first time that we have any kind of an appropriate tool to deal with form defects.

We can generally omit those races where every horse has one kind or another of a form defect. You will find a fair number of these races, and of course, some horse with a form defect will win, which accounts for part of the numbers of winning horses with form defects. However, the discussions that follow will help you compare many of these animals so deficient in good form in case you want to play those races.

Our major concern here, however, is with how we treat a horse that has a form defect as compared to horses without form defects. Some of these defective horses sometimes defeat their apparently more formful rivals. We need to be alert to those situations, especially when it might bring us a good priced winner that we might not otherwise have.

The first defect of lack of recent action is ordinarily so serious that horses with no workouts at all or only a three furlong effort can hardly ever be played. Some of them who are bandaged and cautiously and hopefully entered without a published workout can sometimes survive to stagger past a gang of hapless foes with equally serious physical ailments, but I would never bet on it. You do have to be alert at some tracks, however, to trainers who have access to nearby farms and work their horses there. For example in Maryland, trainer Bill Boniface, who won the Preakness a few years ago, owns and maintains a farm outside the immediate Maryland track area and regularly works his horses there. These works will never show, however, in the Daily Racing Form, which does not send its clockers to outlying farms. When Boniface enters a horse that is absent more than 21 days without a published workout, I automatically assume the horse has worked on the farm and is otherwise as eligible as any other layoff horse.

When we get into form defects in the last race running line because a horse was not up close at the stretch call in his last race, we will encounter a fair number of winners who overcome this detriment. Those are the ones that we must be able to identify. These winners usually are not too far behind the cutoff measure for being up close and are worthy of being considered as serious contenders, as long as they pack some additional punch.

If such a horse has a high PCR as compared to the others in the race, I must look at him again. Then, the last race ability time becomes the most important key. If he shows both a strong PCR and a last race ability time that is one of three highest in the field, he is far from an automatic throw-out because of his form defect. This is especially so if the track surface is running favorable to his style, whether early speed or late speed. As you will find later, when we come to multiple selections, we will often be able to include a horse with this kind of defect in his last race running line (as well as explainable defects in other areas) as a playable contender in the race, because we will find other advantages that will truly compensate.

Stretch Loss. A horse with a form defect because of a stretch loss may have been the victim of a track heavily biased against his running style. Earlier, in showing you races run at Pimlico on Preakness Day, 1987, where the bias against early speed and in favor of closing speed was overwhelming, a sprinter named Roll Dem Bones faded in the stretch, as did every other speed horse that day. When he next ran two weeks later, he brought the form defect of a last race stretch loss with him. This time, however, the bias had faded and the track had returned to its more normal condition where early speed could demonstrate its ordinary effectiveness.

This time it was Roll Dem Bones all the way, wire to wire. Interestingly enough, in that same race two weeks later was Aprils Son, who had defeated him badly on Preakness Day with a closing surge. Aprils Son was back where he belonged this time, well beaten.

But you may not be able to have observed horses in their consecutive races where you could compare the surface bias of the track. You may be forced to rely entirely on the handicapping lines that you have made for today's race. Is there anything in these lines that will help you in deciding that the apparent last race form defect of stretch loss is not a disqualifying factor today?

Showing you the worksheet for that fourth at Pimlico on May 25, 1987 at six furlongs won by Roll Dem Bones may be very instructive for future use, as we focus our efforts on answering the single question of whether we should throw out Roll Dem Bones because of his last race stretch loss.

Horse	PCR							Form	A/Time		
Aprils Son	81/	52	35	+	8/	96	=	84	NNw	47.1 24.4	0/ 72.0
Little Shotgun	65/	42	47	−	10/	79	=	82	NON	47.2 25.0	0/ 72.2
Roll Dem Bones	76/	14	38	+	1/	53	=	143	N+O	46.3 25.4	0/ 72.2
Fun Bunch	x	x							x	x	x
Balloon Meet	74/	43	37	−	5/	75	=	99	NOsg	48.1 25.2	−3/ 73.0
Mortgage Man	69/	40	43	−	9/	74	=	93	NOsg	48.0 24.4	0/ 72.4

Please try to forget that I have already told you who won this race. Let's concentrate on Reading the Numbers to see if we can reach a reasoned conclusion on what to do about Roll Dem Bones, who has a stretch loss form defect in his last race. This same principle will apply to all other horses with the same baggage.

We can start with the reality that the PCR of Roll Dem Bones is far away higher than that of any of the other five. We have omitted figures across the line on Fun Bunch because they were so hopelessly bad we did not want to waste our time in putting them together. Again, we caution, don't do this too often, but where your knowledge and experience tells you a horse has absolutely no chance to have any impact on the race at all, you can omit his handicapping line.

However, in any situation where a horse shows a last race form defect of a stretch loss, you must carefully assess the track's behavior today. In this instance, the track was running normal. If it had favored closers as it did on Preakness Day, we could say goodbye to the stretch losers.

The next reading comes off last race ability times. Even with a stretch loss, Roll Dem Bones, along with Little Shotgun, had the second best figure behind the closer, Aprils Son. Therefore, when you see a stretch loss horse with a last race ability time that is truly competitive, you may have a compensating factor.

Furthermore, you see that the second call time of Roll Dem Bones is three ticks better than that of any other horse. When speed gets its recognition due to track surface tendency, the good second call number thus becomes another powerful compensating factor. Aprils Son, the previous winner, badly imperilled by his closing habits off a front speed track, was hopelessly out of it. The only other low ability time horse, Little Shotgun, had the worst PCR in the field, and was not nearly as strong an early runner as Roll Dem Bones.

Once again, reading all the numbers rather easily led to the winning horse, even with his last race form defect.

We can now summarize as to how we extract our guidelines. When a horse that has a stretch loss defect in his last race has a substantial or even a strong comparative PCR, along with internal figures that are compatible with today's surface—and this is an essential key—or a competitive ability time, he may be able to compensate for this form defect and do well today. He can be played as if he had no form defect at all. This is an important discovery gleaned from development of these new revised rating methods.

(e) *Last Race Winners*

Horses that won their last race with a Big Win receive a plus form factor. Those who win, however, in more ordinary fashion are flagged with a hindrance notation and are considered as facing a difficult task to win two in a row. Part of this comes from the sheer percentages against a horse winning any race, especially where there is a good-sized field entered. But as we all know, some horses do repeat, and our task now is to try to determine if by reading the total handicapping line we can pick up on those that are good candidates to repeat and safely eliminate those that are not.

Again, the first thing we search for is a key advantage somewhere in the total line. A Double Advantage horse sometimes emerges, and we must play him, of course. Another imposing advantage is when a horse possesses a last race ability time that is three ticks or more better than his opponents. If his PCR is substantially higher than that of his rivals, he is a strong candidate to repeat. If his form factors outstrip all the others by a defineable margin, this is another key sign.

Thus, when we are able to find a pronounced competitive advantage when we read the total handicapping line, a last race winner cannot be discarded and may be even an outstanding play. There are several races we could show to demonstrate these features, but we think by now that you can readily identify them when they occur.

With these general guidelines for the selection process now in hand, we are ready to move to the more specific area of finding our prime single selection plays for the profits we must have. Thereafter, we shall deal with the demands of all other kinds of races and betting opportunities that we will find on almost every racing card.

13 Advantages Across the Lines: Social Security

WE ARE NOW ready to set forth a method of play that will bring you Total Victory at the Track, if you exercise the discipline to follow it without deviation. It is not only the most powerful that I have been able to come up with but is so reliable that I am compelled to call it an invitation to Social Security at the race track.

It comes from all that we have set forth to this point. It isolates single selection plays that should be bet to win only. You should regularly and steadily win 50% and more of all the playable races of this kind.

There are four readily identifiable playing situations that are all prime single selection plays. Three of them are infrequent and occasional, but when they do arise, you must take full advantage of them and incorporate them readily into your profit portfolio.

The first situation is the most common, one which will arise on every racing card, and is the bulwark of our method of play. It comes in the race where you are able to find a horse that is among the three highest rated PCR horses, that does not have any form defects, and is among the three highest rated animals in last race ability times. When an entry meets each of those qualifications, he is worth a confident win bet. You will find some Double Advantage horses in this category, but as long as the animal measures up to the three standards required, he is our choice to win.

There is but one other qualification that must be applied, which is in effect throughout this chapter, applying to all our methods of play. The racing surface must not be biased against the horse's running style. If he is an early speed horse, the track must not be biased in favor of closers, and if he is a closing horse, the track must not be biased in favor of early speed. Most of the time, these excessive biases will not exist, and your horse can be played.

A second single play situation arises when there is a favorite that does not meet the test of the first three PCR horses, but has no form defects and is one of the three best in last race ability times. This would apply only when there is no preferred single selection play of first three PCR and first three ability times with no defects or some other greatly advantaged horse.

A primary one of the greatly advantaged horses, of course, is that which we have previously mentioned, which now becomes our third single play selection in sprint races only when a horse has the best last race ability time by·three ticks or more, and the track is not hostile to his running style. He may fall short on both PCR and form factors, but the last race ability time will compensate for it. Unfortunately, there are too many other variables in distance races to allow us to apply this standard when horses go long, although the three-tick advantage is substantial and may lead to a play if other elements are present.

The fourth kind of selection doesn't occur very often, as we also have mentioned before. It is the first time starter, or a very lightly raced horse off a long layoff who meets two essential demands: (1) he must be the favorite, and (2) he must have a recent five furlong workout that is substantially better than the workouts or comparable running lines of any of the others in the race. His handlers and the people who live around the race track must be sufficiently aware of his talents to put enough of their money on his nose to make him the favorite. When they go, we go. But it is the sparkling five furlong workout that is necessary to impress us enough to make the final decision. The price at the window will not be impressive, but we are writing about the essence of financial security at the race track.

An offshoot of this method of play occurs sometimes in the first half of the three-year-old season, when a horse may have run one time many months ago as a two-year-old and is making his return today. He may have run poorly in his only start a long time previously, and if that is so, he must have been either the favorite or at very low odds in the two-year-old race when he ran disappointingly. But if he is coming back today as the favorite and possesses that power workout, then you should be ready for your visit to the cashier.

Let us now concentrate on our bread and butter play: the horse with the substantial big advantage that we always seek. A good example occurred in the sixth race at Pimlico on August 1, 1987, in a mile and a sixteenth allowance race for fillies and mares. I had determined that the track was relatively neutral, with no pronounced leaning either way. There were some powerful, tough competitors entered.

Odds	Horse	PCR Line					Form	Ab/Time
6-5	Smart 'n Quick	78/ 48 32	–	1/79	=	99	N+N	12.2 31.4 0/ 44.1
7-2	Shanghai Square	75/ 31 21	–	/52	=	144	N+N	11.4 32.1 0/ 44.0
7-2	Pot of Antics	87/ 49 37	–	8/78	=	112	N0N	13.0 31.4 0/ 44.4
7	Finder's Reward	72/ 53 44	–	9/88	=	82	L	(12.4 32.0 0/ 44.1)
9-2	Masked Barb	94/ 42 32	–	9/65	=	145	N0g	(12.0 31.3 0/ 43.3)
14	Afflatus	82/ 35 29	–	3/61	=	134	+N0t	n/a

This the kind of race that will cause you some anxious moments because there is so much there. But there is but one animal that meets the required standard. Shanghai Square is one of the first three in PCR, has no form defects, and is right up there in ability times. There is a powerful 6-5 favorite that may cause you to doubt, especially since Smart 'n Quick would otherwise meet a second qualifying single selection play method, because she has no form defects and has one of the top three last race ability times.

But when we are confronted with that situation, our play is on the top PCR horse. That is one reason why we wanted to show you this conflict. Recall in the last chapter there was a race in which the favorite, Judge's Dream, also had no form defects and was within the three last race ability times. We found an outstanding play in that race otherwise. Here, we will stay with Shanghai Square.

Not only are we concerned about Smart 'n Quick, but there is Masked Barb that worries us, too. She brings with her a powerful PCR rating. Her last race was at six furlongs, where she closed with a powerful rush. Nonetheless, there was enough of a form defect to deter us from jumping on her. Her last race ability time is advisory because it is off a sprint race and was converted to a distance, as we showed you earlier in this book.

We also see that every one of these capable animals has a lower finish total than a second call total, indicating they are all slight closers in routes, which is what you might expect when you are dealing with frequent winners. There is one horse, Afflatus, that is such a confirmed grass runner that we are unable to construct any ability time for her. We can be fairly certain she is not a contender in this race.

Consequently, despite the other power in the field, we recognize that Shanghai Square meets our standards for a prime single selection play. When that occurs, we play. Shanghai Square scored an impressive victory at those wholesome 7-2 odds.

Now that the program for Total Victory of the Track has been set forth, you may ask the important question of whether this careful limitation to horses with a distinct advantage found in the total handicapping line really produces the profits and safety sufficient to proclaim a total triumph, and even call it a Social Security method.

Before showing you our own record of these kinds of selections, you may want to reflect upon some statistical realities. For example, favorites, all of them, with no handicapping whatever, normally win one race out of three for a 33% figure. Many of these betting favorites should never be played at all, filled as some of them are with gross defects of one kind or another. Thus, when you realize how many false favorites emerge and the shortcomings that so many of them have, you can appreciate that with some important applications of handicapping factors, you can improve greatly on the percentage of winning favorites if you are able to eliminate many, or most, of those who should never be favorites in the first place.

The prime single selections that we offer here are far better than favorites as a group. These horses go in without defects and must possess strong advantages in addition to merit our support. If they did not perform at the very high level we expect of them, the entire method itself could be called into question.

To evaluate these selections, I carefully studied 200 races at Laurel and Pimlico in the first half of 1987. Imposing the standards set forth above for the kinds of qualifying horses sufficient to meet our standards, but deliberately leaving out first time starters (because at the time of the study, I was analyzing the strength of PCRs), I found 106 plays in the 200 races, a little higher than I expected. At the time I did the study, however, I was not as strict as I should have been about factoring in track surface, which might have reduced the number of plays and surely would have improved the overall win percentage.

What did these 106 key plays reveal? There were 54 winning horses for a 51% winning rate! Frankly, I expected it to do even better, and in the races I have been recording since the study was completed, that is exactly what is happening. A standard $2 bet on these 106 plays would have cost $212; the total gross was $352.80, a splendid 66% return on investment.

Perhaps one of the most enlightening aspects of the study was the incredible consistency of the frequency of winning. From the very beginning, the percentage of winning horses ran at the 50% figure and hardly ever varied. There was an occasional dip below and an occasional rise above, but the end figure of 51% was very near what it was from the outset.

Day by day, the profits rolled in. These 200 races covered 20 racing days, enough to give you the message of whether you're going to win or lose. There were only two days out of the 20 where a loss was shown, thus showing winning results 9 times out of 10. We expect that to continue also. On one of those days, had I included a first time starter that met our standards, there would have been a profit then.

You may once again say this is not enough of a record—you may want to see more than 200 races in 20 trips to the track. Just as a public opinion poll relies upon a selected sampling of a small number of representative citizens, and usually comes out accurate and reliable, if you review 200 races, presenting all kinds of circumstances and situations, and consistently show a certain result, you can readily rely on what you have found.

We come again to the most basic requirement of all, if you are to make this program succeed. You must exercise the sternest self-discipline, which I recognize is difficult to do. There are so many other tempting plays out there that you can hardly resist. But when you draw the line and play only the horses that qualify in the precise situations in this chapter, I can only assure you again that you will have achieved Total Victory at the Track and will have put into play a method that truly deserves to be called Social Security.

The issue of "money management" also arises here. Other writers in the field have set forth three methods of accelerating profits: a percentage of bankroll to be wagered, which increases with profits and declines with losses; a small base bet with an additur of the square root of profits; and the so-called Kelly Criteria, which is based upon betting a percentage of bankroll based upon profit expectancy. Everyone recognizes that no enhancement program of any kind will work unless you are able to consistently show a flat bet profit on your play. The purpose here has been, of course, to demonstrate and solidify that profit. Once you are secure about that, select the money management plan that best fits your own perspectives, and go to it. For good money management, there is a recent work by the hard working racing scholar, Dick Mitchell, entitled, "Thoroughbred Handicapping as an Investment," (Cynthia Publishing Co., 1987) which provides some intelligent guidance on how to wager.

Actually, in our single selection play program, one of your major frustrations may come on days when few of these plays appear. But we look to multiple selection play to cure that drawback. It deals with the major problem area that will include so many of you: those good players who cannot resist all the other enticements found in the races where prime single selections are not to be found. You can either enter the world of risk and disappointment, or turn what we have done so far into a meaningful profit. That, too, can be done—not for social security, but as an arm of Total Victory at the Track. With careful selection, it can be accomplished. We are going to next go into these other methods of play and wagering and into the wonderful world of exactas, with all the possibilities that exist there. Other exotics will be touched upon also.

If you decide to embark upon the second more speculative venture to supplement Total Victory at the Track, you should develop two separate sets of accounts and records. The first should be for prime single selection play for Total Victory as is set forth in this chapter, in order that you may constantly know your degree of success. You may want to fund this portfolio with substantially higher wagers, because of the security involved, as soon as you have established your span of comfort.

For the second venture, likewise using all the tools that are to be found in the total handicapping lines that we have developed, separate records should be kept, again using careful money management once you are sustaining a sound profit level. This second method includes multiple selection play and exacta play as its major ingredients. We are ready to proceed.

14 Multiple Selection Play

WHEN YOU FIND a horse that has met our demanding requirements for PCR, form, last race ability times, and coordination with the track surface, you have already found the advantage we seek in our Total Victory program. Your course of action there is easy and decisive: play the race.

Where that single horse advantage does not exist, which will probably occur in more than half the races and sometimes even more, you enter the far more difficult area of fine-line decision making. The safest and most secure way to protect your Total Victory at the track is not to enter that more perilous arena. But two realities push us ahead: (1) rare is the player indeed that can resolutely hold to these limited situations, and (2) when we are able to make a profit in the second and most frequent kinds of races, and even sometimes score heavily, we should get into it.

The one absolutely vitally necessary element is knowing when to play and when to pass. You will play when you find an advantage of some measurable kind, or series of advantages, based upon the principles in this book. When there is not enough of a defined measurable advantage to override the natural risk involved, you absolutely must pass. That is a mighty key to success: letting the losers go by. When you read all the numbers across the handicapping line, as we have set forth in probably the most important chapter in this book, Chapter 12, you will see the weaknesses of horse after horse, see the relative equalities of contenders, and learn the hazards of trying to "guess" a winner in those races.

If you cannot do this, and are determined to play every race, even when you cannot identify the advantages we must have, you can fold this book now, forget this chapter, and resign yourself not to Total Victory, but to Erratic Defeat. Of course, you will still have your winning days, perhaps even some outstanding ones, but the bottom line when you take stock will be that you will be losing money at the race track.

Old hands may know by sense of "smell" when to pass a race. Their handicapping senses sound out the danger signs. Frequently, I have found that my own sense of smell led me to sensibly pass a number of races. But, upon analysis, it wasn't "smell" at all, but a recognition of the factors that we will now be talking about. The goal is to set forth those factors with sufficient specificity and recognition that you will know when to pass and when to play.

As we come into this area, we are confronted with the necessity of placing your money on more than one horse in many situations or combination of situations. We shall simply call it multiple selection play. We have already fixed the boundaries for the prime single selection play. Anything beyond that brings you to reliance on more than one horse, in one fashion or another.

For example, you may choose to back more than one horse to win in a particular race, as we will often do. You may want to link one or more horses together in a daily double combination, or in any number of kinds of exotic wagers. The most common of these, of course, is the exacta, or perfecta as it is called in some states. The exacta presents the most varied and most challenging and sometimes the most rewarding of all the multiple play opportunities. Remember the race in an earlier chapter where we showed you our powerful play on Gala Gold Dust, who led the way to an exacta that paid $200.80? The careful player today, and that means all of us, must take all these opportunities into account in any campaign to obtain the Total Victory we must have.

In this framework, no matter how you play it, you will be relying upon more than one horse to carry you to profit-land. Let us explore the areas of play, the possibilities, and when to play and when to pass.

(a) *Playing Two Horses to Win*

There has always been a cloud over the idea of playing two different horses to win in a race. The standard, and quite accurate, axiom is that you are sure to lose at least one of your bets, and that is inherently wasteful. Yet, the player who would cringe at the thought of two win bets on different horses may often put two or three and sometimes even four on top in exacta races and think little of it. Many times, that may be far more wasteful than a careful selection of two horses to win only.

In any race where you do not find the solid single selection play that is the foundation of our Total Victory program, you may sometimes find it profitable, based upon how you handle the odds, to play two horses to win. Or, sometimes, even when you have a solid single play, you may want to back a secondary selection as a form of insurance, although this is not too often to be recommended. What your possible return might be, based upon the projected payoff that the tote board indicates, ought to be the first consideration. And the second urge, of course, comes from the understandable need for security. What if Horse A can't make it? Horse B looks pretty good. One of them will surely win. Why not wrap up the "sure thing" and make a smaller, but far safer profit? Be careful, but it can be done.

In races where there are two horses that have nearly comparable PCR ratings which are among the three best, or intermingled with the three top, have no form defects or slight form defects that can be discounted, and have solid last race ability times, you may be compelled to play both of them. You would have to spread your money to make a profit, of course. You would still be looking for the requisite advantage of these two over the rest of the field, and where you would be reasonably confident that one of them would win.

For a play of this kind, as an example, if your base win bet was fixed at $20, you could put $10 to win on each horse, or divide it $12 and $8 according to the odds. You may also want to combine this with an exacta play, or even a combination of a win bet on one horse and an exacta play with the other horse on top.

Obviously, in any two-horse win bet situation, you must be controlled by the odds. Betting on a 7-5 horse and an 8-5 horse in the same race because you are certain that one of the two will win, which is very likely, seems like a foolish way to spend your money when there are so many other better ways of doing it. Another writer has said it quite well: "Bet a little to win a lot but never bet a lot to win a little."

But if there are two horses you like, one at 4-1 and the other at 5-1, with some kind of a recognized advantage over their rivals, and you are reasonably sure, based upon your careful reading of the entire handicapping equation of PCR, form, and ability times, along with track responsiveness, that one of them will win, playing them both can become an important additive to your Total Victory plan. As careful as we may be, we still know that one of these two prime contenders cannot make it because there can be but one winner. Most of you know by now how easy it is to grab the "wrong" one.

Another two-horse wagering variation that has some appeal is to divide your bet in such a way as to use a low odds horse as an insurance investment only.

Let us suppose there is a 6-1 horse that is your first choice, an animal that you really like. There is also a heavy favorite at even money that is most impressive and that might beat your strong selection. Splitting a base bet of $20 to invest $15 on the favorite would give you a $30 return if the favorite won. You would have $5 to bet on your real choice, which would would pay $14 if he won and return a gross $35. You would have a profit either way, but the maximum you would make would be $15 off the risk of the $20 involved. You would be betting a lot to win a little.

But with the confidence you have in your 6-1 horse, because the total handicapping line tells you that with his PCR rating and his form lines, he is indeed a formidable factor, why not split the $20 in half, $10 on the even money favorite and $10 on your real choice? If the favorite wins, you get back $20, with no profit at all. You would have had a free bet, however, on your 6-1 choice. If your prime power selection wins as you expect, your return would be $70, giving you a profit of $50 on the $20 invested, with half of it as insurance against losing.

If neither horse won, of course, you would be experiencing the normal loss that would occur if you placed it all on either one of them. This occurs every time your selection doesn't make it. The insurance "free bet" scenario is only an option for you to consider. I have used it occasionally to this effect.

Primarily, however, playing more than one horse to win is to try to cope with a greater degree of uncertainty than you would otherwise be comfortable about handling. One horse may impress you with his strong advantage, but he may have a slight defect somewhere across his line. Another horse may have won his last race and you are not certain he can repeat, although he does look good today. A horse coming off a layoff may impress you, may look solid as he enters the track, but yet you may have some uncertainty about the effects of his lack of recent action, even though the workouts will qualify him. Because there is another animal out there who appears ready, you may be far more secure with going with both of them, as long as you can spread your money with the odds to maximize your profit.

There may be a particular horse in a tough field that has an outstanding factor that compels you to play him. Yet he may be facing some opponents so dangerous that any one of them might readily win the race, despite the single strong point favoring your primary selection.

Such a situation confronted me at Pimlico on May 2, 1987, in the sixth race on the card at a mile and one-sixteenth for three-year-old fillies in an allowance event. A lightly raced horse named Notastar had turned in an outstanding :58.4 five furlong workout just a few days earlier after running strongly in her last race at six furlongs. Any horse with a five furlong work of that superb caliber absolutely must be played.

Yet this filly had never raced farther than six furlongs. Most of the others in the race had the same limited history. Three of them were getting a stronger play at the windows than Notastar. Projected last race ability times were largely advisory because of the last race sprint history. The advisory times, as you will see, were relatively well bunched, even if we could be sure that they were reliable. While there had to be a decision to play Notastar off that workout, this alone was hardly enough to justify a single selection play. One would have to study the entries carefully to see what else might emerge in this small field of six.

Odds	Horse	Perf. Class Rating					Form	Ab/Time
4	Notastar	26/ 7	5 –	/ 12	= (217)		N+N	(12.3 32.0 0/ 44.3)
5-2	Bal Du Bois	79/ 38	15 –	1/ 52	= 152		L	(12.3 31.4–1/ 44.1)
7-2	Arctic Cloud	77/ 17	20 –	6/ 31	= 245		n/a	(12.3 32.3–1/ 45.0)
5	Daytime Prncss	77/ 28	31 –	14/ 45	= 171		L	(13.1 32.4–1/ 45.4)
6	Release theLyd	83/ 62	44 –	13/ 93	= 89		L	(12.1 30.4–1/ 42.4)
5-2	Doon's Pleasure	38/ 15	8 –	1/ 22	= (173)		N+w	13.2 32.2–2/ 45.2

When there are only six horses running, it is often difficult to make money, and when you consider playing two horses, you have a heavy burden to carry if you are to produce. There was not much to choose among most of the others, except that Release the Lyd, with a very weak PCR and a running pattern that definitely revealed a closer, had an impressive advisory time. But I had already determined that the track was running normal or very slightly speed favoring, which made Release the Lyd's chances very unlikely indeed.

Because Notastar's odds were up to 4-1, this was enough to support a play money-wise. If we wash out Release the Lyd, we have to study the lines on four others to see where the power lies. We are still looking for eliminations, and Doon's Pleasure, with an ability time made last out in a route, becomes a likely candidate. It is a combination of her last race ability time, which is not impressive, and the fact that in her few races, she has demonstrated that she is a closer that makes us decide. Her last race win is another slight detriment.

On the positive side, we blink at the giant PCR of Arctic Cloud. She also runs forwardly, as her lower second call number in her PCR line indicates. Her last race ability time is not applicable, because we are not able to compute it because her last race was at Keeneland at seven furlongs, where no internal times are shown. A projected advisory time is fully competitive, however. Better yet, Arctic Cloud shows four evenly spaced workouts since her last race at Keeneland, two of them at six furlongs. One even reveals a bullet.

The co-favorite, Bal Du Bois, is also off a layoff and is a confirmed closer. Daytime Princess off a layoff has a projected advisory ability time that is the worst in the race. Neither of these two can measure with Arctic Cloud, which then becomes the second horse on which to rely.

Fortunately, in such a short field, there is enough money spread around on all six horses to make the odds more palatable. With Notastar at 4-1 and Arctic Cloud at 7-2, we can play both of them to win and still make a respectable profit.

Not only that, but as we analyze the lines, we can begin to expect that these two will dominate the field and turn it into a two-horse event. I divided my base bet equally between Notastar and Arctic Cloud to win, because there was little difference in the odds. For good measure now, I was confident enough to play them in a two-horse exacta, first and second, back and forth.

That's the way it looked. That's the way it turned out.

Arctic Cloud, with her good early speed, led all the way into the stretch, with Notastar right behind. Notastar then pulled alongside and with the two of them punching it out head to head toward the wire, I could watch with great pleasure, knowing that I was certain to cash both a win bet and an exacta play. Notastar won by a neck, returning $10.00 to win, and keyed a $60.20 exacta with Arctic Cloud off a $4 base investment.

This happy event was derived entirely from reading the numbers and comparing the contenders. The brilliant 5f workout of Notastar was what began the projection. With Arctic Cloud, who almost won the race, and with both of them at good odds, it was an outstanding multiple selection play.

A more common two-horse play would arise when there are two horses with outstanding comparative last race ability times so much better than those of any of the others. Both of them may have a three-tick edge over the nearest next rival. Even if they are low in PCR or have some kind of form blemish, with such a powerful last race, especially in a sprint, you have a play if the odds are right. Neither would be "clean" enough for a single selection play, but where they stand out as a pair to give you an advantage over the rest of the field, you must manage your money properly to do what is necessary.

These are the primary two-horse win bet situations. There are others, of course. But always, as we must stress over and over again, you must ask yourself the critical question: do these horses have a sufficient advantage to warrant making a play? That is the same key inquiry that will concern us also as we enter the enticing field of exacta play, along with continuing to look for the necessary odds opportunity.

(b) *Creative Exacta Play*

One of the great assets flowing from the growth of exacta play in recent years is that it provides so many creative opportunities to increase profits. We have already shown you two such happy bonanzas in the races won by Gala Gold Dust and Notastar, where there were excellent paydays for small risk involved.

And, of course, there is always the other side of the coin: losses can mount up rapidly if mistakes or bad choices or poor racing luck intervenes. One of the perils of exacta play is that it is usually more difficult to pick the second place finisher than it is the winning horse. Many an intrepid exacta player has suffered through the agony of seeing all his bets go down the drain when a rank outsider, with "no chance," winds up in second place.

You will have to learn to stay away, therefore, from those races where it becomes exceedingly difficult to decide who may come in second. In the two events we have previously discussed, where there were short fields, we were able to determine, from reading our handicapping lines, that there were sufficient advantages among the top horses so that we could be reasonably certain that none of the others would surprise us with a second place finish. But in far too many races, that is nearly impossible to do. Sure, you could wheel the field for second, but your investment might then become too costly in relation to what the same amount of money on a win ticket would produce.

The real key to successful exacta play, and the only profitable foundation for it, is to find at least one or more horses with high odds that will run preferably first but no worse than second. You have seen that already in the race examples which we have given, but we will return to it and re-emphasize it shortly.

But before we come to that important point, we would like to detour and bring in' an area of exacta play that, while it will never return nearly as much as our high-profit exacta play, brings with it a measure of security and often a return that may surprise you with its beneficence. It occurs in some races where there is an odds-on favorite that is almost certain to win.

Odds-on horses are normally a poor investment for any player. The major reason is that too many of them lose. And when they do win, the $3.60 or $3.00 ticket hardly seems worth the effort and the risk, which it usually isn't. Even if you won 50% of all your bets on odds-on horses, you would still lose money. A surprising number of them go to the post with form defects; they are the kind that are almost sure to lose.

But out of this ordinarily thin brew, as I have indicated, it is possible to find some plays that are worthwhile. A horse may be so dominant in class and speed and form that the 4-5 you see on the board is almost a fair price, fully justified. Betting against him because of the odds would be a foolish waste of your money when he shows all the victory signs that we recognize so well.

Therefore, when your ratings of PCR, form, last race ability times, class and favorable track surface all come together, as they will from time to time, and 4-5 or 3-5 is what the board tells you will be the return, your best opportunity for profit, if you want to play at all, will come in playing an odds-on horse only in exacta wagering.

Here is where the two critical elements of selecting the second place finisher and managing your money become so important. With an odds-on horse on top in an exacta, you can expect a very low payoff, as all the other people out there can see both the board and what the Racing Form reveals. The goal is to safely get a substantially better payoff than the 4-5 win bet will return, and if you cannot get this in an almost safeproof situation, then you should pass the race.

You can hardly make money unless your "handicapping for second" as you read the lines tells you that no more than two other horses have any realistic chance to finish second. In other words, they must have the same advantage over the remainder of the field that the power horse has over them.

But to play two horses for second in an exacta, you still need a price. Unless the exacta board shows that the lowest return of the two will amount to at least $12 off a $2 ticket, there may not be enough there to warrant a wager. But if one of the two will ring up a good number, you may be back to the "free bet" situation with the other horse. Look for these opportunities.

In 1986, at the first running of the Maryland Million at Laurel, the program was loaded with powerful odds-on horses that stood out above the rest of their rivals. They met the conditions of the races and were shipped in to ring up the good money. In each case, they were positive plays. Many of these races were quite unbalanced, and there was usually no more than two horses that could be counted on to finish second. I had a very profitable day playing these kinds of odds-on exactas, which provided about the only real opportunities of the day. Usually, however, these kinds of races do not occur too often and almost never more than once on a racing card.

But now to return to the more meaningful exacta plays that can build up your profit portfolio. You can stay away from the low payors that carry substantial risks and wait for the paydays that count. For example, every race track crowd is filled with players who box the first three favorites and even if they win, they wind up with a low-paying return that will lead to nowhere. Because so many of these plays are lost, there is no profit at all in playing exactas in this fashion.

Almost as fruitless is the rush by so many players to always include the favorite on top that when the favorite does win, the exacta return is once more too feeble to overcome the pile of losing tickets that such bettors will inevitably have.

There is but one really profitable way to play exactas: concentrate on those races where you have at least one highly advantaged horse that is not one of the three favorites and has reasonably high odds. The Notastar and Arctic Cloud duo at 4-1 and 7-2 is about as low as you should go in odds, and then only where there is a strong possibility of a good payoff. Your key selection must be high in PCR or have an impressive last race ability time or have a powerful workout off a layoff. Your exacta betting should be built around this key horse. He must run first or second for you to make the kind of profits needed to overcome the risk involved.

To look at the realities involved, I recorded the results and payoffs of 1000 exacta races. In that healthy sampling, I found that 652 of the actual winners came from one of the first three favorites, for a 65.2% winning record, reasonably close to the normal result that you would expect.

But in these 652 races won by one of the first three betting choices, the horse that finished second was among those three favored animals only 344 times. If you boxed the first three betting choices in all these 1000 races at $12 a throw, you would have obviously spent $12,000. To break even with your 344 winning tickets, you would have needed an average return of $34.88 per race. This figure is not even close to being attainable when you are boxing the first three favorites. You would lose and lose and lose.

When you subtract the 344 second place winners that were among the first three in the odds from the 652 low priced winners, you can see that there were 318 longer priced horses, which we now identify as any horse not among the first three favorites, that came in second. Your exacta returns will begin to rise, but because low priced horses finished first, they will still be substantially below what you will need.

But when you turn to the other winners in the 1000-race sample, where there were 348 first place finishers that were not among the three lowest priced horses, the picture begins to brighten. In those 348 races where longer priced horses won, the short prices came in second on 299 occasions, or 66% of the time when longer priced horses were winners. Here is where your real exacta profits can be found.

This is what I call the "up and down" effect in exacta play. When a favored horse finishes first, you have almost an even possibility (as the 48% figure demonstrates) of having a longer priced (and thus unexpected) horse finishing second, making it all the more difficult to select the winning exacta. On the other side of the up and down effect, when a longer priced horse wins, you are very likely, two-thirds of the time, to have one of the more favored horses running second. You should handicap accordingly to take advantage of this up and down reality.

We can illustrate how these prices vary, and the effect they have, by looking at what many experienced players already know. Here is the chart from the second race at Churchill Downs on May 1, 1987, the day prior to the Derby.

SECOND RACE Churchill MAY 1, 1987

1⅛ MILES. (1.48⅗) STARTER ALLOWANCE. Purse $8,450. 4-year-olds and upward which have started for a claiming price of $5,000 or less in 1987. Weight, 121 lbs. Non-winners of three races at one mile or over since January 2 allowed 3 lbs.; two such races since February 20, 6 lbs.; one such race since March 27, 9 lbs.

Value of race $8,450; value to winner $5,493; second $1,690; third $845; fourth $422. Mutuel pool $290,826. Exacta pool, $149,895.

Last Raced	Horse	Eqt	A	Wt	PP	St	¼	½	¾	Str	Fin	Jockey	Odds $1
15Apr87 ^{8}Kee^{2}	Grand Illusion II		5	121	1	2	6^{5}	$5^{\frac{1}{2}}$	$3^{1\frac{1}{2}}$	1^{hd}	1^{2}	Montoya D	1.80
10Apr87 ^{10}OP^{5}	Dedicated To Peace	b	5	114	2	1	3^{3}	3^{2}	2^{2}	$2^{\frac{1}{2}}$	2^{4}	Brumfield D	3.60
15Apr87 ^{8}Kee^{6}	Tiger Man		4	118	10	9	$7^{\frac{1}{2}}$	$7^{1\frac{1}{2}}$	6^{1}	5^{4}	3^{hd}	Garcia J J	30.50
4Apr87 ^{8}JnD^{4}	Dese Days	b	4	115	11	4	$1^{\frac{1}{2}}$	1^{hd}	1^{2}	3^{3}	4^{5}	Stevens G L	5.40
19Mar87 ^{2}OP^{1}	Princetonark		5	112	5	5	4^{1}	4^{1}	4^{2}	$4^{\frac{1}{2}}$	$5^{3\frac{1}{2}}$	Day P	4.20
27Apr87 ^{9}CD^{3}	Bold Provocation		5	112	12	12	$11^{2\frac{1}{2}}$	$10^{\frac{1}{2}}$	9^{hd}	$7^{1\frac{1}{2}}$	$6^{\frac{1}{2}}$	McDowell M	91.60
4Apr87 ^{8}Kee^{8}	Seminole Lad	b	4	121	6	10	9^{hd}	8^{3}	8^{4}	$6^{\frac{1}{2}}$	7^{nk}	McKnight J	15.80
29Mar87 ^{12}TP^{3}	Sorocco		4	112	4	6	8^{1}	$9^{1\frac{1}{2}}$	10^{6}	8^{7}	8^{11}	Navedo E	95.40
20Apr87 ^{9}Beu^{4}	Absentee Vote		4	108	7	11	$10^{\frac{1}{2}}$	12	12	$10^{\frac{1}{2}}$	$9^{\frac{1}{2}}$	Miranda L	a-45.20
3Apr87 ^{1}Kee^{3}	Found Pearl Harbor	b	7	114	8	7	5^{1}	6^{3}	7^{1}	$9^{\frac{1}{2}}$	10no	Vasquez J	6.10
9Apr87 ^{8}Beu^{9}	Decoration Day	b	5	115	3	8	12	11^{1}	$11^{1\frac{1}{2}}$	$11^{1\frac{1}{2}}$	11^{2}	Kaenel J L†	a-45.20
15Apr87 ^{1}Kee^{9}	Cruising		5	114	9	3	2^{2}	$2^{3\frac{1}{2}}$	5^{3}	12	12	Bruin J E	103.40

a-Coupled: Absentee Vote and Decoration Day.

OFF AT 1:31. Start good. Won driving. Time, :23⅗, :47⅘, 1:12⅘, 1:38⅘, 1:51⅕ Track fast.

$2 Mutuel Prices:

2-GRAND ILLUSION II	5.60	3.40	2.60
3-DEDICATED TO PEACE		4.20	3.40
9-TIGER MAN			6.40

$2 EXACTA (2–3) PAID $18.60.

The winner paid $5.60 to win, the second choice came in second, and the exacta returned the puny sum of $18.60. This was more than you might expect because of the full 12-horse field and a festival crowd that spread money around more readily than in ordinary times. But look at the very next race, where the winner for the second time in a row paid $5.60 up front.

THIRD RACE Churchill MAY 1, 1987

6½ FURLONGS. (1.16) CLAIMING. Purse $10,450. 4-year-olds and upward. Weight, 122 lbs. Non-winners of two races since February 20 allowed 2 lbs.; a race since April 3, 4 lbs.; two races since Janaury 16, 6 lbs. Claiming price $16,000; for each $500 to $14,000 allowed 1 lb. (Races where entered for $12,000 or less not considered.)

Value of race $10,450; value to winner $6,793; second $2,090; third $1,045; fourth $522. Mutuel pool $380,928. Exacta pool $174,781.

Last Raced	Horse	Eqt	A	Wt	PP	St	¼	½	Str	Fin	Jockey	Cl'g Pr	Odds $1
22Apr87 ^{1}Kee^{2}	So Cavalier		5	114	4	2	3^{2}	3^{2}	$2^{\frac{1}{2}}$	1^{hd}	Day P	15000	1.80
6Mar87 ^{10}OP^{7}	Dusty's Darby		5	116	2	4	4^{5}	4^{6}	4^{7}	$2^{\frac{1}{2}}$	McDowell M	16000	10.20
10Apr87 ^{1}Kee^{1}	Lord Balcony		6	122	1	3	2^{1}	2^{1}	1^{hd}	$3^{1\frac{1}{2}}$	Melancon L	16000	2.70
23Apr87 ^{4}Kee^{6}	For The Gipper	b	4	114	6	1	1^{1}	$1^{2\frac{1}{2}}$	3^{hd}	4^{8}	Allen K K	15000	3.50
11Apr87 ^{7}OP^{3}	Pocket of Miracles		5	116	3	5	6	6	5^{hd}	5^{2}	Shoemaker W	16000	3.20
30Jan87 ^{9}TP^{4}	Satyrically		5	114	5	6	5^{hd}	$5^{\frac{1}{2}}$	6	6	Solomone M	15000	29.30

OFF AT 2:05. Start good. Won driving. Time, :23⅘, :47, 1:11⅘, 1:17⅘ Track fast.

$2 Mutuel Prices:

4-SO CAVALIER	5.60	3.40	2.60
2-DUSTY'S DARBY		7.20	4.00
1-LORD BALCONY			2.80

$2 EXACTA (4–2) PAID $54.40.

This time the exacta returned $54.40 because one of the outsiders came in second. The price was that low because of the short six horse field.

But put that low paying favorite in second place with a longer priced horse on top and see what you get. Here is the chart from the second race at Aqueduct on May 2, 1987.

SECOND RACE **7 FURLONGS. (1.20⅕) MAIDEN CLAIMING. Purse $12,000. 3-year-olds and up. Weights, 3-year-olds, 113 lbs. Older 124 lbs. Claiming Price $35,000.**

Aqueduct

MAY 2, 1987

Value of race $12,000; value to winner $7,200; second $2,640; third $1,440; fourth $720. Mutuel pool $109,986, OTB pool $133,442. ExPl$151,012.OTBExPl$166,433.QuinPl$100,424.OTBQuiPl$137,971

Last Raced	Horse	Eqt.	A.	Wt	PP	St	¼	½	Str	Fin	Jockey	Cl'g Pr	Odds $1
21Apr87 ^{9}Aqu^{3}	Please Pleasure	b	3	109	5	8	2^{hd}	2^{1}	2^{2}	1^{hd}	Graell A	30000	13.50
20Apr87 ^{6}Aqu^{5}	Casual Physician	b	3	114	10	1	1^{1}	1^{2}	1^{1}	2^{3}	Ward W A	35000	1.30
22Apr87 ^{3}Aqu^{8}	Cool It Now		3	113	7	7	$10^{\frac{1}{2}}$	$10^{1\frac{1}{2}}$	9^{1}	3no	Garcia J A	35000	9.40
22Apr87 ^{3}Aqu^{5}	I'm In View	b	5	113	8	4	$3^{\frac{1}{2}}$	4^{3}	3^{hd}	4^{nk}	Heath M J^{7}	30000	17.30
24Apr87 ^{4}Aqu^{4}	Soleri	b	3	113	4	11	6^{1}	$5^{\frac{1}{2}}$	$5^{\frac{1}{2}}$	$5^{\frac{1}{2}}$	Lovato F Jr	35000	7.20
17Apr87 ^{9}Aqu^{6}	Fred the Welder		3	109	11	5	9^{1}	$9^{1\frac{1}{2}}$	$7^{\frac{1}{2}}$	6^{2}	Brown T L	30000	69.50
13Apr87 ^{5}Aqu^{9}	Classwork	b	3	112	9	3	4^{2}	3^{2}	4^{1}	7no	Estrada J C	30000	48.10
17Apr87 ^{9}Aqu^{3}	Celluloid Hero		5	120	2	10	5^{hd}	$6^{\frac{1}{2}}$	10^{5}	$8^{\frac{1}{2}}$	Vasquez M M	30000	6.70
	Proud Dom		3	113	1	13	13	$11^{\frac{1}{2}}$	$8^{\frac{1}{2}}$	9^{nk}	Romero R P	35000	14.30
24Apr87 ^{4}Aqu^{2}	La Sauce		3	113	12	6	$11^{1\frac{1}{2}}$	$8^{1\frac{1}{2}}$	$6^{\frac{1}{2}}$	10^{7}	Samyn J L	35000	a-5.60
16Mar87 ^{1}Aqu^{5}	Ruston		4	120	3	12	$8^{1\frac{1}{2}}$	7^{1}	11^{12}	11^{12}	Messina R	30000	37.40
21Apr87 ^{9}Aqu^{10}	Danielito	b	3	111	13	2	$7^{1\frac{1}{2}}$	$12^{\frac{1}{2}}$	13	12^{4}	DeCarlo C P	32500	a-5.60
10Apr87 ^{2}Aqu^{9}	Mystical Empire		3	109	6	9	$12^{2\frac{1}{2}}$	13	$12^{\frac{1}{2}}$	13	Badamo J J	30000	28.40

a-Coupled: La Sauce and Danielito.

OFF AT 1:31. Start good, Won driving. Time, :22⅘, :45⅘, 1:12, 1:26⅕ Track fast.

$2 Mutuel Prices:				
6-(F)-PLEASE PLEASURE	29.00	8.60	6.20
11-(L)-CASUAL PHYSICIAN		3.40	3.00
8-(H)-COOL IT NOW			5.60

$2 EXACTA 6-11 PAID $117.80. $2 QUINELLA 6-11 PAID $37.20.

The favorite went off at 6-5 on the board. The winner paid $29 up front and brought in an exacta ticket worth $117.80. That is what we are talking about. This is where you must be looking for sound exacta play.

However, you don't need boxcar figures to make good money in exactas, as long as your winning horse leads to a respectable return. Bargains like the Gala Gold Dust payoff at $200 don't lounge around every day, even though they are there to be found. Even the $60 payoff in the race where we had Notastar and Arctic Cloud will help you on your way. Returns in the $50 and $60 range are quite adequate enough, thank you, as long as you are confining your plays to races where you have a realistic chance of winning in that kind of style.

In playing these profit-possible exactas, you will usually find, of course, that you may be compelled to play for protective purposes one of the more heavily backed horses on the board. Your good priced play may not make it for any number of reasons. The two lower priced horses you were compelled to include in your spread may have run first and second, giving you one of those $18 returns that inevitably arise. When this happens, you can again class this as another form of exacta insurance. You accept the reality as a support for the "free bet" that would have brought the payoff that we were really shooting for, and didn't get. When we look at it that way, the $18 ticket isn't all that bad, as long as we know that the returns when our key horse wins will make it all worthwhile.

The road to success is still to always have that longer priced horse that can readily win as an integral part of every serious exacta. And when you can't find such a horse, such as where the low priced animals are so strong that the big prices have little chance at all, that is the time to save your money and leave the exacta alone.

And, of course, there are even those infrequent occasions when you find two powerful horses at long odds that measure up across our handicapping lines and when you can include them both in your exacta play. When they run first and second, as they sometimes do, Santa Claus will be coming early to your house. One of my pleasurable experiences came at Laurel several months back when my two top choices ran first and second to ring up an exacta that paid $447 for a $2 ticket. These needles in haystacks are ordinarily only for "talking" fun; you cannot expect them to occur very often for profit making.

Returning to the difficult assignment of looking for a second place finisher, you are entitled to a little more speculation in this area. You may have two horses with the kind of advantage over the field that you are seeking. Your confidence quotient that one of them will win at good odds may be very high. But the other one of the two may run into trouble, or not just be up to it today, and may finish far back in the pack. If you are going to bring home the big exacta payoff, you must have some other horses to include for second. Again, look hard for some particular advantage or indication that the animal you add in for second money is capable of being there.

The usual standardized play of this kind is to bet two horses to win and three for second, an investment of $12 where exactas cost only $2. Both your selections to win should ordinarily be criss-crossed for second, and then you can add two more to make up your spread.

Here is where we can take a slight chance on the layoff horse, who may show good workouts and have a high PCR. He may not be quite ready to win today, even though he is clearly capable of it. He may be more of a threat to finish second. I have also found that high PCR horses with sufficient defects that we cannot play them to win often begin their return to good form by finishing second. Often their odds are good enough to make playing them in the second hole very worthwhile.

As you study this demanding field of exacta play, the same allowances for risk that you cannot ignore in any exacta race must be factored in. We have spoken of investing $12 in the usual base line form of exacta play. You should always calculate what that $12 invested to win on one of the horses would pay, and compare the risks. The strong possibility that none of your selections for second will make it requires that the exacta return be substantially above what a win ticket would pay. Otherwise, you would be better off going for win only and not worrying about who might come in second.

The greatest hazards of exacta play in this area are the same dangers that occur in any race where there is no single outstanding selection, or where there are not two outstanding plays that are apparent. All of you have seen fields where a majority of the horses have a chance to come in either first or second. Stay away from those situations. And sometimes in short fields, you may properly conclude that every entry is not to be disregarded.

The same kinds of races that are so difficult in straight play present the same perils when you try them in exactas. Stakes races where there are several keen competitors, horses with genuine capabilities of surprise, are usually the kind of poison in exacta races that we want to avoid. Likewise, on the down side, where the entire group of runners is so woeful that anyone can win (only because someone must win) and anyone can run second, the best word is to stay away. These races are as unplayable in exactas as they are in straight play.

In summary then, our first requirement for profitable exacta play is to wager only in those races where two or more horses possess some kind of a distinct advantage across our handicapping lines. You must be able to identify and define these advantages. The second and equally essential requirement is that one of our primary selections must possess odds high enough to become the key ingredient in a high return. Most of the time, this will mean a horse that is not one of the first three favorites, but not always. I have seen many 5-1 and 6-1 horses that stand as the third betting choice on the board, and these are prime candidates to lead to a good exacta payoff.

We have said little about quinella play, which may be called a baby brother to the exacta. You can buy two horses for the same $2 ticket without worrying over who finishes first and who finishes second, as long as they run one-two. The cost is much less, of course, and the payoff likewise is much less, usually in the neighborhood of half the exacta return, but sometimes much less. At many tracks, quinellas, where you choose two horses for first and second without worrying about the exact order of finish, are offered even in the same races where there are exactas, giving the player an option. The same general guidelines should be followed, with again, the key consideration being to find a long priced horse that looks strong enough to finish first or second in order to have a payoff that is commensurate with the risk.

An example of the comparative weakness of quinella play as contrasted to exactas is shown in the second race at Aqueduct on May 2, 1987, which we set forth a few pages back. The $2 exacta returned $117.80 while the $2 quinella on the same two horses brought home only $37.20. The enormous disparity was because the heavy favorite came in second. This is one of the major reasons that I will seldom play quinellas in races where there are exactas also offered.

(c) *The Daily Double*

The Daily Double is not one of my favorite plays. For one thing, at the time you have to place your bet, you can never be sure how the track is running, whether it favors early speed, late speed, or neither. You will often find that one of the first two races on the card is a raggle-taggle event that is more in need of being passed than being played. Too many times, payoffs are ridiculously low for the risk involved, and when boxcars turn up, you wonder how anyone could have been so blind lucky in stabbing a program.

Yet with all this, there are sometimes decent plays to be found. You will have to apply the same standards that are the key ingredients throughout this book. But daily double play is not a part of our regular multiple selection play as a second arm of a program for Total Victory at the Track.

(d) *The Trifecta, or Triple*

Likewise. You are now approaching a form of lottery play when you try to hit the trifecta, or triple, which requires you to select in exact order the first three finishers in the race. The exacta is difficult enough; the trifecta takes you into the arena of pure luck once again. You can buy your lottery tickets at the nearest newstand, toss the dice in a casino (where the odds are far less perilous), enter another sweepstakes, or take any kind of chance you wish. More power to you. All I am saying here is that you can play the trifecta if you wish, but it is not a part of any rational plan that I am able to devise to achieve our profit goals.

(e) *Other Exotics: Pick 'Em All*

The proliferation of exotic play in recent years has spiced the racing scene considerably. The Pick Six, where you must select the winner in six consecutive races, is not altogether impossible, and can bring incredible payoffs if you hit it. At Pimlico not long ago, playing no more than two horses in a race and only one in some, I had the winner eight times in a row. There was no Pick Six offered there, however, and even had it been, I would not likely have been involved. However, if you attend where the Pick Six is offered, and enough races turn up where advantages can be found, then the guidelines in this book should be of inestimable help.

The problem with the Pick Six is always how much you spend in fruitless efforts to strike the big score. The almosts and only ifs and woulda, coulda, shoulda routines can tear you apart. There is no point here for me to try to tell anyone how to play the Pick Six, because I simply don't know. All I am saying is that even if you think you are good at it, it does not fit in with the kind of sound profit program that is stressed in this book.

Then there is the Pick Nine, where you have to find the winner in nine races rather than six. Do we need to say more?

In this category of "crazy" play there is also the Double Triple, which is in vogue in Maryland at the time of this writing. You have to hit two trifectas, or triples, on one racing card to take the jackpot. This kind of play is not worth our serious discussion.

The one type of additional exotic that does have some splendid possibilities is the Daily Triple, as it is called in California, where it is primarily resting at this time. It is a version of the daily double plus one, or one-half the Pick Six, or even a Pick Three, where you select the winner in three consecutive races.

By confining it to three races, the difficulties are decreased enormously. At the same time, the payoffs can be surprisingly high, as California experience reveals. You will have to invest far less money in the Daily Triple than you will in any of the other exotics aside from the double and the exacta. Also, since the three races that must be selected are usually found back in the card, you will have the opportunity to gauge the track surface to find out whether early speed or late speed will do well, and adjust your selections accordingly.

Because I have not had sufficient experience with the Daily Triple to adopt a program for playing it, I will have to stop at this point. If it does come east, as I hope it will, where I can attend tracks where it is offered, I will be out there experimenting and studying and analyzing and trying to determine whether there is a substantial possibility of a safe and secure profit sufficient to add it to our repertoire for Total Victory.

With all this in tow, we are now ready to move to the Performance, to see how the methods in this book can be applied to three different race tracks on the same day, where we take the cards as we find them. Happy days lie ahead.

15 The Performance: Winter Day At The Big A

WE SHALL NOW go through the first of three full racing cards on the same winter day, January 21, 1987, at three tracks where past performances are taken from the western issue of Daily Racing Form of that date. The judgments that have to be made will be demonstrated. The advantages that must be sought in order to make a play will be set forth. Every race that must be passed will be identified, with reasons why.

As we go through these races together, you will have a further opportunity to check the methods of compiling Performance Class Ratings, form factors, and last race ability times. For each race, we will compile a complete handicapping line and make the decision about what should be done in that race based upon what is revealed.

It would unduly lengthen these chapters to go through the mechanics of class ratings and ability time computations for each horse. From what you see in the handicapping line, you can check your own computations. From time to time, as particular problems may arise, I will offer comments as a general guide to the ratings we must make.

In this process, of course, there will be wins and there will be defeats, as you will see. We shall begin in the east, at Aqueduct. You will note that there are only a maximum of eight races shown in each past performance for Aqueduct, rather than the ten races which are normally presented, and which you will find in the west coast races.

1st Aqueduct

1 ⅛ MILES. (InnerDirt). (1.48⅗) CLAIMING. Purse $15,000. Fillies and Mares, 4-year-olds and upward. Weight, 122 lbs. Non-winners of two races at a mile or over since December 15 allowed 3 lbs. Of such a race since then, 5 lbs. Claiming price $17,500; if for $1,000 to $15,500 allowed 2 lbs. (Races when entered to be claimed for $14,000 or less not considered.)

Coupled—Medieval Gem and Out of the Storm.

Ask Directions

Dk. b. or br. f. 4, by Darby Creek Road—Khal On Me, by Vertex
Br.—Elser Mr-Mrs (Ky)
Own.—Adler M R 1085 Tr.—Martello Gene $15,500
Lifetime 42 3 5 7 $70,460

1987	2	0	0	0	$1,620
1986	32	2	3	7	$58,760
Turf	2	0	0	0	

16Jan87-9Aqu	1⅛⊡	:4911:1521:551ft	8¼	1125	63¾	75¼	43	43¼	Baird E T2	Ⓕ 14000	63-18	NtiveDme,NoSuch,MononghlMidn	12
3Jan87-3Aqu	1 1/16⊡	:4721:13 1:463sy	2¼	1125	66½	56¼	57¾	49¼	Baird E T2	Ⓕ 14000	68-16	ProHrmony,RsAndTost,ImptuosCrl	7
22Dec86-9Aqu	1 1/16⊡	:4811:13 1:454ft	11	114	107	109¾	615	613¾	Santagata N2	Ⓕ 22500	67-17	CherokeChill,MtchSpd,Strongbck	12
13Dec86-2Aqu	170⊡	:4831:1421:45 ft	12	1067	106¾	105	46	36	Pabon J C Jr5	Ⓕ 30000	69-20	PuddinTne,TendrYrs,AskDirctions	10
4Dec86-1Aqu	170⊡	:4841:1441:454ft	3	1097	86¼	74½	73¼	44	Nuesch D6	Ⓕ 22500	67-22	KimsIndin,SimpticZenid,Strongbck	9
19Nov86-2Aqu	1	:481 1:141 1:402m	18	1077	85¾	33	2hd	11¾	Nuesch D8	Ⓕ 22500	64-39	AskDirctions,TimlyRis,HonstNickl	10
8Nov86-4Aqu	1	:461 1:112 1:373sy	9	1097	—	77½	711	79½	Ortiz E Jr6	Ⓕ 25000	68-22	TimelyRis,HonstNickl,MistrssDonn	8
8Nov86—Running positions omitted because of weather conditions													
31Oct86-9Aqu	1	:463 1:12 1:38 ft	4½	1097	76	46	36	44¼	Ortiz E Jr6	Ⓕ 25000	72-20	TimlyRis,OutofthStorm,HonstNckl	11

Monongahela Maiden

Ch. m. 5, by Chati—A Reel Diplomat, by Diplomat Way
Br.—Giordano R G (Va)
Own.—Jal Stable 1125 Tr.—Sciacca Gary $17,500
Lifetime 35 3 4 4 $44,480

1987	2	0	0	2	$3,240
1986	23	3	4	1	$39,140
Turf	3	0	0	0	

16Jan87-9Aqu	1⅛⊡	:4911:1521:551ft	8½	119	94	63¾	33	32¼	Lovato F Jr4	Ⓕ c14000	64-18	NtiveDme,NoSuch,MononghlMidn	12
3Jan87-1Aqu	1 1/16⊡	:4731:1331:47 sy	10	119	813	86¼	66¼	37¼	Lovato F Jr6	Ⓕ 14000	68-16	DlcDlcDlc,FrskAndRs,MnnghlMdn	10
22Dec86-1Aqu	1¼⊡	:5031:4332:10 ft	5½	115	64½	2hd	1hd	12¼	Lovato F Jr7	Ⓕ 13000	65-17	MnnghlMdn,Swn'sPrspct,DlcDlcDlc	9
13Dec86-3Aqu	1 1/16⊡	:4911:1511:482ft	3½	115	75¼	52¼	55½	66¾	Lovato F Jr3	Ⓕ 13000	61-20	Kmb,DolcDolcDolc,Swoon'sPrspct	10
5Dec86-1Aqu	1⅛⊡	:4841:14 1:544ft	5¾	115	68¾	55¾	32¼	2½	Lovato F Jr3	Ⓕ 13000	67-21	NtiveDm,MononghlMidn,MyPrincss	9
15Nov86-1Aqu	7f	:231 :463 1:253ft	13	117	73¼	94¼	85¾	811¾	Graell A2	Ⓕ 14000	61-22	LovlyNurs,GunsilII,Swoon'sProspct	9
27Oct86-1Aqu	1	:463 1:112 1:381sy	10	113	108½	810	711	58¼	Davis R G7	Ⓕ 15500	67-20	K.'sSolution,OurTrisha,VisibleMrie	10
22Oct86-9Aqu	7f	:22 :443 1:241ft	2¾	117	812	813	59	57¾	Davis R G7	Ⓕ 14000	72-16	K.'sSolution,IrishPoint,LovlyNurs	10

Nov 26 Bel tr.t 4f gd :49 b

Far East

B. f. 4, by Mr Redoy—China Tea, by Round Table
Br.—Forest Retreat Farms Inc (Ky)
Own.—Asbury T 117 Tr.—Arnold George R II $17,500
Lifetime 10 2 0 4 $22,405

1986	10	2	0	4	$22,405
Turf	1	1	0	0	$7,380

29Dec86-5Aqu	6f	⊡:223 :4621:113ft	27	116	52	62¾	107¼	99¼	Lovato F Jr9	Ⓕ 25000	77-18	ExotcPowr,NoFoolsNoFun,IrshMr	12
20Dec86-1Aqu	6f	⊡:222 :4521:102ft	27	116	97¾	913	916	816	Lovato F Jr9	Ⓕ 50000	76-09	Spiriting, JustGorgeous,Doonesday	9
27Nov86-10CD	6f	:214 :46 1:113ft	21	117	87	108¼	912	911¾	LovtoFJr10	ⒻAw18150	73-23	TnThosndStrs,ScllySt,PltncIntrst	10
14Sep86-9TP	1 1/16	:462 1:113 1:454ft	*9-5	115	57¾	46	44½	32	Smith M E3	ⒻAw10500	79-22	Cafe Brulot, Cristal Dust, FarEast	10
13Aug86-8Cby	170Ⓣ	:4731:12 1:414fm	5	110	21	2½	2½	1no	Smith M E5	ⒻAw12300	— —	Far East, TruLadyRed,MarieofEssa	7
26Jly86-11Cby	1	:472 1:122 1:394ft	2½	110	87	56	45	32	Smith M E7	ⒻAw12300	80-12	Capestele, Comely Castle, Far East	8
29Jun86-3CD	1 1/16	:48 1:131 1:444ft	4¾	110	66	54	44	48¼	Allen K K3	ⒻAw16700	76-16	SongUnsung,CoaxMeMolly,LyClim	6
13Jun86-6CD	7f	:232 :464 1:234ft	3¼	113	43½	33	23½	36	Allen K K4	ⒻAw14320	81-18	Acquire, Lobby, Far East	6

Dec 13 Bel tr.t 4f ft :493 h

Medieval Gem

Dk. b. or br. f. 4, by Medieval Man—Jennie's Gem, by Bold Lark
Br.—Somday Farm Inc (Fla)
Own.—Kogstat H G 113 Tr.—Lake Robert P $15,500
Lifetime 20 2 1 0 $20,980

1987	1	0	0	0	
1986	14	1	0	0	$8,580
Turf	1	0	0	0	

16Jan87-9Aqu	1⅛⊡	:4911:1521:551ft	20	1125	115½	108¾	1011	811¼	Nuesch D3	Ⓕ 14000	55-18	NtiveDme,NoSuch,MononghlMidn	12
15Dec86-2Aqu	6f	⊡:222 :4631:121ft	4½e	116	1214	1117	1013	713¼	Graell A2	Ⓕ 17500	70-20	NoFoolsNoFn,ChrkChll,OtfthStrm	12
4Dec86-1Aqu	170⊡	:4841:1441:454ft	*2¼e	112	53½	63	51¾	54¼	Graell A1	Ⓕ 20000	67-22	KimsIndin,SimpticZenid,Strongbck	9
19Nov86-2Aqu	1	:481 1:141 1:402m	28	1075	54½	67	810	812¼	Badamo J J6	Ⓕ 20000	52-39	AskDirctions,TimlyRis,HonstNickl	10
3Nov86-7Med	1	[T]:4631:1031:363fm	77	112	86¼	108	1012	913	Santagata N2	Ⓕ 28000	82-03	Dve'sKte,SwtContss,RushForGold	10
3Nov86—Slow start													
23Oct86-1Aqu	7f	:224 :454 1:24 ft	29f	116	105	1211	1012	1010¾	Graell A7	Ⓕ 17500	70-17	Berry'sChpter,ChrokChill,TimlyRis	13
14Jun86-1Bel	1 1/16	:482 1:132 1:454ft	28	10610	76¼	714	720	719	Correa C J7	Ⓕ 25000	54-20	MssnOfTrth,AskDrctns,Trmph'sGlr	7
10May86-2Bel	1 1/16	:473 1:13 1:463ft	33	116	87½	64½	58	510¾	Graell A4	Ⓕ 25000	58-13	Out oftheStorm,Kimba,TimelyRaise	8

Jan 5 Aqu ⊡ 4f ft :521 b Dec 24 Aqu ⊡ 4f ft :493 b Nov 29 Aqu 6f ft 1:141 h

Frisky And Risky — B. m. 5, by Cormorant—Sunny Garden, by Sunrise County
Own.—Oak Lane Stables — 113 — Br.—Garbarini W (NY) — Tr.—Levine Bruce — $15,500
1987 1 0 1 0 $2,970
1986 17 4 2 2 $71,580
Lifetime 29 5 5 5 $111,435 — Turf 3 0 0 0

3Jan87-1Aqu 1 1/16 ⊡:473 1:133 1:47 sy *9-5 117 36 21 2hd 23¾ Hernandez R1 (F) 14000 71-16 DlcDlcDlc,FrskAndRs,MnnghlMdn 10
21Nov86-1Aqu 1⅛ :494 1:143 1:53 gd *3-2 117 3½ 21 11½ 14½ Santos J A6 (F) 17500 70-22 FrskyAndRsky,ImbcPntmtr,IrshPnt 6
24Oct86-1Aqu 1⅛ :484 1:14 1:521ft 5 115 1hd 3nk 22 33¾ Migliore R7 (F) 22500 70-20 SoloEnergy,Karabr,FriskyAndRisky 9
1Oct86-1Bel 1 1/16 :483 1:134 1:462ft *4-5 117 1hd 2hd 2½ 22¼ Martens G3 (F) c17500 68-17 VisiblMri,FriskyAndRisky,Bth'sRos 4
18Sep86-2Bel 7f :232 :464 1:251ft 11 117 74½ 78 911 78¾ Martens G2 (F) 25000 67-17 ByFourThirty,HiddenFntsy,Mjnniqu 9
29Aug86-1Bel 7f :231 :463 1:234gd 5¾ 117 64 65 68½ 69¾ Bailey J D7 (F) 35000 73-19 FiguraNaviden,Wench,MissFleming 7
22Aug86-4Sar 1⅛ :471 1:123 1:52 ft 14 115 76½ 74½ 67 512¼ Martens G3 (F) 47500 63-17 BllOfWstviw,MistAStrght,JcqusPrd 8
30Jly86-2Sar 7f :23 :461 1:24 ft 18 113 96 810 56¾ 54½ Martens G1 (F) 30000 77-13 MdyMndy,PrHrmny,MrryWdwWltz 9
30Jly86—Very wide
Dec 21 Aqu ⊡ 5f ft 1:042 b Dec 14 Aqu ⊡ 4f ft :491 b

Swoon's Prospect — B. m. 5, by New Prospect—Swoons Moon, by Swoon's Son
Own.—Silver Mate Stable — 1125 — Br.—O'Quinn Clayton (Fla) — Tr.—Barrera Oscar S Jr — $17,500
1986 25 3 5 3 $47,130
1985 15 1 1 1 $11,460
Lifetime 42 4 6 4 $58,590 — Turf 1 0 0 0

27Dec86-2Aqu 6f ⊡:223 :461 1:112ft 12 1085 1010 1012 912 99¾ Ortiz E Jr10 (F) 20000 77-11 DameDeTrefle,DwnBrek,BbyChris 11
22Dec86-1Aqu 1¼ ⊡:503 1:433 2:10 ft 4½ 1125 33 63½ 42 22¼ Baird E T2 (F) c14000 63-17 MnnghlMdn,Swn'sPrspct,DlcDlcDlc 9
13Dec86-3Aqu 1 1/16 ⊡:491 1:151 1:482ft *3 117 32 1hd 21½ 33½ Maple E7 (F) 14000 64-20 Kmb,DolcDolcDolc,Swoon'sPrspct 10
28Nov86-3Aqu 7f :232 :471 1:252ft 4½ 117 1hd 1hd 22½ 24¼ Maple E5 (F) 14000 70-18 GunsilII,Swoon'sProspect,NtiveDm 7
15Nov86-1Aqu 7f :231 :463 1:253ft 6¾ 117 41½ 41½ 44 38 Maple E7 (F) 14000 65-22 LovlyNurs,GunsilII,Swoon'sProspct 9
4Nov86-2Aqu 1 :452 1:11 1:38 ft 5½e115 1113 1011 811 78 Davis R G5 (F) 22500 68-22 TrulyBest,SoloEnrgy,K.'sSolution 13
24Oct86-1Aqu 1⅛ :484 1:14 1:521ft 16 115 62½ 62¾ 75½ 77¼ Davis R G8 (F) 22500 67-20 SoloEnergy,Karabr,FriskyAndRisky 9
11Oct86-2Bel 1⅛ :472 1:121 1:513ft 11 10710 2hd 53¼ 612 613¼ Correa C J1 (F) c17500 56-19 Karabr,PltinumPoster,HiddenFntsy 8
Jan 16 Bel tr.t 3f ft :38 b Jan 14 Bel tr.t 3f ft :384 b

Out of the Storm — B. f. 4, by Shelter Half—Cyndaira, by Sadair
Own.—C'Est Tout Stable — 117 — Br.—Dick H W Co Inc (WVa) — Tr.—Lake Robert P — $17,500
1987 1 0 0 0
1986 20 3 2 2 $44,520
Lifetime 24 4 3 2 $54,740 — Turf 4 0 0 0 $1,200

14Jan87-9Aqu 6f ⊡:22 :452 1:113ft 21 1125 64 56½ 77 85¾ Baird E T9 (F) 17500 80-16 TmmyDov,PrivtIron,GoodContrrin 12
29Dec86-5Aqu 6f ⊡:223 :462 1:113ft 14 112 104¾ 94½ 118¼ 1110½ Davis R G1 (F) 20000 75-18 ExotcPowr,NoFoolsNoFun,IrshMr 12
15Dec86-2Aqu 6f ⊡:222 :463 1:121ft 4½e1097 46½ 46½ 34 34¾ Nuesch D8 (F) 17500 78-20 NoFoolsNoFn,ChrkChll,OtfthStrm 12
4Dec86-1Aqu 1 70 ⊡:484 1:144 1:454ft *2¼e116 43 3½ 4¾ 78¼ Maple E5 (F) 25000 63-22 KimsIndin,SimpticZenid,Strongbck 9
22Nov86-1Aqu 7f :232 :463 1:25 ft *3½e112 51½ 51¾ 63¼ 67¾ Maple E3 (F) 30000 68-18 Quillo's Love,TorridZone,Pia'sBaby 8
31Oct86-9Aqu 1 :463 1:12 1:38 ft 7 116 32 22 22 23 Maple E4 (F) 25000 73-20 TimlyRis,OutofthStorm,HonstNckl 11
13Oct86-1Bel 1 :463 1:122 1:372ft 5½ 114 54 54 58 [illegible] Maple E9 (F) 25000 68-16 Wench, Solo Energy, HonestNickle 9
25Sep86-5Bel 1 1/16 :471 1:123 1:451ft *2 116 31½ 2hd 1½ 23 Davis R G2 (F) 25000 73-19 AskDrctons,OtofthStorm,HnstNckl 9
Dec 24 Aqu ⊡ 4f ft :48 h

Pro Harmony * — Ch. m. 6, by Pro Consul—Grand Harmony, by Grand Revival
Own.—Ospam Stable — 1125 — Br.—Buttigieg Farms (Ont-C) — Tr.—Hernandez Sandino — $17,500
1987 1 1 0 0 $8,100
1986 23 4 7 2 $68,075
Lifetime 61 9 12 10 $137,699 — Turf 3 0 0 0 $834

3Jan87-3Aqu 1 1/16 ⊡:472 1:13 1:463sy *7-5 1125 3½ 1hd 1hd 1no Nuesch D3 (F) c14000 77-16 ProHrmony,RsAndTost,ImptuosCrl 7
26Dec86-1Aqu 6f ⊡:23 :471 1:123ft 3½ 117 62¼ 52¼ 52¾ 41¼ Maple E7 (F) 17500 80-14 LovlyNrs,Amongthchosnfw,TopSlc 9
14Dec86-1Aqu 6f ⊡:224 :463 1:122ft 3 119 53 53 55½ 54¾ Antley C W4 (F) 25000 77-20 Latin Look, Holly Hagley,OurTrisha 6
4Dec86-2Aqu 6f ⊡:223 :463 1:121ft *8-5 119 1111 96 93¾ 87¾ Antley C W3 (F) 25000 75-22 OurTrisha,Barrancos,KissingBooth 11
4Dec86—Bumped start
27Nov86-2Aqu 1 :48 1:133 1:391gd *1 119 22 21½ 32 24 Romero R P7 (F) 25000 66-29 ImbicPntmtr,ProHrmony,IrishPont 7
22Nov86-2Aqu 6f :223 :462 1:111ft *2½ 119 75½ 52¼ 32 22 Antley C W5 (F) 25000 83-18 AddaGirl,ProHrmony,Berry'sChpter 9
17Nov86-1Aqu 1 :471 1:12 1:382ft *3-2 117 21 2hd 1½ 1nk Antley C W5 (F) 25000 74-20 ProHrmony,PltinumPoster,DwnBrk 7
14Nov86-3Aqu 7f :23 :462 1:251ft 3½ 115 21 31½ 1hd 52½ Antley C W5 (F) 32500 72-23 MerryWidowWltz,Wench,FinlStrok 8
Dec 21 Bel tr.t 3f ft :39 b Dec 13 Bel tr.t 3f ft :39 b

Dolce Dolce Dolce — B. f. 4, by Sweet Candy—Triple Jaylean, by Sailor
Own.—Free W **117** Br.—Free F W (NY) Tr.—Velasquez Alfredo $17,500
1987 1 1 0 0 $8,100
1986 16 2 2 5 $23,445
Lifetime 21 3 2 5 $31,545 Turf 4 1 0 1 $8,685

3Jan87-1Aqu 1 1/16 [•]:4731:1331:47 sy 7½ 1125 915 76 1hd 13¾ Brown T L4 Ⓕ 14000 75-16 DlcDlcDlc,FrskAndRs,MnnghlMdn 10
22Dec86-1Aqu 1¼ [•]:5031:4332:10 ft 7¾ 1065 53½ 3½ 2hd 32¼ Brown T L1 Ⓕ 12000 63-17 MnnghlMdn,Swn'sPrspct,DlcDlcDlc 9
13Dec86-3Aqu 1 1/16 [•]:4911:1511:482ft 21 1065 64½ 4¾ 11½ 2½ Brown T L6 Ⓕ 12000 67-20 Kmb,DolcDolcDolc,Swoon'sPrspct 10
7Nov86-2Aqu 1 :461 1:114 1:38 gd 11 112 55¾ 68 812 815¾ Davis R G2 Ⓕ 12000 60-21 DualRole,IrishPoint,HiddenFantsy 13
23Oct86-1Aqu 7f :224 :454 1:24 ft 33 1115 3nk 4¾ 88¼ 78 Baird E T6 Ⓕ 17500 73-17 Berry'sChpter,ChrokChill,TimlyRis 13
13Oct86-2Bel 1 Ⓣ:47 1:12 1:38 fm 3 114 63½ 97½1012 1014¾ MapleE10 Ⓕ[S]Aw28000 60-33 ‡Tin'sRobin,LibbyDer,Btchelorette 10
15Sep86-3Bel 1 1/16 [T]:4611:1011:42 fm 7 1115 33½ 44 54¾ 58¼ Brown T L8 Ⓕ 35000 83-14 MissSarahJoy,Tinnmon,Colloquium 8
3Sep86-8Med 1 1/16 [T]:4721:1121:442fm *3 1055 89 913 49½ 34¼ Brown T L1 Ⓕ 28000 77-19 MyElnor,SwtstMomm,DolcDolcDlc 9
Dec 7 Bel tr.t 4f ft :49 b

Star of Montana — B. f. 4, by Cougar II—Windrush Star, by Apalachee
Own.—Adelson G H **1085** Br.—Nicholas C E (Ky) Tr.—Woodson Richard $15,500
1987 1 0 0 0
1986 16 1 3 3 $22,050
Lifetime 17 1 3 3 $22,050 Turf 2 0 0 0

4Jan87-9Aqu 6f [•]:223 :4631:122ft 11 117 105¾108¾1215 1116¼ MrquezCHJr5 Ⓕ 17500 66-21 Amongthchosnfw,Tr'sNtiv,Slightd 12
22Dec86-9Aqu 1 1/16 [•]:4811:13 1:454ft 9¾ 1115 96¾1111 1018 916½ Brown T L5 Ⓕ 25000 64-17 CherokeChill,MtchSpd,Strongbck 12
12Dec86-5Aqu 6f [•]:224 :4621:12 m 21 1095 77¼ 65¾ 43½ 2½ Brown T L3 Ⓕ 22500 83-16 GirlishGlee,StrofMontn,ChrokChill 7
21Nov86-1Aqu 1⅛ :494 1:143 1:53 gd 12 1107 56 57 511 417½ BelmonteJF1 Ⓕ c17500 52-22 FrskyAndRsky,ImbcPntmtr,IrshPnt 6
31Oct86-9Aqu 1 :463 1:12 1:38 ft 20 1117 97 911 1013 914¼ Belmonte JF1 Ⓕ 25000 62-20 TimlyRis,OutofthStorm,HonstNckl 11
16Oct86-9Bel 1 1/16 :464 1:122 1:454ft 3¾ 1087 87 55½ 23 12½ BelmonteJF2 ⒻM30000 73-19 StrofMontn,StppnRth,MjorHolbrk 11
20Sep86-9Bel 6f :23 :464 1:114ft 6 1117 1012 89½ 510 510 BelmonteJF7 ⒻM35000 73-20 ZonaRosa,Jen'sDimond,PuddinTne 11
10Sep86-2Bel 1 1/16 :473 1:123 1:453ft 5¾ 1077 74½ 69 410 25½ BelmonteJF5 ⒻM30000 68-20 MstrssDonn,StrofMontn,StppnRuth 9
Dec 6 Bel tr.t 4f ft :482 h

This cheap claiming race at 1 1/8 miles on Aqueduct's inner track, rated as sloppy, is typical of what you may be expected to find at this time of the year. Since most of the horses entered ran their last races at this distance, we will have little difficulty in calculating ability times. Where a horse last ran at 1 1/16 miles, of course, we have to make extensions. And a horse whose last race was in a sprint presents the same problems that are always present when we extend projected times from sprints to routes. With that in hand, we can proceed to see what our worksheet reveals.

Odds	Horse	PCR	Form	Ab/T
9	Ask Directions	79/ 53 33 − 10/ 76 = 104	+NN	16.2 39.2 0/ 55.4
7	Monog. Mdn.	79/ 51 33 + 8/ 92 = 86	++N	16.1 39.3 0/ 55.4
19	Far East	68/ 44 40 − 16/ 68 = 100	NON	(13.2 39.4 0/ 53.1)
e12	Medieval Gem	x	x	x
e12	Out of the Storm	82/ 35 43 − 11/ 67 = 122	+0N	(12.4 39.2+1/ 52.3)
3-2	Frisky and Risky	62/ 37 31 − 8/ 60 = 103	NNO	13.4 40.2+1/ 54.2
10	Swoon's Prospect	76/ 43 39 + 1/ 83 = 92	NON	13.2 39.1+5/ 53.3
4	Pro Harmony	64/ 32 28 − 11/ 49 = 131	N+w	13.0 40.1+1/ 53.2
6	Dolce Dolce	82/ 46 39 + 1/ 86 = 95	NN+	14.4 39.0+1/ 55.0
25	Star of Montana	x	NON	x

On two of the lines, we have not filled in the numbers. You can see that the last races of Medieval Gem, who is coupled with Out of the Storm as a betting entry, and Star of Montana are literally so atrocious that it would be a waste of effort to go through the calculations. We do not lightly omit handicapping lines of any horse, but where they are so obviously and overwhelmingly bad, along with very high odds, we can safely leave them out of our figuring. If a horse shows lower odds on the board than his line would indicate, you should burden yourself with caution and compute the figures.

We are also limited on last race ability times because three horses ran in sprints in their last race. We project them, however, and enter them as advisory, usually to be taken into account if outstanding on one end or abysmal on the other.

Once this work is done, we begin our search for one or more horses with a sufficient advantage to warrant a play. We begin with the three top PCR figures, where Pro Harmony and Out of the Storm are somewhat better than the rest. Pro Harmony has the blemish of having won her last race and Out of the Storm has a running line form defect. Ask Directions, Frisky and Risky, and Far East are virtually bunched for the third highest PCR, since there is no meaningful difference between any of them. If one of the three has some kind of an advantage that we are looking for, there might be play. Since Ask Directions is tied for the poorest ability time in the field, she is a fairly certain no go. Frisky and Risky, as the favorite, bears a form defect, as does Far East, who is coming off a sprint race.

Accordingly, none of the first three PCR horses can meet our standards for a single selection play, unless Pro Harmony can make it. We can see that ability times of many of the horses are reasonably well bunched, which is a clear signal to beware. Actually, Pro Harmony does comparatively well, with much of her competition coming from horses off sprint races. Swoon's Prospect is only one tick behind, and as we have stressed, that means relatively equal. Because Pro Harmony does not stand out insofar as her last race ability time is concerned, and is a cheap horse coming off a win, she cannot possess the kind of advantage we are looking for in a single selection play.

This provides us another opportunity to stress an important handicapping reality about last race winners. Relatively cheap horses, unless they have some kind of clear cut advantage, are very poor prospects to repeat. And this field is near the bottom of the New York barrel.

Where does this leave us? If you see what I see, this is a collection of animals that has nothing at all that stands out above the others. It is one of those races where almost any horse can win, except those with very poor last races. Even some of those we eliminated early might surprise in a group of this kind. When you have a problem race as the first event of the day, this is additional reason to keep your money in your pocket, observe carefully how the track is running, and look for the later races to make your day.

This race is an excellent example of one that should not be played. We pass.

Let's see what happened and how the track appears to be receiving our competitors.

FIRST RACE
Aqueduct
JANUARY 21, 1987

1⅛ MILES.(InnerDirt). (1.48⅘) CLAIMING. Purse $15,000. Fillies and Mares, 4-year-olds and upward. Weight, 122 lbs. Non-winners of two races at a mile or over since December 15 allowed 3 lbs. Of such a race since then, 5 lbs. Claiming price $17,500; if for $1,000 to $15,500 allowed 2 lbs. (Races when entered to be claimed for $14,000 or less not considered.) (18th Day. WEATHER CLOUDY. TEMPERATURE 36 DEGREES).

Value of race $15,000; value to winner $9,000; second $3,300; third $1,800; fourth $900. Mutuel pool $44,403, OTB pool $123,095. Exacta Pool $61,032. OTB Exacta Pool $152,518.

Last Raced	Horse	Eqt.	A.	Wt	PP	St	¼	½	¾	Str	Fin	Jockey	Cl'g Pr	Odds $1
29Dec86 ^{5}Aqu^{9}	Far East		4	117	3	2	$3\frac{1}{2}$	3^{2}	2^{hd}	1^{hd}	$1^{1\frac{3}{4}}$	Lovato F Jr	17500	9.20
3Jan87 ^{1}Aqu^{2}	Frisky And Risky	b	5	115	5	1	$2^{1\frac{1}{2}}$	$2\frac{1}{2}$	1^{hd}	2^{4}	$2^{3\frac{3}{4}}$	Hernandez R	15500	1.50
3Jan87 ^{1}Aqu^{1}	Dolce Dolce Dolce	b	4	117	9	9	7^{1}	8^{2}	$6\frac{1}{2}$	$3\frac{1}{2}$	$3^{1\frac{3}{4}}$	Brown T L	17500	6.80
27Dec86 ^{2}Aqu^{9}	Swoon's Prospect	b	5	112	6	4	10	10	$9\frac{1}{2}$	6^{2}	$4\frac{1}{2}$	Belmonte J F^{5}	17500	10.80
4Jan87 ^{9}Aqu^{11}	Star of Montana		4	109	10	10	9^{1}	$7\frac{1}{2}$	5^{1}	4^{1}	$5^{5\frac{3}{4}}$	Ortiz E Jr^{5}	15500	29.40
16Jan87 ^{9}Aqu^{3}	Monongahela Maiden		5	117	2	3	5^{hd}	$6\frac{1}{2}$	10	$8^{1\frac{1}{2}}$	$6\frac{1}{2}$	Santos J A	17500	7.40
14Jan87 ^{9}Aqu^{8}	Out of the Storm		4	117	7	5	$1\frac{1}{2}$	1^{hd}	$3^{2\frac{1}{2}}$	$5\frac{1}{2}$	$7^{1\frac{3}{4}}$	Antley C W	17500	a-12.40
16Jan87 ^{9}Aqu^{4}	Ask Directions	b	4	109	1	8	$8^{1\frac{1}{2}}$	9^{2}	8^{hd}	$9^{1\frac{1}{2}}$	8^{hd}	Baird E T^{5}	15500	9.50
3Jan87 ^{3}Aqu^{1}	Pro Harmony	b	6	112	8	6	4^{1}	4^{hd}	4^{hd}	7^{2}	9^{1}	Nuesch D^{5}	17500	4.40
16Jan87 ^{9}Aqu^{8}	Medieval Gem	b	4	113	4	7	6^{2}	$5^{1\frac{1}{2}}$	7^{2}	10	10	Santagata N	15500	a-12.40

a-Coupled: Out of the Storm and Medieval Gem.

OFF AT 12:30, Start good, Won driving. Time, :23⅗, :48⅘, 1:14, 1:41, 1:54⅗ Track sloppy.

Official Program Numbers

$2 Mutuel Prices:

4-(C)-FAR EAST	20.40	9.20	5.40
5-(E)-FRISKY AND RISKY		3.60	2.80
9-(J)-DOLCE DOLCE DOLCE			3.60

$2 EXACTA 4-5 PAID $90.60.

It is not too surprising that an outsider, Far East, brought forth a $20.40 winning ticket. There was simply nothing in her record that would have guided us toward this filly with any degree of confidence. The favorite, Frisky and Risky, ran a healthy second, but as we indicated earlier, there were far too many questions marks about her to warrant any kind of a play.

What does this chart tell us about the track today so we can better evaluate the races to follow? This is clearly the most important thing we can glean from this first race. From the chart, we can see that early speed did much better than late speed, as both the first and second finishers stayed ahead of the others through the last three furlongs of the race. The sloppy track was readily pointing the way to a happy afternoon for the quick speed. We would therefore thus rate the track as favoring early speed somewhat, not quite a heavy bias for early speed, but enough to make front speed a formidable factor never to be ignored. We have to keep watching the succeeding races, however, to make sure that this will guide us throughout the afternoon.

We are now ready for the second race at six furlongs, a claiming event with a $50,000 price. We can expect some reasonably good animals at that figure, and since it is a sprint race, we can also expect a reliable guide on the speed of the track.

2nd Aqueduct

6 FURLONGS. (InnerDirt). (1.09%) CLAIMING. Purse $21,000. Filliesand Mares, 4-year-olds and upward. Weight, 122 lbs. Non-winners of two races since December 15 allowed 3 lbs. Of a race since then, 5 lbs. Claiming price $50,000; for each $2,500 to $45,000 allowed 2 lbs. (Races when entered to be claimed for $40,000 or less not considered.)

Dame De Trefle *

B. m. 7, by Tentam—Dame de Pique, by Bolinas Boy
Br.—Levesque J L (Ont-C) 1987 1 1 0 0 $11,400
Own.—Lane G E 108^5 **Tr.—Sedlacek Michael C** $45,000 1986 21 8 2 3 $57,691
Lifetime 66 18 10 7 $133,104

9Jan87-2Aqu	6f	⊡:23	:46^{2}1:11^{4}ft	3	112^5	1hd	1hd	11½	11	Baird E T6	Ⓕ 35000	85-16	DmeDeTrefle,LtinLook,ExoticPowr	9
27Dec86-2Aqu	6f	⊡:22^3	:46^{1}1:11^{2}ft	6¼	117	32½	21	12½	11¼	Lovato F Jr1	Ⓕ c25000	87-11	DameDeTrefle,DwnBrek,BbyChris	11
3Dec86-8Grd	6½f	:24^1	:47^4 1:21^{3}sy	*3¾	117	32	31	1hd	46¾	LeblancJB1	ⒻAw19500	71-36	MdmeTresurer,ClssicAnnie,Bougrin	9
19Nov86-9Grd	6½f	:24	:48^1 1:21 ft	13	114	65	2hd	1hd	3¾	Leblanc J B6	ⒻHcp0	80-32	SwftndBold,DncngRuckus,DmDTrfl	7
12Nov86-6Grd	6½f	:24^2	:48 1:21^{2}ft	7½	117	31½	2½	14	13¼	Leblanc J B6	Ⓕ 19000	79-29	DmeDeTrefl,GoldnSunburst,HrBnt	10
19Oct86-9FE	5½f	:22^3	:46 1:05^{3}ft	9-5e	119	2hd	31½	44	56¾	Grubb R4	Aw5800	85-24	Jimmert, Prince Victor, Bare It All	6
13Oct86-9FE	5½f	:22^4	:47^4 1:07^{4}sy	*2-5e	120	11½	1½	12½	11¾	Grubb R1	Ⓕ®Aw5800	81-35	DmeDeTrefl,LdyStrtgy,SpringSprkl	7
15Sep86-9FE	5f	:23	:47 1:00^{3}sy	3¼	116	21	12½	15½	12¼	Hemsley D L6	Aw6900	83-33	DmeDeTrfl,NorthSKing,GrkQustion	7

Nov 29 Grd 4f gd :51^2 h

Doonesday

B. f. 4, by Doonesbury—Looks Ten, by Raja Baba
Br.—Seaman C O (Ky) 1987 1 0 0 0
Own.—Watral M 108^7 **Tr.—Brida Dennis J Jr** $47,500 1986 8 2 1 1 $13,977
Lifetime 9 2 1 1 $13,977

5Jan87-5Aqu	6f	⊡:22^3	:46^{2}1:11^{4}ft	7¾	117	42¼	42¾	58½	612¾	Maple E4	ⒻAw27000	72-18	Arunji, Ski Bunny, Tops In Taps	9
20Dec86-1Aqu	6f	⊡:22^2	:45^{2}1:10^{2}ft	10e	113	34	34	35	34¾	Maple E3	Ⓕ 45000	87-09	Spiriting, JustGorgeous,Doonesday	9
6Nov86-9Rkm	6f	:23	:47^3 1:13^{4}sy	4	109^5	54½	2	12	17	Bryon T S8	ⒻAw7500	75-27	Doonesday,TintaChina,CarlyleSuite	8
26Oct86-5Rkm	6f	:22^2	:46 1:13^{4}ft	4½	114	42	33½	35½	54¼	Moore D N7	ⒻAw7500	71-27	SilverPitcher,GreatKate,SrtogBelle	8
17Oct86-6Rkm	6f	:22^3	:46^2 1:13 ft	7	108^5	53¼	22	21	21	Bryon T S6	ⒻAw7500	78-29	SeiGesund,Doonesday,QueenAndria	7
11Oct86-9Rkm	1 40	:47^3	1:14 1:46 ft	17	107^5	35½	35	57	67	Bryon T S1	ⒻAw8100	55-28	RelDetrmind,MistyRgin,EnchntdStr	8
5Sep86-8Rkm	6f	:22	:45^4 1:11^{4}ft	8½	118	87¼	85¼	711	711¼	Martin C W5	ⒻAw9000	73-24	MyIrishPrincss,IcyDrlin,SinglKiss	12
26Aug86-5Rkm	6f	:22^4	:46^1 1:12^{1}ft	7	117	22	54	57	59¾	Martin C W2	ⒻAw9000	73-16	Slem'sStrlet,SilverPitcher,SrtogBll	6

26Aug86—Slow start

Dec 30 Bel tr.t 5f ft 1:05 b **Dec 16 Bel tr.t 4f ft :51 b** **●Nov 25 Rkm 3f ft :36^2 h**

Peace Keeper
B. m. 6, by Hold Your Peace—Ain't It A Sham, by Sham
Br.—Westview Stables Inc (Ky) 1986 6 1 3 0 $40,080
Own.—Denmark Muriel 1125 Tr.—Pascuma Warren J $50,000 1985 15 5 1 3 $53,980
Lifetime 22 6 4 3 $94,060

13Dec86-7Aqu 6f [•]:222 :4611:11 ft 8¾ 115 32 42½ 77½ 99½ SantagatN4 ⒻAw40000 79-20 PerfectRoux,Syrianette,Robin'sRob 9
26Nov86-5Aqu 6f :221 :454 1:113sy *6-5 113 2½ 21 32 2nk Santagata N5 Ⓕ 70000 83-19 SkiBunny,PeaceKeeper,MayBeBold 7
4Nov86-5Aqu 6f :221 :46 1:11 ft 7¾ 113 2½ 2hd 1½ 22½ Santagata N2 Ⓕ 70000 84-22 JckieO'Lnternn,PeceKeeper,Arunji 8
12Oct86-7Bel 7f :22 :434 1:23 ft 31 115 27 313 819 817¼ SantagatN3 ⒻAw36000 70-13 ReelEsy,MistressMontgue,Argntrio 8
12Jan86-7Aqu 6f [•]:214 :4521:12 ft 5¾ 115 2½ 1½ 12½ 1½ Graell A6 ⒻAw36000 84-20 PeceKeeper,CherryJubil,FullPromis 7
2Jan86-8Aqu 6f [•]:23 :46 1:112ft 4 115 1½ 2½ 22 23½ Maple E4 ⒻAw36000 83-26 ReglLynco,PeceKeeper,CherryJubil 5
1Dec85-5Aqu 6f :221 :453 1:111sy 15 112 12½ 12½ 13 11½ MacBeth D1 Ⓕ 75000 85-21 Peace Keeper,VeryUltimate,LadyD. 8
1Dec85—Bumped st.,clear
23Nov85-1Aqu 7f :224 :463 1:243m 2¾ 117 2hd 21 33 44 Velasquez J3 Ⓕ c50000 74-14 VeryUltimte,Speier'sImg,MdlinSwti 8
Jan 14 Bel tr.t 6f ft 1:154 b Jan 6 Bel tr.t 6f ft 1:19 b Dec 30 Bel tr.t 6f ft 1:183 b Dec 21 Bel tr.t 4f ft :482 h.

Glady H.
Dk. b. or br. f. 4, by Proud Appeal—Raintree Place, by Bagdad
Br.—Hough S M (Fla) 1987 1 0 0 1 $3,360
Own.—Nagle K 1125 Tr.—Ferriola Peter $50,000 1986 10 1 2 2 $18,865
Lifetime 12 2 2 3 $30,325

11Jan87-7Aqu 1 1/16 [•]:4641:1131:433m 13 117 65 54¾ 56½ 34½ Migliore R4 ⒻAw28000 88-17 Peaches, Cherokee Chill, Glady H. 7
4Dec86-7Crc 1⅛ :493 1:153 1:56 ft 2½ 1095 2½ 2½ 68½ 515½ Paynter L A3 Ⓕ c40000 54-21 AnnieBlueeyes,DeCClhrgr,Rlumbrnt 6
26Nov86-7Crc 1 :494 1:15 1:42 ft *3-2 1075 23 33½ 44 31¾ PaynterLA3 ⒻAw15100 76-17 StutteringSarh,SchoolOfArt,GldyH. 5
12Nov86-8Crc 1 :484 1:143 1:43 ft 2½ 1095 34½ 34½ 2½ 2no Paynter L A3 Ⓕ 40000 73-22 StompinSister,GldyH.,RiseADuchss 7
12Nov86—Bore out
31Oct86-7Crc 1 :49 1:144 1:413ft 3¾e 1077 26 21 32½ 22½ Mancilla O G2 Ⓕ 50000 77-22 She's Content, GladyH.,MerryCathy 6
21Oct86-9Crc 1 :493 1:144 1:421ft 8¾ 1077 1½ 2hd 2hd 32 MancillOG5 ⒻAw19200 75-20 TeaForTop,MaggieGaylord,GladyH. 5
7Aug86-7Crc 6f :221 :453 1:121ft *2 116 52¾ 63½ 611 77 Espinoza J C4 Ⓕ 40000 83-17 DnceRelity,SuprmLuck,KlssyKrystl 8
25Jly86-9Crc 6f :222 :463 1:131sy *6-5 115 3½ 43 65½ 64½ EspinozJC6 ⒻAw12500 81-19 Vale Royale, Shoot For AStar,Dozo 7
Jan 9 Aqu [•] 3f ft :371 b

Miss Scandal
Ch. f. 4, by Inverness Drive—Lady Corniche, by Cornish Prince
Br.—Rutherford M G (Ky) 1987 2 0 0 1 $3,240
Own.—Sabarese T M 115 Tr.—Barrera Oscar S $45,000 1986 7 2 0 1 $34,740
Lifetime 9 2 0 2 $37,980

14Jan87-5Aqu 6f [•]:222 :4521:111ft 19 1175 2½ 32½ 31½ 31½ BelmontJF4 ⒻAw27000 87-16 JustGorgous,Blm'sMjsty,MssScndl 7
5Jan87-5Aqu 6f [•]:223 :4621:114ft 9 122 3nk 32½ 710 917½ Santos J A9 ⒻAw27000 67-18 Arunji, Ski Bunny, Tops In Taps 9
31Dec86-6Aqu 6f [•]:224 :4631:114ft 3¾ 115 31 21½ 1hd 1nk Antley CW1 ⒻAw26000 85-13 MissScndl,RomnticBelle,RinbowAly 8
21Dec86-7Aqu 6f [•]:221 :46 1:112ft 2¾ 115 41½ 4nk 33½ 46½ Antley CW8 ⒻAw26000 81-14 TopsInTps,StgeNtive,NorthrnMido 9
6Dec86-5Aqu 1 1/16 [•]:4831:1341:484ft *4-5 1105 1½ 1hd 2hd 53¾ Baird E T4 ⒻAw27000 62-21 GallantTerms,FstFshion,IdunItToo 7
16Nov86-5Aqu 1 :462 1:12 1:384ft 6¾ 115 11 1hd 2½ 45½ Santos J A8 ⒻAw25000 66-23 UnttenddDt,Rp'sRtton,ExoticPowr 8
10Nov86-7Aqu 7f :223 :461 1:24 gd 2½ 117 2hd 41½ 55½ 810¾ Davis R G1 ⒻAw24000 70-18 MusicOfLove,UnttnddDt,BlnchNig 11
19Oct86-5Bel 7f :23 :462 1:233ft *4-5 119 1½ 1hd 23½ 36½ Davis R G4 ⒻAw24000 77-14 PoelishHills,Rep'sRetton,MissScndl 9

Mother Maloney *
B. m. 6, by Father Hogan—Roma Deb, by Gallant Romeo
Br.—Sea Spray Farm (NY) 1986 12 1 1 3 $32,108
Own.—Briar Patch Farm 1125 Tr.—Vetter Robert C $50,000 1985 16 3 1 1 $49,260
Lifetime 43 6 3 4 $119,948 Turf 1 0 0 0

27Dec86-7Aqu 6f [•]:222 :4541:102ft 18 115 85¾ 87½ 85 76¼ VsquzMM4 ⒻAw40000 86-11 Nasherrico, Saucey Missy,BeSmart 8
7Dec86-8Aqu 170 [•]:4821:1311:444ft 18 114 118½ 97¾ 68 58¼ VsqzMM5 ⒻⓈIroquois 68-18 Anniron,LadyBeRegl,WendyWlker 12
19Nov86-8Aqu 6f :221 :462 1:113gd 4 106 75¾ 65 64 33 VsMM7 ⒻⓈSchnctdH 80-25 Anniron,Advancette,MotherMloney 8
27Oct86-5Aqu 7f :223 :453 1:24 sy *4-5 113 66½ 37½ 26 2¾ Vasquez MM3 Ⓕ 45000 80-20 MissOtni,MotherMloney,BethsSong 8
16Oct86-5Bel 6f :222 :452 1:103ft 17 113 65½ 54 54 32 Vasquez MM2 Ⓕ 45000 87-19 MoodyMondy,Solohi,MotherMlony 7
6Oct86-3Bel 6f :223 :46 1:104ft 18 117 57¼ 714 815 816¼ Vasquez MM6 Ⓕ 35000 72-24 Solohi,ForeverSpecil,ApplyYourself 8
14Aug86-1Sar 7f :224 :46 1:232ft 6½ 117 74½ 66 55¼ 49 Vasquez MM1 Ⓕ 50000 76-20 JckO'Lntrnn,MoodyMndy,PrHrmny 8
24Jly86-1Bel 6f :223 :46 1:104ft 24 113 86¼ 97¾ 57 34 Vasquez MM2 Ⓕ 40000 84-15 TeriyakiStake,Oaxac,MotherMloney 9
Jan 17 Bel tr.t 3f ft :37 h Dec 24 Bel tr.t 3f ft :373 b Dec 2 Bel tr.t 3f ft :37 h

Miss Otani ✕ B. m. 5, by Wajima—Saturday Matinee, by Silent Screen
Br.—Dimauro S A (Ky) 1987 1 0 0 0
Own.—DiMauro S **117** Tr.—DiMauro Stephen L $50,000 1986 10 2 0 3 $31,690
Lifetime 29 4 6 7 $74,650

2Jan87-1Aqu	6f	[•]:22^1 :45^{2}1:11 m	7 112	5$^{3\frac14}$ 7$^{5\frac34}$ 7^{11} 6$^{10\frac12}$	Samyn J L^7	Ⓕ 75000	78-21	JustGorgeous,Robin'sRob,T.V.Snow	8
13Nov86-9Med	6f	:23 :46^3 1:12 ft	4¾ 118	2^1 2$^{1\frac12}$ 2$^{1\frac12}$ 3$^{\frac34}$	MelendzJD^2	ⒻAw17000	81-25	StrBrillint,Eternlsplendor,MissOtni	6
5Nov86-6Med	6f	:23 :46^2 1:12^{2}sy	2¾ 118	4^5 4^9 4^8 4$^{9\frac14}$	MelendzJD^4	ⒻAw17000	71-27	ParisJewel,StarBrilliant,Indistinctly	6
27Oct86-5Aqu	7f	:22^3 :45^3 1:24 sy	3½ 119	1$^{1\frac12}$ 1^6 1^6 1$^{\frac34}$	Samyn J L^5	Ⓕ 50000	81-20	MissOtni,MotherMloney,BethsSong	8
16Oct86-5Bel	6f	:22^2 :45^2 1:10^{3}ft	6 119	3$^{1\frac12}$ 4^1 3$^{1\frac12}$ 4$^{2\frac14}$	Samyn J L^1	Ⓕ 50000	87-19	MoodyMondy,Solobi,MotherMlony	7
3Oct86-10Med	6f	:22^2 :45^2 1:11^{2}sy	7 116	2^1 2^{hd} 2^{hd} 1^{hd}	MelendzJD^7	ⒻAw16000	85-20	MissOtani,PleaseReply,NeedlesLdy	7
13Sep86-8Med	6f	:22^4 :46^3 1:11^{1}ft	20 116	7$^{1\frac34}$ 7$^{4\frac12}$ 7$^{6\frac12}$ 7$^{13\frac14}$	Rocco J^4	ⒻAw16000	73-20	ThirdMrrig,SoclEnggmnt,AnnWngs	7
31Mar86-6Aqu	6f	:23^1 :47^1 1:12^{1}ft	26 112^5	6^3 6^4 8^7 9$^{9\frac14}$	DecarloCP^3	ⒻAw25000	71-20	Mintly, Faster Than Fast, Pondero	9

Jan 12 Bel tr.t 4f ft :47^4 h Dec 24 Bel tr.t 4f ft :48 h ●Dec 14 Bel tr.t 4f ft :47^4 h Nov 29 Bel tr.t 4f ft :48 h

After performing the necessary calculations for PCR lines and last race abilty times, we can now construct our worksheet for the race itself, which looks like this:

Odds	Horse	PCR	Form	Ab/T
3	Dame De Trefle	66/15 17 + 12/44 = 150	N+w	46.2 25.2 + 1/ 72.0
7	Miss Scandal	68/19 37 − 16/40 = 170	++N	46.0 25.3 + 1/ 71.4
15	Doonesday	67/32 35 + 10/77 = 87	NON	47.0 27.2 0/ 74.2
2	Peace Keeper	60/17 29 − 11/35 = 171	L/w	(45.3 25.3 − 1/ 71.0)
6	Glady H	51/27 31 − 2/56 = 91	NON	47.4 24.4 + 1/ 72.4
7-2	Mother Maloney	68/53 35 − 5/83 = 82	00N	47.1 24.2 + 5/ 72.3
7	Miss Otani	58/33 35 − 3/65 = 89	NON	46.3 26.3 − 1/ 73.0

Our major concern begins with the favorite, Peace Keeper, at the top of the PCR ratings, one inconsequential point ahead of Miss Scandal, but off a layoff. Any time you see a horse coming off a layoff to become the favorite, you must take care, because somebody out there believes this horse is ready to run up to full expectations today. We have inserted the notation after the L as a small "w", which stands for the requisite workout. If the workout had any exceptional characteristics, we might insert an exclamation point for one of those burners at 58 or 59 and change, if that occurred. Then we would fully integrate a workout like that into our handicapping.

Ordinarily, a horse off a layoff would rarely, if ever, qualify as a single selection play. However, if its PCR were far above that of any other horse and if it had spectacular workouts, we would take a different view.

What concerns us even more about Peace Keeper is what else we find as we look down her past performances. When a horse's last race ability time cannot be used, such as off a layoff or on one of those occasions where the last race could not in any way be a fair presentation of the horse's form, we must look for advisory times. Ranging down the lines, we need to know how well a horse can do under other conditions, and accordingly, usually look for the best race we can find.

These advisory ability times then become extremely useful. If a horse's reasonably best race down the line turns in a figure that is not competitive in today's field, an elimination is one of the safest handicapping decisions you can make. On the other end, if the horse really stands out above the field, and has the required workouts, he must be considered a substantial factor in today's race. Middle ground, too, is helpful, because if a recorded time is somewhere in the middle of those in today's field, the layoff horse is not a solid prospect, even though he may sometimes surprise you.

When we look at the race of Dec. 1, 1985, which appears to be about her best, even though farther back in her record than we would like to go, we can run a 71.0 ability time. This is far better than what any of the others in today's race are able to show. Now you can see why this horse is a 2-1 favorite in this field.

But we can readily find another strong play, and at good odds, too. Miss Scandal, with a comparatively equal PCR, two strong plus form factors, and the best last race ability time in the field, should attract your attention immediately. This filly is also a strong early runner, as is Peace Keeper.

The third best PCR comes with Dame De Trefle, who won her last race, and has a strong ability time of 72.0, one tick behind Miss Scandal. She, too, cannot be lightly dismissed.

But the others can. Reading the whole handicapping lines enables us to see quickly that this is indeed a three-horse race. All the others are substantially lower in PCRs. All of them have form defects. Not one of them is close to any of the three major contenders in ability times. Mother Maloney, the third favorite, is three full ticks behind Dame De Trefle and with a high second call total, has virtually no chance whatever. The 7-2 odds indicated there was a lot of money on that horse; readers of this book at least will know not to throw away their dollars on such dubious propositions.

Can we find a single selection play? Miss Scandal comes close, but Peace Keeper is too threatening. Dame De Trefle is not out of it, either, but her last race win is a slight impairment. But Miss Scandal, with her plus for recency, is the stronger of the two. Those rather surprisingly good odds make Miss Scandal a required play, along with Peace Keeper, both to win.

We also have an outstanding exacta possibility here, since Miss Scandal as a key horse has those high odds that we require for a regular exacta play. We can play her and Peace Keeper to win, both of them for second, and protect ourselves with Dame De Trefle for second. These horses are so much better than the others, with advantages sticking out all over, that we consider this a very safe play. In addition, it costs no more than $8 base. In New York, there is a quinella also, on which we would have to spend $6 to cover all three horses. Because we know that the payoff is likely to be one-half of the exacta payoff or less, and we have to spend $6 as compared to $8, this is not a sound use of our money. Forget the quinella, and lay it on in the powerful exacta play.

And what a lovely result it was!

SECOND RACE — 6 FURLONGS.(InnerDirt). (1.08%) CLAIMING. Purse $21,000. Fillies and Mares, 4-year-olds and upward. Weight, 122 lbs. Non-winners of two races since December 15 allowed 3 lbs. Of a race since then, 5 lbs. Claiming price $50,000; for each $2,500 to $45,000 allowed 2 lbs. (Races when entered to be claimed for $40,000 or less not considered.)

Aqueduct
JANUARY 21, 1987

Value of race $21,000; value to winner $12,600; second $4,620; third $2,520; fourth $1,260. Mutuel pool $58,579, OTB pool $118,460. Ex Pl $79,897; OTB Pl $136,636. Quin Pl $44,347; OTB Pl $94,178

Last Raced	Horse	Eqt.A.Wt PP St	¼	½	Str	Fin	Jockey	Cl'g Pr	Odds $1
14Jan87 5Aqu3	Miss Scandal	4 115 5 2	4¹	3½	2½	1nk	Antley C W	45000	7.50
13Dec86 7Aqu9	Peace Keeper	6 117 3 4	1¹½	1hd	1hd	2¹½	Santos J At	50000	2.00
27Dec86 7Aqu7	Mother Maloney	6 112 6 3	6³½	4¹½	3³½	35¾	Nuesch D5	50000	3.70
5Jan87 5Aqu6	Doonesday	b 4 108 2 6	5hd	6³½	5¹½	42½	Heath M J7	47500	15.90
2Jan87 1Aqu6	Miss Otani	5 117 7 1	2¹	2¹½	4hd	5³	Samyn J L	50000	7.90
9Jan87 2Aqu1	Dame De Trefle	7 109 1 5	3hd	5hd	6³	6⁴	Baird E T5	45000	3.10
11Jan87 7Aqu3	Glady H.	b 4 117 4 7	7	7	7	7	Migliore Rt	50000	6.30

OFF AT 12:55, Start good, Won driving. Time, :22½, :45½, 1:11½ Track sloppy.

$2 Mutuel Prices:

6-(F)-MISS SCANDAL	17.00	7.60	3.80
4-(D)-PEACE KEEPER		3.60	2.60
7-(I)-MOTHER MALONEY			3.00

$2 EXACTA 6-4 PAID $58.40. $2 QUINELLA 4-6 PAID $25.40.

In the stretch, as you can see, it was our two power horses, head and head, even though Mother Maloney was closer than we thought she might be. Peace Keeper was out in front early, with Miss Scandal holding not too far off the pace. As they put daylight between them and the third place finisher, it was Miss Scandal winning by a neck, paying $17 up front and returning an exacta worth $58.40. No matter what else may occur, our profit for the day is now secure. The second race has also confirmed that early speed is doing quite well, and that will guide us through the remaining races, unless some kind of an abrupt change occurs.

How does the third race fit in with our requirements for playing or passing?

3rd Aqueduct

6 FURLONGS. (InnerDirt). (1.08⅘) MAIDEN CLAIMING. Purse $13,000. 3-year-olds. Weight, 122 lbs. Claiming price $50,000; for each $2,500 to $45,000 allowed 2 lbs.

Lead Man

B. c. 3, by Romantic Lead—Message Received, by Hoist the Flag
Br.—DiMauro S L (NY) 1986 0 M 0 0
Own.—DiMauro S Mrs 122 Tr.—DiMauro Stephen L $50,000
Lifetime 0 0 0 0
Jan 15 Bel tr.t 4f ft :48^3 hg Jan 10 Bel tr.t 5f ft 1:03 b Jan 5 Bel tr.t 5f ft 1:04^3 b Dec 27 Bel tr.t 4f ft :49^3 h

Time to G.

B. g. 3, by Shecky Greene—Sweetest Sound, by Elocutionist
Br.—Hawn W R & Heerman V Jr (Ky) 1987 1 M 0 0
Own.—Kelly W A Mrs 118 Tr.—Kemplon Gary $45,000 1986 0 M 0 0
Lifetime 1 0 0 0
4Jan87-4Aqu 6f [•]:23^1 :47^{4}1:12^{2}gd 4½ 122 6^4 8^8 8^{11} 7^{15}½ Graell A^1 M50000 66-21 Pershing Pach, Jumpski, Yucca 10
4Jan87—Broke slowly
Jan 14 Bel tr.t 4f ft :50 b Jan 1 Bel tr.t 4f ft :48^2 h Dec 27 Bel tr.t 5f ft 1:01^2 h Dec 22 Bel tr.t 5f ft 1:02 bg

Cucumber Picker

Ch. c. 3, by Big Kohinoor—Falling Ruth, by Three Kingdoms
Br.—Mishoe T Neil (SC) 1986 0 M 0 0
Own.—Wright Joanne 118 Tr.—Brida Dennis J $45,000
Lifetime 0 0 0 0
Jan 4 Bel tr.t 5f ft 1:06^4 b Dec 27 Bel tr.t 3f ft :36^3 h Dec 21 Bel tr.t 3f ft :38^1 bg Nov 25 Rkm 5f ft 1:05^4 h

Wise Try

Dk. b. or br. c. 3, by Tri Jet—Wise Duchess, by Bupers
Br.—Burnett R C (Fla) 1986 9 M 1 2 $10,780
Own.—Chevalier Stable 122 Tr.—Shapoff Stanley R $50,000
Lifetime 9 0 1 2 $10,780
26Dec86-5Aqu 6f [•]:22^3 :46^{2}1:11^{4}ft 2½ 118 3^{1}½ 5^5 7^{3}¼ 6^{9}½ Santagata N^4 M50000 75-14 LogicalStan,MenndCrfty,Jumpski 12
7Dec86-5Aqu 6f [•]:22^2 :45^{4}1:12^{2}ft 15 118 2^{hd} 2^2 4^2 5^{5}¾ Santagata N^7 Mdn 76-18 Nphrt,Coco'sDoubl,‡WrongDoctor 11
7Dec86—Placed fourth through disqualification; Steadied
26Oct86-2Aqu 7f :23 :46 1:24^{3}gd *2½ 118 2^{hd} 4^{2}½ 8^{14} 8^{13}¼ Maple E^2 M75000 65-16 Widdum, Slane Hill, Windy Sails 8
12Oct86-9Bel 6f :22^2 :46^1 1:11^{4}ft 5 118 5^7 3^{2}½ 2^4 3^6 Maple E^8 M75000 77-13 Getredyfortheshow,SlnHill,WisTry 11
15Sep86-4Bel 6f :22^3 :46 1:10^{2}ft 7 118 5^{6}½ 4^8 6^{11} 7^{17}½ Maple E^3 Mdn 72-15 Stacked Pack, ItsAcedemic,Yucca 12
6Sep86-5Bel 6f :22^2 :45^3 1:10^{2}gd 13 118 5^{4}½ 4^7 2^6 2^7 Martens G^7 Mdn 83-10 DmscusDrm,WisTry,IronDistncton 12
24Aug86-4Sar 5f :22 :46 :59 m 9 118 4^6 4^6 4^4 3^{2}½ Maple E^3 Mdn 88-13 Pleasure Key,ValidPursuit,WiseTry 9
10Aug86-4Sar 5f :22^2 :46^2 :59 ft 29 118 2^4 3^{2}½ 3^{1}½ 5^{3}½ Maple E^7 Mdn 87-14 GrandRol,CombatHero,PleasureKey 9
Jan 17 Bel tr.t 4f ft :49^4 h Jan 12 Bel tr.t 4f ft :49^3 h Jan 7 Bel tr.t 3f ft :36 h Dec 24 Bel tr.t 3f ft :37 h

Political Analyst

Dk. b. or br. c. 3, by Super Concorde—Stoshka, by Nashua
Br.—Moyglare Stud Farm Ltd (Ky) 1987 1 M 0 0
Own.—Haefner W J 118 Tr.—Nickersen Victor J $45,000 1986 0 M 0 0
Lifetime 1 0 0 0
10Jan87-4Aqu 6f [•]:22^3 :46^{2}1:11^{1}gd 12 122 1^1 2^{1}½ 10^{14} 10^{21}¾ Hernandez R^5 Mdn 66-10 PocktBook,I'mExbrnt,Gnom'sPlsr 10
Jan 4 Aqu [•] 5f ft 1:03^4 b Dec 30 Aqu [•] 3f ft :38^1 b ●Dec 26 Aqu [•] 3f ft :35^4 bg Dec 20 Aqu [•] 5f ft 1:02^4 b

Gallant Fayme

Ch. c. 3, by Play the Gallant—Nayme Fayme, by Imbros
Br.—Rosenthal Frances (NY) 1986 2 M 0 0
Own.—Rosenthal Deborah J 118 Tr.—DiAngelo Joseph T $45,000
Lifetime 2 0 0 0
29Dec86-3Aqu 6f [•]:22^2 :46 1:11^{3}ft 97 118 7^{9}½ 8^{13} 8^{12} 7^{13}¾ Martens G^9 M50000 72-18 B. G.'sTuffy,EbonyRig,Triumvirate 10
28Nov86-6Aqu 1 :46^4 1:12 1:37^{3}ft 62 118 12^{7}½ 11^{12} 11^{18} 11^{25}¼ DeCarlo C P^{11} [S]Mdn 53-18 HudsonNews,OmrKhyym,Tin'sDwn 13
Jan 13 Bel tr.t 4f ft :50^2 b Jan 5 Bel tr.t 4f ft :52^3 b Dec 24 Bel tr.t 3f ft :39 b Dec 15 Bel tr.t 3f ft :39 b

Ride the Rapids

Ch. c. 3, by Red Ryder—Landing Lady, by Irongate
Br.—Singer Craig (Ky) 1986 2 M 0 0
Own.—Singer C B 113^5 Tr.—Tesher Howard M $45,000
Lifetime 2 0 0 0
29Dec86-3Aqu 6f [•]:22^2 :46 1:11^{3}ft 7¾ 114 8^{11} 7^{12} 7^{12} 8^{14} Antley C W^3 M45000 72-18 B. G.'sTuffy,EbonyRig,Triumvirate 10
13Nov86-9Aqu 6f :23^1 :48^1 1:14^{2}gd 4½ 118 3^4 4^{4}½ 4^{3}¾ 5^{3}¾ Santos J A^6 M35000 65-20 Reprocessed, Be a Star,MatzoBrei 10
●Jan 15 Aqu [•] 5f ft 1:00^2 h ●Jan 6 Aqu [•] 3f ft :38 b Dec 15 Aqu [•] 5f ft 1:03 b Dec 6 Aqu [•] 4f ft :49^2 h

Gahairos
B. c. 3, by Ga Hai—Forrest Rose, by Presented
Br.—Alexander Jo Ann D (Pa) 1986 1 M 0 0
Own.—Wemmar J P 1135 Tr.—Smith David $45,000
Lifetime 1 0 0 0
28Nov86-3Med 6f :23 :471 1:131ft 30 1135 8 9½ 9 13 10 14 10 14¼ Murray K C7 M20000 62-21 BrodwySnrs,OrgnlWrk,PrncfNght 12
Jan 14 Aqu [box] 4f ft :531 b Jan 5 Aqu [box] 4f ft :53 b

Winter Freeze
Ro. g. 3, by Arts And Letters—Ice Bird, by Nearctic
Br.—Sea Spray Farms (Fla) 1986 1 M 0 0
Own.—Sea Spray Farms 11210 Tr.—DeBonis Thomas A $50,000
Lifetime 1 0 0 0
18Dec86-4Aqu 6f [box]:223 :47 1:141sy 30 108 10 10 10 11 9 14 7 14 7 10½ O'Hara K A3 M35000 62-21 GoldnMjsty,SpctclrComt,TTghtBt 12
Jan 15 Bel tr.t 3f ft :36 h Jan 10 Bel tr.t 3f ft :373 b Jan 5 Bel tr.t 5f ft 1:023 b Dec 13 Bel tr.t 4f ft :493 h

Casual Physician
Gr. c. 3, by The Cool Virginian—Gun Cotton, by Hagley
Br.—Church Melville III (Va) 1986 3 M 0 0 $480
Own.—Chuckolow Stable 118 Tr.—Galimi P $45,000
Lifetime 3 0 0 0 $480
6Dec86-1Med 6f :23 :471 1:132ft *1 116 6 4¾ 5 4½ 6 8 7 11 Edwards JW5 Mc15000 64-17 FickleWings,SwiftDcision,Mr.Sdir 11
28Nov86-3Med 6f :23 :471 1:131ft 7e118 6 4¼ 5 3½ 5 4 4 4¾ Edwards J W8 M20000 71-21 BrodwySnrs,OrgnlWrk,PrncfNght 12
13Nov86-4Med 6f :233 :481 1:134ft 11 115 10 8¼ 11 17 12 16 12 22 Edwards J W6 M30000 51-25 SuprBumbl,GoHwk,DiplomtcCorps 12
●Jan 8 Aqu [box] 3f ft :361 h Jan 2 Aqu [box] 3f sy :382 b (d) Dec 28 Aqu [box] 6f ft 1:162 hg

Perkins Landing
B. c. 3, by Transworld—Secorissa, by Secretariat
Br.—W. S. Farrish, III&E.J.Hudson (Ky) 1986 0 M 0 0
Own.—Lance R 1135 Tr.—DeStasio Richard T $45,000
Lifetime 0 0 0 0
Jan 15 Bel tr.t 5f ft 1:023 h Jan 12 Bel tr.t 3f ft :36 h Jan 5 Bel tr.t 4f ft :494 b Dec 17 Bel tr.t 4f ft :50 b

There obviously isn't enough here to make handicapping lines, except for one horse, Wise Try, who shows defective form. Maiden claiming races for lightly raced three-year-olds early in the season are notoriously unpredictable. There is nothing there to inspire a bet in anyone. The race must be passed. But it also must be observed, as every race should be, if for no other reason to keep our required watch on the response of the track surface. Therefore, here is the result chart.

THIRD RACE
Aqueduct
JANUARY 21, 1987

6 FURLONGS.(InnerDirt). (1.08⅘) MAIDEN CLAIMING. Purse $13,000. 3-year-olds. Weight, 122 lbs. Claiming price $50,000; for each $2,500 to $45,000 allowed 2 lbs.

Value of race $13,000; value to winner $7,800; second $2,860; third $1,560; fourth $780. Mutuel pool $68,657, OTB pool $99,379. Exacta Pool $141,876. OTB Ex Pool $178,180.

Last Raced	Horse	Eqt.	A.	Wt	PP	St	¼	½	Str	Fin	Jockey	Cl'g Pr	Odds $1
26Dec86 5Aqu6	Wise Try	b	3	122	11	1	3 1½	2 hd	1 ½	1 2½	Santagata N	50000	3.20
10Jan87 4Aqu10	Political Analyst		3	118	4	8	1 1	1 ½	2 7	2 6	Hernandez R	45000	5.30
	Lead Man		3	122	1	11	6 hd	5 2	4 2	3 nk	Migliore R	50000	10.30
6Dec86 1Med7	Casual Physician		3	118	9	2	5 2½	4 2½	3 hd	4 5	McCauley W H	45000	18.00
29Dec86 3Aqu8	Ride the Rapids	b	3	113	6	5	8 hd	7 1½	6 1½	5 ¾	Baird E T5	45000	5.90
18Dec86 4Aqu7	Winter Freeze		3	115	8	7	10 4	10 8	7 5	6 4¾	O'Hara K A†7	50000	40.10
4Jan87 4Aqu7	Time to G.	b	3	118	2	9	2 ½	3 5	5 2	7 2¾	Graell A	45000	6.50
	Cucumber Picker		3	118	3	10	9 5	9 ½	9 6	8 1	Marquez C HJr	45000	25.20
29Dec86 3Aqu7	Gallant Fayme		3	118	5	4	7 ½	8 hd	8 hd	9 6½	Martens G	45000	46.00
28Nov86 3Med10	Gahairos	b	3	113	7	6	11	11	10 hd	10 5½	Badamo J J5	45000	98.90
	Perkins Landing		3	113	10	3	4 3½	6 hd	11	11	Nuesch D5	45000	2.30

OFF AT 1:25 Start good, Won driving. Time, :22⅕, :46⅗, 1:12⅕ Track sloppy.

$2 Mutuel Prices:			
12-(Q)-WISE TRY	8.40	4.40	3.40
4-(E)-POLITICAL ANALYST		6.20	5.20
1-(A)-LEAD MAN			8.00

$2 EXACTA 12-4 PAID $53.00.

Wise Try, the one horse we could have rated, won the race in this nondescript field. After watching the race, noting that the horse was running forwardly throughout, I would then go back to compare internal numbers merely to check whether an early speed running style was still prevailing. We find a total of 29 for the second call position as compared to 39 for the finish, and this is good enough.

The fourth race is for state bred three year olds and we again find the frequent early season story of a flock of first time starters. Is there any way to find a play in this race?

4th Aqueduct

6 FURLONGS. (InnerDirt). (1.08⅘) MAIDEN SPECIAL WEIGHT. Purse $24,000. Fillies, 3-year-olds foaled in New York State and approved by the New York State-bred registry. Weight, 121 lbs.

Coupled—Our Chantei and Restless Gem.

Ms. Jacques

Gr. f. 3, by Jacques Who—Ruling All, by One for All
Br.—Milfer Farm, Inc. (N.Y.)   1986 0 M 0 0.
Own.—Valley Trio Stable   **116**⁵   Tr.—Barbara Robert
Lifetime   0 0 0 0
Dec 28 Bel tr.t 5f ft 1:03⁴ b   Dec 21 Bel tr.t 5f ft 1:03³ b   Nov 23 Bel tr.t 5f ft 1:07 b

Sweetish

Ch. f. 3, by Sir Wimborne—Swift Sweetheart, by Fast Hilarious
Br.—Fairview Farms (NY)   1986 0 M 0 0
Own.—Davidson P   **121**   Tr.—Dunham Bob G
Lifetime   0 0 0 0
Jan 10 Aqu ⊡ 6f ft 1:19 b   Jan 5 Aqu ⊡ 5f ft 1:05² b   Dec 29 Aqu ⊡ 5f ft 1:05³ b   Dec 24 Aqu ⊡ 5f ft 1:05² b

Our Chantei

B. f. 3, by Affiliate—Jo Pe Blue, by Blue Times
Br.—Case Rosemarie (NY)   1987 0 M 0 0
Own.—Hawk Crest Farms   **121**   Tr.—DiAngelo Joseph T   1986 0 M 0 0
Lifetime   0 0 0 0
Jan 17 Bel tr.t 4f ft :50² b   Jan 5 Bel tr.t 5f ft 1:01 hg   Dec 29 Bel tr.t 5f ft 1:02 hg   Dec 20 Bel tr.t 5f m 1:04 b

Francis Manor

Dk. b. or br. f. 3, by Stone Manor—Francis Fair, by Bagdad
Br.—Panorama Farms (NY)   1986 0 M 0 0
Own.—Rosbeck P   **116**⁵   Tr.—Lenzini John J Jr
Lifetime   0 0 0 0
Jan 17 Aqu ⊡ 4f ft :49³ b   Jan 12 Aqu ⊡ 4f ft :49 hg   Jan 6 Aqu ⊡ 4f ft :51 b   Dec 30 Aqu ⊡ 3f ft :37¹ b

I Got A Rumbleseat

Ch. f. 3, by Octavo—I'm Katie, by Spring Double
Br.—Edwards J F (NY)   1987 1 M 0 0
Own.—Old Westbury Farm   **116**⁵   Tr.—Imperio Dominick A   1986 0 M 0 0
Lifetime   1 0 0 0
4Jan87-5Aqu 6f ⊡:23² :48 1:13³gd 16 116⁵ 42 64½ 58 67¾   Baird E T⁸   Ⓕ⒮Mdn 68-21 Peggy'sDrem,Creekr'sGl,Joyr'sZus 10
Dec 6 Bel tr.t 5f ft 1:01 hg   Nov 26 Bel tr.t 4f gd :51 b

Lady Talc

B. f. 3, by Talc—Mardie's Fling, by Barachois
Br.—Pinebourne Farm (N.Y.)   1986 2 M 0 0
Own.—Pinebourne Farm   **121**   Tr.—Campo John P
Lifetime   2 0 0 0
7Nov86-9Aqu 6f :22⁴ :47 1:13²ft 24 117 3½ 41½109 119½   Terry J⁴   Ⓕ⒮Mdn 64-21 BookOfJoy,ArctcHldy,Twlv'clcktls 12
6Oct86-5Bel 7f :23⁴ :48 1:27²ft 6⅞e117 -3½ 32½102²10²9½ Terry J⁵   Ⓕ⒮Mdn 35-24 LondonPass,MissEmpire,GucciGal 12
Jan 18 Bel tr.t 6f ft 1:18⁴ b   Jan 14 Bel tr.t 4f ft :49 hg   Jan 10 Bel tr.t 6f ft 1:18 b   Jan 4 Bel tr.t 5f ft 1:04³ b

Restless Gem — Ch. f. 3, by Restless Restless—Silver Sash, by Craigwood
Own.—Muro R — 1165 — Br.—Big Apple Farms Inc (NY) — 1986 3 M 0 1 $2,880
Tr.—DiAngelo Joseph T
Lifetime 3 0 0 1 $2,880

18Dec86-6Aqu 6f ⊡:232 :4741:133sy 4½ 117 2hd 21½ 81311193/4 Santagata N7 ⒻⓈMdn 57-21 HllyHlllujh,KnDnc,Twlvo'clocktils 12
28Nov86-9Aqu 6f :222 :461 1:113ft 38 117 11½ 2hd 23 38½ Santagata N8 ⒻⓈMdn 74-18 Forlionjuli,HlleyHllelujh,RestlssGm 9
22Nov86-3Aqu 6f :222 :463 1:124ft 24e113 62½126 12151220½ SantagataN7 ⒻM45000 56-18 CzrTrek,GotTheGreenlight.HlfScrt 12
Jan 18 Bel tr.t 4f ft :512 b   Jan 12 Bel tr.t 4f ft :493 b   Jan 5 Bel tr.t 4f ft :493 h   Dec 14 Bel tr.t 5f ft 1:024 h

Sadie Ain't No Lady — B. f. 3, by Weth Nan—Star of Stage, by Sound Stage
Own.—Star Track Farms — 121 — Br.—Star Track Farms (NY) — 1987 0 M 0 0
Tr.—Lambert James — 1986 0 M 0 0
Lifetime 0 0 0 0
Jan 16 Bel tr.t 4f ft :521 b   Jan 7 Bel tr.t 6f ft 1:192 b   Dec 28 Bel tr.t 6f ft 1:163 b   Dec 23 Bel tr.t 6f ft 1:20 b

Fleeting Minim — Ch. f. 3, by Spartan Emperor—Fleeting Second, by Timeless Moment
Own.—Katavolos C — 121 — Br.—Katavolos C (NY) — 1987 0 M 0 0
Tr.—Alaimo R — 1986 0 M 0 0
Lifetime 0 0 0 0
Jan 16 Aqu ⊡ 6f ft 1:171 b   Dec 26 Aqu ⊡ 5f ft 1:032 b   Dec 22 Aqu ⊡ 4f ft :522 bg   Dec 16 Aqu ⊡ 4f ft :524 b

Seymour's Seymone — B. f. 3, by Spruce Needles—Charming Ruthie, by Grey Legion
Own.—Kravet Ruth — 121 — Br.—Kravet Ruth (NY) — 1986 1 M 1 0 $1,826
Tr.—Lake Robert P
Lifetime 1 0 1 0 $1,826
31Aug86-4FL 5½f :232 :481 1:073ft *6-5e117 11½ 11½ 1hd 2nk Cruz C3 ⓈMdn 78-17 Mr.TrtlIn,Symr'sSymn,It'sNtSEsy 10
Jan 15 Aqu ⊡ 6f ft 1:154 b   Jan 10 Aqu ⊡ 5f ft 1:021 h   Jan 5 Aqu ⊡ 6f ft 1:182 bg   Dec 29 Aqu ⊡ 4f ft :49 b

There even isn't very much to say. Pass. Again, however, we must watch the race and on paper here, we look at the result chart. We note speed indeed, an easy wire to wire victory for the third favorite, Ms. Jacques, whose workouts were even somewhat less than mediocre. We do not need to indulge in guessing games in races like this.

FOURTH RACE Aqueduct JANUARY 21, 1987 — 6 FURLONGS.(InnerDirt). (1.08⅘) MAIDEN SPECIAL WEIGHT. Purse $24,000. Fillies, 3-year-olds foaled in New York State and approved by the New York State-bred registry. Weight, 121 lbs.

Value of race $24,000; value to winner $14,400; second $5,280; third $2,880; fourth $1,440. Mutuel pool $67,429, OTB pool $87,021. Ex $88,821. OTB Ex $103,064. Quin $42,476. OTB Quin $73,584.

Last Raced	Horse	Eqt.	A.	Wt	PP	St	¼	½	Str	Fin	Jockey	Odds $1
	Ms. Jacques		3	116	1	6	12	13	16	12	Baird E T5	4.10
	Francis Manor		3	116	4	1	43	43½	25	210½	Ortiz E Jr5	6.20
18Dec86 6Aqu11	Restless Gem	b	3	116	7	4	5hd	63	42	31	Belmonte J F5	a-2.20
4Jan87 5Aqu6	I Got A Rumbleseat		3	116	5	5	21	21½	31½	4hd	Nuesch D5	7.10
	Our Chantei	b	3	121	3	3	71	71½	51½	5hd	Davis R G	a-2.20
7Nov86 9Aqu11	Lady Talc		3	121	6	7	93	93½	6hd	62¼	Lovato F Jr	16.70
	Sweetish		3	121	2	8	81½	81	83½	72¼	Venezia M	13.60
	Sadie Ain't No Lady		3	121	9	10	10	10	92	82¼	McCauley W H	44.50
31Aug86 4FL2	Seymour's Seymone	b	3	121	8	2	32½	31½	7hd	93¾	Antley C W	2.50
	Fleeting Minim		3	121	10	9	63½	5hd	10	10	Santagata N	52.70

a-Coupled: Restless Gem and Our Chantel.

OFF AT 1:51 Start good for all but SADIE AINT NO LADY, Won handily. Time, :22⅖, :46⅖, 1:12⅗ Track sloppy.

$2 Mutuel Prices:

2-(A)-MS. JACQUES	10.20	6.60	3.60
5-(G)-FRANCIS MANOR		6.00	3.20
1-(K)-RESTLESS GEM (a-entry)			2.60

$2 EXACTA 2-5 PAID $85.20. $2 QUINELLA 2-5 PAID $45.80.

Now, we're into the fifth race, a standard sort, where we would expect to find some kind of play, based upon our program for Total Victory.

5th Aqueduct

6 FURLONGS. (InnerDirt). (1.08⅘) CLAIMING. Purse $21,000. 4-year-olds and upward. Weight, 122 lbs. Non-winners of two races since December 15 allowed 3 lbs. Of a race since then, 5 lbs. Claiming price $50,000; for each $2,500 to $45,000 allowed 2 lbs. (Races when entered to be claimed for $40,000 or less not considered.)

Coupled—Proud And Tall and Mr. Meeka; Wandering Feet and Daring.

Aswan High

Ch. h. 5, by Upper Nile—Laraka, by Impressive
Br.—Worswick R J (Ky)
Own.—Pascuma M J   117   Tr.—Pascuma William J $50,000

							1987	2 0 0 0	$1,500
							1986	18 4 6 0	$99,320
						Lifetime	38 6 9 2	$134,520	

14Jan87-7Aqu 6f ⊡:213 :4421:093ft 4½ 1075 32½ 22 32½ 54½ Nuesch D2 75000 91-16 PrisVntur,ShinDulus,LordOfThNght 8
4Jan87-7Aqu 6f ⊡:222 :4611:103ft 7½ 117 53 44 43½ 42½ Murphy D J4 75000 88-21 PrisVenture,MjesticEmpir,CoolJo 10
12Dec86-8Aqu 6f ⊡:222 :45 1:101m 6 1087 33 55½ 57½ 57 Nuesch D5 Aw40000 86-16 Rj'sRvng,Rxson'sBshop,RnnngBold 5
3Dec86-7Aqu 6f ⊡:224 :4521:092gd 9 122 42 43½ 59 711½ Murphy D J6 Aw40000 85-11 ScrtPrspctr,UpPpsAwnnr,Rj'sRvng 7
14Nov86-9Med 6f :222 :451 1:092ft *7-5 117 1hd 1½ 1hd 21½ Murphy D J5 Aw18000 93-12 RnnngBold,AswnHgh,GrndHorzon's 7
4Nov86-6Aqu 6f :222 :452 1:09 ft 2½ 1157 42½ 31 43 57½ Nuesch D4 Aw36000 88-22 SunMster,Rj'sReveng,NwConnction 6
22Oct86-6Aqu 6f :22 :443 1:092ft 6 115 31½ 1hd 12½ 12½ Murphy D J5 Aw36000 94-16 AswnHigh,TonkPss,CleverAllemont 8
17Oct86-2Bel 6f :223 :452 1:092ft 7½ 117 1hd 1½ 1½ 2½ Murphy D J5 75000 94-14 PssingThundr,AswnHigh,SidiBouSd 7
Jan 11 Bel tr.t 5f sy 1:05 b   Dec 30 Bel tr.t 6f ft 1:161 b   Dec 24 Bel tr.t 4f ft :492 h   ●Dec 10 Bel tr.t 3f sy :36 b

Sports Medicine

Dk. b. or br. g. 5, by Hard Work—Bow My Dear, by Knightly Manner
Br.—Oakland Farm Partnership (Ky)
Own.—Bauer R J   113   Tr.—Dutrow Richard E $45,000

							1987	1 0 1 0	$4,620
							1986	29 10 5 2	$53,840
						Lifetime	29 10 5 2	$114,173	Turf 1 0 0 0

10Jan87-3Aqu 6f ⊡:222 :4531:101gd 7½ 113 54½ 53 53¾ 22½ Santos J A5 45000 91-10 Tis Royal, Sports Medicine,Semaj 11
19Dec86-1Aqu 6f ⊡:224 :4631:111m *1 1095 32 32 32 44½ Baird E T6 45000 83-20 Don'tHesitate,HarryL.,FatherRolnd 6
10Dec86-1Aqu 6f ⊡:222 :4541:102m 2½ 1145 37 32 2hd 13¾ Baird E T2 35000 92-13 SportsMedicine,GlintChief,GrnShkl 5
29Nov86-2Aqu 6f :22 :452 1:102ft *4 116 107 66½ 4½ 1no Cordero A Jr11 30000 89-20 SportsMdcn,Scott'sNtv,FinkyHom 13
16Nov86-1Aqu 6f :224 :464 1:113ft 10 117 73½ 82½ 1hd 14 Cordero A Jr2 25000 83-23 SportsMdicin,NorthGld,DrngGroom 8
26Sep86-2Bel 6f :223 :454 1:10 m 5½e113 66½ 64 10111011½ Samyn J L6 c30000 81-19 FlyingSkipper,Charismo,UpperStr 10
11Apr86-2Aqu 1 :453 1:103 1:354ft 3½e117 65½ 68½ 614 717½ Davis R G5 50000 70-27 Boutinierr,GoldnImmigrnt,CpBdgtt 9
6Apr86-6Aqu 7f :224 :453 1:222m 11 113 108 9111106¾108½ Vasquez J5 70000 81-20 Sidi Bou Said, IrishOre,TalcPower 10
●Jan 4 Aqu ⊡ 4f ft :502 b

Engine Chief

B. h. 5, by Satan's Chief—Lady Of The Trees, by Timberlane
Br.—Eissell Jr & Gurkas (NJ)
Own.—Edjys T   117   Tr.—Coletti Edward J $50,000

							1986	6 0 1 1	$5,750
							1985	10 3 2 1	$40,075
						Lifetime	16 3 3 2	$45,825	Turf 1 0 0 1	$1,650

17Dec86-5Pha 6f :221 :451 1:11 ft 10 116 32½ 34 46 68½ Vigliotti M J4 Aw12500 78-20 Danny'sKeys,Trindrus,MickeyBndit 7
25Apr86-8GS 1 :464 1:113 1:374ft 7 112 11 65½ 79½ 711 Wilson R2 ⑤HcpO 75-25 First Sir, Nicajof R., Hi Ideal 9
9Apr86-8GS 6f :222 :454 1:113ft 3 112 14 12½ 1hd 21½ Wilson R7 ⑤HcpO 82-26 Misty Mac, EngineChief,AhSoTony 7
29Mar86-6GS 6f :221 :451 1:11 ft 3½ 116 2hd 3½ 56 59½ Wilson R1 Aw12500 78-20 Gettus Luck, Hiccups, SafeCracker 7
12Mar86-8GS 6f :221 :461 1:121ft 4½ 115 814 65½ 61¾ 31½ Wilson R6 Aw12500 80-29 SunshnPrnc,WntrtmSport,EngnChf 8
12Mar86—Stumbled gate
22Jan86-6Pha 6f¼ :214 :45 1:111ft 4 115 5½ 43½ 69½ 712 Wilson R7 Aw12500 73-21 HemJcMc,ScrdMotion,EmbssyRing 7
20Dec85-6Med 6f :214 :442 1:09 ft ○○ 12 117 41½ 41½ 45 66½ Ferrer J C6 Aw16000 90-06 Irish Ore, Wind Flyer, ARealBuster 7
6Dec85-7Med 6f :222 :454 1:10 ft 2½ 117 42½ 73¾ 75½ 610 Rocco J4 Aw16000 82-15 Hildel,ScredMotion,WintrtmSport 8
Jan 17 Pha 4f ft :50 b   ●Jan 10 Pha 5f gd 1:01 b   Jan 4 Pha 5f ft 1:003 b   Dec 28 Pha 5f ft 1:023 b

Spiderman
Own.—Silvia J **117**

Dk. b. or br. g. 4, by Sir Jinsky—Robber Countess, by No Robbery
Br.—Maraspin L E (NJ) 1987 1 0 0 0
Tr.—Stoklosa Richard $50,000 1986 13 1 0 2 $29,882
Lifetime 23 5 1 4 $91,832 Turf 3 0 0 1 $2,772

1Jan87-6Pha	6f	$:22^1$ $:45^1$ $1:10^3$ft	$9\frac12$	117	$7^{7\frac14}$	7^{12}	7^{19}	—	Lloyd J S^1	Aw15000	— —	SunnyCbin,Dnny'sKeys,JustTerrific	7
1Jan87—Eased													
17Dec86-8Pha	6f	$:22^4$ $:45^4$ $1:10^2$ft	14	117	5^3	$6^{5\frac34}$	$7^{8\frac12}$	$7^{5\frac34}$	Vigliotti M J^5	Aw15000	83-20	LittleBoldJohn,Diapason,HemJcMc	8
29Nov86-8Med	6f	$:22^3$ $:46$ $1:10^4$ft	$8\frac12$	113	7^{11}	$6^{7\frac12}$	$6^{7\frac12}$	$6^{6\frac12}$	SosnsS^3 Rushing Man		81-23	RunningBold,KeyToTheFlg,Huckstr	7
15Nov86-8Med	6f	$:22$ $:44^4$ $1:10^1$ft	19	113	$8^{8\frac12}$	8^5	4^3	1^{hd}	SosonsS^7 Star Gallant		91-13	Spidermn,Thundercrckr,Kryzzchzkk	9
29Oct86-8Med	6f	$:22^1$ $:45^1$ $1:11$ ft	12	115	$9^{8\frac34}$	9^{12}	7^8	$4^{1\frac14}$	Sousonis S^6	40000	86-21	EverAStar,Lumumba,BoogieTheBer	9
7Oct86-8Pha	1	$:47^2$ $1:11^2$ $1:37^2$ft	5	119	6^3	6^{16}	6^{18}	$6^{23\frac14}$	Sousonis S^1	HcpO	64-20	FirePlug,Donneybrook,ClridgeDrive	6
25Sep86-9Med	1^{70}	$:46$ $1:11^1$ $1:41^4$ft	13	111	$8^{7\frac34}$	8^5	8^6	$8^{7\frac14}$	Sousonis S^7	[S]HcpO	80-21	AmericanDibolo,AhSoTony,HiIdel	10
13Sep86-9Med	$1\frac{1}{16}$	Ⓣ$:47^4$ $1:11^4$ $1:41^2$fm	$8\frac12$	115	$1^{\frac12}$	2^{hd}	4^3	$6^{11\frac14}$	EdrdsJW^2 ThndrPuddl		84-07	DoublFint,DncCrdFlld,NudstColony	6

Jan 17 GS 5f ft 1:03^1 b **Jan 13 Pha 3f ft :38^3 b**

Overbought
Own.—Scatuirchio J T **113**

B. g. 5, by Upper Nile—Drop of a Hat, by Midsummer Night
Br.—Hill & Kuster Mr–Mrs T (Ky) 1987 1 0 0 0
Tr.—Forbes John H $45,000 1986 2 1 0 0 $8,700
Lifetime 11 4 1 1 $37,620

10Jan87-3Aqu	6f	[•]$:22^2$ $:45^3$ $1:10^1$gd	$9\frac12$e	112^5	$7^{5\frac14}$	$10^{7\frac34}$	$10^{8\frac14}$	$9^{7\frac34}$	Belmonte J F^6	50000	85-10	Tis Royal, Sports Medicine,Semaj	11
22Nov86-7Med	6f	$:22^2$ $:45^3$ $1:11^3$ft	29	112	$6^{3\frac34}$	$7^{5\frac12}$	$4^{1\frac34}$	$1^{1\frac12}$	Krone J A^6	30000	84-20	Overbought,MjesticEmpire,GrnShkl	8
14Nov86-3Med	6f	$:22^3$ $:46$ $1:09^4$ft	7e	116	$4^{\frac34}$	$4^{\frac34}$	$7^{5\frac12}$	$7^{9\frac14}$	Verge M E^2	35000	84-12	MjstcEmpr,SlntHour,UpPopsThDvl	7
6Dec85-7Med	6f	$:22^2$ $:45^4$ $1:10$ ft	21	115	$8^{5\frac14}$	$8^{5\frac34}$	$8^{5\frac12}$	5^6	Verge M E^1	Aw16000	86-15	HiIdel,ScredMotion,WintrtimSport	8
8Nov85-8Med	6f	$:22^4$ $:45^4$ $1:10^1$ft	14	114	6^2	7^4	6^7	$6^{10\frac34}$	Verge M E^1	Aw17000	80-22	Silver Slate, It's Friesian, Dact Jr.	7
1Apr85-6GS	6f	$:22$ $:45^1$ $1:10^3$ft	$4\frac12$	118	6^5	$7^{5\frac34}$	$7^{4\frac14}$	$5^{6\frac14}$	Verge M E^4	HcpO	— —	Jay Bryan, Julie's Bet, Foligno	9
10Mar85-8Key	6f	$:22^3$ $:46$ $1:11^1$ft	$2\frac34$	117	2^1	$2^{2\frac14}$	1^1	1^3	VergME^5 [R]North Call		85-19	Overbought,SportsMedicin,BroStch	5
3Mar85-2Aqu	6f	[•]$:22^3$ $:46^4$ $1:12$ ft	$6\frac34$	117	3^1	$3^{1\frac12}$	3^2	$3^{1\frac34}$	Verge M E^8	50000	82-17	DeterminedRun,GayDte,Overbought	8

Jan 18 Bel tr.t 5f ft 1:02^1 h **Jan 7 Bel tr.t 5f ft 1:06 b** **Jan 1 Bel tr.t 5f ft 1:04 b** **Dec 28 Bel tr.t 4f ft :49^4 b**

Proud And Tall
Own.—Barrera O S **113**

Ch. c. 4, by Private Account—Deep Dish Pie, by George Lewis
Br.—Jones W L Jr P Farish W S (Ky) 1987 2 1 0 0 $7,800
Tr.—Barrera Oscar S $45,000 1986 23 4 3 2 $68,040
Lifetime 31 6 4 2 $83,660 Turf 2 0 0 0

16Jan87-2Aqu	6f	[•]$:23^1$ $:47^2$ $1:12^1$ft	$8\frac34$	117	8^5	$7^{6\frac14}$	$5^{2\frac34}$	1^{nk}	Murphy D J^7	c17500	83-18	ProudAndTll,Chrsmo,HowofWnloc	10
8Jan87-1Aqu	6f	[•]$:23^1$ $:47$ $1:12^2$ft	20	117	9^9	$9^{5\frac14}$	6^8	$6^{5\frac14}$	Murphy D J^9	17500	77-24	GoldenChief,Strtop,BetterBeSingl	10
31Dec86-2Aqu	$1\frac{3}{16}$	[•]$:47^1$ $1:12^2$ $1:57^2$ft	10	115	$2^{1\frac12}$	5^5	7^{15}	$7^{16\frac34}$	Vasquez M M^5	25000	74-13	ArcticSong,LedTheWy,OurTriumph	9
11Dec86-2Aqu	$1\frac18$	[•]$:48^2$ $1:13$ $1:51^3$ft	20	113	6^6	$10^{8\frac12}$	10^{16}	$10^{18\frac12}$	Vasquez M M^9	45000	65-16	Alioth, Addison Steele, Dalmatian	10
23Nov86-9Aqu	1	$:46^2$ $1:11$ $1:37^1$ft	10	113	$9^{6\frac34}$	8^{10}	7^8	7^9	Vasquez M M^5	45000	71-23	Sky Raider, Lord's Wish,LeVroom	11
9Nov86-3Aqu	$1\frac18$	$:48^1$ $1:12^1$ $1:52$ sy	*3-2	110^7	1^{hd}	1^{hd}	2^2	2no	Nuesch D^4	35000	75-22	Concatinate,ProudAndTll,FlyGryFly	6
20Oct86-5Bel	$1\frac18$	$:46^3$ $1:11^1$ $1:49^2$ft	29	114	3^2	$5^{6\frac12}$	7^{17}	7^{13}	Vasquez M M^5	Aw25000	67-16	WickedWike,Michel'sDncer,Hudcek	8
5Oct86-1Bel	$1\frac{1}{16}$	$:45^4$ $1:10^3$ $1:42^3$ft	$7\frac12$	113	$3^{1\frac12}$	2^1	$6^{7\frac14}$	6^9	Vasquez M M^4	45000	80-18	Michael'sDancer,BoldMruder,Aside	7

Dec 7 Bel tr.t 4f ft :49^3 b

Dale's Folly
Own.—Nagle Kerry **113**

Dk. b. or br. c. 4, by Key To The Mint—Before Bedtime, by Dr Fager
Br.—Taylor E P (Ont-C) 1987 1 0 0 0 $960
Tr.—Ferriola Peter $45,000 1986 18 1 4 3 $37,009
Lifetime 28 2 4 3 $48,949

15Jan87-4Aqu	6f	[•]$:22^2$ $:45^4$ $1:10^2$ft	14	117	6^5	5^3	5^6	4^6	Santagata N^4	c25000	86-19	UpperStar,SaltineWrrior,GoldCrop	11
15Jan87—Broke outward													
8Dec86-5Med	1^{70}	$:47^3$ $1:12^2$ $1:43$ ft	$3\frac14$	115	$2^{\frac12}$	2^{hd}	4^3	$6^{8\frac34}$	Santagata N^5	32000	72-22	MeanJimGreene,Drewster,SlyCindy	7
30Nov86-1Aqu	6f	$:22^3$ $:46^2$ $1:11^2$ft	17	117	$5^{3\frac12}$	$5^{3\frac14}$	5^3	4^3	Davis R G^2	35000	81-24	GallantChief,SwitchInTime,Onnagt	9
10Nov86-2Grd	$6\frac12$f	$:25$ $:49$ $1:21$ ft	8-5	122	$4^{2\frac12}$	$5^{1\frac34}$	$3^{\frac12}$	3^2	Driedger I^3	[S]Aw16500	79-26	Northrnconncton,BldPrsnc,Dl'sFlly	5
30Oct86-9Grd	$6\frac12$f	$:23^1$ $:47^1$ $1:20^3$ft	17	118	$6^{9\frac12}$	6^8	$4^{5\frac12}$	2^{hd}	Driedger I^7	Aw16500	83-28	Lovin Breeze,Dale'sFolly,Spearhead	8
10Oct86-8WO	7f	$:23^3$ $:47$ $1:25^3$ft	15	118	$7^{5\frac14}$	$6^{5\frac12}$	3^4	4^4	Driedger I^2	Aw16500	77-27	Gemsmart, LovinBreeze,NightFight	8
28Sep86-6WO	7f	$:23^2$ $:46^4$ $1:25^1$gd	15	118	$5^{4\frac14}$	3^3	$4^{1\frac12}$	$3^{2\frac12}$	Driedger I^1	[S]Aw16500	80-22	JudicilHumorst,BoldPrsnc,Dl'sFolly	7
14Sep86-7WO	$1\frac{1}{16}$	$:47^1$ $1:12^2$ $1:47$ ft	22	116	$3^{6\frac12}$	2^4	7^{13}	$9^{11\frac34}$	King R Jr^3	[S]Aw18200	62-23	SnipOfLuck,EsternKing,BoldPrsnc	9

Jan 14 Bel tr.t 3f ft :38 b **●Nov 23 Med 6f ft 1:15^2 h**

Flying Skipper

Dk. b. or br. h. 6, by Bold Skipper—Fly Bea Fly, by Cohoes
Own.—Cedar Valle Farm 117 Br.—Cohn S (NY) Tr.—Lenzini John J Jr $50,000
1986 19 4 2 3 $54,120
1985 15 0 1 1 $14,680
Lifetime 58 7 6 9 $194,793 Turf 8 0 0 1 $3,480

3Nov86-5Aqu 7f :222 :451 1:23 ft *2e117 21½ 54½ 98¼ 99¾ Murphy D J5 50000 76-22 HrryL.,StrkSecret,FrontierJustice 12
23Oct86-7Aqu 6f :22 :45 1:10 ft *2¼e113 64 44 24 2nk Romero R P4 45000 91-17 GreenShekl,FlyingSkippr,StrkScrt 10
11Oct86-1Bel 7f :223 :453 1:232ft *7-5e113 45¼ 42 54½ 55¾ Romero R P2 45000 79-19 Frontier Justice,StarkSecret,Semaj 7
11Oct86—Checked str.
26Sep86-2Bel 6f :223 :454 1:10 m 3½ 117 42 41½ 3½ 13 Romero R P3 35000 92-19 FlyingSkipper,Charismo,UpperStr 10
11Sep86-2Bel 1 :47 1:121 1:372ft 3 117 42 52½ 44 33¼ Murphy D J3 c25000 75-21 Will'sFirst,GoldnChif,FlyingSkippr 10
11Sep86—Steadied
4Sep86-2Bel 7f :23 :453 1:233ft *3-2 119 1hd 13 11 2hd Murphy D J4 25000 84-18 Koffkoff,FlyingSkipper,SixthofMay 7
13Aug86-9Sar 6f :221 :453 1:103ft 4¼ 117 32½ 2½ 11½ 13 Murphy D J5 22500 87-17 FlyingSkipper,SixthofMy,PledgCp 11
16Jly86-3Bel 7f :234 :464 1:232ft 7¼ 113 2½ 1½ 1hd 1½ Murphy D J2 20000 85-17 FlyingSkippr,SixthofMy,ArcticSong 7
●Jan 16 Aqu ⊡ 5f ft :593 h Jan 10 Aqu ⊡ 5f ft 1:03 b Jan 5 Aqu ⊡ 4f ft :482 h Dec 30 Aqu ⊡ 4f ft :491 b

Nasty And Tough

B. c. 4, by Nasty And Bold—I Love A Parade, by Hoist The Flag
Own.—Schwartz B K 117 Br.—Stonewall Farm (NY) Tr.—Schmitt William F $50,000
1987 1 0 0 0
1986 5 2 1 1 $62,776
Lifetime 10 3 1 1 $77,776

4Jan87-7Aqu 6f ⊡:222 :4611:103ft 25 117 85¾ 911 1020 1023¾ Samyn J L9 75000 67-21 PrisVenture,MjesticEmpir,CoolJo 10
26Apr86-8Aqu 1 :453 1:101 1:361ft 4e114 74¼ 53½ 43 37¼ VlsqzJ4 [S]Big Apple H 78-16 LndngPlot,I'mYorBy,NstyAndTgh 11
6Apr86-8Aqu 7f :23 :461 1:231m 6½e114 42 51¾ 22½ 24¼ LvtFJr4 [S]D Clinton H 81-20 Tnchn'sPrnc,NstyAndTogh,MdSyn 10
12Mar86-8Aqu 6f :23 :462 1:112ft 12 117 73 54 56 47¼ Lovato FJr2 [S]Catskill 77-26 SltinWrrior,Tinchn'sPrnc,BATyrnt 10
19Feb86-1Aqu 6f ⊡:221 :4541:103gd 5½ 117 55 65 44½ 33¾ Migliore R3 [S]Aw28000 87-13 ‡Tckr'sCbn,‡TrpclFrnt,NstyAndTgh 6
19Feb86—Placed first through disqualification
13Jan86-7Aqu 170⊡:49 1:1521:464ft 5e117 22½ 1hd 11 11½ LovatoFJr1 [S]Aw28000 66-27 NstyAndTough,MjorInvsion,JosHnk 9
29Nov85-9Aqu 6f :231 :464 1:113sy 26 118 1hd 2½ 1½ 11 Lovato F Jr1 [S]Mdn 83-22 NstyAndTogh,Tckr'sCbn,TllRomn 11
28Oct85-6Aqu 1 :482 1:142 1:41 ft 6½ 118 77½ 711 610 610 Santagata N3 [S]Mdn 51-26 HckoryCrk,KpngCompny,MjrInvsn 13
Dec 18 Bel tr.t 4f ft :50 b Nov 23 Bel tr.t 3f ft :371 b

Shear

Dk. b. or br. c. 4, by Private Account—Cracking, by Never Bend
Own.—Sommer Viola 115 Br.—Live Oak Stud (Fla) Tr.—Martin Frank $47,500
1987 1 0 0 0
1986 29 4 3 1 $77,740
Lifetime 30 4 3 1 $77,740 Turf 3 0 0 0 $1,500

8Jan87-8Aqu 6f ⊡:23 :47 1:12 ft 10 119 2hd 32 54½ 69½ Davis R G3 Aw27000 74-24 PssingThunder,Hberdshr,RollingBy 6
20Dec86-6Aqu 6f ⊡:222 :4521:093ft 7 120 1½ 21½ 67½ 810½ Maple E4 Aw27000 85-09 Hrlnghm,PssnThndr,WstrnPrspctr 10
12Dec86-7Aqu 6f ⊡:221 :4531:102m 6¼ 115 12½ 11½ 1hd 11¼ Davis R G2 Aw26000 92-16 Shear, Rolling By, Placid Waters 7
6Nov86-9Aqu 1 :46 1:112 1:381gd 3 117 1hd 3½ 611 715¾ Migliore R7 50000 59-24 Killer Joe, Aside, Sharp Current 8
30Oct86-7Aqu 1 :454 1:104 1:37 ft 5½ 114 44 32½ 43½ 57¼ Migliore R3 Aw25000 74-21 SillyRiffs,SwitchInTime,FicklStorm 7
20Oct86-5Bel 1⅛ :463 1:111 1:492ft *4-5e114 21 31 46 56 Davis R G2 Aw25000 74-16 WickedWike,Michel'sDncer,Hudcek 8
11Oct86-4Bel 1 1/16 :453 1:10 1:43 ft 7 112 64¼ 59 511 613 Cruguet J7 75000 74-19 GoldenOlden,Mcbest,MkeADecision 9
4Oct86-5Bel 6f :222 :453 1:102ft 3 114 53½ 42¼ 53¼ 45 Cruguet J4 Aw24000 85-14 Charismo, Cultivate, Gallic War 6
Jan 16 Bel tr.t 4f ft :474 h Jan 4 Bel tr.t 5f ft 1:03 b ●Dec 29 Bel tr.t 4f ft :472 h ●Dec 9 Bel tr.t 4f gd :472 h

Semaj *

B. h. 8, by Zen—Amber News, by Ambernash
Own.—Abacus Ranch 115 Br.—Whiteoakes Land Corp (NY) Tr.—Frank Maud $47,500
1987 2 0 1 1 $6,700
1986 11 2 2 2 $35,920
Lifetime 51 10 16 5 $243,112 Turf 3 0 0 0 $690

10Jan87-3Aqu 6f ⊡:222 :4531:101gd 5¾ 115 32½ 32 32 32¾ Lovato F Jr8 47500 90-10 Tis Royal, Sports Medicine,Semaj 11
1Jan87-2Aqu 6f ⊡:224 :46 1:103ft 10 117 44½ 44 42 21½ Lovato F Jr8 40000 89-22 Flunky Home,Semaj,FatherRoland 11
1Jan87—Bore out
19Dec86-1Aqu 6f ⊡:224 :4631:111m 5¼ 117 42½ 42¼ 54¼ 58¾ Maple E1 50000 79-20 Don'tHesitate,HarryL.,FatherRolnd 6
11Oct86-1Bel 7f :223 :453 1:232ft 4½ 119 35 32 2hd 31 Martens G5 50000 84-19 Frontier Justice,StarkSecret,Semaj 7
21Sep86-2Bel 7f :224 :46 1:223ft *9-5 117 21½ 21 11½ 11¼ Maple E4 50000 89-12 Semaj,FrontierJustice,FlunkyHome 6
11Sep86-1Bel 6f :223 :46 1:11 ft 2¾ 117 32 1hd 1hd 2hd Maple E1 50000 87-21 National Energy, Semaj,FeuD'enfer 7
20Aug86-1Sar 6f :22 :45 1:093ft 5 113 45 34½ 34 24 Maple E6 45000 88-12 Best By Test, Semaj, Flunky Home 6
18May86-2Bel 6f :223 :452 1:101ft 3 117 1hd 1hd 1hd 1¾ Maple E4 35000 91-15 Semaj, Irish Ore, Super Scope 10
Dec 14 Bel tr.t 6f ft 1:154 h Dec 2 Bel tr.t 5f ft 1:02 b

We are now definitely looking for early speed runners as we begin to compile our worksheet, which reads out like this.

Odds	Horse	PCR							Form	Ab/T		
5-2	Aswan High	58/	21	31	–	11/	41	= 141	+N0	44.4	25.4+1/	70.4
4	Sports Medicine	72/	46	36	+	4/	86	= 84	NOg	46.1	24.3+6/	72.0
24	Engine Chief	60/	24	42	+	8/	84	= 94	L/w	(46.4	26.1–3/	71.2)
22	Spiderman	57/	45	38	–	3/	80	= 71	NON	x		
44	Overbought	63/	48	37	+	2/	87	= 72	NON	47.1	24.3+6/	73.0
10	Proud and Tall	71/	47	46	–	5/	88	= 81	NNw	48.3	23.4+6/	73.3
40	Dale's Folly	64/	34	35	+	9/	78	= 82	+ON	46.2	25.1 0/	71.3
4	Flying Skipper	74/	26	24	+	9/	59	= 125	L/!	(46.1	24.0 0/	70.1)
30	Nasty and Tough	80/	40	25	–	1/	64	= 125	NON	x		
11	Semaj	64/	21	25	+	2/	48	= 133	N+N	46.0	24.4+6/	72.0
7-2	Shear	61/	24	42	–	13/	53	= 115	NON	47.2	26.3–2/	74.3

We shall first look at our top PCR horses, which are Aswan High, Semaj, Flying Skipper and Nasty and Tough. The latter goes out immediately off wretched form and a closing running style.

We can now look at the remaining three, and start with the highest numbered horse, Aswan High. Not only is his PCR strong off an early running style, but he has far and away the best last race ability time of any of the measured horses. In fact, he has a four tick advantage over the next recorded time, that of Dale's Folly, and in a sprint race this may be enough to make him a single selection play. The only defect is the stretch loss in his last race. But before we make that decision, we have to look at the other two.

Semaj with the second best PCR doesn't look bad at all, with no form defects and a good ability time of 72.0. But this is six full ticks behind what Aswan High turned in. This is too much to overcome.

The other horse that has to impress us is Flying Skipper, off since November. But that blistering 5-furlong workout on January 16, along with an advisory ability time off his Sept. 26 effort at Belmont of 70.1, makes him much too tough to cast aside. In fact, we would almost have to say that this is a two-horse race, pure and simple. Aswan High is outstanding, as his superiority over the others in his last race ability time is easily enough to make him a single selection play. But even when a horse qualifies for that kind of confidence, when there is another powerhouse in the field, you may be compelled to make a multiple selection play.

There are no others in this race to challenge these two. Shear was made a strong second choice in the betting, even ahead of Flying Skipper, but when you see his last race ability time, you would now have the advantage over your fellow handicappers because you would know this horse is not likely to win over the Big Two. Others in the race have low PCRs and insufficient ability times. We come back to Aswan High and Flying Skipper.

Our major problem with betting two horses to win here is that the odds are not wholesome enough. But off these lines, I would be as nearly certain as I could be about any outcome that one of them will win. Sure, it's easy enough to know which one after the result is available, but I am trying to leave this in the frame of reference of before the race. I would not be able to confidently pick one over the other at this stage.

If we can build up profits with an exacta in addition to win bets on both horses, we may be getting somewhere. And when two horses have such enormous advantage over the remainder of the field that these do, my exacta play is to box the two at a $4 base, and let it go at that.

Here is what happened:

FIFTH RACE
Aqueduct
JANUARY 21, 1987

6 FURLONGS.(InnerDirt). (1.08$\frac{3}{5}$) CLAIMING. Purse $21,000. 4-year-olds and upward. Weight, 122 lbs. Non-winners of two races since December 15 allowed 3 lbs. Of a race since then, 5 lbs. Claiming price $50,000; for each $2,500 to $45,000 allowed 2 lbs. (Races when entered to be claimed for $40,000 or less not considered.)

Value of race $21,000; value to winner $12,600; second $4,620; third $2,520; fourth $1,260. Mutuel pool $87,738, OTB pool $134,357. Exacta Pool $176,077. OTB Exacta Pool $238,500.

Last Raced	Horse	Eqt.	A.	Wt	PP	St	¼	½	Str	Fin	Jockey	Cl'g Pr	Odds $1
14Jan87 ^{7}Aqu^{5}	Aswan High		5	117	1	3	$1^{1\frac{1}{2}}$	$1^{1\frac{1}{2}}$	1^{3}	$1^{5\frac{1}{4}}$	Antley C W	50000	2.50
3Nov86 ^{5}Aqu^{9}	Flying Skipper		6	117	8	2	2^{hd}	$2^{1\frac{1}{2}}$	2^{hd}	$2^{\frac{1}{2}}$	Migliore R	50000	4.10
15Jan87 ^{4}Aqu^{4}	Dale's Folly	b	4	113	7	10	$6^{1\frac{1}{2}}$	$4^{1\frac{1}{2}}$	3^{4}	3^{5}	Santagata N	45000	42.80
16Jan87 ^{2}Aqu^{1}	Proud And Tall	b	4	113	6	9	10^{4}	9^{hd}	$6^{1\frac{1}{2}}$	4^{nk}	Bailey J D	45000	10.50
10Jan87 ^{3}Aqu^{3}	Semaj		8	115	11	5	$8^{\frac{1}{2}}$	7^{1}	5^{hd}	5^{nk}	Lovato F Jr	47500	11.60
17Dec86 ^{5}Pha^{6}	Engine Chief	b	5	117	3	11	$3^{1\frac{1}{2}}$	3^{hd}	$4^{1\frac{1}{2}}$	$6^{2\frac{3}{4}}$	Hernandez R	50000	24.90
8Jan87 ^{8}Aqu^{6}	Shear		4	115	10	1	$4^{\frac{1}{2}}$	$5^{\frac{1}{2}}$	7^{hd}	$7^{\frac{1}{2}}$	Davis R G	47500	3.60
10Jan87 ^{3}Aqu^{2}	Sports Medicine	b	5	113	2	6	$5^{\frac{1}{2}}$	6^{hd}	$8^{1\frac{1}{2}}$	$8^{\frac{3}{4}}$	Santos J A	45000	4.20
1Jan87 ^{6}Pha	Spiderman	b	4	117	4	7	11	11	$10^{\frac{1}{2}}$	$9^{\frac{1}{2}}$	Graell A	50000	22.40
10Jan87 ^{3}Aqu^{9}	Overbought		5	113	5	4	7^{hd}	10^{5}	$9^{1\frac{1}{2}}$	$10^{2\frac{1}{4}}$	McCauley W H	45000	44.20
4Jan87 ^{7}Aqu^{10}	Nasty And Tough	b	4	117	9	8	$9^{1\frac{1}{2}}$	$8^{1\frac{1}{2}}$	11	11	Samyn J L	50000	30.80

OFF AT 2:18, Start good, Won driving. Time, :22$\frac{4}{5}$, :45$\frac{4}{5}$, 1:10$\frac{1}{5}$ Track sloppy.

$2 Mutuel Prices:

2-(A)-ASWAN HIGH	7.00	4.20	4.00
8-(K)-FLYING SKIPPER		5.20	5.80
7-(I)-DALE'S FOLLY			14.60

$2 EXACTA 2-8 PAID $38.20.

Aswan High was most impressive in his Big Win. His good early speed on a speed-favoring track carried him easily wire to wire. Flying Skipper, as his workout indicated should be the case, was second all the way. Despite his great workout, the absence from competition against a tough horse could have been the slight factor that kept him from winning, even though he was in second place throughout.

The exacta paid a surprising $38.20 for what looked to be, before the race was run, a very secure play.

Again, we think this race is a good illustration of how the full handicapping line, with PCR as a powerful ingredient, leads you to the decisions that must be made for Total Victory at the Track. The early speed of Aswan, with a speed favoring track, combined with his high PCR, coming back in seven days with the strong + for recency, far far overcame the slight stretch loss of his previous race. The ability time concept, even when we are not able to use the preferred last race, provides us with substantial information when we look back to see the capabilities of any horse.

We next come to a short field in the sixth race for nonwinners other than maiden, claiming, or starter, where we have a lightly raced horse that is an overwhelming favorite.

6th Aqueduct

1 1/16 MILES. (InnerDirt). (1.41⅘) ALLOWANCE. Purse $27,000. 3-year-olds which have never won a race other than maiden or claiming. Weight, 122 lbs. Non-winners of a race other than claiming at a mile or over since January 1 allowed 3 lbs. Of such a race since December 15, 5 lbs.

Coupled—Cayman and Looky Dare.

Forest Fair

B. c. 3, by Naskra—Fairest Forest, by Big Spruce
Br.—Meadowhill (Ky) 1986 2 1 0 1 $16,440
Own.—Marano G **117** **Tr.—Lenzini John J Jr**
Lifetime 2 1 0 1 $16,440

29Dec86-4Aqu 6f [•]:221 :4531:111ft *6-5 118 2hd 1½ 11½ 1½ Antley C W1 Mdn 88-18 ForstFir,Gnom'sPlsur,I'mExubrnt 12
17Aug86-6Sar 6f :22 :453 1:103m *6-5 118 31 32 24 38 Cordero A Jr3 Mdn 79-11 Peaceable,ChariotofWar,ForestFir 11
●Jan 14 Aqu [•] 1 ft 1:423 b Jan 8 Aqu [•] 5f ft 1:011 h Dec 24 Aqu [•] 5f ft 1:022 b Dec 18 Aqu [•] 4f ft :48 hg

Mr. J. V.

B. g. 3, by Fantasy 'N Reality—Davlin, by Our Michael
Br.—Farnsworth Farm (Fla) 1987 1 0 0 1 $3,360
Own.—Nagle K **117** **Tr.—Ferriola Peter** 1986 13 2 1 0 $8,465
Lifetime 14 2 1 1 $11,825

14Jan87-1Aqu 1 1/16 [•]:4831:1331:462ft 23 1085 77 75½ 32½ 31¼ Badamo J J2 70000 77-16 Target X., Looky Dare, Mr. J. V. 7
26Dec86-8Crc 1 1/16 :484 1:153 1:52 sy 14 118 915 811 56½ 22 Lee M A4 18000 57-26 Sunbury. Mr. J. V., KrackInflation 11
18Dec86-3Crc 1 1/16 :492 1:161 1:501ft *6-5 114 47 31½ 1½ 11 Danjean R9 c12500 68-23 Mr. J. V.,ExplodingHit,Kleier'sBabe 9
11Dec86-10Crc 1 1/16 :483 1:152 1:492ft 29 114 1010106½ 45¼ 44¾ Danjean R10 20000 67-19 DiamondGalaxia,FlyingAl,Sunbury 10
28Nov86-10Crc 1 1/16 :484 1:144 1:493ft 54 114 10121011 56 54½ Danjean R4 16000 66-22 MicanopyBoy,FireAnimal,Sunbury 10
6Nov86-3Crc 170 :494 1:153 1:473ft 21 114 57 46½ 67½ 66½ Perez O E2 15000 65-20 RtionlEyes,Pet'sFntsy,NoSuchLuck 7
29Oct86-2Crc 170 :494 1:151 1:482ft 37 114 89¾ 815 812 813¼ Perez O E10 20000 55-19 KrackInfltion,ReflecArc,FireAniml 10
3Oct86-6Crc 1 :483 1:143 1:431ft 8 114 11121011 87¾ 68¼ Perez O E4 18000 64-18 Pt'sFntsy,KrckInfltion,ModstRulr 12
Jan 9 Aqu [•] 4f ft :511 b

Target X.

B. c. 3, by Exclusive Native—Target Practice, by Gunflint

Own.—Anchel E **117** Br.—Gailyndel Farms (Ky) 1987 1 1 0 0 $16,800

Tr.—LaBoccetta Frank 1986 13 1 1 3 $22,930

Lifetime 14 2 1 3 $39,730 Turf 1 0 0 0

14Jan87-1Aqu 1 1/16 [•]:483 1:133 1:462ft 14 113 42 41½ 1hd 1no Migliore R3 70000 78-16 Target X., Looky Dare, Mr. J. V. 7

14Dec86-4Aqu 170 [•]:484 1:141 1:451ft 6¾ 114 3nk 2hd 11 1no Hernandez R6 M70000 74-20 Target X., Night Driver,Salvington 10

28Nov86-4Aqu 7f :223 :453 1:234ft 3¾ 1077 53½ 42½ 23 34¾ Ortiz E Jr2 M70000 77-18 Passing Ships, Sting'em, Target X. 8

15Nov86-4Aqu 1 :454 1:113 1:393ft 6 1077 42¼ 1hd 11½ 2hd Ortiz E Jr6 M70000 68-22 Slane Hill, Target X., Jumpski 13

26Oct86-2Aqu 7f :23 :46 1:243gd 3e1077 78¾ 713 59½ 44½ Belmonte J F1 M70000 73-16 Widdum, Slane Hill, Windy Sails 8

9Oct86-3Bel 1 :471 1:124 1:392ft 9 118 1hd 2½ 35 69½ Cruguet J11 M50000 58-18 Cayman,StyintheBuggy,Son'sWish 11

25Sep86-3Bel 1 :472 1:13 1:39 ft 9½ 114 86 56½ 38½ 310½ Cruguet J5 M70000 59-19 TwentyNorth,FoolishPirte,TrgetX. 10

25Sep86—Off slowly, wide

21Sep86-6Bel 1 1/16 (T):48 1:123 1:433hd 27 118 1211 1214 1216 1220¼ Cruguet J12 Mdn 58-20 LightsandMusic,Gunburst,YetWve 12

21Sep86—Broke slowly

Jan 6 Aqu [•] 5f ft 1:033 b

Looky Dare

B. c. 3, by Cathy's Reject—Whoppin, by War Trouble

Own.—Barrera O S **117** Br.—Penn O (Ky) 1987 4 0 1 1 $10,960

Tr.—Barrera Oscar S 1986 8 2 0 1 $12,930

Lifetime 12 2 1 2 $23,890 Turf 1 0 0 0 $720

14Jan87-1Aqu 1 1/16 [•]:483 1:133 1:462ft *9-5 113 32 2½ 2hd 2no Antley C W4 70000 78-16 Target X., Looky Dare, Mr. J. V. 7

10Jan87-5Aqu 170 [•]:473 1:123 1:41 gd 7½ 117 62¼ 53 47¼ 38½ Antley C W7 Aw27000 86-10 Sting'em, Rolls Aly, Looky Dare 9

7Jan87-5Aqu 6f [•]:221 :452 1:112ft 21 117 87¼ 66 44½ 43 Antley C W3 Aw26000 84-21 BstThif,WrongDoctor,LightProspct 9

2Jan87-2Aqu 1 1/16 [•]:472 1:122 1:46 m 9¾ 117 65¾ 46½ 612 612½ Davis R G2 c25000 67-21 LuvThtLibr,SirAmber,BrvndBright 11

21Dec86-2Aqu 1 1/16 [•]:473 1:14 1:46 ft 3¾e1105 127 98¼ 915 918 Nuesch D11 32500 62-14 TurnOnthSpd,Cymn,MghtyChoppr 12

12Dec86-6Med 1 :471 1:124 1:40 sy 2¾ 113 55¼ 55 67 58½ Krone J A1 35000 66-20 TellItHonstly,Sigmundo,Koumbros 7

6Nov86-3Med 170 :473 1:14 1:452m 3½ 113 43 41¾ 3½ 11 Vigliotti M J3 c25000 69-20 Looky Dare, Super Gun, Tocantins 8

22Oct86-8Pha 1 :472 1:121 1:383ft 14 114 1013 811 711 68½ Wilson R6 Aw11500 72-22 WellHonored,Heritnce,SilentLeder 10

Nov 29 Med 5f ft 1:03 b

Do Dat

Dk. b. or br. c. 3, by Verbatim—Show Judge, by Delta Judge

Own.—Murrell J R **1125** Br.—Elmendorf Farm (Ky) 1987 2 1 1 0 $11,040

Tr.—Kempien Gary 1986 8 M 0 0 $2,100

Lifetime 10 1 1 0 $13,140

12Jan87-4Aqu 1 1/16 [•]:481 1:141 1:47 ft 7¼ 1135 94¼ 31½ 12 14 Nuesch D11 M45000 75-19 DoDat,SoftDollars,TooToughtoBet 11

2Jan87-4Aqu 1⅛ [•]:49 1:15 1:553sy 7¾ 118 42 21 21 2no Lovato F Jr8 M30000 64-21 AbsolutAuthorty,DoDt,AcsOvrKngs 8

27Dec86-4Aqu 1⅛ [•]:473 1:131 1:522ft 32 118 79½ 87¾ 812 720¼ Lovato F Jr2 Mdn 60-11 Rolls Aly, Endorse, Bucket Shop 11

7Dec86-5Aqu 6f [•]:222 :454 1:122ft 39 1135 1015 1118 915 817¼ Brown T L5 Mdn 65-18 Nphrt,Coco'sDoubl,‡WrongDoctor 11

2Oct86-9Bel 7f :23 :453 1:242ft 16 1135 119¾ 717 616 415 Brown T L8 M50000 65-09 SonnyVrbtim,Strobt,TurnOnthSpd 11

24Sep86-3Bel 6f :22 :452 1:104ft 13 1095 1118 920 813 69¾ Brown T L8 M45000 78-16 ViolentRelaunch,HighBrite,Caymn 13

4Sep86-5Bel 7f :224 :461 1:242ft 14 118 88¼ 811 716 515¾ Privitera R6 M75000 64-18 QtlyBold,Gtrdyforthshow,B.G.'sTffy 9

17Aug86-6Sar 6f :22 :453 1:103m 33 118 1015 1011 913 915 Lovato F Jr10 Mdn 72-11 Peaceable,ChariotofWar,ForestFir 11

Dec 21 Bel tr.t 4f ft :484 h Dec 15 Bel tr.t 4f ft :494 b Dec 2 Bel tr.t 4f ft :51 b Nov 28 Bel tr.t 6f gd 1:162 b

Coco's Double

Gr. c. 3, by Nodouble—Fearless Queen, by Iron Ruler

Own.—Napolitano Michelina **117** Br.—Napolitano Michelina (Ky) 1987 2 0 1 0 $7,560

Tr.—Johnson Philip G 1986 4 1 1 0 $20,780

Lifetime 6 1 2 0 $28,340

10Jan87-5Aqu 170 [•]:473 1:123 1:41 gd 9¼ 119 31 21½ 37 48½ Samyn J L8 Aw27000 86-10 Sting'em, Rolls Aly, Looky Dare 9

1Jan87-6Aqu 1 1/16 [•]:501 1:151 1:461ft 3e119 31 2hd 32 23¼ Samyn J L7 Aw27000 76-22 Gtrdyforthshow,Coco'sDobl,Stng'm 7

14Dec86-6Aqu 1 1/16 [•]:483 1:131 1:48 ft *9-5 118 42 2hd 12 13 Samyn J L7 Mdn 70-20 Coco'sDouble,Knockon,MdivlMind 11

7Dec86-5Aqu 6f [•]:222 :454 1:122ft 5¾ 118 52¼ 44 32 2hd Skinner K1 Mdn 82-18 Nnhrt,Coco'sDoubl,‡WrongDoctor 11

7Dec86—Bbbld st.-steady

10Nov86-6Aqu 1 :46 1:11 1:37 gd 6¾ 118 47½ 55½ 44 53¾ Samyn J L1 Mdn 77-18 MagicFeet,ParisOffice,FastForward 8

25Oct86-9Aqu 6f :222 :451 1:111ft 26 118 87¾ 613 512 47¾ Samyn J L4 Mdn 77-18 LightProspct,SttlKnight,NishiRdg 10

Dec 29 Bel tr.t 4f ft :484 h Dec 24 Bel tr.t 5f ft 1:03 b Dec 2 Bel tr.t 4f ft :483 h Nov 29 Bel tr.t 3f ft :353 h

Odds	Horse	PCR	Form	Ab/T
6-5	Forest Fair	23/ 4 4 – / 8 =(288)	N+w	(11.1 32.2 0/ 43.3)
5	Mr. J. V.	76/ 60 35 + 15/110 = 69	+NN	14.4 32.1+1/ 47.1
9	Target X	79/ 35 32 – / 67 = 118	++w	14.0 32.3+1/ 46.4
9-2	Looky Dare	73/ 43 36 + 8/ 87 – 84	++N	13.4 32.4+1/ 46.4
10	Do Dat	85/ 58 42 + 8/108 = 79	N++	14.3 32.3 0/ 47.1
5-2	Coco's Double	56/ 21 18 – / 39 = 144	NON	13.0 33.0+6/ 47.1

Seldom will you find a race with such outstanding form factors, loaded with pluses. But for Forest Fair, with only two starts, there is hardly enough to have any kind of meaningful PCR. We even have to extend an advisory ability time because of his previous race at six furlongs. But what we do see is very impressive. We see something else here, too, and that will be the factor that will tell us what to do.

You have seen the front running, early speed victories that have dominated the card from the results charts we have shown. Each of the five rivals to Forest Fair has a higher second call total number than a finish total. Does that tell you enough? This lightly raced youngster has already shown plenty of early speed.

The record shown above is an outstanding example of how an advisory ability time off a sprint race even in a route event that follows is so impressive that a horse must be selected off advisory times this powerful. Even if Forest Fair could not extend his six furlong time to the projected 1 1/16 conversion, he still has an estimated margin of more than three whole seconds, or 16 ticks in all, in which to slump off a bit. This is a single selection play if you ever saw one, as the big advantage in this race literally shrieks for your attention. No one likes to play horses at 6-5, but when you consider the high likelihood that Forest Fair would win, even that is an overlay. The result chart reveals an overwhelming, runaway Big Win.

SIXTH RACE
Aqueduct
JANUARY 21, 1987

1 1/16 MILES.(InnerDirt). (1.41⅗) ALLOWANCE. Purse $27,000. 3-year-olds which have never won a race other than maiden or claiming. Weight, 122 lbs. Non-winners of a race other than claiming at a mile or over since January 1 allowed 3 lbs. Of such a race since December 15, 5 lbs.

Value of race $27,000; value to winner $16,200; second $5,940; third $3,240; fourth $1,620. Mutuel pool $91,609, OTB pool $102,406. Exacta Pool $194,581. OTB Exacta Pool $190,950.

Last Raced	Horse	Eqt.A.Wt	PP	St	¼	½	¾	Str	Fin	Jockey	Odds $1
29Dec86 ^{4}Aqu^1	Forest Fair	3 117	1	1	$1^{1\frac{1}{2}}$	$1^{\frac{1}{2}}$	$1^{\frac{1}{2}}$	1^4	$1^{8\frac{3}{4}}$	Santos J A	1.20
10Jan87 ^{5}Aqu^4	Coco's Double	3 117	6	4	2^3	$2^{4\frac{1}{2}}$	$2^{4\frac{1}{2}}$	2^4	$2^{4\frac{1}{4}}$	Samyn J L	2.80
14Jan87 ^{1}Aqu^1	Target X.	b 3 117	3	5	$4^{1\frac{1}{2}}$	$4^{\frac{1}{2}}$	$4^{\frac{1}{2}}$	3^3	$3^{6\frac{1}{2}}$	Santagata N	9.40
14Jan87 ^{1}Aqu^3	Mr. J. V.	b 3 117	2	3	6	6	5^1	$5^{2\frac{1}{2}}$	4no	Migliore R	5.80
14Jan87 ^{1}Aqu^2	Looky Dare	b 3 117	4	2	$3^{\frac{1}{2}}$	$3^{1\frac{1}{2}}$	$3^{2\frac{1}{2}}$	4^2	$5^{2\frac{1}{4}}$	Antley C W	4.50
12Jan87 ^{4}Aqu^1	Do Dat	b 3 112	5	6	5^{hd}	5^{hd}	6	6	6	Nuesch D^5	10.80

OFF AT 2:45 Start good, Won ridden out. Time, :23⅗, :47⅖, 1:12⅕, 1:38, 1:44⅘ Track sloppy.

$2 Mutuel Prices:				
	2-(B)-FOREST FAIR	4.40	3.00	2.40
	7-(H)-COCO'S DOUBLE		3.40	2.20
	5-(E)-TARGET X.			2.60

$2 EXACTA 2-7 PAID $13.00.

The seventh race brings us another interesting event, a better grade of allowance horse for nonwinners of two other than maiden, claiming, or starter.

7th Aqueduct

1 1/16 MILES. (InnerDirt). (1.41⅘) ALLOWANCE. Purse $28,000. Fillies and Mares, 4-year-olds and upward which have neve won two races other than maiden, claiming or starter. Weight, 122 lbs. Non-winners of a race other than maiden or claiming at a mile or over since January 1 allowed 3 lbs. Of such a race since December 15, 5 lbs.

Proudest Babe *

Own.—Sommer Viola 117
Dk. b. or br. m. 5, by Proudest Roman—Couture, by Burd Alane
Br.—Springtide Inc (Ky) 1987 1 0 0 0
Tr.—Martin Frank 1986 26 6 4 3 $116,560
Lifetime 42 9 4 5 $138,913 Turf 7 0 1 1 $12,065

11Jan87-7Aqu 1 1/16 ⊡:4641:1131:433m *9-5 117 44 31½ 36 55½ MrquezCH7 ⒻAw28000 86-17 Peaches, Cherokee Chill, Glady H. 7
11Jan87—No excuse
22Dec86-5Aqu 1 70 ⊡:4811:1321:423ft *8-5 112 54½ 42½ 1hd 1½ MrquezCHJr2 Ⓕ 75000 87-17 ProudestBabe,BethsSong,T.V.Snow 6
17Dec86-1Aqu 1⅛ ⊡:4811:1331:514ft 7½ 113 46½ 11½ 16 112½ MrquezCHJr1 Ⓕ 45000 83-20 ProudestBb,Blum'sMjsty,MtchSpd 7
3Dec86-9Aqu 1 1/16 ⊡:4811:13 1:452gd *3½ 115 53 3½ 76½ 711 Migliore R9 Ⓕ c32500 72-11 Solo Energy,TrulyBest,RoyalPetII 10
11Nov86-5Aqu 1⅛ :483 1:133 1:514sy 8¼ 1125 64 63¾ 53 54½ Baird E T2 ⒻAw26000 71-21 HappyCherokee,Flantsi,Mrs.Beeton 6
4Nov86-2Aqu 1 :452 1:11 1:38 ft 8¾ 117 10121111 55½ 53¼ Romero RP3 Ⓕ c25000 73-22 TrulyBest,SoloEnrgy,K.'sSolution 13
22Oct85-5Aqu 1 1/16 Ⓣ:4911:1241:443fm 3 113 44 67½ 513 816¼ Romero R P4 Ⓕ 45000 66-18 Queen'sGntlet,AyrshireLss,CertLgis 8
5Sep86-3Bel 1 1/16 Ⓣ:4621:1021:422fm 4½ 117 77¼ 65½ 55 56¼ Venezia M12 Ⓕ 50000 78-11 GwenJohn,CertLegis,FigurNviden 12
Jan 18 Bel tr.t 4f ft :493 b Nov 29 Bel tr.t 4f ft :491 b Nov 23 Bel tr.t 4f ft :50 b

Barely Dancin

Own.—Welsh R W 122
Ch. f. 4, by Nureyev—The Streaker, by Dr Fager
Br.—Reed Dr W O (Ky) 1987 1 1 0 0 $16,200
Tr.—Lukas D Wayne 1986 5 1 0 0 $13,430
Lifetime 6 2 0 0 $29,630

8Jan87-7Aqu 1 1/16 ⊡:4811:1311:464ft 9½ 117 12 12½ 15½ 18½ McClyWH6 ⒻAw27000 76-24 BrlyDncin,ImbicPntmtr,FstFshion 12
21Dec86-7Aqu 6f ⊡:221 :46 1:112ft *9-5 115 1½ 2hd 44 68 CordroAJr1 ⒻAw26000 79-14 TopsInTps,StgeNtive,NorthrnMidn 9
21Dec86—Broke sluggishly
10Nov86-7Aqu 7f :223 :461 1:24 gd *2¼ 120 1hd 1½ 2hd 55 Cruguet J4 ⒻAw24000 76-18 MusicOfLove,UnttnddDt,BlnchNig 11
10Nov86—Bumped st.
31Oct86-3Aqu 7f :223 :453 1:241ft 9 119 11½ 13 13 16½ Cruguet J4 ⒻMdn 80-20 BrelyDncin,DiscreetMtine,LdRunnr 8
5Apr86-2Hia 6f :221 :453 1:114ft 8½ 113 21 2hd 32 58½ Cruguet J6 ⒻMdn 72-13 HoopItUp,OnceMine,RegentGoddss 9
20Jan86-2GP 6f :223 :471 1:134ft 4½ 121 52¾ 62½ 9101113 Cruguet J3 ⒻMdn 57-24 Fappy, Desert View, Betsy Mack 12
Dec 17 Bel tr.t 4f ft :49 b Dec 7 Bel tr.t 4f ft :483 h Nov 30 Bel tr.t 4f ft :50 b

Union Gold

Own.—Julfran Farm 122
Ch. f. 4, by Scythian Gold—Geranyl, by Royal Union
Br.—Julfran Farm (NY) 1987 1 1 0 0 $17,100
Tr.—Garofalo F G 1986 7 1 1 1 $19,720
Lifetime 8 2 1 1 $36,820

12Jan87-5Aqu 1 1/16 ⊡:4911:14 1:461ft 3 119 42½ 51¾ 1hd 16 BaileyJD7 ⒻⓈAw28500 79-19 Union Gold, TenderYears,Vitreace 10
30Dec86-8Aqu 1⅛ ⊡:47 1:1211:521ft 30 108 67 65¾ 73¾ 66 TbRJ2 ⒻⓈTicondrogH 75-16 PltinumPoster,ShSkts,MissFlming 11
21Dec86-5Aqu 6f ⊡:223 :46 1:114ft 16 120 115½11111013 710¾ ThbuRJ11 ⒻⓈAw27000 74-14 Megwtt,LdysMystery,SixRedRoses 12
12Dec86-9Aqu 1⅛ ⊡:4911:1431:533m 5¾ 120 32½ 21½ 1½ 13 Thibeau R J8 ⒻⓈMdn 74-16 Union Gold, Vitreace, Silvie Who 11
27Nov86-9Aqu 7f :234 :474 1:264gd 29 120 74¾ 64¼ 55½ 3nk Thibeau R J6 ⒻⓈMdn 67-29 RunShanaRun,Kiawatha,UnionGold 9
9Jly86-5FL 6f :223 :463 1:132ft 4¾ 115 88¼ 910 811 817¾ Hulet L1 ⒻⓈMdn 64-18 Impious Spirit, Hour Best,AMoral 10
15Jun86-5FL 5½f :222 :461 1:053ft *2½ 113 812 812 815 819½ Doxey D L3 ⒻⓈMdn 68-18 David'sTicket,ImpiousSpirit,AMorl 9
15Jun86—Broke in air
31May86-4FL 6f :23 :471 1:14 ft 7 111 53¼ 43½ 34½ 2¾ Doxey D L4 ⒻⓈMdn 78-18 ClticCross,UnionGold,ImpiousSpirt 8
Jan 8 Bel tr.t 5f ft 1:022 h Dec 27 Bel tr.t 3f ft :39 b

Kathy W.

Gr. f. 4, by Grey Dawn II—Pretty Fresh, by Forli

Own.—Waldman M A 1125 Br.—EatonFrmsInc&RedBullStble (Ky) 1987 1 0 1 0 $4,620

Tr.—Sedlacek Sue 1986 6 2 0 0 $6,582

Lifetime 7 2 1 0 $11,202 Turf 4 2 0 0 $5,322

7Jan87-1Aqu 1 1/16 [•]:50 1:1441:474ft 4¼ 1125 11½ 11 1½ 2hd Ortiz E Jr4 Ⓕ 35000 71-21 Crown Piper, Kathy W., Charsky 7

27Dec86-3Aqu 1 1/16 [•]:4911:1411:46 ft 12 115 41½ 2hd 3½ 43½ Samyn J L8 Ⓕ 35000 76-11 ImbicPentmtr,Chrsky,BllOfWstviw 8

13Dec86-2Aqu 170[•]:4831:1421:45 ft 12 116 74½ 64¼ 96¼ 610¾ Samyn J L7 Ⓕ 35000 64-28 PuddinTne,TendrYrs,AskDirctions 10

13Dec86—Shuffl'd turn

22Aug86♦4Goodwood(Eng) 1½ 2:384gd 3½ 129 [T] 623 CtS TaylorWoodrowTeamHcp Aldino, Dalgadiyr, Plymouth Hoe 8

18Jly86♦3Newbury(Eng) 1¼ 2:101gd 2¾ 128 [T] 46 CuthnS ⒻAlliedDunbarHcp Apply, Red Shoes, Lucky So So 8

24Jun86♦7Pontefract(Eng) 1¼ 2:131gd *1 128 [T] 1½ RynW Mexborough Stakes Kathy W, PokeysPride,KingTefkros 6

26May86♦4Leicester(Eng) 1¼ 2:06 gd 3½ 123 [T] 11½ CthnS Groby Stakes(Mdn) Kathy W, Ensigne, Coinage 16

Dec 5 Aqu [•] 5f ft 1:024 hg Nov 29 Aqu 5f ft 1:022 b

Almost Pure

Ch. f. 4, by Barrera—Lady Jinsky, by Nijinsky II

Own.—Augustin Stable 117 Br.—Strawbridge G Jr (Pa) 1987 1 0 0 0 $345

Tr.—Sheppard Jonathan E 1986 10 2 3 3 $35,155

Lifetime 12 2 4 3 $38,300 Turf 2 0 1 1 $4,265

15Jan87-8Pha 6½f :221 :46 1:201ft *1 115 2hd 31½ 57½ 58¼ Walford J1 ⒻAw11500 64-29 AfllAsm,Bbndsnshs,Mm'sOnAndOnl 7

19Dec86-6Aqu 1⅛[•]:49 1:1321:523m 3½ 115 12 1½ 2hd 31 SantagatN5 ⒻAw28000 78-20 Mrs.Beeton,UnttenddDt,AlmostPur 6

3Dec86-8Pha 6½f :222 :461 1:192gd *1 120 2½ 3nk 43½ 35¼ MdrdAJr1 Ⓕ[S]Aw15600 70-22 St.Cecili,StubbornEsthr,AlmostPur 7

18Nov86-6Med 1 :471 1:123 1:404sy *8-5 115 2½ 21½ 31½ 22¾ Krone J A1 ⒻAw18000 68-25 StatelyBride,AlmostPure,Socialwan 5

29Oct86-7Pha 6½f :221 :452 1:172ft *2-3 119 1½ 13 13½ 14¼ KroneJA4 Ⓕ[S]Aw13500 86-18 AlmostPur,WdsOrRoss,R.DzzlingDri 6

23Oct86-8Pha 170[T]:4621:1221:421fm 6½ 112 64½ 42½ 2½ 31¾ Krone J A3 ⒻAw11500 84-14 Cuc'sLdy,NordenTnzer,AlmostPur 10

16Oct86-9Med 1 1/16[T]:4741:1241:462fm 5½e 114 11½ 11 2½ 21¾ Dufton E11 ⒻAw15000 69-26 SttelyBride,AlmostPure,ShplyLins 11

18Sep86-8Pha 6f :221 :452 1:112ft *1 118 2hd 42 57½ 613 DuftonE2 Ⓕ[S]Aw14500 71-23 PupTent,HeistTheJewls,InThMdow 6

●Jan 13 Pha 3f ft :36 bg Jan 5 Pha 5f fr :592 h ●Dec 31 Pha 5f ft 1:003 b Dec 14 Pha 5f ft 1:00 h

Royal Discovery

B. f. 4, by Tom Tulle—Great Discovery, by Pan Dancer

Own.—Nagle Kerry 117 Br.—Carter Mrs M (Ky) 1987 1 0 1 0 $1,805

Tr.—Ferriola Peter 1986 25 5 5 3 $41,915

Lifetime 32 5 6 6 $47,055 Turf 7 0 0 1 $2,322

2Jan87-5Crc 7f :232 :472 1:263ft *4-5 116 3½ 32½ 2½ 2nk Lester R N8 Ⓕ 40000 83-18 DonIsACrd,RoylDscovry,MllProspct 8

10Dec86-7Crc a1 1/16[T] 1:443fm 5¾ 112 33 33½ 44 75¾ GonzlzMA2 ⒻAw15300 78-22 FrgrntPrincss,Nxos,ShooCityShoo 10

20Nov86-7Crc 6½f :221 :46 1:201ft 2¼ 116 58½ 66½ 55½ 46½ Pezua J M3 ⒻAw13900 77-18 Gentley,DanceRelity,SilveredDncer 7

8Nov86-5Crc 6f :221 :453 1:121ft 8-5 116 46½ 45 42 35 Pezua J M3 ⒻAw20100 85-16 Jos'sBomb,ShnngPrspct,RylDscvry 6

28Oct86-7Crc 6½f :223 :461 1:19 ft *4-5 115 53 41½ 3½ 2no Pezua J M6 ⒻAw16000 90-21 ProudWomn,RoylDiscovry,FlgRlity 6

17Oct86-9Crc 7f :232 :471 1:26 ft 9-5 117 41¼ 51¾ 2½ 21 Pezua J M5 ⒻAw16400 85-22 ProxdPrncss,RoylDscovry,SprmLck 6

20Sep86-7Crc 7f :231 :462 1:244ft *1-2 117 31½ 21 1hd 2hd Lester R N6 ⒻAw14400 92-15 ProxdPrncss,RoylDscvry,FlyngClln 7

17Aug86-5Crc 7f :224 :464 1:243ft *2 114 44 32 1½ 16 Pezua J M8 ⒻAw11500 93-17 RoylDscovry,KlssyKrystl,LollppsRlr 8

Jan 17 Aqu [•] 3f ft :382 b

Unattended Date

B. f. 4, by Far North—Chaperone Rogue, by Hail to Reason

Own.—Warfield T 117 Br.—Welcome Farm (Pa) 1987 1 0 0 0 $1,680

Tr.—Zito Nicholas P 1986 16 2 3 2 $51,520

Lifetime 22 2 3 3 $55,960 Turf 4 0 0 0

11Jan87-7Aqu 1 1/16[•]:4641:1131:433m 4½ 117 33½ 41¾ 46 44¾ Antley CW6 ⒻAw28000 87-17 Peaches, Cherokee Chill, Glady H. 7

19Dec86-6Aqu 1⅛[•]:49 1:1321:523m 14 117 22 2½ 1hd 2nk Bailey J D4 ⒻAw28000 79-20 Mrs.Beeton,UnttenddDt,AlmostPur 6

8Dec86-7Aqu 1 1/16[•]:47 1:1211:454ft 18 120 510 49½ 58 68½ RomeroRP8 ⒻAw28000 72-20 Mine Tonight,Mrs.Beeton,RosaMay 9

28Nov86-8Aqu 1 :462 1:11 1:363ft 6½ 120 21 21 53¾ 58½ Bailey J D6 ⒻAw28000 74-18 Syrian Beauty, Flantasia, Day Off 6

28Nov86—Bled from mouth

16Nov86-5Aqu 1 :462 1:12 1:384ft 12 115 72¾ 52 3½ 1¾ Bailey J D3 ⒻAw25000 72-23 UnttenddDt,Rp'sRtton,ExoticPowr 8

10Nov86-7Aqu 7f :223 :461 1:24 gd 6 115 75¾ 53 42¾ 22¼ Bailey JD11 ⒻAw24000 79-18 MusicOfLove,UnttnddDt,BlnchNig 11

25Oct86-5Aqu 1 :461 1:11 1:37 ft 12 114 31½ 32 34 34¾ Bailey J D7 ⒻAw25000 76-18 RisedInStyl,BrndyButtr,UnttnddDt 8

15Oct86-6Bel 1 1/16 :47 1:113 1:433gd 15 114 21 33½ 35½ 36½ Bailey J D2 ⒻAw25000 77-20 NewDawn,Colophon,UnattendedDte 6

Jan 1 Bel tr.t 4f ft :502 b Dec 16 Bel tr.t 4f ft :50 b Nov 25 Bel 3f sy :38 b

```
Ananas                                  B. m. 5, by Lyphard—Little Nana, by Lithiot
                                        Br.—Caralaine Stable & SchefierA (Ky)      1987 1 0 0 0
Own.—Schefier A D                117    Tr.—Preger Mitchell C                      1986 6 1 0 1        $20,958
                                        Lifetime   8 2 0 1   $23,397               Turf 5 1 0 1         $8,397
14Jan87-5Aqu  6f [•]:222 :4521:111ft  8¾ 117  75¾ 77¼ 77 67¼  Migliore R7 (F)Aw27000 80-16 JustGorgous,Blm'sMjsty,MssScndl 7
15Sep86-7Bel  1 :461 1:111 1:364ft *9-5 117  56 56 57½ 58¾  Migliore R3 (F)Aw26000 72-15 ClaraBow,Flantasia,HappyCherokee 8
6Sep86-6Bel  1 1/16(T):4731:1211:444gd *2¼ 117  31½ 43½ 35½ 48¼  MiglioreR10 (F)Aw26000 64-27 Festivity,FrgrntPrincess,TllPoppy 11
     6Sep86—Bore out.
15Jly86-7Mth  1 1/16(T):4831:1211:431+fm 5 112  12½ 2hd 3nk 52  VlszJ4 (F)Eatontown H 83-18 Mazatleca,CopeOfFlowers,Drbrielle 8
     15Jly86—Run in divisions
3Jly86-9Bel  1 1/16:463 1:11 1:43 ft  3½ 117  31½ 31½ 2hd 17  Migliore R6 (F)Aw25000 87-16 Ananas, Poelish Hills, Flantasia 7
16Jun86-7Bel  1 (T):46 1:1021:35 fm  3½ 117  84 52 22 32¼  Migliore R2 (F)Aw25000 88-15 La Petite Flo, Tres Vrai, Ananas 12
29May86-4Bel  1 1/16(T):4641:1041:412fm *3½ 119  53 98½ 710 715½  Samyn J L3 (F)Aw25000 73-08 Tesd,Robrto'sSocil,LgcvofStrngth 12
     29May86—Rough trip
25Apr85 ♦ 4Pontefract(Eng) 1  1:45 gd*4-5 123  (T) 11½  LA  MileChampionshipQul(Mdn) Ananas, Try Scorer, Happy House 25
  Jan 17 Bel tr.t 3f ft :362 hg    Jan 12 Bel tr.t 4f ft :473 h    Jan 5 Bel tr.t 5f ft 1:012 h    Dec 27 Bel tr.t 5f ft 1:021 h
```

We should next set forth our worksheet lines, and then provide some analytical comments on what we are able to see.

Odds	Horse	PCR	Form	Ab/T
5-2	Proudest Babe	60/ 40 32 + 2/ 74 = 81	NON	12.0 32.4+1/ 45.0
2	Barely Dancin'	61/ 13 29 − 1/ 41 = 149	N+w	13.1 33.2−2/ 46.2
15	Union Gold	80/ 51 36 − 1/ 86 = 93	N++	14.2 32.0 0/ 46.2
9	Kathy W.	25/ 9 12 + 3/ 24 =(104)	N+N	14.4 33.0−1/ 47.3
9	Almost Pure	58/ 19 25 + 10/ 54 = 107	+ON	(15.0 35.3−5/ 49.3)
6	Royal Discovery	58/ 30 23 + 15/ 68 = 85	N+N	(13.2 32.1 0/ 45.3)
8	Unattended Date	63/ 28 26 − 1/ 53 = 119	NON	12.0 32.3+1/ 44.4
7	Ananas	65/ 35 31 − 1/ 65 = 100	NON	(12.4 32.3+1/ 45.3)

When we begin our analysis of the race, we first look as usual at the three highest PCR horses, Unattended Date, Barely Dancin', the 2-1 favorite, and Almost Pure. Do any of them qualify for a single selection play?

The most obvious to the crowd was Barely Dancin' because of her runaway race in her last outing. But it is not obvious at all when you read the kind of handicapping lines that we are developing that will give us as much complete pertinent information as possible in one readable line. Despite that last race runaway victory, when you see a last race ability time that is far behind that of at least two horses, by big margins, you can sense already that trouble is lurking. Even a 15-1 shot, Union Gold, did as well in her last race. Unattended Date with a 44.4 and Proudest Babe at 45.0 are eight and seven ticks ahead of the favored horse. Barely Dancin' is gone already even before we complete our analysis, despite the early speed she has on an early speed day, and despite her high PCR.

In addition, her big lead at the second call in her last race, which led to the runaway, is often a recipe for a next-race shellacking. Remember that we do not award a Big Win to a horse that led at the second call by more than two lengths in its last race and went on to score easily ahead of the pack. The reason is that early speed unchallenged gets a free ride and the recipient will almost always turn in misleading figures. I have seen these kinds of horses lose so many times that I am especially wary of them when they loom up well played in their next race.

The other potential single play is the second highest PCR horse, Unattended Date. While her last race ability time is strong in this weak field, second only to that of Proudest Babe, she does have a very slight form defect by not being within less than five lengths of the lead at the stretch·call of her last race. She did not progress quite enough to meet our requirement for a stretch gain, so we have to pass her momentarily to see what else is in the race.

The other high PCR horse, Almost Pure, has poor form and an extremely high ability time, even if advisory. She is far from a contender.

What about Kathy W. with her strong last race and a showing of early speed? This import from English racing has run but three times in the U.S., making it somewhat difficult to evaluate her. Her last race was by far her best but her ability time is too far off the others unless they allow her to run away and steal the race. Our deceptive favorite, Barely Dancin', is not likely to allow that to happen. No, Kathy, sorry.

A much more impressive horse is Union Gold off a last race Big Win and a decent last race ability time but he is far too much of a closer to have much chance when there is early speed in the race and the track is receptive to the early runners. Royal Discovery, up from Calder, deserves some recognition, but again, we can pass him aside because of his very low PCR, which comes from his weak class standing, which is critical when you get into higher quality horses.

We are back to surveying the field once again to try to find the advantage we seek. It is there, loud and clear, in the last race ability times of Unattended Date and Proudest Babe, which stand so far above those of the others that they can be reasonably played. Their form is not far off, especially that of Unattended Date. Here is another instance where a multiple selection play is in order, even though Unattended Date's better PCR might be a decisive factor in selecting that one. We can play them both, especially when the odds are so high on the horse that we like the best that our profit opportunities are very very good.

The outcome was most pleasing. Unattended Date demolished the field with a Big Win, and Proudest Babe ran well ahead of all the others. This outcome is a powerful tribute to the strength of our new revised ability times. You will find they will bring you winners like this over and over again.

SEVENTH RACE **Aqueduct** **JANUARY 21, 1987** — 1 1/16 MILES.(InnerDirt). (1.41⅗) ALLOWANCE. Purse $28,000. Fillies and Mares, 4-year-olds and upward which have neve won two races other than maiden, claiming or starter. Weight, 122 lbs. Non-winners of a race other than maiden or claiming at a mile or over since January 1 allowed 3 lbs. Of such a race since December 15, 5 lbs.

Value of race $28,000; value to winner $16,800; second $6,160; third $3,360; fourth $1,680. Mutuel pool $88,225, OTB pool $128,614. Exacta Pool $178,338. OTB Exacta Pool $232,052.

Last Raced	Horse	Eqt.	A.	Wt	PP	St	¼	½	¾	Str	Fin	Jockey	Odds $1
11Jan87 7Aqu4	Unattended Date	b	4	117	7	6	7½	7½	4hd	1hd	15	Davis R G	8.00
11Jan87 7Aqu5	Proudest Babe	b	5	117	1	2	3hd	44	2½	25	24	Antley C W	2.60
2Jan87 5Crc2	Royal Discovery		4	117	6	4	6hd	6½	5hd	43½	32¾	Migliore R	6.00
15Jan87 8Pha5	Almost Pure	b	4	117	5	1	12	11½	11½	3½	43	Santos J A	9.20
12Jan87 5Aqu1	Union Gold		4	122	3	7	52	5hd	73½	53½	53	Bailey J D	15.30
14Jan87 5Aqu6	Ananas	b	5	117	8	8	8	8	8	63	611	Santagata N	7.40
8Jan87 7Aqu1	Barely Dancin	b	4	122	2	3	22	22½	32	71½	7¾	McCauley W H	2.20
7Jan87 1Aqu2	Kathy W.	b	4	112	4	5	43½	3hd	6½	8	8	Ortiz E Jr5	9.50

OFF AT 3:12 Start good for all but ANANAS, Won driving. Time, :23, :46⅘, 1:12⅘, 1:40⅕, 1:47 Track sloppy.

$2 Mutuel Prices:			
7-(K)-UNATTENDED DATE	18.00	6.20	4.40
1-(B)-PROUDEST BABE		4.40	3.00
6-(J)-ROYAL DISCOVERY			5.20

$2 EXACTA 7-1 PAID $41.20.

Almost Pure was out there early, with our hapless favorite, Barely Dancin', trying to keep up. Unattended Date, a even-type runner, was easily strong enough to come up on the early speed when those horses did not have enough late punch, as shown by their weak ability times, to hold off in a route race the strength of the two top horses. We will still be required, of course, to pay our usual careful attention to the front runners as we move ahead in the card.

The feature race of the day, with the highest ranking horses of the afternoon, illustrates yet another major aspect of analyzing the lines.

8th Aqueduct

6 FURLONGS. (InnerDirt). (1.08⅘) ALLOWANCE. Purse $29,000. 4-year-olds and upward which have never won three races other than maiden, claiming or starter. Weight, 122 lbs. Non-winners of two races other than maiden or claiming since December 15 allowed 3 lbs. Of such a race since then, 5 lbs.

Faraway Island ✓

Ch. c. 4, by Banquet Table—Tuvalu, by Our Native
Br.—Kimmel & Thomas (Ky) — 1987 1 0 0 0
Own.—Kimmel C P — **117** — Tr.—Toner James J — 1986 17 1 3 5 $55,082
Lifetime 23 3 4 5 $96,292 — Turf 10 0 3 3 $32,512

9Jan87-8Aqu	1 1/16 ⊡:48⁴1:13²1:44	ft	15	117	2hd	2½	45	511¾	Davis R G2	Aw31000	78-16	HrdyGrdyMn,GoldBmby,PrncLyph	11
30Dec86-6Aqu	170 ⊡:48 1:12²1:41	ft	9	115	21	1hd	35	36½	Samyn J L5	Aw31000	88-16	Alioth, I'm Ahead, Faraway Island	6
10Dec86-7Aqu	170 ⊡:46¹1:10⁴1:41	gd	10	113	1½	2½	69¾	613	Samyn J L4	Aw45000	82-08	Misty Mac, Matafao, Khozaam	6
13Nov86-7Aqu	1⅛ :46³ 1:11 1:50³	gd	7½	115	11½	14	1¾	1¾	Samyn J L1	Aw26000	82-20	FarwyIslnd,TheSvge,FbulousMove	10
2Nov86-5Aqu	1⅛ :48² 1:13 1:51²	ft	6½	115	12	12½	2½	31½	Samyn J L4	Aw26000	76-21	SprkofLove,WickedWike,FrwyIslnd	8
19Oct86-7Bel	1 Ⓣ:47 1:11²1:36³	fm	6¾	115	11½	1hd	32	35¾	Samyn J L5	Envoy	76-23	RealCourage,Trubulare,FarwyIslnd	7
3Oct86-7Bel	1 1/16 Ⓣ:46¹1:11¹1:44³	gd	10	114	2hd	67½	615	417½	Romero R P2	Aw26000	55-27	IcyGroom,ChristianHundred,Ioskeh	8
13Sep86-3Bel	1 1/16 Ⓣ:47²1:11 1:41³	fm	25	113	15	11½	12½	2no	Romero R P8	Aw26000	93-09	JackOfClubs,FarwyIslnd,Torquemd	8

Dec 22 Aqu ⊡ 5f ft 1:02² h   Dec 6 Aqu ⊡ 5f ft 1:01² h   Nov 26 Aqu 4f m :50² b

Polar Escapade

Ch. c. 4, by North Pole—Hobo's Lass, by The Willies II
Br.—Heffberger Jerold C (Md) 1987 1 0 0 0
Own.—Patti G Stable **117** **Tr.—Forbes John H** 1986 8 4 1 1 $47,545
Lifetime 12 6 1 1 $55,749

10Jan87-3Aqu	6f	⊡:222 :453 1:101 gd	9½e	113	1½	1½	2hd	54¼	Davis R G1	45000	89-10	Tis Royal, Sports Medicine, Semaj	11
1Dec86-7Med	6f	:223 :454 1:11 ft	6¾	115	3½	42	64	610	Krone J A6	Aw17000	77-23	PrsprFgr,LrdOfThNght,CntStndStll	7
19Nov86-7Med	6f	:223 :46 1:113 ft	7¾	114	3½	2hd	1hd	42½	Krone J A3	Aw18000	81-25	LuckyWhirl,Mr.RunRun,ProsperFgr	6
29Mar86-9Pim	6f	:231 :463 1:12 ft	*2-3	117	11½	12	13½	14½	PinoMG5	[S]Mister Diz	86-23	Polar Escapade, Ascool, Hatta Pro	5
7Mar86-5Aqu	6f	⊡:224 :47 1:123 ft	4½	115	1½	1hd	2hd	3nk	Davis R G2	70000	81-35	Jetsdrem,DistinctEdge,PolrEscpde	7
26Feb86-9GS	6f	:223 :46 1:112 ft	*1	115	2hd	21	1hd	1¾	Verge M E6	Aw10500	85-20	PolarEscapde,BendTheKey,YonSky	7
8Feb86-7Pha	6f	:221 :453 1:11 ft	3	115	31	1hd	1½	24½	Verge M E7	Aw10500	81-18	PickedClen,PolrEscpd,BidForBlnch	9
11Jan86-4Pha	6f	:222 :461 1:114 ft	*3¼	115	21	1hd	1hd	12½	Lloyd J S4	c20000	82-14	PolrEscpd,ErlyHrvst,Slynthropoid	12

●Jan 18 Bel tr.t 5f ft 1:004 h   Jan 7 Bel tr.t 5f ft 1:024 b   Jan 1 Bel tr.t 5f ft 1:031 b   Dec 28 Bel tr.t 5f ft 1:024 b

Steppin Battler

B. h. 6, by Crimson Battle—Steppin Stephanie, by Wa-Wa Cy
Br.—Keller R C (Ky) 1987 1 0 0 0
Own.—Mar-Rich Stable **1125** **Tr.—Kronevich Joseph A** 1986 22 1 1 1 $32,960
Lifetime 63 3 5 5 $98,960 **Turf** 2 0 0 0

10Jan87-1Aqu	6f	⊡:221 :452 1:101 gd	5¼	1125	44	53¾	56	55¼	Nuesch D4	Aw29000	88-10	MjesticEmpir,Mlstrom,HyNowHrry	6
17Dec86-7Aqu	6f	⊡:221 :453 1:111 ft	9	117	59½	57	45½	42	Venezia M4	Aw29000	86-20	BchlorBu,HrdyGrdyMn,HyNowHrry	7
6Dec86-7Aqu	6f	⊡:222 :453 1:11 ft	27	117	511	46	34½	22¼	Venezia M2	Aw29000	87-21	Cool Joe,SteppinBattler,HagleyMill	6
28Nov86-5Aqu	7f	:223 :443 1:22 ft	16	1107	31	43½	59	714¾	Belmonte J F5	50000	76-18	TlcPowr,ForCrtnDoc,UpPopsAwnnr	8
17Nov86-8Aqu	6½f	:221 :453 1:16 ft	54	1107	62¼	64	69	58¾	Belmonte JF6	Aw27000	86-20	Green Knight, I'm Ahead, Synastry	6
9Nov86-1Aqu	6f	:222 :454 1:104 sy	19	117	44	56½	615	616½	Samyn J L4	35000	70-22	Flunky Home, Exmoon, McMichael	7
17Jly86-9Bel	7f	:231 :46 1:232 ft	7½	117	95¾	88½	914	915¾	Davis R G6	50000	69-11	Lucky Belief, Tumbler,SilverStark	11
17Jly86—In tight early													
22Jun86-7Bel	1	Ⓣ:452 1:09 1:343 fm	70	117	46½	913	1117	1119¼	Rojás R I5	Aw29000	72-17	I'm A Banker, Balthazar B ,Attune	11

●Jan 7 Bel tr.t 3f ft :351 b

Slickster *

B. c. 4, by Smarten—Restless Keys, by Restless Wind
Br.—Kerr Mrs D K (Ky) 1986 13 3 1 1 $50,420
Own.—Kluesener Mrs D **117** **Tr.—Nieminski Richard** 1985 2 M 0 0
Lifetime 15 3 1 1 $50,420 **Turf** 1 0 0 0

30Dec86-6Aqu	170	⊡:48 1:122 1:41 ft	15	115	11	31½	58½	613	Antley C W1	Aw31000	82-16	Alioth, I'm Ahead, Faraway Island	6
3Dec86-5Aqu	1 1/16	⊡:471 1:111 1:424 gd	3¼	115	21	42	613	616½	Skinner K3	Aw31000	79-11	SirCorbin,SprkofLov,Tinchn'sPrinc	6
23Nov86-7Aqu	1	:46 1:102 1:36 ft	8	115	1½	2hd	24	310¼	Antley C W4	Aw29000	76-23	Khozaam, Aside, Slickster	7
19Oct86-6Bel	1	:454 1:10 1:342 ft	16	114	43	47½	310	513½	Skinner K7	Aw29000	79-14	Clear Choice, I Rejoice,BalthazarB.	7
18Sep86-8Bel	1 1/16	:451 1:101 1:424 ft	18	113	99½	98¼	77¼	713	Migliore R1	Aw40000	75-17	Carjack,Tinchen'sPrince,WaikikiStr	9
5Sep86-5Bel	1 1/16	:46 1:101 1:424 ft	2½	113	41¾	32	23	23¾	Skinner K1	Aw29000	84-18	Law Talk, Slickster, Doonesbear	6
29Aug86-8Bel	1 1/16	Ⓣ:473 1:121 1:44 gd	10	114	45	59	612	614½	Skinner K4	Aw29000	61-31	WtchForDwn,RelCourg,AlbrtClippr	6
28Jly86-1Bel	1⅛	:453 1:093 1:483 m	7	111	11	1½	14	11	Skinner K2	Aw26000	84-14	Slickster, Gorli, Where's Bob	6

Jan 18 Bel tr.t 3f ft :361 h

Fast Phillip *

B. g. 4, by Giboulee—Table Policy, by Mr Pow Wow
Br.—Taylor Made Farm (Ky) 1987 2 1 0 0 $18,540
Own.—Barrera O S **1145** **Tr.—Barrera Oscar S** 1986 23 4 2 4 $74,520
Lifetime 38 7 3 9 $112,951 **Turf** 2 1 0 0 $15,300

10Jan87-1Aqu	6f	⊡:221 :452 1:101 gd	2¼	1175	54¼	43¼	43	43¼	Ortiz E Jr2	Aw29000	90-10	MjesticEmpir,Mlstrom,HyNowHrry	6
10Jan87—Steadied st.													
5Jan87-7Aqu	1 1/16	⊡:472 1:114 1:44 ft	*9-5e	117	21½	2hd	12½	1½	Lovato F Jr2	Aw28000	90-18	Fast Phillip,Belocolus,WickedWike	9
31Dec86-4Aqu	6f	⊡:221 :46 1:103 ft	*1	115	11	12½	14	14½	Santos J A2	Aw26000	91-13	FastPhillip,DowryDan,PlacidWaters	6
28Dec86-2Aqu	1⅛	⊡:472 1:114 1:501 ft	2¼	1085	1hd	11½	12	14¾	Ortiz E Jr7	30000	91-12	Fast Phillip, Mr. Tatt, Concatinate	8
20Dec86-2Aqu	6f	⊡:221 :452 1:094 ft	4	1065	55	53½	2½	3nk	Nuesch D4	30000	95-09	RiverDemon,FlunkyHom,FstPhillip	7
20Dec86—In tight late													
11Dec86-9Aqu	6f	⊡:223 :461 1:104 ft	4½	1087	41½	42½	23½	36¾	Romero J A5	c14000	83-16	WanderingFeet,BlckOre,FstPhillip	11
26Nov86-1Aqu	1	:46 1:11 1:38 sy	*2¼	1047	41	2hd	2½	32¼	Romero J A6	12000	74-19	BetterBSingl,Tobin'sDrm,FstPhillip	8
15Nov86-5Aqu	1	:453 1:112 1:373 ft	22	115	2½	2hd	1111	1115¾	Santagata N8	Aw25000	62-22	RoundTheStte,ClssicMove,Dlmtin	13

Dec 6 Aqu ⊡ 4f ft :49 h

Shine Diulus — B. g. 5, by Christopher R—Bonnie Maggie, by St Bonaventure
Own.—Davis A — 117 — Br.—Rooney A J (Md) — 1987 2 0 2 0 $10,560
Tr.—Davis Barbara — 1986 9 4 1 0 $32,625
Lifetime 23 9 4 1 $74,705

14Jan87-7Aqu	6f	⊡:21³	:44²	1:09³ft	3½e	108⁷	1¹	1²	1²	2½	Ortiz E Jr⁷	75000	95-16	PrisVntur,ShinDulus,LordOfThNght	8
8Jan87-5Aqu	6f	⊡:22⁴	:46²	1:12 ft	*2¾	113	1²	1¹	2hd	2²	Santagata N⁶	c30000	82-24	BestDefense,ShinDiulus,IrishIrish	10
27Dec86-1Aqu	6f	⊡:22¹	:45³	1:10²ft	4½e	117	1³	1¹½	1½	1no	Santagata N⁶	25000	92-11	ShineDiulus,WndringFt,JollyBrokr	10
18Dec86-9Aqu	6f	⊡:22⁴	:46²	1:11²sy	*2	117	1²½	1¹½	1²	1¹¾	Santagata N⁴	17500	87-21	ShineDiulus,LibertyRex,HaiImpulse	8
12Nov86-6Med	6f	:22²	:45⁴	1:11¹gd	2¼	117	1½	1¹½	1²½	1nk	Edwards J W²	c15000	86-21	ShnDulus,SuprCount,LoqucousLovr	6
1Nov86-3Med	6f	:22³	:45⁴	1:11⁴ft	*2¼	116	1½	1²	1²	1¹¼	Antley C W³	12500	83-21	Shine Diulus, Mister G., Ship Mint	7
14Oct86-8Lrl	6f	:22²	:46³	1:12¹sy	3	115	1hd	1¹½	1hd	2hd	Saumell L⁷	11500	82-26	KpOnStrummng,ShnDls,Bck'sFntsy	7
13Sep86-6Pha	6f	:22¹	:45⁴	1:11¹ft	15	116	1½	1hd	3³½	4⁵¼	Thornburg B³	20000	80-20	Kng'sBluff,KlssyMomnt,RfndOffr	12

Dec 6 Med 5f ft 1:01² h   Dec 2 Med 3f ft :38 b

Maelstrom — B. h. 5, by Red Anchor—Waving Gallery, by Smart
Own.—Flynn J L — 117 — Br.—Flynn J (NY) — 1987 1 0 1 0 $6,380
Tr.—Jerkens H Allen — 1986 9 2 1 0 $50,858
Lifetime 18 3 3 1 $80,378

10Jan87-1Aqu	6f	⊡:22¹	:45²	1:10¹gd	*2	117	3¹½	3nk	2¹½	2¹¾	MrquezCHJr¹	Aw29000	91-10	MjesticEmpir,Mlstrom,HyNowHrry	6
10Dec86-8Aqu	6f	⊡:22¹	:45¹	1:09⁴gd	4¾	117	2hd	1¹½	1³	2²	MrzCHJr¹⁰	Ⓢ J Palmer	93-08	H. T.Willis,Maelstrom,LandingPlot	13
20Oct86-8Bel	1	:45²	1:10³	1:35³ft	13	111	1²	1¹½	4³	6⁹¾	MrCHJr³	Ⓢ AshlyColh	77-16	Fast Step, JudgeCosta,LandingPlot	8
28Sep86-9Bel	7f	:22³	:45³	1:23²m	5½	117	1½	1¹	1⁴	1⁵¼	MrqzCHJr⁵	Ⓢ Aw28000	85-15	Melstrom,CollegeChr,TropiclFront	10
7Sep86-1Bel	6f	:22²	:45⁴	1:09⁴ft	*8-5e	117	1³	1½	2¹½	4⁴½	MrqzCHJr⁵	Ⓢ Aw28000	88-14	Zonter, Flag King, Be A Tyrant	7
28Feb86-7Aqu	6f	⊡:22³	:46³	1:12 ft	*2¾	117⁵	2¹	2²½	4⁴¼	6⁷½	MrqzCHJr⁹	Ⓢ Aw28000	76-29	Ethics Aside, H. T.Willis,R.J.'sHope	9
22Feb86-4Aqu	6f	⊡:22¹	:45²	1:10²gd	3¾	112⁵	1¹½	1¹	1⁶	1⁶½	MrqzCHJr²	Ⓢ Aw26500	92-10	Maelstrom, AuRenor,AprilFoolsBoy	9
14Feb86-7Aqu	6f	⊡:22⁴	:46⁴	1:13¹ft	3¼	119	1²	1²½	1¹½	5³½	Skinner K⁹	Ⓢ Aw26500	74-31	Brni'sBunny,MkKnots,HighTimdty	12

Jan 8 Bel tr.t 3f ft :34⁴ h   Dec 27 Bel tr.t 3f ft :33⁴ h   ●Dec 2 Bel tr.t 5f ft :59 h   ●Nov 25 Bel 5f sy :59¹ h

Hey Now Harry — Dk. b. or br. c. 4, by Well Decorated—Minted, by Key to the Mint
Own.—Schwartz B K — 117 — Br.—Stonewall Farm (Ky) — 1987 1 0 0 1 $3,480
Tr.—Schmitt William F — 1986 14 2 2 3 $53,604
Lifetime 24 4 3 4 $95,222

10Jan87-1Aqu	6f	⊡:22¹	:45²	1:10¹gd	3¼	119	1hd	2hd	3²½	3³¼	Bailey J D⁵	Aw29000	90-10	MjesticEmpir,Mlstrom,HyNowHrry	6
17Dec86-7Aqu	6f	⊡:22¹	:45³	1:11¹ft	3	117	2¹	2hd	2¹	3²	Martens G³	Aw29000	86-20	BchlorBu,HrdyGrdyMn,HyNowHrry	7
10Dec86-6Aqu	6f	⊡:22¹	:45	1:09³gd	18	115	1¹	1³	1³	1³	Martens G⁷	Aw27000	96-08	HeyNowHrry,SillyRiffs,SoundProof	7
6Nov86-5Aqu	6f	:22²	:46¹	1:10²gd	7¾	113⁵	2hd	2¹	6¹⁰	7¹²¾	Belmonte J F¹	90000	76-24	Cultivate, B. C. Sal, Paris Venture	7
19Oct86-3Bel	7f	:23	:46	1:22⁴ft	9	114	1hd	4¹¾	6³½	5⁷¾	Santagata N²	Aw25000	80-14	Green Knight, Uene, I'm Ahead	7
9Oct86-8Med	6f	:23	:46	1:10³ft	3½	113	2hd	2hd	2¹½	2¾	Santagata N³	Aw16000	88-20	LordOfThNght,HyNowHrry,WtrCnn	[illegible]
14Sep86-5Bel	6f	:22³	:45¹	1:09³ft	6½	113	1hd	3⁶½	6¹²	7¹⁰¾	Martens G²	Aw25000	83-11	SecretProspctor,YnkAffir,HglyMill	7
4Sep86-7Bel	7f	:22²	:45¹	1:22²ft	7¾	113	3¹½	3²	3³	3⁴	Bailey J D¹	Aw25000	86-18	ChrgingForbs,WckdWk,HyNowHrry	7

Jan 7 Bel tr.t 4f ft :49 b   Dec 6 Bel tr.t 4f ft :50 b

Here is what our worksheet lines show:

Odds	Horse	PCR	Form	Ab/T
13	Faraway Island	64/ 15 27 – 1/ 41 = 156	NNN	48.4 24.1 + 1/ 73.4
28	Polar Escapade	64/ 13 23 + 2/ 38 = 168	NNO	45.3 25.3 + 6 72.2
12	Steppin Battler	62/ 46 49 – 3/ 98 = 63	NON	46.1 25.1 + 6/ 72.3
15	Slickster	53/ 31 36 – / 67 = 79	NNO	48.0 24.4 + 1/ 73.0
5	Fast Phillip	78/ 21 27 + 6/ 54 = 144	NNN	46.0 24.4 + 6/ 72.0
2	Shine Diulus	68/ 8 14 + 14/ 36 = 189	N+O	44.2 25.2 + 1/ 70.0
2	Maelstrom	74/ 11 27 + 7/ 45 = 164	N+N	45.2 25.1 + 6/ 71.4
5	Hey Now Harry	56/ 19 31 – 1/ 49 = 114	NNN	45.2 25.2 + 6/ 72.0

We are back to a sprint race where early speed, despite the fact that it didn't turn the trick in the seventh race, a distance event, is still likely to be the dominant factor. But as we look at the lines, our eyes pop open at the last race ability time of Shine Diulus. I almost have never seen a sprint race where one horse has a margin of nine ticks over the next best figure in the race. This is simply astonishing.

Not only that, but Shine Diulus has the highest PCR in the field, despite his big plus number for class. His early speed is outstanding, and again, no other horse in the race is even within five ticks of his second call time. The three next best ability times were all turned in on high speed surfaces with low variants, which makes the effort of Shine Diulus all the more impressive.

This race also illustrates the reliability of our artificial manufactured variants. Horses like Maelstrom, who was a co- favorite with Shine Diulus, as well as Fast Phillip and Hey Now Harry, all looked good enough to warrant support at the windows, but when we survey the enormous advantage that Shine Diulus possessed, we were pretty confident of the outcome. In this case, it matters not at all that Shine Diulus had a last race form defect of a loss in the stretch. His blistering times are so outstanding that he could yield even a little more and not be caught. We would expect him, on all the figures we have developed, to win this race wire to wire as our prime single selection. And that, of course, was exactly what he did, putting them all away as he romped to a Big Win.

EIGHTH RACE
Aqueduct
JANUARY 21, 1987

6 FURLONGS.(InnerDirt). (1.08⅘) ALLOWANCE. Purse $29,000. 4-year-olds and upward which have never won three races other than maiden, claiming or starter. Weight, 122 lbs. Non-winners of two races other than maiden or claiming since December 15 allowed 3 lbs. Of such a race since then, 5 lbs.

Value of race $29,000; value to winner $17,400; second $6,380; third $3,480; fourth $1,740. Mutuel pool $76,237, OTB pool $133,639. Exacta Pool $119,169. OTB Exacta Pool $191,135.

Last Raced	Horse	Eqt.	A.	Wt	PP	St	¼	½	Str	Fin	Jockey	Odds $1
14Jan87 ^{7}Aqu^{2}	Shine Diulus	b	5	117	6	1	1^{1}	$1^{1\frac{1}{2}}$	1^{4}	$1^{3\frac{1}{4}}$	Davis R G	2.00
9Jan87 ^{8}Aqu^{5}	Faraway Island	b	4	117	1	4	3^{hd}	3^{hd}	$3^{1\frac{1}{2}}$	$2^{2\frac{1}{2}}$	Samyn J L	13.20
10Jan87 ^{1}Aqu^{3}	Hey Now Harry		4	117	8	2	2^{3}	$2^{3\frac{1}{2}}$	$2^{\frac{1}{2}}$	$3^{\frac{3}{4}}$	Martens G	5.80
10Jan87 ^{1}Aqu^{2}	Maelstrom	b	5	117	7	3	$4^{1\frac{1}{2}}$	$4^{1\frac{1}{2}}$	4^{3}	$4^{\frac{3}{4}}$	Marquez C H	2.00
30Dec86 ^{6}Aqu^{6}	Slickster		4	117	4	7	8	8	7^{hd}	$5^{1\frac{1}{4}}$	Antley C W	15.80
10Jan87 ^{1}Aqu^{4}	Fast Phillip	b	4	114	5	5	5^{hd}	6^{2}	6^{3}	6^{4}	Ortiz E Jr^{5}	5.20
10Jan87 ^{1}Aqu^{5}	Steppin Battler	b	6	112	3	6	7^{5}	7^{6}	8	$7^{1\frac{1}{4}}$	Nuesch D^{5}	12.20
10Jan87 ^{3}Aqu^{5}	Polar Escapade		4	117	2	8	6^{5}	5^{1}	5^{hd}	8	Santos J A	28.40

OFF AT 3:41, Start good, Won ridden out. Time, :21⅘, :45, 1:10⅘ Track sloppy.

$2 Mutuel Prices:			
6-(F)-SHINE DIULUS	6.00	4.60	3.20
1-(A)-FARAWAY ISLAND		13.20	6.20
8-(H)-HEY NOW HARRY			4.00

$2 EXACTA 6-1 PAID $83.00.

We are happy with another winning payoff, even at $6, which was an outstanding bargain considering how much better that Shine

Diulus, with his devastating early speed, was over the others. We can now move to the last race of the day, which, as most races do, presents its own set of new problems.

We are back to a claiming race at the longer distance of 1 3/16 miles, where we have a most lukewarm favorite, Jungleland at 5-2. Because the distance of 1 1/8 miles is the most common among the horses entered, we will be calculating our last race ability times off that distance, and converting those distances that are different.

9th Aqueduct

1 3/16 MILES. (InnerDirt). (1.55⅗) CLAIMING. Purse $15,000. 4-year-olds and upward. Weight, 122 lbs. Non-winners of two races over a mile since December 15 allowed 3 lbs. Of such a race since then, 5 lbs. Claiming price $17,500; for each $1,000 to $15,500 allowed 2 lbs. (Races when entered to be claimed for $14,000 or less not considered.)

Parrell Hill

Own.—Gresch M A **1105**
B. g. 5, by Nonparrell—Hill Sink, by Hillsborough
Br.—Wilson J R (Fla)
Tr.—Hirsch Marilyn $16,500
Lifetime 42 4 5 8 $46,521
1987 1 0 0 0
1986 21 2 1 3 $16,544
Turf 6 1 0 0 $5,304

5Jan87-4Aqu 6f [•]:222 :4611:11 ft 86 113 911 811 613 613¾ Vasquez M M8 20000 75-18 JollyBroker,WnderingFet,GrnShkl 10
14Nov86-6Grd 1 3/16 :503 1:17 2:033ft 13 119 910 911 816 812¾ Grubb R1 19000 54-35 KidShrkin,GrySluth,BobbyLondon 10
6Nov86-3Grd 1 3/16 :533 1:19 2:034ft 6½ 121 21½ 33½ 45 42 Grubb R4 16000 64-29 TnyTtn,BobbyLondon,BldCnnctnII 7
31Oct86-6Grd 6½f :232 :472 1:202ft 46 119 712 711 712 77 Grubb R6 24000 77-29 ApprentiSorcier,Denin,BishopRidly 7
20Oct86-9FE 1 1/16 :47 1:122 1:464ft *7-5 116 714 511 41½ 1no Grubb R4 Aw6400 77-20 PrrellHill,LdyStrtgy,MorVictorious 7
12Oct86-9FE 1 [T]:49 1:1621:454yl 15 119 67½ 89¾ 712 715½ Hemsley D L6 Aw6400 33-75 StgRun,SpctculrBn,DncnOfKnloch 11
21Sep86-1WO 1 1/16 :481 1:141 1:474ft 16 116 66½ 33½ 33½ 33¾ Leblanc J B4 19000 66-30 GraySleuth,StrikingSeson,PrrellHill 7
1Sep86-9FE 1 [T]:4741:1241:383fm 30 122 916 911 87¼ 87½ Grubb R5 Aw7600 77-18 TlkRonTlk,TripleEdge,ClssicRegent 9
Jan 17 Aqu [•] 4f ft :541 b Jan 12 Aqu [•] 7f ft 1:35 h Jan 4 Aqu [•] 3f ft :394 b Dec 29 Aqu [•] 4f ft :484 b

Chubby Babe

Own.—Diprima A **113**
Gr. h. 5, by Jacques Who—Miss Jitters, by Scottsdale
Br.—Grondin J A (NY)
Tr.—DiAngelo Joseph T $15,500
Lifetime 24 3 4 1 $27,535
1987 1 0 0 0
1986 14 1 2 0 $13,670
Turf 3 0 0 0

5Jan87-2Aqu 1 1/16 [•]:4741:1241:453ft *2½ 117 41¾ 31½ 36 89½ Davis R G1 14000 72-18 ShyHughes,NwAdvntur,Mr.Noritk 11
18Dec86-9Aqu 6f [•]:224 :4621:112sy 8 119 46½ 56 514 611¼ Bailey J D8 17500 76-21 ShineDiulus,LibertyRex,HailImpulse 8
3Dec86-2Aqu 1 1/16 [•]:4811:1241:451gd 18 119 52¾ 42 2½ 22½ Romero R P7 17500 81-11 PledgeCp,ChubbyBbe,Tobin'sDrm 10
22Nov86-7FL 170 :472 1:141 1:481sy 5½ 116 37½ 32½ 2½ 1nk RynoldsRL3 [S]Aw10000 60-30 ChubbyBbe,RuknAir,GrdnColletion 8
16Nov86-5FL 6f :224 :46 1:11 ft 4¼ 115 54½ 65½ 64¾ 65¾ Cook R W3 [S] 16000 88-10 MontryCop,ConstttonMn,MchWnd 7
12Nov86-9FL 1 1/16 :48 1:13 1:47 ft *2¾ 116 2hd 22 33 45¼ Cook R W6 [S]Aw10000 76-20 FullCrdt,OrConstlton,GrdnCollcton 7
24Oct86-7Aqu 1 1/16 [T]:4741:1221:444fm 25 117 52¾ 53½ 54½ 711¼ Cruguet J3 [S]Aw29500 70-20 G'DyMte,ExpeditionMoon,RootCnl 8
28Sep86-9Bel 7f :223 :453 1:232m 20 117 76 54½ 37 58½ Maple E6 [S]Aw28000 76-15 Melstrom,CollegeChr,TropiclFront 10
Jan 13 Bel tr.t 3f ft :373 b Dec 31 Bel tr.t 4f gd :482 h Dec 14 Bel tr.t 4f ft :50 h

*Letal

Own.—Perez R **113**
Gr. c. 4, by Legandario—Millingsby, by Hard Tack
Br.—Haras El Ranchero (Uru)
Tr.—Callejas Alfredo $15,500
Lifetime 4 1 0 0 $489
1986 4 1 0 0 $489
1985 0 M 0 0

31Dec86-2Aqu 1 3/16 [•]:4711:1221:572ft 47 111 818 819 925 829¾ Davis R G8 20000 61-13 ArcticSong,LedTheWy,OurTriumph 9
21Dec86-9Aqu 1 1/16 [•]:4721:13 1:451ft 25 115 1220 1223 1120 1127½ Graell A5 22500 57-14 Concatinate, Lemmings, McNaz 12
7Sep86◆5Maronas(Uru) a1 1:383ft 3¾ 123 44¾ MndH GranPolla dePotrillos(Gr1 Ciclo, King, Frenetico 9
10Aug86◆4Maronas(Uru) a5½f 1:083m *1-6 123 15 MndH PremioEldelito(Mdn) Letal, Quietito, Monkish 6
Dec 28 Bel tr.t 4f ft :503 b Dec 6 Bel tr.t 4f ft :50 hg Nov 29 Bel tr.t 4f ft :504 b

Mr. Noritake
Own.—Perroncino J S **113**

B. g. 4, by L'Heureux—Laurob, by Thomasville
Br.—McMakin N (Ky)
Tr.—Widmer Wayne **$15,500**
Lifetime 18 1 2 3 $19,130

1987	2 0 0 1	$1,620
1986	13 1 2 2	$17,510
Turf	2 0 0 0	

5Jan87-2Aqu	1 1/16 ⊡:47^{4}1:12^{4}1:45^{3}ft	10 114	8^7 7$^{7\frac14}$ 5$^{6\frac34}$ 3^6	Lovato F Jr^7	12000	76-18	ShyHughes,NwAdvntur,Mr.Noritk	11
1Jan87-9Aqu	1 1/16 ⊡:48^{3}1:13^{4}1:46 ft	11 113	10^{12}11^9 11^{13}10$^{16\frac34}$	Lovato F Jr^8	15500	63-22	FrnchExprss,YongMnrch,PrntMny	11
17Dec86-9Aqu	1 1/16 ⊡:49 1:15 1:47^{4}ft	6¾ 115	7$^{3\frac34}$ 4¾ 3$^{2\frac12}$ 2$^{2\frac14}$	Lovato F Jr^{10}	14000	69-20	Brasov, Mr. Noritake, Interplay	12
6Dec86-2Aqu	1⅛ ⊡:48^{2}1:13^{3}1:53^{3}ft	7½ 115	9^7 5$^{3\frac34}$ 4^6 4$^{5\frac12}$	Lovato F Jr^9	14000	68-21	VgbondGorg,ButWhoKnows,Brsov	11
6Dec86—Awarded third purse money								
15Nov86-3Aqu	1 :45^1 1:09^4 1:36^{4}ft	20e115	9^{16} 9^{15} 9^{13} 8^{14}	Graell A^9	22500	68-22	RollingBy,RoylPotntl,TinyToShos	10
9Nov86-3Aqu	1⅛ :48^1 1:12^1 1:52 sy	25 113	5$^{6\frac12}$ 5$^{7\frac34}$ 4$^{8\frac12}$ 5$^{7\frac14}$	Graell A^6	30000	68-22	Concatinate,ProudAndTll,FlyGryFly	6
3Nov86-1Aqu	1 :46^4 1:11^3 1:38^{1}ft	7f 113	4¾ 9$^{5\frac12}$10$^{9\frac12}$ 9^8	Graell A^9	20000	67-22	BrillintCsting,RoylPotntt,TllRomn	14
8Aug86-2Sar	1⅛ :48^4 1:13^3 1:52^{3}m	7 113	7$^{6\frac34}$ 7^{15} 7^{18} 7$^{23\frac12}$	Maple E^3	20000	48-17	Lydastar, Fly GaryFly,HawaiiFively	7

Nov 26 Bel tr.t 4f gd :52^2 b

Moss Pond
Own.—Unstable Stable **117**

Ch. g. 4, by Coastal—Dia, by Forli
Br.—Clark S C Jr (Ky)
Tr.—Cotter Mary M **$17,500**
Lifetime 13 1 0 0 $15,720

1987	1 0 0 0	
1986	8 1 0 0	$14,880
Turf	2 0 0 0	

4Jan87-2Aqu	1⅛ ⊡:47 1:12^{4}1:53 gd	12 117	6^9 6$^{7\frac12}$ 5$^{8\frac14}$ 5^{11}	Hernandez R^6	17500	66-21	KeepItEsy,AmricnAngl,EthicsAsid	10
10Dec86-4Aqu	1⅛ ⊡:47^{4}1:12^{3}1:51^{2}m	8¼ 117	6^6 5$^{2\frac12}$ 4^7 4$^{12\frac14}$	Martens G^4	25000	73-13	BrllntCstng,NoQuston,FrnchExprss	7
15Nov86-5Aqu	1 :45^3 1:11^2 1:37^{3}ft	35 117	13^{20}11^{11} 9^{10} 9^{11}	Cruguet J^7	Aw25000	67-22	RoundTheStte,ClssicMove,Dlmtin	13
29Oct86-5Aqu	1⅜ :50 1:39^4 2:20 ft	26 119	4$^{2\frac12}$ 4¾ 1½ 1^1	Martens G^4	Mdn	81-15	MossPond,Hlo'sSplndr,MstrOfArts	7
19Oct86-4Bel	1 1/16 Ⓣ:48^{1}1:12^{4}1:44^{4}fm	30 119	10^{11} 9^{14} 7^9 7^9	Skinner K^{11}	Mdn	63-23	Seattlite,ImperilIdol,TrgetSighted	11
8Oct86-2Bel	1 Ⓣ:46^{4}1:12 1:38^{2}fm	32 119	10$^{8\frac14}$11^{11}10$^{8\frac34}$ 6$^{7\frac12}$	Skinner K^4	Mdn	65-29	FleetingSnow,I'mNoYnke,Snd-Up	12
3Oct86-9Bel	1 :46^1 1:11 1:37 ft	26 119	9$^{9\frac12}$10^{17} 8^{18} 8$^{16\frac14}$	Skinner K^9	M35000	64-17	Free Verse, ByeDad,GallantChamp	12
15Sep86-9Bel	6f :22^4 :46^1 1:11^{2}ft	16 114	10$^{9\frac12}$ 9^{13} 9^{15}10$^{13\frac14}$	Davis R G^4	M30000	72-15	Big Coda, Aptitude, Jeannies Boy	11

Dec 28 Bel tr.t 3f ft :38^1 b **Dec 22 Bel tr.t 4f ft :51^1 b** **Dec 18 Bel tr.t 5f ft 1:05^3 b** **Dec 4 Bel tr.t 4f ft :48^4 b**

Sing With Me
Own.—Lostritto J A **113**

Ch. h. 5, by Singh—Fly With Me, by Misty Flight
Br.—Entenmann Robert (NY)
Tr.—Lostritto Joseph A **$15,500**
Lifetime 36 2 0 1 $39,060

1987	1 0 0 0	
1986	26 2 0 0	$36,060
Turf	6 2 0 0	$32,100

3Jan87-7Aqu	1 1/16 ⊡:48 1:13^{1}1:45 m	6¾e112^5	7$^{8\frac34}$ 7$^{5\frac34}$ 6^9 5$^{8\frac12}$	PabonJCJr^8	[S]Aw29500	76-16	TheSavge,It'sAboutSeven,KillerJoe	9
6Dec86-2Aqu	1⅛ ⊡:48^{2}1:13^{3}1:53^{3}ft	36 108^7	11^{11}11^{11} 9^{16} 9^{16}	Pabon J C Jr^1	13000	58-21	VgbondGorg,ButWhoKnows,Brsov	11
1Dec86-1Aqu	7f :23^1 :47 1:25^{4}ft	50 117	10^{17} 8^{11} 9$^{7\frac34}$ 7$^{7\frac34}$	Ward W A^5	14000	64-25	FlshyDimond,Trberry,WnderingFt	10
15Nov86-2Aqu	1⅛ :47^2 1:12^3 1:52^{3}ft	37 117	11^{20}11^{16}10^{18} 9$^{20\frac34}$	Graell A^9	14000	51-22	PrintMony,ArctcSong,FrdomsEdg	11
11Nov86-2Aqu	1⅛ :48^3 1:13^3 1:53^{1}sy	9 113	5$^{6\frac12}$ 4$^{4\frac12}$ 8$^{7\frac34}$ 8$^{10\frac12}$	Graell A^5	15500	58-21	FrnchExprss,BtWhKnws,Tbn'sDrm	8
2Nov86-6Aqu	7f :23^2 :47^1 1:24^{4}ft	31 112^5	10^{11}10$^{8\frac14}$ 9^{11} 8^{10}	Brown T L^6	[S]Aw28000	67-21	SummerTale,TalcBuster,TheSavge	10
9Oct86-7Bel	1 1/16 Ⓣ:47^{3}1:12 1:44^{2}fm	31 117^5	12^{13}12^{14}12^{11}10$^{11\frac34}$	Brown T L^9	[S]Aw29500	62-26	VtzMtter,ExpditionMoon,RcPoint	12
28Sep86-9Bel	7f :22^3 :45^3 1:23^{2}m	34 117^5	8^8 7^6 4$^{8\frac12}$ 4$^{6\frac34}$	Brown T L^2	[S]Aw28000	78-15	Melstrom,CollegeChr,TropiclFront	10

Dec 16 Bel tr.t 5f ft 1:03^4 b **Nov 25 Bel tr.t 5f m 1:03^1 b**

Classic Deal
Own.—Tall Oaks Farm **117**

B. g. 5, by Victorian Prince—Snow Classic, by Irish Stronghold
Br.—Simmons C E (Ont-C)
Tr.—Trovato Joseph A **$17,500**
Lifetime 40 9 3 3 $57,703

1987	1 0 0 0	$900
1986	20 5 2 2	$35,232

1Jan87-9Aqu	1 1/16 ⊡:48^{3}1:13^{4}1:46 ft	9 112^5	7$^{5\frac12}$ 5$^{2\frac34}$ 5^5 4$^{4\frac12}$	Baird E T^4	17500	75-22	FrnchExprss,YongMnrch,PrntMny	11
1Dec86-9Aqu	1 :47 1:12^1 1:38^{1}ft	13 110^7	6$^{3\frac14}$10^7 11^8 11^9	Nuesch D^4	22500	66-25	SmrtSlnc,SpcyBons,AccountRcvbl	11
1Dec86—Unruly pre-start								
24Nov86-1Aqu	1 :46^4 1:12 1:38^{1}sy	3¼ 119	2^{hd} 3½ 5^4 6$^{6\frac12}$	Santos J A^6	c17500	68-22	CnnonRoyl,LedTheWy,PrintMoney	9
8Nov86-2Grd	1 :48^2 1:14^1 1:40^{4}gd	2½ 121	2$^{1\frac12}$ 2^{hd} 1^{hd} 1$^{1\frac12}$	Lauzon J M^5	20000	76-27	Classic Deal, GraySleuth,Deuterium	6
24Oct86-9WO	1 1/16 :48^3 1:14 1:48^{1}ft	9 116	8$^{5\frac14}$ 4$^{3\frac12}$ 2^2 1½	Lauzon J M^{13}	19000	68-32	ClassicDel,Regent'sOwn,GrySleuth	13
16Oct86-8WO	1 1/16 :48^4 1:14^1 1:48^{3}ft	4¼ 118	4^3 3$^{3\frac12}$ 3½ 2^{nk}	Lauzon J M^5	16000	66-26	Regent'sOwn,ClssicDel,BishopsHill	7
27Sep86-1WO	1 1/16 :47^3 1:13^3 1:47 gd	7¾ 118	7$^{6\frac14}$ 4$^{1\frac12}$ 1½ 1^2	Lauzon J M^{12}	10000	74-20	Classic Deal, Regal Sin,BishopTim	12
13Sep86-1WO	1 1/16 :48^4 1:13^2 1:48 ft	5¾ 119^5	3$^{3\frac12}$ 1^{hd} 1^4 1^4	O'Brien S G J^4	c6250	69-24	ClssicDl,LooksLikACount,RdlyBoy	12

Dec 28 Aqu ⊡ 4f ft :50^2 b

Freedoms Edge

B. h. 5, by Double Edge Sword—Pilgrim's Pride, by First Landing
Own.—Rosenberg Suzanne A 117 **Br.—Quick S E (Md)** **Tr.—Delise Genare J** $17,500
1966 14 0 1 1 $4,875
1985 23 2 4 3 $50,980
Lifetime 39 2 5 5 $56,493 Turf 4 0 0 0

29Dec86-2Aqu 1⅛ [⊡]:48^{1}1:13 1:52^{2}ft 11 115 2^{hd} 31½ 33½ 63½ Thibeau R J^{4} 16500 76-18 ‡Junglelnd,SpiceyBons,CnnonRoyl 12
29Dec86—Placed fifth through disqualification; Impeded
15Nov86-2Aqu 1⅛ :47^{2} 1:12^{3} 1:52^{3}ft 9½ 117 32½ 2^{1} 3^{1} 3^{2} ♦ Lovato F Jr^{2} 14000 70-22 PrintMony,ArctcSong,FrdomsEdg 11
15Nov86—Awarded second purse money; ♦Dead heat
3Nov86-3Aqu 1 :46^{3} 1:11^{1} 1:37^{2}ft 9½ 117 8^{8} 6^{9} 39½ 36¾ Lovato F Jr^{10} 14000 72-22 RiverDemon,LedThWy,FrdomsEdg 12
24Oct86-3Aqu 6f :22^{3} :46^{3} 1:11^{1}ft 39 115 10^{16} 9^{11} 9^{9} 6^{7} Lovato F Jr^{1} 15500 78-20 PledgeCp,SuperScope,CnnonRoyl 10
24Jly86-3Bel 1¼ [T]:49 1:37^{4}2:02^{1}fm 65 117 64¼ 7^{7} 9^{12} 912¼ Saint-Martin E^{4} 35000 70-16 Straight Shot, HisHonour,AllWhite 9
11Jly86-2Bel 1⅜ [T]:48^{2}1:37 2:15 fm 78 117 11^{15}11^{17} 9^{15} 910¾ Skinner K^{10} 35000 71-13 Cloutier,WesternChmp,HisHonour 11
26Jun86-3Bel 1¼ [T]:47^{4}1:37^{4}2:02 fm 47 117 11^{11} 87½ 8^{14} 812¾ Skinner K^{5} 35000 71-17 Temujin,StrightShot,WestrnChmp 11
30May86-7Bel 1 1/16 [T]:47 1:11 1:42^{3}hd 56 119 54½ 6^{5} 6^{9} 612¾ Samyn J L^{7} Aw25000 75-13 RightValue,MoorIndLne,CloverKing 8
Jan 12 Bel tr.t 4f ft :50^{4} b Dec 22 Bel tr.t 5f ft 1:03^{4} b Dec 15 Bel tr.t 3f ft :39 b

Rattlesnake Rogue

B. g. 4, by Native Royalty—Barsa, by Caracolero
Own.—Old Glory Stable 113 **Br.—Stable J J H (Ky)** **Tr.—Sciametta Anthony Jr** $15,500
1987 2 0 0 0
1986 17 2 4 0 $17,398
Lifetime 19 2 4 0 $17,398 Turf 1 0 0 0

15Jan87-2Aqu 1⅛ [⊡]:47^{4}1:12^{3}1:52^{3}ft 25 108^{5} 9^{12} 9^{9} 6^{7} 5^{6} Heath M J^{4} 12000 73-19 BttrBSngl,DubosHnds,StmbotCrk 12
1Jan87-9Aqu 1 1/16 [⊡]:48^{3}1:13^{4}1:46 ft 21 113 98¾ 10^{7} 9^{13} 810¼ Zuniga M^{5} 15500 70-22 FrnchExprss,YongMnrch,PrntMny 11
17Dec86-9Aqu 1 1/16 [⊡]:49 1:15 1:47^{4}ft 22 111 3½ 61¾ 4^{3} 42¾ Zuniga M^{12} 12000 68-20 Brasov, Mr. Noritake, Interplay 12
17Dec86—Checked
29Nov86-2Med 1 1/16 :48^{2} 1:13^{1} 1:46 ft *4-5e 112 73¾ 68½ 4^{11} 47¾ Zuniga M^{5} 10500 65-23 CptinKingwll,ThtAn'tHy,CornshRcp 9
18Nov86-1Med 1 1/16 :48 1:12^{2} 1:45^{2}ft 3¼ 116 5^{5} 36½ 35½ 2^{7} Zuniga M^{8} 10000 69-28 LouiLco,RttlsnkRogu,KlssyButEvl 10
3Nov86-2Med 1 1/16 :47^{4} 1:12^{3} 1:45^{2}ft 17 115 52½ 55½ 57½ 2^{6} Krone J A^{6} 16000 70-26 Koochchng,RttlsnkRogu,GrssWhstl 9
22Oct86-4Med 6f :22^{2} :45^{3} 1:11^{1}ft 21 116 8^{21} 8^{18} 8^{16} 813¾ Antley C W^{4} 16000 72-21 Reygo, Northern Peak,FullStocking 8
22Oct86—Broke slowly
8Oct86-3Med 1^{70}:47 1:12 1:42^{3}ft 7 115 7^{14} 7^{12} 6^{13} 612¾ Moyers L^{7} c12500 70-23 Koochiching,DeltWings,TuxdoJohn 7
Jan 10 Bel tr.t 3f ft :39^{4} b Dec 29 Bel tr.t 3f ft :39 b Dec 8 Med 4f ft :53 b Nov 26 Med 4f sy :52 b

Jungleland

Gr. h. 6, by Warm Front—Olga S, by Terrible Tiger
Own.—Paolangeli F 112^{5} **Br.—Brown J (NY)** **Tr.—Sedlacek Michael C** $17,500
1986 17 2 4 0 $32,016
1985 19 5 1 2 $37,419
Lifetime 63 13 7 5 $122,033 Turf 3 0 0 1 $2,100

29Dec86-2Aqu 1⅛ [⊡]:48^{1}1:13 1:52^{2}ft 29 112^{5} 8^{16} 7^{5} 4^{5} 1^{hd} † Baird E T^{2} 17500 80-18 ‡Junglelnd,SpiceyBons,CnnonRoyl 12
†29Dec86—Disqualified and placed sixth; Ducked out midstr
11Dec86-1Aqu 1⅛ [⊡]:47^{2}1:12^{4}1:50^{3}ft 16 113 89¾ 107¼ 9^{12} 814¾ Murphy D J^{1} 20000 74-16 LeadTheWay,ArcticSong,ClssHero 12
1Dec86-9Aqu 1 :47 1:12^{1} 1:38^{1}ft 15 117 85¾ 86½ 10^{6} 10^{7} Murphy D J^{9} 25000 68-25 SmrtSlnc,SpcyBons,AccountRcvbl 11
20Nov86-1Aqu 1⅜ :50^{1} 2:07 2:19^{4}ft *3½ 117 31½ 31½ 7^{12} 610¾ Murphy D J^{5} 35000 71-20 Stop Light, Oversea, Temujin 9
13Oct86-9FL 1⅛ :48^{3} 1:13^{4} 1:55 sy 5½ 114 7^{9} 65½ 4^{4} 49½ McCrtMJ^{8} WdswrthH 71-27 SprcArrow,CostlyContrct,SmrtSlnc 8
5Oct86-7FL 1^{70}:47 1:11^{2} 1:43^{1}sy *2½ 122 5^{15} 68½ 64¾ 68½ McCarthy M J^{2} 30000 76-18 SpruceArrow,BrberIzzy,CptinMrvel 6
21Sep86-7FL 1 1/16 :47 1:13 1:47 ft 3 114 57½ 4^{3} 2^{hd} 2¾ Hulet L^{4} [S] 27500 80-20 GoldenThreesome,Junglelnd,Tnncy 6
14Sep86-9FL 1^{70}:47^{1} 1:14 1:45^{3}ft 2¾ 115 59¾ 5^{4} 41¼ 1no McCarthy M J^{3} HcpO 73-24 Junglelnd,PostTense,RunOnCourge 5
Jan 16 Aqu [⊡] 4f ft :50^{2} bg Dec 22 Aqu [⊡] 5f ft 1:05^{1} bg

Concealed Identity

B. h. 5, by Masked Dancer—Finest Colleen, by Son Ange
Own.—Still River Farm 113 **Br.—Green Willow Farms (Md)** **Tr.—Puccio Donald** $15,500
1987 2 0 0 1 $1,800
1966 10 0 1 1 $8,280
Lifetime 32 4 4 3 $77,290 Turf 1 0 0 0

11Jan87-9Aqu 1⅛ [⊡]:46 1:11 1:50^{4}gd 62 113 8^{11} 7^{8} 4^{5} 37½ Thibeau R J^{9} 15500 80-12 SoloSportng,PrntMny,CncldIdntty 10
5Jan87-2Aqu 1 1/16 [⊡]:47^{4}1:12^{4}1:45^{3}ft 23 115 9^{7} 119¾ 10^{13} 1015¼ Hernandez R^{3} 13000 67-18 ShyHughes,NwAdvntur,Mr.Noritk 11
6Dec86-2Aqu 1⅛ [⊡]:48^{2}1:13^{3}1:53^{3}ft 31 112^{5} 86¾ 108¼ 10^{16} 1018¼ Brown T L^{4} 14000 56-21 VgbondGorg,ButWhoKnows,Brsov 11
1Dec86-1Aqu 7f :23^{1} :47 1:25^{4}ft 14 112^{5} 9^{16} 10^{12} 109¾ 10^{11} Brown T L^{8} 14000 61-25 FlshyDimond,Trberry,WnderingFt 10
24Nov86-1Aqu 1 :46^{4} 1:12 1:38^{1}sy 11 112^{5} 1^{hd} 2½ 86¾ 99½ Brown T L^{5} 17500 65-22 CnnonRoyl,LedTheWy,PrintMoney 9
13Nov86-2Aqu 1 :46^{3} 1:12^{1} 1:38 gd 27 108^{7} 11^{11} 117¾ 10^{9} 9^{10} Ortiz E Jr^{2} 22500 66-20 EthicsAsid,Tmprtur,AccountRcvbl 13
22Oct86-4Aqu 1 3/16 :48 1:11^{3} 1:56^{4}ft 11 115 42½ 58½ 7^{18} 7^{14} Santagata N^{1} 32500 64-16 Harry L., Our Triumph, Roomie 7
8Oct86-9Bel 7f :22^{4} :46^{1} 1:23^{1}ft 15 117 41¾ 105¼ 11^{11} 1112¾ Messina R^{2} 35000 73-19 FingersIntheTill,Revlrout,TlcPowr 12

```
Class Hero                      Ch. h. 8, by Determined King—Fabulous Rose, by Night Invader
                                Br.—Braman & Pierce (Fla)                      1987 1 0 0 0
Own.—Santangelo Barbara    117  Tr.—Pascuma James J Jr          $17,500        1986 5 0 1 0        $2,800
                            Lifetime  90 10 22 10  $250,700                    Turf 16 1 4 2       $34,890
4Jan87-2Aqu   1⅛[•]:47 1:1241:53 gd    4  1125 45½ 45 48 713¾ Ortiz E Jr5   17500 63-21 KeepItEsy,AmricnAngl,EthicsAsid 10
21Dec86-1Aqu  1 1/16[•]:47 1:12 1:441ft 10 1125 2hd 2½ 53 66½ Ortiz E Jr9   25000 83-14 QuitRoylty,OurTrumph,CnnonRoyl 11
11Dec86-1Aqu  1⅛[•]:4721:1241:503ft    9¼ 1107 46½ 21 44 37½  Ortiz E Jr2   25000 81-16 LeadTheWay,ArcticSong,ClssHero 12
    11Dec86—Disqualified from purse money
28Nov86-1Aqu  1⅛:473 1:12 1:504ft      10 1087 2hd 2½ 65¾ 87¾ Ortiz E Jr7   32500 73-18 How About Now, Askrano, Mr. Tall 8
7Nov86-7Med   1 1/16:474 1:13 1:451gd   7 1087 1hd 1½ 2hd 22  Ortiz E Jr3   32000 75-23 Dirty Birdie, Class Hero, Defarge 5
    7Nov86--Brushed str.
30Oct86-9Aqu  7f :222 :461 1:234ft    42 1087 76¼ 62¾ 95¾ 96  Ortiz E Jr8   32500 76-21 EqulTerms,TlcPower,Vinny'sPride 11
24Nov85-4Aqu  1 :454 1:11 1:361gd     13 117  21½ 31½ 77½ 77¾ McCarron G6   25000 77-15 JunDeFuc,BlzingComt,ShiningOut 11
26Oct85-2Aqu  1 :464 1:121 1:382ft    21 113  41 86¼ 911 910  McCarron G4   30000 64-19 ChicBoutique,Tenifly,HardentLark 10
    26Oct85—Bore out
  Jan 16 Aqu [•] 6f ft 1:163 b      Dec 8 Aqu [•] 4f ft :493 b      ●Nov 25 Aqu 4f sy :49 h
```

How do they rate, and what are their running styles? Our ever trusty worksheet becomes our guide.

Odds	Horse	PCR	Form	Ab/T
20	Parrell Hill	68/ 52 44 – 5/ 91 = 75	NON	x
8	Chubby Babe	69/ 33 39 – 4/ 68 = 101	NON	13.1 41.1 0/ 54.2
50	Letal	x	x	
10	Mr. Noritake	82/ 57 48 – 4/101 = 81	NON	14.1 39.2 0/ 53.3
13	Moss Pond	83/ 65 50 – 3/112 = 74	NON	14.2 41.0 –1/ 54.1
27	Sing With Me	81/ 70 60 – 3/127 = 64	NON	14.2 40.1 +1/ 54.4
3	Classic Deal	81/ 32 27 – 1/ 58 = 140	NON	14.2 40.2 –1/ 54.3
6	Freedom's Edge	84/ 52 50 – 6/ 96 = 88	N+O	13.2 39.4 0/ 53.1
25	Rattlesnake Rogue	78/ 54 39 + 7/100 = 78	+ON	14.2 39.3 0/ 54.1
5-2	Jungleland	69/ 49 38 – 13/ 74 = 93	NNw	14.0 38.3 0/ 52.3
19	Concealed Ident/	83/ 66 69 – 2/133 = 62	NON	12.3 39.4 +4/ 53.1
6	Class Hero	78/ 28 51 – 11/ 68 = 115	NON	13.4 41.0 –1/ 54.3

Here is that very bad, rock bottom kind of field that we see for the second time in the afternoon. There are some truly atrocious horses in this race. Reading the internal numbers can demonstrate how woeful some of them are. Look at Sing With Me, whose second call number of 70 was compiled in total fields of 81. If he had run last at the second call in every race, he could not have exceeded 81, and being so near to that number tells you how he fared most of the time. His finish total is almost as bad. Concealed Identity, in a total field of 83, shows only a 69, extremely bad. Only three horses out of the 12 have a PCR in excess of 100. Eleven of the 12 horses entered all have minus numbers for class, which tells you that they are all drifting downward, rejects from the winning circle.

Despite all this, we must never stop looking for a play if one is to be found. When we make our usual beginning by looking at the three top rated PCR horses, Classic Deal, Class Hero, and Chubby Babe, we can see that all three of them have form defects, although Classic Deal is very close to the line. Classic Deal also has one of the very poor last race ability times in this woeful field. Class Hero and Chubby Babe have PCRs only slightly over the mediocre 100 number and their form defects and poor last race ability times will not allow us to play them either.

The favorite, Jungleland, achieved his measure of support largely because he finished first in his last race, even though he was later disqualified. Since he also turned in the best ability time, is he a play because of being the favorite with no form defects and having one of the three best last race ability times?

This brings up a subject we have not previously discussed: how to deal with horses that won their last race and were disqualified. Most of the time, they are very risky to play in their next race, unless they are high quality horses. In addition, we are back to repeating our earlier caveat that cheap horses that won their last race are very poor prospects to win the next time out, unless they have some form of a strong advantage over the remaining animals in the race. When a winning horse of low class is disqualified, this seems to place yet another burden on his back.

And, of course, the longer a distance that a race is run, the less impact that last race ability times have. The more a race is stretched out, the greater opportunity for a horse to overcome various obstacles. The advantage that Jungleland has in his last race ability time is simply not enough when all these other uncertainties are there. One of our major efforts is to try to avoid as much uncertainty as we can; when we see it, stay away.

There is not one horse in this race that, based upon the kind of handicapping lines we are going to rely on, is worth any kind of a bet. We are required to pass once more. Someone had to win, and someone did.

Our old friend, early speed, carried the day, as Class Hero, despite his very poor last race ability time, went wire to wire without too much difficulty. Perhaps it was predictable, but not with my money on the line, even with the horse's evident early speed style.

We are now ready to summarize the day, where early speed dominated. It made our PCR ratings look very strong, especially where based upon lower second call totals. We can now tally up the races, how we played them, and what were the results, assuming the minimum bet in every playable situation.

NINTH RACE
Aqueduct
JANUARY 21, 1987

$1\frac{1}{16}$ MILES.(InnerDirt). ($1.55\frac{2}{5}$) CLAIMING. Purse $15,000. 4-year-olds and upward. Weight, 122 lbs. Non-winners of two races over a mile since December 15 allowed 3 lbs. Of such a race since then, 5 lbs. Claiming price $17,500; for each $1,000 to $15,500 allowed 2 lbs. (Races when entered to be claimed for $14,000 or less not considered.)

Value of race $15,000; value to winner $9,000; second $3,300; third $1,800; fourth $900. Mutuel pool $59,113, OTB pool $165,631. ExPl $58,505 OTB $141,187. TriPl $146,056 OTB Tri $342,515.

Last Raced	Horse	Eqt.A.Wt	PP	St	¼	½	¾	Str	Fin	Jockey	Cl'g Pr	Odds $1
4Jan87 ^{2}Aqu^{7}	Class Hero	b 8 117	11	5	1^{2}	1^{2}	1^{1}	1^{1}	$1^{2\frac{1}{4}}$	Martens G	17500	6.70
5Jan87 ^{2}Aqu^{8}	Chubby Babe	b 5 113	2	2	$5^{\frac{1}{2}}$	$3^{\frac{1}{2}}$	3^{1}	3^{3}	$2^{\frac{3}{4}}$	Davis R G	15500	8.80
5Jan87 ^{4}Aqu^{6}	Parrell Hill	b 5 110	1	1	2^{hd}	$2^{1\frac{1}{2}}$	$2^{1\frac{1}{2}}$	2^{hd}	3^{5}	Ortiz E Jr^{5}	16500	20.00
1Jan87 ^{9}Aqu^{4}	Classic Deal	b 5 117	7	11	$7^{\frac{1}{2}}$	$5^{1\frac{1}{2}}$	4^{hd}	4^{6}	4^{6}	Santos J A	17500	3.40
5Jan87 ^{2}Aqu^{3}	Mr. Noritake	b 4 113	4	4	$8^{\frac{1}{2}}$	9^{2}	6^{hd}	$5^{1\frac{1}{2}}$	$5^{\frac{1}{2}}$	Santagata N	15500	10.80
11Jan87 ^{9}Aqu^{3}	Concealed Identity	b 5 113	12	9	4^{1}	6^{hd}	7^{2}	7^{1}	6^{nk}	Thibeau R J	15500	19.10
3Jan87 ^{7}Aqu^{5}	Sing With Me	5 113	6	10	12	10^{hd}	9^{hd}	$8^{2\frac{1}{2}}$	7^{1}	Ward W A	15500	27.90
29Dec86 ^{2}Aqu^{6}	Jungleland	b 6 112	10	8	$6^{\frac{1}{2}}$	$4^{1\frac{1}{2}}$	$5^{2\frac{1}{2}}$	6^{hd}	$8^{2\frac{1}{2}}$	Baird E T^{5}	17500	2.60
15Jan87 ^{2}Aqu^{5}	Rattlesnake Rogue	b 4 113	9	12	$11^{\frac{1}{2}}$	12	10^{5}	9^{hd}	$9^{2\frac{1}{2}}$	Zuniga M	15500	25.00
4Jan87 ^{2}Aqu^{5}	Moss Pond	4 117	5	3	9^{3}	$7^{\frac{1}{2}}$	8^{1}	10^{4}	$10^{3\frac{1}{2}}$	Lovato F.Jr	17500	13.00
31Dec86 ^{2}Aqu^{8}	Letal	4 113	3	7	$10^{\frac{1}{2}}$	$11^{\frac{1}{2}}$	11^{4}	11^{10}	11	Rolon E M	15500	52.80
29Dec86 ^{2}Aqu^{5}	Freedoms Edge	5 117	8	6	$3^{\frac{1}{2}}$	$8^{\frac{1}{2}}$	12	12	—	Skinner K	17500	6.70

Freedoms Edge, Eased.

OFF AT 4:06 Start good, Won driving. Time, $:23\frac{2}{5}$, :48, $1:13\frac{1}{5}$, $1:39\frac{1}{5}$, 1:59 Track sloppy.

$2 Mutuel Prices:				
	11-(N)-CLASS HERO	15.40	9.00	8.40
	2-(C)-CHUBBY BABE		10.60	6.80
	1-(A)-PARRELL HILL			11.60

$2 EXACTA 11-2 PAID $134.60. $2 TRIPLE 11-2-1 PAID $2,849.00.

Race	Selection	Bet	Return	P/L
1Aqu	Pass	0		0
2Aqu	Miss Scandal	$ 2	$17.00	+ 15.00
	Peace Keeper	2	0	− 2.00
	Exacta	8	58.40	+ 50.40
3Aqu	Pass	0		0
4Aqu	Pass	0		0
5Aqu	Aswan High	2	7.00	+ 5.00
	Flying Skipper	2	0	− 2.00
	Exacta	4	38.20	+ 34.20
6Aqu	Forest Fair	2	4.40	+ 2.40
7Aqu	Unattended Date	2	18.00	+ 16.00
	Proudest Babe	2	0	− 2.00
8Aqu	Shine Diulus	2	6.00	+ 4.00
9Aqu	Pass	0		0

We made bets in only five of the nine races, fewer than we would normally expect. But we scored in every one of them. Admittedly, this was an unusual result, not likely to happen too many times. But it can, and does occur. Only a few days prior to this writing, I selected 9 winners out of 10 races at Pimlico, combining single selection and multiple selection plays. I admit that I did not play every one of these races, but there were enough that I did play, where there were also some staggering exactas, to make it one of the better days I have ever experienced at the track.

On these figures, and based upon this careful play, we would have invested only $28 and returned the hefty sum of $149.00, an incredibly profitable day. Don't expect to do this well very often, but the major point we can make here is that this is possible, logical, and sound, based upon adherence to the standards that form the foundation of this book.

The day was also a tribute to the power of the PCR ratings. Of the seven races where we could compile PCRs, six races were won by one of the three highest rated horses. In the other, the first race, Far East was within the 7½% numerical span of the third highest PCR horse, making this one for all practical purposes within the same reach.

Where you have a dominant force showing, such as early speed throughout the day, you are almost absolutely certain to make money when you play that speed, backed with high PCRs and strong last race ability times. On the other hand, in the big day I just mentioned at Pimlico, early speed was not dominant at all as the track ran more evenly to a very slight favoring to the late speed horses. Reading the internal numbers, however, allows you to adjust to any situation. When you become accustomed to doing it, as this day at Aqueduct demonstrates, you will be well on your way to Total Victory at the Track.

Finally, we can summarize and repeat some of the important handicapping lessons shown in this chapter, based upon our complete handicapping lines. First of all, and probably as important as anything in this book, we saw clear, decisive examples of when to pass. The first and ninth races on the card, filled with the cheapest horses in New York, were the key candidates for passing, along with the two events filled with horses whose records do not tell us enough to find the advantages that we must have.

A second major showing was in how to rate and integrate a horse coming off a layoff into a competitive field. We went back into the past performances to find a strong race and compare the ability times in it with those of the last race for our measured horses. This provides a sound evaluation of what the horse on layoff can be expected to do.

A third important lesson was in how to consider an advisory ability time made in a sprint race when the horse is running in a distance event. When the sprint time is demonstrably better than the times of the route runners, you can play the sprinter with confidence, as we saw.

A fourth important factor throughout was the strength of the last race ability times as an elimination factor among horses. When these ability times are combined with good PCRs, as we have written earlier, they are potent indeed.

A fifth consideration that was discussed and treated was in how to deal with last race winners.

These and other handicapping factors that are critical to your success will continue to unfold as we move on to the west coast for our other two cards on the same day, both to see how our performance fared and how to utilize the total handicapping equations that make this book unique in any work on thoroughbred racing.

16 The Performance: Same Day At Santa Anita

ON THE SAME day, January 21, 1987, that we went through an entire card at Aqueduct, we moved to the west coast to Santa Anita, one of the nation's favored race tracks, still using the same day's edition of the Daily Racing Form. Santa Anita is the crown jewel of California racing, just as Saratoga stands above all the tracks in the east. We will follow the same principles that we used for the Aqueduct card, making worksheets on all the races and looking for the advantages that we must find in our complete handicapping lines.

We can begin quickly with the first race, a six furlong sprint for some of the cheaper claiming horses on the grounds, typical of what you are certain to find in almost any midweek card wherever you attend.

1st Santa Anita

6 ½ FURLONGS. (1.14) CLAIMING. Purse $13,000. 4-year-olds and upward. Weights, 4-year-olds, 120 lbs.; older, 121 lbs. Non-winners of two races since November 3 allowed 3 lbs.; of a race since then 5 lbs. Claiming price $12,500; if for $10,500 allowed 2 lbs. (Races when entered for $10,000 or less not considered).

M. J.'s Delight — Ch. g. 5, by Vested Power—Little Tirrani, by Mandate
CORDERO A JR 116 — Br.—Mangano & Sons Inc (Cal) — 1986 8 0 2 1 $7,830
Own.—Solvang Stable — Tr.—Greenman Walter $12,500 — 1985 18 4 2 4 $54,530
Lifetime 34 5 4 5 $73,485

16Nov86-9BM	6f	:23	$:45^{4}$	$1:10^{3}$ft	5	114	7^{9}	$7^{7\frac{1}{4}}$	6^{7}	$6^{9\frac{1}{2}}$	Diaz A L^{6}	16000	76-21	BOnGurd,RdwoodBoy,Accptr'sPrnc	7
9Nov86-9BM	6f	$:22^{2}$	$:45^{1}$	1:10 ft	13	114	$3^{2\frac{1}{2}}$	$3^{2\frac{1}{2}}$	11^{19}	$11^{18\frac{3}{4}}$	Gonzalez R M^{5}	20000	70-20	Spccpit,Cool'nScndlous,FirlyOmn	11
19Oct86-4BM	6f	$:22^{3}$	$:45^{2}$	1:10 ft	2¾	115	3^{2}	2^{1}	2^{1}	2^{2}	Castaneda M^{4}	20000	87-17	Cool'nScndlous,M.J.'sDlght,BuDncn	6
5Oct86-7BM	6f	:23	$:45^{4}$	$1:09^{3}$ft	9	115	$7^{5\frac{1}{4}}$	$6^{5\frac{1}{4}}$	$4^{5\frac{1}{2}}$	$3^{5\frac{1}{2}}$	Castaneda M^{3}	20000	85-21	StrodeAMinr,CoolnJck,M.J.'sDlight	8
20Sep86-1BM	6f	$:22^{4}$	:46	1:11 ft	5½	114	6^{5}	$4^{5\frac{1}{4}}$	3^{5}	$5^{7\frac{1}{4}}$	Chapman T M^{5}	20000	77-19	StrodeAMiner,CommercII,°lumGrt	7
14Mar86-7GG	6f	:23	:46	1:10 gd	*2	115	$7^{6\frac{3}{4}}$	$7^{4\frac{1}{4}}$	$7^{4\frac{1}{2}}$	$7^{4\frac{1}{4}}$	Baze R A^{6}	40000	85-23	AuntieRose,BnnttPk,IrishScoundrl	9
1Mar86-6GG	6f	$:22^{4}$	$:45^{3}$	$1:09^{3}$ft	3½	115	4^{2}	$4^{1\frac{3}{4}}$	1^{hd}	$2^{\frac{3}{4}}$	Baze R A^{8}	40000	90-15	PleasntPower,M.J.'sDelight,‡HjjiBb	9
18Jan86-2SA	6½f	$:21^{3}$	:44	$1:15^{2}$ft	*9-5	115	$9^{6\frac{3}{4}}$	$7^{6\frac{3}{4}}$	6^{10}	9^{12}	Stevens G L^{9}	c32000	81-12	Goldy'sCommander,Chevo,Romxe	12
28Dec85-2SA	6f	:22	$:44^{4}$	$1:09^{1}$ft	9½	114	$7^{5\frac{1}{2}}$	6^{5}	4^{5}	$3^{1\frac{3}{4}}$	Baze G^{1}	32000	90-14	Zac K., Larry NGarry,M.J.'sDelight	10
28Dec85—Bumped start; checked, altered course at 1/8															
19Oct85-7SA	6½f	$:21^{3}$	:4[illegible]	$1:15^{4}$ft	18	116	$8^{9\frac{1}{4}}$	8^{11}	8^{11}	8^{13}	Baze G^{4}	Aw32000	78-13	CountryPlsurs,LguHttr,SwrdJncton	8
19Oct85—Bumped start															

Jan 10 SA 6f gd $1:14^{3}$ h   Jan 5 SA 4f sy $:48^{3}$ h   Dec 30 SA 3f ft $:36^{4}$ h

Illuminize — Ch. g. 5, by Star de Naskra—Little Fawn Eyes, by Exclusive Native
SOTO S B 116
Br.—Malmuth Mr-Mrs M (Ky) 1987 1 0 0 0
Tr.—Mayberry Brian A $12,500 1986 11 1 1 1 $17,925
Own.—Siegel Jan-M-Samantha
Lifetime 23 4 2 3 $58,785

1Jan87-1SA 6f :21^{4} :44^{4} 1:11 ft 7½ 116 2½ 2½ 22½ 87½ McHargue D G^{2} 22500 75-19 ClssicQuickie,PtriotGloves,Qurdolit 8
13Dec86-1Hol 6f :21^{4} :45 1:10^{2}ft 17 116 3^{2} 31½ 2^{hd} 2½ Soto S B^{1} 16000 90-09 Neutral Player, Illuminize, Rodney 10
25Oct86-9SA 6f :22 :45^{1} 1:10^{2}ft 5 116 31½ 3^{1} 3^{3} 119¾ Pedroza M A^{1} 20000 76-17 StarOfAmerica,Rodney,SndDigger 11
25Oct86—Veered out, bumped start; lugged out, bumped 3/8 turn
11Oct86-2SA 6f :21^{2} :44^{3} 1:10^{2}ft 28 116 2^{hd} 2^{2} 47½ 7^{13} Pedroza M A^{1} 32000 73-17 Dr. Reality, Gray Pinstripe, Bizeboy 9
11Oct86—Stumbled start; lugged out
4Sep86-7Dmr 6f :21^{4} :45 1:08^{4}ft 33 114 1^{hd} 2½ 32½1014¼ Pedroza M A^{8} 35000 80-14 TeddyNturlly,ToughEnvoy,Dr.Rlity 10
9Aug86-3Dmr 6f :21^{4} :45 1:09^{2}ft 19 118 1^{hd} 1^{hd} 4^{2} 56½ Stevens G L^{6} 40000 84-14 GryPnstrp,MostDtrmnd,PtrotGlvs 10
9Aug86—Bore out 3/8
20Jun86-4Hol 6f :22^{2} :45^{4} 1:10^{1}ft 2½ 119 33½ 41½ 68½ 67¾ Soto S B^{3} 40000 85-11 Ondrty,MsterGregory,BoldTopsider 7
7Jun86-7Hol 1 :45^{3} 1:10 1:37 ft 6½ 116 11½ 1½ 32½ 77½ Soto S B^{5} 50000 70-17 Ono Gummo, Menswear, Paskanell 8
28May86-4Hol 6f :22 :45^{2} 1:10^{1}ft 4¾ 116 3^{3} 3^{1} 22½ 3^{4} Soto S B^{6} 50000 89-15 TeddyNaturally,Dr.Relity,Il'uminize 6
3May86-4Hol 7f :22^{1} :44^{3} 1:23^{3}ft 6¼ 117 1^{hd} 1½ 12½ 11½ Soto S B^{3} 40000 86-16 Illuminize, Rushad, All Wins 6
Nov 21 Hol 5f ft 1:00^{1} h

Lightning Spirit — B. g. 5, by Barbaric Spirit—Golden Balance, by Balance of Power
ARAGON V A 116
Br.—Munger Mr-Mrs D L (Wash) 1987 1 0 0 0 $810
Tr.—Greenman Walter $12,500 1986 4 0 0 0 $1,045
Own.—Lvnsn-Lvnsn-Van Norman
Lifetime 24 5 2 2 $29,985

3Jan87-5BM 6f :22^{2} :45^{4} 1:11^{1}sy 12 115 67½ 77½ 56½ 46 Loseth C^{5} 10000 77-23 BchRomo,BlzingZulu,Acciptr'sPrnc 8
14Dec86-2BM 6f :22^{2} :45^{3} 1:10^{2}ft 13 114 64½ 5^{3} 4^{3} 53¾ Loseth C^{3} 8000 83-17 BeachRomeo,QuietFriend,FireyStar 9
12Jun86-7Lga 6f :21^{2} :43^{4} 1:09 ft 7½ 116 10^{14}10^{15} 9^{20} 9^{8} Delgadillo C^{2} 12500 83-14 SonOfSibirri,NtivePic,BrbricGeorg 10
12Jun86—Broke slowly
24May86-7Lga 6½f :22 :45 1:16^{2}ft *3 116 53½ 5^{5} 8^{11} 78¼ Baze G^{10} 16000 79-21 K.L'sPapa,GalenaSummit,NtivePic 11
27Apr86-7Lga 6f :21^{2} :44^{2} 1:09^{3}sy 11 119 35½ 44½ 55¾ 45¾ Delgadillo C^{1} 20000 82-18 MjstcEffort,Cool'nScndlos,RylMws 7
22Nov85-7BM 6f :22^{1} :45 1:10^{1}ft 19 114 76¾ 77¾11^{13}1213¾ Loseth C^{12} 16000 74-20 FirlyQmn,Stn'sBrthdy,RstYourNtv 12
8Nov85-6BM 6f :22^{2} :45^{1} 1:09^{1}ft 11 114 8^{6} 87¾ 8^{12} 914¼ Ortega L E^{3} 20000 79-25 AppleCke,John'sJove,MrlinOfYork 10
8Nov85—Broke in a tangle
25Oct85-6BM 5½f :22^{3} :45^{4} 1:03^{3}ft 8¼ 114 8^{11} 8^{10} 67½ 65½ Ortega L E^{7} 25000 89-27 BrdrAmbssdr,FlngAdmrl,ShdWtch 11
2Oct85-9Lga 6½f :21^{3} :43^{4} 1:15 ft 6¼ 120 76½ 7^{11} 6^{13} 6^{14} GonsalvesFA^{3} Aw12900 80-17 Mr.HoldHnds,SntorMcGr,Pl'sRmpg 7
21Jun85-9Lga 6½f :21^{4} :45^{1} 1:16^{2}ft *3 120 94¾ 62¼ 5^{4} 63¾ Davidson J R^{3} 40000 83-25 D.J.Lou,KnightsFinale,BonanzaBar 11
Jan 18 BM 4f ft :48^{4} h **Dec 29 BM 5f ft 1:02^{1} h** **●Dec 1 BM 6f ft 1:14 h**

Pickwick Landing * — Ch. g. 5, by Mr Crimson Ruler—Crimson Palace, by Truxton King
PEDROZA M A 116
Br.—Enyart Kathleen M (Ky) 1987 1 1 0 0 $6,600
Tr.—Ivory John C $12,500 1986 16 1 3 1 $20,475
Own.—Caraway-Mathews-Mathews
Lifetime 36 3 7 3 $65,043 Turf 1 0 0 0

4Jan87-1SA 6½f :21^{4} :45 1:17^{3}sy 9¾ 116 11½ 1^{1} 1^{hd} 1no Pedroza M A^{10} 10000 82-22 PckwckLndng,ComtsFlr,SwftMssg 11
30Nov86-2Hol 7f :22^{2} :45^{4} 1:25^{3}ft 8¼ 117 4^{3} 32½106¾11^{10} Pedroza M A^{7} c10000 66-16 Gulfstremer,PinepplеJck,UpThPol 12
30Nov86—Bumped at start
19Nov86-4Hol 7f :23^{1} :46^{3} 1:24^{4}ft 8-5 116 2^{hd} 21½ 4^{4} 38¾ Pedroza M A^{5} 10000 71-21 LndsrII,AncintBlu,PickwickLnding 6
8Nov86-2Hol 6f :22^{3} :46^{3} 1:11^{3}ft 5¼ 116 1^{1} 11½ 2^{hd} 21¾ Pedroza M A^{10} 10000 83-13 GrnPirr,PickwckLndng,Chucklctor 10
8Nov86—Broke in, bumped
4Aug86-3Dmr 6½f :22 :44^{4} 1:16^{1}ft 27 116 97¼ 6^{7} 88½ 7^{9} Soto S B^{12} 12500 82-13 Inquisitive, Jacart, Pride Of Troy 12
4Aug86—Very wide final 3/8
19Jly86-1Hol 6f :22^{2} :46 1:11 ft 3½ 116 67½ 5^{6} 5^{6} 45¼ Stevens G L^{3} c10000 84-15 Snaafy, Wishbone, Mr. Bar Able 7
19Jly86—Hit gate start
11Jly86-9Hol 7f :22^{3} :46 1:23^{3}ft 4¼ 117 79½ 7^{8} 66¼ 69½ Shoemaker W^{3} 16000 76-14 One EyedRomeo,Parlapiano,Eterno 7
11Jly86—Off poorly
29Jun86-4Hol 6f :22^{4} :46 1:09^{4}ft 2½ 116 42½ 44½ 5^{6} 55½ Hernandez R^{5} 20000 89-10 FllFlyr,PrciousBmbino,AffirmdNtiv 6
15Jun86-4Hol 6f :22^{1} :45^{3} 1:11^{1}ft 13 116 88½ 88¾ 7^{7} 51¾ Hernandez R^{6} 20000 86-13 FlyingLessons,SandDigger,DeltTrce 8
10May86-3Hol 7f :22^{2} :45^{2} 1:23^{3}ft 4½ 116 72¾ 53½ 5^{4} 53½ McCarron C J^{3} c16000 82-12 Apprehend, Val De Roi, Pertex 10
10May86—Broke in, bumped
Dec 24 Hol 4f ft :50^{4} h

Melchip B. g. 5, by Our Blue Chip—Melrose Nugget, by Viking Spirit
ORTEGA L E 118 Br.—Millard & Rous Mmes (Cal) 1987 1 0 0 1 $1,950
Own.—Chasteen & De La Merced Jr Tr.—Chasteen William W $12,500 1986 11 2 3 1 $24,390
Lifetime 25 4 4 4 $42,865
9Jan87-9SA 6f :214 :453 1:124sl 5¼ 116 23½ 24 2hd 31 Ortega L E4 12500 73-26 West Boy II, Chagrining, Melchip 11
20Dec86-3Hol 1 :453 1:102 1:364ft 3¼ 116 21½ 21½ 22 25½ Black C A4 12500 73-15 Son Of Raja, Melchip, Parlapiano 7
20Dec86—Awarded first purse money; Lugged out backside
23Nov86-2Hol 6f :221 :454 1:11 ft 3¼ 116 2hd 1hd 1hd 32 Ortega L E8 12500 86-12 HurricaneHec,StrsAtNoon,Melchip 8
23Nov86—Lugged in late
12Nov86-7Hol 6f :214 :452 1:103ft 20 117 66 54 54 64¾ Ortega L E3 16000 85-15 Inqustv,EllsBrvstSong,Rnbow'sCup 8
3Nov86-1SA 6f :213 :444 1:11 ft 8 116 55½ 45 44 2nk Ortega L E1 [S] 12500 83-14 HachalaTachl,Melchip,ShuttleOne 10
25Oct86-1SA 6½f :221 :451 1:171ft 3¼ 118 1hd 2hd 2hd 23½ Castanon A L3 c10000 80-17 Oh Dad, Melchip, Crimaurie 8
13Oct86-1SA 6f :22 :452 1:111ft 2¼ 119 52¼ 34½ 35 49 Castanon A L11 10000 73-19 Reinbow'sCup,PrideOfTroy,KrkLd 11
5Oct86-1SA 6½f :221 :453 1:171ft 2¼ 115 2½ 1hd 11½ 11¼ Castanon A L5 10000 84-15 Melchip, Ancient Blue, Bob'sIntent 7
23Sep86-9Pom 6f :221 :451 1:104ft 5¼ 116 1hd 32 32 2no Vergara O8 10000 97-08 Dominant Roni, Melchip, Singlet 10
8Sep86-2Dmr 6f :214 :454 1:10 ft 13 117 52 62¼ 55½ 53¾ Vergara O1 [S] 12500 84-14 StrOfAmeric,BeThnkful,DollrTrppr 7

Comets Flare Dk. b. or br. g. 4, by Impressive—Confectionate, by Reighs Bull
SIBILLE R 115 Br.—Monteverdi A F (Cal) 1987 1 0 1 0 $2,400
Own.—Anderson-Glick-Thatt Tr.—Pew Karl $12,500 1986 15 3 1 1 $24,400
Lifetime 20 3 4 2 $36,250
4Jan87-1SA 6½f :214 :45 1:173sy *7-5 117 21½ 21 2hd 2no Sibille R3 c10000 82-22 PckwckLndng,ComtsFlr,SwftMssg 11
19Dec86-5Hol 6f :221 :46 1;113ft *9-5 118 2hd 1hd 11½ 31¾ Stevens G L8 12500 83-17 Air Pirate, St. Alexis, Comets Flare 9
5Dec86-7Hol 1 :45 1:102 1:363ft 5¼ 115 1hd 3nk 31½ 78¾ Sibille R1 12500 71-17 Hachi, Son Of Raja,ClassicQuickie 12
19Nov86-6Hol 7f :224 :46 1:241ft 8¼ 117 11 11 12 11¼ Sibille R8 10000 83-21 Comets Flare,Gulfstreamer,Pulsate 9
8Nov86-2Hol 6f :223 :463 1:113ft 11 117 31½ 44½ 77¾ 813½ Meza R Q4 10000 71-13 GrnPirr,PickwckLndng,Chucklctor 10
8Nov86—Lugged in stretch
24Oct86-1SA 7f :224 :454 1:25 ft 5¾ 115 1hd 1hd 2½ 22½ Sibille R9 [S] 10000 72-20 PrideOfTroy,CometsFlre,ShuttleOn 9
13Oct86-1SA 6f :22 :452 1:111ft 10 116 65¾ 711 813 814¼ Sibille R9 10000 68-19 Reinbow'sCup,PrideOfTroy,KrkLd 11
13Oct86—Stumbled, bumped start
25Sep86-5Pom 6½f :223 :47 1:202m 4 116 53 34 11½ 13¼ Sibille R4 10000 78-30 CometsFlre,Brin'sFlying,WterJcket 9
6Sep86-1Dmr 1 1/16 :453 1:112 1:433ft 32 116 43½ 64¼ 914 924¼ Solis A5 20000 58-12 Convincing, Sea And Sew, Mural 10
6Sep86—Broke in, bumped
25Aug86-1Dmr 1 1/16 :452 1:113 1:442ft *6-5 116 2hd 2hd 55 610½ McCarron C J2 c16000 67-16 Ontheemis,VlintGnrtion,Mr.Vlntino 8
25Aug86—Veered in start
Jan 17 SA 4f ft :481 h Dec 29 SA 3f ft :362 h Dec 15 Hol 3f ft :37 h

Buckner B. h. 5, by Riva Ridge—Chinook, by Bold Ruler
BRINKERHOFF D 116 Br.—Beitz Gail P & Honcock (Ky) 1986 6 0 0 0 $1,275
Own.—C D C Racing Stable Inc Tr.—Krikorian George $12,500 1985 4 1 0 0 $7,590
Lifetime 13 1 2 1 $19,625 Turf 2 0 0 0
5Oct86-2SA 6f :213 :443 1:102ft 70 115 116 108¾ 911 1011½ Brinkerhoff D12 20000 74-15 Grenoble, John's Jove, Inquisitive 12
10Sep86-9Dmr 7f :22 :45 1:214ft 22 116 119¾ 117½ 98½ 810 Bonilla R3 25000 86-11 Paskanell,BrndImge,SwiftMessge 12
13Jly86-10Hol 1 :453 1:102 1:35 ft 13 116 32½ 34 49½ 415¼ DelahoussayeE2 32000 73-15 Oricao, Passed The Rule, Elefante 7
5Jly86-7Hol 1⅛ Ⓣ:472 1:113 1:473fm 42 1095 44 51¾ 95¾ 109¾ Black C A2 45000 84-04 Sherkin, Super Noble, Trakady 11
22Jun86-9Hol 1 :444 1:093 1:343ft 16 116 63¼ 66 710 715¾ Kaenel J L7 Aw21000 74-08 Enviro, T. V. Oil, Rafael's Dancer 8
24May86-5Hol 1⅛ Ⓣ:464 1:11 1:482fm 8 116 27 34 54 66¾ ShoemkerW1 Aw22000 83-09 Middlesex, L'Empire, Garrion 7
4May85-2Crc 6f :223 :462 1:13 ft 13 113 44½ 712 1017 1020¼ Velez J AJr11 Aw11000 66-17 GreenCedrs,RoylCrest,MedievlRod 11
16Apr85-8Hia 7f :231 :462 1:234ft 2½ 121 106¾ 73¼ 31½ 63½ Molina V H9 Aw14000 80-18 Slewmobile,MedievalRod,SmrtBsk 10
30Mar85-8Hia 7f :221 :45 1:23 ft 9-5 121 53¼ 31 53 56½ Velasquez J11 Aw14008 81-12 Jeblar, Numeric, Crusher 12
16Mar85-4Hia 7f :23 :453 1:234ft 4 120 32½ 21½ 1½ 11 Molina V H2 Mdn 84-13 Buckner, Buckley Boy, Our Colors 12
Dec 27 SLR tr.t 5f ft 1:02 hg ●Dec 20 SLR tr.t 5f ft 1:01 h

Chagrining — Ch. g. 5, by Blushing Groom—Takebackyourmink, by Raise a Native
MEZA R Q 116 — Br.—Mandell R K (Ky) — 1987 1 0 1 0 $2,600
Tr.—Cleveland Gene $12,500 — 1986 6 0 0 2 $3,600
Own.—Malmuth-Malmuth-Mandell — Lifetime 13 1 1 2 $10,080 — Turf 1 0 0 0

9Jan87-9SA 6f :21^4 :45^3 1:12^{4}sl 8 116 8$^{8\frac{3}{4}}$ 7$^{7\frac{1}{4}}$ 5$^{2\frac{1}{4}}$ 2^1 Meza R Q^1 12500 73-26 West Boy II, Chagrining, Melchip 11
9Jan87—Broke slowly
30Dec86-3SA 6f :21^2 :44^2 1:11^{2}ft 15 116 4^8 4^7 4^7 3^{hd} Meza R Q^6 12500 81-18 LuckyMasadado,VlDeRoi,Chgrining 7
30Dec86—Broke slowly
6Dec86-2Hol 6f :22^1 :46 1:11^{4}gd 27 117 3$^{2\frac{1}{2}}$ 3$^{1\frac{1}{2}}$ 3^2 3$^{2\frac{3}{4}}$ Meza R Q^8 10000 81-16 John's Jove, Cordon, Chagrining 8
6Dec86—Wide backstretch; lugged in stretch
19Nov86-6Hol 7f :22^4 :46 1:24^{1}ft 6 116 6$^{4\frac{1}{2}}$ 6^5 6^8 7^{13} Meza R Q^3 10000 70-21 Comets Flare,Gulfstreamer,Pulsate 9
19Nov86—Broke slowly
2Nov86-1SA 6½f :21^3 :44^2 1:16 ft 23 111^5 3^4 3$^{4\frac{3}{4}}$ 6^8 7$^{11\frac{3}{4}}$ Valenzuela F Z^8 16000 78-10 Rinbow'sCup,WstBoyII,LordPncho 9
17Oct86-9SA 1$\frac{1}{16}$:47 1:12^2 1:45^{3}ft 6½ 112^5 2^{hd} 5$^{2\frac{1}{4}}$ 7$^{7\frac{1}{2}}$ 7$^{10\frac{1}{4}}$ Valenzuela F Z^2 16000 63-21 Espontneo,RinShelter,JupiterTogee 9
5Oct86-2SA 6f :21^3 :44^3 1:10^{2}ft 63 111^5 2^{hd} 2^{hd} 2$^{1\frac{1}{2}}$ 6$^{6\frac{3}{4}}$ Valenzuela F Z^3 20000 79-15 Grenoble, John's Jove, Inquisitive 12
12Oct85-1SA 6½f :21^2 :44^2 1:16^{2}ft 86 117 9$^{8\frac{3}{4}}$ 5^5 5$^{5\frac{1}{2}}$ 5$^{7\frac{1}{2}}$ Valdez S^4 50000 80-18 Mane Magic, D. J. Lou, Dusty Okie 9
30Aug85-5Dmr 6½f :22^1 :45^1 1:16^{3}ft 47 117 7$^{3\frac{1}{4}}$ 7$^{7\frac{1}{2}}$ 7$^{8\frac{3}{4}}$ 7$^{14\frac{3}{4}}$ Meza R Q^7 62500 78-13 AceSimmons,MtthwT.Prkr,QulityJt 8
27Jly85-9Dmr 1$\frac{1}{16}$ Ⓣ:48^{2}1:12^{3}1:43^{4}fm 33 117 2^{hd} 3^{nk} 7$^{6\frac{1}{2}}$ 7$^{7\frac{3}{4}}$ ValenzuelPA^1 Aw19000 81-10 Kingsbury, Creekarosa, Sapient 7
Dec 23 SA 4f ft :48^3 h — Dec 17 SA 4f ft :48 h — ●Dec 4 SA 4f ft :47^1 h

Neutral Player — Dk. b. or br. g. 7, by Triple Bend—Elizabeth Play, by Graphic
STEVENS G L 118 — Br.—Penn O (Ky) — 1987 1 0 1 0 $3,000
Tr.—Murphy Marcus J $12,500 — 1986 19 4 2 3 $50,985
Own.—Dilena & Konis — Lifetime 74 13 11 12 $168,436 — Turf 4 0 0 0 $1,090

4Jan87-3SA 6f :22 :45^1 1:10^{3}sy 3½ 118 5$^{2\frac{1}{2}}$ 3$^{1\frac{1}{2}}$ 3$^{1\frac{1}{2}}$ 2no Stevens G L^3 16000 85-22 Polly'sRuler,NeutralPlyer,Grenoble 8
13Dec86-1Hol 6f :21^4 :45 1:10^{2}ft 7¾ 116 9$^{7\frac{1}{4}}$ 7$^{6\frac{3}{4}}$ 5$^{3\frac{1}{4}}$ 1$^{\frac{1}{2}}$ Stevens G L^6 16000 91-09 Neutral Player, Illuminize, Rodney 10
22Nov86-1Hol 6f :22^2 :46 1:11 ft *6-5 116 2$^{\frac{1}{2}}$ 2^{hd} 1$^{1\frac{1}{2}}$ 1$^{4\frac{1}{2}}$ ValenzuelaPA^1 c10000 88-13 NeutrlPlyr,ChuckIctor,TuscnKnight 5
22Nov86—Lugged in late
9Nov86-4Hol 1 :45^1 1:10^4 1:37^{3}ft *3¾ 116 1$^{1\frac{1}{2}}$ 2$^{\frac{1}{2}}$ 2$^{1\frac{1}{2}}$ 4$^{4\frac{1}{2}}$ ValenzuelaPA^{11} 10000 70-16 Bob'sIntnt,RunningDbonir,Crimuri 11
12Oct86-1SA 6½f :22 :45^2 1:17^{4}ft *3 116 2^{hd} 1^{hd} 4$^{1\frac{1}{2}}$ 8$^{7\frac{1}{2}}$ McCarron C J^2 16000 73-21 Unagloshi,Menswear,StrOfAmeric 12
12Oct86—Bumped start
20Sep86-10Pom 1$\frac{1}{16}$:45^4 1:11^1 1:43^{1}ft 4½ 111^5 4^5 4^5 6^9 7$^{19\frac{1}{4}}$ Black C A^8 20000 76-09 Restage, Hatamoto,LyphardChimes 9
17Aug86-7Dmr 1$\frac{1}{16}$:45^3 1:10^1 1:43^{2}ft 6 111^5 2$^{\frac{1}{2}}$ 2^{hd} 3^2 7$^{5\frac{1}{4}}$ Black C A^8 25000 78-16 BngBngBng,MrkInThSky,OnEdRm 10
27Jly86-9Dmr 1$\frac{1}{16}$:45^4 1:10^2 1:42^{2}ft *3 118 1$^{1\frac{1}{2}}$ 1$^{\frac{1}{2}}$ 1^{hd} 2$^{1\frac{3}{4}}$ McCarron C J^2 25000 86-10 MstrCwston,NutrlPlyr,Rvolutionry 10
4Jly86-3Hol 6f :22 :45^1 1:10 ft 6½ 119 3^2 3^4 4^7 3^7 Stevens G L^4 25000 87-09 FlyngLssons,ToughEnvoy,NutrlPlyr 7
18Jun86-1Hol 1 :45^2 1:10^1 1:35^{3}ft 9½ 111^5 1$^{1\frac{1}{2}}$ 3^{nk} 4$^{2\frac{1}{2}}$ 5$^{5\frac{3}{4}}$ Black C A^1 32000 79-15 PssdThRul,ToughEnvoy,CrystlCort 7
Jan 17 Hol 4f ft :48^2 h — Jan 12 Hol 4f ft :49^2 h — Dec 30 SA 3f ft :36^4 h — Dec 9 Hol 4f ft :49^2 h

Oasis — Dk. b. or br. g. 4, by Skin Head—Desert Eve, by Night Time
KAENEL J L 115 — Br.—Jones O M (Wash) — 1986 7 1 0 2 $6,710
Tr.—Richardson Donald P $12,500 — 1985 0 M 0 0
Own.—Jones O M — Lifetime 7 1 0 2 $6,710

27Dec86-4SA 1$\frac{1}{16}$:47^1 1:11^4 1:45^{1}ft 31 109^5 7$^{5\frac{1}{4}}$ 9^{11} 8$^{9\frac{1}{2}}$ 8$^{11\frac{3}{4}}$ Patton D B^{10} 18000 63-19 ‡ShowrDcr,DckAndHugh,MnyRods 10
6Dec86-6Hol 7f :22^1 :45^2 1:24^{2}gd 49 119 7^{11} 10^{14} 10^{15} 11$^{15\frac{3}{4}}$ Stevens S A^7 16000 66-16 Noon Sun,PineappleJack,VideoSid 12
6Dec86—Checked 5/16
22Oct86-9Lga 6f :21^3 :44^1 1:08^{4}ft 16 112^5 4$^{2\frac{1}{2}}$ 3^4 3$^{9\frac{1}{2}}$ 3$^{9\frac{1}{2}}$ Gibson R G^5 Aw9300 82-20 NorthrnPolicy,JumpingDoctor,Osis 5
12Oct86-1Lga 6f :22^1 :45^1 1:11 ft 8-5 115^5 2^{hd} 2^{hd} 1^1 1^{hd} Gibson R G^3 M32000 81-16 Oasis, Dual Accent, Timely Reply 7
1Oct86-8Lga 6½f :22^2 :46^1 1:19^{4}m 7 109^5 3^2 4$^{3\frac{1}{2}}$ 4^4 3^6 Gibson R G^6 Ⓢ 20000 64-43 Plucky Emperor, ImATrooper,Oasis 6
6Feb86-3SA 6f :22 :45^1 1:11^{1}ft 4 118 8$^{4\frac{3}{4}}$ 10$^{9\frac{3}{4}}$ 8$^{9\frac{1}{2}}$ 7$^{8\frac{1}{4}}$ Stevens G L^7 M32000 74-19 Nashaway,SeAndSew,GelicKnight 12
6Feb86—Hopped at start
15Jan86-2SA 6f :21^4 :44^2 1:09^{4}ft 10 118 9$^{9\frac{1}{4}}$ 7^{12} 7^{14} 5$^{10\frac{3}{4}}$ Stevens G L^5 M32000 78-14 CleverCoin,ImBullt,VoicOfThWind 12
15Jan86—Pinched at start
Jan 15 SA 5f ft 1:01^2 h — Dec 20 SA 6f ft 1:13^1 hg — Dec 14 SA 4f ft :47 h — Nov 25 SA 5f ft 1:00 h

*Navegante
PATTERSON A
Own.—Casella Judy K

116

Ch. h. 9, by Tantoul—Saima, by Penny Post
Br.—Haras Dadinco (Chile)
Tr.—Cassella Judy K $12,500
Lifetime 51 6 14 9 $84,342

1986 14 1 2 2 $21,175
1985   9 0 2 2 $14,015
Turf   3 0 1 0 $8,925

25Jun86-9Hol	1⅛:473 1:121 1:503ft	29 116	86¾ 78½ 68½ 58½	Hernandez R6	12500	76-13	Booster, Post Flag, Hachi 8
25Jun86—Bumped start							
14Jun86-1Hol	1⅛:47 1:122 1:522ft	23 116	107¾ 84¾ 55½ 42½	Warren G5	10000	73-14	Jolly Josh, Billikin, Pocket Heir 11
1Jun86-2Hol	1 :454 1:111 1:37 ft	41 116	85½ 54 45½ 47½	Haire D10	10000	71-14	RefueledII,Billikin,SergeantGerrd 12
25May86-4Hol	1 :453 1:111 1:374ft	7 116	56 55½ 68 61½¾	Kaenel J L6	12500	62-18	CertinTreL,BombyBrtender,Cordon 7
3May86-2Hol	7f :214 :452 1:231ft	11 116	66¾ 53 45 37¾	Kaenel J L3	12500	80-16	Snaafy, I'll Smoke, Navegante 12
18Apr86-9SA	1⅛:471 1:12 1:512ft	7½ 116	42½ 31½ 33 76	McHargue D G4	16000	66-21	SergentGerrd,PolicPursuit CrtinTrt 9
2Apr86-9SA	1 1/16:473 1:121 1:45 ft	14 116	51¾ 74½ 64 47½	McHargue DG10	16000	68-22	Sir Star, Creon, Certain Treat 12
2Apr86—Fanned 5-wide 7/8							
23Mar86-1SA	1⅛:471 1:113 1:494ft	*2½ 116	55½ 44 34½ 26	Castanon A L3	c12500	74-17	Pyramid Zotts, Navegante, Travel 12
15Mar86-5SA	1⅛:46 1:111 1:514m	19 116	47 52½ 44½ 59	Castanon A L2	20000	61-23	GoodThoughtWilly,Muft,WldPlsur 12
22Feb86-2SA	7f :222 :444 1:231ft	4½ 116	67¼ 56¼ 34½ 31	Castanon A L5	16000	83-16	ExclusiveKing,MorseCodeII,Nvegnt 9
Jan 17 SA 5f ft 1:023 h	Jan 11 SA 5f ft 1:022 h	Jan 3 SA 5f ft 1:033 h	Dec 28 SA 4f ft :49 h				

Here is what our worksheet revealed:

Odds	Horse	PCR						Form	Ab/T
12	M. J.'s Delight	87/	54 56	–	19/ 91	=	96	Lw	(46.0 23.4+2/ 70.1)
9-2	Illuminize	85/	22 60	–	19/ 63	=	135	NN0	45.0 27.3 0/ 72.3
45	Lightning Spirit	86/	67 68	–	9/126	=	68	NON	47.2 25.1–2/ 72.1
18	Pickwick Landing	89/	42 49	–	1/ 90	=	99	NNw	45.0 26.0–1/ 70.4
10	Melchip	88/	29 30	+	3/ 62	=	142	NNO	46.2 26.3–3/ 72.2
12	Comets Flare	98/	30 47	+	3/ 80	=	123	N+N	45.1 26.0–1/ 71.0
58	Buckner	x						L	
5	Chagrining	89/	45 52	–	8/ 91	=	98	NNN	47.0 26.1–3/ 72.3
4-5	Neutral Player	89/	28 40	–	11/ 57	=	156	N+N	45.3 25.1–1/ 70.3
45	Oasis	64/	45 38	–	5/ 78	=	82	NON	48.1 25.4 0/ 74.0
65	Navegante	104/	54 43	–	3/ 94	=	111	L	n/a

We start with little awareness of how the track is running today. The tote board calls it "fast," but as every experienced track watcher knows, there are all kinds of varieties of "fast." The heavily speed biased track at Churchill Downs on Derby Day 1987 was labeled fast and the heavily biased closing track at Pimlico on Preakness Day 1987 was also labeled fast. Your first task, before the race is run, is to note who the early speed horses are and who the late speed horses are, and then as the race unfolds, make your analysis of the track based upon what you see.

Regardless of how the track will run, you can quickly make a selection here, even at 4-5. Neutral Player is a double advantage horse all over. He carries the highest PCR, as well as the best last race ability time off an excellent plus running line. He shows a strong early speed style, but with his class and high PCR, he should be able to prevail on a track even if it is not particular conducive to front speed, as long as it is not bogged down in what we might call the Preakness '87 bias.

Before we get to our next step, some comment on our worksheet lines may be instructive. We did not do a PCR line on Buckner because it would have been so hopelessly low. You can see that from the big numbers that leap out at you when you look at his second call and finish totals. His 58-1 odds were quite realistic, thank you. We did run an advisory ability time line on him to see if even at his best he could possibly be competitive in this field. The answer was an easy no.

As for Navegante, we did just the opposite, running a PCR line and omitting an ability time line. The reason was that he showed only one race at a sprint in his past performances. As an old router, it was so obvious that he was coming back off a layoff for conditioning purposes only that we hardly needed his 65-1 odds to convince us he had no chance whatever. We didn't need to do ability times in that situation. Otherwise, we should do as complete a line as we are able to compile.

You would consider Neutral Player, just as I did, not only as near to a "sure thing" as you might expect to find, but that even the 4-5 price that you never like was quite sufficient for a horse that had such a complete advantage over his rivals. If there ever was a case for betting any horse at 4-5, and sometimes we doubt it, this would be the occasion, as we enroll him as a single selection play.

But what happened?

FIRST RACE
Santa Anita
JANUARY 21, 1987

6 ½ FURLONGS. (1.14) CLAIMING. Purse $13,000. 4-year-olds and upward. Weights, 4-year-olds, 120 lbs.; older, 121 lbs. Non-winners of two races since November 3 allowed 3 lbs.; of a race since then 5 lbs. Claiming price $12,500; if for $10,500 allowed 2 lbs. (Races when entered for $10,000 or less not considered). 21st DAY. WEATHER CLEAR. TEMPERATURE 68 DEGREES.

Value of race $13,000; value to winner $7,150; second $2,600; third $1,950; fourth $975; fifth $325. Mutuel pool $225,532.

Last Raced	Horse	Eqt.A.Wt	PP	St	¼	½	Str	Fin	Jockey	Cl'g Pr	Odds $1
9Jan87 ^{9}SA^{3}	Melchip	b 5 118	5	8	5^{2}	5^{2}	$2\frac{1}{2}$	$1^{3\frac{1}{2}}$	Ortega L E	12500	10.10
16Nov86 ^{9}BM^{6}	M. J.'s Delight	5 116	1	5	2^{hd}	$2\frac{1}{2}$	3^{3}	$2\frac{1}{2}$	Cordero A Jr	12500	12.20
4Jan87 ^{3}SA^{2}	Neutral Player	b 7 118	9	1	$6\frac{1}{2}$	6^{1}	4^{hd}	$3\frac{1}{2}$	Stevens G L	12500	.90
1Jan87 ^{1}SA^{8}	Illuminize	b 5 116	2	3	1^{hd}	$1\frac{1}{2}$	1^{hd}	4^{hd}	Soto S B	12500	4.50
9Jan87 ^{9}SA^{2}	Chagrining	b 5 116	8	9	9^{1}	7^{1}	$8^{2\frac{1}{2}}$	$5^{1\frac{1}{4}}$	Meza R Q	12500	5.90
5Oct86 ^{2}SA^{10}	Buckner	b 5 116	7	10	$8\frac{1}{2}$	9^{1}	$5\frac{1}{2}$	6^{2}	Brinkerhoff D	12500	58.40
4Jan87 ^{1}SA^{2}	Comets Flare	b 4 115	6	4	$4^{1\frac{1}{2}}$	$4\frac{1}{2}$	7^{hd}	$7^{1\frac{1}{4}}$	Sibille R	12500	12.70
4Jan87 ^{1}SA^{1}	Pickwick Landing	b 5 116	4	7	$3\frac{1}{2}$	3^{hd}	6^{hd}	$8^{1\frac{3}{4}}$	Pedroza M A	12500	18.80
3Jan87 ^{5}BM^{4}	Lightning Spirit	5 116	3	6	$7^{1\frac{1}{2}}$	8^{hd}	9^{1}	$9\frac{1}{2}$	Aragon V A	12500	45.10
27Dec86 ^{4}SA^{8}	Oasis	4 116	10	11	11	11	11	10^{nk}	Kaenel J L	12500	45.10
25Jun86 ^{9}Hol^{5}	Navegante	b 9 116	11	2	$10^{1\frac{1}{2}}$	$10\frac{1}{2}$	10^{hd}	11	Patterson A	12500	66.90

OFF AT 12:35. Start good. Won driving. Time, :22⅕, :45⅗, 1:11⅕, 1:18 Track fast.

Official Program Numbers↘

$2 Mutuel Prices:			
5-MELCHIP	22.20	11.80	5.00
1-M. J.'S DELIGHT		15.20	5.40
10-NEUTRAL PLAYER			2.60

Surprisingly, this horse, with everything going for him, was off slowly, not up front where we expected him to be. At the second call of the race, he was still back in sixth place. He wound up third as Melchip at 10-1 waltzed away to a Big Win. If you were at Santa Anita that day, you would have seen with your own eyes what happened. But now we can show you by reproducing the chartmaker's comments that followed the results of the race.

MELCHIP, in contention early after being jostled in the initial strides, lodged his bid a furlong out while lugging in and won drawing away. M. J.'S DELIGHT vied for the lead to midstretch, then could not stay with the winner. NEUTRAL PLAYER, outrun early, finished well enough to gain the show, then could not be returned to be unsaddled when pulling up lame following the finish. ILLUMINIZE, a pace factor to midstretch, weakened. CHAGRINING bobbled at the start and was five wide into the stretch. COMETS FLARE, jostled in the opening strides and wide early, was five wide into the stretch. PICKWICK LANDING, jostled in the initial strides, vied for the early advantage, entered the stretch four wide and gave way. LIGHTNING SPIRIT was taken up and pinched back when in close quarters soon after the start, then was four wide into the stretch. OASIS was five wide into the stretch. NEVEGANTE, wide early, was six wide into the stretch. DODO'S LAND (9) WAS SCRATCHED BY THE STEWARDS ON THE ADVICE OF THE VETERINARIAN. ALL WAGERS ON HIM IN THE REGULAR AND DAILY DOUBLE POOLS WERE ORDERED REFUNDED AND ALL OF HIS PICK NINE SELECTIONS WERE SWITCHED TO THE FAVORITE, NEUTRAL PLAYER (10).

This horse pulled up lame after getting across the finish line, so lame in fact that he was not even able to get back to the unsaddling area. That made it apparent that the horse was struggling with his infirmity throughout the race, and, as thoroughbreds often will, kept going to the end and then hobbled around until he was picked up. That was why he was slow out of the gate, laggard early in the race, and not ever able to be the contender that his figures shouted that he would be. We can pay tribute to his gameness, eat our loss, and reflect again upon the uncertainties of the racing game, where bad things can happen to good horses at 4-5. At least the result was no reflection upon our ratings, but that doesn't help with the discarded ticket.

From the result of this race, however, we can still attempt to make our necessary track assessment. There wasn't a lot of early speed in the race, after Neutral Player. Illuminize carried the lowest second call total and led all the way into the stretch before succumbing. The winner, Melchip, with the second highest PCR, showed an even running style and ran exactly that way, fifth at the second call, but only a length and a half out. M. J.'s Delight, another horse with an even running habit, was up early and ran forwardly throughout to finish second.

What does this tell us about the track's receptivity? There is as yet no evidence that closers will have a happy day, but it is far too early to say that they would have no chance at all. Speed did reasonably well and we may leave it that way for a while as we see what the second race brings, and whether it will shed any future light on how we read our internal numbers.

We see that it is a maiden claiming race for state breds, always a risky proposition in itself. But one never knows what may be lurking there, unless one looks.

2nd Santa Anita

6 FURLONGS. (1.07⅗) MAIDEN CLAIMING. Purse $14,000. Fillies. 3-year-olds. Bred in California. Weight, 117 lbs. Claiming price $32,000; if for $28,000 allowed 2 lbs.

Flying Belle — B. f. 3, by Flying Paster—Belle Marais, by Northern Dancer
VALENZUELA P A 117 — Br.—Carver Stable (Cal) 1987 1 M 0 0 $1,050
Own.—Golden Eagle Stable — Tr.—Stute Melvin F $32,000 1986 0 M 0 0
Lifetime 1 0 0 0 $1,050
1Jan87-4SA 6f :22 :46 1:11^{4}ft 13 118 62½ 43 45½ 46¾ CstnnAL^{10} ⒻⓈM32000 72-19 Jan's Swifty, Buy More, Suki 12
1Jan87—Steadied 5 1/2
Jan 9 SA 4f sl :49^1 h Dec 29 SA 5f ft 1:01^2 h Dec 24 SA 5f ft 1:01 h Dec 13 Hol 4f ft :48^4 h

Find My Way — B. f. 3, by Never Tabled—Falcon Way, by Herbager
PEDROZA M A 115 — Br.—Manning J V (Cal) 1986 7 M 1 0 $4,125
Own.—Murphy & Sasselli Mmes — Tr.—Murphy Marcus J $28,000
Lifetime 7 0 1 0 $4,125
18Dec86-2Hol 6f :22^2 :46^2 1:12^{4}ft 11 116 86½ 66½ 56½ 48¾ Meza R Q^2 ⒻM28000 70-17 LfkdinSrnd,Erin'sFun,FlsConcolor 11
12Dec86-1Hol 6f :22^1 :46^2 1:12^{1}ft 20 118 86½ 85½ 58 47 Meza R Q^3 ⒻM32000 75-20 BtflBrook,FlsConcolr,DrlngFnnyfc 11
20Nov86-2Hol 7f :22^3 :46^4 1:26^{2}ft 6 118 21 31 811 813¼ VlenzuelPA^8 ⒻM32000 59-16 SwitchSlips,Sadiya,SouthOfFrnce 12
20Nov86—Lugged in stretch
12Nov86-2Hol 6f :22 :45^4 1:12 ft 8¾ 118 77½ 910 1011 811½ PdrozMA^9 ⒻⓈM32000 71-15 Eghalanda, Buy More,ExaltedJade 12
12Nov86—Erratic backside
9Aug86-6Dmr 6f :22^1 :45^3 1:11^{4}ft 23 117 3½ 74½ 43 76½ Pedroza MA^3 ⒻⓈMdn 73-14 WildManor,Kavalla,HeavyWeather 10
1Aug86-4Dmr 6f :22 :45^3 1:11^{1}ft 12 117 41½ 41½ 31 21¼ PdrozMA^5 ⒻⓈM32000 81-13 CelticLdy,FindMyWy,She'sAllIGot 12
1Aug86—Lugged in drive
10Jly86-6Hol 5½f :22^3 :46^2 1:04^{3}ft 14 118 66½ 66 59½ 514¾ PedrozaMA^2 ⒻM50000 76-18 Footy, Quick Messenger, Beseya 9
10Jly86—Lugged in stretch
Jan 15 Hol 5f ft 1:02^3 h Jan 9 Hol 4f ft :49^1 h Jan 3 Hol 4f ft :50^4 h Dec 10 Hol 4f ft :49 h

Exalted Jade — Dk. b. or br. f. 3, by Exalted Rullah—Lifted Jade, by Wallet Lifter
CASTANON A L 117 — Br.—Pascoe W T III (Cal) 1986 5 M 1 2 $6,750
Own.—Hansen & Neishi — Tr.—Magana Roberto $32,000
Lifetime 5 0 1 2 $6,750
20Dec86-2Hol 6f :23 :46^4 1:11^{4}ft 3¾ 118 3½ 2hd 21½ 24½ CastnonAL^8 ⒻM32000 79-15 Denise, Exalted Jade, Life's Song 9
12Dec86-2Hol 6f :22^2 :46^2 1:12^{1}ft 5½ 118 61¾ 42 32 32¾ Sibille R^2 ⒻM32000 79-20 Davy's Date, Denise, Exalted Jade 10
12Dec86—Lugged in stretch
5Dec86-2Hol 6f :22 :45^4 1:12^{3}ft *2½ 118 41½ 32 32 42¾ PincayLJr^8 ⒻⓈM32000 77-17 JustAsFlt,AWBtIrsh,FllFromGlory 10
20Nov86-2Hol 7f :22^3 :46^4 1:26^{2}ft *9-5 118 11 1hd 21½ 76¾ Pincay L Jr^1 ⒻM32000 65-16 SwitchSlips,Sadiya,SouthOfFrnce 12
12Nov86-2Hol 6f :22 :45^4 1:12 ft 3½ 118 66½ 64¾ 44½ 34¾ PincayLJr^6 ⒻⓈM32000 78-15 Eghalanda, Buy More,ExaltedJade 12
12Nov86—Lugged in stretch
Jan 17 Hol 5f ft 1:01^3 hg Jan 7 SA 5f sy 1:05^2 h (d) Nov 29 Hol 4f ft :47^4 h

Table Bay — B. f. 3, by Never Tabled—Live and Laugh, by Gallant Man
BAZE G 117 — Br.—Stevenson B F (Cal) 1986 3 M 0 1 $1,800
Own.—Patchett Mrs J R — Tr.—Wiseheart Larry $32,000
Lifetime 3 0 0 1 $1,800
5Dec86-6Hol 6f :22^1 :46^1 1:11^{4}ft 8½ 118 31½ 33 34½ 35½ Baze G^5 ⒻⓈM32000 79-17 Heavy Weather,Erin'sFun,TableBay 8
12Nov86-2Hol 6f :22 :45^4 1:12 ft 75 118 89 77½ 68 610 Baze G^{11} ⒻⓈM32000 73-15 Eghalanda, Buy More,ExaltedJade 12
23Oct86-4SA 6f :21^4 :45^4 1:12^{2}ft 79 117 51¾ 53 76½ 75¾ Stevens SA^8 ⒻM32000 70-20 LovbleSlt,HvyWthr,Dr.SockItToM 12
23Oct86—Lugged in stretch
Jan 19 SA 3f ft :36^3 h Jan 11 SA 6f ft 1:15^4 h Jan 3 SA 5f ft 1:04^3 h Nov 28 SA 6f ft 1:14^3 h

Jump At A Bargain B. f. 3, by Bargain Day—Spring Sister, by Sisters Prince
STERLING L J JR 1125 Br.—Layne Mr-Mrs A F (Cal) 1987 1 M 0 0
Own.—Layne & Murray Tr.—Layne Arthur F $32,000 1986 1 M 0 0
Lifetime 2 0 0 0
9Jan87-4SA 6f :221 :462 1:133sl 75 117 87½ 1213 1222 1127½ Kaenel JL2 ⒻⓈM32000 42-26 Time To Call, Divest, Laurentian 12
9Jan87—Stumbled start
18Dec86-2Hol 6f :222 :462 1:124ft 71 1135 76½ 911 911 914¾ Patton DB10 ⒻM32000 64-17 LfkdinSrnd,Erin'sFun,FlsConcolor 11
18Dec86—Broke slowly; wide 3/8
Jan 3 SLR tr.t 5f ft 1:043 h ●Dec 29 SLR tr.t 4f ft :481 h Dec 16 SLR tr.t 4f ft :492 hg Dec 10 SLR tr.t 5f ft 1:032 h

Divest B. f. 3, by Beau's Eagle—Dandish, by Intentionally
PINCAY L JR 117 Br.—Applebaum H (Cal) 1987 1 M 1 0 $2,800
Own.—Relatively Stable Tr.—Rose Larry $32,000 1986 0 M 0 0
Lifetime 1 0 1 0 $2,800
9Jan87-4SA 6f :221 :462 1:133sl 3¾ 117 52½ 33 35½ 26½ PincayLJr3 ⒻⓈM32000 63-26 Time To Call, Divest, Laurentian 12
Jan 18 SA 4f ft :474 h Jan 6 SA 3f gd :361 h Dec 26 SA 6f ft 1:161 hg Dec 19 SA 6f ft 1:16 hg

Fall From Glory B. f. 3, by Never Tabled—Fallen Angel, by Grenfall
COX D W 1105 Br.—Wygod M J (Cal) 1987 1 M 0 0
Own.—Motley D H Tr.—Coffman Mike $28,000 1986 6 M 0 2 $3,350
Lifetime 7 0 0 2 $3,350
9Jan87-4SA 6f :221 :462 1:133sl 6¾ 115 41 43 46 611¼ PttrsonA1 ⒻⓈM28000 59-26 Time To Call, Divest, Laurentian 12
5Dec86-2Hol 6f :22 :454 1:123ft 33 116 1hd 11 1½ 3¾ PttrsonA2 ⒻⓈM28000 79-17 JustAsFlt,AWBtIrsh,FllFromGlory 10
5Dec86—Lugged in 1/8
26Nov86-4Hol 6f :224 :463 1:133ft 141 118 1½ 2hd 2hd 77½ Patterson A2 ⒻM32000 68-20 StrawberryPort,MagicalGal,Jiltble 12
26Nov86—Checked 1/8
14Nov86- Hol 6f :22 :46 1:122ft — 118 3½ 75¾ 1012 1017½ Bonilla R6 ⒻM32000 63-16 PrncssMrcds,Lf'sSng,LvByThSrd 10
14Nov86—No wagering; Broke out, bumped
24Oct86-4SA 6f :22 :461 1:12 ft 20 117 1hd 2hd 41 511¾ VlnzlPA10 ⒻⓈM32000 66-20 TillieTillie,BuyMore,StrwbrryPort 11
24Oct86—Lugged in stretch
13Oct86-4SA 6f :214 :463 1:133ft 16 117 1hd 3nk 811 916½ VlnzlPA12 ⒻⓈM32000 54-19 Our Marge, Eghalanda, Buy More 12
13Oct86—Bumped intervals backstretch; lugged in badly stretch
23Sep86-4Pom 6f :221 :462 1:133ft 29 116 98¼ 712 610 57 White TC9 ⒻⓈM32000 76-08 PrttyPrstgos,‡MntnGld,‡AWBtIrsh 9
23Sep86—Placed third through disqualification
●Jan 14 Hol 4f ft :474 hg Jan 6 Hol 5f gd 1:021 h Dec 30 Hol tr.t 4f ft :541 h Dec 21 Hol 5f ft 1:031 h

Buy More B. f. 3, by Ginistrelli—Jumaireh, by Cornish Prince
SHOEMAKER W 117 Br.—Auerbach E (Cal) 1987 1 M 1 0 $2,800
Own.—Sirkel W D Tr.—Matlow Richard P $32,000 1986 4 M 2 2 $8,750
Lifetime 5 0 3 2 $11,550
1Jan87-4SA 6f :22 :46 1:114ft *2 118 2½ 32 22 2½ DlhossyE9 ⒻⓈM32000 78-19 Jan's Swifty, Buy More, Suki 12
12Nov86-2Hol 6f :22 :454 1:12 ft 4½ 118 55½ 53¾ 24 23 OrtegaLE7 ⒻⓈM32000 80-15 Eghalanda, Buy More,ExaltedJade 12
12Nov86—Wide into stretch
24Oct86-4SA 6f :22 :461 1:12 ft 5½ 117 65¾ 52½ 3½ 22½ OrtegaLE3 ⒻⓈM32000 75-20 TillieTillie,BuyMore,StrwbrryPort 11
24Oct86—Veered in, bumped break; fanned wide into stretch
13Oct86-4SA 6f :214 :463 1:133ft 8 117 1212 105¾ 67½ 35½ OrtegaLE6 ⒻⓈM32000 64-19 Our Marge, Eghalanda, Buy More 12
28Aug86-3Dmr 6f :22 :46 1:104ft 28 117 4¾ 32½ 26 36¾ OrtegaLE3 ⒻⓈM32000 77-18 Zha Zhana, SelectASong,BuyMore 12
Dec 24 Hol 4f ft :501 h

Erin's Fun B. f. 3, by Orbit Ruler—Funs Valentine, by Doc Scott J
SIMPSON B H 117 Br.—J K Houssels Thbd Fm (Cal) 1987 1 M 0 1 $2,100
Own.—Steinmann H Tr.—Gerber Greg D $32,000 1986 8 M 2 2 $10,350
Lifetime 9 0 2 3 $12,450
7Jan87-4SA 6f :22 :46 1:123m *2¾ 117 54½ 54½ 36 38½ Sibille R2 ⒻM32000 66-21 Coron Miss, Aunt Nola, Erin'sFun 10
7Jan87—Broke slowly, wide 3/8
18Dec86-2Hol 6f :222 :462 1:124ft 3½ 118 42½ 32½ 23 23½ Sibille R8 ⒻM32000 75-17 LfkdinSrnd,Erin'sFun,FlsConcolor 11
5Dec86-6Hol 6f :221 :461 1:114ft 9 118 21½ 2½ 21½ 23½ SmpsnBH6 ⒻⓈM32000 80-17 Heavy Weather,Erin'sFun,TableBay 8
14Nov86- Hol 6f :22 :46 1:122ft — 118 51½ 42½ 65¾ 79½ Meza R Q7 ⒻM32000 71-16 PrncssMrcds,Lf'sSng,LvByThSrd 10
14Nov86—No wagering; Bumped start
24Oct86-4SA 6f :22 :461 1:12 ft *9-5 117 43½ 4¾ 63¾ 715 Meza R Q8 ⒻⓈM32000 63-20 TillieTillie,BuyMore,StrwbrryPort 11
24Oct86—Wide into stretch
3Oct86-2SA 6f :214 :453 1:12 gd 5 117 2hd 1½ 1hd 35 Meza R Q1 ⒻM32000 73-17 Chanterella,AutumnGle,Erin'sFun 12
6Sep86-6Dmr 6f :223 :463 1:113ft 4¾ 117 2hd 1¾ 31½ 48¾ Pincay L Jr3 ⒻM50000 71-14 Trcy'sTrck,ItsAlwysSprng,Tmprgz 11
6Sep86—Bumped start; altered path 4 1/2
9Aug86-6Dmr 6f :221 :453 1:114ft 13 117 2hd 3½ 1011 1014¾ Pincay L Jr10 ⒻⓈMdn 64-14 WildManor,Kavalla,HeavyWeather 10
28Jly86-6Dmr 5½f :221 :463 1:054ft 9½ 116 1½ 1hd 2hd 34 Baze R A1 ⒻⓈMdn 78-16 IrishLord'sMiss,Gelicsrch,Erin'sFun 6
28Jly86—Lugged out
Jan 19 SA 4f ft :484 h Dec 30 SA 3f ft :353 h Dec 17 Hol 4f ft :512 h Dec 3 Hol 3f ft :36 h

Hostess Rose
ARAGON V A   117
Own.—Rogers J D

B. f. 3, by Debonair Roger—Polite Khal, by Poleax
Br.—Rogers J D (Cal)
Tr.—Threewitt Noble $32,000

1987   1 M 0 0
1986   1 M 0 0
Lifetime   2 0 0 0

9Jan87-4SA   6f :221 :462 1:133sl   24 117   63 541 815 8201   ArgonVA11 ⑮M32000 50-26 Time To Call, Divest, Laurentian   12
12Dec86-1Hol   6f :221 :462 1:121ft   51 118   53 951 1014 10101   PedrozMA10 ⑰M32000 63-20 BtflBrook,FlsConcolr,DrlngFnnyfc 11
Jan 17 SA 3f ft :352 h   Jan 3 SA 4f ft :48 hg   Dec 28 SA 4f ft :494 h   Dec 5 Hol 4f ft :493 hg

Miss Adios
CORDOVA D W   117
Own.—Wackeen C

Dk. b. or br. f. 3, by Adios—Miss Lynn Marie, by Windy Sands
Br.—Resnick-Lannon-Schrader (Cal)
Tr.—Moerman Gerald C $32,000

1987   1 M 0 0
1986   0 M 0 0
Lifetime   1 0 0 0

7Jan87-4SA   6f :22 :46 1:123m   31 117   66 753 610 812   CordovaDW1 ⑰M32000 63-21 Coron Miss, Aunt Nol- Erin'sFun 10
Jan 19 SA 3f ft :373 h   Dec 30 SA 3f ft :362 hg   Dec 23 SA 7f ft 1:292 hg   Dec 19 SA 6f ft 1:172 h

Making a worksheet on this one becomes rather difficult because of what we don't have. But here is what we managed to produce.

Odds	Horse	PCR						Form	Ab/T		
9-2	Flying Belle	LRH						NON	46.3	6.3	0/ 73.1
55	Find My Way	77/ 43	38	–	/ 81	=	95	Lw	(45.4	25.3 +	3/ 72.0)
7	Exalted Jade	53/ 16	19	–	/ 35	=	151	Lw	(46.4	26.0	0/ 72.4)
19	Table Bay	32/ 15	16	–	/ 31	=	(103)	Lw	(46.4	26.0 +	1/ 73.0)
99	Jump At A Bargain	x						x	x		
2	Divest	LRH						NON	47.0	28.4 –	3/ 75.1
18	Fall From Glory	76/ 25	55	–	/ 80	=	95	NON	47.0	28.4 –	3/ 75.1
2	Buy More	69/ 26	10	–	/ 36	=	192	N+N	46.2	25.3	0/ 73.0
9	Erin's Fun	89/ 29	41	–	/ 70	=	127	NON	46.4	27.2 –	1/ 74.0
99	Miss Adios	LRH						NON	x		
70	Hostess Rose	LRH						NON	x		

This considerable mixture of lightly raced horses and animals off layoffs would cause uncertainty at any time, but in spite of it, you may choose to blink at what you see in this grab bag—a potentially second successive Double Advantage horse. Buy More, with Shoemaker up, seems to have the credentials. With five races, a PCR can be run, and it is extremely high at 192. Coupled with that last race running line and ability time, you may begin to wonder why this horse was only a co-favorite at 2-1 with Divest, who had such a poor last race line that you are constrained to wonder how this horse could be so solidly backed at the windows.

There is a slight nagging concern, however, before we analyze the race further. Buy More has finished second three times in a row. That dread old race track disease, "seconditis," is hard to overcome, and it gives us considerable pause.

There is yet a major hurdle, and this one is far more important. Despite her good last race, Buy More has a second call total that is 2 ½ times greater than her finish total. This is the mark of an habitual closer, as surely as if it were stamped on her forehead. If the track were biased today for closers, this filly would be as much of a sure thing as we believed Neutral Player to be in the first race.

In prior years, before I developed the internal numbers in my PCR lines, and learned how instructive they are insofar as track surface is concerned, I would always play a double advantage horse, without exception. But experience has taught me that even the double advantage animal is an unlikely winner where the track is hostile to his running style. In fact, aside from serious misfortune, which happened to Neutral Player in the first race, most of the infrequent defeats of double advantage horses come when the track is running heavily against their style. We are still wondering about today.

All we have to go on thus far about the track is what we saw in the first race. There were no formidable closers there to show us what they could do. Most of the horses had lower second call totals or were even runners. However, those that ran forwardly in the race did well.

With these doubts and reservations, because the closing habits of Buy More are so critical to how we play the race, we must look at how the others in the field appear. The most pronounced early runner is Fall From Glory, whose last race is atrocious. But even with quick getaway habits, you can get some insight from the ability time readings, where this one turned in a 47.0 at the second call and faded to 28.4 for the last portion. Numbers like this will lead nowhere.

Also very formidable in the early speed department is Exalted Jade, off duty for 32 days, but showing reasonably impressive workouts. We will have to pay attention to an advisory ability line, which is reasonably strong. Erin's Fun, with a 24 against a 41, is also a speed package in the race, but with a last race ability time that inspires no confidence.

What to do? Will this double advantage filly, Buy More, shake off her seconditis and overcome the speedsters to leave the maiden ranks today?

When final decision time comes, all the analytical skills we have learned must come into play. We are not certain about the track, but we see no sign that it favors closers, and if anything, it may run toward being forward or even more neutral. And when a track is running reasonably neutral, the speed merchants can still do relatively well. When there are at least three horses in a sprint race that are almost sure to produce some early foot, the pronounced closer is almost equally sure to have a hard time of it.

On the other hand, the double advantage off such good last race form is such a potent signal that it is hard to ignore. If it were not for the internal numbers that are weighed heavily against Buy More, she would be an outstanding single selection play.

This is the kind of recognizable situation that calls for a multiple selection play, if you can find some other horse with an advantage. Otherwise, you may want to pass altogether. We must now go back and look again to see where there might be a potential play. The second highest PCR horse, Exalted Jade, comes pretty close to obvious, with her good works and an advisory time that is soundly competitive. The other advisory ability time that is impressive belongs to Find My Way if you go back to Del Mar on August 1, 1986. But the low PCR and the 55-1 odds demonstrate that we cannot take this one seriously, especially in view of the fact that all of the later races have been so bad.

What do we do about the co-favorite, Divest? Although lightly raced horses often show startling improvement, a last race ability time that is tied for the worst is a sure formula for a losing ticket. There isn't much else, and it becomes rather easy to add Exalted Jade to our multiple selection list, which has another advantage this early in the afternoon, when we have not yet been able to place a definitive label on how the track is running. We can combine an early speed choice with a closing choice, and of course, find out later where it leads us.

Accordingly, the play is on two horses, Buy More with her double advantage but closing habit, and Exalted Jade with her early speed, good workouts, and her wholesome PCR. At the track, you could have dutched the odds, but for our paper purposes, we'll record the minimum $2 on each of them. Here is the chart of the race.

This one again makes the careful analysis off the worksheet lines look very good. Buy More was an abysmal failure, back in the pack, closing only slightly, never in contention. The early speedster, Fall From Glory, was out in front as expected, and even had a three-length lead as she entered the stretch. Exalted Jade, only four lengths back at the second call, running well, came on impressively to win. The lucrative $17 price came about because of the layoff and the heavy play on Divest, who surprised us by finishing second, and

SECOND RACE **6 FURLONGS. (1.07⅗) MAIDEN CLAIMING. Purse $14,000. Fillies. 3-year-olds. Bred in California. Weight, 117 lbs. Claiming price $32,000; if for $28,000 allowed 2 lbs.**

Santa Anita

JANUARY 21, 1987

Value of race $14,000; value to winner $7,700; second $2,800; third $2,100; fourth $1,050; fifth $350. Mutuel pool $356,112.

Last Raced	Horse	Eqt.	A.	Wt	PP	St	¼	½	Str	Fin	Jockey	Cl'g Pr	Odds $1
20Dec86 2Hol2	Exalted Jade	b	3	117	3	8	5hd	52	42	12	Castanon A L	32000	7.60
9Jan87 4SA2	Divest	b	3	117	6	7	3½	2½	31½	2no	Pincay L Jr	32000	2.00
9Jan87 4SA6	Fall From Glory	b	3	110	7	3	11½	13	13	3nk	Cox D W5	28000	18.60
7Jan87 4SA3	Erin's Fun		3	117	9	5	61½	3½	2hd	41¾	Simpson B H	32000	9.70
18Dec86 2Hol4	Find My Way	b	3	115	2	10	91	81½	6½	5hd	Pedroza M A	28000	55.20
1Jan87 4SA4	Flying Belle		3	117	1	11	81½	7½	71½	62¾	Valenzuela P A	32000	4.70
1Jan87 4SA2	Buy More		3	117	8	4	4½	6hd	85	7½	Shoemaker W	32000	2.00
5Dec86 6Hol3	Table Bay	b	3	117	4	6	2½	4hd	5hd	86½	Baze G	32000	19.20
9Jan87 4SA8	Hostess Rose	b	3	117	10	1	71½	93	96	97¾	Aragon V A	32000	70.60
9Jan87 4SA11	Jump At A Bargain		3	112	5	9	11	11	10hd	10hd	Sterling L J Jr5	32000	113.30
7Jan87 4SA8	Miss Adios		3	117	11	2	101	10hd	11	11	Cordova D W	32000	119.80

OFF AT 1:04. Start good. Won driving. Time, :22, :45⅘, :58⅘, 1:12 Track fast.

$2 Mutuel Prices:			
3-EXALTED JADE	17.20	6.20	5.20
5-DIVEST		3.80	3.60
7-FALL FROM GLORY			7.00

Buy More, which forced the odds upward on the other horses, thank you.

Happy as we are with the result, where are we with our track analysis as far as early or late speed is concerned? Exalted Jade, even with her good early speed, had to rally in the stretch to win. But on the other hand, she was in contention, only four lengths off at the second call. We are left again with "somewhat inconclusive," but you can be sure that early speed is not suffering unduly, despite the folding in the stretch of Fall From Glory. Even if we called the track neutral, front speed would still be a formidable factor.

The third race is one of those incredibly high priced claiming races, with the established tag of $100,000. Does anyone ever claim a horse out of a race like this? There are even horses in there that have run in graded stakes races.

The most immediate problem in computing ability times is the lack of a common last race distance. Today's race is at 7 furlongs, where only one horse ran last time. However, we will still have to convert to the six furlong distance in order to have uniform comparison times, even though this particular race becomes very awkward to figure in a number of ways.

With these problems, we take a look at the field:

3rd Santa Anita

7 FURLONGS. (1.20) CLAIMING. Purse $33,000. 4-year-olds and upward. Weights, 4-year-olds, 120 lbs.; older, 121 lbs. Non-winners of two races since November 3 allowed 3 lbs.; of a race since then 5 lbs. Claiming price $100,000; for each $5,000 to $85,000 allowed 1 lb. (Races when entered for $80,000 or less not considered.)

My Favorite Moment B. h. 6, by Timeless Moment—My Masindi, by Dragante
VALENZUELA P A 116 Br.—Dinnaken Farm (Ky). 1987 1 0 0 0
Own.—Conners W L Tr.—Stute Warren $90,000 1986 4 1 1 1 $31,750
Lifetime 22 8 2 5 $177,640 Turf 1 0 0 0

9Jan87-8SA 6½f :21^{1} :44^{3} 1:18 sl 5¾ 118 3^{6} 5^{6½} 7^{10} 6^{16½} ValenzuelPA^{4} Aw45000 64-26 Innmorto,ProudestHour,GminiDrmr 8
9Jan87—Wide into stretch
21Dec86-5Hol 6f :22^{1} :45^{2} 1:10^{3}ft *1 116 3^{1½} 3^{1½} 3^{1½} 1^{nk} ValenzuelPA^{2} Aw35000 90-15 MFvrtMmnt,McLndn,AmrcnStndrd 6
21Jun86-5Hol 6f :21^{4} :45 1:09^{2}ft 2½ 116 4^{3} 4^{1½} 2½ 2^{1½} DelahoussyeE^{6} 100000 95-09 AmrcnLgn,MyFvrtMmnt,MGllntGm 7
21Jun86—Lost whip start
8Jun86-5Hol 6f :22 :45 1:08^{3}ft 3¾ 117 4^{4½} 4^{5½} 3^{7½} 3^{8} DelhoussyeE^{2} Aw35000 93-11 CsForPs,RgnngCntss,MyFvrtMmnt 6
11Jan86-8SA 7f :21^{4} :43^{4} 1:20^{4}ft 29 116 6^{6½} 6^{11} 6^{16} 5^{13} ᵈ DlhossyE^{6} Sn Crls H 83-11 PhonTrick,TmrityPrinc,MyHbitony 6
11Jan86—Grade II; ᵈDead heat
29Dec85-8SA 6f :21^{2} :43^{3} 1:08 ft 16 116 5^{2¾} 5^{7} 5^{9½} 4^{11½} DlhossyE^{3} Pls Vrds H 86-12 PhoneTrick,FivNorth,DbonirJunior 6
29Dec85—Wide into stretch
13Nov85-8Hol 6f :22^{4} :46^{3} 1:11^{2}gd 7 118 2^{hd} 4^{3} 4^{5½} 5^{9} DlhossyE^{2} Trf Spnt H 78-26 TmrtyPrnc,FrnchLgonr,DbonrJunor 5
28Oct85-10LA 6f :21^{2} :44^{1} 1:08^{3}ft 9-5 117 3^{2½} 3^{3½} 2^{hd} 1½ DlhossyE^{4} Orng Cst H 102-07 MyFvoriteMoment,SilentFox,Mzzo 6
16Oct85-8SA 6f :21^{2} :44 1:09^{1}ft 14 117 5^{2¾} 5^{3½} 5^{5½} 5^{2½} DlhssyE^{1} Anct Title H 89-17 TemerityPrince,DbonirJunior,BidUs 6
14Sep85-11Pom $1\frac{1}{16}$:46 1:11^{4} 1:44 ft *9-5 115 1^{hd} 1½ 2^{hd} 3^{3} HansenRD^{3} P D Shprd — — ApolloFlight,Agul,MyFvortMomnt 11
Jan 20 SA 3f ft :35^{2} h Jan 15 SA 5f ft 1:01^{4} h Jan 7 SA 4f sy :49^{4} h (d) Jan 2 SA 6f ft 1:15^{2} h

Sir Macamillion Ch. h. 8, by MacArthur Park—Peacock Hill, by Bobby's Legacy
CORDOVA D W 116 Br.—Cox & Cleary (Cal) 1987 1 0 0 0
Own.—Wegat & Wegat Tr.—Christin Mark $100,000 1986 10 3 1 2 $95,850
Lifetime 33 10 8 2 $186,575 Turf 5 0 1 0 $4,870

10Jan87-8SA 7f :22^{1} :44^{4} 1:22^{2}gd 39 113 7^{4½} 8^{6} 8^{11} 8^{16¼} CrdvDW^{5} Sn Crlos H 72-20 ZnyTctics,BolderThnBold,Epidurus 8
10Jan87—Grade II; Broke slowly
21Dec86-8BM 6f :22^{4} :46^{2} 1:12^{1}m 4½ 118 3^{3½} 4^{3} 7^{9} 8^{11¼} Loseth C^{3} L Stnfrd H 67-35 BrightAndRight,TripleSec,HolyRscl 8
11Oct86-8BM 7½f Ⓣ:22^{3} :45^{3}1:30^{1}fm 4¾ 112 2^{1½} 2^{2} 6^{3½} 7^{6} HnsnRD^{7} Mrk's Plc H 87-07 PerfcTrvl,NwAtrction,Position'sBst 9
21Sep86-8BM 6f :22^{1} :44^{4} 1:08^{4}ft 11 116 3^{nk} 1^{hd} 1^{1½} 1^{4} HnsenRD^{4} Fall Fstvl H 95-18 SirMcmillion,AmericnLgion,Ondrty 8
6Sep86-9Lga 6f :21^{2} :43^{3} 1:07^{4}ft *8-5 120 5^{5} 4^{4½} 3^{4½} 3^{3} DnRE^{6} W G Mgnsn H 94-13 Mndtory,BigBdBombr,SirMcmillion 7
24Aug86-9Lga 1 :44^{4} 1:08^{4} 1:34^{1}ft 26 116 4^{1½} 3^{2} 4^{4½} 3^{2¼} DmngRE^{1} Lga Mle H 96-14 Skywlkr,BdsidPromis,SirMcmillion 7
24Aug86—Grade II
3Aug86-9Lga 6½f :21^{3} :44^{1} 1:15 ft 9½ 117 5^{2¼} 5^{2¼} 3^{1½} 2½ Dominguez RE^{8} Gov H 93-15 BdsidPromis,SirMcmillion,DustyOk 8
13Jly86-11Sol 5½f :21^{3} :44^{3} 1:02^{2}ft 2½ 117 4^{3½} 4^{3½} 4^{7} 5^{6} DmngzRE^{5} Sol Exp H 93-13 Stn'sBowr,IrishScoundrl,RulrOfFlts 8
13Jly86—Steadied 1/4
12Apr86-8GG $1\frac{1}{16}$ Ⓣ:46^{2}1:11^{1}1:42 fm 5½ 114 2^{hd} 1^{hd} 7^{7} 9^{10½} DnRE^{7} [R]Tly Pp Iv H 81-09 OcenView,Introspective,DrkAccnt 11
28Feb86-8GG 6f :22^{1} :44^{4} 1:08^{4}ft *2½ 118 4^{2½} 2^{1} 1½ 1^{4} DominguzRE^{6} Aw22000 95-22 SirMacamillion,Mr.Brilliant,BigEric 9
Jan 7 SA 3f sy :39^{1} h (d) Jan 2 BM 7f gd 1:27^{1} h Dec 13 BM 6f ft 1:13 h Dec 7 BM 5f sl 1:02^{2} h

Emperdori Ch. h. 5, by Golden Act—Snow Empress, by Young Emperor
PEDROZA M A 116 Br.—Floyd W & M B (Ky) 1987 1 0 0 0
Own.—Brown & Ratzlaff Tr.—Lewis Craig A $100,000 1986 15 2 3 1 $104,355
Lifetime 29 5 6 2 $198,839 Turf 26 4 5 2 $142,659

1Jan87-5SA 1⅛ Ⓣ:47^{1}1:11^{2}1:48^{1}fm 8 118 6^{3} 7^{2¾} 7^{3¾} 7^{5½} Pincay L Jr^{7} 100000 80-14 Steepbank, River Of Kings, Keyala 9
1Jan87—Off slowly, wide
14Dec86-5Hol $1\frac{1}{16}$ Ⓣ:46^{1}1:10 1:40^{2}fm 6½ 119 4^{4½} 3^{3} 3^{2½} 2^{hd} Pincay L Jr^{5} 100000 92-11 Lucky N Green, Emperdori, Keyala 8
22Nov86-5Hol $1\frac{1}{16}$ Ⓣ:47 1:11^{2}1:42^{1}fm 30 116 4^{2½} 4^{1¼} 4^{1} 4^{2½} Pedroza M A^{2} 110000 80-17 NuggetPoint,PolyTest,RivrOfKings 9
17Oct86-8BM $1\frac{1}{16}$:46^{1} 1:09^{3} 1:40^{2}ft 36 115 4^{4} 8^{11} 8^{17} 8^{17} PdrMA^{3} B M Br Cp H 73-16 Hopeful Word, Armin, Bozina 8
28Sep86-11Poma 1⅛ :46^{1} 1:11 1:48^{3}ft 5 115 5^{7} 3^{3½} 3^{3} 2^{5¾} PdrozMA^{3} Pom Inv H 98-09 Epidaurus, Emperdori, Bozina 7
21Sep86-10Pom $1\frac{1}{16}$:46^{1} 1:10^{2} 1:43 ft 12 117 5^{5½} 2^{hd} 1^{5} 1^{7½} PdrzMA^{6} [R]C B Aflrbh 96-07 Emperdori, Estate, Iron Leader 7
3Sep86-7Dmr $1\frac{1}{16}$ Ⓣ:47^{2}1:11^{2}1:42^{3}fm 8½ 118 6^{5½} 7^{4½} 5^{2¼} 3^{1¼} Soto S B^{5} 80000 92-12 ExclusivCpd,RivrOfKings,Emprdori 8
24Aug86-5Dmr $1\frac{1}{16}$ Ⓣ:47^{4}1:11^{4}1:41^{4}fm 22 116 2^{1½} 2½ 4^{3} 5^{6} Soto S B^{8} Aw28000 91-04 Nasib, Glaros, Ascension 8
24Aug86—Broke in, bumped
26Jly86-9Dmr $1\frac{1}{16}$ Ⓣ:47 1:11^{1}1:42 fm 10 120 8^{7¾} 7^{3½} 8^{4¾} 9^{5½} McHargue DG^{2} 100000 90-05 Bshop'sRngII,PttBonhomm,AvtrII 10
26Jly86—Bumped start
5Jly86-4Hol 1⅛ Ⓣ:47^{1}1:10^{3}1:46^{3}fm 17 116 7^{10} 7^{9} 7^{6½} 6^{7½} McHrgueDG^{6} Aw27000 92-04 Raipillan,Diaghlyphard,GllrtArcher 7
Jan 17 SA 4f ft :50^{4} h Dec 24 SA 5f ft 1:00^{4} h Nov 25 Hol 5f ft 1:00 h

Champion Pilot B. h. 6, by Exceller—Jet to Market, by Farm to Market

PINCAY L JR 116 Br.—Hunt N B (Ky) 1986 1 0 1 0 $6,000

Own.—Carothers G Tr.—Blincoe Tom $100,000 1985 14 4 2 0 $164,274

Lifetime 20 5 4 1 $192,949 Turf 8 1 4 0 $58,945

26Dec86-5SA a6½f ⓣ:212 :4411:151fm 6¼ 117 1½ 1½ 2hd 2hd Pincay L Jr11 80000 83-17 Estate, Champion Pilot, Shanaar 12

26Dec86—Broke stride crossing dirt

3Nov85-2Aqu 1 ⓣ:4641:12 1:354fm 20 119 11 1½ 63½ 811¾ Cruguet J6 Shergar 85-01 Win, Solidified, ComeOnTheBlues 10

3Nov85—Run in divisions

26Oct85-8Med 5f ⓣ:214 :442 :562fm*7-5 117 32½ 36 38½ 27 Santos J A4 Aw20000 94-08 Uncnllmmrlck,ChmpnPlt,MdvlScrt 11

17Oct85-8Bel 6f :223 :454 1:101ft 6¾ 115 12 52½ 610 614¾ Santos J A4 HcpO 76-17 PanchoVilla,ChargingFalls,Entropy 6

5Oct85-7Bel 6f :22 :452 1:103m 12 125 12 11½ 42½ 56½ SntosJA10 Fall Hiwt H 83-19 Mt.Livrmor,FightingFit,Zggy'sBoy 10

5Oct85—Grade II

28Jly85-8Dmr 1⅟₁₆ :451 1:091 1:412ft 4 120 1½ 1½ 33 48½ McCrrCJ6 Sn Diego H 84-13 SuprDmond,M.DoublM.,FrnchLgonr 7

28Jly85—Grade III

5Jly85-8Hol 1 ⓣ:4521:0921:341fm 5½ 121 2hd 1hd 2hd 55½ McCrrCJ3 Pretense H 87-09 M. Double M., Zoffany, RetsinaRun 7

15Jun85-8GS 1 :453 1:102 1:353ft 3¾ 118 21 2½ 2hd 44¼ HwlyS7 Carry Back H 93-11 CrrDeNskr,MyHbitony,DrmticDesir 9

26May85-8GG 7½f ⓣ:223 :4541:282fm 3½ 121 11 1½ 2hd 22¼ ChpnTM2 All Amrcn H 95-11 Hegemony, ChampionPilot,NakAck 5

26May85—Grade III

13Apr85-8SA 1⅛ :45 1:09 1:47 ft *4-5e 120 11½ 1½ 33 410½ ShmrW5 Sn Brndno H 84-13 Greinton, Precisionist, Al Mamoon 6

13Apr85—Grade II

●Jan 11 SA 7f ft 1:261 h Dec 23 SA 5f ft 1:01 h Dec 10 Hol 6f ft 1:163 h Dec 6 Hol 6f m 1:14 h

J. R. Johnson B. g. 4, by Jerimi Johnson—Merry Hilarious, by Fast Hilarious

CORDERO A JR 114 Br.—Stevens S E (Tex) 1986 15 6 2 2 $92,175

Own.—Cuadra San Diego Tr.—King Hal $95,000 1985 11 4 4 0 $48,648

Lifetime 26 10 6 2 $140,823 Turf 1 0 0 0

26Dec86-5SA a6½f ⓣ:212 :4411:151fm 11 116 84½ 86½ 89¾ 99½ Valenzuela P A7 80000 73-17 Estate, Champion Pilot, Shanaar 12

26Dec86—Bumped start; lugged out

19Oct86-11Fno 1⅛ :45 1:101 1:482ft 9-5 122 1hd 1½ 1hd 22½ Cruz J B4 Harvest H 87-13 MstrNvjo,J.R.Johnson,U.LuckyShot 8

20Sep86-11Pom 1⅟₁₆ :451 1:103 1:44 ft *2½ 114 2hd 11 1hd 31¼ PdrzMA10 Ⓢ Derby Trl 90-09 BoldBrvoII,Rfl'sDncr,J.R.Johnson 10

11Sep86-11Pom 6½f :22 :454 1:164ft *9-5 117 42½ 3½ 11½ 15 Pedroza M A4 Foothill 96-08 J.R.Johnson,ElCorzon,LghtnngToch 8

11Sep86—Bumped break

15Aug86-7Dmr 7f :221 :45 1:223ft 16 114 2½ 1hd 12 1½ Pedroza MA1 Aw21000 92-12 J. R. Johnson, East Tulip,GoSwiftly 8

15Aug86—Veered in start; lugged in late

3Aug86-7Dmr 6f :213 :444 1:091ft 4½ 114 3½ 1hd 2½ 32¾ Stevens G L5 Aw21000 89-10 Ondarty, High Hook, J. R.Johnson 12

3Aug86—Bumped start

5Jly86-1Hol 6f :214 :45 1:102ft *2½ 116 1hd 2½ 11 1½ Stevens G L4 Aw20000 92-08 J.R.Johnson,SocityRod,LttlRdCloud 7

5Jly86—Drifted out late

26Jun86-1Hol 6f :22 :45 1:094ft 8½ 115 1hd 2hd 1hd 1¾ McCarron C J4 57500 95-12 J. R. Johnson, Totality, Rirnegato 8

15Jun86-3Hol 6f :221 :453 1:111ft *2½ 117 2½ 2hd 1½ 1nk Pincay L Jr1 50000 88-13 J.R.Johnson,AnglArc,EghtyBlowZro 9

6Apr86-9SA 6½f :211 :441 1:163ft 8 1115 23½ 32½ 42½ 57½ Black C A8 62500 79-15 Keen Knight, K. Gibran, GranPierre 8

Jan 8 SA 6f m 1:14 h ●Jan 2 SA 5f ft 1:001 h Dec 23 SA 4f ft :48 h Dec 16 Hol 4f ft :48 h

Metronomic * B. h. 5, by Crozier—Polly N, by Quibu

STEVENS G L 116 Br.—Hooper F W (Fla) 1987 1 0 0 0 $1,125

Own.—Hooper F W Tr.—Fenstermaker L R $100,000 1986 12 1 3 2 $38,890

Lifetime 25 3 5 6 $107,690 Turf 4 0 1 1 $20,200

9Jan87-8SA 6½f :211 :443 1:18 sl 40 114 77½ 78 69 513 Stevens S A7 Aw45000 67-26 Innmorto,ProudestHour,GminiDrmr 8

9Jan87—Wide into stretch

12Nov86-3Hol 7f :221 :451 1:213ft 8½ 117 34½ 53½ 43½ 36½ Stevens G L2 Aw26000 90-15 BoldrThnBold,MyGllntGm,Mtrnmc 6

12Oct86-5SA a6½f ⓣ:214 :44 1:134fm 6 116 65 97¾ 77¼ 610 McHrgueDG7 Aw33000 80-12 PrinceSky,MyGallantGame,Bruiser 12

23Sep86-11Pom 6½f :213 :442 1:151ft 2 116 33 33½ 31 23½ Solis A6 Gvnr Cp H 101-08 BundleOfIron,Mtronomic,SurToFir 7

16Sep86-11Pom 6f :214 :442 1:092ft 8¾ 115 42½ 57 36 2¾ Solis A2 Aprisa H 103-05 BundlOfIron,Mtronomc,ProdstHor 10

27Aug86-7Dmr 7f :224 :452 1:222ft 9 115 1hd 1hd 3nk 31¼ Baze R A1 Aw26000 91-14 Variety Road, Barland, Metronomic 6

13Aug86-3Dmr 6f :213 :443 1:083ft 23 117 45½ 45 35 23¼ Baze R A5 Aw24000 91-15 MneMgic,Metronomic,MyGllntGme 6

28Jun86-11Pln 6f :22 :44 1:083ft 13 113 46 47 47 47¼ GlRM3 Whtng Mem H 91-11 Cardell,Stan'sBower,MchoComcho 6

28Jun86—Bumped start

21Jun86-5Hol 6f :214 :45 1:092ft 38 116 77 64¾ 64¼ 65¾ Sibille R2 100000 91-09 AmrcnLgn,MyFvrtMmnt,MGllntGm 7

1Jun86-9Hol 1 :444 1:092 1:361ft 23 117 58¼ 49½ 48½ 53½ McHrgueDG5 Aw32000 78-14 Koshare, Ultimate Pleasure, Jon O. 7

Jan 19 SA 4f ft :484 hg Jan 6 SA 4f gd :474 h Dec 30 SA 5f ft 1:012 h Dec 18 Hol 5f ft 1:012 h

And here is what our worksheet shows:

Odds	Horse	PCR							Form	Ab/T
5-2	My Favorite Mom't	67/	40	35	–	7/	68	= 99	NON	46.0 28.3–3/ 74.0
7	Sir Macamillion	83/	34	47	–	4/	77	= 108	NON	46.0 26.4 0/ 72.4
8	Emperdori	81/	50	47	–	3/	94	= 86	NNt	n/a
6-5	Champion Pilot	83/	17	42	–	9/	50	= 166	N+N	n/a
9-2	J.R. Johnson	78/	16	18	+	3/	37	= 211	NON	(45.1 25.2+8/ 72.1)
7	Metronomic	75/	48	38	–	1/	85	= 88	NON	46.1 27.4–3/ 73.2

This race is filled with uncertainties. Two of the horses have far and away the best PCRs, J. R. Johnson and the heavily favored Champion Pilot. J. R. Johnson's last race on the turf was very bad, but it was his only experience on the grass, and might well be excused. To go back prior to that race takes us into October in a stakes race at Fresno, and that is too far away to be considered. The question then emerges as to whether the last race on the grass was because the horse couldn't handle the turf or whether he was off form. We are looking for advantages, not uncertainties.

Champion Pilot may be close to a play, having run quite well on the grass in his last effort. But there is no useable last race ability time because of the grass race that began with a run downhill, and which we cannot begin to use for comparison purposes. The last race effort does look good, but there is still that open void in our knowledge. Champion Pilot is loaded with early speed and that might be a considerable asset, but we are not even sure about our reading of the track at this point. We can also see that J. R. Johnson and Sir Macamillion know how to load it on early. We might feel secure about throwing out Metronomic because of his closing habits and weak PCR, but all the others are still around for consideration.

As for early speed, bear in mind that this race is at 7 furlongs, which may be one of the toughest distances for horses to run. It becomes very wearing to sprint all the way and yet it is too short for a route race. I have seen early speed and late speed both do well in similar conditions in 7 furlong races.

There is also the consideration that horses of this quality are often extremely difficult to pick, as we have tried to point out: very good horses and very bad horses often pose equally uncertain choices. More important, in this six horse field, we are only able to compute last race ability times for half the horses, and the other half all have last race form defects. We are confronted with uncertainty at every turn, which carries its own loud message. This is a shining instruction to pass this race. This is exactly what we shall do. Here is what happened:

THIRD RACE
Santa Anita
JANUARY 21, 1987

7 FURLONGS. (1.20) CLAIMING. Purse $33,000. 4-year-olds and upward. Weights, 4-year-olds, 120 lbs.; older, 121 lbs. Non-winners of two races since November 3 allowed 3 lbs.; of a race since then 5 lbs. Claiming price $100,000; for each $5,000 to $85,000 allowed 1 lb. (Races when entered for $80,000 or less not considered.)

Value of race $33,000; value to winner $18,150; second $6,600; third $4,950; fourth $2,475; fifth $825. Mutuel pool $243,455. Exacta pool $315,859.

Last Raced	Horse	Eqt.	A.	Wt	PP	St	¼	½	Str	Fin	Jockey	Cl'g Pr	Odds $1
1Jan87 ^{5}SA^{7}	Emperdori	b	5	116	3	5	6	6	4^{5}	$1^{1\frac{1}{4}}$	Pedroza M A	100000	8.90
9Jan87 ^{8}SA^{5}	Metronomic		5	116	6	1	$3^{1\frac{1}{2}}$	$3^{2\frac{1}{2}}$	$1^{\frac{1}{2}}$	$2^{\frac{1}{2}}$	Stevens G L	100000	7.60
9Jan87 ^{8}SA^{6}	My Favorite Moment		6	116	1	3	1^{hd}	1^{hd}	2^{hd}	$3^{\frac{3}{4}}$	Valenzuela P A	90000	2.80
26Dec86 ^{5}SA^{9}	J. R. Johnson	b	4	114	5	4	2^{hd}	2^{hd}	3^{2}	4^{10}	Cordero A Jr	95000	4.90
10Jan87 ^{8}SA^{8}	Sir Macamillion		8	116	2	2	$4^{2\frac{1}{2}}$	4^{3}	$5^{2\frac{1}{2}}$	$5^{2\frac{1}{2}}$	Cordova D W	100000	7.90
26Dec86 ^{5}SA^{2}	Champion Pilot		6	117	4	6	$5^{1\frac{1}{2}}$	5^{hd}	6	6	Pincay L Jr	100000	1.30

OFF AT 1:38. Start good for all but CHAMPION PILOT. Won driving. Time, :22⅘, :45, 1:10⅕, 1:23⅘ Track fast.

$2 Mutuel Prices:				
	3-EMPERDORI	19.80	9.00	10.40
	6-METRONOMIC		8.00	10.40
	1-MY FAVORITE MOMENT			5.20

$2 EXACTA 3-6 PAID $107.00.

Neither Champion Pilot nor early speed exerted much of an influence on this race. We would not have expected, based on internal numbers, that the early leader, My Favorite Moment, would even be up there. Quite likely, no one was anxious to barrel out front. Emperdori, the winner, five and a half back at the second call, came on nicely to win and bring in another good price. A horse with internal numbers that are relatively even is often a serious threat in a 7 furlong race. We can still rate the track as inconclusive or neutral as we look at the miseries of the fourth race that are laid before us.

4th Santa Anita

6 FURLONGS. (1.07⅗) MAIDEN CLAIMING. Purse $14,000. Fillies. 3-year-olds. Bred in California. Weight, 117 lbs. Claiming price $32,000; if for $28,000 allowed 2 lbs.

Pullybone — Dk. b. or br. f. 3, by Invitado—Cheerful Me, by Lucky Mel
CASTANON A L **117** — Br.—Old McBrayer Farm (Cal) — 1987 1 M 0 0
Tr.—McBrayer C H — $32,000 — 1986 1 M 0 0
Own.—Chami-Hamilton-McBrayer — Lifetime 2 0 0 0

9Jan87-4SA 6f :22^{1} :46^{2} 1:13^{3}sl 109 117 $10^{8\frac{3}{4}}$ 10^{11} 9^{17} $10^{22\frac{1}{2}}$ CstnonAL^{5} ⒻⓈM32000 47-26 Time To Call, Divest, Laurentian 12
12Dec86-1Hol 6f :22^{1} :46^{2} 1:12^{1}ft 106 113^{5} 11^{11} $11^{7\frac{1}{2}}$ 8^{12} 7^{14} Patton D B^{4} ⒻM32000 68-20 BtflBrook,FlsConcolr,DringFnnyfc 11
Jan 3 SLR tr.t 3f ft :37^{4} h Dec 5 SLR tr.t 5f ft 1:01^{2} hg Dec 1 SLR tr.t 6f ft 1:15^{3} h Nov 26 SLR tr.t 5f ft 1:02^{3} h

Pasoneva — Ch. f. 3, by Que Paso—Nevas Date, by Mandate
FERNANDEZ A L **117** — Br.—Dohgel Stables (Cal) — 1987 1 M 0 0
Tr.—Pew Karl — $32,000 — 1986 0 M 0 0
Own.—Doheny T M — Lifetime 1 0 0 0

1Jan87-4SA 6f :22 :46 1:11^{4}ft 7½ 118 $8^{4\frac{1}{2}}$ $7^{6\frac{1}{2}}$ $9^{9\frac{3}{4}}$ $10^{13\frac{1}{2}}$ FrnndzAL^{3} ⒻⓈM32000 65-19 Jan's Swifty, Buy More, Suki 12
Dec 26 SA 5f ft 1:00^{1} h Dec 19 SA 5f ft 1:02^{4} h Dec 12 SA 5f ft 1:00^{2} h Dec 5 SA 5f ft 1:00^{2} h

Natural Star
Ch. f. 3, by L'Natural—Now Starring, by Whodunit
ORTEGA L E 117 **Br.—Whiting Mr-Mrs P J (Cal)** 1987 1 M 0 0
Tr.—West Ted $32,000 1986 2 M 0 0 $825
Own.—Keeler & Michaels **Lifetime** 3 0 0 0 $825
7Jan87-4SA 6f :22 :46 1:12^{3}m 4 117 2½ 3^4 7^{11} — Meza R Q^8 ⒻM32000 — — Coron Miss, Aunt Nola, Er'n'sFun 10
7Jan87—Eased
5Dec86-2Hol 6f :22 :45^4 1:12^{3}ft 3½ 118 $6^{2\frac{3}{4}}$ $7^{7\frac{1}{2}}$ $7^{6\frac{1}{4}}$ 7^8 Baze G^7 Ⓕ[S]M32000 72-17 JustAsFlt,AWBtIrsh,FllFromGlory 10
5Dec86—Wide 3/8 turn
26Nov86-4Hol 6f :22^4 :46^3 1:13^{3}ft 2 118 2½ 1^{hd} 1^{hd} $4^{4\frac{1}{2}}$ Baze G^3 ⒻM32000 71-20 StrawberryPort,MagicalGal,Jiltble 12
26Nov86—Broke slowly; lugged in stretch checked 1/8
Jan 19 SA 3f ft :35^4 hg **Jan 13 SA 3f ft :36 h** **Dec 30 SA 5f ft 1:01^4 hg** **Dec 22 SA 5f ft 1:02^4 h**

Dancers Orbit
Dk. b. or br. f. 3, by Orbit Ruler—Dancer's Model, by Best Dancer
KAENEL J L 117 **Br.—Swindle E E (Cal)** 1987 1 M 0 0
Tr.—Hartgreve Harry R $32,000 1986 0 M 0 0
Own.—Swindle E E **Lifetime** 1 0 0 0
1Jan87-4SA 6f :22 :46 1:11^{4}ft 49 118 4^2 $9^{7\frac{3}{4}}$ 11^{12} $11^{16\frac{1}{2}}$ Kaenel JL^6 Ⓕ[S]M32000 62-19 Jan's Swifty, Buy More, Suki 12
1Jan87—Bumped start, checked at 3 1/2
Jan 17 SA 6f ft 1:17^3 hg **Dec 28 SA 5f ft 1:01^2 h** **Dec 18 SA 5f ft 1:02^3 h**

Miss Vegas Erin
Ch. f. 3, by Star of Erin—Miss Vegas J, by Doc Scott J
STEVENS G L 117 **Br.—Houssels J K (Cal)** 1986 0 M 0 0
Tr.—Headley Bruce $32,000
Own.—Headley & Houssels Jr **Lifetime** 0 0 0 0
Jan 3 SA 6f ft 1:15 hg **Dec 29 SA 6f ft 1:14^3 hg** **Dec 24 SA 6f ft 1:14^4 hg** **Dec 14 SA 4f ft :47 h**

Gina's Tike
B. f. 3, by Fleet Twist—Lotta Tike, by Skin Head
MEZA R Q 117 **Br.—Longden & Gelpar (Cal)** 1987 1 M 0 0 $350
Tr.—Longden Eric J $32,000 1986 0 M 0 0
Own.—Gelpar & Longden **Lifetime** 1 0 0 0 $350
1Jan87-4SA 6f :22 :46 1:11^{4}ft 9½ 118 3^1 2^2 $3^{5\frac{1}{2}}$ $5^{10\frac{1}{4}}$ Meza R Q^7 Ⓕ[S]M32000 69-19 Jan's Swifty, Buy More, Suki 12
1Jan87—Bumped start, green backside
Jan 15 SA 6f ft 1:14^1 h **Jan 9 SA 6f sl 1:16^1 h** **Dec 26 SA 6f ft 1:14^1 hg** **Dec 20 SA 5f ft 1:02^3 h**

Hey Bambino
Dk. b. or br. f. 3, by Caro Bambino—Chrissy Lou, by Aegean Isle
MCHARGUE D G 117 **Br.—Truman-Roub-Stewart (Cal)** 1986 0 M 0 0
Tr.—Truman Eddie $32,000
Own.—Stewart or Truman **Lifetime** 0 0 0 0
Jan 16 SA 6f ft 1:17^1 hg **Jan 10 SA 6f gd 1:17 h** **Jan 2 SA 6f ft 1:18^2 h** **Dec 27 SA 5f ft 1:02^1 h**

Vari Chilly
Ch. f. 3, by Canadian Gil—Villa V, by Olympiad King
COETZEE F 117 **Br.—Relatively & Varium Stables (Cal)** 1987 0 M 0 0
Tr.—Feld Jude T $32,000 1986 0 M 0 0
Own.—Campbell-Feld-Plescia **Lifetime** 0 0 0 0
Jan 17 SA 4f ft :49^3 h **Jan 12 SA 4f ft :49^3 hg** **Jan 7 SA tr.t 4f sy :49^4 h** **Jan 1 SA 4f ft :49^1 hg**

Wings In Orbit
Gr. f. 3, by Orbit Ruler—Born With Wings, by Arcadia Park
SIMPSON B H 117 **Br.—Walsh Mrs Adele (Cal)** 1986 0 M 0 0
Tr.—Gerber Greg D $32,000
Own.—Loewy & Poole **Lifetime** 0 0 0 0
Jan 16 SA 4f ft :50 hg **Jan 9 SA 6f sl 1:19^4 h** **Dec 24 SA 5f ft 1:03^1 h** **Dec 16 Hol 5f ft 1:03^1 h**

Yes Miss Helen
Ch. f. 3, by Be a Native—Girlish Laughter, by Father John
BAZEN J 117 **Br.—Dominguez M M (Cal)** 1986 0 M 0 0
Tr.—Martinez Rafael A $32,000
Own.—Dominguez M M **Lifetime** 0 0 0 0
Jan 17 Hol 5f ft 1:04^1 hg **Jan 9 Hol 5f ft 1:03^2 h** **Jan 3 Hol 5f ft 1:03^4 h** **Dec 16 Hol 5f ft 1:03 h**

Trip The Switch
B. f. 3, by Petrone—Our Advantage, by Fleet Mel
CORDOVA D W 117 **Br.—Matlock D (Cal)** 1986 0 M 0 0
Tr.—Norris Jerry $32,000
Own.—McGee J D **Lifetime** 0 0 0 0
Jan 11 SA 6f ft 1:17^2 hg **Dec 29 SA 5f ft 1:02^3 h** **Dec 22 Hol 4f ft :50^2 hg** **Dec 15 Hol 6f ft 1:17 hg**

Some Sensation
B. f. 3, by Somethingfabulous—Cooky Johnston, by Majestic Prince
WARREN R J JR 117 **Br.—Old English Rancho (Cal)** 1986 0 M 0 0
Tr.—Warren Donald $32,000
Own.—Jhnstn-Jhnstn-Stnbrkr et al **Lifetime** 0 0 0 0
Jan 16 SA 4f ft :47^4 hg **Jan 11 SA 6f ft 1:16^1 hg** **Jan 5 SA 4f sy :48^1 h** **Dec 31 SA 6f ft 1:14^4 h**

With another maiden claiming race for state breds, we have 6 of the 12 horses as first time starters, a peril in itself. Those that have run have turned in wretched performances. The favorite, Miss Vegas Erin, is well played off some passable workout lines, but they are not good enough to tempt us. There is no way handicapping lines could be developed on this race, an easy selection to be passed. For curiosity and track surface watching, here is the result chart:

FOURTH RACE **6 FURLONGS. (1.07⅗) MAIDEN CLAIMING. Purse $14,000. Fillies. 3-year-olds. Bred in California. Weight, 117 lbs. Claiming price $32,000; if for $28,000 allowed 2 lbs.**

Santa Anita
JANUARY 21, 1987

Value of race $14,000; value to winner $7,700; second $2,800; third $2,100; fourth $1,050; fifth $350. Mutuel pool $327,914.

Last Raced	Horse	Eqt.	A.	Wt	PP	St	¼	½	Str	Fin	Jockey	Cl'g Pr	Odds $1
	Some Sensation		3	117	12	2	$6^{2\frac12}$	$6^{1\frac12}$	$4^{\frac12}$	$1^{\frac12}$	Warren R J Jr	32000	5.40
1Jan87 ^{4}SA^5	Gina's Tike	b	3	117	6	1	$4^{2\frac12}$	$3^{1\frac12}$	$1^{\frac12}$	2^3	Meza R Q	32000	4.50
	Yes Miss Helen	b	3	117	10	11	$9^{1\frac12}$	7^3	7^1	$3^{1\frac12}$	Bazan J	32000	80.90
1Jan87 ^{4}SA^{11}	Dancers Orbit	b	3	117	4	12	$11^{3\frac12}$	$10^{3\frac12}$	8^2	$4^{2\frac12}$	Kaenel J L	32000	49.80
	Hey Bambino		3	117	7	7	5^1	5^{hd}	$6^{\frac12}$	$5^{1\frac12}$	McHargue D G	32000	7.20
	Miss Vegas Erin		3	117	5	4	2^1	$2^{\frac12}$	$3^{\frac12}$	6^{nk}	Stevens G L	32000	1.60
1Jan87 ^{4}SA^{10}	Pasoneva		3	117	2	6	3^{hd}	$4^{\frac12}$	5^1	$7^{1\frac12}$	Fernandez A L	32000	23.80
	Vari Chilly		3	117	8	9	$8^{\frac12}$	$9^{\frac12}$	$9^{3\frac12}$	8^1	Coetzee F	32000	24.70
7Jan87 ^{4}SA	Natural Star	b	3	117	3	5	$1^{\frac12}$	1^{hd}	$2^{\frac12}$	$9^{4\frac12}$	Ortega L E	32000	4.40
9Jan87 ^{4}SA^{10}	Pullybone		3	117	1	8	7^{hd}	8^{hd}	10^2	$10^{2\frac12}$	Castanon A L	32000	75.10
	Trip The Switch	b	3	117	11	3	10^1	11^4	11^4	$11^{1\frac12}$	Cordova D W	32000	66.20
	Wings In Orbit		3	117	9	10	12	12	12	12	Simpson B H	32000	45.00

OFF AT 2:11. Start good. Won driving. Time, :21⅘, :45⅘, :59, 1:12⅖ Track fast.

$2 Mutuel Prices:				
	12–SOME SENSATION	12.80	6.40	4.00
	6–GINA'S TIKE		5.40	3.80
	10–YES MISS HELEN			18.00

We learn little, except that early speed has not exerted itself. Once again, a mid-pack runner emerged to win. We can leave this one quickly and see if we can get back to playing in the fifth race, a 6½ furlong claimer for $20,000 horses.

5th Santa Anita

6½ FURLONGS. (1.14) CLAIMING. Purse $17,000. 4-year-olds and upward. Weights, 4-year-olds, 120 lbs.; older, 121 lbs. Non-winners of two races since November 3 allowed 3 lbs.; of a race since then, 5 lbs. Claiming price $20,000; if for $18,000 allowed 2 lbs. (Races when entered for $16,000 or less not considered.)

Pineapple Jack — **Ch. g. 4, by Mister Jacket—Ms B's Doll, by Understanding**
CASTANON A L **115** **Br.—Purcell W (Wash)** 1987 2 0 0 1 $2,550
Own.—Gould E F **Tr.—Stute Warren** **$20,000** 1986 13 2 4 2 $11,546
Lifetime 15 2 4 3 $14,096

10Jan87-2SA	$6\frac12$f	$:22^1$	$:45^2$	$1:18^1$gd	35	115	5^3	3^3	2^2	3^2	Castanon A L^1	20000	77-20	BoldTopsidr,Don'sCo'op,PnpplJck	12
10Jan87—Broke in a tangle															
1Jan87-9SA	$1\frac1{16}$	$:47^1$	1:12	$1:44^3$ft	7	115	10^{10}	$9^{9\frac14}$	9^{11}	$9^{16\frac14}$	Stevens G L^2	c16000	62-19	RoosvltRod,ForgotThRng,Espontn	10
24Dec86-3Hol	7f	:22	$:45^2$	1:24 ft	4	117	$7^{9\frac12}$	$7^{7\frac12}$	4^7	$3^{5\frac14}$	Pincay L Jr^5	18000	79-20	Pilor,Gordon'sCommnd,PineppIJck	7
24Dec86—Wide backside															
6Dec86-6Hol	7f	$:22^1$	$:45^2$	$1:24^2$gd	19	116	6^9	6^9	$5^{6\frac14}$	2^4	Cordero A Jr^5	16000	78-16	Noon Sun,PineappleJack,VideoSid	12
6Dec86—Bumped start															
30Nov86-2Hol	7f	$:22^2$	$:45^4$	$1:25^3$ft	$8\frac12$	115	2^{hd}	2^{hd}	$1^{1\frac12}$	$2^{\frac34}$	Stevens G L^2	c10000	75-16	Gulfstremer,PinepploJck,UpThPol	12
22Nov86-6Hol	6f	$:22^3$	:46	$1:11^1$ft	39	116	$8^{9\frac14}$	$8^{9\frac12}$	$6^{7\frac12}$	$5^{6\frac12}$	Baze G^4	16000	80-13	Manzanero, Pico P., Video Sid	9
22Nov86—Broke slowly															
29Oct86-3SA	$6\frac12$f	$:21^3$	$:44^3$	$1:16^4$ft	19	114	$9^{7\frac14}$	9^{12}	8^{12}	6^{13}	Baze G^6	18000	73-17	Blue Ice, Gran Pierre, Dennis D.	9
23Oct86-1SA	6f	:22	$:45^2$	$1:11^3$ft	4	118	$6^{6\frac34}$	$6^{6\frac12}$	6^4	4^4	Baze G^6	10000	76-20	CeeScoBoy,KarakaLad,Hai'TheEgle	7
23Oct86—Wide into stretch															
28Sep86-7Pla	$6\frac12$f	:23	$:47^3$	$1:22^2$m	$6\frac12$	117	8^{15}	8^{11}	4^7	$2^{1\frac34}$	Freeman W^4	HcpO	67-34	Hydro, Pineapple Jack, Ab'shai	9
17Aug86-6Sal	$5\frac12$f	$:24^4$	$:48^4$	$1:08^1$ft	*3-2	118	4^3	$3^{1\frac12}$	$2^{1\frac12}$	$2^{2\frac34}$	Davidson K J^6	Aw1000	82-18	CrftySilor,PinepplJck,RdWind'sKid	6

Jan 18 SA 5f ft $1:02^2$ h

Doonsport — Dk. b. or br. c. 4, by Matsadoon—Generous Portion, by California Kid
PINCAY L JR 117
Br.—Quality Broodmares (Cal) 1987 1 0 1 0 $3,400
Tr.—Moreno Henry $20,000 1986 11 1 1 2 $19,200
Own.—Finley J L
Lifetime 13 2 2 2 $31,400

7Jan87-9SA 1 :472 1:12 1:38 m *2½ 118 32 22½ 23 24½ Pincay L Jr7 25000 73-21 Danchai, Doonsport, ShowerDecree 9
7Jan87—Bumped hard start
27Dec86-2SA 6½f :214 :444 1:164ft 7 117 67½ 46½ 43½ 11¼ Pincay L Jr6 25000 66-19 Doonsport, BlueIce,ExaltedBubble 10
27Dec86—Broke slowly; wide into stretch
13Dec86-3Hol 7f :222 :452 1:232ft 6 117 64¼ 54½ 54½ 73 Pincay L Jr7 Ⓢ 25000 84-09 Gregson,ManyRoads,ShowerDecree 9
13Dec86—Bumped start; wide backstretch
13Nov86-9Hol 1 :453 1:101 1:353ft 53 114 85½ 67½ 612 614½ Solis A6 45000 70-23 MischievousMtt,CojkMn,BoldDecre 9
23Oct86-7SA 1 :45 1:104 1:38 ft 4 116 911 97¾ 105¾ 1011¾ McHargue D G1 50000 66-20 BoldDecree,TrojnTrick,Bruli'sAnte 10
23Oct86—Rank 7/8
9Oct86-7SA 6f :213 :443 1:111ft 14 116 109½ 108¼ 76¾ 73½ McHrgueDG6 Aw25000 78-21 Salt Dome, Incluso,Harper'sRidge 10
6Sep86-6Dmr 6½f :221 :451 1:161ft 16 116 42½ 33 34½ 21 McHrgueDG6 Aw22000 90-12 Jimed, Doonsport,TommyTheHawk 7
24Aug86-7Dmr 6½f :22 :444 1:153ft 27 116 66½ 57 44½ 37¼ McHrgueDG6 Aw21000 87-12 Our Lordship,HisRoyalty,Doonsport 8
24Aug86—Bore out
7Aug86-7Dmr 6½f :221 :45 1:151ft 15 116 31 22 36½ 310¼ McHrgDG6 ⓈAw19000 85-16 Bzboy,GoodThoghtWlly,Doonsport 6
7Aug86—Lugged out
23Jly86-7Dmr 6f :214 :452 1:093ft 26 115 98 1012 1016 — VlenzulPA8 ⓈAw19000 — — AnothrBloom,Bugrin,FlyingLssons 10
23Jly86—Bled; Bobbled 5 1/2
Jan 13 SA 4f ft :512 h Jan 5 SA 3f sy :384 h Dec 19 Hol 4f ft :492 h Dec 10 Hol 4f ft :494 h

Calabonga — B. g. 9, by Forceten—T V Quiz, by Victoria Park
MEZA R Q 118
Br.—Asbury C A & T H (Ky) 1987 2 0 0 0 $425
Tr.—Parsons Judith $20,000 1986 27 2 6 5 $59,560
Own.—Barberie-Fluder-Sears
Lifetime 106 13 17 26 $267,315 Turf 2 0 0 0 $550

10Jan87-2SA 6½f :221 :452 1:181gd 9½ 118 1211 1210 98¼ 55 Pincay L Jr4 20000 74-20 BoldTopsidr,Don'sCo'op,PnpplJck 12
10Jan87—Very wide into stretch
1Jan87-1SA 6f :214 :444 1:11 ft 12 116 811 88¾ 89 65¾ Ortega L E7 25000 77-19 ClssicQuickie,PtriotGloves,Qurdolit 8
1Jan87—Lugged out 3/8
18Dec86-9Hol 1 :454 1:104 1:364ft 7½ 116 87¾ 79¼ 69 68¼ Sibille R8 25000 71-17 FallFlyer,BrandImage,Revolutionry 8
18Dec86—Wide final 3/8
23Nov86-3Hol 1 :45 1:092 1:354ft 9¾ 116 610 410 411 48¾ Ortega L E5 Aw27000 75-12 Oricao, Breu, Call The Guard 6
5Nov86-3Hol 1 :452 1:111 1:372ft *2¾ 116 710 73¾ 42 11¼ DelahoussayeE5 20000 76-17 Calabonga, Pegus, Vinegarone 7
5Nov86—Wide final 3/8
25Oct86-9SA 6f :22 :451 1:102ft *3¼ 116 108¾ 107¾ 96¼ 52½ DelahoussayeE8 20000 83-17 StarOfAmerica,Rodney,SndDigger 11
25Oct86—Wide stretch
18Oct86-5SA 6f :214 :444 1:11 ft 11 116 911 89¼ 57½ 31 DelahoussayeE6 25000 82-20 Grenoble, Bizeboy, Calabonga 9
18Oct86—Wide final 3/8
5Oct86-2SA 6f :213 :443 1:102ft 4 115 126 119¼ 89¼ 77½ Kaenel J L8 20000 78-15 Grenoble, John's Jove, Inquisitive 12
5Oct86—Wide into stretch
20Sep86-9Pom 6½f :214 :45 1:163ft 4½ 116 74½ 55 54½ 34½ Kaenel J L2 25000 93-09 Yukon's Star, Slugfest, Calabonga 8
1Sep86-3Dmr 6f :213 :444 1:10 ft 3 116 67½ 66¾ 55¼ 2hd Pedroza M A1 c20000 88-13 Down Range, Calabonga, Coyotero 7
1Sep86—Wide into stretch

Pico P. — B. g. 4, by Blue Eyed Davy—Khal Dr Kehr, by Dr Marc R
PEDROZA M A 115
Br.—Sledge Stable (Cal) 1986 10 2 3 0 $23,900
Tr.—Harper David B $20,000 1985 3 M 0 2 $5,400
Own.—Select RacingStable(Lessee)
Lifetime 13 2 3 2 $29,300 Turf 1 0 0 0

6Dec86-6Hol 7f :221 :452 1:242gd *2 119 35½ 35 46 65¾ Pincay L Jr3 c16000 76-16 Noon Sun,PineappleJack,VideoSid 12
6Dec86—Broke out, bumped
22Nov86-6Hol 6f :223 :46 1:111ft *1 119 1hd 1½ 1½ 2hd Pincay L Jr1 16000 87-13 Manzanero, Pico P., Video Sid 9
22Nov86—Lugged out, checked late
26Oct86-1SA 6f :213 :45 1:11 ft 9¼ 116 1½ 1hd 31 66¼ Meza R Q2 32000 77-16 Sebucan, End Play, Fleet Albert 12
26Oct86—Bumped break
16Oct86-3SA 6f :213 :45 1:101ft *6-5 117 2hd 2hd 2hd 12 Pincay L Jr4 25000 87-19 Pico P., New Doc, Premiere 6
3Oct86-3SA 6f :212 :444 1:093ft 3 117 12½ 11 22 23¼ Pincay L Jr2 20000 86-17 MischievousMatt,PicoP.,TrinityHall 9
3Sep86-1Dmr 6f :22 :451 1:101ft *2¾ 115 12 1hd 1hd 2hd McCarron C J3 16000 87-16 Manzanero, Pico P., Czar's Charm 9
3Sep86—Veered in start
21Jly86-5Hol 1 Ⓣ:472 1:113 1:363fm 9½ 1095 52¼ 66½ 610 614½ Black C A5 22500 — — Chief Of Fire, Ridge Flite, Mural 6
12Jly86-7Hol 6f :221 :452 1:104ft 36 116 31½ 88¼ 1118 1120½ Kaenel J L4 32000 69-14 New Doc, Fracoza,NativeForecast 11
26Apr86-1Hol 6f :22 :454 1:12 ft 4 115 1½ 2hd 13½ 1¾ McCarron C J7 M50000 84-18 Pico P., Jimed, Fabulous Sound 7
26Apr86—Veered in, bumped hard break
26Mar86-6SA 6f :212 :451 1:11 ft 24 1125 2hd 21½ 67 88¼ Black C A8 ⓈMdn 75-17 DvilsBrigd,Mrvin'sPolicy,MrkChip 11
●Jan 10 Pom 5f sl 1:032 h Dec 26 SA 3f ft :36 h

Amabeauty's Joy

BAZE G **116**
Own.—Granja Vista Del Rio Stable

Dk. b. or br. h. 5, by Torsion—Amabeauty, by Reverse
Br.—Jackson & Tanners (Ky) 1986 15 1 3 4 $21,570
Tr.—West C R $20,000 1985 18 4 2 1 $28,725
Lifetime 39 7 5 5 $60,375

4Nov86-6CD	6½f	:231	:47	1:19 ft	21	119	63¼	74½	1012	109½	Gomez E R8	25000	75-25	Dr. Dave, Quick Speed, Roenigke	10
26Sep86-9TP	6½f	:231	:46	1:173ft	22	122	22½	22	24	36½	Gomez E R4	Aw11300	83-22	Zeppy, Tajawa, Amabeauty's Joy	6
12Sep86-9TP	1	:454	1:092	1:35 gd	4	115	43½	59	615	729½	Gomez E R4	Aw11700	74-13	Transept, Nik's Okay, CharmingJay	7
1Sep86-9EIP	1⅛	:472	1:12	1:493ft	16	113	65	51½	56½	55½	GomzER5	Tri State H	86-20	McShne,RivermnsPlesur,Rubn'sArt	9
23Aug86-7EIP	6½f	:22	:45	1:17 ft	5	121	66	45½	37	25	Gomez E R5	Aw11500	92-13	MedivlTim,Ambuty'sJoy,Rubn'sArt	8
31Jly86-8EIP	6f	:23	:461	1:113gd	6½	114	43	3nk	2½	11	Gomez E R6	Aw11500	87-20	Amabeuty'sJoy,Cpt.Bold,DoctorEm	6
12Jly86-8EIP	6f	:23	:47	1:123sy	4½	114	3nk	31	46½	48¾	Gomez E R5	Aw11500	73-25	PowerBrk,MrtiniThoughts,Pddlwhl	7
15May86-8Cby	6½f	:232	:462	1:181ft	3	115	53	52	53	53¾	Smith M E2	32000	86-20	Nitap, Indian Licorice, Karchi	5
4May86-7Cby	6f	:221	:443	1:113ft	5	113	55¼	51¾	41½	54¼	Melancon G1	35000	84-17	My Earl, Zeppy, Sense Of Reality	7
25Apr86-6Cby	6f	:224	:452	1:103ft	2½	115	51¾	33	45½	612	Melancon G7	Aw12800	82-09	BlushingGuest,SecondHrvst,Mgicus	7

Jan 20 SA 3f ft :371 h   Jan 16 SA 4f ft :481 h   Jan 6 SA 6f gd 1:143 h   Jan 1 SA 5f ft 1:012 h

Shuttle One

KAENEL J L **116**
Own.—Bisharat S & Virginia

B. g. 6, by Royal Physician—Bishops Pawn, by Determinedly
Br.—Crevolin A J (Cal) 1987 1 0 0 1 $2,700
Tr.—Wilmot William B $20,000 1986 18 1 0 3 $18,415
Lifetime 36 2 6 7 $47,295

4Jan87-9SA	1⅛	:473	1:122	1:514sy	7	116	612	56½	36	37½	Kaenel J L7	20000	62-22	HurricneHec,NewStorm,ShuttleOne	7
26Dec86-9SA	1 1/16	:454	1:102	1:43 ft	11	1095	44½	33½	33½	67	Patton D B1	22500	79-13	Cold,TommyThoms,BoncgBttons	11
11Dec86-7Hol	7f	:222	:46	1:242ft	22	1125	74¾	74½	53½	3½	Patton D B8	20000	81-21	Fall Flyer, Lord Pancho, ShuttleOne	8
11Dec86—Wide															
11Nov86-7Hol	1	:453	1:111	1:371ft	16	1115	54½	31½	33½	43¾	Patton D B3	16000	73-20	Lord Pancho, Oh Dad, Jam Shot	7
3Nov86-1SA	6f	:213	:444	1:11 ft	34	1095	77	66	54½	3nk	Patton D B3 [S]	c10500	83-14	HachalaTachi,Melchip,ShuttleOne	10
3Nov86—Altered path 1/2															
24Oct86-1SA	7f	:224	:454	1:25 ft	26	1115	86	76½	43½	34½	Patton D B5 [S]	10000	71-20	PrideOfTroy,CometsFire,ShuttleOn	9
8Oct86-1SA	1 1/16	:461	1:114	1:443ft	76	1115	43½	76¾	913	917¾	Patton D B11	10000	60-20	I'll Smoke, Oh Dad, Hachi	12
28Sep86-9Pom	6½f	:214	:452	1:171ft	37	1115	98½	1011	1012	710	Patton D B2	12500	84-09	Inqustv,RunnngDbonr,Cody'sChnc	10
22Jun86-7GG	6f	:222	:452	1:102ft	15	115	51½	42	67½	611	Castaneda M6	16000	76-19	Lucky Olympiad, Secular, Galawac	7
15Jun86-7GG	1 1/16	:461	1:104	1:434ft	42	114	1hd	2½	913	1023½	Castaneda M4	16000	60-14	Frivolissimo,OurNordic,GllntMick	11

●Jan 2 SA 3f ft :343 h   Dec 20 SA 5f ft 1:012 h   ●Dec 10 SA 3f ft :352 h   Nov 29 SA 5f ft 1:013 h

Native Captive

CORDERO A JR **115**
Own.—Lewis Marjorie (Lessee)

B. g. 4, by Main Bleu—Captive Audience, by Native Dancer
Br.—Jones B C (Ky) 1986 5 3 0 0 $19,250
Tr.—Harper David B $20,000 1985 0 M 0 0
Lifetime 5 3 0 0 $19,250

8Nov86-4Hol	6f	:22	:453	1:104ft	9½	116	85¾	77½	78	67¾	Solis A2	25000	81-13	SprbMmnt,GrdnsCmmnd,FrBlJns	11
8Nov86—Wide into stretch															
26Oct86-1SA	6f	:213	:45	1:11 ft	5	116	75	95½	63	76¼	Kaenel J L7	32000	77-16	Sebucan, End Play, Fleet Albert	12
26Oct86—Bumped break															
3Oct86-5SA	6f	:221	:452	1:102ft	*4-5	116	1hd	1½	13½	15	ValenzuelaPA2	c20000	86-17	NtvCptv,Nck'sPrnc,JohnsTomrrw	10
3Oct86—Drifted out late															
3Sep86-3Dmr	6f	:22	:452	1:094ft	*1	115	1½	1hd	12½	15½	Valenzuela P A5	16000	89-16	NtiveCptive,ActiveRomn,WterJcket	8
3Sep86—Lugged in stretch															
7May86-3Hol	6f	:223	:462	1:11 ft	9	115	3½	2hd	1½	11	Meza R Q5	M32000	89-12	NtivCptiv,StylishRod,Troy'sAgttor	12

Jan 17 SA 5f ft 1:011 h   Jan 11 SA 6f ft 1:132 h   Jan 2 SA 4f ft :472 h   Dec 29 SA 3f ft :372 h

Music Up

STEVENS G L **116**
Own.—Franks John

Ch. h. 5, by Sharpen Up—Deep Music, by Luthier
Br.—Clerico J (Ky) 1986 13 2 2 0 $21,974
Tr.—Van Berg Jack C $20,000 1985 10 M 1 1 $4,276
Lifetime 23 2 3 1 $26,250 Turf 20 2 3 1 $26,250

31Dec86-5SA	6½f	:22	:453	1:172ft	64	116	52¼	1211	1218	—	Kaenel J L5	40000	— —	Watch'n Win, Angle Arc, Idol	12
31Dec86—Eased															
13Dec86-9Hol	1	Ⓣ:463	1:102	1:342fm	10e	114	64	98½	913	—	Baze G8	57500	— —	AutoCommander,DrkAccert,Dr.Dly	9
13Dec86—Eased															
14Nov86-5Hol	1	:443	1:084	1:344ft	23	116	21½	514	625	—	Valenzuela P A3	62500	— —	Oricao, Silver Hero, Rex Lake	6
14Nov86—Eased															
30Oct86-5SA	a6½f	Ⓣ:214	:444	1:151fm	19	117	21	53½	85¾	108½	Day P7	Aw28000	74-17	Arcadius, Sans Rival, Will Spring	10
18Oct86-7SA	6f	:22	:444	1:092ft	14	115	51½	55½	814	822½	Stevens G L1	Aw28000	68-20	Quip Star, High Touch, High Hook	8
30Jly86♦2Vichy(Fra)	a1			1:403gd	14	119	Ⓣ			2½	Boeuf D	Hcp d l'Allr		BlueBlood, MusicUp, MyOnlyGuest	14
11Jly86♦4Evry(Fra)	a7f			1:273gd	16	119	Ⓣ			2½	Lee C	Px d Mrnvl H		Macmirror, MusicUp, TudorRose	15
29Jun86♦8Longchamp(Fra)	a1			1:374gd	11	119	Ⓣ			94½	Lee C	Px d l'Ete H		Fox Oa,Ventd'Ete,PrinceNeasham	11
24Jun86♦2Chantilly(Fra)	a6f			1:152gd	7½	115	Ⓣ			94¾	Lee C	Px d'Ory H		WiseBird,StrangeBird,KingofAtina	15
14May86♦1Longchamp(Fra)	a7f			1:224gd	6	122	Ⓣ			11½	Caget R	Px Clm c19215		MusicUp, Gus, Kandjar	10

Jan 12 SA 7f ft 1:282 h   Dec 29 Hol tr.t 5f ft 1:05 h   Nov 29 SA 5f ft 1:012 h

Grenoble

Ch. g. 7, by Grenfall—Cheri Meri, by Meritorious

ORTEGA L E		116	Br.—Palmer J F (Cal)			1987 1 0 0 1	$2,250
Own.—De La Merced R A or A A Jr			Tr.—Chasteen William W	$20,000		1986 19 3 5 0	$40,395
			Lifetime 80 9 13 13	$178,981		Turf 2 0 0 0	$3,000

4Jan87-3SA 6f :22 :45¹ 1:10³sy 9½ 116 2¹ 2½ 21½ 3nk Ortega L E⁵ 16000 85-22 Polly'sRuler,NeutralPlyer,Grenoble 8
21Dec86-1Hol 6f :22² :46¹ 1:11¹ft 21 119 74¾ 75½ 65½ 610¾ Castanon A L⁴ 20000 76-15 SndDigger,Polly'sRuler,Andrew'NM 8
  21Dec86—Wide 3/8 turn
13Dec86-1Hol 6f :21⁴ :45 1:10²ft 9½ 122 10101012 99½ 99¾ DelahoussayeE³ 16000 81-09 Neutral Player, Illuminize, Rodney 10
  13Dec86—Broke slowly, wide in stretch
27Nov66-3Hol 6f :21⁴ :45 1:10³ft 10 122 612 68 57 45 Ortega L E² 16000 85-18 Ells Bravest Song, Jacart, FallFlyer 7
  27Nov86—Steadied start
8Nov86-9Hol 6f :22² :45⁴ 1:10³ft 4½ 119 64½ 56 69 612¾ Ortega L E⁶ 25000 77-13 SandDigger,Amarone,Billy'sSpecial 6
  8Nov86—Lugged out badly; wide final 3/8
31Oct86-7SA 7f :22³ :45³ 1:23 ft 9½ 116 74½ 99¾ 913 810½ Ortega L E⁶ 32000 74-16 GryPinstrip,CoursngEgl,Yukon'sStr 9
18Oct86-5SA 6f :21⁴ :44⁴ 1:11 ft 10 116 88½ 58 35½ 1no Ortega L E⁵ 25000 83-20 Grenoble, Bizeboy, Calabonga 9
5Oct86-2SA 6f :21³ :44³ 1:10²ft 11 115 105¾ 76 43½ 11½ Ortega L E¹ 20000 86-15 Grenoble, John's Jove, Inquisitive 12
25Sep86-9Pom 6½f:22¹ :47 1:21¹m 3½ 116 54½ 57 34 2nk Ortega L E⁴ 16000 74-30 DownRnge,Grenobl,DistinctivlyDon 7
  25Sep86—Lugged out 1/2
10Sep86-9Dmr 7f :22 :45 1:21⁴ft 27 116 12141212 86½ 55¾ Ortega L E¹⁰ 25000 90-11 Paskanell,BrndImge,SwiftMessge 12
  10Sep86—Wide 3/8

In constructing our worksheet, we used the 6 furlong time frame that we regularly use in sprint races, because of the ease of converting to it, even though it was not the most common distance in the last races involved.

Odds	Horse	PCR						Form	Ab/T
10	Pineapple Jack	93/ 59	38	+	9/106	=	88	NNN	46.0 26.0 0/ 72.0
6-5	Doonsport	88/ 56	51	–	17/ 90	=	98	NNN	47.4 24.4 – 1/ 72.2
12	Calabonga	88/ 78	42	–	6/114	=	77	NOg	47.2 25.3 0/ 73.0
12	Pico P.	92/ 27	45	–	3/ 69	=	133	Lw	(45.0 25.1 0/ 70.1)
15	Amabeauty's Joy	72/ 42	48	–	13/ 77	=	93	Lw	(46.4 25.3 0/ 72.2)
10	Shuttle One	92/ 55	54	+	10/119	=	77	NON	50.0 24.3 – 1/ 74.2
6	Native Captive	53/ 20	16	–	2/ 34	=	156	Lw	(45.2 25.0 + 1/ 70.3)
16	Music Up	45/ 26	45	–	10/ 51	=	88	NON	x
5	Grenoble	88/ 68	45	–	1/112	=	79	N+N	45.2 25.2 – 1/ 70.3

Two PCRs stand out immediately, Native Captive and Pico P., both of whom are coming off layoffs with workouts. Not only that, but their advisory ability times, compiled in back races, are extremely good. Pico P. is loaded with early speed, while Native Captive runs more evenly toward slight closing. Clearly Pico P. is the more formidable of these two.

Here we have an exceptionally strong 6-5 favorite, with no other horse even near in the betting. Everybody likes Doonsport. That often is a sign that everybody is wrong, but we are required to give this one a close look. He has no form defects, and we know that favorites who have no form defects are usually tough.

As to last race ability times, there are only five that are measurable in this 9-horse field, aside from the layoff horses. Grenoble, the second choice at 5-1, has a far superior figure, but with a very low PCR and a closing running style. Among the horses that we can rate, Doonsport is within the top three on ability times, and that brings him within our standard for a single selection play on favorites with no form defects who are within the first three in last race ability times.

Grenoble's substantial 3-tick and more margin must be dealt with. Internal numbers which show such an enormous second call total makes him much too suspect as a closer. Pico P. also concerns us, but his workouts are not sufficient to show prime readiness. This means that it is doubtful that a layoff horse can run up to his potential, and uncertainty we do not need.

When a horse is such an overwhelming choice as Doonsport, you have to take a further look. The western edition of the Daily Racing Form provides better trouble information than other editions, and we see that Doonsport, running at a mile last out, was "bumped hard start," which may account for his slower internal times. If you look back to his Dec. 27 race, you see some excellent figures, with a 70.4 ability time. That is impressive enough to move any seasoned handicapper.

This allows us to make another observation as to a definitive trouble line. We rely on last race times because they tell us so much about how a horse might run today off his last race form. But when a last race effort is clearly not representative of today's form, we are doing ourselves a disservice by rigidly sticking to the last race. If we throw out the last race for Doonsport, we can use the next-to-last race as advisory, and still see that he compares very favorably with the others.

As Doonsport zeros in on our "favorite plus" rule, we still must see if his running style allows us to accept him. He shows a slight tendency to close, but there is no threatening early speed in the field, aside from Pico P. Doonsport is close enough to an even runner on a track that has not yet shown a forward bias that we can play him, despite our concerns and the very unattractive odds.

Had I been at the track, I would have been tempted to pass this race. But for our records, we are putting down on Doonsport as a single selection play to win only. He not only qualifies, but every other apparent contender carries baggage that need not burden us.

FIFTH RACE
Santa Anita
JANUARY 21, 1987

6 ½ FURLONGS. (1.14) CLAIMING. Purse $17,000. 4-year-olds and upward. Weights, 4-year-olds, 120 lbs.; older, 121 lbs. Non-winners of two races since November 3 allowed 3 lbs.; of a race since then, 5 lbs. Claiming price $20,000; if for $18,000 allowed 2 lbs. (Races when entered for $16,000 or less not considered.)

Value of race $17,000; value to winner $9,350; second $3,400; third $2,550; fourth $1,275; fifth $425. Mutuel pool $255,282. Exacta pool $393,544.

Last Raced	Horse	Eqt.	A.	Wt	PP	St	¼	½	Str	Fin	Jockey	Cl'g Pr	Odds $1
7Jan87 9SA2	Doonsport	b	4	117	2	7	3hd	11½	12½	12½	Pincay L Jr	20000	1.20
8Nov86 4Hol6	Native Captive		4	115	7	3	51	61½	32½	22½	Cordero A Jr	20000	6.00
4Jan87 3SA3	Grenoble		7	116	9	6	72½	7hd	62	3no	Ortega L E	20000	5.60
10Jan87 2SA3	Pineapple Jack	b	4	115	1	4	61	5hd	5½	4hd	Castanon A L	20000	10.00
6Dec86 6Hol6	Pico P.	b	4	115	4	1	2hd	3hd	21	55	Pedroza M A	20000	12.00
10Jan87 2SA5	Calabonga	b	9	118	3	8	81	82½	74	61½	Meza R Q	20000	12.00
4Nov86 6CD10..	Amabeauty's Joy		5	116	5	5	42	41½	4hd	77	Baze G	20000	15.30
4Jan87 9SA3	Shuttle One	b	6	116	6	9	9	9	9	82½	Kaenel J L	20000	10.30
31Dec86 5SA	Music Up		5	116	8	2	11½	2hd	81½	9	Stevens G L	20000	16.10

OFF AT 2:46. Start good for all but SHUTTLE ONE. Won ridden out. Time, :22⅕, :45⅕, 1:10⅕, 1:16⅗ Track fast.

$2 Mutuel Prices:

2-DOONSPORT	4.40	3.00	2.60
7-NATIVE CAPTIVE		5.20	3.40
9-GRENOBLE			3.00

$5 EXACTA 2-7 PAID $53.50.

This time, the power favorite ran just as the crowd expected, as he stayed close up to the speedsters from the outset and won handily. This victory moves us along in the profitbank, even though there was only a $4.40 win ticket.

Moving to the sixth race, we are again confronted with another string of lightly raced maiden state breds. We can see that one of them is an extremely heavy favorite off some impressive workouts as we look over the field.

6th Santa Anita

6 FURLONGS. (1.07⅗) MAIDEN. Purse $21,000. 3-year-olds. Bred in California. Weight, 117 lbs. (Non-starters for a claiming price of $32,000 or less preferred.)

Exceptional Talent — B. c. 3, by Preperantes—Truly Nice, by Selectus
STEVENS G L — 117 — Br.—Old English Rancho (Cal) — 1986 0 M 0 0
Tr.—Headley Bruce
Own.—Jhnstn-Headley-Smpsn et al — Lifetime 0 0 0 0
●Jan 18 SA 4f ft :46^1 h ●Jan 13 SA 5f ft :59^2 h Jan 8 SA 5f m 1:01^2 h Jan 3 SA 5f ft 1:00^4 h

Tellem Ben — B. g. 3, by Tell—Bonne Enfant, by Deck Hand
BAZE G — 117 — Br.—Ballymeehan Farm (Cal) — 1986 0 M 0 0
Tr.—Wright Robert
Own.—Wright R A — Lifetime 0 0 0 0
Jan 15 SA 3f ft :35^4 h Jan 9 SA 5f sl 1:02^1 hg Jan 3 SA 5f ft 1:01^3 h Dec 28 SA 6f ft 1:13^2 h

Auto Focus — B. c. 3, by Somethingfabulous—Soft Focus, by Deck Hand
MEZA R Q — 117 — Br.—Bachecki-Block-Law (Cal) — 1986 1 M 0 0
Tr.—Stepp William T
Own.—Fredericks F L — Lifetime 1 0 0 0
26Dec86-4SA 6½f :21^3 :44^1 1:16^{2}ft 34 117 4^4 10^{13}10^{13} 9^{17} Black C A^1 [S]Mdn 71-13 WindwoodLne,Clvinist,PsDeGuerr 10
●Jan 19 SA 3f ft :35 h Jan 3 SA 4f ft :48^1 b Dec 23 SA 4f ft :47^3 hg Dec 16 SA 5f ft 1:01 h

No Double Deal
MCHARGUE D G
Own.—Siegel-M-Jan-Samantha

B. g. 3, by Nodouble—Peanut Vender, by Native Royalty
Br.—Joan Hadley Investments (Cal)
Tr.—Mayberry Brian A

117

1986   1 M 0 0

Lifetime   1 0 0 0

6Nov86-6Hol   6f :221 :454 1:112ft   11 118   1hd 2hd 21 643   Pedroza M A2 M50000 81-17 ContctGm,WstrlyWind,WsdomDncr 9
Jan 17SA 4fft :51h   Jan 11SA 5fft 1:012h   Dec 30SA 4fft :474h

Hour Willow
VALENZUELA P A
Own.—Majestic & MLM Stables

B. c. 3, by Willow Hour—Alola, by Alto Ribot
Br.—Benford & Whiting Farms (Cal)
Tr.—Mulhall Richard W

117

1986   0 M 0 0

Lifetime   0 0 0 0

Jan 16 SA 3fft :353 bg   Jan 11SA 7fft 1:291h   Jan 3SA 6fft 1:144h   Dec 29SA 6fft 1:142h

Native Nick
CORDERO A JR
Own.—Cavanagh Mr-Mrs T

Ch. c. 3, by Captain Nick—Risque Native, by Native Royalty
Br.—Cavanagh Mr-Mrs T (Cal)
Tr.—Carno Louis R

117

1987   0 M 0 0
1986   0 M 0 0

Lifetime   0 0 0 0

Jan 16 SA 5fft 1:02h   Jan 11SA 5fft 1:004 bg   Jan 6SA 4fgd :494h   Jan 1SA 4fft :504h

President's Port
PINCAY L JR
Own.—Heaton B

Ch. rig. 3, by Hyannis Port—Zamora, by Hill Prince
Br.—Shupe J & Judith (Cal)
Tr.—Heaton Bill

117

1987   1 M 0 0 $1,200
1986   0 M 0 0

Lifetime   1 0 0 0 $1,200

15Jan87-6SA   6f :22 :452 1:114ft   6½ 1135   523 523 523 43   Patton D B7   M50000 78-25 LuckyBer,TrulyRosie,Rconnoitring 12
  15Jan87—Rough trip
Jan 14SA tr.l3fft :352h   Jan 9SA 5f sl 1:011 bg   Dec 17SA 4fft :483 bg   Dec 11SA 4fft :494h

There isn't enough here to make a worksheet. Exceptional Talent reveals a January 13 workout at :59.2 that fits the bill. We like to play first time starters that are favorites off these impressive works, for they usually come through. We see two other reasonably impressive horses in the field, No Double Deal, off a layoff after a strong race at Hollywood, and President's Port with a very impressive last race running line. The only thing we can find wrong, however, with Exceptional Talent is the price as the board shows this youngster at 3-5. I grossly dislike playing 3-5 horses in any situation, no matter how much they fit our standards for having advantages over the others. If you win, you win almost nothing, and losing can never be dismissed as a possibility. Remember Neutral Player in the first race?

Back when we wrote about exacta play with odds on-horses, we demonstrated this kind of situation as a play. We would have ordinarily pegged this race in that vein by settling on two exacta tickets with Exceptional Talent on top and Double Deal and President's Port for second. But fortunately for us, there was no exacta offered in the 6th race at Santa Anita that day. It was either Exceptional Talent at 3-5 or pass. While I admit I would have played exactas had they been available, I also would not play any 3-5 horse to win when there was recognizable strength in the field. While I would have passed at the track, let's stand by our rules for play and enroll Exceptional Talent as if we did play him to win only. You can imagine what happened.

SIXTH RACE **6 FURLONGS. (1.07⅗) MAIDEN. Purse $21,000. 3-year-olds. Bred in California. Weight, 117 lbs. (Non-starters for a claiming price of $32,000 or less preferred.)**

Santa Anita

JANUARY 21, 1987

Value of race $21,000; value to winner $11,550; second $4,200; third $3,150; fourth $1,575; fifth $525. Mutuel pool $341,321.

Last Raced	Horse	Eqt.A.Wt	PP	St	¼	½	Str	Fin	Jockey	Odds $1
6Nov86 6Hol6	No Double Deal	b 3 117	4	1	1hd	12	12½	15½	McHargue D G	7.90
15Jan87 6SA4	President's Port	3 117	7	5	41½	31½	21½	24½	Pincay L Jr	2.30
	Exceptional Talent	3 117	1	7	7	64	4½	3½	Stevens G L	.70
	Tellem Ben	3 117	2	6	5½	4½	53½	41½	Baze G	46.70
26Dec86 4SA9	Auto Focus	3 117	3	2	61	7	61½	52	Meza R Q	23.60
	Native Nick	3 117	6	3	21½	2½	31	65½	Cordero A Jr	15.30
	Hour Willow	3 117	5	4	3hd	5hd	7	7	Valenzuela P A	11.90

OFF AT 3:19 Start good. Won handily. Time, :21⅘, :45, :57⅘, 1:10⅘ Track fast.

$2 Mutuel Prices:			
4-NO DOUBLE DEAL	17.80	6.40	3.00
7-PRESIDENT'S PORT		3.60	2.40
1-EXCEPTIONAL TALENT			2.20

The two others showing good credentials ran away with the race, as our 3-5 favorite barely finished third. No Double Deal, flashing the early speed that his one race revealed could be expected, went wire to wire easily. This strong performance demonstrated that early speed was still a formidable factor when a horse had the capacity to unlimber it.

We are now deep into the card as the seventh race brings us to the turf course at a mile and one-eighth at a claiming price even above what we saw in the third race. This time the price tag is $125,000 for these powerhouse runners.

7th Santa Anita

1 ⅛ MILES. (Turf). (1.45⅘) CLAIMING. Purse $40,000. 4-year-olds and upward. Weights, 4-year-olds, 121 lbs.; older, 122 lbs. Non-winners of two races at one mile or over since December 1 allowed 2 lbs.; of such a race since then 4 lbs. Claiming price $125,000; for each $5,000 to $100,000 allowed 1 lb. (Claiming and starter races for $80,000 or less not considered.)

Steepbank — B. h. 6, by Stage Door Johnny—Favorable View, by Explodent
SHOEMAKER W — 116 — Br.—Little N P (Ky) — 1987 1 1 0 0 $19,800
Tr.—Gregson Edwin — $105,000 — 1986 7 1 1 3 $38,700
Own.—Loblolly Stable — Lifetime 29 7 7 6 $174,200 — Turf 23 6 5 5 $159,160

1Jan87-5SA 1⅛Ⓣ:4711:1121:481fm 10 114 2½ 2hd 1hd 1½ Shoemaker W8 90000 86-14 Steepbank, River Of Kings, Keyala 9
14Dec86-5Hol 1$\frac{1}{16}$Ⓣ:4611:10 1:402fm*9-5 119 2½ 21½ 22½ 61½ Black C A2 100000 90-11 Lucky N Green, Emperdori, Keyala 8
16Nov86-9Hol 1$\frac{1}{16}$Ⓣ:4631:1031:402fm 3½ 116 2½ 2hd 11½ 1½ Shoemaker W5 80000 92-07 Steepbank, Jack Tar, Snowcreek 7
29Oct86-5SA a6½f Ⓣ:212 :4341:151fm 11 1125 88½ 89 54½ 31½ Black C A7 80000 82-17 Stan's Bower, Jack Tar,Steepbank 10
27Mar86-8SA 1⅛Ⓣ:4641:1131:48 fm 4 117 32½ 31½ 64½ 89½ DelahoussyeE2 125000 77-12 EvnngM'Lord,RvrOfKngs,PlAndDc 8
27Mar86—Bumped start
1Mar86-5SA 1⅛Ⓣ:4531:1011:491fm 9½ 116 68¾ 46 43½ 33½ DelahoussyeE3 150000 78-16 Clanrallier,Vulnerability,Steepbnk 10
24Jan86-8SA 1⅛Ⓣ:4541:1021:49 fm 4 116 24 22 41¾ 31 DelhoussyeE2 Aw38000 81-19 Vulnerbility,‡PtitBonhomm,Stpbnk 8
24Jan86—Steadied 1/16
4Jan86-7SA 1⅛Ⓣ:4641:1121:492fm 10 115 21½ 31 1hd 31½ ShoemkerW1 Aw38000 79-23 LuckyNGreen,Vulnerbility,Stpbnk 12
8Dec85-9Hol 1$\frac{1}{16}$Ⓣ:4741:1211:43 fm 8 119 2hd 1hd 11½ 1no † DelahoussyeE8 150000 — — ‡Steepbnk,SuperDupont,Plestiglio 12
† 8Dec85—Disqualified and placed sixth; Drifted out 1/16
16Nov85-9Hol a1⅛Ⓣ 1:454fm 7½ 119 32 41 41½ 22½ DelahoussyeE3 125000 — — Caballo, Steepbank, Cutting Wind 9
16Nov85—Error in placement of starting gate
Jan 15 SA 5f ft 1:004 h — Jan 10 SA 4f gd :492 h — Dec 27 SA 5f ft 1:02 h — Dec 22 SA 4f ft :493 b

Truth
BAZE G **117**
Own.—Bradley-Chndler-Whittinghm

B. c. 4, by Liley—Fact, by Dancing Moss
Br.—Bradley-Whittinghm-Chndler (Ky)
Tr.—Whittingham Charles **$125,000**
Lifetime 15 2 2 0 $36,925

1987	1	0	0	0	
1986	8	1	1	0	$21,225
Turf	9	1	1	0	$21,225

11Jan87-7SA	1⅛Ⓣ	$:47^4 1:36^4 2:02^2$	fm	*7-5e	114	$4^{3\frac{1}{2}}$	$4^{\frac{3}{4}}$	$7^{2\frac{3}{4}}$	$7^{4\frac{3}{4}}$	Baze G^5	Aw31000	70-25	Swink, Dan Thatch, Sly Remark	10
11Jan87—Bumped start														
27Dec86-5SA	1⅛Ⓣ	$:46^2 1:12^1 1:49^2$	fm	7	117	7^9	$8^{3\frac{3}{4}}$	6^5	$5^{4\frac{1}{4}}$	Baze G^7	Aw31000	76-20	MisterWonderfulII,Jota,DanThtch	12
27Dec86—Steadied 1/2														
13Dec86-7Hol	1 1/16Ⓣ	$:47^2 1:11^1 1:41^1$	fm	10	113	$9^{4\frac{1}{2}}$	$7^{4\frac{1}{2}}$	$5^{4\frac{1}{2}}$	$2^{\frac{1}{2}}$	Baze G^{10}	Aw27000	87-08	Rai Den, Truth, Coasting Cougar	10
14Nov86-9Hol	1 1/16Ⓣ	$:46^4 1:10^1 1:41^1$	fm	8½	116	7^{11}	6^9	$4^{5\frac{1}{2}}$	$4^{1\frac{3}{4}}$	Baze R A^7	Aw26000	86-12	Mr. Media, Picatrix II, Rai Den	7
14Nov86—Drifted out late														
2Oct86-5SA	1⅛Ⓣ	$:47\ 1:12\ 1:49^4$	fm	11	115	$8^{6\frac{1}{2}}$	$10^{7\frac{3}{4}}$	9^{11}	8^{10}	ShoemkerW^8	Aw30000	68-22	Kingsbury, Putting, Travet	10
23Aug86-7Dmr	1⅛Ⓣ	$:48^1 1:12^1 1:49^1$	fm	4½	112	$5^{4\frac{1}{2}}$	$5^{3\frac{1}{2}}$	$3^{2\frac{1}{2}}$	1no	ShoemkerW^3	Aw22000	88-11	Truth, Parson John, Never-Rust	7
9Aug86-5Dmr	1 Ⓣ	$:46^2 1:11\ 1:36$	fm	9½	116	$9^{8\frac{3}{4}}$	$9^{6\frac{1}{4}}$	8^7	$5^{4\frac{1}{2}}$	ShoemkerW^6	Aw20000	87-04	BrghtTom,FbulousSond,CtByGlss	10
9Aug86—Wide into stretch														
27Jly86-5Dmr	1 1/16Ⓣ	$:46^4 1:11\ 1:42^3$	fm	8	111	10^{10}	$9^{5\frac{1}{2}}$	$5^{3\frac{1}{4}}$	$5^{2\frac{1}{2}}$	ShoemkrW^{12}	Aw20000	90-04	Travet, Sly Remark, Eliminante	12
4Jly86-9Hol	1 1/16Ⓣ	$:45^4 1:10\ 1:41^3$	fm	9½	116	11^{12}	$10^{8\frac{1}{2}}$	$9^{6\frac{3}{4}}$	$6^{7\frac{1}{4}}$	ShoemkrW^{10}	Aw23000	89 —	Full Charm, Gaelic Knight, Jota	12
22Dec85-3Hol	1	$:46^4 1:12^2 1:37^1$	ft	2½	118	$5^{1\frac{1}{4}}$	$3^{1\frac{1}{2}}$	$1^{\frac{1}{2}}$	$1^{\frac{3}{4}}$	Shoemaker W^1	Mdn	77-17	Truth, We'll See, Frankinstrelli	7

Jan 19 SA 4f ft $:53^2$ h   Jan 2 SA 3f ft :36 h   Dec 21 Hol 5f ft $1:02^3$ h   Dec 12 Hol 3f ft $:37^3$ h

Armin
STEVENS G L **118**
Own.—Jones A U

Gr. h. 6, by Bold Forbes—Molalla, by Gallant Man
Br.—Jones A U (Ky)
Tr.—Barrera Lazaro S **$125,000**
Lifetime 35 7 7 4 $236,353

1986	10	3	5	1	$118,790
1984	20	3	2	2	$99,713
Turf	7	0	3	0	$27,675

7Dec86-8BM	1 1/16Ⓣ	$:47^1 1:11^1 1:42^3$	gd	9¼	114	2^3	2^3	2^6	2^8	Mena F^7	Spr Mmnt H	82-10	Barbery, Armin, Pair Of Aces	9
22Nov86-8BM	7½f Ⓣ	$:23^2\ :47^1 1:29^4$	fm	51	114	$3^{3\frac{1}{2}}$	$3^{1\frac{1}{2}}$	$3^{1\frac{1}{2}}$	$2^{\frac{3}{4}}$	Mena F^9	San Fran H	94-05	Barbery, Armin, Fleet Form	10
8Nov86-8BM	1 1/16	$:45^2\ 1:10\ 1:42^2$	ft	*6-5	119	4^8	3^5	3^6	2^5	BazeRA^5	ⓡSbsct Iv H	75-25	Sidersell, Armin, Don'tFoolWithMe	5
17Oct86-8BM	1 1/16	$:46^1\ 1:09^3\ 1:40^2$	ft	9¼	114	1^2	$1^{1\frac{1}{2}}$	2^2	2^4	BazeRA^4	B M Br Cp H	86-16	Hopeful Word, Armin, Bozina	8
27Sep86-8BM	1⅛	$:47^2\ 1:12\ 1:51$	sl	2¼	116	$1^{1\frac{1}{2}}$	$2^{\frac{1}{2}}$	3^2	3^2	SchctR^6	ⓡS Jqn Iv H	74-27	Ascension,SomthingGorgous,Armin	6
1Sep86-11Sac	1⅛	$:45\ 1:08^3\ 1:47^1$	ft	9-5	121	2^2	2^1	1^3	1^6	Schacht R^1	Gov H	95-09	Armin,TheAyesHaveIt,U.LuckyShot	6
3Aug86-11SR	1 1/16	$:45\ 1:09\ 1:39^4$	ft	*8-5	120	2^{hd}	1^{hd}	$2^{\frac{1}{2}}$	$2^{1\frac{1}{2}}$	Mena F^4	J T Grce H	103-03	Castle Tweed, Armin, Pair Of Aces	7
20Jly86-11Sol	1 1/16	$:46^3\ 1:10^3\ 1:42$	ft	6¼	114	1^2	1^2	1^4	1^7	Mena F^6	Val Dy H	89-14	Armin, Pair Of Aces, Lord Norman	9
12Jly86-9Sol	1	$:47\ 1:10^4\ 1:36^3$	ft	8	115	1^1	1^{hd}	1^{hd}	1^{hd}	Lamance C^3	Aw15000	91-15	Armin, LordNorman,PleasantPower	7
15Jun86-6GG	6f	$:21^4\ :44^4\ 1:09^1$	ft	17	115	3^1	$5^{5\frac{1}{2}}$	$6^{9\frac{1}{2}}$	$5^{12\frac{1}{2}}$	Lamance C^6	Aw22000	81-14	Stan's Bower, Cardell, King Tobin	6

Jan 16 SA 5f ft $1:00^3$ h   Jan 9 SA 5f sl $1:01^1$ h   ●Dec 29 SA 4f ft $:46^3$ h   Dec 2 BM 4f ft $:49^2$ h

***Poly Test**
PINCAY L JR **118**
Own.—Spelling A & Candy

B. h. 7, by Polyfoto—Gaikuresne, by Wordive
Br.—Bordes & Gouyou (Fra)
Tr.—Gosden John H M **$125,000**
Lifetime 46 12 14 5 $293,249

1987	1	0	0	0	$2,700
1986	8	2	3	1	$81,400
Turf	37	11	12	2	$252,440

1Jan87-5SA	1⅛Ⓣ	$:47^1 1:11^2 1:48^1$	fm	*9-5	118	5^2	$4^{1\frac{1}{2}}$	$3^{1\frac{1}{2}}$	$4^{2\frac{3}{4}}$	DelahoussyeE^5	100000	83-14	Steepbank, River Of Kings, Keyala	9
22Nov86-5Hol	1 1/16Ⓣ	$:47\ 1:11^2 1:42^1$	fm	3¼	122	$5^{2\frac{3}{4}}$	2^{hd}	$1^{\frac{1}{2}}$	$2^{\frac{1}{2}}$	DelahoussyeE^9	125000	82-17	NuggetPoint,PolyTest,RivrOfKings	9
16Jly86-8Hol	1 Ⓣ	$:46^4 1:10\ 1:33^3$	fm	3¾	122	$3^{\frac{1}{2}}$	2^2	4^7	$5^{9\frac{3}{4}}$	DelhoussyeE^4	Aw40000	— —	BlueRzor,FlotingReserve,PrinceTru	6
22Jun86-5Hol	1 1/16Ⓣ	$:47^2 1:11\ 1:41$	fm	9-5	117	$2^{\frac{1}{2}}$	2^{hd}	1^{hd}	1no	DelhoussyeE^5	Aw40000	99-02	Poly Test, Floating Reserve, Al Arz	6
6Jun86-7Hol	1 Ⓣ	$:45^3 1:09^1 1:33^2$	fm	3	117	$4^{2\frac{1}{2}}$	1^{hd}	$2^{\frac{1}{2}}$	$2^{2\frac{1}{2}}$	DelhoussyeE^7	Aw40000	— —	Will Dancer, Poly Test, Al Arz	9
9May86-8Hol	1 1/16Ⓣ	$:47^1 1:11^2 1:40^3$	fm	*1	115	1^1	$1^{1\frac{1}{2}}$	1^1	$1^{1\frac{1}{2}}$	DelhoussyeE^1	Aw40000	101 —	Poly Test, Bleding, Mr. Happy	6
23Apr86-8Hol	1 1/16Ⓣ	$:45^1 1:09\ 1:38^4$	fm	6¼	115	3^6	$3^{1\frac{1}{2}}$	$2^{2\frac{1}{2}}$	$2^{3\frac{1}{2}}$	McCrronCJ^2	Prmre H	106 —	ClvrSong,PolyTst,BothEndsBurnng	7
11Apr86-5SA	1⅛Ⓣ	$:45\ 1:09^1 1:46^2$	fm	2¼	116	2^7	2^5	3^{nk}	3^{hd}	McCarron C J^1	125000	95-11	Pol And Dic, HonorMedal,PolyTest	7
11Apr86—Veered out start														
27Mar86-8SA	1⅛Ⓣ	$:46^4 1:11^3 1:48$	fm	2¾	117	2^1	$2^{\frac{1}{2}}$	$3^{1\frac{1}{2}}$	5^4	Pincay L Jr^3	125000	83-12	EvnngM'Lord,RvrOfKngs,PlAndDc	8
27Mar86—Rough trip														
8Dec85-9Hol	1 1/16Ⓣ	$:47^4 1:12^1 1:43$	fm	3¾	117	$3^{1\frac{1}{2}}$	3^{nk}	$2^{1\frac{1}{2}}$	6^2	Pincay L Jr^6	140000	— —	‡Steepbnk,SuperDupont,Plestiglio	12
8Dec85—Took up to avoid heels at 1/16; Placed fifth through disqualification														

Jan 18 SA 4f ft $:47^4$ h   ●Jan 12 SA Ⓣ 6f fm $1:12^4$ h (d)   Dec 29 SA 4f ft $:47^4$ h   ●Dec 22 Hol 1 ft $1:40^1$ h

***Lucky N Green** — B. h. 5, by He Loves Me—Miskish, by Gallant Man
Br.—McCreery L K (Ire) — 1987 1 0 0 0
ORTEGA L E — 120 — Tr.—West Ted — $125,000 — 1986 9 2 0 1 $64,425
Own.—Gonzalez F — Lifetime 30 7 4 4 $220,308 — Turf 11 3 1 2 $120,300

3Jan87-7SA 1⅛ :461 1:11 1:431ft 11 116 107¾ 86½ 75 86¾ Ortega L E5 Aw45000 78-16 PolynsinFlyr,BoldArrngmnt,Bruisr 10
14Dec86-5Hol 1⅛ Ⓣ:4611:10 1:402fm 7¾ 119 89½ 86½ 54½ 1hd Ortega L E1 100000 92-11 Lucky N Green, Emperdori, Keyala 8
22Nov86-5Hol 1⅛ Ⓣ:47 1:1121:421fm 10 122 31 52½ 98¾ 812½ Ortega L E8 125000 70-17 NuggetPoint,PolyTest,RivrOfKings 9
22Nov86—Bumped, steadied 1/4
4May86-4Hol 1 :452 1:101 1:35 ft 11 122 21 31 43 49½ Lipham T4 Aw45000 79-18 SuperDimond,SunMstr,FlotingRsrv 5
4May86—Stumbled break
21Apr86-8SA 1¼ Ⓣ:4521:35 2:00 fm 9½ 115 812 62½ 53 43 LiphmT5 [S]Sn Jcnto H 84-20 Fabbiani, Willingness,PrimeAssett 10
22Mar86-8GG 1 Ⓣ:4541:1111:362fm 16 114 1116 97½ 64½ 35 Lipham T2 S F Mile H 80-15 HilBoldKing,RightCon,LuckyNGrn 12
22Mar86—Broke in tangle; steadied to avoid loose horse early
9Mar86-8SA 1¼ Ⓣ:4731:3712:032yl 21 114 11½ 2½ 32½ 55¾ Lipham T6 Arcadia H 64-30 StrwberryRodII,HilBoldKing,Schillr 7
9Mar86—Grade II
2Feb86-8SA 1¼ :463 1:38 2:033m 47 116 76½ 95½ 810 813½ OrtgLE10 C H Strub 57-28 Nostalgia'sStr,RooArt,FstAccount 12
2Feb86—Grade I
19Jan86-8SA 1⅛ :472 1:112 1:482ft 24 117 42 63¾1011 1012½ OrtegLE9 Sn Frndo 74-12 RightCon,Nostlgi'sStr,FstAccount 10
19Jan86—Grade I; Wide on turns
4Jan86-7SA 1⅛ Ⓣ:4641:1121:492fm 5 118 42½ 2½ 2hd 11½ Ortega L E2 Aw38000 80-23 LuckyNGreen,Vulnerbility,Stpbnk 12
Jan 16 SA 6f ft 1:142 h — Dec 27 SA 7f ft 1:27 h — Dec 20 SA 3f ft :363 h — ●Dec 10 SA 7f ft 1:27 h

Honor Medal * — Ch. g. 6, by Avatar—Honor Maid, by Prince John
Br.—Elmendorf Farm (Ky) — 1986 18 5 3 3 $308,371
CORDERO A JR — 118 — Tr.—Drysdale Neil — $125,000 — 1985 2 0 0 0 $4,275
Own.—Lettuce Farm — Lifetime 39 9 5 10 $413,446 — Turf 22 2 2 6 $114,331

24Dec86-8Hol 1¼ Ⓣ:4841:3612:00 fm 12 115 63¾ 4¾ 41 64½ Sibille R4 500000 S 91-11 Forlitano, Schiller, Skip Out Front 8
24Dec86—Wide stretch
13Dec86-8Hol 1⅛ :461 1:101 1:474ft 33 115 68 43 31½ 42½ Sibille R6 Ntv Dvr H 96-09 HopefulWord,Epidurus,Nostlgi'sStr 7
13Dec86—Grade III
12Oct86-8SA 1½ Ⓣ:4642:0032:26 fm 19 126 77 819 59½ 712½ PncLJr10 Oak Tree Iv 72-12 Estrapade,Theatrical,UptownSwell 10
12Oct86—Grade I
4Oct86-8BM 1⅛ Ⓣ:4841:13 1:483fm 11 115 76½ 74½ 33 33½ Sibille R3 Tanforan H 93-03 TruceMker,CleverSong,HonorMedl 8
4Oct86—Grade III
14Sep86-10LaD 1⅜ Ⓣ:5021:40 2:154fm 7 115 73¾ 61¾ 53 51½ Sibille R7 La D H 85-11 Gallant Archer, Shulich,Nadirpour 14
14Sep86—Grade III
1Sep86-8Dmr 1⅜ Ⓣ:4741:3742:142fm 12 117 104¾116½ 94½ 73¾ PincyLJr8 Dmr Inv H 94-04 Raipillan, Schiller, Shulich 12
1Sep86—Grade II; Steadied at 1/8
3Aug86-9Cby 1⅜ Ⓣ:4831:3642:123fm 17 112 919 2½ 2hd 21½ Skinner K7 Turf Cls H — — Treizieme,HonorMedl,Forkinthrod 12
26Jly86-9Aks 1⅛ :48 1:112 1:492ft 7¾ 114 67¾ 63 32 22½ Baze R A7 Crnhskr H 87-23 Gourami, Honor Medal, Smile 7
26Jly86—Grade II
13Jly86-9Lga 1⅛ :46 1:094 1:472ft *2 116 712 55 21 1½ Sibille R5 Brdrs Cp H 96-12 HonorMedl,BedsidePromis,Shrpnl 10
6Jly86-11Pln 1⅛ :48 1:121 1:494ft *4-5 117 53½ 52½ 11½ 1nk Baze R A3 Almdn H 86-18 HonorMedal,Ascension,Impulsively 7
Jan 18 SA 4f ft :582 h — Jan 8 Hol 5f ft 1:022 h — Dec 30 SA 4f ft :514 h — Dec 20 Hol 5f ft 1:024 h

He's A Saros — B. c. 4, by Saros—The Brig, by Boez
Br.—Green Thumb Farm Stb (Cal) — 1986 18 2 1 2 $52,773
VALENZUELA P A — 115 — Tr.—Manzi Joseph — $115,000 — 1985 4 2 0 1 $5,580
Own.—Green Thumb Farm Stable — Lifetime 22 4 1 3 $58,353 — Turf 12 2 1 2 $51,365

14Dec86-7Hol 1⅛ Ⓣ:4721:11 1:472fm 44 114 52½ 61¾ 32 51½ Cordero A Jr1 HcpO 89-11 Aventino,Bruiser,BoldArrangement 8
7Dec86-7Hol 1 :441 1:093 1:352gd 11 116 43½ 65½ 56 514½ Valenzuela P A1 HcpO 72-18 LateRequest,TheFlts,Thlss'noAsteri 7
30Nov86-7Hol 1 Ⓣ:4631:1011:342fm 21 116 41 31 31 64½ Valenzuela PA12 HcpO 90-12 AnEmprss,Avntno,Cro'sHollywood 12
30Nov86—Wide 7/8
18Oct86-8SA 1⅛ Ⓣ:4711:1121:48 fm 31 115 72¾ 83½ 56½ 58½ VlnzulPA2 Volante H 79-13 Air Display, Armada, Vernon Castle 9
18Oct86—Grade III; Broke out, bumped
7Sep86-7Dmr 1¹⁄₁₆ :452 1:094 1:411ft 24 115 64¾ 55 710 712¾ VlnlPA6 [S]Wndy Snds 81-13 Varick, Epidaurus, Coastliner 8
7Sep86—Broke slowly; wide into stretch
3Aug86-8Dmr 1 Ⓣ:46 1:11 1:351fm 41 115 2hd 2hd 76½ 911 Sibille R7 La Jla Mi H 85-08 VrnonCstl,TrpolShors,Mrvn'sPlcy 12
3Aug86—Grade III; Wide into stretch
23Jly86-8Dmr 1 Ⓣ:4611:1021:341fm 15 115 2½ 21 23½ 34¾ VlnzlPA2 [S]Oceanside 96-04 PrinceBobbyB.,FullChrm,He'sASros 9
5Jly86-8Hol 1 :443 1:08 1:324ft 309 116 106 1112 916 919¾ KaenelJL8 Slvr Scrn H 79-08 Melair, Southern Halo, SnowChief 12
5Jly86—Grade II; Bumped break
21Jun86-8GG 1¹⁄₁₆ Ⓣ:4641:1121:431fm 6 116 76½ 42 52¾ 75¾ ChapmnTM7 Sutter H 80-14 Marvin'sPolicy,Cheapskate,Mercier 9
7Jun86-8Hol 1⅛ Ⓣ:4741:1141:47 fm 29 115 87 64½ 63¾ 55¾ VlnzlPA8 Cinema H 91-02 Manila, Vernon Castle,FullOfStars 10
7Jun86—Grade II
Jan 11 SA 7f ft 1:264 h — Dec 30 SA 5f ft 1:012 h — Dec 24 SA 4f ft :492 h — Nov 23 SA 4f ft :493 h

***Cutting Wind** — Ch. h. 6, by Sharpen Up—Tumble Judy, by Tumble Wind
TORO F 115 — Br.—Kitone Co Ltd (Ire) — 1987 1 0 0 0
Own.—Blincoe & Brown Mmes — Tr.—Blincoe Tom $110,000 — 1986 2 0 1 1 $7,949
Lifetime 26 7 4 3 $120,972 — Turf 25 7 4 3 $119,397

14Jan87-5SA a6½f Ⓣ:214 :4421:151fm 24 116 98¼ 97¼ 87¾ 86¾ McHargue D G2 75000 76-18 Amnotherbrother,StrVideo,Shrkin 10
16Mar86-10TuP 1 1/16 Ⓣ:49 1:1311:432fm*7-5 120 74¾ 53 42 22 CastanedaM9 Gvnrs H 93-05 VirgnPrvtr,CuttngWnd,PolkExcus 11
25Jan86-6BM 1 1/16 Ⓣ:4741:1221:443fm*4-5 115 78¼ 68 35 32 CastanedaM7 Aw22000 83-15 ChicotonBlz,Poston'sBst,CttngWnd 8
25Jan86—Wide into stretch
28Dec85-6BM 1 1/16 Ⓣ:4711:1131:44 fm*8-5 114 510 35½ 1½ 14 CastanedaM2 Aw19000 88-12 Cutting Wind, ‡Dunant, Shayzari 9
8Dec85-9Hol 1 1/16 Ⓣ:4741:1211:43 fm 9¾ 114 117½126½ 95 72½ Baze R A3 135000 — — ‡Steepbnk,SuperDupont,Plestiglio 12
16Nov85-9Hol a1⅛ Ⓣ 1:454fm 7 119 915 84 63¾ 33¼ Solis A9 125000 — — Caballo, Steepbank, Cutting Wind 9
16Nov85—Crowded, steadied early stretch; Error in placement of starting gate
31Oct85-8BM 1 1/16 Ⓣ:4631:1021:413fm*3-2 115 55½ 42½ 32½ 21½ CastanedaM3 Aw20000 98 — VicroyLd,CuttingWind,Frnch'sLuck 8
15Aug85-8Dmr 1 1/16 Ⓣ:48 1:1111:411fm 3 119 58½ 67 67½ 55¼ Solis A6 Aw35000 97 — Zoffany, Pol And Dic, Bold Run 6
1Aug85-8Dmr 1 1/16 Ⓣ:47 1:11 1:422fm 9 115 610 42½ 1hd 12½ Solis A6 Aw35000 96-09 CuttngWnd,BoldRun,PrncFlormund 6
18Jly85-8Hol 1 Ⓣ:49 1:1211:354fm 20 115 66½ 65¼ 52¾ 41¾ Solis A2 Aw45000 82-16 Go Dancer, Bold Run, Ayman 7
Dec 31 SA 4f ft :472 h — Dec 24 SA 1 ft 1:404 h — Dec 12 Hol 7f ft 1:30 h — Nov 30 Hol 6f ft 1:134 h

Every horse in the race except one last ran on the grass, which makes the handicapper's task much easier than when so many of them are in and out from dirt to turf and back. The distance of the race at 1 1/8 was also the most common, and we used that base for the computation of ability times. Here is what our worksheet brought:

Odds	Horse	PCR	Form	Ab/T	
3	Steepbank	93/ 31 31 – / 62 = 150	N+w	11.2 36.4 /	48.1
11	Truth	97/ 71 41 – /112 = 87	NNN	12.4 37.2 /	50.1
6	Armin	73/ 21 21 + 12/ 54 = 135	Lw	(11.4 39.0 /	50.0)
5-2	Poly Test	79/ 22 31 – / 53 = 149	N+O	11.4 37.0 /	48.0
6	Lucky N Green	95/ 58 52 – 6/104 = 91	NON	(11.2 36.0 /	47.2)
7-2	Honor Medal	95/ 58 38 – 6/ 90 = 105	N+N	(14.0 35.2 /	49.2)
15	He's A Saros	98/ 53 61 – 4/110 = 89	Lw	(11.2 36.2 /	47.0)
13	Cutting Wind	86/ 63 36 + 5/104 = 83	NON	(10.2 37.1 /	47.3)

We can begin with some general observations about how we handle handicapping lines for turf racing, although as we have said, it is much easier when you have a field full of established grass runners. Only one horse, Armin, has run as few as seven times on the turf, but he shows only two races in his past performances. Although he has never won on the turf, which would make it very difficult for him to win in a field full of frequent winners on the grass, he has run second three times. For that reason, we would use all his races to calculate his PCR, which we ordinarily do when a horse shows that he can run on either surface.

When you encounter a grass race, you must in each instance compare every horse's turf record with his dirt record. If you find a grass horse that is hopeless on the dirt, you may choose to omit dirt races from your PCR calculations. The same guide in reverse is true in a dirt race where a horse has never performed ably on the grass and where you would choose to ignore his grass races in computing the appropriate numbers. In the race before us, we have no problems of that kind.

Our constant attention to how the dirt track responds may not be nearly so pertinent when we come to turf racing. Many racing cards may have only one grass race for the day, which prevents you from making any judgment on the track. Where there are two or more turf races carded, you can put your observations into play, of course. But we are rarely swayed in a grass race by what the track surface shows on the dirt.

Our major ingredients in looking at grass races are PCRs and class, as well as demonstrated ability to run well. If we know that a grass course is close clipped and baked from the heat, early speed may be a dominant factor, but ordinarily, middle and late runners can be expected to do very well, if they have the credentials. With all this, what do we make of this field?

Steepbank and the favored Poly Test have virtually the same PCRs at the top of the pack. Steepbank, by the notable turf sire, Stage Door Johnny, won his last race but that becomes less and less of a blemish when we encounter higher class horses. His last race ability time is second among those horses off last race ratings. Poly Test, although 3 ticks behind Steepbank, in a long race is far from out of it by this measure. Poly Test lost ground in the stretch in his last race, and that slight form defect may make the difference against him today in this field.

Armin has the next PCR but because most of his efforts came in dirt races, we can discount it slightly. Then there is Honor Medal, the third favorite at 9-2, with the next following PCR. Because his last race was at a mile and a quarter, and he is running a full furlong less today, his stretch call position is the one we center on as he picks up a + running line. Because of the difficult-to-measure distance of a mile and a quarter, with an entirely different running pattern, I find that it is not wise to use compressed ability times as a serious rating. We go back to advisory again, where this horse doesn't fare too well.

While we are somewhat uneasy about this race, application of our rules points to Steepbank as a single selection play. He is in the top third of both PCR and ability times and is without a form defect. We have found that these horses win more than 50% of the time and that is why we play them. We will go that way and see what happens.

SEVENTH RACE
Santa Anita
JANUARY 21, 1987

1 ⅛ MILES.(Turf). (1.45⅗) CLAIMING. Purse $40,000. 4-year-olds and upward. Weights, 4-year-olds, 121 lbs.; older, 122 lbs. Non-winners of two races at one mile or over since December 1 allowed 2 lbs.; of such a race since then 4 lbs. Claiming price $125,000; for each $5,000 to $100,000 allowed 1 lb. (Claiming and starter races for $80,000 or less not considered.)
Value of race $40,000; value to winner $22,000; second $8,000; third $6,000; fourth $3,000; fifth $1,000. Mutuel pool $244,266. Exacta pool $376,438.

Last Raced	Horse	Eqt.A.Wt	PP	St	¼	½	¾	Str	Fin	Jockey	Cl'g Pr	Odds $1
24Dec86 ^{8}Hol^6	Honor Medal	b 6 118	6	8	7^{1½}	6^½	6^½	1^½	1^3	Cordero A Jr	125000	3.60
1Jan87 ^{5}SA^1	Steepbank	6 116	1	3	1^{hd}	1^½	1^½	2^{1½}	2^{1¾}	Shoemaker W	105000	3.10
3Jan87 ^{7}SA^8	Lucky N Green	b 5 120	5	6	4^½	4^1	3^{hd}	4^{hd}	3^{nk}	Ortega L E	125000	6.50
1Jan87 ^{5}SA^4	Poly Test	7 118	4	2	3^2	3^1	2^1	3^2	4^½	Pincay L Jr	125000	2.80
11Jan87 ^{7}SA^7	Truth	b 4 117	2	4	6^½	7^1	7^½	6^{1½}	5^{nk}	Baze G	125000	11.60
14Dec86 ^{7}Hol^5	He's A Saros	4 116	7	5	5^3	5^3	4^½	5^{1½}	6^3	Valenzuela PA	115000	15.90
14Jan87 ^{5}SA^8	Cutting Wind	6 116	8	7	8	8	8	8	7^{nk}	Toro F	110000	13.80
7Dec86 ^{8}BM^2	Armin	b 6 118	3	1	2^½	2^{hd}	5^{1½}	7^½	8	Stevens G L	125000	6.80

OFF AT 3:51. Start good. Won driving. Time, :23⅗, :47⅖, 1:12, 1:36⅘, 1:49 Course firm.

$2 Mutuel Prices:			
6-HONOR MEDAL	9.20	5.00	3.00
1-STEEPBANK		5.20	3.20
5-LUCKY N GREEN			4.40

$5 EXACTA 6-1 PAID $120.50.

Not so good, as the second place finish cannot satisfy us when we play a single horse to win. Honor Medal performed surprisingly well. This race is a good one to illustrate that our selected plays do fail, of course, as all of us recognize. But events like this hardly deter us, as we move along.

We are now at the feature race of the day, the La Centinela Stakes at one mile for three year-old-fillies early in the season. When you see that the lowest priced horse on the board is at 3-1, you can recognize that there is no real favorite at all in this wide open event.

8th Santa Anita

1 MILE. (1.33⅘) 35th Running of THE LA CENTINELA STAKES. $60,000 added. Fillies. 3-year-olds which are non-winners of $50,000 at one mile or over (Allowance). By subscription of $50 each to accompany the nomination and $600 additional to start, with $60,000 added, of which $12,000 to second, $9,000 to third, $4,500 to fourth and $1,500 to fifth. Weight, 120 lbs. Non-winners of $30,000 at one mile or over allowed 2 lbs.; of such a race of $20,000, or a race of $40,000 at any distance 4 lbs.; of a race of $20,000 6 lbs. Starters to be named through the entry box by the closing time of entries. A trophy will be presented to the owner of the winner. Closed Wednesday, January 14, 1987 with 17 nominations.

Foxy Island
KAENEL J L **114**
Own.—Northwest Farms

B. f. 3, by Drum Fire—Run Tara Run, by Run for Nurse
Br.—Northwest Farms (Wash) 1987 1 0 0 0 $4,500
Tr.—McMeans Bob 1986 6 2 3 0 $40,451
Lifetime 7 2 3 0 $44,951

7Jan87-8SA	6f	:21^3	:44^2	1:09^{4}m	4¼	114	2^2	2^7	4^{10}	4^{11¾}	StevnsGL^4	ⒻPasadena	77-21	Very Subtle, Footy, Key Bid	5
18Oct86-9Lga	6½f	:21^2	:43^3	1:15^{3}ft	*2-3	116	1^{1½}	1^2	1^{2½}	1^{1½}	Loseth C^3	Apl Cp H	91-16	FoxyIslnd,Tlk'sChep,DetrmindWritr	9
12Oct86-3Lga	6½f	:21^4	:44^2	1:15^{4}ft	*2-3	118	1^{2½}	1^{3½}	1^6	1^6	Loseth C^3	ⒻMdn	90-16	FoxyIsland,Cokley,ColoredCryons	10
31Aug86-9Lga	6½f	:21^4	:45	1:16^{3}ft	6¼	118	1^{2½}	4^3	—	—	LosthC^1	[S]J Gtstn Fut	— —	O.K.Yet,BobCeeStar,Chan'sDrgon	14
31Aug86—Eased															
9Aug86-9Lga	6f	:21^2	:43^3	1:09 ft	2e	118	1^{3½}	1^{3½}	1^1	2^4	LsthC^5	Ⓕ[S]Bdrk Mem	87-11	SoftCopy,FoxyIsland,NorthernCche	8
26Jly86-9Lga	6f	:21^4	:44^1	1:09^{3}ft	2¾e	118	1^{2½}	1^3	1^{2½}	2^{hd}	LosethC^2	ⒻGrn Rvr H	88-15	Pilot'sPanache,FoxyIslnd,SoftCopy	8
5Jly86-9Lga	5½f	:21^4	:44^3	1:02^{4}ft	4	118	1^{hd}	1^2	2^3	2^4	DmnRE^1	Ⓕ[R]Wsh Stln	94-16	SoftCopy,FoxyIsland,BnchoryFye	10
5Jly86—Bore out 5/16															

Jan 17 SA 5f ft 1:03^2 h **●Dec 31 SA 6f ft 1:12^4 h** **Dec 15 Hol 5f ft 1:03 h** **Dec 9 Hol 5f ft 1:00^4 h**

Timely Assertion — Gr. f. 3, by Assert—Timely Roman, by Sette Bello
Br.—Axmar Stbs & Hubbard (Ky) 1987 1 0 1 0 $9,000
VALENZUELA P A 114 Tr.—Moreno Henry 1986 2 2 0 0 $22,000
Own.—Wichita Equine Inc Lifetime 3 2 1 0 $31,000
4Jan87-8BM 1 :464 1:123 1:382m *4-5 115 32 32 32 21½ ChpTM6 ©Hail Hilars 74-30 ChicShrn,TmlyAssrton,QuckMssngr 8
4Jan87—Bumped hard start
11Dec86-5Hol 6f :22 :46 1:112ft *4-5 120 63¾ 51½ 2½ 12½ Pincay LJr4 ©Aw22000 86-21 TmlyAssrton,IncConnctn,SlctASng 7
11Dec86—Lugged in 1/16
15Nov86-6Hol 6f :22 :462 1:114ft *7-5 118 63¾ 41¾ 11½ 15 Pincay L Jr6 ©Mdn 84-14 TimelyAssertion,HiloBb,LivlyMiss 11
15Nov86—Crowded, steadied 1/4
Jan 15 SA 7f ft 1:281 h Jan 10 SA 4f gd :502 h Dec 29 SA 4f ft :473 h Dec 26 SA 6f ft 1:13 h

Footy — B. f. 3, by Topsider—Obstetrician, by Dr Fager
Br.—Chry Vly Fm Inc & GamelyCp (Ky) 1987 1 0 1 0 $12,000
SHOEMAKER W 116 Tr.—Proctor Willard L 1986 6 2 1 1 $73,325
Own.—Cherry Valley Fm (Lessee) Lifetime 7 2 2 1 $85,325
7Jan87-8SA 6f :213 :442 1:094m 3½ 118 56½ 49 39½ 25 ShmkrW3 ©Pasadena 84-21 Very Subtle, Footy, Key Bid 5
7Jan87—Lugged in stretch
30Oct86-8SA 7f :22 :444 1:223ft 2 121 42 32 23 23¾ ShrW3 ©ⓇSprtng Ls 83-18 VerySubtle,Footy,PerchnceToDrem 7
30Oct86—Lugged in stretch
31Aug86-8Dmr 1 :452 1:102 1:354ft 9¾ 117 1hd 1½ 31½ 47 SotSB2 ©Dmr Deb 82-12 BraveRaj,RodToHppiness,SoftCopy 7
31Aug86—Grade II; Lugged out backstretch
18Aug86-8Dmr 7f :22 :443 1:223ft 5 121 42 31½ 41½ 33¾ McCrrCJ1 ©Sorrento 88-14 Brave Raj, Breech, Footy 10
18Aug86—Grade III
6Aug86-8Dmr 6f :213 :444 1:10 ft 2¾ 114 41½ 2½ 21½ 1¾ McCrronCJ6 ©Jr Miss 88-13 Footy, Brave Raj, Evil Elaine 10
6Aug86—Veered in start
10Jly86-6Hol 5½f :223 :462 1:043ft 3½ 118 11½ 11 13 16½ McCrronCJ5 ©M50000 91-18 Footy, Quick Messenger, Beseya 9
27Jun86-3Hol 5½f :222 :45 1:042ft 19 118 63¾ 66 67½ 69¾ Patterson A7 ©Mdn 82-12 DebutnteLinRose,Ros'sCntin,KyBid 9
Jan 20 SA 3f ft :382 h Dec 31 SA 6f ft 1:131 h Dec 25 SA 6f ft 1:133 h Dec 18 Hol 6f ft 1:151 h

Alyaffirm ✻ — Ch. f. 3, by Alydar—Crafty Alice, by Crafty Admiral
Br.—Harbor View Farm (Ky) 1987 1 1 0 0 $15,400
STEVENS G L 114 Tr.—Lukas D Wayne 1986 3 1 1 0 $19,140
Own.—Harbor View Farm Lifetime 4 2 1 0 $34,540
8Jan87-7SA 1 :473 1:132 1:413m 2¾ 116 11½ 12½ 1½ 13 StevensGL1 ©Aw28000 60-30 Alyaffirm, Infringe, French Etoile 7
8Jan87—Propped near 3/16; very wide into drive, green in stretch
30Nov86-2Aqu 1 :471 1:123 1:383ft 3¾ 116 1hd 11½ 2½ 22¾ LovtoFJr10 ©Aw27000 70-24 MissileMgic,Alyffirm,GrcefulDrby 11
20Nov86-3Aqu 7f :23 :461 1:242ft 13 117 1½ 11 11½ 13¾ Lovato F10 ©Mdn 79-20 Alyffrm,Koluctoo'sRby,SpctclrDn 11
2Nov86-4Aqu 6f :223 :462 1:121ft 2¾ 117 31½ 44½ 1221 1226¾ Romero R P1 ©Mdn 53-21 GrecianFlight,SomeHome,Tchaika 12
2Nov86—Off slowly
Jan 17 Hol 4f ft :473 h Jan 3 Hol 5f ft 1:033 h Dec 29 SA 6f ft 1:133 h Dec 18 Hol 5f ft 1:003 h

French Etoile — Ch. f. 3, by Score Twenty Four—French Tout, by Tout
Br.—Cale-Capehart-Liebau (Cal) 1987 1 0 0 1 $4,200
BAZE G 114 Tr.—Mulhall Richard W 1986 4 1 0 0 $9,050
Own.—Arnold-Clark-Cirmm et al Lifetime 5 1 0 1 $13,250
8Jan87-7SA 1 :473 1:132 1:413m 40 114 21½ 22½ 32 36 Meza R Q3 ©Aw28000 54-30 Alyaffirm, Infringe, French Etoile 7
8Jan87—Stumbled start; lugged in stretch
11Nov86-1Hol 1 :47 1:13 1:392ft 11 118 2½ 2hd 11½ 11¾ DelhoussyE6 ©M50000 66-20 FrnchEtoil,SouthOfFrnc,SwtchSlps 7
24Oct86-6SA 6f :221 :46 1:11 ft 14 117 95½ 75½ 78 815 DelhoussyE8 ©ⓈMdn 68-20 LyriclPirte,DnceAllSummer,Lurntin 9
10Oct86-6SA 6f :222 :461 1:112ft 4½ 117 73¾ 76½ 916 918½ DelhoussyE6 ©ⓈMdn 62-24 FlyingHghr,LyrclPrt,DncAllSummr 11
10Oct86—Broke poorly
3Sep86-6Dmr 6f :221 :454 1:111ft 9½ 117 97½ 97½ 77 44½ DelahoussyeE3 ©Mdn 78-16 Breakable, Gritty Bid, Tou'ange 9
3Sep86—Broke slowly
Jan 3 SA 6f ft 1:163 h Dec 29 SA 6f ft 1:141 h Dec 24 SA 5f ft 1:02 h Dec 18 SA 7f ft 1:29 h

Key Bid

SIMPSON B H **116**
Own.—Ryehill Farm
B. f. 3, by Key to the Mint—Delta Bid, by Delta Judge
Br.—Ryehill Farm (Md) 1987 1 0 0 1 $9,000
Tr.—Barrera Lazaro S 1986 9 3 0 2 $118,137
Lifetime 10 3 0 3 $127,137

7Jan87-8SA 6f :21^{3} :44^{2} 1:09^{4}m 6¼ 118 3$^{4\frac{1}{2}}$ 3$^{8\frac{1}{2}}$ 2^{8} 3^{9} PincyLJr^{1} ⒻPasadena 80-21 Very Subtle, Footy, Key Bid 5
7Jan87—Rough start
30Nov86-8Hol 1 :45^{4} 1:10^{1} 1:36 ft 36 120 4$^{2\frac{1}{2}}$ 4$^{6\frac{1}{2}}$ 3$^{9\frac{1}{2}}$ 4$^{12\frac{3}{4}}$ VergarO^{5} ⒻHol Strlt 70-16 Very Subtle, Sacahuista, Infringe 6
30Nov86—Grade I
26Oct86-8BM 6f :22^{1} :45^{3} 1:11^{1}ft *1 115 4$^{1\frac{1}{2}}$ 3$^{1\frac{1}{2}}$ 1$^{1\frac{1}{2}}$ 1$^{\frac{3}{4}}$ Vergara O^{7} ⒻBrlngme 83-20 Key Bid, Geisha Fan,WindyTripleK. 9
2Oct86-7SA 6f :21^{3} :45 1:11^{1}sy *1 116 2$^{1\frac{1}{2}}$ 2^{1} 1^{2} 1$^{1\frac{1}{2}}$ StevensGL^{2} ⒻAw25000 82-21 Key Bid, Sellemall, Tracey's Trick 5
2Oct86—Bumped 3/8, 3/16
8Sep86-8Dmr 6f :22 :45^{1} 1:09^{3}ft 9¼ 117 2^{1} 2^{2} 3$^{4\frac{1}{2}}$ 3$^{5\frac{3}{4}}$ Solis A^{3} ⒻⓇCoronado 84-14 EvilEline,PerchnceToDrem,KeyBid 9
18Aug86-8Dmr 7f :22 :44^{3} 1:22^{3}ft 18 117 3^{1} 5$^{3\frac{1}{2}}$ 6$^{4\frac{1}{2}}$ 6$^{7\frac{1}{2}}$ StnsGL^{4} ⒻSorrento 84-14 Brave Raj, Breech, Footy 10
18Aug86—Grade III
6Aug86-8Dmr 6f :21^{3} :44^{4} 1:10 ft 6¼ 117 3^{1} 3^{2} 3^{3} 4$^{3\frac{1}{4}}$ Stevens GL^{4} ⒻJr Miss 85-13 Footy, Brave Raj, Evil Elaine 10
6Aug86—Bumped hard start
19Jly86-3Hol 5½f :22^{3} :46^{3} 1:05^{3}ft *1 118 1$^{\frac{1}{2}}$ 1^{hd} 1$^{1\frac{1}{2}}$ 1^{2} Stevens G L^{4} ⒻMdn 86-15 Key Bid, Miss Endicott, SuperCook 7
4Jly86-7Hol 6f :21^{2} :45 1:10 ft 74 114 4^{3} 4$^{2\frac{1}{2}}$ 4$^{5\frac{1}{2}}$ 4$^{8\frac{1}{2}}$ Solis A^{1} ⒻLandaluce 85-09 DlictVin,AnythingForLov,PurduQun 9
4Jly86—Grade III
27Jun86-3Hol 5½f :22^{2} :45 1:04^{2}ft *8-5 118 3^{2} 2^{1} 2^{2} 3$^{2\frac{1}{2}}$ Stevens G L^{1} ⒻMdn 89-12 DebutnteLinRose,Ros'sCntin,KyBid 9
Jan 20 SA 3f ft :35^{2} h   Jan 2 SA 5f ft 1:02^{2} h   Dec 27 SA 5f ft 1:00^{3} h   Dec 20 Hol 5f ft 1:01^{3} h

Infringe

SIBILLE R **114**
Own.—Hibbert R E
Dk. b. or br. f. 3, by Irish River—Stargard, by Tell
Br.—Hibbert R E (Ky) 1987 1 0 1 0 $5,600
Tr.—Manzi Joseph 1986 3 1 1 1 $88,625
Lifetime 4 1 2 1 $94,225

8Jan87-7SA 1 :47^{3} 1:13^{2} 1:41^{3}m *1 117 3^{2} 3^{3} 2$^{\frac{1}{2}}$ 2^{3} Pincay LJr^{4} ⒻAw28000 57-30 Alyaffirm, Infringe, French Etoile 7
8Jan87—Checked at 7/8
30Nov86-8Hol 1 :45^{4} 1:10^{1} 1:36 ft 7¼ 120 6$^{5\frac{1}{2}}$ 6$^{9\frac{1}{2}}$ 5^{11} 3$^{11\frac{1}{2}}$ DlhssyE^{1} ⒻHol Strlt 71-16 Very Subtle, Sacahuista, Infringe 6
30Nov86—Grade I; Wide into stretch
14Nov86-8Hol 1 :46^{1} 1:11 1:36^{2}ft 7 120 3^{2} 4^{1} 4$^{\frac{3}{4}}$ 2$^{1\frac{1}{4}}$ VlenzulPA^{4} ⒻAw24000 80-16 Rose'sCantina,Infringe,YoungFlyer 6
14Nov86—Bumped, steadied 1/16
25Oct86-4SA 6f :21^{2} :44^{3} 1:12^{1}ft *3¾ 117 10^{11} 8$^{9\frac{3}{4}}$ 5$^{6\frac{3}{4}}$ 1$^{\frac{3}{4}}$ ValenzuelPA^{11} ⒻMdn 77-17 Infringe, Folia,YouMakeMeHappy 12
25Oct86—Broke slowly; wide into, through stretch
●Jan 16 SA 5f ft 1:00 h   Jan 2 SA 6f ft 1:14^{4} h   Dec 28 SA 7f ft 1:30^{1} h   Dec 21 SA 5f ft 1:01 h

Devil's Bride

MEZA R Q **114**
Own.—Oak Cliff Stable
Gr. f. 3, by Caro—Satan's Pride, by Crimson Satan
Br.—Oak Cliff Thbds Ltd (Ky) 1986 3 2 0 0 $24,200
Tr.—Gosden John H M
Lifetime 3 2 0 0 $24,200

28Dec86-7SA 6f :21^{2} :44^{1} 1:10 ft *2¼ 120 1^{2} 1^{6} 1^{5} 1$^{3\frac{1}{2}}$ Meza R Q^{7} ⒻAw26000 88-14 Dvl'sBrd,PrchncToDrm,Buryyorblf 10
30Nov86-6Hol 6f :21^{3} :45^{2} 1:10^{4}ft 3¼ 118 2^{hd} 1^{1} 1$^{3\frac{1}{2}}$ 1^{6} Meza R Q^{1} ⒻMdn 89-16 Dvl'sBrd,SmmrSonds,DncAllSmmr 12
18Oct86-6SA 6½f :21^{3} :45^{2} 1:19^{1}ft 2¼ 117 3^{1} 4$^{2\frac{1}{4}}$ 6^{8} 6$^{10\frac{3}{4}}$ Pincay L Jr^{6} ⒻMdn 63-20 ExprssElvtor,GlfstrmFlyr,Contrctd 7
Jan 15 SA 7f ft 1:27^{3} h   Jan 10 SA 5f gd 1:01^{3} h   Dec 22 Hol 5f ft 1:01^{3} h   Dec 16 Hol 5f ft 1:00^{2} h

Chic Shirine *

CORDERO A JR **120**
Own.—Alexander E G
B. f. 3, by Mr Prospector—Teo Chic, by Blushing Groom
Br.—Alexander E (Ky) 1987 1 1 0 0 $31,950
Tr.—Lukas D Wayne 1986 3 1 0 0 $10,450
Lifetime 4 2 0 0 $42,400

4Jan87-8BM 1 :46^{4} 1:12^{3} 1:38^{2}m 4 114 1$^{1\frac{1}{2}}$ 1^{hd} 1$^{\frac{1}{2}}$ 1$^{1\frac{1}{2}}$ BazeRA^{3} ⒻHail Hilars 76-30 ChicShrn,TmlyAssrton,QuckMssngr 8
20Dec86-6Hol 7f :22^{1} :45^{4} 1:24 ft 3¾ 118 1^{1} 1$^{1\frac{1}{2}}$ 1$^{2\frac{1}{2}}$ 1$^{2\frac{3}{4}}$ Pincay L Jr^{8} ⒻMdn 84-15 Chic Shirine, Hilo Baba, Cee'sVigor 8
13Nov86-5Aqu 6f :23^{1} :47^{1} 1:12 gd 10 117 5$^{2\frac{3}{4}}$ 7$^{5\frac{1}{4}}$ 7$^{8\frac{1}{2}}$ 9$^{16\frac{1}{4}}$ Cordero A Jr^{5} ⒻMdn 65-20 Fine Timing, Starita, Finalmente 13
26Oct86-9Aqu 6f :22^{2} :46 1:11^{3}sy 4½ 117 6^{3} 4$^{2\frac{1}{2}}$ 8^{13} 10$^{18\frac{1}{2}}$ Romero R P^{11} ⒻMdn 64-18 DoublsPrtnr,SunstCloud,FinTimng 11
Jan 17 Hol 4f ft :49^{2} h   Jan 1 SA 4f ft :49^{3} h   Dec 13 Hol 5f ft 1:00^{2} h   Dec 5 Hol 5f ft 1:02^{1} h

Saros Brig

B. f. 3, by Saros—The Brig, by Boez
Br.—Green Thumb Farm Stable (Cal)   1986 8 2 1 1 $203,868

PINCAY L JR   **116**   Tr.—Manzi Joseph

Own.—Green Thumb Farm Stable   Lifetime 8 2 1 1 $203,868

27Dec86-8SA	7f :22² :453 1:24 ft	3 121	7⁴ 63½ 2³ 2²	PncyLJr⁷ ⒻⓈCl Brdrs	78-19 YoungFlyer,SrosBrig,DncAllSummr 9
27Dec86—Broke slowly
30Nov86-8Hol	1 :454 1:10¹ 1:36 ft	6 120	5³ 5⁸ 6¹² 513¾	ShmkrW⁴ ⒽHol Strlt	69-16 Very Subtle, Sacahuista, Infringe 6
30Nov86—Grade I; Lugged in late
1Nov86-2SA	1 1/16 :453 1:10¹ 1:43 ft	23 119	78½ 6⁷ 51¹ 3⁹	ShrW³ ⒻBr Cp Juv F	76-13 Brave Raj, Tappiano, Saros Brig 12
1Nov86—Grade I; Bore out, rank 7/8; lugged in stretch
5Oct86-8SA	1 1/16 :453 1:10² 1:443 ft	18 115	6⁶ 64½ 5⁵ 42¾	ShmrW² ⒻOak Leaf	75-15 Sacahuista, Silk'sLady,DelicateVine 7
5Oct86—Grade I; Broke in a tangle; bumped; wide into stretch
31Aug86-8Dmr	1 :452 1:10² 1:354 ft	6 117	7³ 5⁴ 5⁶ 58½	ShrW⁴ ⒻDmr Deb	81-12 BraveRaj,RodToHppiness,SoftCopy 7
31Aug86—Grade II; Broke slowly, wide into stretch
18Aug86-8Dmr	7f :443 1:223 ft	3½ 121	84½ 76½ 5⁴ 56½	PncLJr³ ⒻSorrento	86-14 Brave Raj, Breech, Fooly 10
18Aug86—Grade III
25Jly86-8Dmr	6f :22 :452 1:11 ft	*9-5 117	8⁴ 42½ 31½ 1½	PincyLJr⁶ ⒻⓈC T B A	83-18 SrosBrig,JoeyTheTrip,WindyTriplK. 8
25Jly86—Broke slowly; bore out, wide
26Jun86-3Hol	5f :22² :462 :59 ft	3 118	5⁵ 43½ 2½ 12½	Pincay LJr¹⁰ ⒻM50000	91-12 SrosBrig,Prind'sPride,MountinGld 10
Jan 18 SA 4f ft :48² h	Jan 13 SA 7f ft 1:29⁴ h	Jan 8 SA 4f m :49¹ h	Dec 21 SA 6f ft 1:13³ h

Young Flyer

Dk. b. or br. f. 3, by Flying Paster—Youthful Lady, by Youth
Br.—Mabee Mr—Mrs J C (Cal)   1986 4 2 0 1 $83,000

TORO F   **118**   Tr.—French Neil

Own.—Golden Eagle Farm   Lifetime 4 2 0 1 $83,000

27Dec86-8SA	7f :22² :453 1:24 ft	3 116	2½ 1¹ 1³ 1²	DlhssyE⁵ ⒻⓈCl Brdrs	80-19 YoungFlyer,SrosBrig,DncAllSummr 9
30Nov86-8Hol	1 :454 1:10¹ 1:36 ft	8 120	3¹ 35½ 4¹⁰ 615½	StvnsGL² ⒽHol Strlt	67-16 Very Subtle, Sacahuista, Infringe 6
30Nov86—Grade I
14Nov86-8Hol	1 :46¹ 1:11 1:362 ft	*1-3 120	1¹ 2ⁿᵈ 2ⁿᵈ 3²	StevensGL¹ ⒻAw24000	79-16 Rose'sCantina,Infringe,YoungFlyer 6
14Nov86—Bumped, steadied 1/16
2Nov86-4SA	6½f :21³ :441 1:16 ft	*1e 117	1½ 11½ 1⁵ 1⁵	Stevens G L² ⒻMdn	90-10 Young Flyer, Afloat, CharmedOne 10
●Jan 17 SA 5f ft :59 h	Jan 12 SA 5f ft :59¹ h	Jan 6 SA 4f gd :47³ h	Dec 21 SA 6f ft 1:12² h

A reading of our worksheet may tell you why.

Odds	Horse	PCR	Form	Ab/T
39	Foxy Island	64/ 7 14 + 10/ 31 = 206	NON	12/1 26.2–1/ 38.2
9-2	Timely Assertion	26/ 12 4 – / 16 =(163)	N+N	13.0 25.4–5/ 37.4
3	Footy	57/ 20 19 – 2/ 37 = 154	NON	(10.4 24.3–1/ 35.1)
9-2	Alyaffirm	46/ 7 16 + 2/ 25 =(164)	N++	13.2 28.1–5/ 40.3
98	French Etoile	43/ 27 25 + 2/ 54 = 80	NNO	14.1 28.4–5/ 42.0
39	Key Bid	79/ 29 30 – 5/ 54 = 146	NON	11.3 25.3–1/ 37.0)
11	Infringe	31/ 21 8 – 2/ 27 =(115)	NNO	14.0 28.0–5/ 41.0
3	Devil's Bride	29/ 6 8 – 1/ 13 =(223)	N++	(10.1 25.4+2/ 36.2)
12	Chic Shirine	40/ 13 21 – 1/ 33 =(121)	N+w	12.3 26.0–5/ 37.3
5	Saros Brig	69/ 43 26 – 7/ 62 = 111	NNN	(11.2 25.1 0/ 36.3)

Half the field consists of lightly raced horses whose PCRs are thus not fulfilled, even though we do have measurable last races from each of them. The horse with the highest PCR, Foxy Island, ran at a much lower class up at Longacres and acquired her numbers against much lesser competition. The 39-1 odds accurately reflect her chances. Two other established runners with high PCRs, Footy and Key Bid, both have form defects. Key Bid is soft enough in the ability time department to cause us to discount her chances.

Since none of the three highest PCR horses qualify as a single selection play, we can ask what else is in the field. If there is no single selection play, can we narrow it down to two horses with decent odds that look strong enough to prevail?

When we come to our powerful ability times, we have another problem: four of our entries have advisory times off sprint races. Since this is a one mile event, we can place more reliance on these times. The co-favorites at a high 3-1 are Footy and Devil's Bride. While Footy has substantially the best last race time off a race on a muddy track where she was never in real contention, she has a form defect off that race. Devil's Bride ran on a fast track with a low variant and racked up a double plus form reading with a Big Win, always a powerful sign.

Both of them are even to early runners and certainly have no disadvantage in running style.

The other candidate that cannot be overlooked is Saros Brig because of her strong last race at 7f and the impressive class credentials she brings to the race. If this were an exacta event, here might be the perfect place to box three horses, but it isn't. If we can't find enough of an advantage in two horses we will have to pass the race.

Here again is where our total handicapping lines are so helpful. Based on these lines, we are down to three horses in a talented field, Footy, Devil's Bride, and Saros Brig. We have to do a double check here on the others to see if there is a real threat in the rest of the field. A case might be made for some of the others, but comparing them over and over again, the three we have centered on really do look as if the winner will come from one of them. Alyaffirm off a good race has an ability time that is simply not competitive, and for that reason, she cannot be viewed as a serious threat.

We have to be able to discard one of the final three with enough confidence to justify a play. Who goes out, if anyone? Footy's powerhouse ability time, even at 6f, cannot be ignored. Devil's Bride is off a splendid last race. And Saros Brig with a good ability time and with strong class experience is still right in there.

The decisive factor comes down to PCR and running style. Saros Brig, even with her class points, is quite low in PCR and shows a 43 over 26 for internal numbers. She will not have the early speed at one mile to compete with much of the early foot in the race.

This is how we make our eliminations. Saros Brig, although very solid, is a shade below Footy and Devil's Bride. The odds are juicy enough to allow us to bet them both and expect to have a winning ticket.

And that is exactly what happened, as the chart reveals. Devil's Bride showed the early speed, out wire to wire all the way to win decisively.

EIGHTH RACE

Santa Anita

JANUARY 21, 1987

1 MILE. (1.33⅗) 35th Running of THE LA CENTINELA STAKES. $60,000 added. Fillies. 3-year-olds which are non-winners of $50,000 at one mile or over (Allowance). By subscription of $50 each to accompany the nomination and $600 additional to start, with $60,000 added, of which $12,000 to second, $9,000 to third, $4,500 to fourth and $1,500 to fifth. Weight, 120 lbs. Non-winners of $30,000 at one mile or over allowed 2 lbs.; of such a race of $20,000, or a race of $40,000 at any distance 4 lbs.; of a race of $20,000 6 lbs. Starters to be named through the entry box by the closing time of entries. A trophy will be presented to the owner of the winner. Closed Wednesday, January 14, 1987 with 17 nominations. Value of race $66,850; value to winner $39,850; second $12,000; third $9,000; fourth $4,500; fifth $1,500. Mutuel pool $465,916.

Last Raced	Horse	Eqt.A.Wt	PP	St	¼	½	¾	Str	Fin	Jockey	Odds $1
28Dec86 7SA¹	Devil's Bride	3 114	8	1	11½	12	12½	13½	13½	Meza R Q	3.30
27Dec86 8SA²	Saros Brig	3 116	10	10	7¹	6½	5½	4hd	2nk	Pincay L Jr	5.80
4Jan87 8BM¹	Chic Shirine	3 120	9	5	4¹	4¹	2hd	2hd	3¹	Cordero A Jr	12.60
4Jan87 8BM²	Timely Assertion	3 116	2	9	8½	8²	6¹	5½½	42½	Valenzuela P A	4.70
7Jan87 8SA³	Key Bid	3 116	6	2	2²	3½	3½½	3¹	5hd	Simpson B H	39.60
7Jan87 8SA²	Footy	b 3 116	3	6	6¹	5½½	4hd	65	64½	Shoemaker W	3.20
8Jan87 7SA²	Infringe	3 115	7	8	9½	92½	85	89	72	Sibille R	11.70
8Jan87 7SA¹	Alyaffirm	3 114	4	3	3½	2½	73½	7½	8	Stevens G L	4.50
8Jan87 7SA³	French Etoile	b 3 114	5	7	10	10	10	92½	—	Baze G	98.00
7Jan87 8SA⁴	Foxy Island	b 3 116	1	4	5hd	71	9½	10	—	Kaenel J L	39.70

French Etoile, Eased; Foxy Island, Eased.

OFF AT 4:24. Start good. Won ridden out. Time, :22⅖, :46⅘, 1:11, 1:23⅘, 1:37⅖ Track fast.

$2 Mutuel Prices:

8-DEVIL'S BRIDE	8.60	5.20	4.60
10-SAROS BRIG		5.60	4.00
9-CHIC SHIRINE			5.80

Alyaffirm, as expected, showed early but her weak last portion figure was too much to overcome. Footy's poor form showed again, despite her numbers. Saros Brig, who tantalized us to the end, was back in the field early, of course, but was up at the wire to gain the place. The $8.60 ticket was a solid play for a profit builder.

As the ninth and last race of the day approaches, we're back to the lowest claiming price on the grounds, $10,000 for older horses at a mile and a sixteenth. Like races for the topnotch animals which are often too competitive to find a play, we approach this one with similar wariness because nobody may be able to win. As always, we continue our search for horses with the advantage, for even in these low priced events, there are sometimes bargains to be found.

9th Santa Anita

1 1-16 MILES
SANTA ANITA
START • • FINISH

1 1/16 MILES. (1.40½) CLAIMING. Purse $13,000. 4-year-olds and upward. Weights, 4-year-olds, 121 lbs.; older, 122 lbs. Non-winners of two races at one mile or over since November 3 allowed 3 lbs.; of such a race since December 1, 5 lbs.; since November 3, 7 lbs. Claiming price $10,000. (Claiming and starter races for $8,500 or less not considered.)

Universal Dream — Dk. b. or br. g. 4, by Universal—Carrie's Angel, by Fleet Host
STEVENS G L 114 — Br.—Popik R (Cal) — 1987 1 0 0 0
Own.—Gellman or Gellman — Tr.—Lewis Gary $10,000 — 1986 18 4 0 3 $32,183
Lifetime 20 4 1 3 $34,383

8Jan87-1SA 1 1/16 :473 1:132 1:48 m 5 115 11 1hd 66 916½ Stevens G L7 10000 44-30 Menswer,Herts'NRoss,LottHistory 12
12Dec86-9BM 1 3/16 :444 1:093 1:55 ft 2½ 114 18 14 2½ 66¾ SchvneveldtCP2 A6250 82-23 Procurer, Longpo Free, Mt. Elba 8
23Nov86-10BM 1⅛ :461 1:11 1:503ft 11 114 14 12 16 16 SchvneveldtCP10 6250 78-20 UniversalDream,RpidAct,JetRoyle 12
13Nov86-9BM 1⅛ :46 1:102 1:50 ft 11 1095 34½ 915 1125 1121½ Sherman A B10 8000 59-24 Trjet,NobleAndGentle,BckToDnvr 12
25Oct86-1BM 1 1/16 :46 1:112 1:441ft 8 1065 13 3½ 44 37 Sherman A B2 8000 64-21 SprtnConqust,RdDusty,UnivrslDrm 8
16Oct86-9SA 1 1/16 :472 1:122 1:44 ft 13 114 11 43½ 812 917 Hernandez R6 18000 64-19 CojakMan,ResonToStudy,Averted 10
2Oct86-9SA 1 1/16 :463 1:12 1:45 sy *8-5 118 46 913 1022 — Pincay L Jr2 16000 — — Cinderhoof, Rey Sol, WaterJacket 10
2Oct86—Eased
20Sep86-10Pom 1 1/16 :454 1:111 1:431ft 16 1085 2hd 22 35 617½ Sterling L J Jr3 20000 77-09 Restage, Hatamoto,LyphardChimes 9
20Sep86—Bore out on turns
28Aug86-7Dmr 1 1/16 :45 1:104 1:442ft 3 116 1hd 23 47½ 611¾ Sibille R3 25000 66-18 Averted,ILoveRacing,MiamiDream 11
28Aug86—Broke in a tangle
18Aug86-9Dmr 1 1/16 :451 1:11 1:434ft *7-5 116 1½ 2hd 52½ 69½ Stevens G L6 32000 71-14 Halo Express, Joab. PeacefulImage 8
18Aug86—Rough start; returned bleeding from mouth
Jan 17 SA 4f ft :481 h Dec 27 SA 5f ft 1:002 h Dec 6 BM 6f m 1:154 h

***Estoc** — B. g. 6, by Gay Mecene—Eastern Silk, by Zeddaan
WARREN R J JR 115 — Br.—Bonnefoy & Nicol (Fra) — 1987 2 0 0 0 $975
Own.—Hatley-Klein-Lukas — Tr.—Lukas D Wayne $10,000 — 1986 6 1 0 0 $19,600
Lifetime 27 5 1 2 $42,344 — Turf 24 5 1 2 $41,369

8Jan87-1SA 1 1/16 :473 1:132 1:48 m 23 116 98 85¾ 54½ 46½ Warren R J Jr4 10000 54-30 Menswer,Herts'NRoss,LottHistory 12
8Jan87—Broke slowly
4Jan87-9SA 1⅛ :473 1:122 1:514sy 14 114 715 712 626 — Meza R Q3 18000 — — HurricneHec,NewStorm,ShuttleOne 7
4Jan87—Eased
26Dec86-9SA 1 1/16 :454 1:102 1:43 ft 36 116 66½ 65 912 913¾ Stevens S A4 25000 72-13 Cold,TommyThoms,BoncngBttons 11
8Jun86-4Hol 1 1/16 Ⓣ:454 1:094 1:404fm 4 116 1112 1112 89 65½ McCarron C J3 50000 94 — Sndy'sEgle,EmprdorAlNor,Rushd 11
26May86-6Hol 1¼ Ⓣ:49 1:371 2:02 fm 6¼ 1115 32 2hd 42 55¼ Black C A1 50000 92 — Crony, Tio Nino, Killyglen 9
25Jan86-5SA 1¼ Ⓣ:462 1:364 2:021fm 10 114 21 108¾ 913 916½ McCarron C J6 75000 59-23 PolAndDic,DonnyK.,Morry'sChmp 10
17Jan86-5SA 1⅛ Ⓣ:482 1:123 1:49 fm 7½ 116 85¼ 54¼ 46½ 45¼ McCarron C J4 80000 77-15 Bishop'sRngII,PolAndDc,Snowcrk 10
17Jan86—Wide into stretch
5Jan86-5SA 1⅛ Ⓣ:47 1:114 1:512gd 9½ 114 65¼ 63½ 41½ 11½ McCarron C J11 57500 70-25 Estoc,RoyalCouncillor,FlyingGene 12
22Dec85-6Hol 1¼ Ⓣ:503 1:392 2:04 fm 37 116 1½ 1hd 2½ 31¾ Valenzuela P A9 50000 — — Allowance, Vigorous Vigors,Estoc 12
22Dec85—Lost whip 1/8
13Oct85-4Bel 1¼ [T]:503 1:40 2:052gd 12 117 99½ 914 914 912½ Velasquez J7 75000 54-25 Red Brigade, Ski Fleet, Cloutier 9
Jan 17 SA 5f ft 1:041 h Dec 18 SA 7f ft 1:284 h Dec 9 SA 6f ft 1:162 h

Gallant Minded — B. g. 7, by Gallant Romeo—Broadside, by Stage Door Johnny
VERGARA O 119 — Br.—Greentree Stud (Ky) — 1987 2 0 0 0 $400
Own.—Limelight Stables — Tr.—Barrera Albert S $10,000 — 1986 15 1 1 1 $16,300
Lifetime 56 9 4 4 $158,390 — Turf 10 0 0 1 $9,465

11Jan87-2SA 1 1/16 :47 1:121 1:451ft 19 115 810 910 89½ 611 Vergara O2 14000 64-21 Julie'sMrk,Slugfest,LyphrdChimes 11
1Jan87-9SA 1 1/16 :471 1:12 1:443ft 27 115 78 56 66 58½ Vergara O3 14000 69-19 RoosvltRod,ForgotThRng,Espontn 10
1Jan87—Wide into stretch
7Dec86-4Hol 1⅛ :474 1:132 1:531gd 8¾ 116 76 33 1hd 12 Vergara O8 10000 71-18 GllntMinded,FelthorpMrinr,Crimuri 8
26Nov86-3Hol 1 :454 1:112 1:373ft 48 116 66¾ 53¾ 43 43¾ Vergara O2 12500 71-20 Oh Dad, Digga Dee, Hearts 'NRoses 9
26Nov86—Bumped start; wide into stretch
9Nov86-4Hol 1 :451 1:104 1:373ft 16 116 910 99¾ 98¾ 810 McCauley W H8 10000 65-16 Bob'sIntnt,RunningDbonir,Crimuri 11
9Nov86—Wide in stretch
26Oct86-2SA 1 1/16 :453 1:102 1:434ft 6¾ 116 820 916 615 68½ Estrada J Jr10 12500 74-16 Jam Shot, Son Of Raja,AmorousII 12
12Oct86-1SA 6½f :22 :452 1:174ft 97 117 128¾ 129½ 109½ 65¾ Estrada J Jr10 16000 75-21 Unagloshi,Menswear,StrOfAmeric 12
16Jly86-9Hol 1⅛ :47 1:12 1:51 ft 5¼ 116 46½ 57 67½ 610¼ Patterson A4 c16000 72-15 Booster, Travet, March Speed 7
11Jun86-9Hol 1⅛ :464 1:111 1:504ft 3 116 33 32½ 43½ 45¾ Patterson A1 16000 77-16 Certain Treat, ‡Sirtaki, Eterno 8
11Jun86—Placed third through disqualification; Impeded at 3/16
17May86-4Hol 1⅛ :47 1:11 1:494ft *3½ 116 35 35 46 46½ Soto S B2 25000 82-14 Neutral Player,WhidbeyTea,SirStar 8
Jan 7 SA 4f sy :521 h (d) Dec 27 SA 5f ft 1:014 h Dec 4 Hol 5f ft 1:024 h Nov 23 Hol 5f ft 1:011 h

Boondoggler B. h. 5, by Nantequos—Nashville Ollie, by Nashville
Br.—White Rose Ranch (Cal) 1987 1 0 0 0
BAZAN J **115** Tr.—Martinez Rafael A $10,000 1986 8 1 1 1 $4,695
Own.—Hernandez & Taylor Lifetime 13 1 1 2 $8,620
2Jan87-1SA 6½f :221 :451 1:174ft 67 116 1111 1113 711 910½ Bazan J11 10000 70-22 GallantChairman,OhDd,WithSpirit 12
21Dec86-3Hol 1 1/16 :464 1:12 1:45 ft 74 116 98¾ 69 511 416 Bazan J4 10000 68-15 Jam Shot, In Natural Form,Booster 9
21Dec86—Rough start
7Dec86-4Hol 1⅛ :474 1:132 1:531gd 48 116 810 89½ 67½ 611¾ Sibille R4 10000 59-18 GllntMinded,FelthorpMrinr,Crimuri 8
7Dec86—Wide final 3/8
30Nov86-2Hol 7f :222 :454 1:253ft 27 119 98½ 85 84¾ 96½ Meza R Q12 10000 69-16 Gulfstremer,PinepepleJck,UpThPol 12
30Nov86—Wide
19Nov86-4Hol 7f :231 :463 1:244ft 6¾ 119 4¾ 42 33½ 49½ Douglas R R1 10000 71-21 LndsrII,AncintBlu,PickwickLnding 6
2Nov86-2AC 6f :221 :443 1:09 ft 9½ 120 67 55 53 4½ Mares A M5 Aw4500 93-12 Prieta's Beau, SilverTicket,Quantus 6
26Oct86-8AC 6f :231 :454 1:104ft 9-5 120 78 74½ 63½ 1nk Mares A M4 M10000 85-15 Boondoggler, Justinian, Quiso 8
18Oct86-4AC 6f :222 :442 1:102ft 8-5 1137 64½ 66¾ 55 33½ Rodriguez R G4 AlwM 83-13 Sobreslint,ElGtoPscdo,Boondogglr 8
5Oct86-8AC 6f :223 :444 1:092ft 5½ 1147 64½ 55 35 24 Rodriguez R G8 AlwM 88-17 SilverTicket,Boondoggler,PrNone 12
2Nov85-10SA 6f :22 :45 1:094ft 19 118 31½ 33 34 36¾ Castanon A L4 Mdn 82-13 Genrliztion,CoolPhilbrt,Boondogglr 7
Jan 12 Hol 5f ft 1:012 h Dec 16 Hol 5f ft 1:022 h

Visible Asset B. g. 5, by Majestic Light—Premised Woman, by Premised Land
Br.—Gentry T (Ky) 1987 1 0 0 0
BLACK C A **115** Tr.—Mulhall Richard W $10,000 1986 12 3 0 1 $20,235
Own.—Rancho Rio Hondo Lifetime 23 3 0 3 $24,855
1Jan87-9SA 1 1/16 :471 1:12 1:443ft 27 116 42 1011 1014 1020¾ Black C A4 16000 57-19 RoosvltRod,ForgotThRng,Espontn 10
16Oct86-1SA 1 :461 1:113 1:381ft 9¾ 1115 12½ 12 13½ 14½ Black C A2 10000 77-19 VisibleAsset,BombyBrtndr,BstLdr 10
8Oct86-1SA 1 1/16 :461 1:114 1:443ft 5 1115 2½ 1hd 32½ 58 Black C A1 10000 70-20 I'll Smoke, Oh Dad, Hachi 12
22Sep86-13Pom 1 1/16 :461 1:112 1:443ft *9-5 1175 32½ 21½ 23 31½ Black C A7 8500 87-19 ScheerBob,Orn'sBllrd,VisibleAsset 10
13Sep86-9Pom 1 1/16 :462 1:112 1:443ft 4 1105 2hd 1hd 11 12¾ Black C A6 8500 88-10 VisblAsst,Swpround,ClsscEndvour 10
21Aug86-9Dmr 1⅛ :46 1:102 1:503ft 46 116 12 2hd 31 65½ Kaenel J L1 10000 71-17 TheWaliOfSwt,WhidbeyTe,SonOfRj 9
28Jly86-9Dmr 1 1/16 :452 1:112 1:441ft 22 1115 1hd 3½ 912 1013 Black C A5 10000 66-16 Police Pursuit, Le Carluret, Hachi 12
11Jly86-9LA 1 1/16 :453 1:104 1:432ft 29 1115 43 53¾ 610 616½ Black C A2 Aw15000 75-14 Arcadius, Dubai Tornado, Fairfax 7
18Jun86-7Hol 7f :222 :454 1:234ft 10 116 11 2½ 89½ 810¾ Kaenel J L9 16000 74-15 Parlapiano,ColdNose,SirEdgarAllan 9
11Jun86-9Hol 1⅛ :464 1:111 1:504ft 15 1115 1½ 21 56½ 68 Black C A4 16000 75-16 Certain Treat,‡Sirtaki, Eterno 8
Jan 16 SA 3f ft :35 h Jan 11 SA 4f ft :48 h Dec 29 SA 4f ft :474 h Dec 24 SA 6f ft 1:132 h

Son Of Raja Ch. g. 7, by Raja Baba—Couronne de Fer, by Iron Ruler
Br.—Whitney T P (Ky) 1987 2 0 0 0 $1,600
VALENZUELA P A **117** Tr.—Palma Hector O $10,000 1986 18 3 3 3 $44,125
Own.—Abrams S A Lifetime 70 4 10 9 $57,942 Turf 48 1 7 6 $18,867
11Jan87-2SA 1 1/16 :47 1:121 1:451ft 7½ 1095 31 1hd 22 59 Patton D B10 14000 66-21 Julie'sMrk,Slugfest,LyphrdChimes 11
1Jan87-9SA 1 1/16 :471 1:12 1:443ft 5½ 1115 65½ 67 54½ 48½ Patton D B5 16000 69-19 RoosvltRod,ForgotThRng,Espontn 10
20Dec86-3Hol 1 :453 1:102 1:364ft *2½ 1115 11½ 11½ 12 15½ † Patton D B1 12500 79-15 Son Of Raja, Melchip, Parlapiano 7
20Dec86—Disqualified from purse money; Lugged out drive
5Dec86-7Hol 1 :45 1:102 1:363ft 6 1095 77 52¼ 1½ 2¾ Patton D B6 10500 79-17 Hachi, Son Of Raja,ClassicQuickie 12
5Dec86—Broke against bit
22Nov86-3Hol 1⅛ :47 1:12 1:511ft 2½ 1115 1½ 11 13 13 Patton D B2 10000 81-13 SonOfRaj,Stemed,Lighthevyholme 5
22Nov86—Lugged out stretch
15Nov86-2Hol 1⅛ :47 1:12 1:51 ft *2½ 119 63½ 53 46 49¾ Soto S B9 10000 72-14 Steamed,Antigua,BombayBrtender 9
15Nov86—Wide into drive
26Oct86-2SA 1 1/16 :453 1:102 1:434ft 17 119 612 49 36½ 2¾ Soto S B8 12500 81-16 Jam Shot, Son Of Raja,AmorousII 12
17Oct86-9SA 1 1/16 :47 1:122 1:453ft 7 115 64½ 41¾ 31½ 43¾ Soto S B4 14000 69-21 Espontneo,RinShelter,JupiterTogee 9
10Oct86-9SA 1⅛ :463 1:12 1:514ft 7½ 1135 43½ 1hd 1hd 32¾ Black C A7 12500 67-24 PassPssPssed,RinShelter,SonOfRj 11
26Sep86-10Pom 1 1/16 :48 1:141 1:473sl 3½ 1145 63½ 21½ 23 39½ Black C A3 12500 63-29 InNaturlForm,UpThePole,SonOfRj 10
Dec 28 SA 4f ft :501 h Dec 14 Hol 4f ft :494 h Dec 1 Hol 4f ft :484 h

Diabolo Royale
CASTANON A L **114**
Own.—Garelick Stables

B. g. 4, by Diabolo—Cookie Puddin, by Our Native
Br.—Udouj Mr–Mrs H J (Ark)
Tr.—Kenney Martin **$10,000**
Lifetime 25 3 5 2 $18,447

1987	1	0	0	0
1986	21	3	5	2	$17,487
Turf	2	0	2	0	$2,160

10Jan87-1SA	6f	:222	:461	1:114gd	76	115	96¾	76½	86¾	89¼	Castanon A L4	10000	70-20	ValDeRoi,Dodo'sLand,GllntChirmn	10
13Dec86-5TuP	1 1/16	:47	1:121	1:454ft	5	1095	55½	98¾	913	914¾	Ortiz M V Jr8	8000	54-23	RoyalBargin,ClssicComfrey,Wihru	10
3Dec86-7TuP	1	:461	1:11	1:371ft	3¾	114	84¾	63¼	73¾	73¾	Jones D D2	10000	79-17	Wiharu,‡RidentSpirit,BoldCdence	10
21Nov86-10TuP	a1 1/16 Ⓣ	:474	1:131	1:472fm	6	1075	46	43	21½	2½	Pineda G8	14000	94-05	SolarRiver,DiboloRoyle,Snsotomy	10
19Oct86-8TuP	1	:463	1:11	1:374ft	2¾	113	41	54	66½	88¾	Jones D D5	10000	71-19	Jerell'sGuy,AgitatedLad,KnightSil	10
1Oct86-9TuP	1 Ⓣ	:474	1:121	1:382fm	5	115	45½	3½	2hd	21	Jones D D2	16000	89-10	NativeFella,DiboloRoyle,SierrGold	12
30Aug86-10Cby	1	:464	1:111	1:382ft	5¾	1105	57½	510	510	412½	Pineda G R6	20000	76-08	SocillyRotten,CowboyBill,Jinkinson	6
17Aug86-6Cby	1	:464	1:12	1:391ft	*2-3	115	612	65½	45½	34¼	Melancon L2	c16000	81-14	SocillyRotten,Jinkinson,DiboloRoyl	8
8Aug86-6Cby	1	:472	1:121	1:394ft	*2	111	56½	33½	1hd	15	Melancon L J3	12500	82-16	DiboloRoyle,Kmloops,SmoothSport	8
31Jly86-9Cby	1 1/16	:481	1:131	1:464ft	6¾	121	73¾	51¾	21½	12	Melancon L J1	10000	77-17	DblRyl,StrctlyFrnch,McGnty'sRvng	9

Jan 19 SA 3f ft :372 h

***Booster**
PEDROZA M A **115**
Own.—Hillcrest Stable

Dk. b. or br. g. 8, by Lecris—Berdoada, by Buru
Br.—Haras Sideral (Brzl)
Tr.—Fanning Jerry **$10,000**
Lifetime 68 10 5 7 $73,026

1986	22	2	2	4	$30,825
1985	19	1	3	0	$24,800
Turf	14	3	0	2	$6,070

21Dec86-3Hol	1 1/16	:464	1:12	1:45 ft	7¾	116	67	47	39½	312	Valenzuela P A7	10000	72-15	Jam Shot, In Natural Form,Booster	9
7Dec86-4Hol	1⅛	:474	1:132	1:531gd	31	116	43	54	43	46¼	Pedroza M A3	10000	65-18	GllntMinded,FelthorpMrinr,Crimuri	8
7Dec86—Lugged out 1/2, bumped															
15Nov86-2Hol	1⅛	:47	1:12	1:51 ft	17	116	87¾	86½	712	714¾	Baze G5	10000	67-14	Steamed,Antigua,BombayBrtender	9
5Nov86-6Hol	1⅛	:463	1:11	1:49 ft	5	116	45½	47½	515	522¼	Stevens G L1	10000	70-17	Amorous II, Steamed, A Right Idea	9
16Oct86-1SA	1	:461	1:113	1:381ft	10	116	710	912	914	814¼	Lipham T4	10000	63-19	VisibleAsset,BombyBrtndr,BstLdr	10
16Oct86—Wide 7/8 turn															
26Sep86-10Pom	1 1/16	:48	1:141	1:473sl	7¼	116	76¼	88¾	815	716¾	Dominguez RE7	12500	56-29	InNaturlForm,UpThePole,SonOfRj	10
26Sep86—Wide															
6Sep86-9Dmr	1	:452	1:104	1:364ft	11	118	97½	86¾	912	811¼	Garrido O L4	12500	72-12	CptinDouble,He'sNoMistress,Hchi	10
20Aug86-9Dmr	1 1/16	:453	1:102	1:421ft	4	120	97	97	79½	710¾	Stevens G L7	16000	78-11	OlimpicBingo,RedDusty,Hatamoto	10
20Aug86—Wide into stretch															
3Aug86-9Dmr	1 1/16	:46	1:101	1:42 ft	2¾	116	106¾	116¾	118¾	88½	Stevens G L6	20000	81-10	OnEydRomo,FlthorpMrnr,RsvltRd	12
3Aug86—Wide															
16Jly86-9Hol	1⅛	:47	1:12	1:51 ft	3¼	116	33½	21½	13½	14	Stevens G L7	16000	82-15	Booster, Travel, March Speed	7

Jan 17 SA 5f ft 1:032 h **Jan 10 SA 5f gd 1:032 h** **Dec 30 SA 4f ft :501 h** **Nov 30 Hol 4f ft :503 h**

Erin's Glory
ORTEGA L E **115**
Own.—Guest W D

Dk. b. or br. g. 5, by Reflected Glory—Spanish Lark, by My Lark
Br.—Guest B (Cal)
Tr.—West Ted **$10,000**
Lifetime 28 1 5 7 $21,952

1987	2	0	0	0	$600
1986	11	1	2	4	$8,171

10Jan87-1SA	6f	:222	:461	1:114gd	12e	116	41¾	43½	63¾	55½	Baze G7	10000	73-20	ValDeRoi,Dodo'sLand,GllntChirmn	10
4Jan87-1SA	6½f	:214	:45	1:173sy	18	116	74¾	75½	75¼	55½	Baze G9	10000	76-22	PckwckLndng,ComtsFlr,SwftMssg	11
22Nov86-5BM	6f	:23	:461	1:111ft	27	114	97¼	109¾	99¾	1211	Caballero R4	10000	72-24	DustyTrader,DownRange,FireyStr	12
22Nov86—Bumped start															
8Nov86-3BM	6f	:221	:453	1:112ft	7¼	115	69	67½	64	55	Hummel C R3 Ⓢ	10000	77-25	AvengingWrrior,FltWvr,PcosExprss	8
30Oct86-3BM	6f	:224	:462	1:112ft	*4-5	120	63¾	42	1½	11½	Hummel CR5 Ⓢ	M12500	82-24	Erin'sGlory,BrdN'Bruce,Muskogee	12
16Oct86-3BM	6f	:22	:45	1:09 ft	13	120	53¾	21	21½	22½	Hummel C R5	M12500	91-18	GntlmnDon,Erin'sGlory,Wdsworth	12
1Oct86-1BM	1 1/16	:472	1:123	1:454ft	5¾	120	54½	41¾	31½	31	Hummel C R1	M12500	62-20	WindAtHisBck,BigRki,Erin'sGlory	11
19Sep86-1BM	1 1/16	:472	1:13	1:473ft	7¾	120	711	56½	55¾	54¾	Hummel CR2 Ⓢ	M16000	49-28	Charlie Feldman, TropicalHill,Blake	8
19Sep86—Wide into lane															
6Sep86-3Bmf	1 1/16	:483	1:13	1:451ft	4	122	55	69	99¾	1012½	Caballero R2 Ⓢ	M12500	53-18	OlRobbr,Alld'sBloomng,ThGoldGy	11
13Aug86-4Stk	1	:47	1:121	1:372ft	4½	121	611	45½	45½	26	Caballero R2	M16000	85-12	TorngStr,Ern'sGlory,ALttlGodNws	10

Jan 18 SA 4f ft :501 h **Dec 26 SA 5f ft 1:012 h** **Dec 21 SA 5f ft 1:004 h** **Dec 15 SA 3f ft :363 h**

In Natural Form — Ch. h. 6, by L'Natural—In Rare Form, by Run for Nurse
SIBILLE R — 115 — Br.—Hardcastle Linda L (Cal) — 1987 1 0 0 0
Tr.—Landers Dale — $10,000 — 1986 12 1 2 1 $16,505
Own.—Scheidecker Dorothy N — Lifetime 33 3 6 5 $62,467

8Jan87-1SA 1 1/16 :473 1:132 1:48 m 8½ 116 31½ 2hd 22½ 711¾ Sibille R5 10000 49-30 Menswer,Herts'NRoss,LottHistory 12
21Dec86-3Hol 1 1/16 :464 1:12 1:45 ft 5¾ 116 11½ 1½ 21½ 26½ Sibille R1 10000 77-15 Jam Shot, In Natural Form,Booster 9
26Nov86-3Hol 1 :454 1:112 1:373ft 8½ 119 53¼ 42¾ 87 89¼ Olivares F1 12500 66-20 Oh Dad, Digga Dee, Hearts 'NRoses 9
26Nov86—Veered out, bumped start; lugged out stretch
15Nov86-1Hol 6f :223 :46 1:104ft 7 119 31½ 32 34 35½ Olivares F5 [S] 12500 83-14 Polly'sRulr,SolidSpirit,InN'turlForm 6
17Oct86-9SA 1 1/16 :47 1:122 1:453ft 8 117 54 86¾ 915 922¾ Olivares F8 16000 50-21 Espontneo,RinShelter,Jupi'erTogee 9
17Oct86—Wide
26Sep86-10Pom 1 1/16 :48 1:141 1:473sl *9-5 116 12 11½ 13 16¾ Olivares F10 12500 73-29 InNaturlForm,UpThePole,SonOfRj 10
19Sep86-12Pom 1 1/16 :454 1:111 1:46 ft 4½ 116 15 12 11 2nk Olivares F7 12500 81-09 A. J.Ruler,InNaturalForm,RedDusty 9
3Sep86-9Dmr 1 1/16 :462 1:111 1:43 ft 16 116 95¼ 73¼ 44½ 86½ Olivares F5 16000 78-16 Nami, Espontaneo, Susumu 9
3Sep86—Wide 3/8 turn
20Aug86-9Dmr 1 1/16 :453 1:102 1:421ft 20 116 86½ 63½ 54 55¾ Olivares F8 16000 83-11 OlimpicBingo,RedDusty,Hatamoto 10
6Aug86-9Dmr 1 1/16 :452 1:094 1:414ft 12 116 68½ 510 49½ 410¼ Ortega L E7 16000 81-13 AmorousII,ParsonJohn,Never-Rust 7
Dec 10 Hol 4f ft :484 h — Dec 9 Hol 3f ft :38 h

A Right Idea — Dk. b. or br. g. 7, by Bagdad—Fleet Courage, by Fleet Nasrullah
DOUGLAS R R — 115 — Br.—Helmore Farm (Ky) — 1987 2 0 0 0
Tr.—Chavez Tony — $10,000 — 1986 16 0 0 5 $18,000
Own.—Estrada E & J — Lifetime 45 1 5 8 $67,525 — Turf 5 0 0 0 $2,505

8Jan87-1SA 1 1/16 :473 1:132 1:48 m 18 116 75½ 64½ 86¾ 69¾ Douglas R R6 10000 52-30 Menswer,Herts'NRoss,LottHistory 12
8Jan87—Wide into stretch
1Jan87-9SA 1 1/16 :471 1:12 1:443ft 37 114 97 87¾ 87¾ 810¾ Soto S B9 14000 67-19 RoosvltRod,ForgotThRng,Espontn 10
13Dec86-2Hol 7f :22 :451 1:233ft 18 117 108¾ 107¾ 96¼ 66¼ Pedroza M A5 10000 80-09 Cordon, Parlapiano, Ancient Blue 12
30Nov86-2Hol 7f :222 :454 1:253ft 14 117 119¼ 118½ 95¼ 42¾ ValenzuelaPA11 10000 74-16 Gulfstremer,PinepplеJck,UpThPol 12
30Nov86—Wide backside
15Nov86-2Hol 1 1/8 :47 1:12 1:51 ft 7½ 116 53½ 65½ 915 919¾ Valenzuela P A3 10000 62-14 Steamed,Antigua,BombayPrtender 9
15Nov86—Lugged out late
5Nov86-6Hol 1 1/8 :463 1:11 1:49 ft 5¾ 116 22 23 39 317½ Valenzuela P A9 10000 74-17 Amorous II, Steamed, A Right Idea 9
5Nov86—Wide 7/8
23Oct86-9SA 1 1/8 :463 1:113 1:504ft 6 115 12 11½ 32 35¼ Valenzuela P A7 10000 70-20 Hachi, Bob's Intent, A Right Idea 8
23Oct86—Checked early stretch, altered course
10Oct86-9SA 1 1/8 :463 1:12 1:514ft 7½ 116 55½ 76½ 911 911½ Meza R Q8 12500 58-24 PassPssPssed,RinShelter,SonOfRj 11
10Oct86—Wide into stretch
1Oct86-9SA 1 1/16 :461 1:10 1:443ft 21 114 46½ 45½ 45 35¾ Meza R Q5 14000 73-18 PlntyConscous,CptnDoubt,ARghtId 8
28Aug86-9Dmr 1 1/16 :452 1:11 1:45 ft 6 116 919 1012 813 77 Baze R A4 c12500 68-18 Jam Shot,Angleman,PolicePursuit 10
28Aug86—Lugged out badly, bumped 7/8
Dec 18 SA 3f ft :361 h — Nov 26 SA 4f ft :47 h

From these past performances, we can construct our worksheet:

Odds	Horse	PCR	Form	Ab/T
6	Universal Dream	90/ 25 57 – 2/ 80 = 113	NON	13.2 38.0–5/ 50.2
6	Estoc	96/ 58 50 – 16/ 92 = 104	NON	14.3 34.4–5/ 48.2
4	Gallant Minded	96/ 63 50 – 14/ 99 = 97	NON	14.1 33.1–1/ 47.1
55	Boondoggler	88/ 63 45 + 5/113 = 78	NON	(13.3 32.4–1/ 46.1)
9	Visible Asset	93/ 29 56 – 4/ 81 = 115	NON	14.1 34.3 0/ 47.4
2	Son of Raja	96/ 30 29 – 10/ 49 = 196	N0cd	12.1 34.1–1/ 46.1
60	Diabolo Royale	93/ 53 45 – / 98 = 95	NON	(13.3 33.1 0/ 46.4)
19	Booster	94/ 68 58 – 7/119 = 79	Lw	13.2 33.0 0/ 46.4
12	Erin's Glory	105/ 52 60 + 2/114 = 92	NON	(13.0 32.4 0/ 45.4)
9	In Natural Form	90/ 38 49 – 10/ 77 = 117	NNO	14.0 37.0–5/ 50.0
34	A Right Idea	101/ 65 58 – 6/117 = 86	NON	14.2 35.3–5/ 49.0

One horse has a PCR so much higher than any of the others that you take a second look. Son of Raja, the favorite at 2-1, has run strongly both early and late and can be labeled off his line as an "even runner" that still possesses up front speed, as most even runners do. He is dropping in class today to tangle with the cheaper stock, but the fact that he ran only 10 days ago is a good sign. He showed early speed off his last race, which enables us to rate his form as "Nescd," meaning a neutral running line because of his early speed and class drop. Readers of How Will Your Horse Run Today? will recall that horses fitting this exact pattern were always serious contenders if they had other credentials.

But is what is even more impressive is his last race ability time made in a race where he lost enormous ground near the end of the race. Among the rateable times, leaving aside the advisory figures, he has the best last race ability time in the field, a full three ticks ahead of the longshot, Booster. When you look at the advisory times compiled in sprints, you can be sure that none of the lower numbered horses have much of a chance today. Boondoggler at 99-1 off a horrible race and Erin's Glory off a lackluster sprint are not likely to be serious threats in this race.

Is Son of Raja a single selection play? With PCR and last race ability time, he is indeed outstanding. The only blemish of the last race fall back is compensated for with the drop in class and the early speed showing for this even runner. He is indeed an outstanding single selection play because he does possess the big advantage that we must have. You could have even greater confidence in the outcome of this race than you could in the eighth race, where we were reasonably sure one of our two strong selections would be there to win.

There it is, as easy as we thought. There really wasn't very much to challenge this exceptionally strong play, as we rack up a $6.00 win ticket to close out the afternoon.

Before we tally up how well we did, some reflections on the entire card may be most useful, particularly as related to our repeated search for track tendencies, which is even a better term than "bias." We were finding it difficult to put any kind of a defined label on the track throughout the afternoon. Now, let us take the winners in six of the eight races run on the dirt, omitting only the two where there were no measurable internal numbers. In these six races, we will now repeat only the winning horse's totals at the second call and at the finish.

NINTH RACE
Santa Anita
JANUARY 21, 1987

1 $\frac{1}{16}$ MILES. (1.40⅗) CLAIMING. Purse $13,000. 4-year-olds and upward. Weights, 4-year-olds, 121 lbs.; older, 122 lbs. Non-winners of two races at one mile or over since November 3 allowed 3 lbs.; of such a race since December 1, 5 lbs.; since November 3, 7 lbs. Claiming price $10,000. (Claiming and starter races for $8,500 or less not considered.)
Value of race $13,000; value to winner $7,150; second $2,600; third $1,950; fourth $975; fifth $325. Mutuel pool $203,830. Exacta pool $408,572.

Last Raced	Horse	Eqt.A.Wt	PP	St	¼	½	¾	Str	Fin	Jockey	Cl'g Pr	Odds $1
11Jan87 ^{2}SA^{5}	Son Of Raja	b 7 117	6	3	3^{2}	$3^{\frac{1}{2}}$	1^{hd}	$1^{3\frac{1}{2}}$	$1^{2\frac{1}{2}}$	Valenzuela P A	10000	2.00
8Jan87 ^{1}SA^{7}	In Natural Form	b 6 115	10	4	4^{3}	4^{3}	$4^{2\frac{1}{2}}$	2^{2}	2^{1}	Sibille R	10000	9.50
21Dec86 ^{3}Hol^{3}	Booster	b 8 115	8	9	10^{2}	$9^{\frac{1}{2}}$	$5^{\frac{1}{2}}$	$3^{1\frac{1}{2}}$	$3^{2\frac{1}{2}}$	Pedroza M A	10000	19.10
11Jan87 ^{2}SA^{6}	Gallant Minded	b 7 119	3	5	$7^{2\frac{1}{2}}$	$7^{1\frac{1}{2}}$	$7^{\frac{1}{2}}$	4^{1}	$4^{1\frac{3}{4}}$	Cordero A Jr	10000	4.00
2Jan87 ^{1}SA^{9}	Boondoggler	5 115	4	10	8^{1}	$8^{\frac{1}{2}}$	$9^{1\frac{1}{2}}$	$7^{\frac{1}{2}}$	$5^{1\frac{1}{2}}$	Bazan J	10000	55.50
8Jan87 ^{1}SA^{4}	Estoc	b 6 115	2	11	11	$10^{2\frac{1}{2}}$	10^{2}	9^{3}	$6^{\frac{3}{4}}$	Warren R J Jr	10000	6.50
8Jan87 ^{1}SA^{6}	A Right Idea	b 7 115	11	8	$6^{\frac{1}{2}}$	5^{1}	8^{1}	$8^{\frac{1}{2}}$	$7^{1\frac{1}{4}}$	Douglas R R	10000	34.10
10Jan87 ^{1}SA^{5}	Erin's Glory	b 5 115	9	6	5^{hd}	6^{1}	6^{hd}	$6^{1\frac{1}{2}}$	8^{2}	Ortega L E	10000	12.20
8Jan87 ^{1}SA^{9}	Universal Dream	b 4 114	1	1	$2^{1\frac{1}{2}}$	2^{1}	2^{1}	5^{1}	$9^{1\frac{3}{4}}$	Stevens G L	10000	6.00
10Jan87 ^{1}SA^{8}	Diabolo Royale	b 4 114	7	7	$9^{\frac{1}{2}}$	11	11	11	$10^{3\frac{1}{2}}$	Castanon A L	10000	61.30
1Jan87 ^{9}SA^{10}	Visible Asset	b 5 115	5	2	$1^{1\frac{1}{2}}$	$1^{\frac{1}{2}}$	$3^{\frac{1}{2}}$	$10^{1\frac{1}{2}}$	11	Black C A	10000	9.40

OFF AT 4:57. Start good. Won ridden out. Time, :22⅘, :47, 1:12⅘, 1:38⅕, 1:45 Track fast.

$2 Mutuel Prices:

6-SON OF RAJA	6.00	4.20	3.40
10-IN NATURAL FORM		7.40	6.80
8-BOOSTER			7.00

$5 EXACTA 6-10 PAID $133.50.

1SA	Meldrip	29	30
2SA	Exalted Jade	16	19
3SA	Emperdori	50	47
5SA	Doonsport	56	51
8SA	Devil's Bride	6	8
9SA	Son of Raja	30	29

I have rarely seen such consistency of similarity of internal numbers among a whole card of winning horses. Every one of those winners could be called an "even" runner, even though there was considerable early speed in the low numbers when compared to the number of horses total.

The lesson to be learned is that when a track is inconclusive as to tendency, neither biased toward early speed nor closing speed, the even runner may be formidable indeed. You will find this particularly so at distances like seven furlongs and one mile, and even at a mile sixteenth. The horse that shows internal numbers that are relatively equal may be able to show strength early in the race or late in the race.

There is something more than can be added to that, as demonstrated by what happened. Where the even runner has a high PCR as compared to the others, then he is indeed formidable. Among these six winning horses, only one, Emperdori, lacked one of the first three highest PCRs. Three of the six, if we include lightly raced Devil's Bride, had the highest of any in their field, and one other, Meldrip, was second highest.

Please do not believe that I am relying upon one racing card to make a point. What happened on this day at Santa Anita does occur frequently, and that is why this particular card has turned out to be so instructive, although I had no way of knowing that when I decided to choose one unknown day and apply it to three racetracks. I have observed what was revealed here many, many times. I repeat: on days when the track tendency is inconclusive and does not particularly favor either early or late speed, horses who may be called even runners because of the similarity of the second call and finish totals and who are among the highest PCR horses in the race may always be considered strong contenders, as long as they have any reasonable semblance of decent form.

Let's now summarize the play we have set forth in this chapter:

Race	Play	Bet	Result	P/L
1SA	Neutral Player	$ 2	0	− 2
2SA	Buy More	2	0	− 2
	Exalted Jade	2	17.20	+15.20
3SA	Pass	0		0
4SA	Pass	0		0
5SA	Doonsport	2	4.40	+ 2.40
6SA	Exceptional Talent	2	0	− 2
7SA	Steepbank	2	0	− 2
8SA	Footy	2	0	− 2
	Devil's Bride	2	8.60	+ 6.60
9SA	Son of Raja	2	6.00	4.00
	Totals	$ 18	$36.20	+18.20

There were not as many single selection plays as we would like to find, as we turned up with four. Two won and two lost, but there was a profit nevertheless, as there will always be as long as you turn in 50% winners. In seven playable races, our methods showed four winning horses. Only one of them carried a reasonably good sized ticket, but there was still profit all over the place, which is what we seek. We stayed away from exactas here, as none of the possibilities seemed safe enough, although one could make a strong argument in a couple of instances.

Multiple selection play yielded a stronger profit than our low priced single selection plays, as is usually the case when you are able to score.

But it was a most satisfactory and instructive day indeed, as we move up the coast to the San Francisco area to see how we would have fared at Bay Meadows on the same day.

17 The Performance: On To Bay Meadows

For the same Wednesday, January 21, 1987, that we played the card at Aqueduct in New York and Santa Anita in Los Angeles, we moved up the coast to San Francisco to take on the card at Bay Meadows, again from the same edition of the Daily Racing Form. This track is at an approximate one level below the southern California circuit, just as the good eastern tracks in New Jersey and Maryland are a level below the prime New York circuit. There is quality racing at Bay Meadows, however, with reasonably good purses and horses with ability.

The chapter you are about to read is remarkably illustrative of the strength of the methods in this book. Situation after situation arises that requires analyses that come from our internal numbers and the form factors that have been developed. What occurred here is beautifully consistent with what we have set forth. Let's get on with it.

The first race is a lower priced claiming event for fillies at one mile, always a tough proposition for horses in outside post positions because the starting gate is so near to the first turn on a one-mile track. Because most of the measureable runners, as you will see, last ran at 6 furlongs, we will calculate our ability times for that distance. Here is how the seven runners entered looked in their past performances:

1st BayMeadows

1 MILE. (1.33⅗) CLAIMING. Purse $6,800. Fillies. 4-year-olds. Weight, 120 lbs. Non-winners of two races at one mile or over since December 1 allowed 3 lbs.; one such race since then, 6 lbs. Claiming price $6,250. (Maiden, starter and claiming races for $5,000 or less not considered.) (Cal breds preferred.)

Georgia Smith B. f. 4, by Just Right Mike—Secret Amor, by Tom Tulle
SAITO S T 1095 Br.—Straggas R (Cal) 1987 1 0 0 0 $540
Own.—Keefe & Smith Tr.—Buckridge Gloria $6,250 1986 10 1 0 2 $4,370
Lifetime 14 1 0 2 $5,185
7Jan87-2BM 6f :231 :472 1:14 m 12 116 42½ 31½ 43½ 42½ Hummel C R4 Ⓕ 6250 66-35 Ivorette,Jo'sDughter,AlwysElegnt 10
31Dec86-2BM 6f :223 :462 1:131gd 3 115 68½ 77 76 54½ Hummel C R8 Ⓕ 6250 68-32 Exit's Lady, Stan's Belle, Les Rae 10
5Dec86-2BM 6f :222 :453 1:122sl 23 114 75¾ 79 58½ 34½ Aragon V A8 Ⓕ 8000 72-26 Days Bet, Vickarick,GeorgiaSmith 11
24Oct86-9SA 1 1/16 :463 1:124 1:454ft 147 111 53½ 83¾111511122¾ Gomez E A10 Ⓕ 10500 49-20 FrindlyCrowd,BrooksPl,SuprisGift 12
15Oct86-9SA 1 1/16 :463 1:124 1:462ft 100 114 79 107¼ 913 920¼ FernandezAL7 Ⓕ 14000 48-18 Julin'sDrm,Mistingutt,DvlishDzzlr 11
15Oct86—Veered out start
26Sep86-9Pom 6½f :222 :47 1:212sl 45 114 108¾ 915 919 311 FernandezAL8 Ⓕ 10500 62-29 OhMrie,GoldenTwntis,GorgiSmith 10
26Sep86—Bumped break; wide 1st turn
17Sep86-9Pom 6½f :22 :46 1:192ft *8-5 112 43½ 32 45½ 63 Stevens S A3 Ⓕ 8500 80-13 True To You, Pirate's Miss, Fonta 10
17Sep86—Steadied on turn
31Aug86-1Dmr 6f :222 :454 1:103ft 31 115 52½ 55 89½ 715 Castanon AL3 Ⓕ 14000 70-12 JazzyLisa,IndinFlower,OrientlChmp 9
31Aug86—Bumped start; lugged in backstretch
27Jly86-2AC 6f :221 :443 1:103ft 8 114 11 11½ 11½ 1hd Gomez E A10 ⒻMdn 86-12 GeorgiSmith,GrcisEscrow,MorMin 11
6Feb86-4SA 1 :47 1:124 1:391ft 23 117 86½ 77¼ 78¾ 711¾ Sibille R3 ⒻⓈM32000 60-19 Mush, Michcari, Petite Bicker 10
6Feb86—Steadied 1/4
Jan 18 BM 4f ft :482 h Dec 20 BM 5f sy 1:052 h (d) Dec 3 BM 3f ft :363 h Nov 26 BM 6f ft 1:14 h

Chris's Glamor Gr. f. 4, by Top Crowd—Sisters Glamor, by Glamor Kid
HANSEN R D 114 Br.—Wiemken L C (Cal) 1987 2 0 0 0
Own.—Bean Barn-Scannell-Scannell Tr.—Bean Robert A $6,250 1986 11 1 1 1 $13,405
Lifetime 21 3 3 1 $31,430
17Jan87-10BM 1 :463 1:124 1:394ft 9½ 115 35 33 69½ 915½ Hansen R D3 Ⓕ 10000 54 — Mlingring,BitARoni,WndyCtyWhrl 10
2Jan87-9BM 1 1/16 :474 1:131 1:473gd 26 114 811 88 88 67½ Schacht R5 Ⓕ 16000 46-33 La Major, Star Dream, Tante Bleue 9
18Dec86-7BM 6f :224 :46 1:13 m 23 115 12171017 815 811¾ Hansen R D1 Ⓕ 10000 62-41 Days Bet, L'Indian, Long Yardage 12
27Nov86-5BM 6f :223 :454 1:103ft 27 114 95¾ 98½ 95¾ 67½ ♦ Aragon V A12 Ⓕ 12500 79-23 CriMyHrt,ExcutivPosition,Crst'sIc 12
♦27Nov86—Dead heat
13Nov86-7BM 6f :224 :461 1:113ft 11 114 109¾ 88¾ 66 58½ Aragon VA10 Ⓕ c10000 72-24 Nyrc,PlsntlyNuty,ExecutivPosition 12
13Nov86—Ducked in start
2Nov86-2BM 6f :222 :46 1:11 ft 12 114 11131011 79¼ 49 Judice J C4 Ⓕ 12500 75-21 AlphRttMurphy,Ivortt,PlsntlyNuty 11
2Nov86—Broke slowly
16Oct86-1BM 1 :464 1:111 1:37 ft 3½ 114 57 55 42½ 58 Judice J C6 Ⓕ 16000 75-18 Haida Star,Forumstar,SpecialEagle 6
9Oct86-5BM 6f :23 :461 1:11 ft 10 114 1011 84½ 67½ 57 Judice J C10 Ⓕ 16000 77-19 HotCche,IWlkAlone,DoubleDcortd 11
9Oct86—Ducked in start
25Sep86-9BM 1 1/16 :481 1:142 1:493sl *2½ 114 1011 87½ 35 37½ Judice J C5 Ⓕ 16000 36-35 NowNowNcl,DblDcrtd,Chrs'sGlmr 10
12Sep86-10Bmf 6f :221 :453 1:12 ft 9½ 115 119¾1111 84½ 21½ Judice J C8 Ⓕ 16000 77-29 Blke'sDncr,Chris'sGlmor,Forumstr 11
5Sep86-10Bmf 6f :222 :451 1:112ft 7½ 115 66½ 69½ 68½ 56½ Judice J C3 Ⓕ 25000 75-30 MysteryMaid,HollyAnn,LovableFlirt 8
Jan 16 BM 4f ft :54 h Jan 10 BM 5f gd 1:014 h Dec 27 BM 4f gd :473 h Dec 13 BM 4f ft :502 h

Taniwa Ch. f. 4, by First Back—Royal Pixie, by Rideabout
CABALLERO R 114 Br.—Qvale K M (Cal) 1986 9 1 1 0 $2,279
Own.—Qvale K M Tr.—Seeley Pat $6,250 1985 0 M 0 0
Lifetime 9 1 1 0 $2,279
31Dec86-2BM 6f :223 :462 1:131gd 30 114 1018101910181018 Caballero R1 Ⓕ 6250 55-32 Exit's Lady, Stan's Belle, Les Rae 10
13Nov86-7BM 6f :224 :461 1:113ft 144 114 1110121411171017 Caballero R12 Ⓕ 10000 64-24 Nyrc,PlsntlyNuty,ExcutivPosition 12
6Nov86-7BM 1 1/16 :463 1:114 1:45 ft 23 114 69 79 916 925¼ Caballero R9 Ⓕ 12500 41-22 OutOfMind,FlyingPstis,StltownGirl 9
13Oct86-3Fno 1 :454 1:112 1:374ft 2½ 114 34 11½ 13 16 CblleroR10 ⒻⓈM12500 81-13 Taniwa, Boitrillion, SweetChastity 10
6Oct86-3Fno 1 :464 1:134 1:394ft 27 114 85 64 2½ 21 CablleroR4 ⒻⓈM12500 70-17 SumHoney,Taniw,Dimggio'sWorld 10
6Oct86—Broke out, bumped
5Sep86-3Bmf 6f :232 :472 1:131ft 31 117 107½ 97 78½ 77¾ Tohill K S7 ⒻⓈM12500 65-30 Donbelor,MidgetMessenger,LtFoli 12
5Sep86—Bumped start
20Aug86-8Sac 6f :224 :461 1:122ft 83 117 85½ 911 84¾ 51¾ Tohill K S8 ⒻM12500 75-16 SprklingLight,LottPlot,SilverLind 10
11Jly86-6SR 1 1/16 :46 1:114 1:442ft 38 116 35½ 47 717 823½ Tohill K S8 ⒻM16000 58-09 Cutenss,NtivDwn,WindyCityWhirl 10
17Jly86-4Sol 6f :221 :453 1:114ft 34 1115 10101011 912 813½ Barton J9 ⒻⓈM12500 70-14 HoneyHollow,Wnd'sGift,Propriety 10
Jan 17 BM 7f ft 1:323 h ●Jan 10 BM 7f gd 1:32 h Dec 29 Pla 4f ft :49 h Dec 18 Pln 6f ft 1:161 h

Gala Prevue *
WHITE T C 114
Own.—Bellasis & Tschanz
Ch. f. 4, by No Prevue—Impetuosa, by Juanro
Br.—Boyens Irene E (Cal) 1987 2 0 0 0
Tr.—Bellasis Richard L $6,250 1986 17 0 5 2 $13,529
Lifetime 26 1 6 3 $22,577

8Jan87-2BM $1\frac{1}{16}$:48 1:13^{4} 1:48^{2}sl 22 114 5^{7} 7^{7½} 6^{9} 7^{10¾} Yamamoto TJ^{2} Ⓕ 8000 39-33 BitARoni,Mlingring,TllMTomorrow 8
1Jan87-5BM 6f :22^{3} :46^{4} 1:13 gd 24 114 12^{14}12^{15}11^{13} 8^{8} Tohill K S^{3} Ⓕ[S] 8000 66-30 Creista's Ice, Misty Silk,Vickarick 12
11Dec86-5BM $1\frac{1}{16}$:46^{4} 1:12^{1} 1:45^{2}ft 60 114 10^{10}10^{9¼}10^{12}10^{10½} Yamamoto TJ^{5} Ⓕ 6250 54-24 NativeDawn,HaceComida,HelpGirl 12
27Nov86-4BM $1\frac{1}{16}$:46^{2} 1:12 1:44^{4}ft 17 114 9^{12}10^{8½} 9^{11} 7^{12½} YammotoTJ^{2} Ⓕ[S] 8000 55-23 FirstFiveStr,Mlingering,NtiveDwn 11
6Nov86-7BM $1\frac{1}{16}$:46^{3} 1:11^{4} 1:45 ft 21 114 9^{18} 9^{12} 7^{7½} 6^{11½} Hamilton M^{4} Ⓕ 12500 55-22 OutOfMind,FlyingPstis,StltownGirl 9
6Nov86—Ducked in start
24Oct86-2BM 6f :22^{3} :46^{3} 1:12^{4}ft *2¾ 114 12^{11}10^{8} 6^{4½} 4^{2¾} ChapmanTM^{6} Ⓕ c8000 72-25 Prima'sBest,Moneyjy,PointOfFith 12
16Oct86-9BM $1\frac{1}{16}$:47^{2} 1:12^{1} 1:43^{4}ft 4¼ 114 5^{2¾} 4^{2½} 4^{4} 4^{7} ChapmnTM^{7} Ⓕ[S] 8000 66-18 Michl'sSpcil,FirstFivStr,OutOfMind 8
25Sep86-7BM 6f :23 :47^{4} 1:15^{1}sl 5 114 8^{6¼} 5^{5} 3^{4½} 2^{1} Chapman T M^{3} Ⓕ 8000 62-35 BoisHon,GalaPrevue,EveningWalk 11
12Sep86-9Bmf 6f :22^{1} :44^{4} 1:11^{3}ft 6¼ 113 10^{12}10^{11} 6^{11} 6^{5¼} Chapman T M^{5} Ⓕ 8000 76-29 Windian, Stan's Belle, Atacada 10
12Sep86—Broke slowly
16Jly86-10Sol 1 :47^{1} 1:12^{1} 1:39^{3}ft 3¼ 114 7^{12} 7^{7½} 4^{1¼} 2^{½} Chapman T M^{7} Ⓕ 8000 75-13 Rajwa, Gala Prevue, Iluvembee 10
Jan 20 GG 3f ft :36^{1} h Dec 29 GG 4f hy :52^{4} h Dec 10 GG 3f ft :36^{1} h ●Nov 21 GG 6f ft 1:14^{1} h

Mean Lizzie
JUDICE J C 114
Own.—Owens G
Ch. f. 4, by Maheras—Note of Pleasure, by Second Pleasure
Br.—Owens & McLuen (Wash) 1987 1 0 0 0 $540
Tr.—Roberts Tom $6,250 1986 11 2 2 2 $4,444
Lifetime 12 2 2 2 $4,984

15Jan87-5BM 6f :23 :47 1:13 ft 16 114 10^{12} 9^{11} 7^{9½} 4^{2} Judice J C^{2} Ⓕ 6250 72-30 Vickarick,TripleChange,She'sAHit 12
15Jan87—Broke slowly
11Dec86-5BM $1\frac{1}{16}$:46^{4} 1:12^{1} 1:45^{2}ft 7¼ 115 6^{6½} 4^{2½} 3^{3} 4^{4½} ♦ Baze R A^{11} Ⓕ 6250 60-24 NativeDawn,HaceComida,HelpGirl 12
♦11Dec86—Dead heat
15Nov86-8YM 6f :22^{2} :45^{2} 1:10^{3}ft 5 120 6^{11} 6^{5} 4^{5½} 3^{5} MtschbcrT^{1} ⒻAw1000 84-14 RoanyRainy,LadyLuKay,MeanLizzie 9
1Nov86-2Lga $1\frac{1}{16}$:47^{4} 1:13^{1} 1:46^{2}m 11 118 8^{10} 7^{7¾} 4^{3½} 2^{3} Gonsalves F A^{2} Ⓕ 8000 64-30 Bit ARonie,MeanLizzie,TableAnne 10
25Oct86-3Lga $1\frac{1}{16}$:49 1:14^{3} 1:48 ft 45 113 11^{16}10^{6} 4^{2½} 4^{1¾} Johnson B G^{7} Ⓕ 10000 57-41 DuchssOfRoni,FghtnLI,AlwysElgnt 11
19Oct86-5Pla 6f :22^{2} :46^{1} 1:11^{4}ft *9-5 120 8^{7¾} 8^{5¾} 6^{6} 6^{7¼} Thibert T^{4} Ⓕ[S] 5000 83-13 PulsCutie,JnuryJnnifr,Dsh'sPrincss 8
8Oct86-7Pla 1 :48^{1} 1:12^{4} 1:38 ft 15 120 4^{3} 4^{8} 3^{9½} 2^{12} Thibert T^{9} Ⓕ 5000 75-14 LilliansDebut,MenLizzie,BerzoMiss 9
1Oct86-5Pla 6f :23^{3} :48^{3} 1:16^{1}m 5½ 119 7^{8½} 8^{7¾} 4^{3½} 4^{3¼} Freeman W^{4} Ⓕ[S] 4000 65-35 Ebony Ice, Starting Line, AlaVelle 10
12Sep86-7Pla 1 :48 1:13^{1} 1:39^{3}ft 2¾ 120 6^{6} 6^{5} 5^{6} 5^{6½} Thibert T^{7} Ⓕ 4000 72-16 Jillioniress,BerzoMiss,GllntActress 10
5Sep86-6Pla 6f :22^{2} :46^{4} 1:12^{2}ft *6-5 120 4^{5} 3^{1½} 2^{hd} 1^{3} Thibert T^{4} Ⓕ 4000 87-17 Mean Lizzie, Miss Pupcup, StarEnu 7
Jan 10 BM 5f gd 1:03^{4} h Jan 4 BM 4f sy :52^{3} h (d) Dec 30 GG 3f hy :38^{4} h Dec 20 GG 3f m :39^{3} h

Vitascope
SANCHEZ K W 109^{5}
Own.—Brock R J
B. f. 4, by Tell—Viability, by Envoy
Br.—Dryer D (Cal) 1987 1 0 0 0 $150
Tr.—Roberts Tom $6,250 1986 8 2 1 0 $9,398
Lifetime 13 2 1 0 $11,798

15Jan87-5BM 6f :23 :47 1:13 ft *2 116 5^{3½} 4^{3} 4^{5} 5^{2½} Hansen R D^{7} Ⓕ 6250 71-30 Vickarick,TripleChange,She'sAHit 12
29Dec86-6BM 6f :22 :45^{1} 1:10^{2}ft 13 115 3^{3½} 2^{4} 7^{9½} 6^{11} Hansen R D^{4} Ⓕ 10000 76-15 DysBet,ExcutivPosition,MystryMid 8
29Dec86—Bumped, steadied start
8May86-2GG 6f :22 :45^{3} 1:12^{3}ft 5¾ 115 8^{11} 9^{14} 9^{15} 7^{11½} Hummel C R^{8} Ⓕ 16000 64-22 MysteryMaid,MoveAwy,Ms.LdyFox 9
2May86-2GG 6f :22 :45 1:11^{3}ft 7½ 115 5^{5¼} 5^{2¾} 2^{hd} 1^{2} HummelCR^{5} Ⓕ[S] 12500 81-15 Vitscop,OnGoodAnswr,GoldN'Snow 7
11Apr86-3GG 6f :22^{3} :46 1:11^{4}ft 3¾ 117 1^{hd} 1^{hd} 1^{1½} 1^{3} HmmlCR^{6} Ⓕ[S]M12500 80-20 Vitascope, Light As Day, Les Rae 12
12Mar86-2GG 6f :22^{3} :46^{2} 1:12^{3}m 5 117 7^{7} 7^{8½} 6^{7¼} 6^{7½} HmmlCR^{11} Ⓕ[S]M16000 68-21 FrndlyBrtchs,LghtAsDy,BBc'sLdy 12
28Feb86-3GG 6f :22^{3} :46^{2} 1:12^{2}ft 2 117 4^{2½} 5^{2} 3^{4½} 2^{1½} HmmlCR^{4} Ⓕ[S]M12500 75-22 CretivFun,Vitscop,DistntThoughts 12
28Feb86—Steadied 1/4
5Feb86-3SA 6f :21^{4} :45^{4} 1:12^{1}gd 11 113^{5} 3^{1½} 3^{2} 3^{3} 5^{7} Alvarez A^{6} ⒻM32000 70-19 DncHllHssy,PrvtPtty,DstntCmmnd 12
5Feb86—Lugged in backstretch
2Jan86-4SA $1\frac{1}{16}$:46^{3} 1:11^{4} 1:45 ft 8¼ 115 1^{hd} 2^{2½} 5^{12} 8^{22½} Ortega L E^{2} ⒻM35000 53-16 Velveteen, La Puerta, Rajwa 11
11Dec85-3Hol 6f :22^{2} :46^{3} 1:13 gd 7¼ 118 2^{hd} 2^{1} 3^{4½} 4^{7¼} OrtegaLE^{4} Ⓕ[S]M32000 72-19 Oak Portal,Pastreil,MusicalTheme 12
●Jan 10 BM 3f gd :35 h Jan 5 BM 4f m :49^{3} h Dec 7 BM 4f sl :49^{4} h ●Dec 1 GG 5f ft 1:01^{2} h

A Chocolateholic

YAMAMOTO T J
Own.—Bach & Widroe

114

Dk. b. or br. f. 4, by Walker's—Chocolate Ripple, by Windy Sands
Br.—Bach & Widroe (Cal)
Tr.—Lewis Richard J

					1986	10	0	0	1	$2,520
			$6,250		1985	8	1	1	0	$6,854
			Lifetime	18	1	1	1	$9,374

31Dec86-2BM	6f :22³ :46² 1:13¹gd	31 114	8¹⁴ 9¹⁵ 9¹³ 9¹³	Yamamoto TJ⁷ ⓑ 6250	60-32 Exit's Lady, Stan's Belle, Les Rae 10
2Jly86-6Pln	17⁰:47 1:11³ 1:43 ft	10 1095	7¹² 7¹⁵ 7¹⁷ 7¹⁹	YamamotoTJ² ⓑ 12500	60-18 Fly So Far,KuteZoot,LittleMissLori 7
2Jly86—Bumped 7 1/2					
19Jun86-2GG	1¹⁄₁₆:47 1:11³ 1:44³ft	16 114	8⁶½ 8⁹½ 7⁶½ 5⁵	Segundo MA⁷ ⓑ 10000	75-15 Sarah Aaron, Rajwa, Lifters Last 9
5Jun86-2GG	1¹⁄₁₆:46¹ 1:10⁴ 1:45¹ft	37 114	7⁷½ 8⁹½ 7⁶½ 4³½	Segundo MA¹ ⓑ 10000	73-14 Lady Of Destiny,Rajwa,SarahAaron 9
24Apr86-7GG	1¹⁄₁₆:46⁴ 1:12⁴ 1:45 ft	72 114	10¹¹10⁸½ 8⁹ 8⁸	Segundo MA⁷ ⓑ 12500	70-16 Lemana, Kaviot'sFlight,MissDolby 11
1Apr86-1GG	1¹⁄₁₆:48³ 1:13⁴ 1:47¹ft	8½ 114	6⁶ 6⁷½ 7¹⁴ 7¹⁹½	Diaz A L² ⓑ 10000	47-23 SrhAron,SinfullSiest,Jenny'sPetron 7
19Mar86-1GG	1¹⁄₁₆:48 1:13⁴ 1:47¹ft	11 114	7⁸½ 5⁴½ 4⁴ 3⁵½	Diaz A L⁵ ⓑ 10000	61-21 Chrgin,JudcousDmon,AChocolthok 7
19Mar86—Broke in a tangle					
6Feb86-9GG	1 :47² 1:12² 1:38³ft	12 1095	7¹⁰ 7⁹½ 7¹¹ 5¹⁴	YamamotoTJ⁴ ⓑ 16000	61-22 Selected Princess,Manale,Chargina 7
6Feb86—Broke in air					
23Jan86-1BM	1¹⁄₁₆:48³ 1:13² 1:45³ft	11 1105	3¹ 7⁵½ 7⁹½ 6¹¹½	YamamotoTJ⁴ ⓑ 16000	52-24 BrennMorn,NovelSprit,ClssicQulity 8
6Jan86-6BM	1 :49¹ 1:15³ 1:44⁴sl	12 1095	8⁷½ 7¹¹ 6¹² 6¹⁶½	Shaw K⁴ ⓑ 25000	27-42 Chris'sGlamor,GlPrevue,BitARonie 8
Jan 14 3M 3f ft :41² h	Dec 28 BM 4f ft :49 h	Dec 21 BM 4f m :51² h	Dec 11 BM 6f ft 1:14³ h		

We are able to compile the following worksheet:

Odds	Horse	PCR					Form	Ab/T
9-2	Georgia Smith	104/ 60 56	–	10/106	=	98	NNN	47.4 26.4 – 8/ 73.0
19	A Chocolateholic	83/ 74 60	–	18/116	=	72	NON	x
5	Chris's Glamor	112/ 86 58	–	20/124	=	90	+ON	x
24	Taniwa	93/ 68 60	–	4/124	=	75	NON	x
24	Gala Preview	103/ 84 56	–	9/131	=	75	NON	49.2 26.0 – 7/ 74.0
6-5	Mean Lizzie	98/ 65 35	+	5/105	=	93	+Og	49.1 25.0 – 5/ 73.1
2	Vitascope	107/ 40 45	–	9/ 76	=	141	NON	47.3 26.0 – 5/ 72.3

This group of fillies reveals only one with a good PCR, Vitascope, the second favorite at 2-1, with all the others far behind. Two of the extremely high odds horses in this small field, Taniwa and Gala Preview, have last race running lines so bad that they can be dismissed out of hand. A Chocolateholic is almost as weak, with a PCR that is so low that the internal numbers alone tell us the graphic words, "no chance." Look at them for a moment. Against a field of 83, this horse scores a 74 at the second call, which means that in every race shown, she was always relatively near the end of the pack. If it were not for the minus 18 for class, this horse would show a PCR that would approach a record low. In addition, she has a last race running line that is likewise pathetic, off which it nearly takes a miracle for a horse to win in any field where there is any other contender that is alive and well. Yet people bet enough on this filly to make her odds to win only 19-1, which, although still very high, do require more than a handful of dollars. These are distorted odds: 500-1 would be more like it, and I wouldn't waste anything even at that.

Little effort is required to find yet another horse that has relatively little chance to win. Chris's Glamor, off a substantial drop in class, has run very badly in recent races, with her last performance being extremely woeful. We did not compute a last race ability time because there was no variant to factor in, relegating us to bad form to discard this horse.

Now, we are quickly down to three horses. When you have 4/7ths of a field that has absolutely no chance whatever, the others possess a big advantage already. We can now study the remaining horses to see if one or more rises above the others sufficient to allow us to bet in this very first unknown race of the day. This situation also lends itself to a multiple selection play of enormous security, as long as one of the three remaining horses falls below the other two, and if the odds are not prohibitive.

We can begin our analysis with Vitascope, the high PCR horse, which has a number that in itself is a distinct advantage over the others. That alone makes it almost imperative that we include her in if we play the race. She also has the best last race ability time, but it is not enough better than that of Georgia Smith, whose effort was made in the mud, to warrant a single selection play. It is her form defect, reinforced by the fact that one horse passed her in the stretch, that requires us to eliminate her as a single selection play and weakens our over all confidence in her.

Another uncertainty is one that we have said very little about to this point. A horse in an outside post position in a race that starts literally at the beginning of a turn is at a distinct disadvantage unless that horse has exceptional early speed sufficient to break out of the gate, cut over in front of the others without causing interference, and not be forced wide at the turn. A slow starting closing horse may also compensate by drifting quickly inward to the rail as his rivals get out ahead of him. But a horse that is neither early nor late, as is Vitascope, based upon our good internal numbers, is likely to encounter problems at the very outset of the race.

With these reservations, we next look at the strong 6-5 favorite, Mean Lizzie, coming back in six days off an impressive stretch gain and a comment, "Broke slowly." But look at those internal numbers: 65 against 35. This filly doesn't do anything much but close. Unless the track is bogged down today enough to kill off anything out in front, Mean Lizzie's 6-5 odds appear to be much lower than is realistic. We may also note here that when a substantial part of the field shows such bad form you will see odds on other horses forced down much lower than you would otherwise expect.

Where does that leave us? The best last race form clearly belongs to Georgia Smith, at 9-2, who gets an N rating with her reasonably close run along with a fall-back-gain pattern that cannot ever be ignored. In today's race, she has the more favorable inside post position flanked by starters in the 2-hole and 3-hole that have no early speed and thus are not likely to box her in.

This brings us back to another comment on post position, which I believe ordinarily is vastly overrated as an influence on the outcome of races, including the Kentucky Derby. I repeat: post position is indeed a factor in at least two kinds of situations: (1) where a race starts so near a turn that outside horses are penalized because they are so likely to be forced wide at the beginning, and (2) where there is a strong position bias at a track, such as the rail being very fast or very slow, which can truly occur. In each instance, you are compelled to do some "post position handicapping," and when you do, the internal numbers in your PCR provide an excellent guide. This race illustrates that point.

What about early speed? Where is it? Not much at all, we may conclude, with Vitascope the only horse in the race that even has a lower second call number, and even that is not by much, not enough to be called early speed. But Georgia Smith can be rated as an even runner, with the 60 over the 56 with a field total of 104 bringing her numbers very close together. Even runners are always a threat on neutral tracks, as we saw in our last chapter at Santa Anita, and where there is an absence of strong early speed.

It is now decision time. If we are to play, we must discard one of the three contenders in the race. Vitascope must be retained because of her PCR and last race ability time, even with her other detriments. That reduces our choice to either Georgia Smith or Mean Lizzie. There are two key considerations here that help us establish the advantage that we must have in any situation. The first is last race form, where Georgia Smith rates well above Mean Lizzie. The second, and perhaps even more influential, is the imbalance of the internal numbers—the 65 over 35 for Mean Lizzie stamps her as too much of a closer against a more even runner on the inside. We therefore are able to throw out Mean Lizzie with her 6-5 odds that allow us to take home a little more on the other two.

The result did not make us unhappy at all.

FIRST RACE
BayMeadows
JANUARY 21, 1987

1 MILE. (1.33⅗) CLAIMING. Purse $6,000. Fillies. 4-year-olds. Weight, 120 lbs. Non-winners of two races at one mile or over since December 1 allowed 3 lbs.; one such race since then, 6 lbs. Claiming price $6,250. (Maiden, starter and claiming races for $5,000 or less not considered.) (Cal breds preferred.) 72nd DAY. WEATHER CLEAR. TEMPERATURE 64 DEGREES.

Value of race $6,000; value to winner $3,300; second $1,170; third $840; fourth $540; fifth $150. Mutuel pool $62,809.

Last Raced	Horse	Eqt.	A.Wt	PP	St	¼	½	¾	Str	Fin	Jockey	Cl'g Pr	Odds $1
7Jan87 ^{2}BM^4	Georgia Smith		4 114	1	4	1^{hd}	2^5	2^5	1^4	1^1	Doocy T T	6250	4.90
17Jan87 ^{10}BM^9	Chris's Glamor	b	4 116	3	7	7	7	6^3	3^2	2^5	Hansen R D	6250	5.20
15Jan87 ^{5}BM^5	Vitascope	b	4 109	7	3	2^4	$1^{\frac{1}{2}}$	1^{hd}	2^2	3^2	Sanchez K W^5	6250	2.30
31Dec86 ^{2}BM^9	A Chocolateholic		4 114	2	5	$3^{\frac{1}{2}}$	$4^{1\frac{1}{2}}$	4^3	4^1	$4^{1\frac{1}{2}}$	Yamamoto T J	6250	19.80
8Jan87 ^{2}BM^7	Gala Prevue		4 114	5	2	6^6	6^4	5^2	6	5^2	White T C	6250	24.40
15Jan87 ^{5}BM^4	Mean Lizzie	b	4 115	6	6	$5^{\frac{1}{2}}$	3^2	3^2	$5^{1\frac{1}{2}}$	6	Judice J C	6250	1.30
31Dec86 ^{2}BM^{10}	Taniwa		4 114	4	1	4^2	5^3	7	—	—	Caballero R	6250	24.10

Taniwa, Eased.

OFF AT 12:31. Start good. Won driving. Time, :22⅗, :46⅕, 1:12⅗, 1:26⅕, 1:39⅗ Track fast.

Official Program Numbers

$2 Mutuel Prices:

1-GEORGIA SMITH	11.80	5.40	4.00
3-CHRIS'S GLAMOR		5.60	4.60
7-VITASCOPE			3.60

The victory of Georgia Smith with a return of $11.80 is a good start for the day. You can see from reading the chart that Vitascope surely suffered from her outside post position, as she was forced to use her energy to get out ahead of the others and then fall back drastically in the stretch. Mean Lizzie was far back all the way, the hapless closer that her record revealed, a dreadful waste of money at 6-5. There is no confirmed judgment as to track tendency out of this race, and as we go to the second event, we can keep watching off what thus far appears to approach "normal."

The next race is a maiden claimer for young fillies, which will leave us with a lot of blanks as we survey the field.

2nd BayMeadows

6 FURLONGS. (1.07⅗) MAIDEN CLAIMING. Purse $6,000. Fillies. 3-year-olds. Weight, 117 lbs. Claiming price $12,500.

Perfect Ternary
CASTANEDA M **117**
Own.—Buell J R

B. f. 3, by Peregrinator—Miss Triple Win, by Triple Bend
Br.—Helle II (Cal) **1986 0 M 0 0**
Tr.—Henderson Frances **$12,500**
Lifetime 0 0 0 0

●Jan 19 GG 3f ft :35³ h ●Jan 12 GG 5f gd 1:03² h Jan 6 GG 5f m 1:07 hg Dec 29 GG 5f hy 1:07⁴ h

Percussionist
CHAPMAN T M **117**
Own.—Braiman W

Ch. f. 3, by Drums and Fife—Indian Tales, by Dusty Canyon
Br.—Dorazio Dr-Mrs A (Cal) **1986 0 M 0 0**
Tr.—Ramirez Octavio **$12,500**
Lifetime 0 0 0 0

Jan 15 GG 5f ft 1:04³ h Jan 12 GG 3f gd :39 h Jan 6 GG 4f m :53² hg Dec 30 GG 4f hy :53 hg

Kris's Peach
B. f. 3, by Kris S—Perfect Peach, by Sir Gaylord
HANSEN R D
Br.—Meadowbrook Farms Inc (Fla) 1986 4 M 0 0 $450
117
Own.—La Croix Barbara
Tr.—La Croix David $12,500
Lifetime 4 0 0 0 $450
10Sep86-6Bmf 6f :224 :462 1:121ft 7¾ 117 53½ 54 510 717¼ GonzlezRM4 ⒻM12500 61-22 Apres Sol, Gay Ho, Next Hit 12
16Aug86-5Cby 6f :224 :461 1:121ft 6¾e 1095 52½ 44 35½ 47½ Murray K C3 ⒻM22500 78-07 BttyBinBd,TurnndTun,Finl'yProvd 10
18Jly86-5Cby 5½f :223 :464 1:063ft 13 1115 75½ 711 69½ 512½ Murray K C2 ⒻM25000 74-12 DessertMidn,Bbymysid,ImpccblLdy 9
6Jly86-3Cby 5f :223 :46 :594gd 13 1115 811 89½ 811 710¼ Murray K C8 ⒻMdn 80-15 MoonshnMshp,HommdCock,Lproyr 8
●Jan 16 BM 4f ft :464 hg Jan 10 BM 6f gd 1:18 h Jan 2 BM 6f gd 1:163 h Dec 13 BM 4f ft :483 h

Fleet Gee Gee
B. f. 3, by Fleet Allied—Gaelic Girl, by Gaelic Dancer
LOZOYA D A
Br.—Wood Nancy F (Cal) 1987 1 M 0 0
117
Tr.—Knight Tom $12,500 1986 4 M 0 3 $1,844
Own.—Freitas A J or W
Lifetime 5 0 0 3 $1,844
8Jan87-3BM 6f :23 :472 1:142sl 7¼ 117 85 54 34 64 McGurn C7 ⒻM12500 63-33 DixieRon,ChocolteLnd,VegsScore 12
18Dec86-1BM 1 1/16 :484 1:152 1:521sy 5¼ 117 42½ 47 414 516¾ Rinne C E3 ⒻM12500 — — FinllyProved,Zulu'sPride,PhyllisHill 8
18Dec86—Broke in a tangle
5Dec86-1BM 6f :23 :471 1:134sl 8¼ 117 21 3½ 32 33½ Rinne C E5 ⒻM12500 67-26 LoyolCorners,KeeliH.,FleetGeeGee 12
18Oct86-7Fno 5f :22 :454 :592ft 2¼ 118 54½ 55 74¼ 45½ Burns S6 ⒻM20000 75-15 ‡I'llcriyours,MissWindySky,CmlTos 8
18Oct86—Placed third through disqualification; Bumped hard start
9Oct86-6Fno 5f :221 :452 :582ft 16 118 42 44½ 42 32½ Burns S4 ⒻⓈM16000 82-14 PetiteZoot,JpneseBeetle,F'eetGeeG 9
Jan 6 BM 3f sy :39 h (d) Dec 1 Pln 5f ft 1:021 h Nov 24 Pln 5f ft 1:024 h

Holy Smokes
B. f. 3, by Holy War—Summershine, by Olympiad King
YAMAMOTO T J
Br.—Weigel M J (Cal) 1986 5 M 2 2 $4,850
117
Own.—Schuering & Schuering Jr
Tr.—Steele Roy $12,500
Lifetime 5 0 2 2 $4,850
18Dec86-3BM 6f :223 :463 1:141sy [illegible] 117 88½ 81½ 13 3½ YmmotTJ9 ⒻⓈM16000 61-41 FleetBrgin,VegsScore,HolySmoks 12
21Nov86-3BM 6f :222 :462 1:134ft 3 117 87½ 86½ 32½ 22½ YmmotTJ4 ⒻⓈM12500 67-23 CallMrie,HolySmokes,ChrgingFree 12
16Oct86-4BM 1 :462 1:113 1:383ft 4¼ 117 31½ 21½ 22 55¼ CastnedM3 ⒻMc16000 70-18 OutOfDarkness,NextHit,Denmorlin 10
2Oct86-4BM 6f :224 :461 1:111ft 6¼ 117 66 47 46 37 Judice JC9 ⒻⓈM16000 76-19 DrsHope,OutOfDrknss,HolySmoks 11
18Sep86-4BM 6f :23 :471 1:14 ft 4 117 52½ 2½ 1½ 22 Judice J C7 ⒻM16000 67-27 TroisAmis,HolySmoks,Gigcl'sDlight 7
Jan 19 BM 3f ft :362 h Jan 14 BM 4f ft :493 h Dec 13 BM 5f ft 1:013 h Dec 3 BM 3f ft :361 h

Happy Hacker
Dk. b. or br. f. 3, by Sumarlid—Sharp Spirit, by Inverness Drive
BAZE R A
Br.—Hibbert R E (Ky) 1986 0 M 0 0
117
Own.—Hibbert R E
Tr.—Retherford N J $12,500
Lifetime 0 0 0 0
Jan 15 BM 6f ft 1:172 h Jan 8 BM 5f m 1:023 h Dec 28 BM 4f ft :483 hg Dec 24 BM 3f m :384 h

Alotagas
B. f. 3, by Master Jorge—Utalk, by Stable Talk
LOSETH C
Br.—Andersen D A (Wash) 1987 1 M 0 0
117
Own.—Anderson D A
Tr.—Anderson Dennis $12,500 1986 2 M 0 0 $225
Lifetime 3 0 0 0 $225
8Jan87-3BM 6f :23 :472 1:142sl 29 117 63 1011 1116 1013¼ CastanedM2 ⒻM12500 53-33 DixieRon,ChocolteLnd,VegsScore 12
6Jun86-4Lga 5f :214 :461 :591ft 30 118 68¾ 617 611 710¾ Drexler H7 ⒻM25000 69-25 Spring Trooper,ShotPut,WayofFire 9
4May86-4Lga 5f :221 :454 :574ft 18 118 75½ 79½ 616 517½ Steiner J J1 ⒻMdn 69-21 SoftCopy,PopsciclTos,SprngTroopr 9
Jan 6 GG 3f m :38 h Dec 31 GG 5f hy 1:004 h (d) Dec 16 GG 5f m 1:073 h Dec 9 GG 4f ft :513 h

Naughty Pine
Dk. b. or br. f. 3, by Pine Supreme—Nona Dari Sumatra, by Irepeat
MILLS J W
Br.—Prineville Stud Company (Ore) 1986 3 M 0 0
117
Own.—Merrill & Rhoden
Tr.—Merrill Doris $12,500
Lifetime 3 0 0 0
24Dec86-4BM 6f :231 :472 1:141hy 61 117 65 714 720 723 FuentesFP10 ⒻM12500 45-39 Yung Yang,KeeliH.,JackcirLeader 12
3Dec86-4BM 6f :224 :461 1:12 ft 70 117 98½ 1013 1015 1019½ Mills J W9 ⒻM25000 59-19 MeMir,BzrBrod,FunnymonyBunny 10
16Nov86-2BM 6f :23 :463 1:124ft 65 117 911 1017 915 913 Fuentes FP6 ⒻM25000 62-21 PorMPdr,GoodStppr,ComfltlyIrsh 11
●Jan 16 GG 5f ft 1:012 h Jan 10 GG 5f sl 1:052 h Jan 2 GG 4f hy :542 h (d) Dec 22 GG 3f sy :38 h

Restless Regatta
Ch. f. 3, by Restless Run—First Sailing, by Promised Land
JOHNSON B G
Br.—Lanphere R D (Wash) 1986 0 M 0 0
117
Own.—Lanphere Farm
Tr.—McLean Bill $12,500
Lifetime 0 0 0 0
Jan 12 GG 6f gd 1:174 h Dec 9 GG 5f ft 1:031 h Dec 2 GG 4f ft :511 hg

We can hardly make a worksheet on this race. Only two horses have run at least five times, and there is nothing in the field without form defects. As we acknowledge that someone must win, this is an easy pass situation. We look at the race, however, as we do with all of them, to see what we can learn from how the track is responding.

SECOND RACE **6 FURLONGS. (1.07⅘) MAIDEN CLAIMING. Purse $6,000. Fillies. 3-year-olds. Weight, 117 lbs. Claiming price $12,500.**

BayMeadows

JANUARY 21, 1987

Value of race $6,000; value to winner $3,300; second $1,170; third $840; fourth $540; fifth $150. Mutuel pool $90,611.

Last Raced	Horse	Eqt.	A.	Wt	PP	St	¼	½	Str	Fin	Jockey	Cl'g Pr	Odds $1
18Dec86 3BM3	Holy Smokes		3	117	5	4	7^{hd}	$6^{1\frac{1}{2}}$	$4^{\frac{1}{2}}$	$1^{\frac{1}{2}}$	Yamamoto T J	12500	3.20
	Happy Hacker		3	117	6	9	9	$7^{\frac{1}{2}}$	7^{5}	2^{2}	Baze R A	12500	2.50
	Restless Regatta		3	117	9	8	$4^{\frac{1}{2}}$	3^{hd}	$3^{\frac{1}{2}}$	3no	Johnson B G	12500	19.80
8Jan87 3BM6	Fleet Gee Gee	b	3	117	4	3	$2^{\frac{1}{2}}$	$2^{1\frac{1}{2}}$	1^{hd}	4^{nk}	Lozoya D A	12500	6.00
10Sep86 6Bmf7	Kris's Peach	b	3	117	3	2	1^{hd}	1^{hd}	2^{1}	5^{1}	Hansen R D	12500	4.80
	Perfect Ternary		3	117	1	7	5^{1}	5^{1}	$6^{1\frac{1}{2}}$	6^{1}	Castaneda M	12500	3.80
24Dec86 4BM7	Naughty Pine	b	3	117	8	1	$3^{1\frac{1}{2}}$	4^{2}	5^{hd}	7^{6}	Mills J W	12500	37.20
8Jan87 3BM10	Alotagas		3	117	7	5	8^{2}	9	9	8^{2}	Loseth C	12500	29.80
	Percussionist		3	117	2	6	6^{hd}	8^{2}	8^{2}	9	Chapman T M	12500	30.50

OFF AT 1:00. Start good. Won driving. Time, :23⅕, :47⅕, 1:00⅖, 1:13⅗ Track fast.

$2 Mutuel Prices:				
	5–HOLY SMOKES	8.40	3.60	2.40
	6–HAPPY HACKER		3.60	3.00
	9–RESTLESS REGATTA			5.80

Once again, we learn little, outside of the fact that no one had any demonstrable early speed. The winner, Holy Smokes, wasn't too far behind at the second call and was only a length and a half behind at the head of the stretch, which does not tell us too much about closing, either. But races like this on tracks that are not yet defined, or may not be defined at all, occur over and over again. Prospects for the third race, which is a twin of the second for maiden fillies at the same claiming price, and equally filled with the same uncertainties, are hardly any better.

3rd BayMeadows

6 FURLONGS. (1.07⅘) MAIDEN CLAIMING. Purse $6,000. Fillies. 3-year-olds. Weight, 117 lbs. Claiming price $12,500.

Magic Recipe — **Ro. f. 3, by Hookano—Little Bit Swaps, by Hy Swaps**
JUDICE J C **117** — **Br.—Dickey Molly (Cal)** — **1987 1 M 0 0**
Tr.—Roberts Tom **$12,500** — **1986 4 M 2 1 $3,180**
Own.—Love & Tulving J R — **Lifetime 5 0 2 1 $3,180**

16Jan87-3BM	6f	:22^{4}	:46^{4}	1:13 ft	$4^{\frac{1}{2}}$	117	10^{7}	$8^{9\frac{3}{4}}$	$6^{8\frac{1}{2}}$	$6^{8\frac{1}{2}}$	Maple S7	Ⓕ[S]M12500	65-30	ADringDbut,CroDOro,KingsburgGl	12
24Dec86-1BM	6f	:22^{3}	:48	1:17^{2}hy	$3^{\frac{1}{4}}$	117	5^{4}	$4^{4\frac{1}{2}}$	3^{1}	$2^{\frac{1}{2}}$	Maple S6	ⒻM12500	51-39	Pul'sFunDte,MgicRcip,FrindlyPtsy	12
7Nov86-3BM	6f	:22^{4}	:47	1:13^{4}ft	*3-2	117	$7^{6\frac{1}{2}}$	$3^{3\frac{1}{2}}$	3^{2}	$3^{2\frac{3}{4}}$	Baze R A7	ⒻM12500	67-24	PromisingNote,FltBrgin,MgicRcip	12
8Oct86-1BM	6f	:23^{2}	:47^{3}	1:14^{2}ft	$7^{\frac{1}{4}}$	117	$6^{4\frac{1}{2}}$	$3^{1\frac{1}{2}}$	2^{1}	2^{3}	Grable T C5	ⒻM12500	64-25	Frisky Me,MagicRecipe,Tisnotlove	12
11Sep86-4Lga	6f	:22^{4}	:47^{2}	1:14^{1}gd	*$2^{\frac{1}{2}}$	113	2^{hd}	2^{1}	$3^{2\frac{1}{2}}$	6^{4}	Aragon V A1	ⒻM12500	61-24	Tear Ash,LaFleur,Doc'sSugarBabe	12

Dec 17 BM 3f gd :36^{2} h   Dec 10 BM 5f ft 1:02^{2} h   Dec 2 BM 3f ft :37^{1} h

Battling Broad Ch. f. 3, by Sure Fire—Altalice, by Orbit Ruler
LOZOYA D A 117 Br.—Houssels & Ham (Cal) 1986 3 M 0 0 $288
Own.—Matos G Tr.—Matos Gil $12,500
Lifetime 3 0 0 0 $288
18Oct86-7Fno 5f :22 :454 :592ft 15 118 3½ 41 21 56¼ Furlong K1 ⒻM20000 74-15 ‡I'llcriyours,MissWindySky,CmlTos 8
18Oct86—Placed fourth through disqualification
10Oct86-7Fno 6f :224 :454 1:112ft 8 118 55 b7 83¾ 914¼ White T C4 ⒻM20000 68-15 Iland Lass, Ai Nui,MichelleLaBelle 10
10Oct86—Broke in, bumped
4Sep86-4Dmr 6f :221 :461 1:122ft 50 117 85¾1112111412173 PttersonA10 ⒻM32000 58-14 EstsTwlv,Dr.SockItToM,MontnGld 12
4Sep86—Bumped hard start
●Jan 15 BM 5f ft 1:021 hg Jan 11 BM 4f gd :522 h Jan 3 BM 3f sy :37 hg Dec 30 BM 5f ft 1:041 h

Fali Quick B. f. 3, by Faliraki—Miss Laissez Faire, by Rising Market
CAMPBELL B C 117 Br.—Rowan L R (Cal) 1987 2 M 0 0
Own.—Delaplane E E Tr.—Jackson Monty $12,500 1986 1 M 0 0
Lifetime 3 0 0 0
14Jan87-1BM 6f :224 :471 1:141ft 42 114 42 55½ 69½ 64½ Campbell BC2 Ⓕ 12500 63-27 Aldaba, Frisky Me, Camosun 8
14Jan87—Bumped start
2Jan87-3BM 1 1/16 :482 1:142 1:503gd 11 117 67½ 611 718 717 Tohill K S8 ⒻM12500 — — PssEllen,OnMorDwdrop,PhyllisHill 10
24Dec86-4BM 6f :231 :472 1:141hy 20 117 2½ 36 412 618 Tohill K S3 ⒻM12500 50-39 Yung Yang,KeeliH.,JackcinLeader 12
Jan 10 BM 4f gd :514 h Dec 20 BM 6f sy 1:213 h (d) Dec 13 BM 5f ft 1:013 hg Dec 7 BM 5f sl 1:064 h

Jo's Little Lady Dk. b. or br. f. 3, by Fort Calgary—Little Bigjo, by War Emperor
GONZALEZ R M 117 Br.—Dante T C (Cal) 1986 0 M 0 0
Own.—Dante-Dante-Dante Tr.—Retherford N J $12,500
Lifetime 0 0 0 0
●Jan 19 BM 3f ft :352 h Jan 15 BM 5f ft 1:051 h Jan 10 BM 5f gd 1:061 h Jan 5 BM 5f m 1:03 h

Laughing Native Ch. f. 3, by Talented Native—Wafa, by Vertexas
ESSMAN D W 117 Br.—Metz Mr-Mrs J H (Cal) 1987 1 M 0 0
Own.—Elm Tree Farm Tr.—Lefort Michel $12,500 1986 0 M 0 0
Lifetime 1 0 0 0
8Jan87-3BM 6f :23 :472 1:142sl 67 117 107 99¾1015 912½ EssmnDW11 ⒻM12500 54-33 DixieRon,ChocolteLnd,VegsScore 12
Jan 5 Pln 3f sy :371 h Dec 22 Pln 6f m 1:153 h

Great Renown Dk. b. or br. f. 3, by Angle Light—Western Idol, by Western Sky II
VALERA T G 1125 Br.—Morgan Nancy Penn (Ky) 1986 3 M 0 0 $160
Own.—Phillips & Stuart Tr.—Prospero Floyd J $12,500
Lifetime 3 0 0 0 $160
20Nov86-2Hol 7f :223 :464 1:262ft 149 1115 98½1111111911122½ Cisneros JE6 ⒻM28000 50-16 SwitchSlips,Sadiya,SouthOfFrnce 12
20Nov86—Bumped start; wide final 3/8
3Oct86-2SA 6f :214 :453 1:12 gd 159 117 121211111110 915 Bonilla R11 ⒻM32000 63-17 Chanterella,AutumnGle,Erin'sFun 12
3Oct86—Broke slowly
11Sep86-4Pom 6f :223 :463 1:12 ft 127 116 97½1013 820 820 Bonilla R6 ⒻMdn 71-08 Stembold, GrittyBid,ThanksToJ.P. 10
11Sep86—Pinched at break
Jan 9 BM 5f gd 1:032 hg Dec 28 BM tr.t 4f sl :54 h

Pink Deli Gr. f. 3, by Raise an Orphan—Delicious Pinkie, by Donut King
BAZE R A 117 Br.—Eaton & Kratz (La) 1987 1 M 0 0
Own.—Dutton & Eaton Tr.—Dutton Jerry $12,500 1986 4 M 0 0 $540
Lifetime 5 0 0 0 $540
14Jan87-1BM 6f :224 :471 1:141ft 24 115 52½ 44½ 710 76½ Razo E6 Ⓕ 12500 61-27 Aldaba, Frisky Me, Camosun 8
24Dec86-1BM 6f :223 :48 1:172hy *3 117 44 34½ 54 63½ GonzlezRM7 ⒻM12500 48-39 Pul'sFunDte,MgicRcip,FrindlyPtsy 12
11Dec86-4BM 1 :462 1:124 1:391ft 9 114 1½ 55½ 717 927 Gonzalez RM1 Ⓕ 12500 45-24 Twisting Silver,Aldaba,LovelyRuler 9
7Nov86-3BM 6f :224 :47 1:134ft 7¾ 117 65½ 44½ 44 46¾ Hansen R D2 ⒻM12500 63-24 PromisingNote,FltBrgin,MgicRcip 12
7Nov86—Bumped hard start
13Oct86-1BM 6f :223 :463 1:13 ft *2½ 117 3½ 21 56½ 710½ Hansen R D6 ⒻM16000 63-21 BcksColMss,KngsbrgGl,EcsttcMss 10
Jan 10 BM 4f gd :523 h Jan 2 BM 3f gd :391 h Dec 19 BM 3f m :372 h (d) Dec 6 BM 6f m 1:181 h

Verneda Dk. b. or br. f. 3, by Caro Bambino—Easter Lilly, by Three Quarters
CHAPMAN T M 117 Br.—Brasil & Karlowitsch (Cal) 1987 0 M 0 0
Own.—Brasil-Karlowitsch-Murphy Tr.—Murphy G T $12,500 1986 0 M 0 0
Lifetime 0 0 0 0
Jan 17 BM 5f ft 1:02 h Jan 11 BM 5f gd 1:04 h Dec 29 BM 6f ft 1:141 h Dec 24 BM 5f m 1:05 h

Bring Flowers — Ch. f. 3, by Hereditary—Go Courting, by Lucky Mel
DOOCY T T — 117 — Br.—P. K. G. Industries (Cal) — $12,500 — 1987 1 M 0 0
Tr.—Marsh Gordon — 1986 2 M 0 0
Own.—Murray Creek Rch & Girdner — Lifetime 3 0 0 0

17Jan87-3BM 6f $:22^3$ $:46^2$ 1:12 ft 14 117 10^{13} 9^{15} 9^{19} $7^{18\frac{3}{4}}$ Doocy T T^6 ⒻM12500 60 — OnStgMinni,HobbsChoic,SwtSnsy 11
24Dec86-4BM 6f $:23^1$ $:47^2$ $1:14^1$hy 7 117 10^{10} 11^{18} 9^{23} 8^{23} Doocy T T^1 ⒻM12500 45-39 Yung Yang,KeeliH.,JackcinLeader 12
24Dec86—Broke slowly
23Aug86-5Bil 6½f $:25^1$ $:50^1$ $1:26^3$ft *8-5e117 2^3 $2^{1\frac{1}{2}}$ $2^{1\frac{1}{2}}$ $1^{1\frac{1}{2}}$ Halajian R^1 Fut Trl 62-25 BringFlowrs,sullyCrk'sRg,‡BinnPkn 8
23Aug86—Disqualified from purse money
Jan 12 GG 4f gd $:51^4$ h — Dec 9 GG 5f ft $1:03^3$ h — ●Nov 28 GG 4f ft $:47^4$ h

Just as we were unable to construct a meaningful work sheet on the second race, we meet the same fate in this same kind of event. Again, there are only two horses where we can even have a PCR. Form defects and weak workouts are everywhere. This is equally another pass situation. We often encounter inaction in early races on a card where you have these conditions with lightly raced animals. Here is where your patience is useful, along with the knowledge that something better is sure to come along.

We take our usual look at how the race was run, which we do here with a study of the chart. Was there any reason why anyone would have had this $57 winner who was coming back in four days off truly atrocious form? Results like this do occur in these kinds of races, which further adds to our resolve to stay far away unless there is a true standout.

THIRD RACE — 6 FURLONGS. (1.07⅘) MAIDEN CLAIMING. Purse $6,000. Fillies. 3-year-olds. Weight, 117 lbs. Claiming price $12,500.

BayMeadows
JANUARY 21, 1987

Value of race $6,000; value to winner $3,300; second $1,170; third $840; fourth $540; fifth $150. Mutuel pool $70,081. Exacta pool $91,148.

Last Raced	Horse	Eqt.	A.Wt	PP	St	¼	½	Str	Fin	Jockey	Cl'g Pr	Odds $1
17Jan87 3BM7	Bring Flowers		3 117	9	1	2^3	2^3	1^1	$1^{4\frac{1}{2}}$	Doocy T T	12500	27.60
	Verneda		3 117	8	9	$5^{1\frac{1}{2}}$	$3^{\frac{1}{2}}$	3^3	$2^{\frac{1}{2}}$	Chapman T M	12500	3.50
18Oct86 7Fno4	Battling Broad	b	3 117	2	3	1^{hd}	1^{hd}	2^3	3^1	Lozoya D A	12500	4.70
14Jan87 1BM6	Fali Quick		3 117	3	4	6^5	6^2	$5^{\frac{1}{2}}$	$4^{\frac{1}{2}}$	Campbell B C	12500	8.00
16Jan87 3BM6	Magic Recipe	b	3 117	1	6	7^2	7^4	$6^{1\frac{1}{2}}$	5^4	Judice J C	12500	3.60
	Jo's Little Lady	b	3 117	4	5	3^{hd}	$4^{\frac{1}{2}}$	4^{hd}	6^{nk}	Gonzalez R M	12500	3.70
14Jan87 1BM7	Pink Deli	b	3 117	7	2	4^2	5^2	7^4	7^{nk}	Baze R A	12500	5.10
20Nov86 2Hol11	Great Renown	b	3 112	6	8	9	9	8^1	$8^{2\frac{1}{2}}$	Valera A G^5	12500	23.80
8Jan87 3BM9	Laughing Native		3 117	5	7	$8^{\frac{1}{2}}$	$8^{\frac{1}{2}}$	9	9	Essman D W	12500	81.10

OFF AT 1:30. Start good for all but VERNEDA. Won driving. Time, :22⅗, :46⅗, :59⅗, 1:13 Track fast.

$2 Mutuel Prices:			
9-BRING FLOWERS	57.20	19.60	9.60
8-VERNEDA		6.80	4.60
2-BATTLING BROAD			4.20

$2 EXACTA 9-8 PAID $295.40.

At least there is an indication that up front running is faring reasonably well, but once again, the quality of the field leaves little to rely upon.

The fourth race is the third successive maiden claimer for young three year olds on the card, as we may be getting a little restless by now. We have a short field of six, stretching out to a mile and a sixteenth, but at least there is a slightly better quality of horse.

4th BayMeadows

1 1/16 MILES. (1.38⅘) MAIDEN CLAIMING. Purse $8,000. 3-year-olds. Weight, 118 lbs. Claiming price $20,000.

Chris Zanthe

B. g. 3, by Zanthe—Pleasant Chris, by Dewan

BAZE R A 118 **Br.—Tam R (Cal)** 1987 1 M 1 0 $1,560

Own.—Tam R **Tr.—Mason Lloyd C** $20,000 1986 5 M 0 0 $325

Lifetime 6 0 1 0 $1,885

7Jan87-4BM 1 1/16 :471 1:133 1:493sl 3¼ 118 79¾ 67½ 45 2no Baze R A4 M20000 44-35 SocilVilln,ChrisZnthe,LeftSpchlss 10

7Jan87—Ducked out start

24Dec86-4Hol 1 :453 1:111 1:381ft 26 118 31 64¼ 612 616¼ Black C A4 M32000 56-20 Tell J. C., Royal Blurr, Versing 9

24Dec86—Broke stride 5/8

4Dec86-1Hol 1 :461 1:123 1:401ft 22 1135 41¾ 43½ 55 58¼ Patton D B8 M32000 54-25 Sky Warrior, Versing,CrystalCutter 9

13Nov86-2Hol 1 :451 1:11 1:383ft 96 1135 78 109¾ 78½ 89 Patton D B11 M32000 61-23 SuperAction,You'reGlorious,TkOn 12

3Nov86-6SA 1 :472 1:113 1:371ft 101 117 911 814 718 719¾ Bonilla R1 ⓈMdn 62-14 FastDelivery,NstyNskr,HilriousFlirt 9

16Oct86-2SA 6f :221 :454 1:122ft 142 118 97¼ 711 710 811¼ Bonilla R11 ⓈM32000 65-19 TheQuipper,TakeOne,NeverSmoke 12

Dec 20 SA 6f ft 1:141 hg ●Nov 27 SA 4f ft :462 h

Prince Tulyar

Dk. b. or br. c. 3, by Historically—Tulyann, by Tulyar

SCHVANEVELDT C P 118 **Br.—Boneau P (Cal)** 1987 1 M 0 0 $720

Own.—Valley Farm **Tr.—Slot Troy** $20,000 1986 5 M 1 0 $1,613

Lifetime 6 0 1 0 $2,333

7Jan87-4BM 1 1/16 :471 1:133 1:493sl 14 118 913 711 55½ 4nk Doocy T T5 M20000 44-35 SocilVilln,ChrisZnthe,LeftSpchlss 10

7Jan87—Off slowly; wide

11Nov86-4BM 6f :23 :471 1:111ft 9 118 810 711 69 610½ Hansen R D2 ⓈM25000 72-21 Court Wizard, Danbo,GildedCajun 11

29Oct86-4BM 6f :223 :46 1:122ft 24 118 911 57 42½ 2no Hansen R D9 M16000 77-22 He'sAnOfficer,PrinceTulyar,Rassit 10

17Sep86-1BM 5½f :224 :464 1:064gd 26 118 89½ 811 813 611 Judice J C6 ⓈM16000 67-31 Princeps, Kid Zuni, I'm Notorious 8

17Sep86—Broke in a tangle

4Sep86-6Bmf 6f :224 :463 1:121ft 22 118 65¼ 64½ 1010 1011¾ Hummel C R9 M20000 66-19 CmlDrivr,QutARmndr,CountyGrov 11

23Aug86-6Sac 5½f :221 :454 1:04 ft 10 117 52¾ 32 55¼ 510½ Baze D5 Mdn 77-12 Big Boi, Quite AReminder,Tonopah 7

Jan 17 GG 4f ft :481 h Dec 29 GG 6f hy 1:224 h Dec 22 GG 5f sy 1:054 h Dec 10 GG 4f ft :493 h

El Ancon

B. c. 3, by Full of Hope—Our Lorie, by Researching

SAITO S T 1135 **Br.—Pearlstein L (Cal)** 1986 0 M 0 0

Own.—Luby & Pearlstein **Tr.—Severinsen Allen** $20,000

Lifetime 0 0 0 0

Jan 16 BM 3f ft :41 h Jan 4 BM 6f sy 1:244 h (d) Dec 30 BM 4f ft :48 h Dec 14 BM Tr. 5f ft 1:032 hg

Sleepy Brigadier

Dk. b. or br. g. 3, by Light Cavalry—Sleepy Sis, by Advocator

RAZO E 118 **Br.—Penn O (Ky)** 1987 1 M 0 0 $540

Own.—Bruce R **Tr.—Specht Steve** $20,000 1986 3 M 0 0 $187

Lifetime 4 0 0 0 $727

9Jan87-4BM 6f :23 :474 1:141sl 63 118 1215 1014 68 46¼ Razo E1 12500 62-34 JstRghtLck,SprmLgnd,CowbyFrnk 12

24Dec86-3BM 6f :224 :473 1:144hy 24 118 1118 1018 715 613 Razo E2 M12500 52-39 SpnishTony,Dncer'sSong,RodTest 12

29Oct86-4BM 6f :223 :46 1:122ft 62 118 78½ 811 79 98 Razo E10 M16000 69-22 He'sAnOfficer,PrinceTulyar,Rassit 10

15Oct86-1BM 6f :223 :454 1:113ft 28 118 99¼ 88¼ 711 59¼ Razo E7 M16000 72-17 PaddyMuldoon,Hulgar,SndyPririe 12

Jan 19 BM 4f ft :492 h Jan 8 BM 3f m :381 h Dec 20 BM 6f sy 1:204 h (d) Dec 4 BM 5f ft 1:02 h

Make A Pocketful — Dk. b. or br. g. 3, by Pocketful in Vail—Kazuko, by Envoy
DOOCY T T 118 — Br.—Fitzgerald J R (Cal) — 1987 1 M 0 0
Tr.—Fanning Jerry $20,000 — 1986 10 M 0 1 $3,125
Own.—Bandura-Bw Ww St-Gls et al — Lifetime 11 0 0 1 $3,125

8Jan87-4SA 1 :474 1:14 1:413m 6¼ 117 54¾ 88 810 917 PedrozaMA8 [S]M32000 43-30 SixTwoAndEvn,SomHittr,RidngBy 10
8Jan87—Lugged in
31Dec86-6SA 1$\frac{1}{16}$:47 1:124 1:454ft 68 115 55 52¼ 76¼ 513½ Pedroza M A12 M35000 58-20 Darion, Synergist,SixTwoAndEven 12
31Dec86—Bumped hard start
14Dec86-2Hol 6f :223 :462 1:123ft 21 118 96¾1111 910 911¼ Pedroza M A8 M32000 69-18 WisdomDancer,VikingBlue,TellJ.C. 12
23Nov86-4Hol 6f :221 :454 1:114ft 20 118 1213 1010 79½ 79 DominguezRE8 M32000 75-12 NvrSmok,TurnBckJohn,Promoting 12
8Oct86-2SA 6f :221 :461 1:123ft 9½ 117 108 96¼ 65 64 DomngzRE10 [S]M32000 71-20 SecretScore,Panuco,UniversalMan 12
8Oct86—Wide; lugged in stretch
27Sep86-4Pom 6f :221 :462 1:132ft 10 118 86 814 711 43¼ DomngzRE8 [S]M32000 81-10 Forcefully, Fastly, Panzer Value 9
27Sep86—Wide 1st turn, backstretch
5Sep86-4Dmr 1 :463 1:123 1:393ft 46 118 32 32½ 33 42¼ Garrido O L8 M32000 68-16 FrstShootr,EghtIsEnough,Jck'sLnd 8
8Aug86-4Dmr 6f :222 :461 1:113ft 23 117 129½ 129¾ 1012 1013¼ Garrido O L2 [S]M32000 67-13 JzzPlyer,FirstShooter,Tht'sBlrney 12
24Jly86-4Dmr 6f :223 :47 1:12 ft 24 117 77 811 912 913¼ Garrido OL10 [S]M32000 65-15 SprAdos,FrstShootr,SoldGoldSnd 12
24Jly86—Stumbled start
7Jly86-5LA 6f :224 :47 1:121ft 10 118 2hd 31 34½ 35¾ Garrido O L2 [S]M32000 77-15 TissrsBsl,FirstShootr,MkAPocktful 7
Dec 22 SA 5f ft 1:04 h   Dec 8 SA 4f gd :504 h

Ninepoundhammer — Dk. b. or br. g. 3, by Pappagallo—Sweet Lori Ann, by Bendbersandal
HANSEN R D 118 — Br.—Hallowell Mr-Mrs A L (Wash) — 1987 1 M 0 0 $200
Tr.—Wright Richard $20,000 — 1986 6 M 4 0 $5,575
Own.—Hallowell A L — Lifetime 7 0 4 0 $5,775

7Jan87-4BM 1$\frac{1}{16}$:471 1:133 1:493sl *2¾ 118 13 12 12 5¾ Hansen R D1 M20000 43-35 SocilVilln,ChrisZnthe,LeftSpchlss 10
29Dec86-4BM 6f :222 :453 1:111ft *8-5 118 42½ 43½ 66½ 97 Hansen R D7 M20000 76-15 CrystlCttr,BttrflyBoy,NwGoldDrm 12
29Dec86—Ducked out start
10Dec86-3BM 6f :23 :462 1:123ft 6¾ 118 62¼ 52¼ 32 22 Aragon V A1 M25000 74-21 SltyShos,Nnpondhmmr,SpnshGllnt 12
10Dec86—Broke in a tangle
2Nov86-6Lga 6f :221 :462 1:131m *3½ 120 31½ 32 21 22 Mills J W5 M25000 68-31 FiryFinsh,Nnpoundhmmr,SltyShos 11
11Oct86-3Lga 6f :214 :451 1:111ft *3e 120 54 42 33½ 21 Wentz M10 M25000 79-16 SwpSvn,Ninpoundhmmr,AgittdNtv 12
27Jun86-3Lga 5f :221 :454 :574ft 3½ 120 53¾ 67¾ 811 811½ Steiner J J7 M25000 75-20 SarajevoMerit,Utewin,AppleMrket 10
27Jun86—Wide 3/8 turn
23May86-4Lga 5f :223 :463 :59 ft *2½ 120 21 22 33½ 23 Steiner J J3 M25000 78-29 TlkTMBnr,Nnpndhmmr,Emprr'sTrn 8
●Dec 27 BM 3f gd :342 h   Dec 20 BM 4f sy :522 h (d)   Dec 2 GG 4f ft :494 h   Nov 21 GG 5f ft 1:012 h

At least we are able to construct a worksheet, which reads like this:

Odds	Horse	PCR	Form	Ab/T
9-5	Chris Zanthe	61/ 41 36 – 5/ 72 = 85	NNg	15.1 34.4–8/ 48.2
4	Prince Tulyar	57/ 36 33 – / 69 = 83	NOg	15.4 34.4–8/ 49.0
30	El Ancon	FT	w	
19	Sleepy Brigadier	46/ 36 24 – 2/ 58 = (79)	NON	(15.2 34.4–7/ 48.4)
9-2	Make A Pocketful	106/ 77 66 – 10/133 = 80	NON	15.3 36.0–5/ 50.3
3-2	Ninepoundhammer	75/ 25 30 – / 55 = 136	N+O	13.3 36.1–8/ 48.1

We can begin with two major considerations. The first is that in any field where there are two horses under 2-1 you can almost surely rely upon one of these two to win, unless there is some other notably strong competitor lingering not far off. The second is that we are able to eliminate the rest of this short field almost at a glance. Very low PCRs and very weak ability times wipe out Prince Tulyar, Sleepy Brigadier, and Make A Pocketful. El Ancon, a first time starter with no monetary support at 30-1, cannot be taken seriously.

We are back to the two low-priced horses where there is little profit to be had and a good chance that one could easily pick the wrong horse. It happens all the time. But we have tried to build a sufficient foundation with our total handicapping line, from PCR to form to last race ability times, to give you enough to be able to weed out the one that will lose and make your profit on the winner. Can we do it here?

The slight favorite is Ninepoundhammer, who begins with the advantage of having a PCR that is far above any of the others. His last race ability time is a shade better by one, but we consider that relatively equal, and essentially no advantage at all. Our next comparative factor is running style, where we see that Ninepoundhammer runs more forwardly than Chris Zanthe, who is a slight closer. Chris Zanthe gained in the stretch in his last race while Ninepoundhammer had the form defect of a stretch loss. Does this tip the scales?

They both ran in the same last race on a slow track with a wicked variant of 35. It was apparently a field day for closers, which we can see from looking at Prince Tulyar, who also finished with a strong gain in the same race.

This is where the internal numbers and the responsiveness of the track surface give us the clue to finding the advantage we must have to play the race. If the track were heavy and slow and favored closers, it would have to be Chris Zanthe. On the other hand, if the track runs reasonably normal, Ninepoundhammer with his high PCR and superior early speed, will be the winner.

The three races we have observed thus far tell us the answer. In the two that can be presumed to be reasonably reliable, the winner was never worse than second at any call. This means that at least there is no pronounced bias for closers. This has to make our choice: Ninepoundhammer.

The major point of this book is to find a big advantage if we are to make a single selection play. Ninepoundhammer falls short of our normal standards because of his stretch loss defect in his last race. But here, we have essentially a two-horse race and must only decide between one or the other. It is less difficult to find an advantage there, as we weigh all factors, one by one across the line. PCR and running style give us that advantage here. Yes, we can safely play Ninepoundhammer and accept the 3-2 odds that come with the risk. The result makes our sound analysis look as good as it appeared beforehand.

FOURTH RACE **1 1/16 MILES. (1.38⅘) MAIDEN CLAIMING. Purse $8,000. 3-year-olds. Weight, 118 lbs. Claiming price $20,000.**

BayMeadows

JANUARY 21, 1987

Value of race $8,000; value to winner $4,400; second $1,560; third $1,120; fourth $720; fifth $200. Mutuel pool $73,862. Expacta pool $80,086.

Last Raced	Horse	Eqt.A.Wt	PP	St	¼	½	¾	Str	Fin	Jockey	Cl'g Pr	Odds $1
7Jan87 ^{4}BM^5	Ninepoundhammer	b 3 118	6	1	1^5	1^6	1^3	1^3	1^6	Hansen R D	20000	1.50
7Jan87 ^{4}BM^4	Prince Tulyar	b 3 118	2	6	$5^{1\frac{1}{2}}$	$3^{\frac{1}{2}}$	$2^{1\frac{1}{2}}$	2^3	2^2	SchvneveldtCP	20000	4.10
7Jan87 ^{4}BM^2	Chris Zanthe	b 3 118	1	4	2^1	2^1	3^2	4^6	3^{nk}	Baze R A	20000	1.90
9Jan87 ^{4}BM^4	Sleepy Brigadier	b 3 118	4	5	6	6	4^3	3^{hd}	4^6	Razo E Jr	20000	19.40
	El Ancon	b 3 113	3	3	$3^{\frac{1}{2}}$	5^2	6	5^{hd}	5^2	Valera A G^5	20000	30.80
8Jan87 ^{4}SA^9	Make A Pocketful	b 3 118	5	2	4^1	$4^{\frac{1}{2}}$	5^3	6	6	Doocy T T	20000	4.50

OFF AT 1:58. Start good. Won ridden out. Time, :23⅕, :46⅘, 1:12⅕, 1:39⅕, 1:46⅕ Track fast.

$2 Mutuel Prices:

7-NINEPOUNDHAMMER	5.00	2.80	2.10
3-PRINCE TULYAR		3.80	2.20
1-CHRIS ZANTHE			2.20

$2 EXACTA 7-3 PAID $22.40.

We can now take off our hat to front speed. Ninepoundhammer literally destroyed the field. We can establish our conclusion that the track is favoring early speed somewhat, which should help us for the remainder of the afternoon. We have some much sounder foundations as we begin to look closely at the fifth race, a 6 furlong affair for fillies, to see what it may bring.

5th BayMeadows

6 FURLONGS. (1.07⅘) CLAIMING. Purse $7,000. Fillies. 4-year-olds. Weight, 120 lbs. Non-winners of two races since December 1 allowed 3 lbs.; a race since then, 6 lbs. Claiming price $8,000. (Maiden, starter and claiming races for $6,250 or less not considered.)

Double Surprise — Ro. f. 4, by Hawkin's Special—Double Path, by Double Double

DOOCY T T **114** Br.—Chase Archie C (Colo) 1986 18 2 3 3 $16,409

Tr.—Offield Duane $8,000 1985 2 1 0 0 $2,220

Own.—Stein D M Lifetime 20 3 3 3 $18,629

11Dec86-5BM	1 1/16	:46^4	1:12^1	1:45^{2}ft	4½	114	2^3	$3^{\frac{1}{2}}$	4^4	6^6	Doocy T T^1	Ⓕ c6250	59-24	NativeDawn,HaceComida,HelpGirl	12
4Dec86-9BM	6f	:22^1	:45^1	1:11^{1}ft	3¾	117	$7^{4\frac{1}{2}}$	$7^{5\frac{1}{4}}$	5^6	$4^{2\frac{1}{4}}$	Schrick D E^{12}	Ⓕ 6250	81-20	Atcd,HppyMgee,FlyMeToThMoon	12
22Oct86-2BM	6f	:22^2	:45^3	1:11^{2}ft	15	115	$10^{9\frac{1}{2}}$	8^{12}	8^{11}	8^7	Hansen R D^7	Ⓕ 10000	75-23	Stan's Belle,BoisHon,CariMyHeart	11
9Oct86-5BM	6f	:23	:46^1	1:11 ft	35	115	11^{11}	11^{10}	11^{14}	11^{14}	McGurn C^5	Ⓕ 16000	70-19	HotCche,IWlkAlone,DoubleDcortd	11
9Oct86—Bumped start															
16Aug86-4Aks	6f	:22^3	:45^3	1:11^{1}ft	11	113	4^4	$5^{3\frac{1}{2}}$	$7^{6\frac{1}{2}}$	$7^{10\frac{3}{4}}$	Walker B JJr^6	Ⓕ 18500	70-17	DiamondJenie,EpicBlue,Perception	7
1Aug86-6Aks	6f	:22^2	:46^1	1:12^{3}ft	*1	118	$6^{3\frac{3}{4}}$	7^5	$8^{7\frac{1}{4}}$	7^5	Cordova D W^5	Ⓕ 18000	69-24	Dance East, Calle De, Wind Castle	8
17Jly86-7Aks	6f	:22^3	:45^3	1:12^{2}ft	2½	118	$6^{4\frac{1}{2}}$	$5^{3\frac{3}{4}}$	$4^{3\frac{1}{4}}$	2^{nk}	Lively J^6	Ⓕ 18000	75-26	DimondJenie,DoubleSurpris,MoHul	6
25Jun86-7Aks	6f	:22^1	:45	1:11 ft	15	111	5^5	6^5	8^{12}	$8^{10\frac{3}{4}}$	PttersonG^3	ⒻAw13800	71-20	Im Stunning, WonInCourt,BlueImp	8
13Jun86-4Aks	6f	:22^3	:45^4	1:11 ft	3	116	$3^{1\frac{1}{2}}$	$5^{1\frac{3}{4}}$	$4^{\frac{3}{4}}$	$1^{1\frac{1}{4}}$	Lively J^1	Ⓕ 18000	82-16	DoubleSurpris,Olympic'sBst,BtsLss	7
4Jun86-2Aks	6f	:22^2	:45^3	1:12 ft	2½	112	4^2	$3^{\frac{1}{2}}$	3^2	2^{nk}	Lively J^1	Ⓕ 16000	77-20	BetsLss,DoubleSurpris,PrincssRoqu	8

Jan 18 BM 4f ft :48 h   Jan 8 BM 5f m 1:02^2 h   Dec 30 BM 4f ft :47^3 h   Nov 29 GG 4f ft :48^1 h

Bois Hon *
TOHILL K S — 114
Own.—Alaskan Stable

Ch. f. 4, by Boitron—Heather Honey, by Bold Combatant
Br.—Mann & Vescera (Cal) — 1986 13 3 2 1 $20,750
Tr.—Orr Ike — $8,000 — 1985 0 M 0 0
Lifetime 13 3 2 1 $20,750

5Dec86-2BM 6f :222 :453 1:122sl 3 114 33 33 47½ 811 Lamance C5 Ⓕ 8000 66-26 Days Bet, Vickarick,GeorgiaSmith 11
13Nov86-7BM 6f :224 :461 1:113ft 3½ 117 43 78½1017 1220 Lamance C1 Ⓕ 10000 61-24 Nyrc,PlsntlyNuty,ExcutivPosition 12
22Oct86-2BM 6f :222 :453 1:112ft *6-5 117 31 1hd 1½ 2no Lamance C6 Ⓕ 10000 82-23 Stan's Belle,BoisHon,CariMyHeart 11
10Oct86-9BM 5½f :214 :454 1:034ft *2½ 114 43½ 3nk 12 13 Lamance C5 Ⓕ 10000 93-18 BoisHon,ExcutivPosition,ClssicCon 8
25Sep86-7BM 6f :23 :474 1:151sl *7-5 114 2hd 1½ 14 11 Lamance C6 Ⓕ 8000 63-35 BoisHon,GalaPrevue,EveningWalk 11
1Sep86-7Bmf 6f :22 :45 1:11 ft 3 113 21½ 2½ 2½ 42 Lamance C5 Ⓕ 12500 82-16 Creist'sIce,DoubleDecortd,HotCch 10
7Aug86-10Stk 6f :221 :451 1:10 ft *9-5 115 2½ 22 1½ 2½ Hummel C R4 Ⓕ 12500 99-08 Kegani, Bois Hon, Haute Affair 9
7Aug86—Broke slowly
18Jly86-8Sol 5½f :214 :453 1:04 ft 2½ 114 2½ 21 32 36 Lamance C6 Ⓕ 12500 85-12 PleasantlyNuty,MoveAwy,BoisHon 10
18Jly86—Veered in, bumped start; lugged in 5/8
2Jly86-11Pln 5½f :221 :461 1:05 ft 32 115 63½ 21 31½ 42½ HummlCR6 ⒻAw16000 82-18 EstrgglLbth,MrnngstrLn,NrthrnIsl 10
19Jun86-7GG 6f :22 :443 1:103ft 4½ 114 2½ 1hd 2hd 42 Campbell BC3 Ⓕ 16000 84-15 Profila, Lovable Flirt, Move Away 11
Jan 12 BM 5f ft 1:042 h Nov 30 BM 5f ft 1:01 h

Royal Defense
MUNOZ R — 1095
Own.—Pickens & Bean Barn

B. f. 4, by Tarboosh—Firm Defense, by Bold Ruler
Br.—Kuehne E W (Tex) — 1987 1 0 0 0
Tr.—Bean Robert A — $8,000 — 1986 13 1 2 3 $7,997
Lifetime 16 1 2 4 $8,767

7Jan87-2BM 6f :231 :472 1:14 m 68 1095 53½ 42½ 67½ 68½ Munoz R10 Ⓕ 6250 60-35 Ivorette,Jo'sDughter,AlwysElegnt 10
5Dec86-2BM 6f :222 :453 1:122sl 56 114 109 1012 1117 912 Loseth C7 Ⓕ 8000 65-26 Days Bet, Vickarick,GeorgiaSmith 11
19Nov86-5BM 6f :224 :461 1:111ft 61 114 43½ 55½ 511 611½ Loseth C2 Ⓕ 6250 71-22 Dr. Anne, Renew, Mizanthe 10
24Oct86-2BM 6f :223 :463 1:124ft 40 114 1110 1212 1112 1010¾ Fuentes F P8 Ⓕ 8000 64-25 Prima'sBest,Moneyjy,PointOfFith 12
24Oct86—Hopped in air
10Oct86-9BM 5½f :214 :454 1:034ft 17 114 88¾ 78¾ 59½ 511½ Chapman TM2 Ⓕ 10000 81-18 BoisHon,ExcutivPosition,ClssicCon 8
25Sep86-7BM 6f :23 :474 1:151sl 8 115 1112 1111 59 45½ Hansen R D5 Ⓕ 8000 57-35 BoisHon,GalaPrevue,EveningWalk 11
25Sep86—Broke in air
5Sep86-9Bmf 6f :224 :461 1:12 ft 5 115 54 32½ 32 33½ Baze R A3 Ⓕ 6250 75-30 ShdyDilly,GoldGlimmer,RoylDefens 9
28Aug86-8Sac 6f :22 :45 1:103ft 7½ 1095 712 816 76 65¾ Righter J A3 Ⓕ 6250 80-13 Littleblurrr, Atacada, GoldGlimmer 8
26Apr86-4Sun 5½f :223 :471 1:072ft 5½ 1105 55 55½ 35 34½ Clark M D2 ⒻAw2500 71-26 ScoutsPrtnr,MissDhioLdy,RoylDfns 6
30Mar86-11Sun 6f :222 :46 1:123ft 6½ 116 53½ 54 52½ 23 RivsC4 ⒻCty Lscrcs H 76-23 ClssicQulity,RoylDefense,Bsktstmp 7
Jan 13 BM 5f gd 1:021 h Jan 5 BM 3f m :372 h

Lovable Flirt
MAPLE S — 114
Own.—Skriver Mr-Mrs D

B. f. 4, by Just Right Mike—Greta Gearhart, by War Flirt
Br.—Skriver & Argante (Cal) — 1986 13 2 2 2 $15,850
Tr.—Argante James E — $8,000 — 1985 0 M 0 0
Lifetime 13 2 2 2 $15,850

27Dec86-2BM 6f :221 :454 1:11 ft 8½ 115 1½ 1hd 42½ 711½ Maple S8 Ⓕ 16000 73-14 AShdeFster,DetermineCne,RisAHill 8
27Nov86-5BM 6f :223 :454 1:103ft 7 114 106 86¾ 73¾ 108¾ Ochoa A9 Ⓕ 12500 78-23 CriMyHrt,ExcutivPosition,Crst'sIc 12
27Nov86—Broke in a tangle
20Nov86-5BM 6f :223 :454 1:122ft 18 114 1½ 1½ 21 86½ Ochoa A1 Ⓕ 16000 71-22 AlphRttMrphy,DblDcrtd,AmblAngl 12
29Oct86-7BM 6f :22 :451 1:102ft 34 114 1hd 1hd 57 914½ Ochoa A1 Ⓕ 25000 72-22 Hot Cache,OneDrum,LongYardage 10
5Sep86-10Bmf 6f :222 :451 1:112ft 7 114 1½ 12 13 32 Ochoa A4 Ⓕ 25000 80-30 MysteryMaid,HollyAnn,LovableFlirt 8
20Aug86-11Sac 6f :221 :45 1:111ft 14 114 11 12 13 11 Ochoa A4 Ⓕ 16000 83-16 Lovable Flirt, Scurley, MoveAway 11
30Jly86-9SR 6f :214 :441 1:091ft 7½ 114 42 34½ 513 718 Ochoa A5 Ⓕ 25000 78-09 IllicitJoy,Creista'sIce,AirForceBaby 8
9Jly86-9Sol 5½f :214 :452 1:043ft 8½ 114 22 2hd 2hd 32½ Ochoa A4 ⒻAw13000 85-17 FltAndFrosty,NorthrnIsl,LovblFlirt 8
19Jun86-7GG 6f :22 :443 1:103ft 12 114 31½ 33 31½ 21½ Ochoa A9 Ⓕ 16000 84-15 Profila, Lovable Flirt, Move Away 11
19Jun86—Lugged out turn
4Jun86-2GG 6f :22 :444 1:111ft 26 114 1hd 1hd 1hd 2nk Ochoa A11 ⒻⓈ 12500 83-17 Tennessouri,LovbleFlirt,KuteZoot 12
Jan 11 BM 3f gd :364 h Dec 21 BM 3f m :39 h

Majestic Jessie
GONZALEZ R M — 114
Own.—Kay P P

Dk. b. or br. f. 4, by Big Jess—Kazuko, by Envoy
Br.—Goodwin J & Joan (Cal) — 1986 3 1 0 1 $1,380
Tr.—Utley Doug — $8,000 — 1985 0 M 0 0
Lifetime 3 1 0 1 $1,380

21May86-9GG 6f :223 :462 1:112ft 15 1095 54½ 78¾ 812 814 Moore C A4 ⒻⓈ 8000 68-17 Annie'sWorld,DnceDb,Molly'sDrm 10
8May86-3Fno 6f :222 :462 1:12 ft 9¾ 1135 11 13 13 15 Moore C A6 ⒻM12500 80-15 MjsticJssi,BrookLyntt,HughtyKys 10
25Apr86-3Fno 5f :222 :453 :582ft 3½ 1135 53½ 55½ 56¾ 39½ Moore C A5 ⒻM12500 75-19 DrkRoom,SweetChstity,MjsticJssi 10
Jan 19 GG 3f ft :361 h ●Jan 14 GG 6f gd 1:16 h Jan 9 GG 5f my 1:034 h (d) Dec 30 GG 5f my 1:074 h

Ivorette — Dk. b. or br. f. 4, by Sir Iversen—Pizzaz, by Pilot John
BAZE R A 114
Br.—Kosterman W J (Wash) 1987 1 1 0 0 $3,300
Tr.—Arterburn Lonnie $8,000 1986 16 2 3 3 $15,920
Own.—All American Stable
Lifetime 22 4 3 3 $22,530

7Jan87-2BM 6f :231 :472 1:14 m 2¼ 115 2½ 1hd 1½ 11 Baze R A6 (F) 6250 69-35 Ivorette,Jo'sDughter,AlwysElegnt 10
10Dec86-9BM 6f :221 :454 1:121ft *8-5 114 98¼ 97½ 57 52½ Baze R A9 (F) 10000 75-21 DrkSombr,PlsntlyNuty,BnkMssngr 11
21Nov86-2BM 1 1/16 :48 1:131 1:462ft 8¼ 114 13 42½ 67¾ 712 Tohill K S2 (F) 16000 48-23 Campti, All Decked Out,TanteBleue 9
2Nov86-2BM 6f :222 :46 1:11 ft 6¼ 114 1011 98¾ 56¾ 26 Tohill K S2 (F) c12500 78-21 AlphRttMurphy,Ivortt,PlsntlyNuty 11
2Nov86—Forced wide turn
16Oct86-1BM 1 :464 1:111 1:37 ft *2¾ 114 34½ 43½ 52¾ 47 Tohill K S4 (F) 16000 76-18 Haida Star,Forumstar,SpecialEagle 6
12Oct86-2BM 6f :214 :443 1:111ft 6¼ 114 914 917 712 41¾ Pfau R K4 (F) 12500 81-19 B.Mgic,ErniesChoice,ThinkOfHome 9
12Oct86—Broke slowly
31Aug86-6Lga 1 1/16 :472 1:13 1:444ft *2¼ 118 46 23 24 37 Steiner J J3 (F) 12500 68-22 OurBrian'sKelly,TableTies,Ivorette 10
22Aug86-6Lga 1 :464 1:121 1:374ft 4 115 2½ 12½ 32 32¾ Steiner J J6 (F) 16000 77-17 Club Dancer, Fightin Lil, Ivorette 8
6Aug86-6Lga 6f :222 :46 1:11 ft 4 118 106½ 64¾ 45½ 21½ Steiner J J3 (F) c10000 79-22 LughingDuchess,Ivorett,Prim'sBst 12
25Jly86-6Lga 6½f :213 :442 1:163ft 20 118 64¾ 68 46½ 22 Steiner J J5 (F) 12500 84-21 Rosie'sCommnd,Ivorette,BitARonie 9
Jan 17 BM 4f ft :533 h Dec 31 GG 4f hy :47 h (d)

Misty Silk ✻ — Dk. b. or br. f. 4, by Les Aspres—Queen April, by Donut King
NICOLO P 114
Br.—Summer Farms (Cal) 1987 2 0 1 0 $1,566
Tr.—King Robert $8,000 1986 10 2 0 0 $5,060
Own.—Sarmento E M
Lifetime 12 2 1 0 $6,626

14Jan87-7BM 6f :224 :471 1:132ft 8¾ 114 2hd 2½ 1hd 56 Nicolo P2 (F) 8000 66-27 SeptmbrMgic,Dubinnt,Jn'sProspct 1
1Jan87-5BM 6f :223 :464 1:13 gd 7 114 2½ 3½ 21 21 Nicolo P9 (F)[S] 8000 73-30 Creista's Ice, Misty Silk,Vickarick 1
18Dec86-2BM 6f :223 :48 1:151sy 34 114 54½ 21 13 14 Nicolo P1 (F) 6250 63-41 MistySilk,ClstilOrphn,DmondOystr 1
4Dec86-9BM 6f :221 :451 1:111ft 38 114 63¾ 63¾ 68 97 Nicolo P7 (F) 6250 76-20 Atcd,HppyMgee,FlyMeToThMoon 1
6Nov86-5BM 6f :223 :461 1:122ft 49 115 65½ 54½ 67½ 77¾ HummelCR11 (F)[S] 8000 69-22 IfNotNowWhn,Vickrck,RpplngRdg 1
24Oct86-2BM 6f :223 :463 1:124ft 32 116 76¼ 97 109½ 89¼ Hummel C R2 (F) 8000 66-25 Prima'sBest,Moneyjy,PointOfFith 1
24Oct86—Broke slowly
9Aug86-4Stk 6f :221 :463 1:12 ft 4¾ 118 52½ 54½ 34 1hd CmpbellBC2 (F)M12500 90-07 MistySilk,PortsideMolly,Celi'sDrm 1
2Jly86-8Pln 6f :222 :452 1:114ft 15 114 3½ 3½ 45½ 717 Mena F4 (F)M16000 66-18 PnnyDvlin,MissJimyJon,LovBound 1
8Jun86-3GG 6f :221 :453 1:104ft 32 115 2hd 31½ 46 713½ Mena F10 (F)[S]M25000 71-11 EdnN.,CountyWexford,MufftsSun 1
15May86-3GG 1 1/16 :463 1:12 1:454ft 51 117 11 2hd 75¾ 815¼ HmmlCR8 (F)[S]M12500 59-15 SpecialEgle,MrysCse,Merry'sBest 1
Jan 10 BM 4f gd :502 h Dec 28 BM 3f ft :373 h Dec 14 BM 4f ft :482 h Nov 29 BM 4f ft :481 h

Molly Ida — B. f. 4, by Advocator—Chuckle Patch, by Vent Du Nord
CHAPMAN T M 114
Br.—Webb T W (Ont-C) 1986 15 1 0 2 $10,035
Tr.—Ramirez Octavio $8,000 1985 10 1 1 0 $3,256
Own.—Braiman & Thomas
Lifetime 25 2 1 2 $13,301 Turf 2 0 0 0

18Dec86-9BM 1 1/16 :482 1:14 1:472m 29 115 78 — — — Aragon J5 (F) 12500 — — Bargain Queen,LaMajor,TanteBleue
18Dec86—Eased; Ducked in start
3Dec86-5BM 6f :224 :46 1:112ft 126 114 97¼ 1113 1114 1114¼ Aragon J11 (F) 12500 68-19 PrncssSplndr,SssyErryn,StrChngr 1
23Nov86-2BM 6f :222 :453 1:111ft 61 114 88½ 810 915 917¾ Aragon J7 (F) 12500 65-20 WptRgn,ScondhndRs,PrncssSplndr
2Jly86-9Pln 170 :463 1:11 1:421ft 33 115 11 811 — — Hummel C R3 (F) 25000 — — She's So Bold, Menaevia, Decorata
2Jly86—Eased
26Jun86-8Pln 170 :443 1:103 1:40 ft 19 115 35 513 — — HummlCR5 (F)Aw15000 — — NotSoDistant,Blake'sDancer,Patng
26Jun86—Eased
5Jun86-9GG 6f :22 :444 1:103ft 27 115 76½ 712 712 66½ Hummel C R1 (F) 20000 80-14 AboyThkst,ChmpgnBby,MystryMid
24May86-4GG 7½f (T):223 :472 1:31 fm 36 1095 1½ 2hd 89 710¾ Pfau R K5 (F)Aw17000 74-15 Kvngh,SuprciliousSu,Amy'sOwnGirl
14May86-6GG 1 1/16 :462 1:104 1:45 ft 11 1095 2hd 58 512 514¾ Pfau R K4 (F)Aw16000 63-17 Transgogo, Patang, Foolish Ice
14May86—Bobbled start
3May86-8GG 1 1/16 (T):473 1:121 1:442fm 102 112 41¾ 811 817 814¼ Pfau R K9 (F)Cal Oaks 66-17 TopCorsge,NovelSprite,LdyMxinD. 1
3Apr86-9GG 1 1/16 :48 1:134 1:493ft 41 1095 13 11½ 1½ 12 Pfau R K7 (F) 16000 55-30 Molly Ida, Virgin Miss, GalaPrevue
Jan 16 GG 3f ft :381 h Jan 10 GG 4f sl :55 h Jan 3 GG 4f sy :55 h (d) Dec 11 GG 1 ft 1:464 h

```
Manale                         Dk. b. or br. f. 4, by Tell—Lilda, by Boldnesian
                               Br.—Hi Card Ranch (Cal)                   1986  5 0 1 0      $3,475
  SCHACHT R A             114  Tr.—Gilchrist Greg           $8,000       1985  6 2 0 1      $9,865
Own.—Anderson R & Sylvia       Lifetime   11 2 1 1   $13,340
21Mar86-1GG  1  :47^4 1:13^1 1:40^3ft  5 114  5^1¾ 5^2¼ 5^3 5^3½  Diaz A L^4 Ⓕ 16000 61-22 Blke'sDncer,Molly'sDrem,GlPrevue 8
    21Mar86—Jumped in air; steadied 3/8
5Mar86-4GG  1 1/16 :48^4 1:12^4 1:45^3ft  8½ 114  1^hd 2^1½ 4^8 7^16½  Gonzalez RM^5 Ⓕ 25000 58-19 Novel Sprite, Faye, Kaviot's Flight 9
    5Mar86—Placed fifth through disqualification
6Feb86-9GG  1  :47^2 1:12^2 1:38^3ft  5½ 114  3^2 2^hd 1^hd 2^2½  Gonzalez RM^7 Ⓕ 16000 72-22 Selected Princess,Manale,Chargina 7
23Jan86-1BM  1 1/16 :48^3 1:13^2 1:45^3ft  15 114  4^1½ 3^nk 3½ 4^4  Chapman TM^7 Ⓕ 16000 60-24 BrennMorn,NovelSprit,ClssicQulity 8
13Jan86-5BM  6f :22^3 :45^3 1:11^1ft  23 115  6^3¼ 9^7¼ 8^7¼ 7^6½  McGurn C^1 Ⓕ 16000 76-15 Forumstar,DysBet,KnightsControl 12
30Dec85-2BM  6f :22^4 :46^2 1:12 sl  19 114  6^4 6^4¾ 6^6½ 5^9  Loseth C^1 Ⓕ 25000 70-21 PttiPerkins,Chris'sGlmor,IWlkAlon 7
    30Dec85—Broke slowly
19Dec85-5BM  6f :22^4 :46^2 1:12^2ft  4¼ 114  6^3¼ 6^3¼ 4^1¾ 1^1  Chapman TM^9 Ⓕ 12500 77-20 Manale, Foolish Ice, EveningWalk 12
5Dec85-4BM  6f :23^2 :47^1 1:13^3m  16 114  10^7¼ 11^20 8^17 7^11½  Fuentes F P^4 Ⓕ 16000 59-33 Days Bet,BarrengerBay,FoolishIce 12
    5Dec85—Bumped at start
21Nov85-5BM  6f :22^4 :46^3 1:12^1ft  14 114  1½ 1½ 1^1½ 3^1¼  Fuentes F P^5 Ⓕ 16000 77-22 OlympicClassic,FoolishIce,Manale 11
31Oct85-4BM  6f :22^4 :46^2 1:12 ft  5½ 114  4^5 5^5 6^8½ 6^9½  Gonzalez RM^5 Ⓕ 25000 69-21 GoldGlimmer,BarrengerBay,DysBet 7
  Jan 18 BM 4f ft :48^4 hg    Jan 11 BM 6f gd 1:15^4 h    Jan 5 BM 6f m 1:15^4 h    Dec 29 BM 5f ft 1:01^3 h
```

Our worksheet shows some potential power here.

Odds	Horse	PCR	Form	Ab/T
6	Double Surprise	90/ 60 56 – 13/103 = 87	Lw	(47.2 25.1–2/ 72.1)
9	Bois Hon	103/ 24 41 – 13/ 52 = 198	Lw	(45.3 25.4–2/ 71.0)
77	Royal Defense	92/ 70 54 – 6/118 = 78	NON	48.0 27.4–8/ 74.1
5	Lovable Flirt	100/ 22 52 – 20/ 54 = 185	OON	45.4 27.2+2/ 73.3
30	Majestic Jessie	30/ 13 12 + 2/ 27 =(111)	Lw	x
3-2	Ivorette	95/ 55 33 – 16/ 72 = 132	N+w	47.2 26.3–8/ 72.2
5	Misty Silk	111/ 40 55 + 4/ 99 = 99	+NO	47.1 27.2–4/ 73.4
40	Molly Ida	x		x
7-2	Manale	93/ 50 47 – 20/ 77 = 131	Lw	(47.4 24.3–1/ 72.1)

The top PCR animals are Bois Hon off a layoff and Lovable Flirt, both far ahead of the others. The two top betting choices, Ivorette and Manale, are next bunched together considerably above the rest of them. Lovable Flirt can go out quickly with the most serious form defect of all, lack of recent action. She shows only one three furlong workout since her last race 25 days ago, and a work that short does not qualify.

While we can reserve momentarily on the three remaining top PCR horses, we can find some other quick eliminations that narrow our field. Royal Defense at 77-1 and the poorest last race ability time is easily discarded. Molly Ida, too wretched to calculate, and Majestic Jessie can be discarded without even a second thought. We can concentrate a little better on the five that are left.

We can return to the strong favorite, Ivorette, to see if she is worthy of a single selection play. She turned in a good winning race last out at a lower class, but has been running reasonably well in the past against stronger competition. Because there are a number of unrated last race numbers, her ability time stands among the first three. But the great rap against this one is her running style: the 55 over 33, which despite her being up early in her last race, is a most distrustful sign. For this reason, we must be wary and keep looking before making any money decision.

The second favorite, Manale, returns off a long layoff. As we have tried to indicate, any time a horse is returning off a long layoff and is well played, that horse must be given careful consideration. We go almost a year to pick up an advisory ability time off the 6Feb86 Golden Gate effort, but this is not totally reassuring.

The one who really catches our attention, however, is Bois Hon, the high PCR horse. Here is the early speed that can cause great trouble for the others. She has a requisite 5-furlong workout. And her advisory ability time is so far ahead of anything else in the field that we wonder why she shows on the board at 9-1. If she can run back anywhere near to her capabilities, she can win this race.

We are basically dealing again with only three horses. Misty Silk has both a low PCR and a weak last race ability time, which rules her out. While each of our three remaining animals carries a question mark of one kind or another, they do stand out enough over the rest of the field to find the advantage we seek. The only remaining task is to weed out one of them and again make a multiple selection of two horses to win.

There isn't much doubt about it. Bois Hon, with her credentials, must be kept in our contention. Between Ivorette and Manale,

FIFTH RACE
BayMeadows
JANUARY 21, 1987

6 FURLONGS. (1.07$\frac{4}{5}$) CLAIMING. Purse $7,000. Fillies. 4-year-olds. Weight, 120 lbs. Non-winners of two races since December 1 allowed 3 lbs.; a race since then, 6 lbs. Claiming price $8,000. (Maiden, starter and claiming races for $6,250 or less not considered.)

Value of race $7,000; value to winner $3,850; second $1,366; third $980; fourth $630; fifth $174. Mutuel pool $83,163. Exacta pool $95,713.

Last Raced	Horse	Eqt.A.Wt	PP	St	¼	½	Str	Fin	Jockey	Cl'g Pr	Odds $1
5Dec86 ^{2}BM^{8}	Bois Hon	4 114	2	3	$3^{1\frac{1}{2}}$	3^{1}	3^{4}	$1^{2\frac{1}{2}}$	Tohill K S	8000	9.40
14Jan87 ^{7}BM^{5}	Misty Silk	b 4 114	7	2	2^{1}	2^{2}	2^{hd}	$2^{\frac{1}{2}}$	Nicolo P	8000	5.80
7Jan87 ^{2}BM^{1}	Ivorette	b 4 115	6	8	$7^{1\frac{1}{2}}$	6^{2}	5^{2}	3^{2}	Baze R A	8000	1.60
21Mar86 ^{1}GG^{5}	Manale	4 114	9	5	5^{2}	4^{3}	4^{hd}	4^{hd}	Schacht R	8000	3.90
11Dec86 ^{5}BM^{6}	Double Surprise	b 4 114	1	6	$6^{\frac{1}{2}}$	5^{hd}	6^{3}	5no	Doocy T T	8000	6.40
27Dec86 ^{2}BM^{7}	Lovable Flirt	4 115	4	1	$1^{\frac{1}{2}}$	$1^{1\frac{1}{2}}$	$1^{\frac{1}{2}}$	$6^{\frac{1}{2}}$	Maple S	8000	5.60
7Jan87 ^{2}BM^{6}	Royal Defense	b 4 109	3	7	8^{2}	8^{1}	7^{3}	7^{3}	Munoz O R^{5}	8000	77.50
21May86 ^{9}GG^{8}	Majestic Jessie	4 114	5	9	9	9	8^{hd}	$8^{\frac{1}{2}}$	Gonzalez R M	8000	30.40
18Dec86 ^{9}BM	Molly Ida	b 4 114	8	4	$4^{\frac{1}{2}}$	7^{2}	9	9	Chapman T M	8000	40.20

OFF AT 2:29. Start good. Won driving. Time, :22$\frac{3}{5}$, :46, :58$\frac{4}{5}$, 1:11$\frac{1}{5}$ Track fast.

$2 Mutuel Prices:			
2-BOIS HON	20.80	10.20	4.20
7-MISTY SILK		7.40	3.20
6-IVORETTE			2.40

$2 EXACTA 2-7 PAID $134.20.

Ivorette, off her last race, is less risky and thus becomes our second selection.

We got what we wanted, the high odds horse on top, as we so often will off our numbers that regularly do so well.

Speed indeed is now well established as the order of the day. Lovable Flirt, with her low second call number, led all the way into the stretch before fading under the burden of her lack of recent action. Bois Hon, hanging close, only a half-length out when they hit the stretch, was an easy winner. Ivorette, just as the numbers said she would do, was back in the pack, gaining in the stretch, of course, but in no way could overcome the front running receptivity of Bay Meadows today.

With that splendid $20.80 return, we are now ready for another sprint in the sixth for better claiming horses.

6th BayMeadows

6 FURLONGS. (1.07⅘) CLAIMING. Purse $11,000. 4-year-olds. Weight, 120 lbs. Non-winners of two races since December 1 allowed 3 lbs.; a race since then, 6 lbs. Claiming price $20,000. (Maiden, starter and claiming races for $16,000 or less not considered.)

Exotic Motion *
JUDICE J C — **114**
Own.—Lamoureux & Pagano
Dk. b. or br. g. 4, by Spec o' Motion—Exotic Pulse, by Gallant Host
Br.—Schilz L (Cal) — 1987 2 2 0 0 $10,450
Tr.—Delia William — $20,000 — 1986 10 3 0 1 $16,390
Lifetime 12 5 0 1 $26,840

11Jan87-7BM	6f	:23	:46^4	1:12^{1}gd	*9-5	114	$4^{3/4}$	$1^{1/2}$	1^1	1no	Judice J C^8		16000	78-27	ExoticMotion,Mr.Cane,LarryRoland	8
4Jan87-9BM	6f	:22^1	:46^1	1:11^{3}m	8½	114	2^{hd}	1^{hd}	1^3	1^7	Judice J C^4	[S]	12500	81-30	ExoticMotion,Mr.Cne,Let'sGoLong	8
14Dec86-5BM	6f	:22^1	:45	1:10^{1}ft	18	115	$7^{5 1/2}$	5^6	$5^{8 1/2}$	6^6	Judice J C^7		16000	82-17	TheFitest,SteadyPrty,PeruvinBlde	10
30Nov86-5BM	6f	:22	:44^4	1:09^{3}ft	5½	114	4^4	7^6	$8^{9 3/4}$	$8^{7 1/4}$	Chapman T M^4		c12500	84-14	CourgousNght,StrongSt,StdyPrty	12
9Nov86-3BM	6f	:22^3	:45^1	1:10^{1}ft	7½	117	$4^{2 1/2}$	$5^{6 1/2}$	$5^{8 1/2}$	$4^{6 1/2}$	Chapman T M^1		16000	81-20	TheFitest,Shmazam,GentlemnDon	11
24Oct86-7BM	6f	:22^2	:45^2	1:10 ft	8¼	117	$9^{7 3/4}$	9^8	9^{12}	$9^{12 3/4}$	Barton J^7		25000	76-25	Cpt.Pddy,WestListing,ClipprSkippr	9
10Oct86-1BM	6f	:22^2	:45	1:10^{1}ft	4¾	109^5	$3^{3 1/2}$	$3^{3 1/2}$	2^{hd}	1no	Barton J^6		25000	88-18	ExotcMoton,WstLstng,Bkr'sBounty	6
28Sep86-4BM	6f	:22^4	:45^4	1:10^{2}ft	7½	109^5	$5^{2 1/4}$	5^6	5^7	4^6	Barton J^1		35000	81-18	RoylAlloy,Percentstr,ClipperSkippr	6
13Sep86-4Bmf	6f	:22^4	:46^1	1:10^{4}ft	9½	109^5	$4^{2 1/4}$	$3^{1/2}$	1^2	1^7	Barton J^7		12500	85-31	ExoticMotion,See'sBest,OrderOrdr	8
31Aug86-12Bmf	1	:45	1:11	1:36^{4}ft	26	109^5	6^6	7^5	$8^{8 1/2}$	6^8	Barton J^4		16000	76-15	VictoryCalibre,Snedigar,Bill'sFntsy	9

Jan 3 BM 3f sy :40^1 h ●Dec 12 BM 3f ft :35 hg Nov 28 BM 3f ft :36^2 h Nov 22 BM 4f ft :49^4 h

Mr. Hugh
WINLAND W M — **114**
Own.—Aglieto-Recchedy-Waters
Dk. b. or br. g. 4, by Poly Host—Bit of Stakes, by Claim Staker
Br.—Weeks D (Cal) — 1987 1 0 0 0 $900
Tr.—Orr Ike — $20,000 — 1986 9 2 3 1 $14,583
Lifetime 13 2 3 1 $15,978

11Jan87-7BM	6f	:23	:46^4	1:12^{1}gd	6	117	3^{nk}	$2^{1/2}$	3^3	4^6	Winland W M^6		16000	72-27	ExoticMotion,Mr.Cane,LarryRoland	8
5Dec86-10BM	1 1/16	:46^1	1:12^1	1:45^{3}sl	5½	117	$3^{8 1/2}$	$4^{4 1/2}$	$6^{7 1/2}$	$6^{13 1/2}$	Winland W M^1		16000	50-26	Boundround,CloudBstr,Ddthbllrng	11
21Nov86-10BM	1 1/16	:46^3	1:11^3	1:43^{2}ft	14	115	2^{hd}	2^{hd}	$1^{1/2}$	1^{nk}	Winland W M^9		16000	75-23	Mr.Hugh,CutHimFree,Didthbllring	12
6Nov86-9BM	6f	:22^4	:45^2	1:10^{3}ft	7½	115	$4^{3/4}$	4^1	$2^{1 1/2}$	2^{nk}	Winland W M^4		8000	86-22	SteadyParty,Mr.Hugh,KingApache	11
29Oct86-3BM	6f	:22^3	:45^3	1:11^{2}ft	12	115	$6^{3 1/4}$	5^3	$4^{2 1/4}$	$4^{1 3/4}$	Winland W M^7	[S]	8000	80-22	HelOfAspr,LotPric,Acrotrion'sEdg	10
29Oct86—Bumped start																
10Oct86-2BM	6f	:22^3	:46	1:12^{1}ft	3½	117	4^2	$4^{1 1/2}$	3^1	1^{nk}	SchvnevldtCP^9		M12500	78-18	Mr. Hugh, Tellemana, RightBayou	12
1Sep86-3Bmf	6f	:22^3	:45^4	1:11^{3}ft	3¾	118	$2^{1/2}$	2^2	2^1	3^1	SchvnldtCP^3	[S]	M16000	80-16	HappyToTell,B.Traditionl,Mr.Hugh	11
15Aug86-6Stk	5½f	:22^2	:46	1:04^{3}ft	3¾	118	$4^{1 1/2}$	5^6	4^{11}	4^{13}	Campbell B C^5		M12500	81-09	Another Juan, Will He B., DonRan	10
19Jly86-4Sol	6f	:22^1	:45^2	1:10^{3}ft	6	117	2^2	2^5	2^5	2^7	Tohill K S^3	[S]	M12500	83 —	ErniAndWill,Mr.Hugh,ExotcMoton	10
20Jan86-3BM	6f	:22^4	:46^2	1:11^{4}gd	6½	118	$2^{1/2}$	2^2	2^2	2^2	Campbell B C^3		M12500	78-20	GrkChmpgn,Mr.Hugh,WildHorsmn	12

Jan 17 BM 5f ft 1:02^2 h Jan 9 BM 4f gd :48^1 h Jan 2 BM 5f gd 1:01 h Dec 28 BM 4f ft :51 h

Sun Vest — Ch. g. 4, by Sunday Guest—Miss Raedine, by Vested Power
DIAZ A L — 114 — Br.—Wood Prairie Farm (Wash) — 1987 1 0 0 1 $1,540
Own.—Vatne R — Tr.—Leonard Jack R — $20,000 — 1986 19 2 5 2 $23,460
Lifetime 24 4 5 4 $27,720

4Jan87-7BM 6f :222 :46 1:112m 11 114 42½ 41½ 2hd 31 Diaz A L1 20000 81-30 Acceptance Final, Zacbee, SunVest 9
4Jan87—Crowded on turn
21Dec86-6BM 6f :224 :461 1:114m 6¾ 114 41½ 22 23 25 Judice J C7 20000 75-35 MeYouAndQ.,SunVest,AccptncFinl 7
10Dec86-6BM 1 1/16 :46 1:103 1:442ft 8¾ 114 1hd 2½ 33 66½ Judice J C4 25000 63-21 IvnPhilps,BonVvntDottor,ClWyHlm 7
23Nov86-9BM 1 1/16 :464 1:113 1:434ft 4½ 114 11 1½ 1½ 21½ Judice J C1 25000 71-20 LuckyCretion,SunVst,PirdAndPintd 9
30Oct86-9BM 1 1/16 :451 1:101 1:433ft 19 114 23 22 1hd 41½ Judice J C3 20000 72-24 CptnO'Dsy,SnstvCopy,RtnlApprch 11
18Sep86-7Lga 6f :214 :444 1:092ft 5 120 42 33 34½ 25 Moore D1 16000 84-23 Timothy Pat, SunVest,HijoElToro 10
7Sep86-4Lga 6½f :213 :44 1:151ft 9 118 2hd 2½ 25 48 Moore D4 20000 85-14 NrthrnPlcy,PlckyEmprr,BlzngThng 7
30Aug86-7Lga 6½f :221 :45 1:18 gd 6½ 120 2½ 1hd 11 2hd Moore D2 16000 79-22 Joe'sMmoris,SunVst,TmpstDTmpo 10
23Aug86-7Lga 6½f :212 :432 1:143ft 11 116 22½ 22½ 45 47 Moore D7 20000 89-15 AgntTodd,PlckyEmpror,NrthrnPlcy 9
16Aug86-4Lga 6f :22 :451 1:101ft 6 120 1hd 1½ 2hd 1½ Moore D7 16000 85-14 Sun Vest, Merry Yanky, Tar War 8
Jan 16 BM 6f ft 1:194 h — Dec 28 BM 3f sy :392 h (d)

Larry Roland — B. g. 4, by Danzig—Triple A, by Limit to Reason
MOORE C A — 1095 — Br.—Glencrest Farm & Headley Jr (Ky) — 1987 1 0 0 1 $1,400
Own.—4-FunStbl-Mybury-Pdrencili — Tr.—Murphy Chuck — $20,000 — 1986 11 1 0 1 $13,300
Lifetime 12 1 0 2 $14,700

11Jan87-7BM 6f :23 :464 1:121gd 24 1095 88½ 87½ 67½ 34½ Moore C A2 16000 73-27 ExoticMotion,Mr.Cane,LarryRoland 8
21Dec86-7BM 1 1/8 :463 1:124 1:473m 22 115 36½ 610 716 720 Maple S3 25000 34-35 Bondrnd,NblAndGntl,PrdAndPntd 10
29Nov86-7BM 1 1/16 :454 1:101 1:42 ft 47 114 912 79½ 714 714½ Olivares F4 Aw16000 68-17 Arbitrte,Petrone'sKismet,NwStorm 9
15Nov86-9BM 1 1/16 :461 1:11 1:44 ft 36 112 44 43½ 89¾ 812½ Tohill K S1 Aw17000 59-21 Planter, Midnight Ice, New Storm 12
1Nov86-13BM 1 1/16 :464 1:113 1:444ft 36 112 63¾ 42½ 43½ 44 YammotoTJ2 Aw17000 64-21 Throw Home, Ghaza,FrereJacques 10
1Nov86—Bumped at start
28Sep86-4BM 6f :224 :454 1:102ft 7½ 114 65½ 67½ 69 57½ Yamamoto T J2 35000 79-18 RoylAlloy,Percentstr,ClipperSkippr 6
19Sep86-9BM 1 1/16 :472 1:121 1:454ft *2½ 115 42 41¾ 31 3½ Castaneda M5 c25000 62-28 BonVvntDottor,CchCnwy,LrryRlnd 7
9Sep86-10Bmf 1 :453 1:103 1:371ft 39 115 63¾ 3½ 21½ 42½ ChapmanTM8 Aw17000 79-21 PassPassPssed,ClvryChrge,Plnter 10
18Jly86-3Sol 1 :462 1:112 1:36 ft 9½ 114 43½ 31½ 43 58 CastanedaM5 Aw13000 86-12 BuckRoyl,LondonExprss,BigDnRyn 7
3Jly86-6Pln 1 1/16 :473 1:12 1:444ft *8-5 115 41 1½ 14 11 Baze R A9 Mdn 80-23 Larry Roland, Curl Out, Keawewai 10
Jan 5 BM 4f m :484 h — Dec 14 BM 4f ft :484 h

Zacbee — B. g. 4, by Gallant Best—Repeatable, by Irepeat
MILLS J W — 114 — Br.—Leckbee M & Roberta (Wash) — 1987 2 0 1 0 $2,445
Own.—Smith R W — Tr.—Cummings William R — $20,000 — 1986 14 0 2 1 $7,218
Lifetime 27 1 4 4 $20,148

11Jan87-10BM 1 1/16 :464 1:123 1:464gd 9½ 114 49 47½ 67 57 Mills J W7 25000 51-27 AckLikeM,CutHimFr,PirdAndPintd 8
4Jan87-7BM 6f :222 :46 1:112m 28 114 66¾ 54½ 64 2½ Mills J W6 20000 81-30 Acceptance Final, Zacbee, SunVest 9
10Dec86-6BM 1 1/16 :46 1:103 1:442ft 30 115 54 713 — — SchvneveldtCP1 25000 — — IvnPhilps,BonVvntDottor,ClWyHlm 7
10Dec86—Eased
23Nov86-9BM 1 1/16 :464 1:113 1:434ft 37 114 21 2½ 2½ 45½ ‡ Tohill K S2 25000 67-20 LuckyCretion,SunVst,PirdAndPintd 9
‡23Nov86—Dead heat
14Nov86-7BM 1 1/16 :464 1:111 1:43 ft 65 114 42½ 53¾ 813 814¾ Tohill K S6 40000 62-20 Arbitrate,DoctorDakota,GreekNtive 8
17Oct86-9Lga 6½f :214 :441 1:144ft 9½ 116 33½ 33 33 33¾ Hanna M A2 40000 91-18 Northern Policy, Mr. Spade,Zacbee 7
8Oct86-9Lga 1 1/16 :462 1:112 1:434ft 16 117 98¾ 94½ 513 57½ Hanna M A6 Aw9300 73-19 ImATrooper,SenorSpanish,BigDuke 9
20Sep86-9Lga 1 1/8 :464 1:104 1:49 ft 41 115 79¾ 97½ 820 812½ HMA3 [S]B Mrcs Prt H 76-18 Sssy'sHllr,GllntSlor,CrrncyControl 11
12Sep86-9Lga 1 :461 1:103 1:353ft 20e 115 77 87½ 816 77½ Hanna M A7 Aw10000 84-19 CrrncyControl,Sssy'sHllr,SnrSpnsh 9
22Aug86-9Lga 1 :453 1:101 1:351ft 37 114 66 76½ 917 810¾ Hanna M A7 Aw10000 82-17 Sssy'sHllr,CrrncyContrl,BrndyRsrv 10
Dec 29 BM 4f ft :482 h

Forget The Money — B. g. 4, by Nantequos—Forgotten One, by Whodunnit
CHAPMAN T M — 114 — Br.—Harris Farm Inc (Cal) — 1987 1 0 0 0
Own.—BmStb-HrrsFrmInc-Goodmn — Tr.—Hayden Marie E — $20,000 — 1986 4 2 0 1 $35,290
Lifetime 6 3 0 1 $40,790

7Jan87-8BM 1 :464 1:121 1:401sl 7½ 114 32 67¾ 612 616 ChapmanTM6 Aw17000 51-35 AllTheBucks,Crdell,Petrone'sKismt 6
13Dec86-6BM 6f :224 :46 1:10 ft 6¾ 113 63¾ 65½ 68½ 69¾ ChapmanTM3 Aw19000 79-19 Infantryman, CariJillHajji,Verboten 6
13Dec86—Broke in a tangle
4Feb86-8GG 6f :22 :442 1:10 gd 4 117 43½ 43 2½ 11 ChpnTM3 [R]Gldn Bear 89-18 ForgtThMony,J.R.Johnson,TllFloHll 5
24Jan86-8BM 6f :222 :454 1:104ft 2½ 120 43½ 42½ 35 32½ ChapmanTM3 Aw16000 83-21 Donnaskr,JySwift,ForgetTheMoney 8
13Jan86-8BM 6f :224 :451 1:093ft 2½ 114 1½ 1hd 1hd 11 ChapmanTM2 Aw16000 91-15 ForgtThMony,StolnMmors,DstntBy 6
21Dec85-2BM 6f :224 :452 1:102ft 3½ 118 63½ 32½ 2hd 1½ ChapmnTM8 [S]M25000 87-14 ForgtThMony,LordBlodgtt,Dfndbl 12
Jan 20 GG 3f ft :354 h — Jan 14 GG 5f gd 1:023 h — ●Jan 6 GG 3f m :37 h — Dec 20 GG 7f m 1:364 h

Our worksheet reads this way:

Odds	Horse	PCR									Form	Ab/T
4	Exotic Motion	87/	46	41	+	6/	93	=		94	N+w	46.4 25.2–4/ 71.2
8	Mr. Hugh	107/	32	29	+	17/	78	=		137	NON	47.0 26.3–4/ 72.4
2	Sun Vest	87/	20	30	+	1/	51	=		171	N+O	46.2 25.2–5/ 70.4
15	Larry Roland	89/	46	47	–	14/	79	=		113	NOg	48.1 25.0–4/ 72.2
7	Zacbee	87/	59	57	–	15/101		=		86	NON	48.3 25.4–4/ 73.3
8-5	Forget the Money	43/	24	18	–	0/	42	=		102	NON	47.1 26.3–8/ 72.1

There is nothing that an investing player should like better than a short sprint field where one horse has the highest last race ability time with a three tick advantage over the next closest animal and even more on the others, especially when one of them is an 8-5 favorite. And of course, when that same horse has by far and away the best PCR also, that is icing on the cake. No matter that he shows a form defect of a stretch loss in his last race off a plus running line. With those credentials, he can be played as a single selection even with that slight burden.

The beauty of this race is that so much money went on the nose of Forget the Money, aptly named for this race. The reason was apparently due to his victory almost a year earlier in a restricted stakes race, but what has he done for us lately? His last race ability time, still the single most reliable number in our total line, tells us that he is very, very unlikely to win.

The only horse that has any real chance of beating Sun Vest is the third favorite, Exotic Motion, who has an impressive last race ability time, three ticks off that of Sun Vest. His last race victory was impressive.

Sun Vest looks almost too good to be true. Horses who have this kind of advantage over a short field, unless the jockey falls off or they break down, can hardly avoid finishing at least second, assuming some other horse turns in an unusual performance. In situations of this kind, hearken back to our discussion of the insurance exacta. If you would play Sun Vest for win and place, skim $2 off the place ticket and turn it into an exacta with the only horse in the race with any kind of chance on top and your power horse on second, you will have truly purchased inexpensive and sound insurance. This is what we almost always do in these situations. To make this workable, you should have a minimum of $10 to win on your choice, $8 to place, and a $2 exacta. We will do it this way and when we have the result, we can reduce the bet proportionately to a $2 sum for the purpose of keeping our books straight.

I was happy to find this race on the day's card because it so beautifully illustrates what can happen and what uncertainties lurk with such a strong play as Sun Vest. Almost unbelievably, he finished second. Our insurance saved us.

SIXTH RACE
BayMeadows
JANUARY 21, 1987

6 FURLONGS. (1.07⅘) CLAIMING. Purse $11,000. 4-year-olds. Weight, 120 lbs. Non-winners of two races since December 1 allowed 3 lbs.; a race since then, 6 lbs. Claiming price $20,000. (Maiden, starter and claiming races for $16,000 or less not considered.)

Value of race $11,000; value to winner $6,050; second $2,145; third $1,540; fourth $990; fifth $275. Mutuel pool $90,618. Exacta pool $86,540.

Last Raced	Horse	Eqt.A.Wt	PP	St	¼	½	Str	Fin	Jockey	Cl'g Pr	Odds $1
11Jan87 ^{7}BM^{1}	Exotic Motion	b 4 114	1	2	1^{2}	1^{2}	1^{1}	$1^{3\frac{1}{2}}$	Judice J C	20000	4.30
4Jan87 ^{7}BM^{3}	Sun Vest	4 114	3	1	2^{hd}	2^{2}	$2^{1\frac{1}{2}}$	$2^{1\frac{1}{2}}$	Diaz A L	20000	2.00
11Jan87 ^{7}BM^{4}	Mr. Hugh	b 4 117	2	3	$3^{1\frac{1}{2}}$	$3^{1\frac{1}{2}}$	3^{5}	3^{4}	Winland W M	20000	8.20
7Jan87 ^{8}BM^{6}	Forget The Money	4 114	6	6	4^{2}	4^{4}	4^{2}	4^{1}	Chapman T M	20000	1.60
11Jan87 ^{7}BM^{3}	Larry Roland	b 4 109	4	5	$5^{\frac{1}{2}}$	$5^{\frac{1}{2}}$	5^{2}	5^{4}	Moore C A^{5}	20000	15.60
11Jan87 ^{10}BM^{5}	Zacbee	4 114	5	4	6	6	6	6	Mills J W	20000	7.50

OFF AT 2:58. Start good. Won ridden out. Time, :22⅗, :45⅘, :58, 1:10 Track fast.

$2 Mutuel Prices:			
2-EXOTIC MOTION	10.60	4.60	3.40
4-SUN VEST		3.40	3.60
3-MR. HUGH			5.40

$2 EXACTA 2-4 PAID $26.00.

There was nothing wrong with early speed. Exotic Motion had it all, wire to wire, pulling out for a Big Win. Sun Vest was second all the way, but could never catch up. Forget The Money, so heavily backed, did just what we expected, running in the second tier all the way, out of the money.

But did our internal numbers fail us this time? Exotic Motion showed a 46 over a 41, indicating his tendency to be a closer. But here is where we must be watchful indeed. Earlier in this book, I showed you an example where a horse named Hawaiian Cop went wire to wire off bigger second call numbers. His early speed showed in his last few races, while his older outings revealed big numbers that distorted his current form. The same is true here with Exotic Motion.

This horse had arrived in his last two races, up close all the way to win them both. In fact, in his next to last race, he turned in an ability time of 70.3, even better than the figure for Sun Vest. It is easy to overlook something like this. But the last two races told us enough about early speed to allow us to discount the high second call number. Because Sun Vest was a sound single selection play under our rules, we stuck to him. We did say that it would take something very exceptional to beat him, and on this day, Exotic Motion had it. Our insurance bet was well played.

Because we are capitulating our records on $2 bets and were forced to increase the number five times to get the $10 figure, we will decrease the returns by five times for our end-of-the-day summary. We would do this by making two mythical $2 bets, one to win and the other split between place and the insurance exacta. This would allow us to recoup one-fifth of the exacta return and four-fifths of the place return. This would reduce the value of our exacta to $5.20 and the value of the $3.40 place ticket to $2.72. We would have a total return of $7.92 for the $4 wagered. In real money track terms, for our $20 investment, we would have recouped $26.00 on the exacta and 4x3.40, or $13.60 on the place ticket, or $39.60 for $20 for a profit of $19.60—almost an even money return off an insured "sure thing." The final figures off $2/2 or $10/10 come out proportionately the same.

The seventh race is a rather ordinary low-priced claiming event at 1 1/16, similar to what you may find at most American tracks below the level of the two dominant circuits of New York and southern California. There are no age conditions, but the card is filled with 4-year-olds who have just passed over from the 3-year-old ranks with the beginning of a new calendar year.

7th BayMeadows

$1\frac{1}{16}$ MILES. (1.38⅗) CLAIMING. Purse $8,000. 4-year-olds. Weight, 120 lbs. Non-winners of two races at one mile or over since December 1 allowed 3 lbs.; one such race since then, 6 lbs. Claiming price $10,000. (Maiden, starter and claiming races for $8,000 or less not considered.)

El Puntero — **B. c. 4, by Inkerman—Lead Lady, by Windy Sea**
MCGURN C — **114** — **Br.—Safari Stable (Cal)** — **1987 2 0 0 0 $810**
Own.—Haley F E — **Tr.—Mejia Hugo** — **$10,000** — **1986 16 5 2 2 $12,312**
Lifetime 18 5 2 2 $13,122

10Jan87-5BM	6f	$:22^2$	$:46^1$	1:12 sl	49	115	2^2	$4^{6\frac{1}{2}}$	5^{11}	$6^{11\frac{3}{4}}$	McGurn C1	12500	67-34	Cool'nScndlous,BlzingZulu,MoveFr	9
10Jan87—Lugged out 4 1/2															
4Jan87-9BM	6f	$:22^1$	$:46^1$	$1:11^3$m	16	115	$4^{3\frac{1}{4}}$	3^2	3^5	4^{10}	McGurn C7	[S] 12500	71-30	ExoticMotion,Mr.Cne,Let'sGoLong	8
21Dec86-7BM	$1\frac{1}{16}$	$:46^3$	$1:12^4$	$1:47^3$m	28	115	7^{14}	—	—	—	McGurn C7	25000	— —	Bondrnd,NblAndGntl,PrdAndPntd	10
21Dec86—Eased; Lugged out backside															
7Dec86-10PM	6f	$:02^2$	:46	1:12 gd	8	119	4^2	$6^{3\frac{3}{4}}$	$6^{8\frac{3}{4}}$	7^{12}	Ortega JA7	Gov Spd H	75-27	ClockrsChoc,MongoDrms,Mckiddn	7
7Nov86-9PM	6f	$:22^3$	$:46^2$	1:13 ft	$2\frac{1}{2}$	120	$2^{\frac{1}{2}}$	1^{hd}	2^1	2^1	Ortega J A3	Aw2900	81-24	Mongo Drums,ElPuntero,NotInJest	6
25Oct86-10PM	6f	$:22^1$	$:46^3$	$1:13^4$sy	18	115	$1^{\frac{1}{2}}$	$1^{\frac{1}{2}}$	$1^{\frac{1}{2}}$	$1^{\frac{3}{4}}$	CrntsED1	Inaugural H	78-31	ElPuntero,OnaLuckyStrek,E.Z.Zulu	9
5Oct86-8Pla	170	$:46^4$	$1:11^4$	$1:41^2$ft	$5\frac{1}{2}$	121	$1^{\frac{1}{2}}$	$1^{1\frac{1}{2}}$	1^2	1^3	Hadley R M4	Aw2400	92-17	El Puntero, Tandika, Royal Actor	6
28Sep86-7Pla	$6\frac{1}{2}$f	:23	$:47^3$	$1:22^2$m	9	118	2^1	$3^{4\frac{1}{2}}$	9^{18}	$9^{26\frac{3}{4}}$	Hadley R M8	HcpO	42-34	Hydro, Pineapple Jack, Abishai	9
21Sep86-8Pla	$1\frac{1}{8}$	$:47^4$	$1:13^2$	$1:52^2$ft	$8\frac{1}{2}$	116	1^{hd}	1^{hd}	1^2	$1^{\frac{1}{2}}$	Hadley R M3	Dby Con	83-20	El Puntero, Tandika, Indian Coach	6
7Sep86-8Pla	1	$:46^2$	1:12	$1:38^2$ft	25	116	$5^{3\frac{1}{4}}$	$5^{2\frac{1}{2}}$	3^2	3^2	Hadley R M6	10000	83-13	StrongN'Gallant,Tandika,ElPuntero	9

Jan 2 GG 3f hy :42¹ h (d)   Dec 29 GG 5f hy 1:07⁴ h   Dec 4 PM 3f ft :37 b   Nov 26 PM 5f gd 1:04 b

Abercrombie

DOOCY T T **114**
Own.—Barron–Cleary–Massey

B. c. 4, by Petrone—Place Card, by Windy Sands
Br.—Schaffer-Schaffer-Howe (Cal) 1987 1 0 0 0
Tr.—Christiansen Albert **$10,000** 1986 7 1 0 2 $7,675
Lifetime 8 1 0 2 $7,675

4Jan87-5BM	$1\frac{1}{16}$	:46^3 1:12 1:46	m	20	114	9^{14} 10^{12} 8^{6} $7^{7\frac{1}{4}}$	Mena F^3	16000	55-30	WonderPlum,YeahMeDo,ChinaSag	10
19Dec86-9BM	$1\frac{1}{16}$	:48^2 1:13^3 1:47	m	$9\frac{3}{4}$	114	$8^{8\frac{3}{4}}$ 8^{8} 9^{11} $8^{6\frac{1}{4}}$	Mena F^2	16000	51-29	YehMeDo,NightSwope,CptinO'Dsy	11
19Dec86—Crowded 5/16											
29Nov86-7BM	$1\frac{1}{16}$	:45^4 1:10^1 1:42	ft	12	114	7^{11} 8^{10} 6^{13} $5^{11\frac{3}{4}}$	Mena F^5	Aw16000	70-17	Arbitrte,Petrone'sKismet,NwStorm	9
20Nov86-6BM	6f	:22^3 :45^3 1:10^1	ft	37	114	7^{12} 6^{7} $3^{4\frac{1}{2}}$ 3^{3}	Mena F^4	Aw17000	85-22	JustTooMuch,RisdOnStg,Abrcromb	7
25May86-3GG	$1\frac{1}{16}$	:47^3 1:12^1 1:45	ft	$5\frac{1}{2}$	114	$8^{7\frac{1}{2}}$ $9^{3\frac{3}{4}}$ 5^{4} 1no	Mena F^3	M16000	78 —	Abercrombie,Telarhyme,Schoenith	12
25May86—Ducked in start											
15May86-2GG	$1\frac{1}{16}$	:46^3 1:11^1 1:44	ft	$5\frac{1}{2}$	114	10^{11} $8^{8\frac{1}{4}}$ $5^{8\frac{1}{2}}$ $3^{4\frac{1}{2}}$	Mena F^4	M12500	78-15	Trajet, Oil Robber, Abercrombie	12
15May86—Ducked in start; rank 1st turn											
26Apr86-1GG	6f	:22^1 :45^2 1:11^1	ft	21	118	11^{12} 9^{18} 8^{12} $8^{6\frac{1}{2}}$	Mena F^2	M25000	76-12	Bkhit,DustyFether,OregonSummer	12
26Apr86—Broke slowly											
12Apr86-2GG	6f	:23^1 :46^3 1:12^1	ft	17	118	$9^{7\frac{1}{4}}$ $8^{7\frac{1}{2}}$ $8^{9\frac{1}{2}}$ 6^{4}	Mena F^4	[S]M25000	74-17	Nu Guy,TheGoldGuy,ArrogantHeir	11
12Apr86—Bumped start											

Dec 15 BM 5f ft 1:04^1 h

Cumberland Dancer

CAMPBELL B C **114**
Own.—Snell & Van Berg

Dk. b. or br. g. 4, by Sovereign Dancer—Showyourself, by Sir Gaylord
Br.—Sprague Phineas (Fla) 1987 1 0 0 0 $720
Tr.—Van Berg Jack C **$10,000** 1986 13 1 0 2 $8,775
Lifetime 14 1 0 2 $9,495

7Jan87-7BM	$1\frac{1}{16}$	:47^2 1:12^3 1:46^2	sl	18	116	$3^{1\frac{1}{2}}$ 3^{3} 2^{1} $4^{3\frac{1}{4}}$	Maple S^8	10000	57-35	Mostccioli,HloExpress,Mr.Vlntino	10
28Dec86-9SA	$1\frac{1}{16}$	:47 1:12 1:44	ft	85	117	$7^{6\frac{1}{4}}$ $8^{8\frac{3}{4}}$ 8^{12} $8^{15\frac{1}{2}}$	Sibille R^3	32000	65-14	Chili Hill, Cojak Man, Bruli's Ante	8
27Nov86-5Hol	1	:45^2 1:10^3 1:36^4	ft	105	119	$4^{2\frac{1}{2}}$ $8^{5\frac{3}{4}}$ 8^{8} $8^{12\frac{1}{4}}$	Vergara O^6	40000	67-18	Sebucan, Split Winners,BoldDecree	8
27Nov86—Lugged in backstretch, green through stretch											
13Nov86-9Hol	1	:45^3 1:10^1 1:35^3	ft	118	119	$9^{8\frac{1}{4}}$ 8^{12} 8^{21} $8^{27\frac{1}{2}}$	Meza R Q^5	50000	57-23	MischievousMtt,CojkMn,BoldDecre	9
26Oct86-2LaD	170	:48^1 1:13^2 1:45^2	ft	$3\frac{1}{4}$	119	2^{hd} 1^{hd} 1^{1} 1^{1}	Faul J H^1	Mdn	70-23	CumbrlndDncr,Smokhous,ErlyExit	10
17Oct86-5LaD	170	:46^2 1:12^2 1:45^1	ft	16	118	4^{9} $4^{8\frac{1}{2}}$ 4^{7} $3^{4\frac{1}{2}}$	Faul J H^7	Mdn	66-23	FctsOfLf,CddoDncr,CmbrlndDncr	12
28Aug86-9AP	$6\frac{1}{2}$f	:23 :47 1:19^1	ft	*2	118	$3^{2\frac{1}{2}}$ $2^{\frac{1}{2}}$ $4^{2\frac{1}{2}}$ $5^{7\frac{1}{4}}$	Fires E^2	Mdn	72-19	AkureyriKid,LynchMob,TrdingBord	9
19Aug86-1AP	6f	:23 :47^2 1:12^1	ft	$4\frac{3}{4}$	118	6^{5} $5^{1\frac{3}{4}}$ 2^{2} $4^{7\frac{1}{2}}$	Romero R P^1	Mdn	73-18	Nimoy, Burglar Alarm, AkureyriKid	9
25Jly86-3Aks	6f	:23 :45^3 1:11^1	ft	11	116	$3^{2\frac{1}{2}}$ 3^{4} 3^{5} $4^{8\frac{1}{4}}$	Doocy T T^7	Mdn	72-24	Casa Dante, StarFighter,SilkySham	7
25Jly86—Bore in											
3Jly86-1Aks	6f	:22^2 :45^1 1:10^3	ft	$4\frac{1}{2}$	116	4^{5} $4^{6\frac{1}{4}}$ 3^{8} $4^{13\frac{1}{2}}$	Doocy T T^6	Mdn	70-24	Lequori, Casa Dante, Indian Action	8

Jan 17 BM 5f ft 1:02^1 hg **Dec 27 SA 3f ft :36^2 hg**

Tropical Hill

MILLS J W **114**
Own.—Cardiff Stud Farm

B. c. 4, by Bold Tropic—Hil Race, by Hillary
Br.—Cardiff Stud Farm (Cal) 1986 10 1 1 0 $6,453
Tr.—McAnally Ronald **$10,000** 1985 0 M 0 0
Lifetime 10 1 1 0 $6,453

14Dec86-5BM	6f	:22^1 :45 1:10^1	ft	34	114	10^{16} 10^{12} 8^{12} $7^{7\frac{1}{2}}$	Loseth C^3	16000	80-17	TheFitest,SteadyPrty,PeruvinBlde	10
14Dec86—Broke in a tangle											
23Nov86-9BM	$1\frac{1}{16}$	:46^4 1:11^3 1:43^4	ft	19	115	8^{11} 8^{7} $8^{8\frac{1}{2}}$ $8^{11\frac{1}{2}}$	Castaneda M^8	25000	61-20	LuckyCretion,SunVst,PirdAndPintd	9
31Oct86-9BM	$1\frac{1}{16}$	:47^3 1:12^1 1:43^3	ft	44	114	7^{10} 6^{7} $5^{6\frac{1}{2}}$ $4^{9\frac{1}{2}}$	Judice J C^3	40000	64-21	Arbitrte,LordBlodgtt,HilHollywood	7
15Oct86-3BM	6f	:22^2 :45^3 1:11	ft	13	117	$12^{9\frac{1}{4}}$ $9^{8\frac{1}{2}}$ 5^{5} 1^{1}	CastnedM^{11}	[S]M12500	84-17	TropiclHill,RoylRogue,BrndyTruffl	12
15Oct86—Ducked out start											
3Oct86-4BM	$1\frac{1}{16}$	:46^3 1:11^4 1:44^3	ft	$5\frac{3}{4}$	116	$7^{9\frac{1}{2}}$ $9^{6\frac{1}{4}}$ 8^{12} $7^{11\frac{3}{4}}$	Maple S^1	M16000	57-21	TheRammer,SuperCharge,Zafirino	10
19Sep86-1BM	$1\frac{1}{16}$	:47^2 1:13 1:47^3	ft	4	115	$6^{8\frac{1}{2}}$ 3^{5} 3^{5} 2^{1}	ChapmnTM^7	[S]M16000	53-28	Charlie Feldman, TropicalHill,Blake	8
30Aug86-7Bmf	6f	:22^1 :45 1:09^4	ft	36	118	9^{11} 9^{12} 9^{14} $9^{14\frac{1}{4}}$	Yamamoto T J^{10}	Mdn	76-12	ColonelGay,ChinaSag,CrystoMono	10
13Jly86-7Sol	1	:46^2 1:11^2 1:38^4	ft	4	116	9^{16} 8^{12} $6^{6\frac{3}{4}}$ 5^{5}	Chapman T M^7	Mdn	75-13	Laderack, Count Ridge, Hizaam	9
28Jun86-3Pln	6f	:22^2 :45^2 1:11	ft	14	115	8^{8} 8^{9} 7^{11} 6^{7}	Judice J C^2	Mdn	80-11	‡StrongSut,Cptton,HndfulOfDmond	9
14Jun86-4GG	6f	:22 :45 1:09^4	ft	31	114	8^{11} $8^{7\frac{1}{2}}$ $7^{8\frac{1}{4}}$ $6^{6\frac{1}{4}}$	Judice J C^1	Mdn	84-09	NotableHost,Cpittion,KeyPurchse	11
14Jun86—Broke slowly											

Jan 15 BM 4f ft :48^1 h **Jan 6 BM 3f sy :38^2 h (d)** **Dec 30 BM 3f ft :36^3 h** **Dec 24 BM 3f m :39^1 h**

Abatis — Ch. g. 4, by Ruken—Windsor Rush, by Windsor Ruler
NICOLO P 114 — Br.—Currin W (Cal) — 1987 1 0 0 0
Tr.—Bonde Jeff $10,000 — 1986 12 3 2 1 $29,340
Own.—N R W Stable-Bonde-Yorn — Lifetime 19 4 4 1 $37,182

11Jan87-7BM	6f	:23	:46^4	1:12^{1}gd	9½	114	2^{hd}	41½	54½	78½	Nicolo P^1	16000	69-27	ExoticMotion,Mr.Cane,LarryRoland	8
21Dec86-2BM	6f	:22^1	:46	1:12^{2}m	*2¼	114	59½	58½	59½	47	Baze R A^3	c12500	70-35	WillHB.,Mostcciol,HrmonyAtThTop	7
21Dec86—Ducked out start															
14Aug86-9Dmr	1$\frac{1}{16}$	:46^2	1:11^3	1:44^{3}ft	9¾	116	2½	3^1	8^{11}	8^{15}	Shoemaker W^2	20000	62-17	ReasonToStudy,MimiDrem,Averted	9
14Aug86—Lugged out															
18Jly86-4Aks	1^{70}	:46^2	1:11^2	1:45^{2}ft	*2½	116	2^1	2^{hd}	1^{hd}	42½	Lively J^3	22500	67-26	PowrPct,WdnDtchkWn,ChckInfltn	6
12Jly86-3Aks	6f	:23	:46^2	1:12^{1}ft	*3-2	118	5^3	42¼	34½	2^5	Lively J^4	18000	71-25	Super Jag, Abatis, Crews Coterie	7
14Jun86-7Aks	1^{70}	:47	1:12^3	1:43^{2}ft	*4-5	116	45½	5^3	59½	516¾	Doocy T T^2	25000	63-21	Adios Madre, CheckInflation,Slider	6
24May86-9Aks	1^{70}	:47^1	1:11^2	1:43^{2}ft	7	114	68½	68½	6^9	78¾	DoocyTT^8 His Maj Cnl		71-24	RisethBoy,Tobin'sMinMn,Lif'sBst	10
14May86-7Aks	1^{70}	:49^1	1:14^3	1:44^{1}ft	*3-2	121	1½	1½	1^{hd}	1^3	Doocy T T^2	Aw16900	76-24	Abatis, Dusty Terra, Bruli's Ante	6
15Apr86-7GG	1$\frac{1}{16}$	:47^2	1:12^2	1:44^{4}gd	*2¾	114	3^1	2^{hd}	11½	12½	Gonzalez R M^2	25000	79-25	Abatis, Bud Bell, Natural Rush	7
19Mar86-2GG	1$\frac{1}{16}$	:47^3	1:12^2	1:45 ft	9¾	114	2^{hd}	1^{hd}	1^3	1^5	Judice J C^3	16000	78-21	Abatis,EndangeredSpirit,CptinChd	10

Jan 4 BM 1 sy 1:47^2 h (d) — Dec 29 BM 3f ft :35^4 h — Dec 13 BM 5f ft 1:00^1 h — Dec 4 BM 6f ft 1:15^1 h

Didthebellring * — B. g. 4, by Les Aspres—Ring a Bell, by Nantallah
CHAPMAN T M 114 — Br.—Bachman T W (Cal) — 1986 11 1 1 2 $10,805
Tr.—Retherford N J $10,000 — 1985 1 1 0 0 $7,150
Own.—Bachman & Bettinelli — Lifetime 12 2 1 2 $17,955

20Dec86-10BM	1$\frac{1}{16}$	:47^2	1:12^4	1:46^{4}m	5	114	66½	44½	9^{14}	10^{17}	Maple S^5	12500	41-30	Frivolissimo, Down Range,Kampur	12
5Dec86-10BM	1$\frac{1}{16}$	:46^1	1:12^1	1:45^{3}sl	16	115	9^{17}	7^8	32½	33½	Maple S^4	16000	60-26	Boundround,CloudBstr,Ddthbllrng	11
21Nov86-10BM	1$\frac{1}{16}$	:46^3	1:11^3	1:43^{2}ft	6¾	114	3^2	3^1	2½	34¼	Chapman T M^2	16000	71-23	Mr.Hugh,CutHimFree,Didthbllring	12
30Oct86-9BM	1$\frac{1}{16}$	:45^1	1:10^1	1:43^{3}ft	13	114	6^{11}	4^6	52½	6^4	Chapman T M^{11}	20000	70-24	CptnO'Dsy,SnstvCopy,RtnlApprch	11
10Oct86-10BM	1$\frac{1}{16}$	:47^1	1:11^3	1:43^{4}ft	8½	114	1½	1½	1^{hd}	2^1	Chapman T M^8	12500	72-18	CutHimFree,Didthebellring,Se'sBst	9
24Sep86-5BM	6f	:23	:46^3	1:13 sl	5½	114	1½	2^{hd}	1½	1½	Chapman T M^1	10000	74-31	Didthebellring,LotaPrice,CptinChd	9
6Sep86-4Bmf	6f	:22^3	:45^2	1:10 ft	13	114	2^{hd}	41¼	42½	42½	Chapman T M^1	10000	86-18	DonThln,CourgousNght,Bc'sInfront	6
6Sep86—Off slowly															
14May86-9GG	6f	:22^1	:45^3	1:10^{3}ft	23	114	2^2	75¼	7^{11}	910½	Chapman T M^6	16000	75-17	AccptncFnl,Crmylttr,ThrBngASprt	11
23Apr86-9GG	1$\frac{1}{16}$	:47	1:10^4	1:43^{2}ft	12	114	5^4	5^8	8^{15}	1016½	Campbell B C^8	16000	69-15	SilntSmil,EndngrdSprt,SnstvCopy	10
15Apr86-1GG	6f	:22^2	:46^1	1:12 gd	8¼	114	53¾	67¼	65½	46½	Chapman T M^3	16000	72-25	FlagOfTruce,DrkMence,LittleMhers	7
15Apr86—Raced greenly															

Jan 9 BM 5f gd 1:02^3 h

Halo Express — B. g. 4, by Halo—Destructora, by Atlas
BAZE R A 114 — Br.—Wilson Constance (Cal) — 1987 1 0 1 0 $1,560
Tr.—Sherman Art $10,000 — 1986 14 2 1 1 $21,810
Own.—Sokolow L — Lifetime 15 2 2 1 $23,370 — Turf 1 0 0 0

7Jan87-7BM	1$\frac{1}{16}$	:47^2	1:12^3	1:46^{2}sl	2½	115	9^{15}	9^{11}	6^4	2^{hd}	Baze R A^2	10000	60-35	Mostccioli,HloExpress,Mr.Vlntino	10
7Jan87—Very wide stretch															
19Dec86-9BM	1$\frac{1}{16}$	:48^2	1:13^3	1:47 m	7½	115	99¾	10^{11}	79½	76¼	Castaneda M^8	16000	51-29	YehMeDo,NightSwope,CptinO'Dsy	11
11Dec86-7BM	1$\frac{1}{16}$	:46^2	1:11^2	1:43^{2}ft	*3½	115	99¼	64¼	5^5	21½	Castaneda M^1	10000	73-24	SecretGene,HaloExpress,VitalMte	10
21Nov86-10BM	1$\frac{1}{16}$	:46^3	1:11^3	1:43^{2}ft	5¼	115	11^{16}	11^{10}	89½	810¾	Hansen R D^{12}	16000	64-23	Mr.Hugh,CutHimFree,Didthbllring	12
13Nov86-7Hol	1⅛	:47^2	1:12^2	1:52^{1}ft	5	116	10^{19}	10^{16}	98½	74¾	DelahoussayeE^5	20000	71-23	HertbrkDncr,JupitrTog,DoublQust	10
16Oct86-9SA	1$\frac{1}{16}$	:47^2	1:12^2	1:44 ft	6	118	87¾	9^7	7^9	79½	Olivares F^9	20000	71-19	CojakMan,ResonToStudy,Averted	10
16Oct86—Wide into stretch															
9Oct86-9SA	1$\frac{1}{16}$	:47^2	1:12^2	1:45^{1}ft	4¼	118	7^6	7^3	63¼	6^7	Stevens G L^7	25000	68-21	ILoveRcing,MimiDrem,HrtbrkDncr	12
9Oct86—Bumped hard start															
30Aug86-3Dmr	1$\frac{1}{16}$	:45^1	1:09^2	1:41^{3}ft	19	112	8^{15}	8^{16}	8^{14}	714¾	Ortega L E^3	40000	77-10	ForHimslf,NorthrnProvidr,DnliRidg	8
30Aug86—Broke slowly, erratic backstretch															
18Aug86-9Dmr	1$\frac{1}{16}$	:45^1	1:11	1:43^{4}ft	4	116	8^{11}	83¼	2^1	11¼	DelahoussyeE^5	c32000	81-14	Halo Express, Joab, PeacefulImage	8
7Aug86-3Dmr	1	:46^3	1:11^3	1:36^{4}ft	3	115	41¼	41¾	43½	44¼	Stevens G L^4	40000	80-16	Exuberant's Image, Tai High, Joab	7

Jan 15 BM 5f ft 1:03^3 h — Dec 30 BM 5f ft 1:01^2 h — Nov 26 SA 5f ft :58^2 h

Mr. Valentino ✻

DIAZ A L   **114**

Own.—Hobby Hrse Fms & Vannatta

B. g. 4, by Nantequos—Sultry Siren, by Herbalist
Br.—Forsythe J (Cal)
Tr.—Greenman Walter   **$10,000**

| 1987 | 1 | 0 | 0 | 1 | $1,120 |
| 1986 | 12 | 2 | 0 | 2 | $17,840 |

Lifetime ' 17 3 0 3 $23,710

| 7Jan87-7BM | 1₁₆:47² 1:12³ 1:46²sl | 6 114 | 8¹⁵ 67½ 31½ 3¾ | Diaz A L⁶ | 10000 59-35 Mostccioli,HloExpress,Mr.Vlntino 10 |
| 28Dec86-3BM | 6f :22¹ :45 1:09³ft | 41 114 | 10¹⁹10¹⁸10¹⁹10²² | Diaz A L⁴ | 16000 69-14 LodThWgon,ClipprSkippr,WillHB. 10 |
| 28Dec86—Bumped, steadied start |
| 24Oct86-10BM | 1₁₆:46² 1:12³ 1:45 ft | 5½ 114 | 9¹⁶ 78½ 57½ 65½ | Diaz A L¹⁰ | 12500 62-25 Boundround,Bill'sFntsy,ChrlFldmn 10 |
| 20Oct86-1BM | 1₁₆:47¹ 1:12¹ 1:43³ft | 5 114 | 6⁷ 63¾ 5⁵ 54½ | Yamamoto T J⁵ | 16000 69-19 VictoryCalibre,Bill'sFantsy,Snedigr 6 |
| 20Oct86—Broke slowly |
| 18Sep86-7BM | 1 :47 1:11⁴ 1:38 ft | *3 114 | 7⁸ 6⁹ 5⁸ 55½ | Yamamoto TJ¹⁰ | 16000 72-27 CptinO'Dsy,StrckngFury,‡RdCrdnl 10 |
| 18Sep86—Placed fourth through disqualification |
| 6Sep86-1Dmr | 1₁₆:45³ 1:11² 1:43³ft | 5½ 115 | 9⁹ 84¾ 6⁶ 4⁸ | McCarron C J¹⁰ | 18000 74-12 Convincing, Sea And Sew, Mural 10 |
| 6Sep86—Broke slowly, checked start |
| 25Aug86-1Dmr | 1₁₆:45² 1:11³ 1:44²ft | 2½ 117 | 8¹² 86½ 44½ 3² | Pincay L Jr⁶ | 16000 76-16 Ontheemis,VlintGnrtion,Mr.Vlntino 8 |
| 25Aug86—Wide 3/8 turn; lugged in stretch |
| 14Aug86-9Dmr | 1₁₆:46² 1:11³ 1:43³ft | 5½ 109⁵ | 8⁶ 51¾ 4⁵ 55½ | Black C A⁸ | 18000 72-17 ReasonToStudy,MimiDrem,Averted 9 |
| 14Aug86—Wide 3/8 turn |

Jan 4 BM 3f sy :41³ h (d)   Dec 19 BM 4f m :51² h (d)   Dec 13 GG 4f ft :49³ h   ●Dec 8 GG 3f ft :35³ h

And now for the worksheet.

Odds	Horse	PCR			Form	Ab/T
15	El Puntero	79/ 25 44 –	2/ 67	= 118	NON	(14.2 33.4–7/ 46.4)
6	Abercrombie	84/ 66 41 –	7/100	= 84	NON	14.2 33.4–5/ 47.1
5	Cumberland Dncr	90/ 46 49 –	13/ 82	= 110	NNO	13.1 33.4–8/ 45.3
19	Tropical Hill	95/ 78 55 –	4/129	= 74	Lw	(11.4 32.0+1/ 44.0)
5	Abatis	76/ 33 40 –	19/ 52	= 146	NON	(14.0 33.3–4/ 46.4)
6	Didthebellring	99/ 41 52 –	14/ 79	= 115	0–	(11.4 32.2–2/ 43.4)
9-5	Halo Express	98/ 82 51 –	16/117	= 84	NNg	14.4 32.3–8/ 45.4
6	Mr. Valentino	73/ 56 41 –	13/ 87	= 84	NNN	14.1 32.4–8/ 45.2

As in many races, you will quickly come into what may appear at first to be two conflicting key situations. You have already seen the power of early runners on a track favoring early speed somewhat. Among the eight horses, there are only three whose second call numbers are significantly lower than their finish position numbers. These three also have the three highest PCRs. Two of them, El Puntero and Abatis, are coming off sprint races with such bad form that it would be difficult to take them too seriously. The other, Didthebellring, had a very slight layoff off miserable form and a workout that is in itself not recent enough to avoid a zero defect for recency. If it were not for the early speed factor that we must consider, you would quickly dismiss all three of them. Cumberland Dancer runs more to evenly, but has a good class factor number.

But with speed doing so well, you have to look further. The strong horse in the race is the heavy favorite, Halo Express, at 9-5, where the next lowest on the board shows at 5-1. This is an exceptional odds spread in a medium sized field. You may be immediately repelled by the very low PCR of Halo Express and his habit of lagging behind the field, which makes him the most pronounced closer in the race. Thus, the apparent questionable conflict arises, can the late running closer overtake the speed horses on a day when the track is clearly running fast early?

Halo Express is one of two in the race with no form defects. His last race ability time among the measured horses is fully competitive. The other, Mr. Valentino, is another closer with another very low PCR, and likewise a competitive last race ability time.

You will recall that one of our key rules for single selection play is a favorite with no form defects who has one of the three best last race ability times, even if his PCR is low. That fits Halo's Express. But there is always one further step: the constant caveat that the track must not be contrary to the horse's running style, which brings us back to our apparent conflict.

When we are confronted with these kinds of conflicting situations, we must weigh one against the other and decide, based upon what we have tried to set forth in this book, whether there is enough of an advantage in one or the other to warrant a play or a pass.

The key element here is that our three earlier speed horses are so weak. You simply cannot expect any one of them to win. Didthebellring has a sparkling advisory time, but in our form studies, we have stressed that the recency form defect is so severe that a horse with it cannot be played. That means throw them out. And if they can be genuinely and confidently discarded, almost as if they did not exist, you are left with a kind of vacuum on one side of a possibly conflicting situation, which leaves the other element as dominant.

Based upon the studies that we provided earlier that in route races, early speed is not nearly as compelling as late speed, which is generally known to every experienced player, you can be even more confident that the closers will indeed come on to pass the weak frontrunners.

Because of this, we can elevate Halo Express back into a single selection play as the favorite with no form defects and a strong quali- fying last race ability time. Now, that wasn't too hard, was it?

Neither difficult nor surprising. Once again, the race was run almost precisely as the internal numbers and the form factors would indicate. At the first call at four furlongs, Abatis, Cumberland Dancer, and Didthebellring, all with lower internal numbers, were running one-two-three. At the second call at the 6-furlong point, the front

SEVENTH RACE
BayMeadows
JANUARY 21, 1987

$1\frac{1}{16}$ MILES. (1.38⅘) CLAIMING. Purse $8,000. 4–year–olds. Weight, 120 lbs. Non–winners of two races at one mile or over since December 1 allowed 3 lbs.; one such race since then, 6 lbs. Claiming price $10,000. (Maiden, starter and claiming races for $8,000 or less not considered.)

Value of race $8,000; value to winner $4,400; second $1,560; third $1,120; fourth $720; fifth $200. Mutuel pool $85,896. Exacta Pool $114,845.

Last Raced	Horse	Eqt.	A.	Wt	PP	St	¼	½	¾	Str	Fin	Jockey	Cl'g Pr	Odds $1
7Jan87 ^{7}BM^{2}	Halo Express	b	4	115	7	7	7^{2}	7^{2}	7^{hd}	3^{1}	$1^{1\frac{1}{2}}$	Baze R A	10000	1.80
7Jan87 ^{7}BM^{3}	Mr. Valentino	b	4	114	8	8	8	8	8	$5^{1\frac{1}{2}}$	2^{hd}	Diaz A L	10000	6.30
7Jan87 ^{7}BM^{4}	Cumberland Dancer	b	4	114	3	3	$2^{\frac{1}{2}}$	$2^{\frac{1}{2}}$	$2^{\frac{1}{2}}$	1^{1}	3^{4}	Campbell B C	10000	5.30
11Jan87 ^{7}BM^{7}	Abatis	b	4	114	5	2	1^{3}	$1^{1\frac{1}{2}}$	$1^{\frac{1}{2}}$	2^{hd}	4^{1}	Nicolo P	10000	5.80
20Dec86 ^{10}BM^{10}	Didthebellring		4	114	6	1	$3^{\frac{1}{2}}$	4^{3}	3^{3}	4^{hd}	5^{nk}	Chapman T M	10000	6.00
4Jan87 ^{5}BM^{7}	Abercrombie		4	114	2	4	6^{4}	$5^{\frac{1}{2}}$	5^{hd}	6^{2}	$6^{1\frac{1}{2}}$	Doocy T T	10000	6.80
14Dec86 ^{5}BM^{7}	Tropical Hill		4	114	4	5	5^{hd}	6^{5}	6^{2}	7^{10}	7^{15}	Mills J W	10000	19.80
10Jan87 ^{5}BM^{6}	El Puntero		4	115	1	6	4^{3}	3^{hd}	4^{1}	8	8	McGurn C	10000	13.70

OFF AT 3:28. Start good. Won driving. Time, :23⅗, :47⅕, 1:12⅕, 1:38, 1:44⅕ Track fast.

$2 Mutuel Prices:				
	9–HALO EXPRESS	5.60	3.00	2.40
	10–MR. VALENTINO		4.80	3.00
	4–CUMBERLAND DANCER			3.00

$2 EXACTA 9–10 PAID $20.00.

runners were still prominent. But the end was near. Halo Express and Mr. Valentino, the two big closers, were running next to last and last even at the second call, when almost three-quarters of the race had been run. At the head of the stretch, their moves had been made. It was no trouble at all for Halo Express to win and return a $5.60 mutuel that was about right in the circumstances. The high PCR early speed horses were simply too far off form to win even with a track that so readily favored them.

Thus, you must be aware that you cannot be wedded to the early speed concept even when it is running so well if the form of the ranking horses is simply so bad that it becomes a major impediment that will defeat these animals. This is especially so in route races. If this race had been a sprint, Abatis or Cumberland Dancer might have hung on because there might not have been enough time for Halo Express to get there, but even then, I would be fearful.

Again, this is the beauty of the full handicapping equation of integrating Performance Class Ratings with form as almost equal partners in the process. We can achieve our successes in two situations, one, when there is a semblance of harmony between them, and two, when one simply overpowers the other, as the last race illustrates. Both of them give us the big advantage that is so necessary to achieve the profits we will have as long as we play this method.

The eighth and feature race brings the very short field of five that we intensely dislike because of how it curtails our opportunities. But again, races with only five horses occur from time to time, as late scratches and changing circumstances leave the racing secretary with little choice. There are times when we can do well, but with wariness.

Here is the field in this one-mile event, a classified allowance race for older horses.

8th BayMeadows

1 MILE. (1:33⅗) CLASSIFIED ALLOWANCE. Purse $20,000. 4-year-olds and upward, non-winners of $9,500 twice at one mile or over since July 15. Weights, 4-year-olds, 120 lbs.; older, 121 lbs. Non-winners of $11,500 at one mile or over since November 1 allowed 3 lbs.; $10,500 at one mile or over since September 1, 6 lbs. (Maiden, starter and claiming races not considered.)

Don't Fool With Me

B. h. 5, by Tanthem—Varsity Hostess, by Forward Pass
LAMANCE C **121** **Br.—Sea Spray Farm (Ky)** 1987 1 0 0 0 $1,750
Tr.—Offield Duane 1986 12 2 2 4 $52,782
Own.—Worswick R **Lifetime 37 7 5 9 $149,599** **Turf 21 3 5 5 $90,955**

3Jan87-8BM 1 :461 1:111 1:372sy 5 113 1hd 31 44½ 510 Lamance C6 Bart H 71-23 Right Con, Barbery, Retsina Run 7
20Dec86-7BM 1 :452 1:114 1:384m 3 113 11 12 1½ 11 Lamance C7 HcpO 74-30 Don'tFoolWithMe,Ascension,BunJf 7
20Dec86—Run in divisions
8Nov86-8BM 1 1/16 :452 1:10 1:422ft 27 114 13 11 22 35½ Maple S3 [R]Sbsct Iv H 75-25 Sidersell, Armin, Don'tFoolWithMe 5
31Oct86-8BM 5½f :222 :453 1:04 ft 34 115 42½ 44½ 812 812¾ Maple S3 Aw20000 79-21 Holy Rascal,Cardell,TeddyNaturally 9
11Oct86-8BM 7½f (T):223 :4531:301fm 13 113 31½ 32½ 31½ 54½ LmnceC2 Mrk's Plc H 88-07 PerfcTrvl,NwAtrction,Position'sBst 9
1Sep86-9LaD 1 1/16 (T):46 1:1031:413fm 23 112 12½ 1½ 73½ 93½ FrzierRL9 Sport Cty H 89-12 Miss Aggie Lue, Jamie Joe,Catane 11
8Aug86-9LaD a7½f (T) 1:282fm 3 114 13 15 12½ 1nk Frazier R L1 Aw15000 97-03 Don'tFoolWithMe,BrbedNl,Frightnr 6
25Jly86-9LaD a1 (T) 1:35 fm 2 114 17 12 1½ 2nk Faul J H1 Aw15000 92-08 Nonno,Don'tFoolWithM,KnofSpots 6
4Jly86-10LaD 1 1/16 (T):47 1:1041:413fm 9¾ 114 11 2hd 32 56½ TejeiraJ8 Indepence H 87-15 Jamie Joe, Mimir, Tricky Bond 10
21Jun86-9LaD a1 1/16 (T) 1:413fm 7½ 114 31½ 2½ 31½ 31 Tejeira J1 Aw17000 92-06 TrickyBond,Mimir,Don'tFoolWithM 8
21Jun86—Hand Timed
●Jan 18 BM 5f ft :593 h ●Jan 13 BM 4f gd :464 h ●Dec 29 BM 4f ft :452 h ●Dec 13 BM 7f ft 1:24 h

*Dormello

B. h. 6, by Liloy—Perusa, by Pardallo
CASTANEDA M **115** **Br.—Haras Santa Maria de Araras (Arg)** 1987 1 0 0 1 $6,500
Tr.—McAnally Ronald 1986 9 0 1 1 $17,332
Own.—Paulson A E **Lifetime 24 5 2 3 $42,698** **Turf 15 5 2 1 $29,132**

1Jan87-8BM 1 1/16 :461 1:104 1:441gd 10 114 55¼ 55½ 43 32½ LosthC8 [R]Nw Yr Iv H 68 — CalvaryCharge,OnRetiner,Dormello 8
20Dec86-6BM 1 :462 1:114 1:384m 3½ 114 22 34 38 510¼ Loseth C7 HcpO 64-30 RetsinaRun,Waitin'ForBever,Plnter 8
20Dec86—Run in divisions
29Nov86-4BM 6f :221 :444 1:09 ft *6-5e 114 46 56½ 54½ 43½ Loseth C1 Aw20000 90-17 BrghtAndRght,ProudstHor,RtsnRn 6
26Oct86-6BM 7½f (T):231 :4641:294fm 8½ 114 35 42½ 55¼ 46 Judice J C2 Aw22000 89-05 PairOfAces,NewAtraction,ReglBrek 6
21Sep86-8BM 6f :221 :444 1:084ft 13 113 75¾ 88¼ 89 810¼ ChpnTM3 Fall Fstvl H 85-18 SirMcmillion,AmericnLgion,Ondrty 8
21Sep86—Broke slowly
30Aug86-11Bmf 6f :222 :444 1:083ft 13 114 31 32½ 33 32 ChpnTM1 Ormndle H 94-12 PrinceDonB.,Stan'sBower,Dormello 4
11May86-9Hia 7f :231 :453 1:221ft 19 112 2hd 2½ 76½ 714¾ LeeMA7 Sprint Chp H 77-24 LordByron,JustAMnr,WrdOffTrobl 7
21Apr86-8Hia 1⅛ :47 1:11 1:491ft 31 115 76¾ 713 721 727¾ Sellers M S8 Aw15000 58-18 LnchAPgss,BoldSothrnr,CrystlGblt 8
11Apr86-9Hia a1 1/16 (T) 1:412fm 12 115 65¼ 64¾ 914 812½ Lee M A10 Aw17200 78-09 Tri For Size,Ronbra,Aristocratical 10
1Feb85♦6SanIsidro(Arg) a1 1:322gd 9¾ 130 (T) 1nk †VldsJ GP JS deAncrn(Gr1) Dormllo,GoodChmpgn,GoodDnzyl 21
† 1Feb86—Disqualified and placed second for bearing out final yards
●Jan 11 BM 4f gd :472 h ●Dec 29 BM 3f ft :343 h Dec 13 BM 5f ft :592 h ●Dec 6 BM 3f m :351 h

Retsina Run

Ch. h. 7, by Windy Sands—Retsina Star, by Pia Star
SCHVANEVELDT C P **121** **Br.—Oldknow & Phipps (Ky)** 1987 1 0 0 1 $6,500
Tr.—Martin R L 1986 13 1 2 1 $44,300
Own.—Oldknow & Phipps **Lifetime 50 7 12 6 $295,050** **Turf 16 1 3 2 $82,850**

3Jan87-8BM 1 :461 1:111 1:372sy 4¼ 114 31 21 33 38 SchvnevldtCP7 Bart H 73-23 Right Con, Barbery, Retsina Run 7
20Dec86-6BM 1 :462 1:114 1:384m *3¼ 114 12 13 14 14 SchvneveldtCP1 HcpO 74-30 RetsinaRun,Waitin'ForBever,Plnter 8
20Dec86—Run in divisions
7Dec86-8BM 1 1/16 (T):4711:1111:423gd 16 114 34 33 511 515 ScldtCP3 Spr Mmnt H 75-10 Barbery, Armin, Pair Of Aces 9
29Nov86-4BM 6f :221 :444 1:09 ft 6½ 115 33 32 32½ 33½ SchvnvldtCP6 Aw20000 90-17 BrghtAndRght,ProudstHor,RtsnRn 6
7Sep86-7Dmr 1 1/16 :452 1:094 1:411ft 21 116 43½ 77½ 812 813¼ McHrDG4 [R]WndSnds 81-13 Varick, Epidaurus, Coastliner 8
27Jly86-7Dmr 1 (T):4611:1011:343fm 20 116 11 1hd 2hd 42¼ McHrgueDG3 Aw35000 96-04 Corridor Key, Estate, Raipillan 9
13Jly86-3Hol 6f (T):224 :4521:081fm 11 116 54 45½ 45 44¾ DelahoussayeE2 HcpO 96-03 Ice Hot,RiverDrummer,LincolnPark 6
13Jly86—Bumped start
28Jun86-7Hol 6f (T):22 :4431:08 fm 3¾ 115 75¼ 75¼ 63¾ 44¾ Shoemaker W7 HcpO 97-05 River Drummer,LincolnPark,Estate 7
6Jun86-7Hol 1 (T):4531:0911:332fm 5¼ 115 1½ 2hd 31 64¾ Toro F8 Aw40000 — — Will Dancer, Poly Test, Al Arz 9
18May86-5Hol 6f (T):212 :4341:083fm 25 115 109¾105½ 63¼ 2½ DlhssyE4 Nght Mvr H 98-03 ZanyTactics,RetsinaRun,StrVideo 10
18May86—Stumbled start
Jan 17 BM 5f ft 1:02 h Dec 31 BM (T) 4f fm :51 h (d) Dec 18 BM 4f sy :524 h (d) ●Nov 22 BM 6f ft 1:11 h

Soldat Bleu B. h. 5, by Lyphard—Summer Mark, by Summer Tan
BAZE R A 115 Br.—Gainesway Fm & CrescentFm (Ky) 1986 7 2 1 0 $33,980
Tr.—Drysdale Neil 1985 3 0 1 1 $2,706
Own.—SheikManaBnRshdAlMktoum Lifetime 14 3 3 1 $43,684 Turf 14 3 3 1 $43,684
26Dec86-7SA 1⅛Ⓣ:48 1:1221:49 fm 14 116 31½ 52½ 77 78½ DelhoussyeE7 Aw48000 73-17 Hermes, Catane, Rivlia 8
23Nov86-6BM a1⅛Ⓣ 1:483fm*8-5 115 2hd 11 11½ 1no CastanedaM6 Aw19000 92-08 SoldatBleu,DiplomatRuler,JaySwift 9
23Nov86—Bothered by loose horse 2nd turn
22Oct86-7SA 1⅛Ⓣ:4541:1021:471fm *3 117 43½ 51½ 85 77¾ Pincay L Jr3 Aw35000 83-12 Nugget Point, Catane, Schiller 10
22Oct86—Steadied 1/8
11Oct86-7SA 1⅛Ⓣ:4631:1031:481fm 4½ 115 46 35½ 44 53¾ Stevens G L6 Aw45000 82-21 Nasib, Skip Out Front, Pudahuel 8
28Sep86-6BM 1 Ⓣ:4641:1111:372gd *2½ 115 812 87 45 21 CastanedaM5 Aw19000 92-08 WellRelated,SoldtBleu,OrindOriginl 8
28Sep86—Stumbled at start
12Apr86-5SA 1⅛Ⓣ:4711:1131:473fm 5½ 119 31 3½ 32 64 Pincay L Jr5 Aw35000 85-14 Rich Earth, Snowcreek, Rivlia 8
23Feb86-7SA 1⅛Ⓣ:4711:12 1:504fm 8½ 117 97¼ 85½ 21½ 1hd Pincay L Jr2 Aw34000 73-24 Soldat Bleu, Kala Dancer, Solstein 9
23Feb86—Wide into stretch
27Jly85♦1Ascot(Eng) 1 1:433fm 5½ 129 Ⓣ 21½ JusterM Hope Diamnd Field Hand, SoldatBleu,SheerCliff 24
9May85♦4Chester(Eng) a1¼ 2:131gd 3½ 124 Ⓣ 634 Piggott L Dee(Gr3) Infantry, Trucidator, Vertige 7
1May85♦4Ascot(Eng) 1¼ 2:093gd *2½ 126 Ⓣ 34 SnbrnWR White Rose Vertige, Trojan Prince, Soldat Bleu 7
Jan 15 SA 5f ft 1:012 h ●Jan 10 SA tr.t 4f gd :481 h Dec 20 SA 7f ft 1:301 h Dec 15 Hol 6f ft 1:143 h

***Aras An Uachtarain** Dk. b. or br. h. 7, by Habitat—Galletto, by Nijinsky II
MAPLE S 115 Br.—Lyonstown House Stud (Ire) 1987 1 0 0 0
Tr.—Kiesner James R 1986 2 0 0 0 $500
Own.—Dmpsy-Solomon-Wlson(Lss) Lifetime 22 4 2 7 $131,792 Turf 17 4 2 6 $70,342
1Jan87-8BM 1$\frac{1}{16}$:461 1:104 1:441gd 6 115 2hd 3½ 56 711½ MapleS5 ⓇNw Yr Iv H 59 — CalvaryCharge,OnRetiner,Dormello 8
7Dec86-8BM 1$\frac{1}{16}$Ⓣ:4711:1111:423gd 19 114 514 616 821 724 Diaz AL9 Spr Mmnt H 66-10 Barbery, Armin, Pair Of Aces 9
7Dec86—Broke slowly
21Nov86-8BM 6f :22 :443 1:083ft 12 115 66 54½ 48½ 511¾ Hansen R D7 Aw20000 84-23 BuenJef,WhipUpThTmpo,HolyRscl 7
21Aug85-8Dmr a1¼:461 1:352 1:581ft 3¾ 119 64½ 42½ 66½ 57 Toro F1 ⓇCabrillo H 79-12 LstCommnd,ExecutivePrid,IronLdr 8
11Aug85-8Dmr 1⅛Ⓣ:4811:1131:464fm 18 113 66½ 66½ 78¼ 78¾ Toro F7 E Read H 95-05 TsnmSlw,AlMmoon,BthEndsBrnng 7
11Aug85—Grade II
28Jly85-7Dmr 1$\frac{1}{16}$Ⓣ:4841:1231:433fm*6-5 120 84½ 73¼ 43 11½ Toro F6 Aw26000 90-09 ArsAnUchtrn,ExplosvPssr,Snowcrk 9
28Jly85—Wide into stretch
19Jly85-8Hol 1$\frac{1}{16}$Ⓣ:4641:1041:411fm*9-5 119 76½ 54½ 41¾ 3¾ ShoemkerW3 Aw36000 92-13 ExecutivePrid,Psknll,ArsAnUchtrin 7
29Jun85-9Hol 1$\frac{1}{16}$Ⓣ:4641:1041:414fm*8-5 117 68¾ 66½ 4nk 11 ShoemkerW6 Aw38000 90-13 ArsAnUchtrn,WtchForDwn,AllzBrtn 9
13Jun85-9Hol 1 :444 1:091 1:333ft 3 116 31 2hd 1½ 32 ShoemkerW5 Aw38000 103-06 LotsHony,RoylConcllr,ArsAnUchtrn 7
1Dec84-7Hol 1$\frac{1}{16}$Ⓣ:4711:11 1:414fm *2½ 116 31½ 2½ 1hd 21½ McCrronCJ10 Aw28000 88-14 PrncGrd,ArsAnUchtrn,EprdrAlNrt 12
1Dec84—Wide
Jan 18 BM 4f ft :471 h Jan 11 BM 7f gd 1:28 h Dec 29 BM 3f ft :351 h Dec 17 BM 4f gd :484 h

We have the following worksheet:

Odds	Horse	PCR	Form	Ab/T
7-2	Don't Fool W/Me	78/ 19 42 – 6/ 55 = 142	NNO	11.2 28.0−2/ 39.0
5-2	Dormello	65/ 43 49 – 7/ 85 = 76	NNN	(09.4 23.3+1/ 33.3)
2	Retsina Run	79/ 40 40 – 13/ 67 = 118	NNO	11.2 27.3−2/ 38.0
5-2	Soldat Bleu	60/ 33 29 – 7/ 55 = 109	NOt	n/a
9	Aras An Uacht/	83/ 46 41 – 17/ 70 = 119	NON	–

Immediately we are struck with the gaps in information that make selection so difficult. When we have blanks before us, we enter the realm of guesswork. Take Dormello, for example, who ran well in his last race. But we have no published variant to compute, and this leaves us out of a last race ability time. When we go back to earlier races, we work off a sprint on Nov. 29, and this, despite its splendid figure, is still very speculative.

Soldat Bleu is a turf horse and there is nothing on the dirt that allows us to do figures on him. Aras An Uachtarain is likewise an unknown. The high PCR horse, Don't Fool With Me, with good early speed, has a woeful last race ability time. Retsina Run, the favorite, carries a form defect and an ability time that does not inspire confidence.

This race beautifully illustrates the value of passing. Not enough information is too much of a handicap if we are to succeed; guesswork is the evil we must avoid. I could not urge more strongly the passing of a race like this. We were not too surprised that Dormello won at a fair price in this field, but it was simply too risky for us.

EIGHTH RACE
BayMeadows
JANUARY 21, 1987

1 MILE. (1.33⅘) CLASSIFIED ALLOWANCE. Purse $20,000. 4-year-olds and upward, non-winners of $9,500 twice at one mile or over since July 15. Weights, 4-year-olds, 120 lbs.; older, 121 lbs. Non-winners of $11,500 at one mile or over since November 1 allowed 3 lbs.; $10,500 at one mile or over since September 1, 6 lbs. (Maiden, starter and claiming races not considered.)

Value of race $20,000; value to winner $11,000; second $3,900; third $2,800; fourth $1,800; fifth $500. Mutuel pool $78,024. Exacta pool $66,593.

Last Raced	Horse	Eqt.A.Wt	PP	St	¼	½	¾	Str	Fin	Jockey	Odds $1
1Jan87 ^{8}BM^{3}	Dormello	6 115	2	3	5	5	$4^{\frac{1}{2}}$	3^{2}	$1^{1\frac{1}{4}}$	Castaneda M	2.60
3Jan87 ^{8}BM^{5}	Don't Fool With Me	5 121	1	1	$1^{1\frac{1}{2}}$	1^{1}	1^{hd}	1^{1}	2^{4}	Lamance C	3.70
3Jan87 ^{8}BM^{3}	Retsina Run	b 7 121	3	2	2^{3}	2^{3}	2^{3}	2^{hd}	$3^{1\frac{1}{2}}$	Schvaneveldt C P	2.00
1Jan87 ^{8}BM^{7}	Aras An Uachtarain	7 115	5	4	3^{hd}	$4^{\frac{1}{2}}$	3^{hd}	4^{3}	4^{2}	Maple S	9.00
26Dec86 ^{7}SA^{7}	Soldat Bleu	b 5 115	4	5	4^{3}	$3^{1\frac{1}{2}}$	5	5	5	Baze R A	2.70

OFF AT 3:56 Start good. Won driving. Time, :22⅗, :45⅗, 1:10⅖, 1:23⅖, 1:36⅕ Track fast.

$2 Mutuel Prices:

2-DORMELLO	7.20	3.80	2.40
1-DON'T FOOL WITH ME		4.60	2.40
3-RETSINA RUN			2.20

$2 EXACTA 2-1 PAID $36.60.

Early speed runner Don't Fool With Me led into the stretch, as might have been expected, and faded, as might have been expected. Dormello, off his good form and a smidgeon of early speed, betrayed his style by running slightly behind the others for a short time and then coming on to win without undue difficulty. In looking back over the race, you could rather easily make a strong case for this one after it was over, but playing the red board is no way to fool ourselves.

Therefore, on to the ninth and last race on the card, where we have a six furlong sprint for fillies and mares of lower echelon quality. Another small field leaves us with the usual perplexities at the outset.

9th BayMeadows

6 FURLONGS. (1.07⅘) CLAIMING. Purse $10,000. Fillies and mares. 4-year-olds and upward. Weights, 4-year-olds, 120 lbs.; older, 121 lbs. Non-winners of two races since December 1 allowed 3 lbs.; a race since then, 6 lbs. Claiming price $12,500. (Maiden, starter and claiming races for $10,000 or less not considered.)

Miss Muffet

LOSETH C — **115**
Own.—Van Kempen Diane E

B. m. 5, by Plaster—Mrs Batchelor, by Magic Hope II
Br.—Van Kempen D (Cal) — 1986 6 0 1 1 $4,400
Tr.—White Dan — $12,500 — 1985 5 1 1 1 $10,750
Lifetime 11 1 2 2 $15,150

3Dec86-1Hol 6f :22^1 :46^2 1:12^{2}ft 16 116 1^{hd} 3½ 3^{3½} 5^{12} Sibille R^1 Ⓕ 12500 69-18 SweetJspry,Ms.CrookdRod,NigrLdy 8
3Dec86—Bumped at break
1Aug86-1Dmr 6f :22 :45^1 1:11 ft 6¼ 111^5 2^{hd} 2½ 5^{5½} 7^{8½} Cisneros J E^5 Ⓕ 12500 74-13 JazzyLisa,TrendyPress,Wlker'sLdy 10
1Aug86—Steadied at 3/16
8Jly86-8LA 6f :22^2 :46^1 1:12^{1}ft 3-2 111^5 9^{11} 9^{17} 9^{29} 9^{39} Cisneros J E^3 Ⓕ 12500 43-14 Walker'sLady,Intentional,MinAsset 9
14Jun86-3Hol 6f :22^1 :46^1 1:11^{3}ft 9¾ 111^5 4^{2¼} 6^{6¼} 7^8 7^{13¼} Cisneros J E^7 Ⓕ 20000 73-14 Sweet Winkle,AmecaJ.,MyGirlBeck 9
14Jun86—Unruly;rough trip
24May86-3Hol 6f :22^3 :46^2 1:12^{3}ft 9½ 111^5 1½ 1^{hd} 2^{1½} 3^{1¾} Cisneros J E^9 Ⓕ 20000 79-16 RdFrnchy,Rogr'sScrtry,MissMufft 12
24May86—Lugged out drive
8May86-3Hol 6f :22^1 :45^4 1:11^{3}ft 6 111^5 1^2 1½ 2½ 2^{hd} Cisneros J E^2 Ⓕ 10000 86-14 PrincesaElvir,MissMuffet,JnisViol 10
8May86—Lugged out drive
17Jly85-2Hol 6f :22^2 :46 1:11^{4}ft *2¼ 115 1^{1½} 1^1 1½ 1¾ Sibille R^{11} ⒻM32000 88-09 Miss Muffet, SugarTrail,HydroJet 11
21Jun85-2Hol 6f :22^4 :46^2 1:11^{4}ft 17 115 1^{1½} 1^{1½} 1^1 2½ Sibille R^3 ⒻⓈM32000 87-05 Gorgi'sRinbow,MissMufft,ProprM 12
8May85-1Hol 6f :22^1 :46^2 1:11^{3}ft 38 116 1½ 2½ 2^2 3^{5½} ♦ Sibille R^9 ⒻⓈM32000 83-10 ThirdMrrige,IRemmbrWhn,SwtDD 11
♦ 8May85—Dead heat
19Apr85-1SA 6f :21^3 :44^4 1:11 ft 37 117 3^{1½} 3^5 8^{14} 11^{12¼} Sibille R^{11} ⒻM32000 71-16 ClgryConnction,SugrTrl,ArctcHrss 12
Jan 11 BM 5f gd 1:04^1 h — Jan 3 Hol 3f ft :35^2 h — Dec 24 Hol 5f ft 1:05 h — ●Dec 19 Hol 3f ft :36 h

Mystery Maid

TOHILL K S — **114**
Own.—Sherry Ann Stable

Ch. f. 4, by Persian Emperor—Class Factor, by First Balcony
Br.—Wiggins Mr-Mrs G K (Wash) — 1987 1 1 0 0 $4,400
Tr.—Orr Ike — $12,500 — 1986 20 3 2 3 $33,780
Lifetime 26 5 4 4 $43,760 — Turf 1 0 0 0 $325

8Jan87-7BM 6f :22^4 :46^4 1:12^{4}sl 7¾ 114 9^{9¼} 9^{7¼} 5^4 1^{hd} Tohill K S^{10} Ⓕ 10000 75-33 MystryMd,FllngFthr,ExctvPoston 12
8Jan87—Ducked in start
29Dec86-6BM 6f :22 :45^1 1:10^{2}ft 6 115 6^5 4^{5½} 2^6 3^4 Campbell BC^8 Ⓕ 10000 83-15 DysBet,ExcutivPosition,MystryMid 8
4Dec86-6BM 6f :22^2 :45^1 1:10^{3}ft 28 114 4^2 4^3 5^{5½} 5^{6¼} Campbell BC^4 Ⓕ 16000 80-20 NturlBlonde,Blke'sDncer,IllicitJoy 10
27Nov86-5BM 6f :22^3 :45^4 1:10^{3}ft 7¼ 114 3^2 4^{2½} 5^3 9^{8¼} Tohill K S^8 Ⓕ 12500 78-23 CriMyHrt,ExcutivPosition,Crst'sIc 12
27Nov86—Bumped start
11Nov86-7BM 6f :22^2 :45^2 1:11^{3}ft 41 114 9^{8¼} 9^{17} 9^{19} 9^{20½} Gonzalez RM^8 Ⓕ 25000 60-21 Hot Cache, Patti Perkins, E'Mirage 9
23Oct86-6BM 6f :22 :45^2 1:10^{3}ft 5¼ 114 6^7 6^{3½} 4^{2½} 3^4 Campbell BC^7 Ⓕ 16000 82-21 ReysBrbizon,FullAcclim,MystryMid 9
15Oct86-7BM 6f :22 :45 1:09^{3}ft 5 117 8^9 8^{13} 8^{14} 8^{13} Campbell BC^2 Ⓕ 25000 78-17 MyLdiesTiger,Drumscell,PttiPrkins 8
19Sep86-8BM 6f :22 :45^1 1:11^{4}ft 9 114 8^{7¼} 7^8 5^{5½} 5^{7¾} CmpbllBC^8 ⒻAw16000 72-28 ByAnyOtherName,EdnaN.,Sobrnie 10
5Sep86-10Bmf 6f :22^2 :45^1 1:11^{2}ft 7¼ 114 4^5 4^7 3^4 1^2 Campbell BC^5 Ⓕ 25000 82-30 MysteryMaid,HollyAnn,LovableFlirt 8
30Jly86-9SR 6f :21^4 :44^1 1:09^{1}ft 4½ 114 8^{6¼} 7^8 4^{11} 4^{7½} Campbell BC^8 Ⓕ 25000 88-09 IllicitJoy,Creista'sIce,AirForceBaby 8
Jan 18 BM 4f ft :51^2 h — Jan 5 BM 4f m :51^4 h — Dec 28 BM 3f ft :37^1 h — Dec 20 BM 5f sy 1:07^4 h (d)

She's Fit

GONZALEZ R M — **118**
Own.—A H Enterprises

B. m. 5, by Maheras—Raging Fit, by Raja Baba
Br.—Roberts Mr-Mrs G C (Wash) — 1987 1 1 0 0 $5,500
Tr.—Greenman Walter — $12,500 — 1986 15 1 6 0 $15,685
Lifetime 31 5 9 5 $35,995

7Jan87-6BM 6f :22^3 :46^1 1:12^{2}sl 7 115 2^2 1^{hd} 1^{1½} 1^2 Gonzalez RM^8 Ⓕ 12500 77-35 She's Fit, Verbal, L'Indian 8
7Jan87—Lugged out late
17Dec86-7BM 6f :22^3 :46^3 1:13 sl 9¾ 114 2^4 3^3 2^4 2^4 Aragon VA^{11} Ⓕ c10000 70-36 Kims Benz, She'sFit,MissCalabash 11
3Dec86-5BM 6f :22^4 :46 1:11^{2}ft 19 114 1^{hd} 2^{hd} 2½ 5^4 Loseth C^1 Ⓕ 12500 78-19 PrncssSplndr,SssyErryn,StrChngr 11
19Nov86-4BM 6f :22^3 :46^3 1:11^{3}ft 10 114 3^5 3^7 4^{7½} 5^{9½} Loseth C^5 Ⓕ 16000 71-22 B. Magic, Ritzy Chick,RudeInvader 8
12Oct86-8Lga 6f :21^4 :44^2 1:09^{3}ft 9 115 3^{2½} 3^{3½} 3^5 4^{5½} Delgadillo C^4 Ⓕ 20000 82-16 Angel'sHalo,ParisinLce,MissMonco 6
27Sep86-8Lga 1$\frac{1}{16}$:48^2 1:14^1 1:49^{2}sl 3¼ 115 2^2 2^2 2^2 2^{3½} Delgadillo C^3 Ⓕ 16000 48-43 Super Tea, She's Fit, Hunter'sFirst 8
13Sep86-8Lga 6f :22 :45^3 1:11^{1}m 7½ 115 2^2 2^{1½} 2^{2½} 2^3 Best F^2 Ⓕ 20000 77-32 BarbaricNell,She'sFit,Ms.SatusWay 8
1Sep86-5Lga 6½f :22^2 :45^3 1:16^{3}ft 7½ 116 2^1 2½ 1^{1½} 1^{1½} Best F^8 Ⓕ 12500 86-19 She's Fit, Cast In Silver, Mug Shot 8
22Aug86-8Lga 6f :22 :45^1 1:09^{3}ft 17 115 3^2 5^5 6^{8¾} 5^{8½} Best F^4 Ⓕ 25000 79-17 MissMonaco,Renee'sLark,SpnishKy 6
8Aug86-9Lga 6f :21^2 :44^3 1:09^{2}ft 14 116 4^{2½} 6^5 7^{17} 7^{13½} Estrada J Jr^7 Ⓕ 25000 75-20 ParisianLace,SpanishKy,Angel'sHlo 7
Jan 4 BM 3f sy :37^3 h (d)

Secondhand Rosee *

CAMPBELL B C **115**
Own.—Fobert A

Dk. b. or br. m. 6, by Black Mackee—Miss Posey Patch, by Cup Race
Br.—McDonald M L (Wash) 1987 1 0 0 0 $250
Tr.—Clements John $12,500 1986 9 0 2 3 $10,855
Lifetime 47 6 13 7 $55,748

7Jan87-6BM	6f	:22^{3}	:46^{1}	1:12^{2}sl	6½	115	33½	41¼	46	58½	Campbell BC^{3}	Ⓕ 12500	68-35	She's Fit, Verbal, L'Indian	8
23Nov86-2BM	6f	:22^{2}	:45^{3}	1:11^{1}ft	10	114	1^{hd}	2½	2½	2^{2}	Campbell BC^{4}	Ⓕ 12500	81-20	WptRgn,ScondhndRs,PrncssSplndr	9
11Nov86-5BM	6f	:22^{4}	:46^{1}	1:11^{4}ft	8½	114	62½	41½	3^{2}	33¾	Baze R A^{7}	Ⓕ c8000	76-21	ScotchPips,KmsBnz,ScondhndRos	12
11Nov86—Lugged backside, on turn															
22Oct86-7BM	6f	:22^{1}	:45^{2}	1:11 ft	13	114	5^{4}	3^{3}	46½	711¾	Lamance C^{10}	Ⓕ 12500	72-23	RudInvdr,PrincssSplndor,O.K.Klly	10
18Apr86-7GG	6f	:22^{1}	:45^{3}	1:11^{1}ft	3¾	115	42½	3^{4}	46½	4^{12}	Hummel C R^{6}	Ⓕ 16000	71-22	Torkatue, Peggy Dee, Verbal	8
18Apr86—Ducked in start															
8Apr86-2GG	6f	:22^{2}	:46^{1}	1:12^{1}sl	5	114	5^{3}	42½	3^{1}	3¾	Lamance C^{8}	Ⓕ 16000	77-31	Verbal,Mizanthe,SecondhndRosee	10
25Mar86-7GG	6f	:22^{2}	:45^{2}	1:10^{4}ft	13	115	4^{2}	42½	42½	63½	Hummel C R^{1}	Ⓕ 25000	81-20	MchoFogoso,MornngstrLn,Mvmnt	10
27Feb86-7GG	6f	:22^{1}	:45^{2}	1:10^{4}ft	10	115	3^{nk}	1^{hd}	1^{1}	2^{2}	Hummel C R^{7}	Ⓕ 25000	83-20	PetiteShirh,ScondhndRos,FirMliss	11
11Feb86-5GG	6f	:22	:44^{3}	1:10 ft	4	115	51¾	3^{1}	6^{5}	76¾	Hummel C R^{7}	Ⓕ 25000	82-18	Fusayso, Verbal, Diamond Favor	9
11Feb86—Wide on turn															
5Jan86-1BM	6f	:22^{4}	:46^{3}	1:13^{1}sy	*1	121	2^{hd}	2^{hd}	3½	32½	Long B^{4}	Ⓕ c25000	70-32	MchoFogos,SnwyWngs,ScndhndRs	6

Jan 4 BM 3f sy :39^{3} h (d) Dec 20 BM 5f sy 1:05 h (d)

Ballet Shoes

DOOCY T T **115**
Own.—Fouts R

B. m. 6, by Landish—Recreation Time, by A-Okay
Br.—Bachman T W (Cal) 1986 5 2 0 0 $8,377
Tr.—Hollendorfer Jerry $12,500 1985 1 1 0 0 $3,025
Lifetime 6 3 0 0 $11,402

29Dec86-7BM	6f	:22^{2}	:45^{3}	1:10^{2}ft	4¼	114	96¼	4^{3}	2^{hd}	11½	Doocy T T^{2}	Ⓕ 8000	87-15	BalletShoes,PrideOfWindy,Capitol	11
29Dec86—Broke slowly															
12Dec86-5BM	6f	:22^{3}	:45^{4}	1:11^{2}ft	31	114	72¾	52¾	3^{1}	11½	Doocy T T^{8}	Ⓕ 6250	82-23	BalletShoes,Mizanthe,Inexplicable	12
20Feb86-9GG	6f	:22^{3}	:46^{2}	1:12^{1}m	*2½	110^{5}	77¼	76½	45½	65¼	Aragon V A^{6}	Ⓕ 5000	73-20	RchMonns,GntlMomnt,FutrOpton	10
20Feb86—Awarded fifth purse money															
5Feb86-1GG	6f	:22^{2}	:45^{2}	1:11^{3}gd	4	115	56½	5^{6}	54¾	4^{3}	Mena F^{5}	Ⓕ 6250	78-19	Tweed, Delta Magic, Sara Dulce	7
5Feb86—Off slowly, bobbled															
24Jan86-2BM	6f	:22^{3}	:46	1:12 ft	4¼	115	66½	97¾	85¾	84¾	Mena F^{1}	Ⓕ 10000	74-21	Brbck,Dixie'sPrise,Junction'sOrbit	10
23Dec85-3BM	6f	:22^{3}	:46	1:11^{1}ft	3½	120	3^{3}	31½	1^{2}	1^{5}	Baze R A^{3}	ⒻM12500	83-18	BlletShoes,DncSuziDnc,PlomrPrk	12

Jan 15 BM 3f ft :37^{1} h Dec 24 BM 4f m :51^{1} h Dec 4 BM 5f ft 1:02^{1} h Nov 29 Stk 7f ft 1:28^{1} h

Tyre Not

HANSEN R D **114**
Own.—Parks D

Ch. f. 4, by Tyrant—Conciegerie, by Banner Sport
Br.—Smith D D & Edith (Fla) 1986 17 4 2 1 $19,870
Tr.—Velasquez Danny $12,500 1985 1 1 0 0 $3,600
Lifetime 18 5 2 1 $23,470

3Dec86-7Tam	6f	:23^{3}	:47^{3}	1:13^{3}ft	3½	114	1½	2½	35½	712¾	Allen R D Jr^{1}	Ⓕ 12500	64-25	Gem Tex, La Rusee, Inaha	9
9Nov86-9Tdn	1$\frac{1}{16}$	:48^{3}	1:15^{3}	1:50 ft	8½	117	11½	1^{hd}	31½	7^{9}	Picon J^{2}	Ⓕ 14500	50-31	MssSlvr,Ncky'sMFthr,PlntAlgnmnt	7
29Oct86-9Tdn	1$\frac{1}{16}$	:48^{3}	1:15	1:49 ft	4¾	119	2^{1}	1^{2}	41¼	45¾	LondonOA^{2}	ⒻAw12600	58-31	OurKtherin,PlntAlignmnt,PlumTim	6
23Oct86-9Tdn	6f	:22^{4}	:47	1:13^{1}ft	3	122	2^{hd}	2^{hd}	2^{hd}	2^{1}	LondonoOA^{10}	Ⓕ 14500	77-27	AngeltDwn,TyreNot,Stnmdemdoit	12
10Oct86-8Tdn	1$\frac{1}{16}$	:48^{2}	1:14	1:48 ft	7¼	122	1^{1}	1^{1}	3^{6}	35½	LondonOA^{1}	ⒻAw12600	63-25	BeLikeJmiC.,Rggi'sPrincss,TyrNot	11
3Oct86-9Tdn	6f	:23	:47^{3}	1:14^{2}m	*6-5	122	2^{hd}	2^{1}	2^{2}	73¾	Londono O A^{7}	Ⓕ 14500	68-30	AngelatDawn,NewProspective,Lnde	7
17Sep86-8Tdn	6f	:22^{3}	:45^{4}	1:12 ft	*2	116	2^{hd}	1^{hd}	1^{3}	13½	Londono O A^{4}	Ⓕ 14500	84-25	TyreNot,AngeltDwn,PrincessHether	7
1Sep86-4Tdn	6f	:22^{3}	:46^{4}	1:13^{1}ft	*6-5	122	2^{hd}	11½	1^{4}	1^{6}	Londono O A^{2}	Ⓕ 6500	78-27	TyreNot,StarlightMiden,Forlidonte	8
17Aug86-5Tdn	6f	:22	:45^{4}	1:12^{2}ft	2½	119	31½	1^{2}	1^{4}	1^{1}	Londono O A^{6}	Ⓕ 6500	82-19	Tyre Not, PurpleDustII,Forlidonte	10
7Aug86-8Tdn	6f	:22^{2}	:46^{4}	1:14^{1}ft	*1	116	2½	1^{5}	1^{4}	4^{nk}	Londono O A^{1}	Ⓕ 11500	73-28	DustMop,StrlightMiden,AppleSwift	7

Jan 14 SA 5f ft 1:02^{2} h Jan 9 SA tr.t 4f gd :52 h

Natural Squaw

SCHACHT R **115**
Own.—Stewball Stable

B. m. 6, by L'Natural—Indian Bend, by Triple Bend
Br.—Warwick G (Cal) 1987 1 0 0 0 $720
Tr.—Arterburn Lonnie $12,500 1986 12 4 0 3 $19,987
Lifetime 33 8 4 5 $59,847

8Jan87-5BM	6f	:23	:47	1:13^{4}sl	2¼	115	10^{10}	10^{15}	10^{9}	4^{1}	Schacht R^{2}	Ⓕ 8000	69-33	Phetlle,MyChoosing,I'llHveTheTb	10
10Dec86-2BM	6f	:22^{3}	:46	1:11 ft	2¾	114	21½	3^{2}	2^{4}	36½	Schacht R^{2}	Ⓕ 8000	77-21	TbleStrek,Jn'sProspect,NturlSquw	8
28Nov86-2BM	6f	:22	:45^{1}	1:10^{1}ft	5½	114	3^{2}	2½	1^{3}	1^{5}	Schacht R^{2}	ⒻⓈ 6250	88-20	NaturalSquaw,NotAStraw,ThePntry	8
14Nov86-5BM	6f	:22^{3}	:45^{3}	1:11^{2}ft	3½	114	12^{22}	12^{21}	10^{16}	37½	Schacht R^{5}	Ⓕ 6250	74-20	TableStreak,Anotamar,NturlSquw	12
14Nov86—Took up start															
15Oct86-5BM	6f	:22^{3}	:45^{4}	1:10^{4}ft	4¾	117	2^{hd}	1^{hd}	2^{2}	3^{6}	Chapman T M^{4}	Ⓕ 6250	79-17	Renew, Mizanthe, Natural Squaw	10
3Oct86-2BM	6f	:22^{4}	:46^{2}	1:11^{3}ft	5½	114	7^{4}	99½	9^{12}	89½	Chapman T M^{1}	Ⓕ 8000	72-21	ThLdyWh,Tmy'sDrn,PrncssSplndr	11
19Sep86-2BM	6f	:22^{2}	:46^{2}	1:13^{1}ft	5	114	63¾	52¾	2^{1}	1½	Chapman T M^{6}	Ⓕ 6250	73-28	Natural Squaw, Mizanthe, Just Us	11
23Jly86-10SR	5½f	:22^{1}	:46^{1}	1:04^{4}ft	*2	116	3^{5}	34½	3^{2}	6^{7}	Olguin M^{5}	Ⓕ 6250	80-14	Kegani,DebestStake,‡ReginCnyon	10
23Jly86—Took up sharply 1/16; Placed fifth through disqualification															
3Jly86-10Pln	6f	:22^{2}	:46^{1}	1:11 ft	7	113^{5}	1^{1}	2^{3}	8^{17}	10^{17}	Giacobbe DL^{3}	Ⓕ 12500	70-23	MdonnBlue,RoylFrpp,Bcky'sRunnr	10
14Jun86-2GG	6f	:22	:44^{4}	1:09^{3}ft	*2½	114	11½	1½	34½	8^{13}	Hummel C R^{4}	Ⓕ 16000	78-09	Bold Rumor, Last Hit, Tributeena	9

Jan 17 BM 4f ft :51^{2} h Jan 3 BM 4f sy :53^{3} h Dec 29 BM 5f ft 1:01^{2} h Dec 20 BM 4f sy :52^{4} h (d)

For a worksheet, this is what we find:

Odds	Horse	PCR							Form	Ab/T
7	Miss Muffet	106/	29	48	−	6/	71	= 149	Lw	(45.1 25.4 = 2/ 72.0)
8	Mystery Maid	94/	62	48	−	15/	95	= 99	NNN	48.1 24.4 − 7/ 71.3
3	She's Fit	81/	29	34	−	5/	58	= 140	N+w	46.1 26.1 − 8/ 70.4
9	Secondhand Rosee	93/	30	42	−	6/	66	= 141	NON	46.2 27.3 − 8/ 72.2
3-2	Ballet Shoes	63/	33	21	+	10/	64	= 97	NNw	46.1 24.1 + 2/ 70.4
16	Tyre Not	84/	13	37	−	4/	46	= 183	Lw	(45.4 26.1 − 3/ 71.2)
4	Natural Squaw	99/	48	47	+	15/110		= 86	NOg	50.2 25.3 − 7/ 74.1

We can begin with some very good PCRs, with the longest price in the field, Tyre Not, leading at 140, and also possessed of good early speed which is so fashionable today. This horse is off a layoff with only average works, which would immediately negate a single selection play. She's Fit, also with some front speed, and having a last race victory with a good effort, has 169. Miss Muffet, off a layoff and slow works, has 149 and Secondhand Rosee at 141 has bad form and a last race ability time that is not likely to challenge anyone in this race. She can be discarded rather quickly.

There are two horses, however, that command quick attention. Ballet Shoes, the strong 3-2 favorite, has the second lowest PCR, but comes off a powerful race with a splendid 70.4 last race ability time. This one cannot be ignored. And then there is our last race winner with the strong PCR, She's Fit, the second favorite, also with the same 70.4 last race ability time.

These two are three ticks better than any of their rivals. This is the margin we require for the distinct advantage that we seek in sprint races. Is either one of them a single selection play? The only blemish on either horse is a last race win, not enough to totally disqualify unless at the bottom rung of the class ladder without compensating credentials. Under the standards in this book, both of them could be single selection plays—She's Fit because she is one of the first three in PCR and last race ability times and has no form defects; Ballet Shoes because she is the favorite with no form defects and one of the best three last race ability times.

We are now again approaching near certainty that one of the two will this race.

Does track tendency separate them sufficiently? She's Fit is geared toward fairly early while Ballet Shoes is indeed a closer, with a 33 over 21 for the two key internal numbers. Class, PCR, and early speed all weigh in the direction of She's Fit. I would have to bite the bullet here and go with She's Fit, because that's what our lessons tell us to do.

Did we succeed this time?

NINTH RACE
BayMeadows
JANUARY 21, 1987

6 FURLONGS. (1.07⅘) CLAIMING. Purse $10,000. Fillies and mares. 4-year-olds and upward. Weights, 4-year-olds, 120 lbs.; older, 121 lbs. Non-winners of two races since December 1 allowed 3 lbs.; a race since then, 6 lbs. Claiming price $12,500. (Maiden, starter and claiming races for $10,000 or less not considered.)

Value of race $10,000; value to winner $5,500; second $1,950; third $1,400; fourth $900; fifth $250. Mutuel pool $89,883. Exacta pool $129,251.

Last Raced	Horse	Eqt.	A.Wt	PP	St	¼	½	Str	Fin	Jockey	Cl'g Pr	Odds $1
29Dec86 ^{7}BM^{1}	Ballet Shoes		6 115	5	5	6^{3}	6^{5}	$2^{\frac{1}{2}}$	$1^{1\frac{1}{2}}$	Doocy T T	12500	1.50
7Jan87 ^{6}BM^{1}	She's Fit		5 118	3	2	2^{1}	2^{2}	1^{3}	$2^{2\frac{1}{2}}$	Gonzalez R M	12500	3.40
7Jan87 ^{6}BM^{5}	D Secondhand Rosee	b	6 115	4	4	4^{hd}	5^{2}	3^{hd}	3no	Campbell B C	12500	9.80
8Jan87 ^{7}BM^{1}	Mystery Maid		4 114	2	7	5^{2}	4^{hd}	6^{6}	4^{3}	Tohill K S	12500	8.30
3Dec86 ^{7}Tam^{7}	Tyre Not	b	4 116	6	1	$3^{1\frac{1}{2}}$	$3^{1\frac{1}{2}}$	5^{1}	$5^{1\frac{1}{2}}$	Hansen R D	12500	16.40
3Dec86 ^{1}Hol^{5}	Miss Muffet		5 115	1	3	1^{2}	1^{hd}	4^{hd}	$6^{1\frac{1}{2}}$	Loseth C	12500	7.30
8Jan87 ^{5}BM^{4}	Natural Squaw		6 115	7	6	7	7	7	7	Schacht R	12500	4.30

D-Secondhand Rosee Disqualified and placed fourth.

OFF AT 4:27. Start good. Won driving. Time, :22⅗, :46, :58⅖, 1:11⅗ Track fast.

$2 Mutuel Prices:			
5-BALLET SHOES	5.00	3.00	2.40
3-SHE'S FIT		3.60	2.80
2-MYSTERY MAID			2.80

$2 EXACTA 5-3 PAID $18.20

Almost, but not quite. That isn't good enough. We don't like to end on a losing note, but that's what occurred. Strong front speed did not prevail, as Ballet Shoes continued her power sweep in the stretch to beat She's Fit and make us tear up our ticket. We could have considered another insurance exacta in this apparent two-horse race, but these plays are far better when we like the lower priced horse to win.

This race went somewhat contrary to the internal numbers at the finish, even though the first half of it was the usual pattern of what we would expect. Miss Muffet and She's Fit, the demonstrated early runners, were right up there. She's Fit was easily better than the rest of them, but Ballet Shoes had enough late kick today to make it. Whether the track was leveling off at the end of the day, as it sometimes does in either direction, we cannot know. What we can say is that even the most sound and rational of playing methods is not infallible. On speed favoring days, some horses with later running styles do get there, but these tardy runners must not show too much of that kind of disability. Everything can't go the way we expect it all the time.

This turned out to be a very satisfying day, another powerful performer all the way. Here's how the totals looked.

Race	Horse	Bet	Return	Net P/L	Cum.P/L
1	Georgia Smith	$2	$11.80	+ $9.80	+ $9.80
	Vitascope	2	0	− 2.00	+ 7.80
2	PASS	0			+ 7.80
3	PASS	0			+ 7.80
4	Ninepoundhammer	2	5.00	+ 3.00	+ 10.80
5	Bois Hon	2	20.80	+ 18.80	+ 29.60
	Ivorette	2	0	− 2.00	+ 27.60
6	Sun Vest	2	0	− 2.00	+ 25.60
	Place/Exacta	2	7.92	+ 5.92	+ 31.52
7	Halo Express	2	5.60	+ 3.60	+ 35.12
8	PASS	0			+ 35.12
9	She's Fit	2	0	− 2.00	+ 33.12

This was another splendid day, cashing a ticket in five of the six races that we played. When you are able to find horses that stand out over the remainder of the field, and can narrow the serious threats down to three horses, where you can eliminate one of them, you will score time and time again. In our single selection plays there were two winners out of three. Our long priced big profit horses came in the races where we could play two of them when odds were high.

Let me assure you that these kinds of days, while rather obviously not occurring at every turn, will happen over and over again. These are the ones where you must spring with the advantages that we can find. These are the kinds of days that will build your profit potential to its fullest, making up for the thin line days when our profit margin is relatively small, or even those rare ones where we fall slightly in the red.

With this performance, we leave you to your own successes. Most assuredly, we have shown you some very good days, but as we have indicated, we did not know what these efforts would produce when we began. We tried to adhere strictly to the rules and guidelines that you have found in this book, because they are sound and they work.

When you follow them, you, too, will capitalize on these kinds of days that will bring you the Total Victory at the Track that this work is designed to do. The promise has been made and the performance has been demonstrated. The rest is up to you.